Thomas Thomson, Charles MacFarlane

The Comprehensive History of England

civil and military, religious, intellectual, and social, from the earliest period to the

suppression of the Sepoy revolt - Vol. 3

Thomas Thomson, Charles MacFarlane

The Comprehensive History of England

civil and military, religious, intellectual, and social, from the earliest period to the suppression of the Sepoy revolt - Vol. 3

ISBN/EAN: 9783337369125

Printed in Europe, USA, Canada, Australia, Japan

Cover: Foto ©ninafisch / pixelio.de

More available books at **www.hansebooks.com**

THE COMPREHENSIVE
HISTORY OF ENGLAND;

CIVIL AND MILITARY,
RELIGIOUS, INTELLECTUAL, AND SOCIAL.

FROM THE EARLIEST PERIOD

TO THE CLOSE OF THE RUSSIAN WAR.

WITH NUMEROUS ANNOTATIONS

FROM THE WRITINGS OF RECENT DISTINGUISHED HISTORIANS.

EDITED BY THE

Rev. THOS THOMSON,

AUTHOR OF "A HISTORY OF SCOTLAND FOR THE USE OF SCHOOLS," AND OF THE SUPPLEMENT TO THE
"BIOGRAPHICAL DICTIONARY OF EMINENT SCOTSMEN," ETC.

ILLUSTRATED BY ABOVE ONE THOUSAND ENGRAVINGS.

DIVISION III.

BLACKIE AND SON:
GLASGOW, EDINBURGH, LONDON, AND NEW YORK.

MDCCCLIX.

GLASGOW:
W. G. BLACKIE AND CO., PRINTERS,
VILLAFIELD.

perhaps have rendered that king's return to his country highly dangerous to himself. The positions of the great houses of the Earls of March and of Douglas were reversed: March had been restored to his forfeited estates and honours by the Duke of Albany, without consulting the parliament of Scotland; and Douglas declined in influence. The regent had sent troops into France to assist the dauphin without declaring war against England; and while some of the barons approved of the measure, foreseeing in the conquest of France the subjugation of Scotland, others strongly condemned it. Archibald, Earl of Douglas, who had been for several years a prisoner in England in the time of Henry IV., readily listened to proposals which were sanctioned, and even warmly recommended, by his captive sovereign. He engaged to serve the King of England all his life against all men, except the King of Scotland, and to follow him to France with 200 men-at-arms and 200 archers, to whom Henry was to pay the usual wages, allowing Douglas £200 a-year for himself. The gallant king also agreed to serve in that war, Henry engaging to allow him to revisit Scotland three months after their return from France. Out of affection for James, Alexander, Lord Forbes, Alexander de Seton, Lord of Gordon, William Blair, and two other Scottish knights, each with a certain number of men, joined Henry's standard at Dover, where, by the beginning of June, 4000 choice men-at-arms, and about 24,000 archers, were collected in admirable array. These forces were landed, on the 11th and 12th of June, at Calais, whence 1200 men-at-arms were sent, by forced marches, to Paris, to reinforce the Duke of Exeter. Henry marched more leisurely to Montreuil, where he had a long conference with his ally, the young Duke of Burgundy, who soon after, while the English were employed near the banks of the Loire, defeated the Dauphinists at Mons-en-Vimeu, in the marches of Picardy, and took Saintraille and some others of the bravest knights of that party. This victory was followed by the surrender of several places in the north-west. When Henry reached Paris, the dauphin was besieging Chartres, and some of his partizans were scouring the whole country between Chartres and the capital. But all this soon came to an end: the siege of Chartres was raised at the approach of Henry; Beaugency was taken by the English, and the dauphin was driven behind the Loire. Leaving the King of Scotland, in whom he appears to have had the fullest confidence, to prosecute the siege of Dreux, which capitulated on the 20th of August, Henry followed up the flying dauphin until he again took refuge in the strong town of Bourges in Berry. He then recrossed the Loire and returned to Paris. Allowing himself a very short repose, he proceeded, in the month of October, to lay siege to Meaux, about thirty miles to the north-east of Paris. Within that place, which was one of the strongest in all France, was a chief who had made himself remarkable for his atrocities, and an object of wonderment even in those atrocious times, when cruelties were committed in all parts of the kingdom. The Bastard of Vaurus had been an adherent of the old Count of Armagnac, and to avenge his master's death, he became more ferocious and blood-thirsty than a tiger. Whenever a Bourguignon or an Englishman fell into his hands, he was massacred on the spot, or put to death by execrable torture. Henry carried the town by assault in ten weeks; but the Bastard and his garrison, who could expect little mercy, retired to a sort of acropolis, called the market-place, where they made a long and a most desperate resistance. The dauphin wished to do something for the relief of these worthy allies, but he was not very courageous or adventurous; his troops, however numerous, dreaded to meet their adversaries in the field, and all that he did was to send the Sire d'Affemont to steal by night with some reinforcements into the besieged place. D'Affemont was taken prisoner by the English; and at last, in the beginning of the month of May, the place surrendered at discretion, and the Bastard of Vaurus was hanged. During this siege of seven months, Henry lost a considerable number of his brave warriors: the Earl of Worcester and Lord Clifford were killed by the enemy's artillery; others perished of an epidemic sickness; but the conquest of that important place left the English undisputed masters of the whole of France north of the Loire. While he was prosecuting the siege with wonderful perseverance, he was gladdened with the news that his wife Catherine had borne him a son, in Windsor Castle, on the 6th of December. On the 21st of May the queen, escorted by the Duke of Bedford, landed at Harfleur, whence she proceeded, with still increasing troops of noblemen, by way of Rouen, to the Bois de Vincennes, where she was received as some angelical person. On the great festival of Whitsuntide the two courts of Henry and Charles made a grand entry into Paris, and on that day King Henry and Queen Catherine kept their court in the palace of the Louvre, where they sat in their royal robes, with their imperial crowns on their heads.

Meanwhile the dauphin had collected in the south an army of 20,000 men, the command of which he intrusted to the Earl of Buchan, who still retained a considerable Scottish force. From Bourges Buchan advanced to the Loire, and, crossing that river, took the town of La Charité; then descending the right bank of the river, he laid siege to the important town of Cosne, and reduced it to such straits that the garrison agreed to surrender if they were not relieved by a given day. Before Cosne, Buchan was joined by the dauphin. The Duke of Burgundy pressed Henry to march to the relief of the besieged place. The King of England never required much pressing on occasions like these, and though he was labouring under a severe illness, he left Paris at the end of July. As soon as the dauphin heard that he was in motion, he caused the siege to be raised, recrossed the Loire, and again threw himself into Bourges. But Henry's strength failed him on the march, and halting at Corbeil, about twenty miles to the south of Paris, he gave the command of his army to his brother, the Duke of Bedford, and throwing himself into a litter, was conveyed back to the Bois de Vincennes in the neighbourhood of the capital. The Duke of Bedford was about to cross the Loire when he was recalled by the unexpected news that the king his brother was dying. The duke arrived at Vincennes in time to receive his instructions and his last farewell.

Henry had much to attach him to life; his grand scheme of conquest seemed to be approaching a happy completion; he was King of France in fact, and the crown was within his grasp, for his wretched father-in-law was at last dying; he was the happy husband of a young and beautiful wife; he was a father; he was young himself, and until recently, when a mysterious malady attacked him, in the enjoyment of vigorous health and buoyant spirits. Yet, in spite of all this, he saw death approach with calmness. He felt no remorse for the blood he had shed in France, believing to the last that he had rights to the crown, and that he had been but an instrument in the hand of Providence. He felt some natural anxiety on account of his infant son, but even on this head he was supported by a confident hope in the wisdom, valour, and fidelity of his brothers and of his English subjects. On the day of his death, he summoned the Duke of Bedford, the Earl of Warwick, and some other great lords, to his bedside, and told them he saw it was the will of his Creator that he should quit this world: he bade them be of good cheer, and be comforted them with kind words, yet grave and full of meaning. He exhorted them to be true to his son as they had been to him, and to keep peace and amity among themselves during the long minority. He most earnestly recommended them to cultivate the friendship of his ally the Duke of Burgundy. He told them never to make a peace with Charles, calling himself dauphin, which did not stipulate for his surrender of all claims to the crown of France, or, at worst, for the grant to England of the duchies of Normandy and Aquitaine in full sovereignty. He cautiously warned them not to release the Duke of Orleans, or any of the French princes of the blood taken at Azincourt. During the minority of his son, he signified his wish that his brother the Duke of Gloucester should be regent or protector in England, and that his brother the Duke of Bedford, with the advice of the Duke of Burgundy, should be regent in France. His hearers, who did not share his equanimity, wept and sobbed while they vowed obedience to his dying injunctions, and promised to protect his wife and child. Feeling his end approach, he sent for his confessor and his chaplains, whom he directed to chant the seven penitential Psalms. When they came to the verse "Thou shalt build up the walls of Jerusalem," he stopped them, and said aloud, that he always intended, after he had wholly subdued the realm of France and restored it to peace and good order, to go and conquer the Holy City from the Saracens. Having expressed this intention, he allowed the priests to proceed, and a few minutes after, he calmly breathed his last, in the thirty-fourth year of his age and the tenth of his reign, on the last day of August, 1422.

It had been very usual to abandon the king as soon as the breath was out of his body, and even to treat his unconscious remains with disrespect; but Henry's nobles and officers resolved to give him a most magnificent funeral. In the first place, they caused the body to be embalmed, and then to be carried in great pomp to the church of Nôtre Dame, in Paris, where a solemn service was performed. The funeral procession, blackening all the way, then proceeded to Rouen, whither some of the nobles had previously conducted Queen Catherine, who had been kept in ignorance of the danger of the king, and knew not of his death until some days after it had happened. At Rouen it lay in state for several days. The coffin was then placed within a car drawn by four splendid horses. In this state the body was conveyed by slow journeys from Rouen to Abbeville, where it was placed in the cathedral of St. Ulfran, with rows of priests on each side of the coffin to chaunt requiems all through the night. During the slow, sad progress from town to town, the funeral car was preceded and flanked by heralds, persons bearing banners and achievements, and a host of men, all clad in white sheets, and carrying lighted torches in their hands; it was followed by the royal household in deep mourning, by some hundreds of knights and esquires in black armour, and plumes, with their lances reversed, and by the princes of the blood, and the King of Scotland, who acted as chief mourner. At about a league in the rear of all travelled the youthful widow, with a numerous retinue. The night after leaving Abbeville, they rested at Hesdin, the next night at Montreuil, the next at Boulogne, and then at Calais, where a fleet was in readiness to convey them to Dover. From Dover they travelled by the usual road to London, where they arrived on Martinmas Day. As the melancholy procession approached London, fifteen bishops in their pontifical attire, many mitred abbots and churchmen, with a vast multitude of persons of all conditions, went out to meet it. The churchmen chanted the service for the dead as it passed over London bridge and through the street of the Lombards to St. Paul's. After the obsequies had been performed at St. Paul's in presence of the whole parliament, the body was carried to Westminster Abbey, and there interred near the shrine of Edward the Confessor.[1] "At this funeral," continues Monstrelet, who wrote some years later, "greater pomp and expense were made than had been done for 200 years at the burying of any King of England; and even now, as much reverence and honour are paid every day to his tomb as if it were certain that he is a saint in heaven."

We take this strong popular feeling as one proof that Henry had many fine qualities besides those of a mere warrior and conqueror.[2]

CHAPTER III.—CIVIL AND MILITARY HISTORY.—A.D. 1422—1431.

HENRY VI., SURNAMED OF WINDSOR.—ACCESSION, A.D. 1422—DEPOSITION, A.D. 1461.

Henry VI., infant son of Henry V., proclaimed king—The Duke of Gloucester appointed Protector of England, and the Duke of Bedford Regent of France—Henry VI. proclaimed King of France—Charles the dauphin also proclaimed King of France—Victory of the English over the French and Scots at Crevant—They are again victorious at Vernueil—The successes of the Duke of Bedford impaired by the folly of the Duke of Gloucester—Marriage of Gloucester to Jacqueline of Hainault—Umbrage of the Duke of Burgundy at the marriage—Dissensions in the court of Charles, the French king—Orleans besieged by the English—Victory of the English over the French and Scots at Rouvrai—Orleans reduced to the last extremity—Joan of Arc appears—Her early history—Her application to Charles—The examination held upon her claim to a Divine commission—She marches to the relief of Orleans—Dismay of the English at her coming—They are defeated, and compelled to raise the siege—Successes of Joan of Arc—Victory of the French over the English at Patay—Triumphant march of Charles to Rheims—His coronation—Appeal of Joan to the Duke of Burgundy—Perplexities of the Duke of Bedford—He is reinforced by Cardinal Beaufort—Indecisive operations in the field—Declining influence of Joan of Arc—Bedford resigns the regency of France to the Duke of Burgundy—Joan of Arc taken prisoner—She is tried as a sorceress—Her unjust and oppressive treatment—She is condemned and executed.

HE son of Henry and Catherine was not quite nine months old. As soon as his father's death was known in England, some of the bishops and lay lords issued commissions, in the name of Henry VI., to the judges, sheriffs, and other officers, authorizing them to continue their respective duties, and summoned a parliament to meet in November. As soon as parliament was assembled, it laid claim to the right of regulating the regency. The Duke of Gloucester claimed the post of regent, because, in the absence of his elder brother, the Duke of Bedford, he was nearest in blood,

---

[1] Monstrelet: Walsing.
[2] "Power deemed to be ill gotten is naturally precarious; and the instance of Henry IV. has been well quoted to prove that public liberty flourishes with a bad title in the sovereign. None of our kings seems to have been less beloved, and indeed he had little claim to affection. But what men denied to the reigning king, they poured in full measure upon the heir of his throne. The virtues of the Prince of Wales [Henry V.] are almost invidiously eulogized by those parliaments who treat harshly his father; and those records afford a strong presumption that some early petulance or riot has been much exaggerated by the vulgar minds of our chroniclers. One can scarcely understand, at least, that a prince who was three years engaged in quelling the dangerous insurrection of Glendower, and who, in the latter time of his father's reign, presided at the council, was so lost in a cloud of low debauchery as common fame represents. Loved he certainly was throughout his life, as so intrepid, affable, and generous a temper well deserved; and this sentiment was heightened to admiration by successes still more rapid and dazzling than those of Edward III. During his reign there scarcely appears any vestige of dissatisfaction in parliament—a circumstance very honourable, whether we ascribe it to the justice of his administration or to the affection of his people. Perhaps two exceptions, though they are rather one in spirit, might be made:—The first, a petition to the Duke of Gloucester, then holding parliament as Guardian of England, that he would move the king and queen to return as speedily as might please them, in relief and comfort of the commons; the second, a petition that their petitions might not be sent to the king beyond sea, but altogether determined 'within the kingdom of England during this parliament,' and that this ordinance might be of force in all future parliaments to be held in England. This prayer, to which the guardian declined to accede, evidently sprung from the apprehensions excited in their minds by the treaty of Troyes, that England might become a province of the French crown, which led them to obtain a renewal of the statute of Edward III., declaring the independence of this kingdom."—Hallam, *State of Europe during the Middle Ages*, vol. iii. pp. 143, 144.

and because the late king had named him regent on his death-bed. The lords, after searching the rolls and consulting with the judges, told the duke that this demand was contrary to the constitution, and that the late king had no power whatever to appoint a regent without the consent of parliament. They offered to appoint him president of the council in the absence of the Duke of Bedford, and to give him, not the title of regent, lieutenant, or tutor, but that of Protector of the realm and church of England—which title, they said, would serve to remind him of his duty. A few days after they proceeded to name a chancellor, a treasurer, a keeper of the privy seal, and a permanent council, which consisted of sixteen members, with the Duke of Bedford for president, the Duke of Gloucester to act for him, and to receive the salary of £5333 during his brother's absence from England. All these regulations and nominations received the assent of the commons, and the Duke of Gloucester was obliged to be satisfied with them. The care of the person and education of the young prince was afterwards intrusted to the Earl of Warwick and to Henry Beaufort, Bishop of Winchester, a half-brother of King Henry IV., who had also a high seat in the council.[1] After voting the continuance of the duty on wool, and tonnage and poundage for two years, the parliament was dissolved. With the exception of some movements on the Welsh borders, the accession of the infant king was perfectly peaceful.

In France, where there were no constitutional delicacies to be managed, the Duke of Bedford, who was deservedly popular with the army, was at once recognized as regent, and succeeded to the power, and nearly to all the consideration of his deceased brother.[2] He remained at Paris, or in the neighbourhood, surrounded by the Earls of Somerset, Warwick, Salisbury, Suffolk, and Arundel, Sir John Talbot, Sir John Fastolfe, and the other distinguished captains who had carried the military fame of England to so high a pitch in the preceding reign. In the month of October, Charles VI. expired at Paris. The dauphin, who was now in his twenty-first year, was in Auvergne, and in a very poor and reduced condition. As soon as the knights of his party received the news, they conducted him to a little chapel, raised a banner with the arms of France upon it, and saluted him with cries of "Long live the king!" Such was the inauguration of Charles VII., who at the time was not master of a fourth part of the kingdom. The death of his father, however, gave him an immediate increase of moral strength, and he soon proceeded to the city of Poictiers, where he was crowned and anointed with some solemnity.

The Duke of Bedford, with the consent of the parliament of Paris, had proclaimed the infant Henry King of France; and while Charles was being crowned at Poictiers he held a great assembly in the capital, where the parliament, the university, the archbishop, the metropolitan clergy, the magistrates, and principal burghers, swore fealty to Henry. The same ceremony was performed in all the other great towns of France in subjection to the English, or to their ally the Duke of Burgundy. To secure the friendship of this prince, whose power nearly equalled that of the King of France, even when France was undivided, Bedford strictly adhered to the instructions of his dying brother, consulting the Duke of Burgundy upon all important affairs, and paying a politic deference to his judgment and better acquaintance with the feelings and habits of the French. He married the Duke's sister, Anne of Burgundy; and, by negotiating a marriage between another sister of the duke's, the widow of the deceased dauphin, and Arthur, Count of Richemont, brother of the Duke of Brittany, he hoped to secure the support and co-operation of the Bretons, who, in the time of Henry V., had been only neutral. A sort of congress was held by these great personages at Amiens, in the month of April, 1423, and there Bedford received the most gratifying assurances of continued support from his two allies. But, at the same time, and without the knowledge of the Duke of Bedford, the Dukes of Burgundy and Brittany made a separate treaty with one another; and some embarrassing discussions arose concerning the flight into England of Jacqueline, Countess of Hainault, whose marriage with the Duke of Gloucester struck the first great blow at the power of the English in France.[3] But, for the moment, that power seemed to be on the increase, and Bedford soon gained two great vic-

---

[1] Beaufort was the second of the sons of John of Gaunt, by his third wife Catherine Ruet, Roet, or Rowet, widow of Sir Otes Swynford, generally supposed to have been the sister of Philippa Rowet, who is said to have been the wife of the poet Chaucer. There are considerable doubts, however, both as to the reality of this connection, and even as to the fact of Chaucer having been married at all. Catherine Rowet, who was the daughter of Sir Paine Rowet, a knight of Hainault, had long been the duke's mistress, having been originally brought over to wait upon his first wife, Blanche of Lancaster. The children of John of Gaunt and Catherine Rowet—three sons and a daughter—were all born before their marriage, which took place in 1397, but were legitimated that year by a patent which is entered on the rolls of parliament. They took the name of Beaufort from the castle of Beaufort in France, where they were born; a property that came into the possession of their father by his first wife. The patent of legitimation entitled them and their descendants to hold all honours and estates, such as duchies, principalities, earldoms, &c.; and in some copies of it there is an express reservation of the right of inheriting the crown. Henry VII. descended from the oldest of these Beauforts, John, created (A.D. 1397) Earl of Somerset.

[2] *Rot. Parl.; Rymer; Walsingham.*

[3] *Barante; Daru, Hist. de la Bretagne.*

tories, which were compared to the glorious affairs of Crecy, Poictiers, and Azincourt. Charles VII. gave himself up to indolence and selfish indulgence, loitering away his time, not with his beautiful wife, Mary of Anjou, but with his mistresses. He had, however, about him many men of great energy: they roused him from his inglorious ease and forced him into the field. Crossing the Loire once more, Charles now fixed his head-quarters at Gien, a small town close on the right bank of that river, and there he remained while the mass of his forces, under James Stuart, Lord Darnley, and the Marshal of Severac, struck off to the east, fell upon Burgundy, and laid siege to Crevant, a very important place. The Duke of Burgundy had some forces on foot in that direction, but they were very inconsiderable, and he again eagerly pressed the English to save his fertile province. The Duke of Bedford instantly despatched the Earls of Salisbury and Suffolk to the relief of Crevant, and as the French, relying on their great superiority of numbers and the determined valour of their Scottish allies, stood their ground outside the town, a general battle was resolved upon. At Auxerre the English were joined by the Burgundians; but their force was still very inferior, and they had to pass the river Yonne in face of the enemy. Having forced the passage, they found the main body drawn up in good position on the right bank. While the English attacked in front, the Burgundians attacked in flank, and then made a movement to the rear. By this disposition the English were opposed to the Scots; the Burgundians to the French, their own countrymen. The French soon gave way, and then fled in a disgraceful manner, leaving their Scottish allies to shift for themselves. Though thus abandoned by all save a few honourable knights, the Scots gallantly defended themselves for a long time, and the victory was not decided till more than 3000 of them were killed or taken prisoners.[1]

Charles VII. received about this time a body of auxiliaries from the Duke of Milan, and gave encouragement to an insurrection in Maine and Anjou, and in other places north of the Loire. We must pass over a number of petty combats and sieges. In the affair of La Gravelle, John de la Pole, brother to the Duke of Suffolk, was surprised by a great force under Harcourt, Count of Aumale, and was obliged to retreat with considerable loss.

In another direction a detachment of the Duke of Burgundy was defeated by the Italian and Scottish auxiliaries of King Charles. The spirit of the French people had gained one great advantage for this *roi-fainéant;* they had gradually thrown off the yoke in several parts of the north and the north-west; they had got possession of several towns in Normandy; and thus the English, instead of crossing the Loire, were obliged to fight in the country between that river and the Seine. Their alliance with the Duke of Brittany rested on hollow foundations from the first, and a quarrel with his brother, the Count of Richemont, was followed by bad effects. The count, who was refused the separate command of an army, for which Bedford judged him unfit, would not be soothed by the offer of a liberal pension—lands and honours he had received already—and, stealing away secretly, he withdrew to Brittany, hoping to induce his brother to declare against the English. Bedford laboured the more earnestly to gratify the Duke of Burgundy; but he did not yet know the secret treaty existing between that prince and the Duke of Brittany. In the course of 1423, the auxiliary force of Scotland had been greatly increased by fresh arrivals; and Archibald, Earl of Douglas, lately the adherent of Henry V., went and joined Charles, who made him a French duke, by the title of the Duke of Touraine. Here, again, the regent Bedford acted with all possible good policy; he negotiated with King James of Scotland, and released him from his imprisonment in England in the spring of 1424, by which further reinforcements from Scotland to France were prevented.

In the summer of 1424 the Duke of Bedford laid siege to the strong town of Ivry. Charles resolved to relieve the place, and to that end sent his whole army into Normandy. This army consisted of about 7000 Scots and 7000 Italians and French. The command was nominally given to the Earls of Douglas and Buchan; but the Counts of Alençon, Aumale, and Narbonne, and the other French nobles who marched with them, would take no orders from Scottish adventurers —for such they termed the bravest and noblest of their allies. This ill-assorted army marched within sight of Ivry, but they halted in dismay on seeing the excellent position of the English, and presently retreated without drawing a sword. Upon this failure Ivry surrendered. Either by an ingenious stratagem of their own, or by a rising in their favour of the inhabitants, Charles' army got possession of the important town of Verneuil, situated about thirty miles to the south-west of Ivry; but they were scarcely there when the Duke of Bedford presented himself before the walls. A tumultuary council was held, and as they could not possibly remain where they were on account of a scarcity, it was resolved to go out and fight the English in an open field. They had every advantage of position: the town covered one of their flanks, they had also learned

---

[1] *Monstrelet.*

something from experience, and, leaving their baggage and their horses within the walls, they formed on foot, leaving only about 2000 men-at-arms, part of whom were Italians, to fight on horseback. The Duke of Bedford, whose army was inferior in numbers, followed the old tactics of Crecy and Azincourt: he made all his cavalry dismount; he placed his horses and his baggage in the rear, under a guard of archers; and he stationed the rest of the bowmen on his flanks and in his van, where they stuck their sharp stakes into the ground. There was a brief pause. The Earl of Douglas wished to wait for the attack of the English, but the French nobles would not listen to his prudence, and the Count of Narbonne rushed forward, shouting "Mountjoye St. Denis!" The whole line followed him in hurry and confusion; and by the time they got up to the English stakes, they were both out of breath and out of order. Their number, however, was imposing, for van, rear, and reserve, came up altogether. The English stood firm, shouting "St. George for Bedford!" But some of the archers were borne down and driven towards the baggage—a fortunate circumstance, for they seem to have arrived just in time to support their comrades there, who were charged in the rear by the 2000 horse, led on by La Hire and Saintrualle. This cavalry was repeatedly repulsed, and at last completely driven from the field. Then the English archers in the rear (above 2000 men) advanced to the main body and decided the victory, which had been fiercely and at times very equally disputed for upwards of three hours. The loss of the allies was tremendous. The Earl of Douglas and his son, Lord James Douglas, the Earl of Buchan, Sir Alexander Meldrum, with many Scottish knights, were slain. The French lost the Counts Narbonne, Tonnère, and Vantadour, the Sires of Roche-baron and Gamaches, with many other great lords, and nearly 300 knights. The Duke of Alençon, the Marshal de la Fayette, the Sires de Maucourt, and Charles de Longueval, with many other lords, were taken prisoners. The Duke of Bedford cut off the heads of Maucourt and Longueval, because they had formerly taken the oath of fealty to his nephew; and he did the same to several knights of Normandy, because they had deserted from his standard on the eve of the battle.[1] The great loss he had himself sustained probably had something to do with these executions. Sixteen hundred Englishmen lay dead on that bloody field, mixed with 3000 or 4000 Scots, French, and Italians. The town of Verneuil immediately surrendered to the conqueror. Such was the battle of Verneuil, the last great victory obtained by the Duke of Bedford; it was fought on the 17th of August, 1424.

The cause of Charles now seemed hopeless; his army was destroyed, he had no money or credit, and many of his friends began to complain of his want of activity and valour, for he still kept away from the scene of danger. But circumstances operated wonderfully in his favour, and made him King of all France in spite of his follies. Dissension had broken out in the English council, where the Duke of Gloucester could never agree with his uncle Beaufort, Bishop of Winchester; and the English people had grown weary of this long war, which had once been exceedingly popular. At this moment (and we are disposed to believe on *most* occasions afterwards) Beaufort advocated measures of prudence and cautious policy, which were defeated by the impetuous will of Gloucester.

Jacqueline of Hainault, only daughter of the Count of Hainault, brother-in-law of Jean Sans-peur, inherited at a very early age the states of Hainault, Holland, and Zealand. Her succession was disputed by her uncle, John the Merciless, Bishop of Liége, who invaded Holland. After a long war, the Duke of Burgundy, Jean Sans-peur, interfered, and concluded a treaty, by which the Bishop of Liége was to enjoy the revenues of Holland and Zealand. John the Merciless had previously shed a great deal of Christian blood in order to remain Bishop of Liége. But soon after this arrangement he got himself secularized by the pope, and throwing away crozier and stole, married Elizabeth of Luxemburg, the widow of the Duke of Brabant, who had perished at Azincourt. This Elizabeth had a son, now Duke of Brabant, and the ex-bishop proposed that he should be married to his niece Jacqueline. This union, as tending to unite the different branches of the house of Burgundy, was strongly recommended by Jean Sans-peur and other members of the family; but the young lady had a great aversion to the match. John of Brabant was younger than she: they were cousins-german; and she, besides, had been the boy's god-mother. The pope, however, gave his dispensation, and Jacqueline was tormented into a compliance with the family scheme. But her antipathies were never overcome: she was of a womanly age, beautiful, bold, and not deficient in wit and understanding; her husband was a puny boy of fifteen, weak in mind as in body, fond of the society of low favourites, and entirely led by them. Shortly after their marriage they quarrelled violently; and Madame Jacqueline, who had a summary way of proceeding, sent her half-brother, called the Bastard of Hainault, to punish her husband's chief favourite, William le Begue, who had insulted her. The Bastard killed the favou-

---

[1] *Monstrelet.*

rite in his bed. But the young duke chose a new confident, and continued to be ruled by a set of vulgar servants; and the court was continually disgraced by domestic broils. On an unlucky day the young duke, by the advice of his favourite, drove away all the ladies that waited upon his wife, and exiled them to Holland. On this insult, Jacqueline withdrew to Valenciennes, and thence to Calais, where the English received her with great honour. From Calais she passed over to England, and sought an asylum and the protection of the court. This was in 1421, while Henry V. was still living; and at the end of that year she was residing in great friendship with Henry's wife Catherine at Windsor Castle. Jacqueline had not been long in England when she became enamoured of the king's brother, the Duke of Gloucester; and the duke, rather out of ambition than affection, proposed himself as her husband. Here another dispensation was necessary. On applying to Pope Martin V. it was found that he had been applied to by the powerful princes of the house of Burgundy, and was not disposed to annul the marriage with the Duke of Brabant, although Jacqueline alleged that she had been driven into that union by deceit and force. But it happened that there was another pope living; for Benedict XIII. would not submit to the decision of the council of Constance, and he readily enough granted a dispensation to the duchess. Jacqueline then married the Duke of Gloucester; on which the duke claimed as his own Hainault, Holland, and Zealand—all the states, castles, and towns which his wife inherited from her father. For some time no open measures were adopted for the recovery of Jacqueline's patrimony; and the Duke of Bedford, who had married the Duke of Burgundy's sister, contrived to keep that prince in apparent good humour, though in reality Philip had many misgivings, and intrigued under-hand long before venturing upon any overt act. A few weeks after the great battle of Vernenil, Gloucester and Jacqueline, with an English army of 5000 or 6000 men, landed at Calais; and, contrary to the advice of Beaufort, Bishop of Winchester, and in spite of the earnest representations of the Regent Bedford, these two ardent spirits led their forces through the territories of the Duke of Burgundy, and fell upon his cousin, the Duke of Brabant, in Hainault. At this time Jacqueline's uncle, John, ex-Bishop of Liége, died, and she was accused of having induced some of her partizans to poison him. Gloucester and his daring wife soon got possession of Mons, the capital of Hainault, where a strong party declared for her. At first the Duke of Burgundy thought that Gloucester was coming to reinforce his brother in France; but when he knew the direction he had taken he became perfectly furious, and sent orders to all his vassals to assist his beloved nephew the Duke of Brabant, and oppose the duchess and her new husband to the utmost. Gloucester, upon this, wrote to Duke Philip, telling him that if the Duke of Brabant was his cousin, his companion and wife Jacqueline was twice his cousin—that he (Gloucester) had not broken the peace or the treaties existing between him and his very dear cousin of Burgundy—that he was only taking possession of what lawfully belonged to him by his marriage—and he hinted, truly or falsely, that the Duke of Burgundy had formerly encouraged his projects. The duke replied by giving Gloucester the lie, and defying him to single combat. Gloucester readily accepted the challenge, and named St. George's Day for the duel, which Philip had no intention to fight. He sent a great part of the forces which he had engaged to keep on foot for the service of the Regent Bedford, into the Low Countries, against his brother, and at the same time the Duke of Gloucester obtained the English reinforcements intended for Bedford. Philip did not cool on reflection. He even employed troops and many knights that had been in the service of his great enemy Charles VII., the murderer of his father; and among these warriors was the celebrated Saintraille. The Burgundians thus began to listen to their old foes, and to join them in attributing (incorrectly) the origin of all the evils France was suffering to the English. Proposals were suggested for an accommodation with King Charles by the pope, the Duke of Savoy, and others; and though the Duke of Burgundy did not think, as yet, he had taken sufficient vengeance for his father's death, and though he did not openly abandon his brother-in-law the Duke of Bedford till eight years later, he was from this moment a lukewarm and suspected ally. For about a year and a half Gloucester defied all the power of Burgundy, and maintained himself in Hainault; but then want of money, and a jealousy of his uncle Beaufort, induced him to return to England. His departure was fatal to the interests of his wife: Valenciennes, Condé, and Bouchain opened their gates to Duke Philip; and Jacqueline was besieged in Mons, the citizens of which soon delivered her up to the duke, who committed her to a close imprisonment in his palace at Ghent.[1]

Gloucester's return to England was attended by other disastrous circumstances. His quarrel with Beaufort rose to such a height that a civil war seemed imminent; and the Duke of Bedford was obliged to leave France at a very critical moment, and come over to London at the end of

---

[1] *Monstrelet; P. Henin; Barante.*

1425. By his authority and influence a reconciliation was effected, and the uncle and nephew were made to shake hands in the presence of a parliament assembled at Leicester. But the bishop immediately resigned the seals and prepared to go abroad.

During Bedford's absence the Duke of Brittany declared for the King of France, being induced thereto by his brother the Count of Richemont, whom Charles had recently named Constable of France. The constable was out of his reach, in the country beyond the Loire; but soon after Bedford's return to France he severely punished the duke by sending a formidable army into Brittany, that repeatedly defeated his forces, and compelled him to abandon his treaty with the King of France, and resume his allegiance to England.[1]

Meanwhile the errant court of Charles continued to be the scene of disgraceful intrigues, jealousies, and dissensions. Arthur, Count of Richemont, the new constable, complained, not without reason, of the conduct of the king's ignoble favourites; but the system which he adopted to correct this evil was truly atrocious. When he first joined the king the chief favourite was the Sire de Giac, who, with his wife, had had so great a share in the murder of Jean Sans-peur at Montereau. This wretched man he seized by night in his bed, set him half naked upon a horse, and gave him over to George de la Tremoille, Count of Guines, who carried him to Dun-le-Roi, and there had him thrown into the river with a great stone tied to his neck. Camus de Beaulieu succeeded to the now dangerous post of prime favourite, and the constable got rid of him by assassination. Seeing that Charles could not live without a favourite, the constable then recommended to his notice George de la Tremoille, a person whom he thought entirely devoted to his interest, and incapable of making himself too formidable. But Count Arthur was mistaken in his man: George de la Tremoille, who had married Madame de Giac, whose husband he had just murdered, because she was still very beautiful and very rich, was the most accomplished rogue in that profligate court. He was witty, insinuating, experienced in business and in war; and he soon obtained a greater ascendency over the frivolous king than any preceding favourite. As soon as the constable discovered his mistake, he made a league with the Count of Clermont, the Count of la Marche, the Marshal of Boussac, and others, to destroy him; but La Tremoille was well versed in the ways of treachery: he declined an interview to which they invited him, kept himself with the king close in a strong castle, and laughed at the conspirators, who were obliged to disperse at the approach of winter. Charles then passed a sentence of banishment against the constable, who thereupon took up arms against him in conjunction with several princes of the blood. In the spring of 1428 these allies surprised the town of Bourges, but neither the king nor Tremoille was there. The constable retired into Poictou, and there kept up the civil war. At the same time another great royalist and patriot, the Marshal of Severac, threatened to desolate Languedoc with fire and sword unless the king paid him certain arrears; and the king and the treasurer had only four crowns between them. The Count of Foix took forcible possession of Beziers, and René of Anjou, a brother of the queen, negotiated on his own account with the English.

These brief details will render it perfectly intelligible how, during the six years that Charles had been a king, no progress had been made against the English, who were now determined to cross the Loire, and carry their conquests farther than Henry V. had ever penetrated.[2] The miserable state of weakness to which their recent chastisement had reduced him, more than any reliance on the treaty which he had signed, made the English feel sure of the Duke of Brittany, whose states extended along the right bank of the Lower Loire, and whose forces, under other circumstances, might have embarrassed them on their right flank and on their rear. At the same time, they felt a renewed confidence in the Bourguignon party; for Duke Philip returned to Paris, and had a friendly interview with the Duke of Bedford, being much pleased at having been permitted to settle the affairs of Madame Jacqueline after his own fashion. That wife of two husbands, who had some of the essentials of a heroine of romance, escaped from her prison in Ghent, and fled, disguised as a man, into Holland, where a strong party immediately took up arms for her. The Duke of Burgundy soon pursued her in the name of his cousin and her husband, the Duke of Brabant. The Duke of Gloucester contrived to send some money and a small force of archers to her aid. The archers landed on one of the islands of Zealand, and were well nigh taking the Duke Philip prisoner; but they were overwhelmed by superior force, and after a fierce battle, in which the duke lost many of his best knights, they were driven back to their ships. Philip took may towns—for he also had a faction in his favour— and then withdrew into Flanders to collect a great army. Jacqueline tried to retake the towns; and she commanded in person at several sieges and in several battles, making

---

[1] Rymer; Daru.

[2] Monstrelet; Juvenal; P. Hênin; Villaret; Barante.

knights and performing all the offices of a warrior and a prince. Her party however declined; the Duke of Bedford and the council prevented Gloucester from lending any further assistance; the Duke of Burgundy advanced again into Holland with an immense force well provided with artillery; town fell after town, and she was obliged to retire into Friesland. At the same time the thunders of the Vatican rolled over her head. The pope Martin V., whose authority was now generally recognized by the Christian world, declared that her marriage with Gloucester was null and void; and that, even in case of the death of her first husband, the Duke of Brabant, she could never lawfully be the wife of the English prince. The Duke of Gloucester consoled himself for this disappointment by marrying Eleanor Cobham, daughter to Lord Reginald Cobham—"which Eleanor before was his wanton paramour, to his great reproach, as was then noted."[1] But, though abandoned by her plighted knight, the husband of her choice, and threatened by the pope, the daring Jacqueline maintained the struggle; nor did her first husband, the object of her hatred, live to triumph over her. The Duke of Brabant died in the month of April, 1427; he was succeeded in his hereditary state of Brabant by his brother; but the Duke of Burgundy kept his hold of Holland and Hainault, the inheritance of Madame Jacqueline. A great naval victory, which the duke gained over William de Brederade, Jacqueline's admiral, completed the ruin of her affairs: and in the summer of 1428 she was obliged to submit to a harsh treaty. She agreed to recognize her dear cousin as direct heir to all her dominions—to give him the government of them all immediately—never to marry without his consent—and to satisfy herself with the revenues of Ostrevand, Veveland, and Brille. Duke Philip rejoiced in the success of his arms and his policy; and as he could not but feel that the English might have frustrated his scheme, he for a while was in good humour with them, engaging to furnish troops for the great enterprise of subduing the country beyond the Loire.

Ever since the English had been in possession of Paris, the city of Orleans, advantageously situated on the Loire, had been considered as the centre of the kingdom. Whatever fragments of prosperity remained were gathered within its walls; its fall would have the most fatal effects on the cause of independence; and the best road to the provinces of the south lay through it. It was, therefore, determined to reduce it by siege or blockade; but this project had been imprudently divulged, and the Earl of Salisbury lost many weeks in reducing a number of insignificant places in the neighbourhood, instead of marching at once to his object; and the French people, who were fully sensible of the life-and-death importance of the town, made the best use of this time in preparing for its defence. The season was far advanced before Salisbury appeared; but at last, on the 12th of October, he took up his positions both on the right and left bank, and began the difficult operation of girding in a large and populous town, in the best possible state of preparation, with a small army of 8000 or 9000 men. The inhabitants had provided themselves with all sorts of warlike stores and provisions, being determined to defend the place to the last extremity. The people of Orleans were well seconded by the inhabitants of other towns upon the Loire or behind it; for the burghers generally were good Frenchmen, and did not, like the princes of the blood and the great lords, lose their patriotism in jealousies and broils. Bourges, Poitiers, La Rochelle, and other places, sent provisions, money, and troops. The three estates met at Chinon, and voted an aid of 400,000 francs. The king also was roused from his lethargy; and as La Tremoille, and all the royalists about him believed that the fall of Orleans would be followed by the loss of all France, very unusual exertions were made. Charles named the Sire de Gaucourt governor of Orleans; and Saintraille, De Guitry, Villars, and many other captains of name, threw themselves into the town before the English appeared.[2]

Unappalled by all these circumstances, the Earl of Salisbury began the attack of the place, and his first plan seems to have been to take it by assault. A strong bridge communicated between the left bank of the river and the town, and the entrance to this bridge was defended by a fortress called the Tourelles, of which Salisbury determined to make himself master. The English scaled the walls, but were repulsed more than once with considerable loss. Salisbury, however, persevered, and, on the 23d of October, he carried the Tourelles by storm. But, in the interval, the besieged had broken down an arch of the bridge, and raised a new fort at the other end of it in advance of the city walls. Why the English general should have chosen to make his attack on this side, with a wide river between him and the town, when two sides of the triangle on the right bank[3] presented no such obstacle, we are at a loss to determine; but the bridge, as a passage, was now given up. The Bastard of Orleans,[4] the bravest and best officer in Charles'

---

[1] *Stow.*

[2] *Monstrelet; Journal du Siège; Barante; Villaret.*
[3] Then, as now, Orleans covered an irregular triangle, the base of which was along the river bank.
[4] He was the natural son of the Duke of Orleans, killed by order of Jean Sans-peur.

service, broke through the English lines on the opposite side of the river, and got into the town with numerous reinforcements, composed of French, Scots, Italians, and Spaniards. Salisbury saw that he must proceed by blockade. A few days after, as he was examining the town from the tower of the Tourelles, he was wounded in the face by a stone-shot, which killed the gentleman behind him on the spot. The earl survived a week, and then died, to the great regret of the army, who considered him as one of the most skilful and fortunate in arms of all the English captains. The Earl of Suffolk succeeded to the vacant command. It was now the month of November, and the weather was inclement; but the English built themselves huts, which were covered from the fire of the town by banks of earth, and there they were tolerably well supplied with provisions, and occasionally reinforced. But their number was insufficient to surround the whole town, and maintain constantly the passage of the river; boats occasionally ascended or descended with provisions for the besieged, and convoys of stores and fresh troops stole from time to time into the city.

Thus passed the winter months. Early in February, the Duke of Bedford collected about 500 carts and waggons from the borders of Normandy, and the country round Paris; and these the merchants were ordered to load with provisions, stores, and other things for the use of the army before Orleans. When all was ready, Sir John Fastolfe was appointed to escort the convoy with 1600 men. Sir John marched out of Paris on Ash Wednesday, and proceeded in good order until he came near to the village of Rouvrai, between Genville and Orleans. Here he was brought to a halt by intelligence that an army of French and Scots, 4000 strong, occupied the road before him. Making the best use of a short notice, Fastolfe formed a square with his carts and waggons, leaving but two openings; he posted his archers in these two gaps, the men-at-arms standing hard by to support them. In this situation Sir John waited two hours for the coming of the enemy, who at last arrived with a great noise. It seemed to them, that, considering their superior numbers, and that the convoy consisted of not more than 600 real Englishmen—the rest being people of Paris and other parts—they could not fail of destroying them speedily, and making prize of the stores. Others, however, had their doubts and misgivings, seeing that their captains did not well agree as to how the battle should be fought; for the Scots insisted that they ought all to dismount and fight on foot, while the French were all for fighting on horseback. At last, each nation resolved to fight in its own way. The Constable of Scotland, his son Lord William Stewart, and all the Scots, dismounted and advanced impetuously to force the openings of the square; but the English archers shot so well and stiffly, that they were slain almost to a man. The Constable of Scotland and his son were killed fighting side by side; many Scottish knights of high repute also perished; and the Sires of Rochechouart, D'Albret, and other French lords, shared their fate. The defeat was perfect: the French who were on their horses, galloped from the field, upon which there remained about 600 dead, nearly all Scots. Sir John Fastolfe then refreshed his men, and marched on to Rouvrai, and from Rouvrai they departed in handsome array, with their convoy and artillery, armed with all accoutrements becoming warriors; and so they arrived in triumph before the walls of Orleans.[1]

King Charles, on learning the news of this defeat, was sick at heart; and the great vigour with which the English now pressed the blockade of Orleans made most of his party despair. At certain intervals, the Earl of Suffolk had erected strong posts called bastilles, and he now sunk ditches and drew lines from one bastille to the other, until the circumvallation was almost complete. Thus those within the garrison could no longer pass with the ease they had done between the bastilles, and their friends without could no longer throw in provisions. At the hideous prospect of famine, the citizens, with the consent of Charles, proposed to deliver the town into the hands of the Duke of Burgundy. They despatched, as their ambassador to the duke, a knight who was his personal friend, and who had recently fought for him in Hainault against Jacqueline. This was Saintraille, who, as well as his proposition, was joyfully received by Philip. But when they opened their project to the regent Bedford, he would not listen to it, saying that the prize ought to belong to the valour of those who had reduced Orleans to these straits. The Duke of Burgundy smiled, and acquiesced, but he immediately after left Paris in a very ill humour with the English.

In Orleans the patriotic citizens now felt the sharp pangs of hunger. In Chinon, where the court was residing, the greatest consternation prevailed; many of the lords withdrew; and if Charles himself did not flee into Auvergne, or the more distant province of Provence or Languedoc, it was owing to the counsels of his ill-treated but magnanimous wife, Mary of Anjou,

---

[1] Hume, following some of the French historians, lays the blame of this mischance on the Scots, who, he says, would not wait the sure effect of the artillery which the French had with them, but insisted upon charging. It does not, however, appear that the French had a single cannon; whereas Monstrelet particularly mentions Fastolfe's artillery, though he does not say it was used during the battle.

and the stormy opposition of the brave Bastard of Orleans. One day in the end of February, shortly after the battle of Rouvrai, when Charles' affairs were at the lowest ebb, there came messengers from the town of Fierbois, about five leagues from Chinon, to tell him that the deliverer of France was at hand, and only waited at Fierbois for permission to be admitted into his presence. This deliverer was neither prince, warrior, nor statesman; it was a poor country girl—Joan of Arc.

It would be marvellous, indeed, if the story of a miraculous interposition and a succession of miracles were not embarrassed with much doubt and confusion. We may, however, safely assume the following positions, which have been held by most modern historians:—1. That there was no supernatural agency in the case, though Joan thoroughly believed that there was. 2. That her heated imagination, acted upon by the miseries of France, by current superstitions, and aided by a peculiar temperament of body, raised the visions she saw and the voices she heard. 3. That her object was pure and glorious, entitling her in all ages to the name of a patriot and liberator. 4. That there was no previous collusion between Joan and King Charles, or between her and any of the king's friends, though some of the latter wisely determined to make the most of a delusion in which they themselves never believed.

On first receiving the strange message from Fierbois, Charles burst into a fit of laughter. He, however, consented that the wonderful maiden should come to him at Chinon; and Joan arrived in man's attire, attended by two squires and four servants. But, in the interval, the people about Charles had forced some serious reflections upon him, and he refused to admit her into his presence. For three days consultations were held on the subject: some said that if he accepted such unusual aid, the English would instantly accuse him of putting faith in sorcery, and leaguing himself with the devil; others said, that it would be dishonourable to the noble kingdom of France, and productive of mockery, to send forth a peasant wench as their champion. Some maintained that the king ought not to trust himself in a personal interview with a mad woman; but others thought that it would be well to hear what she could say, and to send trusty messengers into the district she came from, in order to ascertain the particulars of her history and previous conduct. All this time, Joan was lodged in the town of Chinon, where her strict morality and fervent devotion greatly edified the people, and made some impression even upon the immoral court. Her story, at the same time, spread far and wide; and, strange as was the narrative, there was little in it very startling to the common people in a credulous age; and there were six witnesses at Chinon to corroborate parts of it. Joan, who was then in her twentieth year, was a native of a wild and hilly district in Lorraine, on the borders of Champagne; she was born in the little hamlet of Domremy, about three leagues south of the town of Vaucouleurs. Her parents were poor peasants; and, from her earliest days, she shared in their rustic labours, receiving no other education than lessons of simple piety. The whole district was remarkable for the simplicity of manners and the devotion of the people. The curse of faction had extended even to that remote spot. Domremy was Armagnac; but the next village was Bourguignon; and the children of the two

HAMLET OF DOMREMY, AND HOUSE OF JOAN OF ARC.—From Laborde, Monumens de la France.

places used to fight and pelt each other with stones for the sake of these names. As Joan grew up from infancy, she was famed all over the canton for her great piety; and passing much of her time among the hills, tending flocks and herds, she there mused in solitude over the wondrous legends of saints and virgin martyrs. The passing traveller frequently brought news of the triumphs and oppressions of the English, and of the cruel war that was desolating the fertile plains of France; and occasionally the quiet marches of Lorraine witnessed the destructive progress of hostile bands. From her infancy, Joan had listened to these tales of horror, and the miseries of the land became mixed with her dreams of heaven. When she approached the age of womanhood, several singularities, both moral and physical, were observed in her, and she began to talk of visions and voices from another world. At first she saw a great light, and heard a voice, which merely told her to be wise and virtuous, and go frequently to mass. At this first warning, as she said afterwards, she took the vow of perpetual chastity. Then she saw the bright light again, and heard the voice, but the light at this time displayed angelic figures with wings on their shoulders; and one of these bright essences told her to go and succour the Dauphin of France. There was an old prophecy in the country, that France, after being ruined by a wicked woman, should be restored by a spotless virgin: it was easy to fix the character of the destroyer on Queen Isabella—Joan thought herself called to be the virgin deliverer. She represented, however, to the voices that she was but a lowly maiden, not knowing how to ride a war-horse or to conduct men of war; but the great voice who made himself known to her as St. Michael, assured her that faith and aid would be lent to her for that great end, and that she would be assisted by St. Catherine and St. Margaret. When her imagination reached this point, the two female saints appeared to her in the midst of the great light; she saw their heads crowned with glittering jewels —she heard their voices, mild and modest, and sweeter than music. The visions returned, but less frequently than the invisible voices, which she was very apt to hear when the bells of the church were ringing. When the voices had ceased, or the visions had departed, she was often found weeping, for that the angels of paradise had not carried her away with them. For a long time her parents had little faith in her visions, and they wished to cure her of them, by giving her a husband; but all proposals of this kind Joan rejected with horror. On a certain day, a troop of Bourguignons drove all the good people from Domremy, and burned their church. Joan with her family took refuge for a short time in a humble inn in the town of Neufchâteau, where she heard many more relations of the sad events that were passing in France. From this time her visions became more frequent; she said that her voices told her that she was the veritable virgin of the prophecy, and that she must go and conduct the dauphin —for so, according to her account, Charles was to be called until he was crowned—to Rheims. The voices had already instructed her to proceed, in the first instance, to the Sire de Baudricourt, commander at Vaucouleurs, who would provide her with the means of travelling to Charles beyond the Loire; and, in the summer of 1428, she resolved to go to that governor. Her honest father would as soon have seen her thrown into the Meuse, as travelling the country among wicked men-at-arms and camp-followers; but she had made a convert of one of her uncles, and in his company she travelled to Vaucouleurs. Baudricourt took her for one crazed, or for a vagabond impostor, and at first refused to see her, saying that she ought to be sent back to her father, in order to be well whipped. Joan, however, was not easily repulsed; and as the object of her coming made a great noise all over the country, the governor was in a manner obliged to grant her an audience. She told the worthy knight that she was sent to him by her Lord. "And who is your Lord?" said the governor. "The King of Heaven," replied Joan. This confirmed Baudricourt in his opinion that she was crazed, and he dismissed her with very little ceremony. The Maid remained with her uncle, who was a cartwright in the town of Vaucouleurs; and still the fame of her sanctity grew and spread, for she passed whole days in the churches—she fasted with great austerity—her life was spotless; and still she continued to assert that her voices urged her night and day to go and succour the noble dauphin, and conduct him to Rheims, there to be crowned and consecrated. At length Baudricourt con-

HOUSE IN WHICH JOAN OF ARC WAS BORN, as existing in 1812.—From Laborde.

fronted her with a priest well armed with stole, crucifix, and holy water; and this clerk adjured her, if she were an evil spirit, to depart from them. Joan crawled on her knees to embrace the cross—a sure sign that she was no witch or sorceress. A short time after this, John of Nouvelourpont, surnamed De Metz, a gentleman of the neighbourhood, met her, and said it was time to think of seeing the king driven out of France, and of becoming every man an Englishman. Joan answered, in a tone of inspiration, that since the Sire of Baudricourt would not give ear unto her, she must make the journey to Charles on foot, even though she wore her legs down to her knees on the road; for, she added, it is neither kings nor dukes, nor yet the daughter of the King of Scotland, that can raise up this suffering France. "There is no help but in me. My *voices* have said it. And yet, in sooth, would I rather stay at home and spin at my mother's side; for this is not work that I have been used to; but I must go, and I must do, since my Lord so wills it." "Who is your Lord?" asked De Metz. "He is God!" answered Joan. De Metz was converted by her enthusiasm, and so was his friend Bertrand de Poulengi: the town's-people had been believers long before. There were some other portents and signs given by Joan, and nearly all Lorraine believed that she was deputed by Heaven; but Baudricourt, even to the last, seems to have doubted of her sanctity. Things, however, were at that desperate pass which makes men catch at straws. He gave permission to John of Metz and Bertrand of Poulengi to conduct her to Charles. The people of Vaucouleurs eagerly furnished Joan with everything she wished. The voices had long before told the Maiden to put on man's attire; and this she now did, and put spurs to her heels. They bought her a horse, and Baudricourt gave her a sword. When everything was ready for her departure, the governor received the oaths of the two squires, that they would faithfully conduct her to the king. Then Joan mounted her horse, and rode away, followed by the squires and four servants mounted.

It was on the 15th of February when the Maid began her long and dangerous march through a country almost entirely occupied by the English or by the Bourguignons, and many were the perils she encountered. The servants, weary and vexed, had some misgivings as to the holiness of her mission; they fancied that, after all, she might be a sorceress; and more than once they thought of throwing her over a precipice. But she got safely to Chinon, as we have seen; and the accomplishment of such a journey seemed in itself a miracle. After three days of doubt, Charles consented to receive her; for messages had been brought from Orleans, imploring, for the last time, that he would aid his faithful city, and he saw no earthly means at hand. In this first interview, unabashed by the sneers of the court, Joan spoke with firmness, and in a tone which sounded very like prophecy, even to many incredulous ears. "Gentle dauphin," said she, "I am Joan the Maid. I come with a commission from the King of Heaven, to drive out your enemies, and conduct you to Rheims, where you shall receive the crown of France, which is your right." Charles took her aside, and spoke with her for a considerable time, in an under-tone of voice; and when she departed from him, he felt or feigned a conviction that it had pleased Providence to place the fate of France in the hands of that peasant girl. And from this moment it is clear that efforts were made, not only to spread her fame, but to add, by ingenious inventions, to the marvellousness of her whole story. Here lay the tricky part of the business; but it scarcely needed, for popular credulity might now be safely left to its own imaginings. Still, however, Charles or his ministers hesitated ere they would commit themselves by proclaiming that Joan was to be their deliverer. In order to ascertain that there was no magic or sorcery in the case (for the least credulous seemed to have entertained a dread of this kind from the beginning), they delivered Joan over to a commission of priests, among whom were some who boasted that they could detect the devil under any disguise. These seekers found no diabolical indications. But Tremoille and the chancellor had still some doubts. Charles, therefore, went from Chinon to Poictiers, where his parliament was assembled, and where there was besides a learned university. The king ordered that the Maid should be conveyed thither. Joan was growing weary of these long processes, and she had some dread of the doctors' bonnets; but, saying that she trusted in God to give her speech to convince the doctors, she went willingly to Poictiers. The monomania of this wonderful creature was free from all extraneous extravagance; she never varied in her story; she spoke with a natural eloquence and (admitting only her premises) with much good sense. She had an excellent notion of what was meant by heavenly assistance. "But," said one of the doctors, "if God wishes and intends to deliver France from her enemies, where is the use of our fighting?" "Let us fight," said Joan, "the help will come while we are fighting." They then asked her to give them some signs of her miraculous mission. "Not here," said Joan; "Poictiers is not the place: but send me to Orleans with as small a number of men-at-arms as you will, and I will give you a sure sign—the sign that I am to give is the raising of the siege of Orleans." When her examiners brought down their ponderous learning upon her, she said that she was an unlettered peasant—that she knew not the difference between letter A and letter B —but this she *did* know, God had sent her to raise the siege of Orleans, and to conduct the dauphin to Rheims. The doctors of both faculties were convinced or silenced. Then the bishops of the south of France were consulted; and Jacques Gelu, Archbishop of Embrun, composed a very learned tractate to prove by quotations from Scripture that God might still interfere directly in the affairs of kingdoms—that there was nothing wicked in Joan's wearing the culotte and the whole garb of a man, though it was contrary to a law in Deuteronomy, provided such things were pre-ordained, and necessary to the end in view—that it was not wonderful, when miracles had been wrought by means of beasts (witness Balaam's ass), that they should be wrought by a virgin, albeit of lowly condition. Indeed, he said, that God had very frequently intrusted his secrets to virgins in preference to other conditions of mankind; and here the erudite archbishop, as proofs, placed in curious juxtaposition the Virgin Mary and the Sibyls. It appears that it was well known in those days that a virgin could have no dealings with the devil: and a last and delicate proof was intrusted by Charles to the matronly inspection of his queen's mother and Madame Gaucourt. The report of the doctors to the council of state was, that they had neither seen, known, nor discovered any particular in that virgin that was not conformable with the character of a good Christian and true Catholic. When bishops, doctors, lawyers, ladies, had all made their inquiries, the soldiers would see how the Maid could sit a horse and wield a lance. Here Joan's early occupations, and the address they had given, stood her in good stead. They mounted her upon a charger, and she kept a firm seat; they put a lance into her hand, and she showed that she had a vigorous grasp and a good eye. Here, however, some little instruction was necessary, and this it appears was given to her.

As the English pressed the siege, and the people of Orleans still implored for aid, and requested that the miraculous Maiden might be sent to them, it was at last resolved to give entire faith to her mission, and adopt Joan as the forlorn hope of France. They gave her the rank and the proper staff of a general officer. John Daulon, a brave and experienced knight, who had long served the king, was placed near her person as her esquire; two pages and two heralds were added; and a chosen squadron of horse was placed under her immediate orders. They caused to be made a complete suit of new armour to fit her person; her sword was an ancient blade bearing the mark of five crosses, which she was said to have miraculously discovered in the church of St. Catherine at Fierbois. Her standard, which was made to her order, was white, dotted with *fleurs-de-lis;* on one side was figured the Almighty, on the other side were inscribed the words *Jhesus Maria.* Her charger was a snow-white steed; and when Joan first showed herself, mounted upon it, in her bright, new armour, and with her banner spread before her, the people could not sufficiently admire her noble and martial appearance. By this time the army of Charles was greatly reinforced; men flocked from all parts to have sight of the inspired Maiden; and a new enthusiasm, half patriotic, half religious, was awakened by the sight of Joan. The Maid set a bold and uncompromising face against the prevailing dissoluteness of manners; she drove away all the camp-followers, she made the men-at-arms confess their sins and take the sacrament, and she would not allow a soldier to follow her that had not performed these religious duties.

A great convoy of provisions was got together at Blois, and thither repaired, with the determination of escorting it to Orleans, Saintraille, Gaucourt, the Marshal of Boussac, the Sire de Raiz, La Hire, Ambroise de Lorré, and the Admiral de Culant. Joan of Arc joined these renowned men of war in the month of April, and insisted that they should shape their manœuvres according to the inspirations which she had received, or which she might receive, from her voices. The captains, however, thought that a little military precaution would not be amiss; and, while they pretended to obey her, they had recourse in most things to their own science and experience. Joan said that her voices ordered her to march straight on from Blois by the right bank of the Loire; but the chiefs, who knew that the English troops were more numerous and better posted on that side, deceived the Maid, passed the troops over to the left bank, and got ready a convoy of boats to carry the provisions; and while Joan and the miraculous part of the expedition made way by water, they were flanked by an immense body of horse that kept close to the river. As they approached Orleans the garrison sallied out, and fell upon the besiegers with unusual vigour, shouting "The Maid! the Maid is come!" Favoured by this diversion, Joan, with the provisions and a powerful reinforcement, got into the town a little after night-fall, and Orleans was saved.

The English camp was now as sad as the city of Orleans was joyous: the soldiers had borne the risks and privations of a long siege without murmuring, but their bold hearts were not proof against the terrors of superstition. For two months they had heard of nothing but the miraculous Maid; they knew that she had caused a letter to be written to their chiefs, telling them that she was coming, commissioned by Heaven to drive them out of France; and she had come at last, and by provisioning Orleans, had already performed one of her miracles. It was in vain that the Earl of Suffolk and the other captains tried to check this despondency—in vain represented the whole affair as a miserable juggle got up by their enemies—in vain spoke of the disgrace the dauphin and his people incurred in setting up a low-born woman as their champion. When the best of their knights had been beaten in every battle, could the fools hope to turn the fortune of war, and overcome English valour, by means of a cow-driving girl? These and the like arguments had no effect; but it was otherwise with another assertion they made. They said that Joan was not an envoy from heaven, but from hell—that she was a foul sorceress, working by spell and witchcraft. This had a very bad effect, for it agreed with their notions of things; and the men said, that, as brave soldiers, they would fight any earthly enemy, but that they were unequal to a contest with the powers of darkness. The consequence was inevitable; they began to see strange sights in the clouds; the sentinels were startled at night by strange sounds; some saw figures on horseback galloping through the air; others were quite sure that the moon and the stars were getting out of order. But, at the same time, there were other material causes working on the side of this supernatural dread. Flemings, Burgundians, Picards, nearly all the people of Duke Philip had stolen away from the siege; when the lines were once broken or overawed, continual reinforcements poured into the town until there were many more fighting men within it than without. An army constantly recruited lay at Blois. The English, receiving no succour, must evidently from besiegers become besieged; and this soon took place. The Maid of Orleans —for such was the title now given to Joan— would have sallied in full force the very day after her arrival, to fall pell-mell on all their positions; but this was opposed by the Bastard of Orleans. A large reinforcement was expected from Blois; and the garrisons of all the places which held for King Charles received orders to march out, to unite their forces, and to fall upon the English lines. The Bastard and the Sire Daulon undertook to go to Blois to hasten the march of the forces assembled there. On the following day, Joan, with La Hire, and a good part of the garrison, rode out of Orleans to escort them on the road to Blois. The bewildered English let them pass; indeed, they no longer attacked anything, but remained in their wooden towers or bastilles. In this manner the Maid was permitted to re-enter Orleans as freely as if there had been no siege. She had already caused to be written, in her name, a strange letter to the enemy, and now she determined to address them by word of mouth. Mounting on the wall opposite to the tower at the end of the bridge, which was occupied by the English, she raised her voice like a prophet of old, and bade them all begone out of France, or woe and shame would befall them. Sir William Gladesdale, who commanded in the tower, replied with words of abuse, calling her a leman, and the French miscreants, to follow such a base leader, and telling Joan to go back and take care of her cows. Within the town Joan was still revered as an angel from heaven—at least by the common people—and her conduct was calculated to preserve and strengthen this feeling. She took extreme pains to check the immoralities and indecencies of the town and army; and certes, says one of her chroniclers, there was much to do in this way. At times, she paraded through the city mounted on her white charger, preceded by the sacred banner, and followed by her chaplain and a long line of priests bearing crosses and relics. The poor people who came trooping in from all the country round about crowded upon her path; and when they could not have the felicity of touching her hand, or knee, or foot, they were happy at being able to touch the horse she rode on.

All warlike operations were wisely suspended until the return of the Bastard, who, in a few days, was seen marching along the right bank of the Loire with a complete army. At this welcome sight Joan made a sortie with a great part of the garrison to meet him, and make his way more easy. The English remained motionless in their bastilles, and let her pass. Some of the men cried "There goes the witch;" but others began to think that, after all, her marvellous power might be from above. The Bastard's reinforcement entered Orleans preceded by Joan and the priests. The Maid was told that Sir John Fastolfe was again on his way to Orleans with troops and provisions for the besiegers. "Bastard," said the Maid, "in God's name let me know when he cometh, that I may deal with him." The Bastard assured her that she should receive timely notice. "If I do not," said Joan, "and if this Fastolfe pass without my knowing it, I will cut off your head." On the same day, Joan, who had lain down to rest, suddenly awoke, sprung from her bed, and called for her arms. Her voices, she said, told her to go out and fight the English, but whether they meant the reinforcements under Fastolfe, or the English in the bastilles, she knew not. She took her banner in her own hand, and rode to one of the gates. Here she saw a wounded man brought in. "Ha!" she exclaimed, "I can never see the blood of a Frenchman without my hair standing on end." Here also she learned that an irregular sortie had been made, and that the French had been repulsed in an attack on one of the bastilles. She instantly resolved to head a fresh attack in person; and, as the moment was favourable, the Bastard hurried to join her in force. The Maid led the assault; the French followed her with enthusiasm: and, after a desperate fight of three hours, the bastille of Saint-Loup was carried. No quarter was given; but Joan tenderly regretted that so many English should perish without confession and absolution. On the next day there was no fighting, because it was the festival of the Assumption of the Blessed Virgin; but Joan caused another letter to be thrown into the English lines, and stood on the ramparts to hear what they would say to it. They called her so many foul names, that she wept with shame and vexation; but she presently said, that her invisible voices spoke comfort to her ear, and brought her news from heaven. The plan now adopted proceeded, however, not from her miraculous inspiration, but from a council of war. It was resolved to make a feigned attack on the right bank; and while the English were gathering on that side, to fall suddenly upon the bastilles on the left bank. Although this combined movement was awkwardly executed, Joan crossed the river, took one of the bastilles by assault, and passed the night on the left bank. On the following day she had a furious quarrel with Gaucourt, the governor of Orleans, and other great captains, who still wished to proceed cautiously, while Joan insisted, that, without caring for the right bank, the whole might of the French should be poured out on the left to reduce the formidable position of the Tourelles. Gaucourt would have opposed her will by open force, but the people of the town and the common soldiers, who were all for the Maid, rose against him, threatening him with death. Joan, therefore, had her way; and while she fell upon the Tourelles from the land-side with an overwhelming force, the citizens attacked from the side of the river in boats and from the bridge, which they had repaired with planks and trunks of trees. The grand assault commenced two hours before noon; but notwithstanding their superstitious fears, the English fought most bravely, and repulsed their countless assailants. Another assault was made; but again the French were slaughtered in the breach, or hurled from the wall. The fire of their guns, and still more the flight of the English arrows, several times cleared both bank and bridge. About two hours after noon, when the French seemed quite disheartened, Joan herself planted a scaling ladder, and mounted the wall: she was struck by an arrow in the neck, and fell as if dead into the ditch. The difference of half an inch would have made all the difference between victory and defeat: the arrow wound was not mortal, and Joan was drawn out of the ditch by a valiant knight, and carried to the rear. While they were drawing out the arrow, she yielded to the weakness of her sex, and shrieked and wept; but when the first anguish was assuaged, she fell into earnest prayer, and then she heard over all the din of battle those voices that were sweeter than music. The English, who believed her dead, were confounded at seeing her presenting herself again at the edge of the ditch, urging on the French to the assault. They now felt assured that she was more than mortal; and as the superstitious panic spread, some of the men fancied they saw St. Michael the archangel, the patron saint of the city of Orleans, riding on a white horse, and fighting for the French. But what, perhaps, was even worse than this, in a military point of view, was the notable circumstance that they had used nearly all the gunpowder and arrows they had with them in the fort. Thus reduced to comparative inaction, the English were assaulted from the bank and from the bridge at the same moment. After defending the post like lions, Sir William Gladesdale and all his knights were slain. Then the French became masters of the tottering walls of the Tourelles, which were heaped within and without with piles of dead bodies. Scarcely an Englishman of any condition whatever escaped, but for every one that fell, there had fallen at least ten Frenchmen; so that Joan's miracle was not achieved without cost. That night a council of war was held in the English camp; and the Earl of Suffolk, Talbot, and the other captains, agreed that the siege should be raised. They were, however, most anxious to preserve the high military reputation of their country which had been won in so many fields; and as morning dawned, they left their towers and entrenchments, and drew out in open array, hoping to tempt the triumphant army within Orleans to come forth and give them battle. Inferior as they were in numbers, they were quite ready to face Joan—whether harlot, witch, or prophetess—if she would meet them on a fair field. Joan was willing enough to gratify them in this respect, but she was suffering from her wounds, and had no intimation from her celestial voices. After waiting for some time, the English burned or blew up their works, and marched on the road to Paris. retiring in perfect order with their colours proudly flying. Thus was raised the memorable siege of Orleans, on the 8th of May, 1429.[1]

Suffolk did not retreat far. Leaving the Paris road, he threw his men into different castles in the neighbourhood of the Loire, and then, trusting

---

[1] Hist. de la Pucelle; Monstrelet; Villaret; Barante.

to the arrival of reinforcements from the Duke of Bedford, he shut himself up in Jargeau, only a few miles from Orleans. But he was attacked sooner than he expected. As soon as the siege was raised, Joan went from Orleans to meet King Charles. She was received with great honour by the court; and the courtiers proposed to regale her with feasts and entertainments. But Joan told them it was no season for piping and dancing—that there was much work to do—and that she had but a short time upon earth to do it. It is said she predicted that she would die within a year.

Charles now was induced to put on his armour, and to show himself to his people as an active soldier for the first time in his life. He collected all his forces on the right bank of the Loire. Within four weeks, the white banner of the Maid was unfurled before Jargeau, and in ten days it was planted on the tower of that fortress. In this affair the Earl of Suffolk was made prisoner, and Joan had another narrow escape; for, as she mounted to the assault, she was struck on the head, and precipitated into the ditch. The Lord Talbot drew out the troops from the castles and garrisons in which they had been placed by Suffolk, and continued the retreat towards Paris. After taking possession of the places thus vacated, the French pursued him. Being met by a reinforcement of 4000 men, Talbot halted at Patay, but the French also were reinforced from every side, and even the disgraced constable, the Count Richemont, marched with an army of Bretons to join the king, against whom he had so recently waged war. Charles remembered how the count had murdered his favourites; and Tremoille was still with the king, and the chief director of his council. So violent was the feeling against Richemont, that the king at first refused to receive him, and even sent him word, that if he approached, he would cause him and his troops to be attacked as though they were English. There were, however, prudent men in the royal camp, who thought that past grievances ought to be forgotten; and most of the knights and esquires began to say that they would much rather follow an approved warrior like the Breton count than all the Maids in the world. It was therefore decided, in spite of the king and Tremoille, that the constable should be welcome. There had been a whisper that Joan had undertaken to attack him in the name of Charles. When they met, the constable said to her, "Joan, they say you wish to fight me; I am ignorant whether you are from God or not; if you are from God, I fear you not—if you are from the devil, I fear you still less." These words made a great impression; for it was known that Richemont had a keen eye in matters of witchcraft, and that he had burned a great many witches in Brittany.

The majority of the French captains were still rather unwilling to risk a pitched battle with the English in the open field; they were awed by the great skill of the enemy in disposing their troops in such encounters, and by the recollection of Azincourt, Crevant, and Verneuil. "We had better wait," said they, "for more horse." "Have you good spurs?" said Joan—"ride on, in the name of the Lord, and conquer! The English are delivered over into my hands—you have but to smite them." And it was owing to the absolute will of the Maid, and the confidence the common men had in her, that the French were induced to fight the battle of Patay. Sir John Fastolfe, who had brought up the reinforcements, was of opinion that the English ought to decline the battle, and retreat to some strong fortress in their rear; and this because the men were disheartened by the recent occurrences at Orleans, and had not yet recovered from their superstitious fears. But Talbot thought it would be ridiculous and disgraceful to turn their backs upon the French, whom they had so constantly seen flying before them. The country about Patay was level and open, with nothing but a village or a young wood scattered here and there. Talbot, when aware that the French were approaching, made a movement, in order to derive advantage from a village and some thick hedges; but he was too late, and before he could gain the position his skilful eye had chosen, the van of the French army, led on by La Hire and Saintraille, charged into the midst of his moving columns, allowing them no time to form. The archers could not even fix their stakes, and they were mixed up with the enemy's horse before they could bend their bows. The main body of the French closely followed the van; and when they saw that it was not repulsed, and that the English were in such a disorder as they had never seen before, they also charged with great spirit and confidence. The division under Sir John Fastolfe turned and retreated without fighting. Those that remained with Talbot could never recover themselves or form with any effect. The archers were slaughtered in heaps; the horsemen spurred from the field, seeking safety in flight. The brave Talbot, who scorned such an expedient, was made prisoner, and with him were taken Lords Scales, Hungerford, and many other noble captains. Twelve hundred English remained dead on the field. The French were intoxicated with their unwonted success, and as proud of the battle of Patay as if they had gained it with an inferior force.[1]

Immediately after the battle, the Maid of Orleans rode to the king, who, though he had taken the field, still kept his person far from the scenes

---

[1] *Monstrelet; Mémoires de Richemont; Villaret: Sism.*

of actual warfare. She now insisted on his undertaking the journey to Rheims. Charles still hesitated, and many of the persons about him found good reasons for delaying the journey. It would be wiser, they said, to make sure of the ground they had gained, and reduce several strong fortresses on the right bank of the Loire which the English still held. They represented that the wide tract of country which lay between them and Rheims was almost entirely in obedience to the King of England or the Duke of Burgundy, and that such an expedition would be full of danger and difficulty. The Maid reproved them for their lack of faith: she told them that the relieving of Orleans was not an easy task, that Orleans had been relieved; that none of them expected to take the Earl of Suffolk, and yet Suffolk was their prisoner; that they had been afraid of fighting the battle of Patay, and yet that battle had been won; and, finally, she repeated her old assurances that she was guided by heavenly counsels, and that the powers intrusted to her knew no limits, as they were the powers of heaven. Seeing that no reinforcements arrived from England, and that Bedford was beginning to concentrate near Paris all the army that remained to him, Charles took heart, and resolved to follow the Maid to Rheims. He set out on his flying expedition with a considerable array, composed entirely of horse. La Hire and Saintraille led the van; the rear was formed of provincial gentlemen of no great name, and of respectable burghers from the cities of the south, who all rode their own small horses, and brought their own provisions. The important town of Auxerre made a submissive treaty. From Auxerre Charles marched to Troyes, in the hope that the weak garrison of 500 or 600 Bourguignons would surrender to his army of 800 or 900 men. But the Bourguignons shut the gates of Troyes, and bade him defiance. Charles was not provided with artillery, and his troops were not inclined to make an assault by sealing the walls. For five days he lay before the town doing nothing. During this time, most of his troops suffered cruelly from want of provisions; and the ill humour which arose had well nigh proved fatal not only to the expedition, but also to the Maid of Orleans, whom the men began to apostrophize as a foul impostor. Even many of the captains advised Charles to return, and the Archbishop of Rheims, who had never thought much of Joan's supernatural mission, now openly expressed his doubts and misgivings. The Maid was summoned almost like a criminal to the bar to give an account of herself to the royal council; but her earnest eloquence again relieved her from all dangerous suspicions, and she made the leaders of the army agree to storm the walls as best they could. On the sixth day they began to fill the ditch with bags of earth and faggots, and to prepare scaling ladders; but the citizens of Troyes were lukewarm in the cause of the Duke of Burgundy, and the priests of the town were numerous, influential, and inclined to the cause of the king. Chiefly by means of a certain Friar Richard, negotiations were opened with the besiegers, and Troyes was quietly surrendered to Charles. When Joan was about to enter the town, she was met by Brother Richard, who rapidly made many signs of the cross, and sprinkled holy water on the threshold of the gate; for the friar was not quite certain that she might not be an evil spirit, and the good people were sorely afraid of her. But as the Maid stood this proof, she was instantly proclaimed as an angel. Friar Richard then attached himself to the king's service, and induced, by his eloquent preaching, the people of several towns to declare for Charles. From Troyes, Charles marched to Rheims, where the people, greatly alarmed at all they heard of the miraculous Maid, rose in his favour, expelled all the officers and friends of Bedford and Burgundy, and threw open their gates at his approach. On the 15th of July, 1429, escorted by Joan and a host of priests, the French king made his solemn entrance into Rheims; and, two days after, he was anointed and crowned in the cathedral church. Next to himself, the most conspicuous figure in this ceremony was Joan of Arc, who stood close by his side, bearing aloft her white standard. When the king was crowned, she threw herself at his feet in tears, and all present wept when they heard the words she uttered:—"Gentle king, now is accomplished the will of God, who would have you come hither to Rheims, to receive your consecration, and show you that you are the true king, to whom the kingdom of France rightly belongs." Not one of the peers of France was present at this coronation; but the spontaneous joy and enthusiasm of the people gave to it the character of a national celebration.[1]

Joan had caused a letter to be written to the Duke of Burgundy a few weeks before, requesting or commanding him to attend the coronation of his lawful sovereign; and on the day after that ceremony, she again addressed Philip, with the full consent of Charles' ministers, who knew the differences and jealousies that existed between the duke and Bedford, and who hoped that he might be detached from the English alliance. Joan's letter, like all those written in her name, began with the words "Jhesus Maria," written under a cross. On the part of the King of Heaven, she required the duke to make peace, and live in friendship with the King of France:

[1] *Monstrelet; Chron. de la Pucelle; Documents and Original MSS.* quoted by Lebrun des Charmettes and Laverdy.

she told him that it was monstrous in him to make war against his cousin and liege lord, and to shed the blood of loyal and Christian Frenchmen—that if he loved war, there were the Turks whom he might go and fight. She added, in the name of the gentle king, that he, Charles, was ready and willing to be reconciled on any conditions saving his honour, and that the peace and happiness of France depended entirely upon him, Duke Philip. The duke was probably not much affected by this letter, but many of his soldiers were uneasy at a prediction in it—that they would never gain another victory so long as they fought on the English side. Joan and Friar Richard gained more towns and fortresses for the king than several brave armies could have done in the same short space of time. Wherever Joan carried her white banner, the people saw swarms of beautiful white butterflies fluttering about it, and so they opened their gates to the miraculous visitant. The friar was scarcely less prevalent—sometimes winning a triad of towns by one eloquent discourse in the pulpit.

Soon after his coronation, instead of being obliged to return to the Loire as he had expected, Charles was enabled to march from Champagne into the Isle of France. Town after town surrendered to him as he advanced. Where, however, the garrison was composed of native English, matters were not quite so easily managed, for their ignorance of his language made them proof against the sermons of Friar Richard, and they still held the Maid as a foul witch. At several places Joan narrowly escaped being made prisoner and burned. At the same time, notwithstanding the accomplishment of all her prophecies and the advantages they still gained through her, many of the French captains treated her with great coldness, and even with harshness; for they were weary of hearing every success attributed not to them, the flower of the chivalry of France, but to the Maid of Orleans. Some foul attempts were made to commit her character for modesty and chastity, but these Joan defeated with the rage of a tigress. It appears clearly that she now kept the field against her inclination, and an inward conviction that she had done all that she had been appointed to do. Immediately after the coronation, she besought Charles to let her depart in peace, now that he was consecrated at Rheims and her mission fulfilled. She several times repeated the request with tears in her eyes, but Charles always found good arguments to detain her; he resolved not to part with the Maid as long as her name and presence could be of any use to him. When Joan was asked what she proposed to do with herself, she said that she would return to her native village, to her father and mother, who longed to see her again, and that there she would tend the flocks and herds as she had done before. This modesty—this absence of all worldly ambition—gained her fresh consideration, and touched the hearts of some who had been disposed to consider her as a lucky impostor hunting after wealth and honours. Her voices, however, made themselves less frequently heard, and, as the operations became more complicated, they gave her contradictory suggestions; at least Joan frequently hesitated and varied in her opinions, which she had never done before.[1]

The Regent Bedford had done his best to prop the fast-falling dominion won by his great brother, but he was badly seconded by the government in England. In the council there was perpetual discord and dissension, kept up chiefly by the jealousy and hatred which existed between the regent's brother, the Duke of Gloucester, and his great uncle Cardinal Beaufort, Bishop of Winchester, who, after a short retirement, had resumed his post in the government. The national exchequer was poor and embarrassed. As there was no raising of troops without money, Bedford got no reinforcements, and he was obliged to weaken his garrisons in Normandy in order to keep on foot a respectable force at Paris. Now, however, he received a small army, which Beaufort had raised by his own means, and for a very different purpose. The cry for religious reform, which had been raised in England by Wyckliffe, was echoed in Bohemia and part of Germany, a few years after his death, by John Huss, an eloquent preacher, who formed a sect too powerful to be put down at once by the ordinary means of the gibbet, the block, and the faggot. The pope excommunicated them in a mass, and preached a crusade against them. All the Christian princes and people of Europe were invited to embark in this holy war, and the zealous Cardinal Beaufort got together 250 men-at-arms, and about 2000 stout English archers, whom, in spite of his years, he determined to lead in person into Bohemia for the uprooting of heresy. But when the cardinal landed on the Continent and saw the difficulties to which Bedford was reduced, he agreed, after some feigned hesitation, to join this force to the army of the regent. The coffers of the regent were empty. To fill them Bedford cast an eye on the rich possessions of the Church of France.[2] It was but a glance, and seeing the difficulties, he did absolutely nothing except give the alarm to a sensitive body. Hitherto he had had a strong party among the bishops and great abbots (the poor clergy were better patriots), but his friends now began to fall from his side, although at first secretly. The Duchess of Bedford, who

---

[1] *Monstrelet; Barante.*   [2] *Monstrelet.*

was sister to the Duke of Burgundy, exerted her influence to reconcile her husband and brother. Duke Philip went to Paris, and had another long and friendly conference with the regent: by mutual consent, the solemn treaties which bound them to one another were read in public, and so also was a circumstantial account of the atrocious murder of Jean Sans-peur on the bridge of Montereau. After a short visit, Duke Philip quitted Paris, leaving only a weak reinforcement of 700 men with the regent; and very soon after, when Charles was approaching Paris, he received an embassy from him at Arras, and listened anew to overtures for a separate peace. He found, however, that he could not yet make a sufficiently advantageous bargain, and many of his most powerful adherents were not yet in a state of mind to tolerate a reconciliation with the detested Armagnacs. Philip's plan now appears to have been to afford Bedford just such a degree of support as would prevent his being crushed, and never to give him force sufficient to strike a decisive blow. The regent could never collect more than 10,000 men; at times his army did not amount to half that number. The consequences of his weakening the garrisons in Normandy, and of Charles' advance to the same quarter, were inevitable. Insurrections broke out; great lords, who had made separate treaties with the English, took up arms for Charles; some towns overpowered their garrisons; others were taken by assault; and the banner of independence was planted in several important places on the Norman coast. Bedford had been obliged to make more than one march into Normandy to provide for the security of that most important conquest; but the time was now come when he must face King Charles, whose forces made incursions to the very gates of Paris. As he advanced from the capital, the French retreated and fled so rapidly that there was no coming up with them. There was a great want of money on that side also, and Charles proposed retreating to his old positions on the Loire, but his wife and the Maid reasoned against this measure, and the Bastard of Orleans and other captains vowed that they would not follow the king in that direction. Being unable to find Charles, Bedford sent him a letter. He reproached him with deluding the ignorant people by means of a female—an impostor and prostitute—and an apostate friar; he required him to give him a personal meeting: if it could be proved that any reliance could be put in the word of one who had betrayed the late Duke of Burgundy, and stained himself foully with blood, then he, Bedford, would be ready to conclude a peace on reasonable conditions; but otherwise he would fight him in single combat, in order that the quarrel might end, and the world see whose cause was the just one. To this letter Charles sent no answer. About the middle of August, when neither force expected it, the two armies came suddenly in sight of each other near Senlis. The English, who were very inferior in number, took up positions in front of the French. The French kept their ground, but would not attack, and the English were determined not to begin the battle. The French had become cautious in the field, had condescended to employ large bodies of archers, and had adopted much of the tactics and discipline of their enemy. Many of the hot-headed French knights wanted to attack, but when the more prudent captains cast their eyes along the English lines, and observed the firm countenance of the men, and the masterly arrangements of Bedford, they declared that this was not a thing to be thought of. Some cavalry was detached to skirmish round the positions of the English, in the vain hope of tempting the troops to leave them. Troops of horse rode out to meet these assailants, and many fierce encounters took place; but the rest of Bedford's army, though eager for the fight, obeyed the voice of their general, and remained motionless. Then the Maid was asked whether the French might quit their posts and engage; but her voices gave no consistent advice; and still Charles was unwilling to risk his crown in a general engagement of any kind. For three days the two armies thus lay facing each other, and then each marched off the field by its own road.

Bedford marched again into Normandy, which was invaded by the Constable Richemont. When he was at some distance, Charles turned round upon Paris, with the hope of taking it during the regent's absence. Beauvais, St. Denis, and other places in the neighbourhood of the capital, opened their gates to him, and, with the view of inducing the people of Paris to do the same, he published a general amnesty, and made the most brilliant promises to his good and loyal city. But the walls of Paris were defended by a small but determined garrison of English, and the populace had not yet made up their minds to receive the Armagnacs. It was then resolved to try the effect of force, and on the 12th of September an assault was made on the faubourg or suburb of St. Honoré. The Maid of Orleans was foremost in scaling the walls, but her white banner was no longer victorious; she was wounded and thrown down into the ditch, where her repulsed companions basely abandoned her. She crawled out of the ditch, and lay for some time alone among the dead. Then rising, she waved her banner, and cheered on the men to a fresh assault. The soldiers lost heart, and soon fell back by troops, until she was again left alone. Some better spirits, ashamed to see a woman stand her ground while the mass of the army skulked behind some mounds of earth, where they were safe from the enemy's fire, moved forward and tried another assault, but they were driven back in the greatest confusion and fled, forcing the Maid with them.[1] It was evident that Joan's influence was fast declining, and that even the common soldiers were no longer for her. A few days before the unsuccessful attack on Paris she had found some of the men committing shameful disorders, and she beat them soundly with the flat of her sword until the weapon broke in her hand. It was the miraculous blade marked with the five crosses, which she had discovered in the church of St. Catherine at Fierbois, and which she had worn ever since. She was grieved at the accident; but as for the soldiers, they were disposed to think that her virtue lay in her sword, and that it departed from her when that sword was broken. Besides, they were weary of her rigid system of morals. Captains as well as men laid the whole blame of their recent failure upon her. "You are a false prophetess!" they cried: "you said we should have slept this night in Paris." "And so you would," said Joan, "if you fought as I fought!" But she was not blind to what was passing; and smarting with her wound, and a keener pang within, she again resolved to withdraw from an army and court where she had experienced little else than ingratitude. She even went to the abbey church and hung up her suit of white armour before the shrine of St. Denis; but again Charles found arguments to convince her that she ought to remain, for he fancied that she might still be of some little use. The miscarriage before Paris was sure to produce a moral effect detrimental to his interests. Charles had always drawn his main supplies from the country beyond the Loire, and he began to find a difficulty in subsisting at a distance from those provinces. Money was as scarce as ever; for want of it his troops were deserting; and Bedford, having done his business in Normandy, was advancing by forced marches. Charles therefore began a retreat, and scarcely halted until he had the Loire between him and the English regent. Bedford, who reached St. Denis soon after Charles' departure, marched into Paris in triumph, and there he was soon joined by his brother-in-law of Burgundy, who gave him the most consoling assurances of fidelity, and kept up a correspondence with the friends of Charles in the neighbourhood, at one and the same time. Soon after Bedford found himself obliged to resign the regency of France to Philip, who was further gratified by the payment of a large sum of money.

Bedford withdrew to Normandy, where he retained the supreme command; and at the close of the year Philip left Paris for Flanders.

A.D. 1430. During the winter months there was a nominal truce between the Bourguignons and the party of King Charles; and negotiations for the settlement of all differences were carried on by means of the Count of Savoy, some envoys of the emperor, and other agents.[2]

Meanwhile Charles lay inactive at Bourges. Another miraculous woman was now presented, whose inspiration was wholly of a financial description. This was Catherine of La Rochelle, who promised the king an abundance of riches. Catherine did not pretend to fight, like Joan; her *forte* lay in preaching, and in extracting money for the use of the king from those who possessed any. She announced that she could tell at a glance all those who had hidden treasures. She also had her visions, but these were rude and material compared with the celestial visitations of Joan, for she saw nothing but the figure of a single lady covered all over with massive gold. In truth, the whole affair was a vulgar parody of Joan's ideal and glorious monomania. Joan accused Catherine of imposture; but Friar Richard, that other great warrior in this unmanly struggle, supported the new prophetess, and both declared a deadly enmity to the Maid of Orleans. During the winter months Joan laid siege to St. Pierre-le-Moutier and La Charité. The first she took after the display of all her former valour and enthusiasm, but she was repulsed at the latter.[3] At the opening of spring Charles moved from Bourges, and his army prepared to advance once more from the Loire to the Seine. It was accompanied by two prophetesses; for he did not think proper to dismiss Catherine of La Rochelle; and Joan, with banner and lance, marched with the van of the army to the neighbourhood of Paris.

After some unimportant skirmishes in the immediate neighbourhood of Paris, Joan marched to the relief of Compiegne, which was besieged by the people of Duke Philip. On approaching the town she found that the duke had come up in person, and that he was pressing the siege with his whole army, assisted by a body of English. She, however, fought her way into Compiegne. On the same day, the 25th of May, promising herself the same brilliant success which had attended her at Orleans, she made a *sortie*, and fell upon the enemy's lines. She surprised one of their positions and killed a great many men; but

---

[1] *Monstrelet; Lenglet; Hist. de la Pucelle; Barante.*

[2] *Barante; Villaret.*

[3] During the winter Charles had ennobled the family of Joan, and had declared that her native village of Domremy should be for ever exempt from taxes.

the whole Bourguignon force collected to a point and bore her back. With her usual intrepidity she threw herself in the rear of her now flying host, and she several times drew rein, and, rallying some of her men, faced about and fought, in order to check the pursuers. In this manner, fighting and retreating, she had nearly reached the edge of the town ditch, but there she was pulled from her horse by an archer, and her troops, without pausing to rescue her, fled over the drawbridge and closed the gate upon her. Joan rose and tried to defend herself, but her efforts were fruitless; she was surrounded by her enemies, her friends made no sally to save her, and so, at last, she surrendered to the Bastard of Vendôme, who carried her in triumph to the quarters of the Bourguignons. All the captains of the army ran to gaze at the prisoner, nor was Duke Philip the last. This prince went to the lodgings where she was confined, and spoke many words with her; "but what they were," adds Monstrelet, "I do not now recollect, although I was present." The wonderful news spread with the rapidity of lightning; the Bourguignons and the English sung *Te Deum*, as if a great victory had been obtained; the ungrateful French made no effort to effect the release of the heroine by ransom, exchange of prisoners, or any other means. Three days after her seizure she was claimed, not by the Duke of Bedford, as generally stated, but by Friar Martin, doctor in theology, vicar-general of the inquisitor of the faith in the kingdom of France. Martin, in right of the office he held under the pope, required that Joan, called the Maid, should be instantly sent to him, that she might be tried by the Holy Inquisition. The Bastard of Vendôme, to whom Joan surrendered, had sold his prisoner to John of Luxemburg, who, without heeding Friar Martin's letter, sent Joan to his strong castle in Picardy. The university of Paris then took up the cause, and wrote to the Duke of Burgundy, imploring him to cause the Maid to be delivered to the Bishop of Beauvais, in whose diocese she had been taken. The duke took no more heed of the letter of the university than the count had taken of that of the inquisitor. Then the Bishop of Beauvais, who was a great foe to witchcraft and a great friend of the English, took the cause into his own hands and sent apostolic notaries to signify to the Duke of Burgundy, in presence of his captains, that he must deliver up the Maid. A similar notification was served in the same manner on John of Luxemburg, who, after some months, sold Joan to the bishop for 10,000 francs.

In the interval Duke Philip had returned into Flanders, leaving the Sires de Brimeu, De Lannoy, and De Saveuse to prosecute the siege of Compiegne. But that place was strong, and well defended, and the siege was raised by the Marshal of Boussac, who came up with the principal army of Charles. The duke was detained in the Low Countries till the approach of winter. The emissaries of King Charles had stirred up his subjects of Liége to revolt; and when Philip, not without great loss, had reduced these to obedience, he became occupied by another disputed succession. As he was the strongest, he had the best of the argument, and he annexed Brabant to his other vast possessions. But while he was gaining these advantages in Flanders, he suffered defeat in France. He had concluded a treaty with the Count of Savoy, that former friend of Charles, who agreed to march an army into France, and to divide the south of that kingdom with the Duke of Burgundy. Philip sent an army into the provinces beyond the Loire, under the command of the Prince of Orange, who carried everything before him, and threatened Dauphiny, the Lyonnois, and even Languedoc. Those provinces, which had been so devoted to Charles, were exhausted by the long war, and could offer little resistance; but the royalists had secured the services of the celebrated Spanish adventurer Villandrada, who threw himself into the south with some companies composed of Spaniards, Portuguese, Italians, and Germans. These companies of adventure obtained a splendid victory over the Prince of Orange, who was obliged to evacuate the southern provinces. This defeat wholly disconcerted the scheme formed with the Count of Savoy. In the month of November the Duke of Burgundy returned into France, but he undertook no great enterprise, and winter was passed in petty skirmishes or in idleness.

A.D. 1431. Meanwhile Joan languished in prison; her friends forgot her; her enemies longed to reduce her to ashes. All the English, and at least one-half of the French, firmly believed that all she had done had been by the direct aid of the devil. So strong was this feeling in Paris, that they burned alive a poor woman of Brittany for merely saying that she believed Joan's inspiration proceeded from heaven. After being confined successively in the castles of Beaurevoir, Arras, and Crotoy, she was transferred, at the end of six months, to Rouen. The Bourguignons, as well as the English, clamoured for her death, and the learned doctors of the university of Paris represented that religion would be in danger if sorcery and dealing with the devil were permitted to go unpunished. The Bishop of Beauvais claimed the right of conducting her trial, and this claim was formally admitted and confirmed by the clergy of Rouen and the university of Paris. The Duke of Bedford was desirous that the trial should be conducted in such a manner as to make a great impression on the whole kingdom, and the Bishop of Beauvais summoned priests, and lawyers, and lettered men from far and near. Upwards of 100 doctors assembled to exercise their ingenuity in detecting impossible crimes; but some of these men grew weary of the long business, others were excluded by the bishop, and, towards the end, not more than forty sat in judgment. For sixteen days Joan was sharply interrogated by men who were ready to detect a lurking devil in everything she said, and who cross-examined her and twisted her words with all the adroitness of the schools. Though frequently puzzled by the long hard words they used, and by polemical demonstrations, to her perfectly unintelligible, Joan, unsupported by any one, pleaded her cause with great spirit, at times confounding the doctors with her prompt and clear replies and her plain good sense; for still, on all points but one, she was perfectly rational. Whenever the Bishop of Beauvais saw that her simple eloquence was producing an effect, he raised his voice angrily and silenced her. The principal object in view was to terrify or entrap her into an avowal that she had been labouring under an illusion, and that she now knew that the spirits which had appeared to her were spirits of darkness; but Joan maintained that they were angels from heaven, and that neither the devil, nor any of his ministers, could have power over a virgin like herself. Her judges thought that there must have been a deal of magic in her white banner, which had so often led the troops of Charles to victory, and raised such a panic among the bravest of the English and Bourguignons. Joan said that there was nothing about the banner but the blessing of God, and that she had used it fairly in battle as other combatants used their lances. When questioned touching her attachment to mother church, she said that her whole life bore witness in her favour; but they drew from her an assertion that she could not submit to the ministers of that church when her voices ordered the contrary. This was considered the worst heresy of all. The court drew up articles of condemnation and despatched them to the university of Paris, and to several French prelates of the highest rank. All the faculties of the university, and all the bishops consulted, agreed that Joan was heretical, and an impious impostor, and, as such, deserving death by fire. Several of her judges were, however, averse to burning, and, though the French writers pretty generally accuse the English of pressing for this execution, there is more evidence to show that they would have been satisfied with a public exposure and imprisonment for life. From the beginning, Joan's own countrymen of the Bourguignon faction were by far the most eager for her destruction.

After undergoing trying examinations in the court, the Maid was tormented in her cell by monks and confessors, who constantly represented that the church, which had tried her, was infallible in matters of faith, and that it was most merciful to those who recanted and submitted to its authority. These reasonings had their effect, and Joan was staggered at the array of bishops, doctors, and devout priests. She could hardly understand how such holy men could err; and though there was plenty of time for such a measure, the bishops and priests of her own or the royalist party, never set up a plea in her favour, or made any attempt to prove that she was a good Catholic. Indeed, Charles and his friends forgot her at once, as a thing that had answered its purpose and was no longer of any use. It was infamous in her enemies to burn her, but it was more infamous in her friends to abandon her in this manner. On the 24th of May, Joan was brought up to hear her sentence. It was known that her mind was already wavering, and every means was adopted to render the scene imposing and terrific, in order to induce her publicly to acknowledge her errors. She was placed on a scaffold in the cemetery of Saint-Ouen, and at a short distance stood a stake surrounded by faggots; the bishops and doctors sat in a gallery opposite to her, a Dominican friar mounted a high pulpit to preach, and the executioner stood close by with his cart. The church-yard was crowded with French and English soldiers and citizens of Rouen. The preacher dwelt with vehement oratory upon the damnable sin of heresy, hitherto so little known in France, and he expressed his horror and astonishment that so Christian a people as the French should have followed the delusions of an infamous loose woman. Joan listened in silence so long as the sermon turned upon her own character, but it was otherwise when the preacher attacked Charles, the man who "called himself king." "Speak of me," said the noble-minded enthusiast, "but sully not the fame of the king; he is good and royal; he is a Christian—the best in France." In the end Joan submitted; a paper, containing a confession and renunciation of errors was put into her hand, and, not knowing how to write, she signed it with a cross. Her punishment was commuted into perpetual imprisonment, and a penitentiary diet on the "bread of sorrow and the water of affliction." After being made to thank the church for its tender mercies, Joan was reconducted to her dungeon, where she put on the dress of her sex, as she had agreed to do, her male attire being considered as one of the most detestable features of her heresy. But when bishops, doctors, friars, executioner, and stake had disappeared, her cell was again illumined by the miraculous light, the saints and angels again appeared to her, and again she heard their voices floating on the stillness of night. She examined her own heart and felt that she was still unconvinced by the arguments of the church; that she had meanly yielded to force and terror. She recalled all her former glories—she longed again to have her foot in the stirrup and her hand on the white banner—to be once more fighting for the independence of her country. By accident or design, the dress of a soldier was left in her prison, and one morning Joan was discovered wearing it. This circumstance was considered a sufficient proof that she had relapsed into heresy, and then it was determined that she should die. Her firmness again forsook her when she was told that they were going to burn her alive; she said that she did not fear death by the sword, or the axe, or the rope, but that to be burned was too horrible; and she tore her hair and made loud lamentations. The Bishop of Beauvais asked her if she had heard her voices again? She replied that she heard them, and that they had told her she had done wrong to sign the paper presented to her by the churchmen. Even if it had been usual to show mercy to relapsed heretics, this would have been fatal to her. She was delivered over to the secular arm. On the 30th of May, seven days after her abjuration, she was put into the executioner's cart and carried to the old market-place of Rouen, in the centre of which was a stake, and on the sides of which were scaffoldings and galleries erected for the bishops, doctors, priests, captains, and other select spectators. At sight of the stake, and the faggots which they were heaping round it, she shuddered and wept; but by degrees she recovered her self-possession, and said that she hoped to be that night in paradise. The cart halted under the wooden gallery,

THE OLD MARKET-PLACE, ROUEN.[1]—From France Monumentale et Pittoresque.

on which were seated the great Cardinal Beaufort and the French bishops. A monk delivered a short discourse, which reproached her with her backsliding, and which ended with these words:—"Go in peace, Joan; the church can no longer defend thee!" She knelt and prayed aloud, fervidly, though in tears. Cardinal Beaufort could not bear this lamentable spectacle; he rose from his seat and left the market-place, followed by several bishops, all shedding tears like himself. They covered her with the infernal livery of the Inquisition, and fixed on her head a black cap, which bore this inscription, "Heretic, Relapsed, Apostate, Idolater." They then forced her to the centre of the square, tied her to the stake, and set fire to the faggots. As the smoke and flames rose round her, Joan[2] was seen embracing a crucifix, and the last word that she was heard to utter was the name of "Jesus."[3]

---

[1] This little square is now called *Place de la Pucelle*, in honour of Joan of Arc. A fountain in its centre, surmounted by a statue of the Maid, marks the spot where she was burned.

[2] "It is easy to trace the true character of Joan. A thorough and earnest persuasion that hers was the right cause—that in all she had said she had spoken the truth—that in all she did she was doing her duty—a courage that did not sink before embattled armies and beleaguered walls, or judges thirsting for her blood—a serenity amidst wounds and sufferings, such as the great poet of Tuscany ascribes to the dauntless Usurper of Naples—a most resolute will on all points that were connected with her mission, perfect meekness and humility on all that were not—a clear, plain sense that could confound the casuistry of sophists—an ardent loyalty, such as our own Charles I. inspired—a dutiful devotion on all points to her country and her God. Nowhere do modern annals display a character more pure, more generous, more humble, amidst fancied visions and undoubted victories—more free from all taint of selfishness, more akin to the champions of old times."—*Lord Mahon.*

[3] *Monstrel.; Chron. de la Pucelle; Villaret; Lebrun des Charmettes; Laverdy.* . . . . . M. Laverdy's work consists chiefly of extracts from ancient manuscripts in the Bibliothèque du Roi, at Paris, and contains full accounts of Joan's trials. The works of different kinds relating to the Maid are very numerous: M. Chaussard enumerates upwards of 400 expressly devoted to her life, or including details of her history. The fullest accounts of the Maid are derived from the revision of her trial, which took place twenty four years after her death, by command of the pope, who had been petitioned by Joan's mother Isabella. Many of the Maid's companions of all ranks, from the lowest to the highest, were at this time living, and bore witness to the purity of her life and the marvellousness of her exploits. As a strong reaction had taken place, and as no English witnesses were heard, the accounts of this trial may afford some room for cavil, but most of the facts may be safely admitted after a little deduction on the score of oratory and amplification. As a continuous narrative, full of the spirit and colour of the times, without any sceptical inquiry, and vividly dramatic, we know nothing superior to the story of Joan given by Barante in his *Histoire des Ducs de Bourgogne.*

CHAPTER IV.—CIVIL AND MILITARY HISTORY.—A.D. 1431—1461.

HENRY VI., SURNAMED OF WINDSOR.—ACCESSION, A.D. 1422—DEPOSITION, A.D. 1461.

Coronation of Henry VI. as King of France at Paris—The pageant unsuccessful—The Duke of Burgundy withdraws his alliance from England—His reconciliation with Charles the French king—Death of the Duke of Bedford—He is succeeded as English Regent of France by the Duke of York—Fresh victories of the English in France—Exploits of Talbot, Earl of Shrewsbury—Imbecile character of Henry VI. on reaching manhood—His marriage with Margaret of Anjou—Quarrels and factions in the English court—The Duchess of Gloucester tried and punished for sorcery—The Duke of Gloucester murdered—Death of Cardinal Beaufort—English reverses in France—The French recover the whole of their country except Calais—Causes of their success—Unpopularity of the Duke of Suffolk in England—He is banished, and irregularly executed—John Cade's insurrection—He effects an entrance into London—His defeat and death—Revival of the claims of the house of York—The Duke of York appears in arms—He is apparently pacified—Defeat and death in France of Talbot, Earl of Shrewsbury—Increasing imbecility of Henry VI.—The Duke of York appointed protector of the realm—Commencement of the wars of York and Lancaster—Victory of the Yorkists at St. Alban's—Political intrigues and insincere treaties that followed—The civil war renewed—Victory of the Yorkists at Bloreheath—Warwick, the "king-maker," their principal champion—The Duke of York openly claims the crown—He is satisfied with a compromise—His defeat and death at Wakefield—Atrocities of the Lancastrians after the battle—Edward, eldest son of the Duke of York, succeeds to his father's claims—He defeats the Lancastrians at Mortimer's Cross—Defeat of the Earl of Warwick by the Lancastrians upon Barnet Common—The Yorkists rally—Popularity of Edward—He enters London in triumph—He is proclaimed king.

THE affairs of the English were not mended by the burning of the Maid of Orleans. Thinking to please the people of Paris and to counteract some of the effects of the coronation at Rheims, they determined to get up another ceremony of the same kind. Young Henry, who had been crowned King of England at Westminster in the preceding year, was brought over to Paris to be crowned as King of France. At one time it was proposed to conduct him from Paris to Rheims, where the regal unction was supposed to have more virtue; but this project was abandoned, owing to the dangerous state of the country, and, after many delays, he was crowned in the church of Nôtre Dame, at Paris, in the month of November, 1431. The ceremony was splendid, but there was no joy on the part of the people: few of the great French lords attended; even the Duke of Burgundy was absent; and, instead of a French prelate, Henry's relative, Cardinal Beaufort, placed the crown on his head. Another discouraging symptom was that the royal boy—the son of a hero—though now nine years old, was spiritless and unpromising.

The utter disorder of affairs in England still prevented the sending of money or any considerable reinforcements to the Duke of Bedford; and the incurable madness of the French nobles clogged and impeded the opposite party, who were still poorer than the English. Charles led an errant life, apparently indifferent to the fate of his country, which suffered more from a lingering, irregular war, than it had done during more decisive conflicts. He was gay in the midst of his mistresses, and his courtiers were only made unhappy by the rancorous jealousies they entertained of one another. Now and then the scene was darkened by an assassination, such as we have already described. The only consistent plan acted upon was that of detaching the Duke of Burgundy from his English alliance; and here a circumstance upon which they had no reason to count played into their hands. The Duchess of Bedford, the strongest connecting link between her husband and her brother, died in November, 1432. In the month of May of the following year Bedford espoused Jacquetta of Luxemburg. The Duke of Burgundy complained that Bedford had acted unfairly in marrying Jacquetta, his vassal, without asking his consent; and that by marrying so soon he had shown a shameful disrespect to the deceased duchess, his very dear sister. The Duke of Bedford could not tolerate the harsh reproaches of his ally, and the less so from his knowing that Philip had courteously received fresh envoys from Charles immediately after the death of his sister. Some attempts at reconciliation were made by Cardinal Beaufort, but they were of no avail; Philip wanted a pretext for quarrelling, having at last almost concluded a satisfactory bargain with King Charles. To crown all, the Duke of Bedford's health was declining; and sickness, disappointment, and the daily exhibition of treachery, rendered him peevish and suspicious. Philip, however, affected scruples of conscience as to breaking the solemn oaths which bound him to the English. His brothers-in-law, the Duke of Bourbon and the Constable Richemont, who were now steady in the interests of Charles, suggested that the pope could remove this difficulty; and, in a private conference, they induced Philip to agree to the general mediation of the Church of Rome, which had made several fruitless endeavours to promote a peace. By degrees the English were persuaded to refer their cause to the same arbitration. Eugenius IV. entered actively into the business, and arranged a grand European congress, which assembled at Arras in 1435. The Duke of Burgundy summoned the nobility of all his states to

The Hôtel-de-Ville, Arras.—From Coney's Ancient Cathedrals, &c.

his fair city of Arras; King Charles sent twenty-nine of his lords and ministers, the Duke of Bourbon and the constable being at the head of them: the interests of England were defended by Cardinal Beaufort and twenty-six lords, one-half of whom were English, the rest French: the great council of Basil despatched the Cardinal of Cyprus, and the pope was represented by the Cardinal of Santa Croce. In addition to all these negotiators there were ambassadors from the Emperor Sigismund, from the Kings of Castile, Aragon, Portugal, Navarre, Naples, Sicily, Cyprus, Poland, Denmark, and the Dukes of Brittany and Milan. The Duke of Savoy, who had played a conspicuous part in former negotiations as well as wars, sent no ambassadors, because he had lately grown weary of the sins of the world, and had retired to a sort of hermitage. Europe had not yet seen any assembly of the kind half so magnificent; and, before the diplomatists proceeded to business, Duke Philip entertained them with jousts, tournaments, mysteries, and feasts. After the feasting came a course of sermons suited to the occasion; and then the Cardinal of Santa Croce opened the congress with a long speech, in which he dwelt on the duty of Christian nations to live in peace and harmony with one another. It was soon made evident that the representative of the pope was wholly biassed in favour of King Charles; at the same time the English, though they saw the rapidly growing friendship between the Bourguignons and the French, maintained a high tone, and at last Cardinal Beaufort disavowed the authority of the congress, and retired in disgust. Matters then proceeded smoothly with those who remained. Fifteen days after the departure of the English negotiators the Duke of Burgundy concluded a treaty with Charles: the terms were, of course, most favourable to Philip. In the first article Charles expressed his regret and penitence for the murder of Duke John. By the second article he agreed to abandon the men who had done that wicked deed, in order that they might be punished in person and in property —to do all that was possible to arrest them —and, failing in this, to banish them for ever from his dominions. By the fourth article, Charles engaged to build a chapel at Montereau for the good of the soul of Duke John; and, besides other pious foundations, a stone cross upon the bridge over the very spot where the duke had fallen. But these articles were insignificant preludes to those which followed. Charles engaged to pay Philip the sum of 400,000 crowns, and to put him in immediate possession of sundry fortresses as security for this money; he also ceded to Philip and his heirs the county of Mâcon, Boulogne, the towns and castles of Péronne, Roye, and Montdidier, together with several other towns and castles on the river Somme.

As soon as the treaty was sealed the congress repaired to the church of St. Waast. When mass had been sung, the Cardinal of Santa Croce ordered the treaty to be read. Then Jean Tudert, a dean of Paris, advanced, and threw himself at the feet of the Duke of Burgundy, and begged pardon publicly, on the part of King Charles, for the murder of his father. Then the Cardinal of Santa Croce, having placed a golden cross and the holy sacrament upon a cushion, made the Duke of Burgundy swear to forget and forgive the death of his father, and to live evermore in peace and friendship with the King of France. Then the two cardinals laid their hands upon the duke's head, and gave him full absolution for all the oaths he had sworn to the English. The Duke of Bourbon and the constable swore upon the crucifix for Charles; and then followed a long process of swearing in the French and Burgundian lords, who to a man had taken many contrary oaths on former occasions.[1]

The Duke of Bedford did not live to see the conclusion of the memorable congress of Arras; he died at Rouen on the 14th of September, and was buried there in the cathedral.[2] The French hoped that his death, and the secession of the Duke of Burgundy, would lead to an immediate conclusion of the war; but in part through their own miserable follies, in part through the valour of those with whom they had to contend, it took them fifteen more long years to drive the English out of their kingdom. The troops of Charles took Meulan, Pontoise, and other places on the Seine, while the English were left without a chief. In Normandy, Dieppe was surprised; and the people in several places were excited to insurrection by Richemont. When the French ventured too frankly into the open field they were several times defeated; but the English found enemies rising on every side, and they could no longer trust any of their sworn allies. The Duke of Burgundy soon declared open war against them. He sent some troops to join the army of Charles, and began to make immense preparations in Flanders for the siege of Calais, which place he intended to appropriate. He made use of all his influence over the people of Paris, in order to induce them to forget their old quarrel with the Armagnacs and declare for the king. In the month of April, 1436, the Parisians opened their gates to the famous Burgundian chief L'Isle Adam; and the weak English garrison, surprised and betrayed, was compelled to capitulate.

When the capital was lost, a successor to the Duke of Bedford arrived in the person of the Duke of York, who brought with him a reinforcement of 7000 or 8000 men; but the war no longer excited the English nation with dazzling visions of conquest and glory; the imprudent and impoverished government could no longer afford the same liberal pay to the soldiers; the hardy and respectable yeomen who had followed Henry V. with such enthusiasm, and who had filled the ranks of his archers with good will and merry hearts, no longer presented themselves, and the recruits were chiefly drawn from very inferior classes or conditions of men. But, inferior as they were to the picked men that fought at Azincourt, they were not destitute of the hardy national spirit; and in the course of the ten following years the French were frequently made sensible of this fact. The gallant Talbot, afterwards Earl of Shrewsbury, soon reduced the revolted towns in Normandy; he defeated a French army near Rouen; he retook Pontoise in the depth of winter; he cleared the whole country round Paris; and, at one moment, nearly succeeded in retaking that capital. The Duke of Burgundy, who was supposed to have learned the art of war from the English, did not practise that art against them with any effect; and he never ventured personally to face them in the field. The annals of war scarcely present a more miserable and ridiculous exhibition than Philip's siege of Calais, in the prosecution of which he spent immense sums. The Duke of Gloucester, formerly protector, now head of the council, who was getting ready reinforcements for Calais, sent a challenge to Philip, telling him that he would fight him and his whole army outside of Calais, as soon as the wind should serve for his voyage; and that if Philip would not await him there, he would follow him into his states of Flanders. Philip replied, that he would abide where he was; but four days before Gloucester landed, his army fled in a panic; and knights, men-at-arms, and all—30,000 men wearing helmets —followed their example, leaving an enormous quantity of baggage and all their artillery and engines of war behind them. Philip was swept away by the rush of the fugitives, and the Constable Richemont, who had gone to share in the glory of capturing Calais, partook in his disgrace and vexation. The English, who had not waited for the raising of the siege to make incursions into Flanders, now fell with fury upon that country, taking several towns, and carrying off an immense booty. Gloucester soon followed Philip into the heart of Flanders, sending the most provoking messages after him; but Philip would not meet this army, small

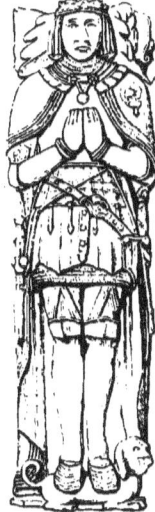

JOHN TALBOT, EARL OF SHREWSBURY.[3]

---

[1] *Monstrel.; Rym.; Olivier de la Marche; Rot. Parl.; Barante.*
[2] The French wished Louis XI., the son of Charles VII., to destroy the monument, and throw the remains of the great warrior out of the church; but Louis rejected the brutal proposal, saying that he would not wage war against the dead, or insult the remains of one who had made his father tremble so often, and who, were he alive, might yet make all France tremble.
[3] The figure represents his monumental effigy at Whitchurch, Shropshire. Talbot inscribed on his sword this motto:—
"Sum Talboti pro vincere inimicos meos."

as it was. Gloucester, who owed him many grudges on account of the affair of Madame Jacqueline, had now taken upon himself the title of the Earl of Flanders, pretending that Philip had forfeited those states by his treasons, and that his nephew Henry, as king of France, had bestowed them upon him.

If Duke Philip's ardour for the war had been but lukewarm before the siege of Calais, it cooled almost to the freezing point after that disgraceful miscarriage; and a similar failure in the following year (1437), before the walls of Crotoy, in the neighbourhood of Crecy, did not tend to revive his spirits. Ghent and Bruges had openly revolted, and the subjects of all his states complained that they were beggared by the war. From this time he can scarcely be said to have taken a part in the struggle; but his neutrality alone was sufficient to turn the scales in favour of the French, who gradually regained possession of the provinces north of the Loire, though not without many a check. In Normandy and the neighbouring countries of Maine and Anjou, the English long presented a bold front. The Duke of York was recalled in 1437, and then the difficult command was given to the Earl of Warwick. Warwick died in two years, on which, after a considerable interval, the Duke of York was reappointed. There was now a pause in the horrors of war occasioned by famine and the plague, which visited both England and France at the same time. In 1439 Talbot recovered Harfleur, the first conquest of Henry V., which had been wrested from the English. The valour of the nation never shone with a more brilliant light than during the siege, when Talbot, with a strong garrison before him, was attacked in the rear by an army far superior in number to his own, and annoyed at the same time by a fleet of ships which lay in the river and on the coast.* Two years later Talbot displayed admirable generalship in relieving Pontoise, which was besieged by an army of 12,000 men; but all his skill and the valour of his troops could not long preserve that isolated position. In the course of the years 1442 and 1443 the French turned their arms against Henry's possessions in the south; but while they were gaining some fortresses in Guienne, the English took others in the north, and overran Picardy and Anjou. Soon after this, the Duke of Burgundy turned a ready ear to proposals for an armistice; and negotiations were opened for a general peace. In the end all parties agreed to a truce for two years, to terminate April 1, 1446.

Henry of Windsor was now in his twenty-fourth year, but it had long been apparent that no increase of years would bring him the spirit of a man or the capability of managing his own affairs. Gentle, timid, submissive, and superstitious, he would have made a tolerably good monk, but he had not one of the qualities which constitute a good king. Parliament, which settled the regency, and apportioned and nicely limited the power and authority of its members, gave no authority whatever to the queen-mother, Catherine of France, the youthful widow of Henry V. This lady appears to have had little ambition; as three or four years after the death of the hero of Azincourt she married Owen Tudor, an obscure gentleman of Wales, who, however, boasted a most ancient and even a royal descent; but what, perhaps, had more influence over Catherine's choice was, the circumstance of his being one of the handsomest men in England, besides being "garnished with many godly gifts." In her affection for her promising family by this second marriage, from which sprung the royal line of Tudor, she may have somewhat neglected the care of the sickly and unpromising Henry, But all her cares had long ceased; for she died in 1437, and had now been buried nearly seven years in Westminster Abbey, by the side of her first husband.[1]

In an evil hour part of the council took up the notion that Henry's miserable deficiencies might be all supplied by marrying him to a princess of intelligence and spirit; and for the execution of this precious scheme they fixed their eyes (of all the princesses in Europe!) upon Margaret of Anjou, the cousin of the French queen, and the devoted friend of Charles, in whose court she had passed much of her time. Margaret was handsome, of a womanly age, and noted for ability and decision of character; and she had not yet been intoxicated by power, or allowed opportunities of showing her pride, envy, and vindictiveness. The Earl of Suffolk, who negotiated the truce, and who was in high favour with the French court, also negotiated this fatal marriage.

---

[1] By an *ex post facto* law, passed in the sixth year of Henry VI., though not now found on the rolls of parliament, having apparently been torn out, such marriages as those of Catherine with Owen Tudor were declared presumptuous, derogatory to the royal dignity, and illegal, without the express consent of the sovereign. After Catherine's death, Tudor was apprehended and put in ward, but he was allowed to escape from the Tower. He was afterwards beheaded for his adherence to Henry VI. Jacquetta of Luxemburg, the widow of the great Duke of Bedford, followed Catherine's example, and married, to the great annoyance of the English court, Sir Richard Woodville, who was only a knight. She and her husband, however, after some persecution and payment of a fine of £1000, were allowed to live in peace. Catherine, besides a daughter, had three sons by Owen Tudor. During the reign of their half-brother Henry VI., Edmund, the eldest, was created Earl of Richmond; and Jasper, the second, was made Earl of Pembroke. The first of these, by his marriage with the only daughter of John, Duke of Somerset, had Henry, who succeeded to the earldom of Richmond, and who afterwards ascended the throne as Henry VII.

It appears that the original notion was his, but that, though opposed most strenuously by the Duke of Gloucester, who here spoke the sense of the English people, he was supported by Cardinal Beaufort and other members of the government. The father of Margaret, though titular King of Sicily and Jerusalem, was deplorably poor—a very Lackland. Suffolk, instead of asking, as usual in such cases, for a dower in money or in territory, consented to pay a price for the young lady's hand, and finally agreed to resign Anjou and Maine, which were wholly or in greater part in possession of the English, to her father, whose hereditary states they were. This was giving up, by a stroke of the pen, that which the French had not been able to obtain by the sword; and, from the geographical position of the territories ceded, it was putting the keys of Normandy into the hands of the enemy. If Suffolk and Beaufort had made up their minds to end the ruinous struggle, and to give up the whole of the English conquests in France, we might perhaps, abstractedly, and in the cool philosophy of a better period, applaud both the justice and the wisdom of the cession; but such notions were not suited to the fifteenth century, nor to the conquerors of any other time—the nation was bent on preserving at least a portion of what they had obtained at an enormous expense of blood and treasure, and the minister that had dared to propose any such measure would have been torn to pieces by the English people. The cession, in the circumstances of the times, savoured strongly either of treachery or fatuity. Beaufort was now nearly fourscore years old, and it is more charitable to suspect him of dotage than to accuse him of treachery.

As soon as the Earl of Suffolk returned to England with the bride, he was elevated to the rank of a marquis, and from that moment he and the queen began to monopolize and divide between them the whole authority of government. They were constantly together, and people said that Suffolk looked more like her husband and King of England than the unfortunate Henry. There was a strong popular prejudice against French queens of any kind; nor did Margaret's conduct at all tend to remove it. She applied doctrines of government which she had learned in France to a country wholly and happily different, and incensed the people by her arrogant despotic conduct. The friends and admirers of the Duke of Gloucester, among whom the citizens of London were very conspicuous, said everywhere that he would have found them a better queen, and taken better measures for the preservation of the English conquests; but the duke, either from fear of the prevalent faction at court, or from some other motive, gave his approval, in a very marked manner, in parliament to all the negotiations concluded by Suffolk.[1] It is quite clear, however, that there was no sincerity in these outward demonstrations, and that the duke—"the good Duke Humphrey," as he was called by the people—would, on account of his great popularity, be a formidable obstacle in the way of the queen and her favourite. Besides, the passionate and vindictive Margaret was not likely to forget that Gloucester had at first strongly opposed the measures which made her a queen and gave to her father a respectable existence.

In 1441, after an altercation with the cardinal, in which the duke was defeated and humiliated,[2] a strange prosecution was got up against his wife the duchess, Eleanor Cobham, who, it will be remembered, had the misfortune of being Gloucester's mistress before she became his wife, and could never wholly efface the unfavourable impression made by this circumstance. She is represented as an avaricious, grasping, ambitious, and dissolute woman; but her enemies drew this portrait, and whatever she might be, she was dear to the duke, although he was not the most faithful of husbands. The duke was much devoted to all the learning then in vogue, and exceedingly fond of the society of learned men. Among other doctors and clerks whom he entertained was one Roger Bolingbroke, whom he kept constantly in his house as chaplain. This Bolingbroke was much given to the sciences, especially to astronomy, and astronomy in those days was generally made to include astrology. Gloucester's wife, aware that Henry was sickly, and that her husband stood next in succession, was probably anxious to know whether the stars would tell when the king would die; and she had frequent consultations with the chaplain and others. On a sudden, soon after her husband's last violent quarrel with Cardinal Beaufort, she was accused of treason, "for that she, by sorcery and enchantment, intended to destroy the king, to the intent to advance and to promote her husband to the crown." The duchess and Bolingbroke were arrested, together with Southwell, priest and canon of St. Stephen's, Westminster; John Hum, priest; and Margery Jourdayn, commonly called the Witch of Eye. The duchess was examined in St. Stephen's Chapel before the Archbishop of Canterbury: she was condemned to do public penance in three places within the city of London, and afterwards to pass her life a prisoner in the Isle of Man, under charge of Sir John Stanley. Roger Bolingbroke, the learned astronomer, who died protesting his innocence of all

---
[1] *Rot. Parl.; Rymer; Hall.*
[2] The subject of the quarrel was the liberation (upon ransom) of the Duke of Orleans and other prisoners taken at Azincourt. Gloucester opposed their liberation.

evil intentions, was drawn and quartered at Tyburn; Margery Jourdayn was burned in Smithfield; Southwell died in prison before the time of execution; and John Hum received the royal pardon. The worst thing proved against the duchess was, that she had sought for love-philters to secure the constancy of her husband. The worst thing attempted to be proved against her was, that she kept by her a wax figure, made by the "cunning necromancers," and endowed with this remarkable quality, that, in proportion as it was sweated and melted before a fire, it would, by magical sympathy, cause the flesh and substance of the king to wither and melt away, and his marrow to be dried up in his bones. "The Duke of Gloucester," says the chronicler,[1] "bore these things patiently and said little." But his enemies were now preparing for him the safe silence of the grave. A parliament was summoned to meet in February, 1447, not in the usual place at Westminster, because the Londoners were devoted to the erring but generous-hearted victim, but at Bury St. Edmunds, in Suffolk, where the favourite was in the midst of his dependents. Orders were given to the knights of the shire to come armed, and the men of Suffolk were collected and crowded in the town and neighbourhood. The king was conveyed to the town, and, as if his sacred person was in danger, a numerous guard was placed round the house he occupied. Gloucester, who was at his strong castle of Devizes, went to attend this parliament, and fell unsuspectingly into the snare. On the 11th of February, the day after the opening of the session, he was arrested on a charge of high treason, and, on the 28th day of the same month, he was found dead in his bed. The whole nation believed that the duke was foully murdered, and, with a single but striking exception,[2] all the writers living at or near the time hint, more or less openly, that this was the case. The body of the duke was shown to the people at Bury St. Edmunds, and there were no marks of violence upon it; but all men remembered that the bodies of Edward II., of Richard II., and of the other great Duke of Gloucester, who had been taken off at Calais during the reign of Richard II., had been exposed to view in the same manner, and bore no signs of the murderous hands of their enemies. Suffolk's party wished it to be believed that he had died of apoplexy. Some said he had died of a broken heart; but, even in the latter case, Suffolk and the queen were his murderers. Humphrey, however, was not a man likely to die of grief and despair, for he knew his great popularity, which in all probability must have assured him that the parliament, however composed, would not venture to proceed to extremities against him. What followed was a miserable show designed to furnish a plausible justification of his arrest. Five of his retainers were seized, and accused of plotting to release the Duchess of Gloucester from her confinement—to come to the parliament in arms—to murder the king, and proclaim the duke, their master, in his stead. They were convicted and condemned to die the horrible death of traitors; but when they were only half hanged, they were cut down, and, before the executioner could proceed in the bloody task of cutting up their bodies, Suffolk produced the royal pardon, and the men were easily restored to animation.[3]

As if he had not already created odium enough, the Marquis of Suffolk seized all the estates of the deceased duke, and, after keeping what best suited him, divided nearly all the remainder among his own family and most devoted partizans.[4] The good Duke Humphrey left no legitimate children, and, on account of her conviction, Dame Eleanor could not claim any part of his property. The duke's friends in parliament boldly asserted his perfect innocence of treason, and laboured, session after session, to clear his memory from the imputation of his enemies. His old rival, his uncle Cardinal Beaufort, did not long survive him. He had for some time withdrawn from political affairs to his see of Winchester, where, however, in spite of his age and infirmities, he was still cherishing projects of ecclesiastical ambition, and dreaming of the triple crown of Rome which had so long eluded his grasp, but which he fancied was at last within his reach. He died in his palace of Walvesey on the 11th day of April, and the *sign*[5] he gave of Christian feeling was shown in his will, whereby he bequeathed the mass of his property to charitable purposes.[6]

When the truce expired, the King of France consented several times to renew it for short periods; but this suited his own purposes, and he knew that many of his lords would not permit their operations to be hampered by any ar-

---

[1] Hall.
[2] This is Whethamstede, who was abbot of St. Alban's at the time, a warm friend of Gloucester, and a declared enemy of the Suffolk party, whom he calls "dogs, scorpions, and impious noisers." He asserts that the duke died of grief and sickness. It appears that the abbot could have no motive for concealing the truth if he knew it.
[3] Rymer; Rot. Parl.; Whethamstede; Hall; Grafton.
[4] Rymer.
[5] "Lord Cardinal, if thou think'st on heaven's bliss, Hold up thy hand; make signal of thy hope: He dies, and makes no sign."—*Henry VI.*, part ii.
It is almost impossible to remove the impression made by Shakspeare's terrific death-bed scene; but that it is historically incorrect there can be little doubt. The great cardinal died almost in public, surrounded by the clergy of his diocese.
[6] Hall; Continuation Hist. Croyland; Nichols, Royal and Noble Wills; Milner's Hist. Winchester.

mistice, in case of a favourable opportunity for attacking the troops of Henry. The fact was, Charles had another civil war in the south upon his hands: the Count of Armagnac, favoured by the now discarded minister La Tremoille, had organized a formidable league against him. France, indeed, was for some time in such a distracted condition that she must again have fallen under the yoke, if the government of England had been able and willing to press her; but that government was now influenced by Margaret of Anjou, whose father, brothers, cousins, and a host of relatives were to benefit by its folly, weakness, and vacillation.

A.D. 1449. Maine, which lay so conveniently along the southern frontier of Normandy, and which Suffolk had so liberally surrendered to the queen's father, Réné of Anjou, had gradually been filled with French troops and companies of adventure in the service of King Charles, who insulted the English lines almost with impunity. The Duke of York had been for some time recalled. In vain his successor, the Duke of Somerset, represented to his government that he had no money—no efficient army—and that all the fortresses in Normandy were falling into ruin from want of proper repairs. Charles wanted a decent pretext for breaking the armistice, and such pretexts are always found when sought for. Some English soldiers, who had been expelled from their houses in Maine, plundered a town in Brittany, just as the French had plundered many a place in Normandy during the truce. Somerset, conscious of his weakness, offered a reparation in money; but Charles named a sum which it was impossible for him to pay, and then threw his troops across the frontiers of Maine, and called up his columns from all sides to fall upon both Lower and Upper Normandy. While the English were negotiating about the damage done in Brittany, Vernenil and Pont de l'Arche were surprised or betrayed. The Bastard of Orleans, now Count of Dunois, led the main body of the army to Rouen, within the walls of which he had many secret agents. His force was immense, but the capital of Normandy was taken rather through the treachery of the inhabitants than the valour of his troops. The Duke of Somerset had been obliged to shut himself up in Rouen, and all that he had to oppose to an army without, and to a vast and disaffected population within, was a weak garrison of 1200 men; but the brave Talbot was with him, and where Talbot was the English were sure to do something to save their honour. But the situation of the English was too desperate to be saved even by the heroism of a Talbot: the whole town rose against them, opened their gates to the Bastard, and drove the garrison into the citadel, where Somerset capitulated on the 4th of November, 1449, being obliged to order the surrender of several other important fortresses as the price of his own liberty and that of his brave men. Talbot was given as an hostage—Somerset retired to Caen.[1]

A.D. 1450. Popular indignation obliged the minister Suffolk to do something; but all that he did, and it might be all that he could do, was to send a reinforcement of 3000 men into Normandy. Sir Thomas Kyriel, the leader of these men, had the old confidence of a captain of Henry V. and Bedford; and he did not doubt that, in case of the French meeting him in the open field, he could give a satisfactory account of them, however superior their numbers. He accordingly gladly joined battle at Fourmigni with an army under the command of the Count of Clermont; but, while he was engaged, a second army, led on by the Constable of France, closed upon him in flank and rear. Some of his men then broke and fled, but more remained to fight desperately, and die with their swords in their hands. The victory of the French was complete, and they boasted of it without any reference to the enormous disparity of numbers.[2] Bayeux, Avranches, and other towns, immediately surrendered to them; and soon after, the Duke of Somerset was driven out of Caen. The last siege the English sustained was at Cherbourg; but that place being furiously assailed both by sea and land, surrendered on the 12th of August; and the whole of Normandy was lost.[3]

The Count of Dunois and other captains had already made an impression on the English possessions on the Garonne: the Count of Penthièvre had recently been despatched with an army in that direction, and, soon after the conquest or submission of Normandy, the mass of Charles' forces marched against Guienne, where there were scarcely any English troops, and where the people, though not much attached to the French, from whom they still differed materially in language and habits, were wavering and divided. The nobles generally had declared against the English: when the French army began their campaign in earnest, in 1451, the castles were surrendered to them without any fighting. The English, collecting their weak and scattered detachments, retired to Bordeaux and the places in the neighbourhood of that fair and flourishing city, where their flag had floated for 300 years. Castillon, St. Emilion, Libourne, Rions, were carried by assault; and the Sire d'Orval advanced with a

---
[1] *Monstrelet; Hall.*
[2] *Monstrelet; Villaret.* Sir Thomas Kyriel had drawn some troops from the garrisons, and joined them to his 3000; but his force was still very inferior to the army of Clermont, to say nothing of the second French army under Richemont.
[3] *Monstrelet.*

body of horse to the environs of Bordeaux. At his approach the English garrison and 8000 or 10,000 of the citizens, with the mayor at their head, made a sortie with more spirit than discipline: D'Orval charged them rudely at several points, broke them, covered the roads with their wounded and their dead, and carried off a considerable number of prisoners. But Bordeaux was not lost by an unlucky sally; and this year the French were awed by its formidable attitude. In the following summer the Counts of Dunois, Penthièvre, Foix, and Armagnac penetrated into Guienne from four different sides: the important town of Blaye surrendered to them; other places declared for Charles; and, hemmed in or crushed by numerous and still increasing forces, the Eng-

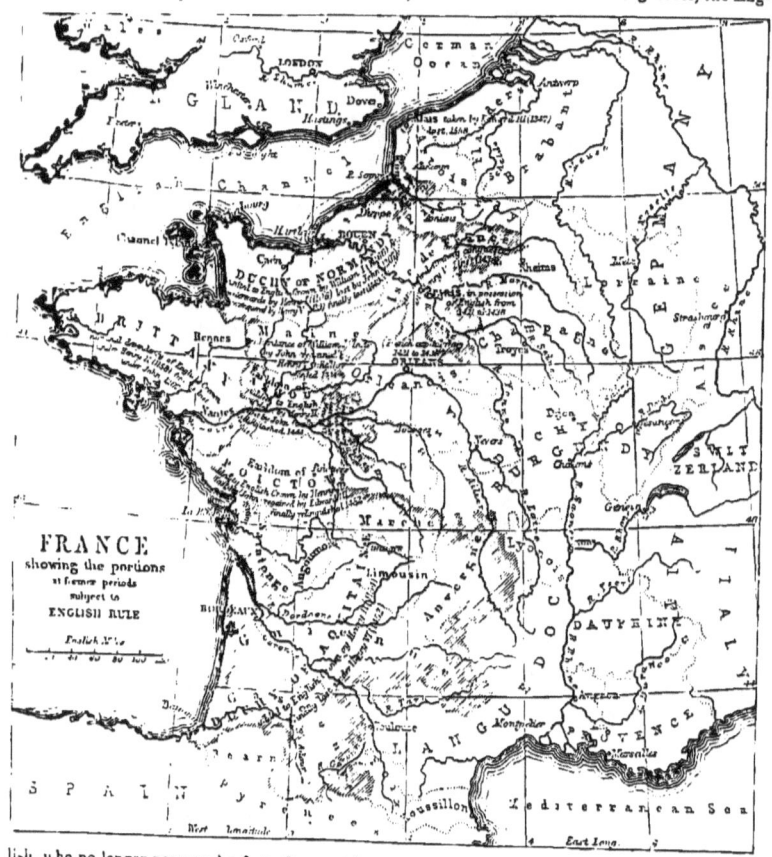

FRANCE showing the portions at former periods subject to ENGLISH RULE

lish, who no longer possessed a foot of ground in the province except Fronsac, Bayonne, and Bordeaux, were forced to consent to give up those places by the festival of St. John, if they were not previously relieved and reinforced by troops from England. The time passed; not a man was sent to their succour; and on the appointed day the garrisons of Fronsac and Bordeaux opened their gates to the officers of Charles. Notwithstanding their stipulation, the garrison of Bayonne still attempted to defend that place; but they were compelled to capitulate soon after to Count Gaston de Foix.[1]

Thus was lost the last fragment of the brilliant heritage of Eleanor of Aquitaine, which had been secured by the policy and valour of Henry II. Nothing now remained to the English in France

[1] The connection, at once political and commercial, which bound England by the closest ties with Guienne and Languedoc, during whole centuries, at times, too, when northern and west-

save Calais and a strip of marshy land commanded by its batteries. In Normandy and other parts of France their expulsion was hailed with a general though not unanimous joy; but it was far different in Guienne, where the people, who did not consider themselves Frenchmen, and who were strongly attached to their old franchises, which the English, accustomed to liberties of the same sort, had respected, felt that they had much to lose and little to gain by being included in that national system and placed under French governors. Forgetting all their former complaints against the pride of the Islanders, the people of Guienne long continued to regret the days when the red cross of England waved over their thriving cities and sea-ports. Nor did they submit to their new masters without an effort to restore the dominion of their old ones.[1]

The tables had been turned: the English began, under Henry V., to make their conquest of France when that country was cursed with a mad king, an intriguing and vindictive queen, and a factious nobility; and they finished losing all they gained, and a great deal more, when the same curses fell upon their own country. But the shame of those losses was not to be borne patiently by a high-spirited people, and before the final closing of the account of defeat and expulsion, they took a terrible vengeance on the *Duke* of Suffolk—for such was the title which this minister, rising as his country sank, had now taken to himself.

Bitter complaints had been repeatedly made in parliament by a spirited minority, and as misfortunes thickened this minority became a majority, whose indignation was overwhelming. Towards the end of 1449, while the public mind was exasperated by the recent loss of Rouen, Suffolk was attacked in both houses. He had a short breathing-time during the Christmas recess,[2] but the popular clamour rose louder and louder; and when parliament met, early in January, 1450, he complained of the accusations made against him, defended his loyalty and patriotism, and challenged his accusers to the proof. This challenge was readily accepted. Four days after, the commons requested the lords to commit him to the Tower. The lords replied that they could not commit a peer without some specific charge. The commons took only two days to get up a direct charge, and, when they produced it, it was neither honest nor ingenious. It simply charged the duke with having furnished the castle of Wallingford with provisions and military stores, with the object of assisting the King of France, who, they asserted, was preparing to invade England. The lords, however, without hesitation, ordered the arrest of the obnoxious minister, and he was seized and conveyed to the Tower. The bill of impeachment, which the commons prepared in ten days, contained several additional charges. For example, they charged Suffolk with the design of destroying both Henry and his partial mistress Margaret, and placing the crown on the head of his own son; and they said that he had contracted engagements with the French, in the view of obtaining their assistance for these ends. To the charges of liberating the Duke of Orleans, and of ceding Maine and Anjou, he was certainly amenable as a minister; and these charges were now preferred against him. But the commons were still wavering and uncertain as to their proofs; and on the 7th of March, a month after laying their first impeachment of eight articles, they presented a new impeachment of a very different kind, which contained sixteen articles, some of which seem probable enough, but none of them amounted to absolute treason.

On the 13th day of March, Suffolk was brought to the bar of the lords, and falling on his knees before the king, he vowed that he was innocent of any treason. In pleading, he kept to the absurd impeachment in eight articles, never alluding to the charges of waste of money, improvidence, and corruption, or indeed to any other of the sixteen charges contained in the second bill of impeachment. As to the article relating to his project to secure the crown for his own son, he maintained that it was absurd, and the pro-

---

orn France was at war both with England and what are now her own southern provinces, must have greatly promoted the intellectual and social development of England. Thierry speaks thus of Languedoc:—"The county of Toulouse, and the great lordships which in the thirteenth century were its dependencies, either as allies or vassals, were infinitely more civilized than any other territories comprised within the limits of ancient Gaul. They drove a great trade with the ports of the Levant. Their cities enjoyed municipal constitutions, and even resembled in some measure the Italian republics. The wealthy burgesses had each his own mansion-house, flanked with towers; and their sons might be knighted if they chose, and joust at tournaments like noblemen. This love of political equality, which scandalized the knights of France, Burgundy, and Germany, bringing all classes of the population into free intercourse with each other, inspired the Gallic inhabitants of the coasts of the Mediterranean with a spirit of activity which displayed itself in all kinds of moral culture. Their literature was the most refined in Europe, and the language of that literature was classical in Italy and Spain. Their Christianity was ardent and exalted; for they were by nature impassioned, and it did not consist in an implicit belief of the dogmas, and a mechanical observance of the practices of the Roman church. Without openly revolting against that church, they had at that remote period anticipated, and in some sort had even exceeded, the religious reformation which the sixteenth century saw burst into light in other countries. All this was effected amongst them insensibly, without a religious war—without any burst of fanaticism—without their having themselves exactly measured the degree of their dissent from the Catholic church." Many traits in this description seem to have been transplanted into England at an early date.

[1] *Monstrelet;* A. Thierry, *Hist. Guyenne; Hall; Stow.*

[2] During this interval the Bishop of Chichester, a friend of Suffolk and keeper of the privy seal, was massacred by the people of Portsmouth for the part he had taken in the negotiations about Maine and Anjou.

ject impossible. He could not deny the cession of Maine and Anjou; but he urged that he was not alone in that guilt (if guilt it were), for the other lords of the council had authorized that measure, and the peers in parliament had afterwards sanctioned it. The commons were determined that he should not escape, and refused to vote any supplies; the court, by which could be meant little but the queen, were equally resolved that he should not be convicted; and the whole proceeding ended, as it began, in irregularity.

On the 17th of March, Suffolk was again called up to the lords, the king being present. The chancellor[1] observed to the duke that he had not claimed the privilege of a peer, and asked him whether he had more to say in defence of his conduct. Suffolk said that he thought he had said enough to establish his innocence: and he threw himself upon the will of the king, his master. The scene had been arranged beforehand; the chancellor instantly rejoined, saying that, as the duke did not put himself upon his peerage for trial, the king would not declare him either innocent or guilty; but with respect to the second impeachment (to which Suffolk had given no answer), the king, not as a judge taking council of the lords, but as one to whose authority the prisoner had submitted of his own free will, commanded him to quit England before the 1st of May, and to remain in banishment for the space of five years.

If parliament had entered into this compromise, and were satisfied with it, it was far otherwise with the people of London. These were furious that the traitor, the cause of all the disgrace abroad, as they considered him, should be allowed to escape so easily; and, on the day of his enlargement, upwards of 2000 persons collected to take his life. Suffolk, however, evaded the rage of this mob, and went to his estates, where he summoned his relatives, friends, and dependents. In their presence he swore upon the host that he was a wronged and innocent man; and then he went to Ipswich, and embarked for the Continent. On the 2d of May, as they were sailing between Dover and Calais, the two small vessels which carried the exile and his retinue were brought-to by the *Nicholas of the Tower*, a great ship of war. The duke was ordered on board the *Nicholas*, the captain of which said to him, as he stepped upon the deck, "Welcome, traitor!" He was kept on board two days, during which the ship stood off and on, probably communicating with some great movers in the business on shore, and the duke employed himself with his confessor. On the third day a cock-boat came alongside, and in the boat were a block, an axe, and an executioner. Suffolk was handed over to the latter, who cut off his head. A general cry had been raised that Suffolk still retained the confidence of Margaret, and that it was insupportable to see the "queen's darling" escape with a certainty of being soon recalled to power and to vengeance; but who were the great directors of his assassination was never clearly proved. No investigation took place; the people rejoiced at the death, and their minds were soon excited by other events which were the faint prelude to the wars of the Roses.[2]

John Cade was a native of Ireland, who had passed some time in France as a soldier of the English, or, according to other authorities, as an outlaw. It appears, however, that he had returned to his own country, and that he came from Ireland, then governed by the Duke of York, into England, at the moment when the excitement against the government was at the highest. Insurrections had broken out in several parts of the kingdom before Suffolk's fall, and Cade put himself at the head of a popular movement immediately after that event. He assumed the noble name of Mortimer, and claimed a descent which made him a relation (though illegitimately) of the Duke of York. None but very questionable evidence was ever brought to show that this prince had employed him, yet it is certain that Cade, or rather the peculiar circumstances of the times, without which Cade would have been nothing, played the game of the duke, and encouraged the hopes which York had long entertained of grasping the royal power. The men of Kent[3] had long been noted for their determined spirit; they were the boldest and least vicious of the insurgents who, under Wat Tyler, nearly overturned a former weak government; they were probably better informed than the people of the inland counties of what was passing in France; and they were now more violent in their complaints than the rest of the nation. It was said that the queen held them guilty of the recent murder of her favourite, whose headless body lay for some time exposed on the beach near Dover, and that she had threatened to take a sanguinary vengeance. Cade threw himself among these men, who se-

---

[1] This was the Archbishop of York. Suffolk's chancellor, the Archbishop of Canterbury, resigned the seals at the first blush of the prosecution. According to some accounts, the present scene passed in the king's apartment, to which all the lords, spiritual and temporal, were summoned.

[2] *Hall; Continuation Hist. Croyland; Stow.*

[3] Thierry ascribes the readiness of the men of Kent to take the lead in popular insurrections to their having preserved some remembrance of their fathers having made terms with William the Conqueror. A much more likely cause lay in the law of gavelkind prevailing in that county. This "incensate custome of gavelkind," as it is called in the *Glory of Generosity*, "tendeth to the destruction of auncient and gentle houses," and hence also to the multiplication of small democratic proprietors.—P. 94.

lected him to be their captain. He led them towards the capital; and about the middle of June, a great multitude, estimated at 15,000 or 20,000, encamped at Blackheath, from which point Cade kept up a correspondence with the Londoners. The court sent to demand why the good men of Kent had quitted their homes. Cade gave their reasons in a paper entitled "The Complaint of the Commons of Kent." After alluding to the report that Kent was to be destroyed by a royal power, and made a hunting forest, "for the death of the Duke of Suffolk, of which the commons of Kent were never guilty," Cade, or the pens that wrote for him, went on to complain that justice and prosperity had been put out of the land by misgovernment; that the king was stirred to live only on the substance of the commons, while other men fattened on the lands and revenues of the crown; that the people of the realm were not paid for stuff and purveyance forcibly taken for the king's use; that the princes of the royal blood were excluded from the court and government, which were filled exclusively by mean and corrupt persons, who plundered and oppressed the people; that it was noised that the king's lands in France had been alienated and put away from the crown, and the lords and people there destroyed with untrue means of treason; that the commons of Kent had been especially overtaxed and ill-treated; that their sheriffs and collectors had been guilty of infamous extortion; and that the free election of knights of the shire had been hindered. The court pretended to be preparing a proper answer to this startling list of grievances, but it employed the time thus gained in collecting troops in London. In this interval Cade sent in another paper, headed "The requests by the captain of the great assembly in Kent." This document, though conceived in respectful language, went more directly to the point. It required that the king should resume the grants of the crown, so that he might reign like a king royal; that he should instantly dismiss all the false progeny and affinity of the Duke of Suffolk, and take about his noble person the true lords of his royal blood, namely, the high and mighty prince the Duke of York, long exiled from the king's presence, and the mighty princes the Dukes of Exeter, Buckingham, and Norfolk; that he should punish the false traitors who had contrived and imagined the death of that excellent prince the Duke of Gloucester, of their holy father the cardinal,[1] and others, and who had promoted and caused the loss of Anjou, Maine, Normandy, and other parts of France. The court had now levied a considerable army; and this force was sent out to give the rebels their answer. Cade fell back from Blackheath to Sevenoaks, where, in a good position, he halted, and waited the attack of a detachment of the royal army. This detachment was defeated on the 24th of June, and the commander, Sir Humphrey Stafford, was slain. The soldiers had not fought with good will at Sevenoaks; and when their main body, still at Blackheath, got intelligence of that affair, they began to say that they liked not to fight against their own countrymen, who only called for a reasonable redress of grievances. The court now found that concession was expedient: and they sent Lord Say, a very obnoxious minister, and some other individuals, who had been closely connected with the Duke of Suffolk, to the Tower, which Lord Scales undertook to maintain for the king. The army was disbanded, and the king was conveyed for safety to the strong castle of Kenilworth. While this was doing, Cade re-appeared at Blackheath; and by the end of June, he had made himself master of all the right bank of the Thames, from Lambeth and Southwark to Greenwich. From Southwark he sent to demand entrance into the city of London; and this, after a debate in the common council, was freely granted to him by the lord-mayor. On the 3d of July, Cade led his followers into the heart of the capital. He seemed anxious to preserve the strictest discipline—he issued proclamations forbidding plunder, and in the evening he led his host back to the Borough. The next day he returned in the same good order; but he forced the mayor and judges to sit in Guildhall, and pass judgment upon Lord Say, of whose person he had, by some means, obtained possession. Say demanded a trial by his peers, but Cade's men hurried him to the standard at Cheapside, and cut off his head. Soon after, they did the same by Say's son-in-law, Cromer, the sheriff of Kent.[2] When this was over, they retired quietly to the Borough for the night. In the course of the following day a few houses were pillaged. The citizens now took counsel with Lord Scales, who had 1000 soldiers in the Tower; and it was resolved that they should prevent Cade from entering the city on the morrow. The insurgents got news of this intention in the night, and instantly made an attack on the bridge. The citizens resolutely defended it, and, after a nocturnal fight, which lasted six hours, and cost many lives, they remained masters of the passage.

---

[1] This murder of old Beaufort was the most absurd statement in these documents. Surely it was natural enough for a man to die at the age of eighty; and the cardinal, as we have said, died almost in public.

[2] Bills of indictment were also found against the Duchess of Suffolk, the Bishop of Salisbury, Thomas Daniel, and several other friends of the deceased minister, who, fortunately, were out of reach of the insurgents.

The insurgents retired into Southwark, and, in concert with the irritated citizens, it was resolved to delude them by promises of pardon, as had been practised with the followers of Wat Tyler. Both the chancellor and the ex-chancellor, the Archbishops of York and Canterbury, had taken refuge in the Tower, whence they despatched the Bishop of Winchester with a general pardon, under the great seal, to all such as should return to their homes. It appears that the prelate also promised a redress of grievances. His mission had the immediate effect of creating a division among the insurgents—one party being of opinion that they ought to accept the conditions; the other, that there was no faith to be put in them. Some began to retire into Kent: Cade accepted the pardon, and then the whole force began to disperse. But in two days Cade was again in Southwark, with a considerable host, who maintained that it would be folly to lay down their arms until they had obtained some security from government for the performance of its promises. Dissension, however, broke out afresh, and being awed by the warlike attitude of the Londoners, they retreated to Blackheath, and thence marched to Rochester, where their feuds terrified their leader. Cade, who expected to be murdered or delivered up to government, which had proclaimed him a traitor, and offered 1000 marks for his apprehension, got secretly to horse, and galloped across the country towards the Sussex coast. He was closely followed by one Alexander Iden, an esquire, who overtook him and attacked him sword in hand. After a desperate fight, the squire proved the better man. The head of Cade was stuck upon London bridge, with the face turned towards the pleasant hills of Kent; and Iden was made happy with the 1000 marks. Pursuit was then made after Cade's companions,[1] and many were taken and executed as traitors.[2] It was stated in a subsequent act of attainder, that some of these men confessed that their object had been to place Richard, Duke of York, on the throne; but this evidence is open to suspicion; and, moreover, it was not affirmed that the insurgents had been employed by the duke.[3] But whatever may have been the caution, prudence, and patience of the Duke of York, that prince's name was certainly put prominently forward at this time; and it is equally certain, if the question was to be decided by descent and birth, that York had a preferable right to the throne.

We have shown in what manner the claims of the old line of the Plantagenets rested in Edmund Mortimer, Earl of March.[4] This Edmund, after faithfully serving the house of Lancaster in peace and in war, died in 1424; upon which, as he left no issue, and as his brother Roger and his sister Eleanor had died childless, his rights passed to his sister Anne, married to the Earl of Cambridge, who had been condemned and executed for treason in the beginning of the reign of Henry V. Anne Mortimer had a son, the present Prince Richard, who succeeded to the titles of his paternal uncle the Duke of York, as also to the lineal rights of his maternal uncle Edmund Mortimer, Earl of March. But notwithstanding the growth of the doctrine of hereditary right—a doctrine which had gradually made way in Europe—it may

---

[1] *Stowe; Fabyan; Paston Letters.*

[2] Thierry contrasts this insurrection with that under Wat Tyler, seventy years before. The latter he considers as chiefly one of the Anglo-Saxon race, represented by the serfs, against the Anglo-Norman, represented by the *gentilhommes*—the gentry —and to have been the final term of the series of Saxon revolts, and the first of a new order of political movements. Had it succeeded, as an historian of that period expresses himself, all nobility and gentry might have disappeared from England. What really followed M. Thierry describes thus:—

" A. D. 1381-1450. But, instead of this, matters remained as formerly established by the Conquest; and the serfs, after their defeat, continued to be treated according to the terms of the proclamation, which told them:—' Villains you were, and still are, and in bondage you shall remain.' Notwithstanding the failure of the great effort they had made to escape at once from bondage, and to obliterate the distinction of conditions which had succeeded that of races, the natural process by which that distinction became gradually less visible and revolting went on uninterrupted; and the enfranchisement of individuals, which had begun long before, became more and more frequent. The idea of the specific injustice of serfdom and prædial bondage whatever its origin, and whether of ancient or recent institution—this great idea, which had formed the grand tie uniting the conspirators of 1381, and which the instinct of freedom had implanted in the souls of the peasantry before it had reached the higher ranks, came at length to be owned as a true principle by the gentry themselves. In those moments of thoughtfulness when reflection becomes calmer and deeper—when reason prevails over interest and avarice—in the hour of domestic sorrow, of sickness, and of impending death—the nobles of that age repented in such moments of doubt of their holding property in bondmen, as a thing displeasing to that God who had created all men after his own image. Many deeds of manumission, dated in the fourteenth and fifteenth centuries, have the following preamble:—' Inasmuch as in the beginning, God made all men by nature free, and as the law of nations placed some afterwards under the yoke of bondage, we think it would be pious and meritorious in the sight of God to liberate such persons to us subjected in villanage, and to free them entirely from such services: Know therefore that we have freed and liberated from all yoke of servitude —, our knaves, of the manor of —, them and all their children, born and to be born.' Jack Cade, who in 1448 played the same part as Wat Tyler in 1381, did not, like the latter, make himself the representative of the rights of the common people in opposition to the gentlemen; but, connecting his own and the popular cause with the aristocratical factions which then divided England, he went so far as to announce himself as one of the royal family, unjustly excluded from the succession to the throne. The influence which this imposture had on the minds of the people in the northern provinces, and in that very county of Kent which, seventy years before, had chosen tilers, bakers, and carters for its leaders, proves that a rapid amalgamation was in progress between the political interests and passions of the different classes of men in England, and that a certain order of ideas and sympathies was no longer attached, in a fixed and invariable manner, to a certain descent or social condition."—*The Norman Conquest.*

[3] The act here alluded to was an act of attainder passed against the Yorkists in November, 1459, when their enemies were triumphant.

[4] See vol. i. p. 637.

be questioned whether the nation would have paid much attention to the genealogy of the Duke of York, if the notorious and still increasing incapacity of Henry, and the odium which his wife incurred, had not forced the subject upon their attention. The duke had been recalled from the command in France through the influence of Queen Margaret, and his post in Ireland was considered by his friends as a kind of exile. He had, however, acquired great popularity among the English and the descendants of the English in that country; and recently (in the year 1449) he had gained much credit by the ability he displayed in the suppression of an insurrection of the native Irish. Resigning his command there, he suddenly appeared in England in the end of August, 1451. After paying a short visit to the king in London, he retired to his castle of Fotheringay. He was mute as to his intentions, but the court took the alarm, and sought to oppose him by the Duke of Somerset, the nearest male relation to King Henry, and the head of the younger branch of the house of Lancaster. But it was under Somerset's government in France that the loss of Normandy was completed; and this circumstance, added to that of his being in high favour with the queen, rendered him almost as unpopular as the Duke of Suffolk had been.[1] Two years were spent in noisy discontent and silent intrigues. Each party stood in awe of the other, and measured its ground before proceeding to extremities. Some dark deeds were committed by both factions, but the scale of guilt seemed rather to incline to the side of the court. Tresham, the speaker of the House of Commons which had prosecuted the Duke of Suffolk, was assassinated by some friends of the queen.

A member of the commons boldly proposed that, as Henry had no children, and was not likely to have any, the Duke of York ought to be declared heir to the throne; but the proposer was committed to the Tower. The commons, however, passed a bill of attainder against the deceased Duke of Suffolk, and agreed in a request that the king would be pleased to dismiss from office and from the court the new minister the Duke of Somerset, and several lords and ladies related to Suffolk. The court resisted or evaded both measures. Violent quarrels arose between the adherents of government and the Yorkists; the former asserting that there was treason afloat —the latter, that there were projects for depriving Duke Richard of his liberty, and treating him as the Duke of Gloucester had been treated at Bury St. Edmunds. In the beginning of the year 1452, the Duke of York repaired to his castle of Ludlow, in Shropshire, the neighbourhood of which was devoted to the Mortimer family. He collected a considerable armed force, but, by proclamation, declared that he had no evil intentions against the king, to whom he offered to swear fealty upon the sacrament. A royal army was sent against him; but while that force went westward by one road, York marched eastward by another, and appeared before the gates of London, which were shut in his face. He then marched to the borders of Kent, where he probably expected to be joined by the malcontents who had been out with Cade. It appears, however, that few joined him, and when Henry came up with him, at Dartford, he agreed to a peaceful negotiation. Two bishops were the negotiators on the part of the king; and when they asked why York was in arms, he asserted that it was for his own safety, seeing that repeated attempts had been made to work his ruin. Henry said that he cleared York of all treason, and esteemed him as a true man and his own well-beloved cousin. Notwithstanding the coyness of the men of Kent, it may be presumed, from the high tone maintained by the duke, that his force was considerable. He insisted that all persons who had trespassed and offended against the laws, especially such as were indicted of treason, should be arrested and put upon their trial. The king, or those who directed him, promised all this, and more. A mock order was given for the apprehension of the minister, the Duke of Somerset, and York was assured that a new council, in which he should have a seat, should be appointed forthwith. Upon this Duke Richard disbanded his army, and agreed to a personal interview. With singular confidence he went unarmed and almost alone to the king's tent. One of the first persons he saw there was the Duke of Somerset, who called him felon and traitor, epithets which were retorted with interest. When York turned to depart, he was told that he was the king's prisoner. Somerset, it is said, would have proceeded to a summary trial and execution, but this was prevented by the fears of the other ministers and courtiers. York was then sent to London, and held partly as a prisoner, and "straighter would have been kept, but it was noised that Sir Edward, Earl of March, son to the said Duke of York, was coming towards London with a strong power of Welshmen, which feared so the queen and council that the duke was set at full liberty; and on the 10th of March he made his submission, and took his oath in St. Paul's to be a true, faithful, and obedient subject to the king, there being present King Henry and most of the nobility."[2] York retired to his castle of Wigmore, and remained

---

[1] Rot. Parl.; Wm. Worcest.; Hall; Stow.   [2] Stow.

perfectly quiet till he was brought forward by the movements in parliament.

We have said that the people of Guienne did not submit without a struggle to the oppressive government of Charles VII. Soon after the pacification of the Duke of York,[1] they sent a deputation into England to request the assistance of a small army, to express their bitter regret at all the changes which had taken place, and to promise the most perfect loyalty and attachment to King Henry if he would enable them to throw off the French yoke.[2] Nearly all the lords of the Bordelais were equally irritated against the French, and they united with the citizens in the project of recalling the English. The chief of these nobles—the men of the highest rank in the country—the Sires of Duras, L'Esparre, Monferrand, Rauzan, and L'Auglade, repaired secretly to London, where they treated with good effect, for, weak as was the government, it was determined to make an effort to recover what had been lost by miserable negligence. Four or five thousand good soldiers were collected and equipped, and the command was offered to the brave old Talbot, who, notwithstanding the weight of nearly eighty years, accepted it joyfully. At his approach to Bordeaux the nobles of the country crowded to his honoured standard—the people caught the flame of insurrection—and in a brief space of time the red cross of England was again raised in nearly every town in Guienne. Charles, at the moment, was engaged in a senseless war with the Count of Savoy; but these startling events recalled him from the neighbourhood of the Alps to the hills of Gascony. Having failed in his attempts to win over the people by promises of better government, he advanced against the towns on the Dordogne and the Garonne with fire and sword. Some of them he took by assault; and in these cases his troops were even more merciless than is usual on such occasions. In the summer following he laid siege to the important town of Castillon. Talbot determined to relieve this place. On the 20th of July, between night and morning, he surprised and cut to pieces a considerable force, drove in the outposts, and fell upon the French in their intrenchments. Their position was strong, and defended by bombards that discharged stone shot; but Talbot had nearly

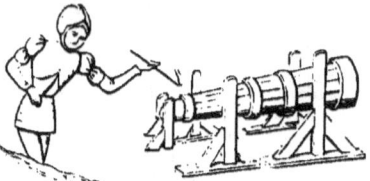

BOMBARD.—Froissart MS. Bib. Royale, Paris.

carried it when the Count of Penthièvre came up with another army. The English withdrew from the works, formed in good order, and even then did not despair of fighting their way back to Bordeaux; but their brave "octogenarian chief" was slain, and his son was killed in attempting to save him; and then the troops fled. About 1000 men were made prisoners. There was no second army—there was no Talbot to prolong the struggle. The French army soon appeared before Bordeaux, which, after a bold resistance of nearly two months, was compelled by famine to capitulate on the 10th of October.[3]

A.D. 1454. The uneasiness shown by parliament at the increasing incapacity of the king, and at the power of the queen and the Duke of Somerset, brought about the recall of the Duke of York to the council; and this measure was soon followed by the committal of Somerset, who was sent to the Tower at the end of the year 1453. On the 14th of February, 1454, parliament was opened by the Duke of York, as lieutenant or commissioner of the king. For some time the court had endeavoured to conceal Henry's real condition; but the lords were now resolved to ascertain it, and an accidental circumstance afforded them a good reason for forcing the privacy of Windsor Castle. Kemp, Archbishop of Canter-

---

[1] *Paston Letters; Whethamstede; Rot. Parl.*

[2] The inveterate dislike and contempt of the Aquitanian provinces for France and Frenchmen, and their attachment to England, were both of old standing, and had their root in very various causes. The influence of the Duchess Eleanor, Henry II.'s queen, in preserving her own vassals from falling away from the Anglo-Norman rule, was powerfully seconded by natural feelings and material interests pervading the whole southern provinces of France, from Marseilles to Bayonne. "By a singular destiny," says Thierry, "while Normandy, the old land of the kings and nobles of England, became to them a hostile territory, Aquitaine, from the Bay of Rochelle to the Pyrenees, seemed not unwilling to remain subject to their authority. It has already been seen how the latter country was preserved under the Anglo-Norman dominion by the influence of Henry II.'s widow, the Duchess Eleanor. After her death, the Aquitanians remained true to her grandson, through fear of becoming direct vassals of the king of France, now, as master of Poictou, their immediate neighbour. Pursuing a policy that was thought wise in the middle ages, they would rather, setting aside all other considerations, have for their lord paramount a distant king, as in that case the country was commonly allowed to govern itself according to its own local customs, and by a native administration—advantages hardly to be expected under a sovereign whose immediate domains lay close at hand." The industrial and commercial interests of Languedoc, also, favoured a connection between that province and England, for the wools of England were transported across the country from Bordeaux to the seats of the woollen manufacture on the Rhone and its tributaries, the returns being probably made in the silks, spices, &c., of the East, imported at Marseilles, and in the drugs and sweetmeats of Montpellier.

Had we but sufficient ground upon which to proceed, it would be a curious subject of inquiry how far intercourse with the peaceful and industrious Albigenses in the early part of the thirteenth century may not, through this channel, have first transmitted Lollard opinions into England.

[3] *Monstrelet; A. Thierry, Hist. de Guyenne; Hall.*

bury and chancellor of the kingdom, died; and as it was usual for the House of Lords to confer personally with the sovereign on such high occasions, a deputation of twelve peers went to Windsor, and would not be refused entry into the castle. They found Henry incapable of answering them or understanding them: in the words of their report to the house, "they could get no answer nor sign from him, for no prayer nor desire," though they presented themselves to him three several times. This report of the deputation was, at their prayer, entered on record in parliament, and was reasonably considered as authentic a testimony as could be procured of their sovereign's infirmity (of which there was no kind of doubt in the country); and after adjourning two days, they "elected and nominated Richard, Duke of York, to be protector and defender of the realm of England." York, still advancing no hereditary claim to the crown, accepted of the humbler office, with all the limitations put upon it by parliament; but a weighty circumstance probably this time contributed to his moderation. Queen Margaret had been delivered of a son about a year before, and, though the outcry seems to have been almost universal that this was no child of Henry, the legislature could not entertain the popular clamour, but recognized the infant Edward by creating him Prince of Wales and Earl of Chester. In accepting this post as protector, York took care to obtain the most explicit declarations from the peers that he only followed their "noble commandments." In about nine months Henry recovered his memory and some degree of reason—perhaps as much as he had usually possessed. The court instantly claimed for him the full exercise of royalty, and York at once gave up the protectorate. The first use made of this resumed authority by the king was to liberate the Duke of Somerset.[1] This step and some others, which showed that it was the intention of the court to restore the unpopular minister, irritated a great part of the nation, and induced York once more to take up arms. He retired again to Ludlow, where he was joined by the Duke of Norfolk, the Earls of Warwick and Salisbury, and other men of rank. Again Henry went, or was carried, with an army, towards Ludlow; but this time the duke, instead of avoiding him by taking a different road, anticipated his movements, and met him near to the capital with an army equal to his own. On the 22d of May, as the royalists were about to continue their march from St. Alban's, they saw the hills in their front covered with armed men, who were moving forward, and who did not stop till they came near to the barriers of the town. The duke sent a herald into the town, professing great loyalty and affection for the king, but demanding the person of the Duke of Somerset. It was replied by or for the king, that he would rather perish in battle than abandon his friends. Upon this, battle was joined. York was kept in check at the barriers, but another way into the town was pointed out; and, winding round part of the hill on which it stands, and crossing some gardens, the Earl of Warwick entered St. Alban's, and attacked the royalists in the streets. York then forced the barriers, and after a very short contest, the royalists gave way, rushed out of the town, and fled in the greatest disorder.[2] The Duke of Somerset, the Earl of Northumberland, and the Lord Clifford were slain: the Duke of Buckingham, Lord Sudeley, the Earl of Stafford, and the unfortunate king were wounded—all by arrows. The Duke of York found Henry concealed in the house of a tanner: his wound, though in the neck, was not serious. He was treated with mildness and outward respect; his conqueror conducted him to the noble abbey of St. Alban's, where they prayed

ABBEY OF ST. ALBAN'S.—From an old drawing in the British Museum.

together before the shrine of England's first martyr. When parliament met in the month of

---

[1] Rot. Parl.; Rymer; Whethamstede; Paston Letters.

[2] The number of the Lancastrians killed in this affair has been absurdly exaggerated in most of our old histories. One of the Paston Letters, written immediately after the fight, says that only six score were slain.

July, it did little else than renew the protestations of allegiance to Henry and his son. After a prorogation, parliament met again on the 12th of November, when the Duke of York was appointed by commission to open the proceedings as lieutenant of the king. The commons, thereupon, sent up a message to the lords, stating, that as the Duke of York had been appointed to represent the king on this occasion, so "it was thought by the commons, that if the king hereafter could not attend to the protection of the country, an able person should be appointed protector, to whom they might have recourse for redress of injuries, especially as great disturbances had lately arisen in the west through the feuds of the Earl of Devonshire and Lord Bonvile." The new Archbishop of Canterbury, in his quality of chancellor, said that the subject would be taken into consideration by the lords. Two days after, the commons repeated their request—refusing to proceed with any other business until it should be granted. York, therefore, was again declared protector; and he was to hold his authority till discharged of it by the lords in parliament. Still, however, parliament respected the rights of the infant prince, and it was declared in this session, as in the preceding year, that the protectorate should cease, in all cases, as soon as Edward attained his majority.[1] The ostensible reason for superseding Henry was his acknowledged incapacity, derived from physical maladies attended by mental derangement. There is no positive proof that he was worse than he had been a few months before; but if he were no better, the step need not surprise us. It happened to him, as to his reputed grandfather, the unhappy Charles VI.; being known to suffer fits of insanity, people could never count with any certainty on his lucid intervals, or put any trust in a king who was alternately declared to be sane or insane according to the rise or fall of a party. The House of Commons and the people would certainly have gone farther in the way of revolution; but the prelates, with one or two exceptions, and most of the lay lords, were still averse to a change of dynasty. The duke gave some of the most important offices to his tried friends. No acts of vengeance were committed: it was considered that the Somerset faction had suffered sufficiently in the deaths of the lords in the affair of St. Alban's. Not a drop of blood was spilt, not a single attainder passed.

Queen Margaret was not idle during this second short protectorate, and the powerful party of the court was put in motion. When parliament met, after the Christmas recess, in 1456, Henry, to the surprise of most people, attended, and demanded back, and received from the lords, all his authority as king. No doubt was raised touching his malady, and York resigned the protectorate without a struggle—apparently without a murmur. All the officers he had appointed were dismissed and replaced by persons devoted to the queen. Then York thought it time to look after the personal safety of himself, his sons, and adherents. He retired to his estates, where he kept his vassals on the alert; and most of the great lords of his party did the same. This was the more necessary, as the families and friends of Somerset and Northumberland, and the other lords who had fallen at St. Alban's, openly expressed their determination to take a sanguinary vengeance.

In the end of February a great council was held at Coventry, and a sort of pacification was there effected between the Yorkists and the court party, the duke and his friend Warwick being compelled to give fresh assurances and oaths of fidelity. The king, who was no doubt sincere, whatever may have been the feelings of his wife and the courtiers, then endeavoured to reconcile York and his friends with the avengers of Somerset and Northumberland. London was chosen, by mutual consent, to be the scene of this great peace-making. After some days spent in deliberation, the king, who had assumed the character of umpire, gave his award, signifying that the Duke of York and the Earls of Warwick and Salisbury should build a chapel for the good of the souls of the lords they had killed at St. Alban's; that both those who were killed there and those who had killed them should be held loyal subjects; that the Duke of York should pay to the widow and children of the Duke of Somerset the sum of 5000 marks; that the Earl of Warwick should pay to Lord Clifford the sum of 1000 marks, and that the Earl of Salisbury should release Percy Lord Egremont from the damages he had obtained against him for an assault, upon condition of Percy's giving securities to keep the peace for ten years. This award was accepted; the court came into the city; and king, queen, Duke of York, and all, walked lovingly together in procession to St. Paul's.[2]

This was on the 25th day of March. In the month of May, Warwick, who had been allowed to retain the command at Calais, engaged, with great bravery, but without a due regard to the laws of nations, a strong fleet belonging to the Hanse towns, captured five or six ships, and carried them into Calais. The powerful Hanseatic league complained to the English court, which

---

[1] Rot. Parl.

[2] Whethamstede; Rot. Parl. Long accounts of the procession to St. Paul's are given in Hall, Stow, and Holinshed. The Duke of York and the queen walked hand in hand. The great quarrel was between these two.

called upon Warwick for explanations. Warwick presented himself at Westminster; but in a few days he fled, alleging that his life was aimed at by the malice of the courtiers, who had set on men wearing the king's livery to assassinate him.[1] He joined his father, the Earl of Salisbury, and soon after they had a conference with the Duke of York and his friends. He then hastened over to Calais, where he was so popular, that his recall or dismissal by the government of Henry would have been but an idle ceremony. During the winter months he collected some veteran troops who had served in the French wars. In England the Yorkists were not less active; and as the court was raising an army as fast as the embarrassment of its finances would permit, it became evident that a fierce conflict was inevitable. The Yorkists asserted, as before, that they only armed for their own security. In the month of September, 1459, the Earl of Salisbury moved from Middleham Castle in Yorkshire, to join his forces to those of Duke Richard, who lay in the Welsh marches. At Bloreheath, near Drayton, in Shropshire, he found himself in presence of a Lancastrian army, commanded by Lord Audley, who had thrown himself between the earl and the duke with the view of preventing their junction. The Lancastrians were far superior in number; but Salisbury, by superior generalship, and the better discipline of his troops, gained a complete victory Two thousand of the Lancastrians were slain, and Lord Audley himself was included in the number.

Salisbury joined the duke at Ludlow Castle, and Warwick, the true hero of these unhappy times, appeared there soon after with the fine troops he had raised at Calais.[2] The Lancastrians were not unprepared : 60,000 men had been collected from different parts, and Henry was at Worcester with this force. After some fruitless negotiations, the Lancastrians advanced from Worcester against their enemies, who, notwithstanding the comparative smallness of their numbers, boldly awaited their attack. The positions occupied by the Yorkists showed the military science of Warwick and his father Salisbury. As the Lancastrians approached, they were cannonaded with some effect; the lines of the enemy were imposing; and it was resolved to put off the battle for that day. During the night, Sir Andrew Trollop, who was marshal of the Yorkist camp, and who had the immediate command of most of the men brought from Calais, deserted with all his veterans to the standard of Henry. This defection was so important that it finished the campaign: the Yorkists broke up from the intrenched camp near Ludlow, and retreated in different directions without being followed.

All this happened on the 13th and 14th of October, 1459. On the 20th of November a parliament met at Coventry, and attainted the Duke of York, his duchess, his sons, the Earl and Countess of Salisbury, their son the Earl of Warwick, the Lord Clinton, and many others. The Duke of York had got safely to Ireland, where he was still popular. The Earl of Warwick had retired to his sure asylum of Calais, conducting with him his father, the Earl of Salisbury, and the young Earl of March, the Duke Richard's heir. The court appointed the Duke of Somerset to the command of Calais; but when that obnoxious nobleman appeared before the port, the batteries opened upon him, and he was glad to escape to Guisnes. While he lay there, the

WAR-SHIPS OF THE FIFTEENTH CENTURY.[3]

mariners of his fleet deserted to a man, and went over to their great favourite, Warwick, carrying all the ships with them. This gave the "king-maker" the command of the Channel, and after taking two small fleets, fitted out by the Lancas-

[1] As Warwick was leaving the court, one of his retinue was struck by a servant of the royal household, and a dreadful affray followed. It is not proved that there was a design to murder the earl; but it is quite clear that the parties were in such a state that any accident must bring them to a collision.
[2] Whethamstede; Hall; Stow.

[3] The nearer vessel is restored from the ship of Beauchamp, Earl of Warwick, Cotton MS. Julius E. IV.; the distant from Froissart MS. in the British Museum.

trians, he sailed to Dublin.¹ From Ireland he returned to Calais, and then, crossing the Channel, he landed in Kent towards the end of June, 1460. He only brought 1500 men with him; but manifestoes had been previously circulated, and the men of Kent crowded to his banner. As he approached Canterbury, the archbishop, who had been promoted during the first protectorate of the Duke of York, went out to meet him and welcome him. The Lord Cobham and all the knights and gentlemen in the neighbourhood soon joined his army, which was swelled to 30,000 men before he reached Blackheath. On the 2d of July, the city of London welcomed him as a friend and deliverer; and he rode through the city accompanied by his father and Edward the heir of York, to whose beautiful person and promising appearance all eyes were turned. Five bishops followed in the train of Warwick, who, without losing time, continued his march into the midland counties. He found the Lancastrians at Northampton, occupying an intrenched camp, not unlike that which he and his friends had formed at Ludlow in the preceding year. There were other points of resemblance between these two affairs, for Lord Grey de Ruthyn now deserted the Lancastrians as Sir Andrew Trollop had deserted the Yorkists. The former, however, were not so fortunate in their retreat: they lost 300 knights and gentlemen, besides the Duke of Buckingham, the Earl of Shrewsbury, and the Lords Beaumont and Egremont.² The unhappy Henry was taken prisoner a second time, but Margaret escaped with her son Edward, and, after many adventures, got into Scotland. The victors marched back to the capital and summoned a new parliament, to meet at Westminster. This parliament repealed all the acts passed at Coventry the year before, alleging that that parliament had not been duly and freely elected. Then the Duke of York, who had come over from Ireland, entered London with a splendid retinue. From the city he rode to Westminster, where he dismounted and entered the House of Lords. It was an exciting moment: he walked straight to the throne and laid his hand upon the gold cloth which covered it; but there he paused—looked round—and did not seat himself on the throne. He had, however, at last made up his mind to claim it. His friend, the Archbishop of Canterbury, asked him if he would not visit the king, who was in the palace hard by? The duke replied that Henry ought rather to wait upon him —that he was subject to no man in that realm— but, under God, was entitled to all sovereignty and respect. The peers maintained a dead silence, and the duke, leaving the house, took possession of the royal palace as his own.³ In less than a week —on the 16th of October—the duke sent a formal demand of the crown to the lords, requiring their immediate answer. The lords told him that they refused justice to no man, but that they could give no answer without the advice and consent of the king. They, however, were forced to attend to the duke's paper, in which he traced his descent, and claimed as the representative of Roger Mortimer, whose right he maintained was according to all law preferable to that of a descendant of Henry of Bolingbroke, who had entered upon the thrones of England and France against all manner of right. Many of the great lords had attained to their greatness under Henry of Bolingbroke, his son, and grandson, whom it was now proposed to declare usurpers; and the Yorkists had irritated the tenderest susceptibilities of many of the lords by their repeated threats of resuming the estates and grants of the crown. At the same time, no doubt, they felt some sympathy for the inoffensive king, who, now that the queen was away, was pitied by the people at large. Indeed, a notion had gone forth that Henry was very likely to become a saint, and to be canonized, like his predecessor Edward the Confessor, whom he resembled in many respects. As the Duke of York would not brook delay, the lords waited upon Henry on the following morning. The captive king, or those who advised him, made a spirited reply, reminding the lords that he, as an infant, had inherited the crown which had been worn with honour by his father and his father's father—that he himself had been permitted to wear it without challenge for nearly forty years, and that the lords and princes had repeatedly sworn fealty to him. The lords were then requested to make search for arguments and proofs against the duke's right. The lords, greatly embarrassed, wished to have the opinion of the judges, but the judges asserted that such high matters could be decided only by the princes of the blood and the parliament, and refused to attend. The upper house then summoned the king's serjeants and attorneys, who were obliged to attend against their will, the lords holding them as bound by their office to give advice to the house. The lords deliberated and voted with an appearance of perfect freedom, just as if Warwick had not been nigh at the head of a victorious army; and, on the 23d of October, they presented their objections to Richard's title. These were—1. The duke's oaths of fealty and the oaths they had all taken to Henry; 2. Many acts of parliament passed since the accession of the house of Lancaster; 3. That entails had been made of the crown on the male line only, whereas he claimed

---

¹ *Whetham.: Poston letters.* ² *Whetham.: Stow; Hall.* ³ *Whetham.: Hall; Rot. Parl.*

through a female. The other two objections were thoroughly ridiculous; they referred to York not having borne his proper coat-of-arms, and to a declaration made by Henry IV., which everybody knew to be utterly false. The duke's counsel had an easy task in replying to these objections. Nothing was of much weight except the oaths, and these the duke offered to refer to the consideration of the highest spiritual court. The lords were compelled to acknowledge that the hereditary law was wholly in favour of York. At the end of this curious inquiry, they suggested a compromise, which York had the moderation to accept. Henry was to retain the crown during his life; but at his death it was to devolve to Richard, and to be vested in him and his heirs, to the exclusion of Prince Edward, the son of Margaret of Anjou.¹

But there was a powerful party whose voices were not heard in these deliberations, and the energetic Margaret was at large exciting them to take up arms for her son. Soon the gentle hills of England glittered again with hostile lances; and hostile bands, collecting from all quarters, advanced to meet in two great armies, the one under the Duke of Somerset, the Earls of Northumberland and Devon, and the Lords Clifford, Dacres, and Nevil; the other under the Duke of York, the Earl of Salisbury, and other lords. They met, on the last day but one of the year, at Wakefield, in Yorkshire, where Richard imprudently gave battle with forces very inferior in number. The onslaught was terrific; the men on both sides fought with savage fury, for the people had entered into the delicate questions of right and legitimacy, and their passions were worked up to frenzy. For a time the Yorkists maintained the conflict with a good hope of victory, but a sudden charge in their rear, made by some troops of Borderers who had been brought up by Queen Margaret, proved fatal to them. The duke himself was slain; and of 5000 men who had followed him to Wakefield, 2000 remained upon the field. The Earl of Salisbury was pursued and taken during the night: he was carried to Pontefract Castle, where he lost his head. York's second son, the Earl of Rutland, a beautiful boy only twelve or thirteen years old, was stopped at Wakefield bridge, as he was flee-

ing with a priest "called Sir Robert Aspall, who was chaplain and schoolmaster to the young earl." The poor boy fell on his knees to pray for mercy, but as soon as he was known, Lord Clifford,

WAKEFIELD BRIDGE AND CHAPEL.²—From an old view in the British Museum.

whose father had been killed by the Yorkists at St. Alban's, plunged his dagger into his heart, vowing, by God's blood, that he would do the like to all of kin to York; and then the savage bade Aspall go on and tell his mother, the duchess, what had happened. England was not yet accustomed to such deeds, and a cry of horror ran through the land. Margaret vented what spite she could upon the lifeless body of Duke Richard: by her orders his head was stuck over a gate of the city of York, and a paper crown was put upon it in cruel mockery. Nearly all the officers and persons of note died fighting at Wakefield, where no quarter was given; but a few knights and esquires who escaped from the field were taken and executed by order of the queen at Pontefract and other places. This vindictive woman was mad for blood, and her fury was but too well seconded by such of the Lancastrians as had lost friends and relations in the war.

A.D. 1461. Edward, Earl of March, now Duke of York, was lying at Gloucester when he received news of the death of his father, brother, and friends: he had raised a body

---

¹ *Rot. Parl.*; *Whethom.*; *Hall.*

² Wakefield bridge was built in the reign of Edward III. It has eight arches. Leland notices it in his *Itinerary* as "a fair bridge of stone built over the Calder;" "and on the est side of the bridge," he says, "is a right goodly chapel of our Ladye." The chapel, which was removed not long since, stood upon the site of a chapel built by Edward III. (1327-77), which appears to have been pulled down and rebuilt by Edward IV. (1461-83), in memory of his father. The architecture is in the florid Gothic style of the fifteenth century. As the endowments were withdrawn at the dissolution it fell into decay, and was for some time used as the counting-house of a corn-factor. It is now set up in the grounds of a gentleman in the neighbourhood of Wakefield.

of troops to reinforce the army in the north, but, being too late for that operation, he moved towards the south-east, with the intention of throwing himself between the queen's army and the capital, within the walls of which was the main strength of his party. The fate of Duke Richard, which was proclaimed in manifestoes, greatly irritated the vassals of the house of Mortimer, and thousands who had not moved before, now left the Welsh marches and followed the standard of his son. Upon this Edward was encouraged to proceed directly towards the queen; but he found an enemy sooner than he expected, for a great force of Welsh and Irish had been detached under Jasper Tudor, King Henry's half-brother, and a dreadful conflict took place on the 1st of February, at Mortimer's Cross, near Hereford. Edward gained a complete victory: 3600 of his enemies were left on the field; Owen Tudor, the second husband of Catherine of France, was taken, and, with eight other Lancastrians of rank, was beheaded at Hereford a few days after, as a retaliation for the queen's executions at Wakefield, Pontefract, and other parts in Yorkshire. Jasper, Owen Tudor's son, had the good fortune to escape out of the battle.

Before Edward could join him in the east, the Earl of Warwick was attacked and routed by the queen, who had followed the high northern road with good hopes of reaching London. At the town of St. Alban's, which was held by the Yorkists, she experienced a severe check; but, turning that position, she fell upon the army of Warwick, which occupied the hills to the south-east of the town. The combat was prolonged over the undulating country that lies between St. Alban's and Barnet; and the last stand was made by the men of Kent upon Barnet Common. At night-fall, Warwick found himself beaten at all points; and so precipitate was his retreat, that he left King Henry behind him at Barnet. The queen and her son found this helpless man in his tent, attended only by the Lord Montague, his chamberlain. In this running fight the Yorkists lost nearly 2000 men, and on the following day the Lord Bonvile and the brave Sir Thomas Kyriel, who had been made prisoners, were executed in retaliation for the beheading of Owen Tudor and his companions at Hereford. On the 17th of February King Henry was freed again from the hands of his enemies: five days after, a proclamation was issued in his name, stating that he had consented to the late arrangement respecting the succession to the crown only through force and fear. Edward, "late Earl of March," was declared a traitor anew, and rewards were offered for his apprehension.

But Edward was now in a situation to proclaim traitors, and to put a price upon other men's heads himself. His victory at Mortimer's Cross produced a great effect. As he marched eastward, every town and every village reinforced him, and when he joined the Earl of Warwick and collected that nobleman's scattered forces, he had an army more than equal to that of the queen. The favour of the Londoners, the cruelties of the queen, and the conduct of the undisciplined troops which she had brought from the north, made the balance incline wholly to the side of the Yorkists. It appears that Margaret and her party had no money, and that their troops subsisted by plunder. Wherever they stopped they laid the country bare, making free by the way with whatever they could carry off. After the battle, they not only plundered the town of St. Alban's, but also stripped the rich abbey.[1] At the same time the Londoners were told that Margaret had threatened to wreak her vengeance upon them for the favour they had so constantly shown to her enemies. She sent from Barnet to the city, demanding supplies of provisions; and the mayor, not knowing as yet what Edward was at hand, loaded some carts with "lenten stuff" for the refreshing of her army; but the people would not suffer them to pass, and, after an affray, stopped them at Cripplegate. During this disturbance some 400 of the queen's horse, who had ridden from Barnet, plundered the northern suburbs of the city, and would have entered one of the gates, had they not been stoutly met and repulsed by the common people. A day or two after, on the 25th of February, the united forces of Edward and Warwick appeared in view, and were received as friends and deliverers. The northern army was in full retreat from St. Alban's, and Edward, who was a stranger to the scruples and indecision of his more amiable father, was fully resolved to seize the throne at once. He rode through the city like a king and a conqueror; and he was carried forward to his object by a high stream of popularity and the enthusiastic feelings of the people, who could not sufficiently admire his youth, beauty, and spirit, or pity his family misfortunes.

The Lord Falconberg got up a grand review of part of the army in St. John's Field; and a great number of the substantial citizens assembled with the multitude to witness this sight. Of a sudden, Falconberg and the Bishop of Exeter, one of Warwick's brothers, addressed the multitude thus assembled, touching the offences, crimes, and deceits of the late government—the long-proved incapacity of Henry—the usurpation and false title through which he had obtained the throne; and then the orators asked if they

---

[1] The plunder of the abbey entirely changed the worthy abbot's politics, and, from a zealous Lancastrian, Whethamstede became a Yorkist.

would have this Henry to reign over them any longer. The people with one voice cried "Nay, nay." Falconberg or the bishop then expounded the just title of Edward, formerly Earl of March, and drew a flattering, but not untrue picture of his valour, activity, and abilities. Then they asked the people if they would serve, love, and obey Edward; and the people of course shouted "Yea, yea;" crying "King Edward! King Edward!" with much shouting and clapping of hands. On the following day, the 2d of March, a great council, consisting of lords spiritual and temporal, deliberated and declared, without any reference to the authority of parliament, which never met till eight months after, that Henry of Lancaster, by joining the queen's forces, had broken faith and violated the award of the preceding year, and thereby forfeited the crown to the heir of the late Duke of York, whose rights by birth had been proved and established. On the 4th of March, Edward rode royally to Westminster, followed by an immense procession. There he at once mounted the throne which his father had only touched with a faltering hand; and from that vantage ground he explained to a favourable audience the doctrine of hereditary right and the claims of his family. The people frequently interrupted him with their acclamations. He then proceeded to the Abbey church, where he repeated the same discourse, and where he was again interrupted by shouts of "Long live King Edward!" On the same day he was proclaimed in the usual manner in different parts of the city.[1]

At the time he took these bold steps Edward was not twenty-one years old.

CHAPTER V.—CIVIL AND MILITARY HISTORY.

EDWARD IV.—ACCESSION, A.D. 1461—DEATH, A.D. 1483.

Edward IV., on his accession, prosecutes the war—He defeats the Lancastrians at Towton—His coronation—His claims confirmed—Queen Margaret's exertions, in Scotland and France, to restore her party—They rally and are defeated—Henry VI. imprisoned in the Tower—Edward IV. marries Lady Elizabeth Gray—Indignation of Edward's supporters at the marriage—Rapacity of the new queen's relations—Rupture between Edward and the Earl of Warwick—Marriage of the Duke of Clarence with Warwick's daughter—Disturbances in England—Quarrels between Edward and Warwick—Warwick and Clarence obliged to leave England—Reconciliation between Warwick and Margaret of Anjou—Warwick resolves to restore Henry VI.—Unexpected landing of the earl in England—Flight of Edward to the Continent—Henry VI. led back from prison to the throne—Edward's sudden return—His pacific professions on landing—His welcome in London—Battle of Barnet, and defeat and death of Warwick—Landing of Queen Margaret in England—Her total defeat by Edward at Tewkesbury—Atrocious murder of Prince Edward, son of Henry VI.—Sanguinary proceedings of the victors—Death of Henry VI. in the Tower—Quarrels between the Dukes of Clarence and Gloucester—Edward sends a defiance to the King of France—He invades France—Interview between Edward and King Louis—Edward's campaign turned into jollity and revel—His inglorious return to England—Continuing dissension among Edward's brothers—Clarence accused of sorcery and treason—His mysterious death in the Tower—Disturbances in Scotland—The Duke of Gloucester invades Scotland—Indecisive results of his campaign—Louis of France violates his engagements to Edward—His politic aggressions on Burgundy—Death of Edward IV.

INSTEAD of staying in London to enjoy the pageant and festivity of a coronation, Edward was obliged to take the field instantly, and face the horrors of a war which became more and more merciless. The Lancastrians, after their retreat from St. Alban's, had gathered in greater force than ever behind the Trent and the Humber; and, by the middle of March, they took up ground in the neighbourhood of the city of York, being, horse and foot together, 60,000 strong. Their chief commander was the Duke of Somerset, who acted in concert with Queen Margaret; for Henry still lay helpless at York, and the Prince Edward, Margaret's son, was only eight years old. Instead of awaiting their attack in the southern counties, the Yorkists determined to meet them on their own ground in the north. This resolution was adopted by the advice of the Earl of Warwick, who set out at once with the van of the army. Edward closely followed him; and, partly through good-will to him and his cause, and still more from an anxious wish to prevent a second visit from the northern army, the men of the south flocked to his advancing banner, and by the time he reached Pontefract Castle, he was at the head of an army of 49,000 men.

England had never before witnessed such a

[1] *Whetham.; Stowe; Hall.*

campaign as this. There was no generalship displayed; the ordinary precautions and manoeuvres of war were despised, and Yorkists and Lancastrians moved on in furious masses, with no other plan than to meet and strike. They met in full force at Towton, on the 28th of March, and began a general combat in the midst of a terrible snow-storm. They fought from nine o'clock in the morning till three in the afternoon, when the Lancastrians, who were more numerous than their adversaries, but not so well armed and equipped, were driven from the field, upon which they left 28,000 dead—a far greater number than had fallen in battle on the side of the English during the whole French war. Edward, who had none of the generous or merciful feelings of youth, had ordered that no quarter should be given. The Earl of Northumberland and six northern barons died fighting; the Earls of Devonshire and Wiltshire were taken prisoners and beheaded as traitors. The Duke of Somerset, the commander-in-chief, escaped with the Duke of Exeter to York, whence they fled rapidly to the Scottish borders, carrying with them Queen Margaret, her son, and her husband. The previous battles of the Roses sink into insignificance when compared with this mighty slaughter: the loss on both sides had hitherto usually ranged between the moderate numbers of three hundred and five or six thousand; but at Towton there perished, between Yorkists and Lancastrians, thirty-eight thousand men.[1]

Edward entered York a very short time after the flight of Henry, and having decapitated some of his prisoners, and stuck their heads upon the walls, from which he took down the heads of his father and young brother, he continued his march as far north as Newcastle. The people submitted to the conqueror, whose hands were yet reeking with the blood shed at Towton; but the Scots, who had contracted a close alliance with Henry, were disposed to give him further trouble. But Edward, confident in his officers, and impatient for his coronation, soon left the army and returned to London. On the 29th of June he was crowned at Westminster with the usual solemnities; and he then created his brother George Duke of Clarence, and his brother Richard Duke of Gloucester.

The Scots, who had been gratified by the gift of their old town of Berwick, laid siege to Carlisle, and assisted Margaret in making an incursion into the county of Durham: but both these operations were unsuccessful. Henry, who was carried about by the Lancastrians, had a narrow escape from being made prisoner near Durham; and the Scottish army before Carlisle was defeated with great loss by Lord Montague, one of Edward's commanders. By the time the new king assembled his first parliament, which was not till the 4th of November, all opposition had disappeared, and there was no armed force on foot in England, except such bands of his victorious army as he could afford to keep embodied. As the chiefs of the Lancastrian party were all proscribed, or about to be so, as some of the peers were absent, and others intimidated, and as the House of Commons and the city of London were declared and enthusiastic Yorkists, no opposition was to be apprehended. An act was passed to declare Edward's just title. No allusion was made to the mental derangement or incapacity of Henry, or to any of those demerits in the late government which might have justified this revolution. The position assumed was the high ground of legitimacy. After stating Edward's right by descent, the act proceeded to declare the three kings of the Lancastrian line tyrants and usurpers, and to recite how, upon the 4th day of the month of March last past, Edward had "taken upon him the realm of England and lordship of Ireland, and entered into the exercise of the royal estate, dignity, and pre-eminence, having on the same 4th day of March, amoved Henry, late called Henry VI., son to Henry, son to the said Henry, late Earl of Derby, son to John of Gaunt, from the occupation, intrusion, reign, and government of the realm."[2] The act thus confirmed Edward's

EDWARD IV.—From a rare print by R. Elstrachs.

---

[1] *Paston Letters; Cont. Hist. Croy.*

[2] *Rot. Parl.*

title, and fixed the commencement of his reign from the 4th of March, the day on which he had been proclaimed. The other proceedings of the parliament were in keeping with this act: the grants made by the three Henries were resumed, with certain exceptions, and bills of attainder were passed against the expelled king, the queen, Prince Edward, the Dukes of Somerset and Exeter, the Earls of Northumberland, Devonshire, Wiltshire, and Pembroke, the Lords Beaumont, De Roos, Nevil, Rougemont, Dacres, and Hungerford, and 150 knights, esquires, and priests. Considering the fearful thinning the party had undergone on the bloody field of Towton, this proscription must have included most of the great heads of the Lancastrian faction. As usual in such cases, the loyalty of the Yorkists was gratified and enlivened with gifts of the forfeited estates. Before the dissolution Edward made a gracious speech to the commons, thanking them for the "tender and true hearts" they had shown unto him, and promising to be unto them a "very right wise and loving lord."¹

If the deposed Henry had been left to himself, he would have found peace, and as much happiness as he was susceptible of, within the walls of some religious house; but Margaret was as resolute and as active as ever, and nothing was left to the proscribed nobles but their desperate swords. The queen, on finding her intrigues in Scotland counteracted by the money and the large promises of Edward, passed over to France, to see what assistance might be obtained from family affection, and gratitude for past services. The Duke of Brittany, pitying her forlorn condition, gave her a little money; but Louis XI., who had succeeded in the preceding year to his father Charles VII., was a most cunning, cautious prince—one that never gave anything without an equivalent, immediate or prospective, and who had even less family affection than the generality of kings. Louis explained how poor he was, how distracted the state of his kingdom; but when Margaret spoke of delivering up Calais as the price of his aid, he turned a more ready ear. He was not, however, in a condition to do much; and all that the fugitive queen obtained from him was the sum of 20,000 crowns, and about 2000 men, under the command of Peter de Brezé, seneschal of Normandy, who, it appears, raised most of the men at his own expense. Such a reinforcement was not likely to turn the tide of victory. Margaret, however, returned to England, and threw herself into Northumberland, where she was joined by the English exiles and some troops from the borders of Scotland. She even obtained some trifling successes, taking the castles of Alnwick, Bamborough, and Dunstanburgh; but she was obliged to flee when the Earl of Warwick advanced with 20,000 men: the French got back to their ships, all but 500, who were cut to pieces at Holy Island. A storm assailed her flying ships; the vessels that bore her money and stores were wrecked on the coast, and she and De Brezé reached Berwick in a wretched fishing-boat. This was in the month of November. In December, Warwick reduced Bamborough and Dunstanburgh; or rather those places surrendered, on condition that the Duke of Somerset, Sir Richard Percy, and some others, should be restored to their estates and honours, upon taking oaths of allegiance to Edward; and that the Earl of Pembroke, the Lord de Roos, and the rest of the garrisons of the two places should be allowed to retire in safety to Scotland. Alnwick Castle was garrisoned by more determined men; and an attempt was made by a Lancastrian

DUNSTANBURGH CASTLE.²—Finden's Ports and Harbours.

force to relieve it; but Warwick got possession of it by capitulation early in January.

A.D. 1463. Edward gave Alnwick to Sir John Ashley; and this circumstance converted Sir Ralph Gray from a very violent Yorkist into a very violent Lancastrian;

---

¹ Rot. Parl.

² Dunstanburgh Castle is not recorded earlier than the beginning of the fourteenth century, when it was rebuilt by Thomas, Earl of Lancaster, who likewise owned Pontefract Castle. It was taken and dismantled by Edward IV., but its extensive ruins still inclose an area, nearly square, of about nine acres. There is no appearance of the keep, the remains consisting only of the outworks. Dunstanburgh Castle is situated six miles north-east from Alnwick.

for Gray had expected to get Alnwick for himself. This kind of sudden political conversion became very prevalent. Somerset and Percy got back their lands, and their attainders were reversed in parliament. King Henry was now conveyed for safety to one of the strongest castles in Wales. Margaret sailed once more from Scotland, to solicit foreign aid. She landed at Sluis, in Flanders, attended by De Brezé, the Duke of Exeter, and a small body of English exiles. Philip, Duke of Burgundy and Lord of Flanders, with all the adjoining country, was the same Duke Philip that had so long been the ally of the Lancastrians, and that had repeatedly sworn oaths of fealty to Henry; but the whole political system of his early life had changed, and in his old age he had become cautious and reserved. He had no wish to quarrel with the predominant faction in England; his subjects of Flanders were intolerant of all measures likely to interrupt their trade with the English; the duke therefore gave Margaret some money to supply her immediate wants, and sent her with an honourable escort to her father in Lorraine, counselling her to wait events and be patient. But patience was a virtue little known to Margaret of Anjou, who, though she remained some years on the Continent, never remitted her endeavours to raise up enemies against Edward, and stir the people of England to fresh revolts.

A.D. 1464. As early as the month of April the Lancastrians were again in the field. The Duke of Somerset, in spite of his recent submission, flew to the north, where Percy had raised the banner of King Henry, who had been brought from Wales to give the sanction of his presence to this ill-arranged insurrection. The Lord Montague, brother to the Earl of Warwick, scattered their forces or prevented their joining: he defeated Percy on the 25th of April, at Hedgley Moor, near Wooler; he surprised Somerset on the 15th of May, at Hexham. Percy died fighting; the Duke of Somerset and the Lords de Roos and Hungerford were taken and beheaded; and their deaths were followed by a series of executions at Newcastle, Durham, and York. Sir Ralph Gray, who had been out in this affair with the Lancastrians, was taken by the Earl of Warwick in the castle of Bamborough some weeks after, and carried to King Edward, who, during the short, murderous campaign, had been detained at Doncaster by an illness. Edward treated Gray with the utmost severity; his knightly spurs were stricken off by the king's cook; his coat-of-arms was torn from his body, and another coat, reversed, put upon his back: he was sent bare-foot to the town's end, and then he was laid down on a hurdle, and drawn to a scaffold, where his head was struck off. King Henry lurked for a long time among the moors of Lancashire and Westmoreland. About a year after the battle of Hexham he removed into

PERCY'S CROSS ON HEDGLEY MOOR.[1]—Scott's Border Antiquities.

Yorkshire, where he was recognized by some persons of the opposite faction, or, as some say, betrayed by a monk. In the month of July he was seized in Waddington Hall, as he was sitting at dinner, by the servants of Sir James Harrington, who, with his associates, the Tempests, Talbots, and other Yorkists of those parts, forwarded the royal prisoner with a good guard to the capital. As the captive king rode through Islington, he was met by the Earl of Warwick, who lodged him safely in the Tower.

The destruction of the greatest of his enemies, the flight of Queen Margaret, the captivity of her husband, the truces and treaties he had concluded with Scotland, with the King of France, with the Duke of Burgundy, the Duke of Brittany, the Kings of Denmark, Poland, Castile, and Aragon, and the congratulations of the pope on his accession, seemed to prove that Edward's throne was safe and unassailable; but a sudden passion for a beautiful woman—the least dishonourable and ungenerous passion he ever indulged in—shook the throne until it fell; and he, in his turn, became, for a season, a fugitive in foreign lands. Jacquetta, once Duchess of Bed-

[1] This monument, to commemorate the death of Sir Richard Percy, stands on Hedgley Moor, in Northumberland, about sixty paces east of the road which runs from Morpeth to Wooler. It consists of a stone pillar fixed in a pedestal, having the arms of Percy and Lucy cut upon it in relief.

ford, was still living with her second husband, Sir Richard Woodville, or Wydeville. One day Edward paid this lady a visit at her manor of Grafton, near Stony-Stratford. By accident or design, Jacquetta had with her at the time of this visit, her beautiful daughter Elizabeth, who was widow of Sir John Gray, a Lancastrian, who had been slain in the second battle of St. Alban's, and whose estates had been forfeited. This young widow threw herself at the feet of the young and amorous sovereign, imploring him to reverse the attainder of Sir John Gray, in favour of her innocent and helpless children. Whether the effect of this touching appeal was foreseen or not, it seems quite certain that the experienced Jacquetta contrived to turn it to the best account for the advantage of her daughter, and that it was through her ingenious manœuvres that the impetuous Edward was induced to contract a private marriage with Elizabeth at Grafton on the morning of the 1st of May, 1464. The fears of Edward induced him to keep this union a profound secret for some months; but on the 29th of September, having prepared his friends and gathered around him the relations and connections of his wife, who, notwithstanding their having been all of them Lancastrians, were not slow in changing their politics when Elizabeth became queen, he summoned a great council of the prelates and lay lords to meet in the royal abbey of Reading. There the king's brother, the Duke of Clarence, and the Earl of Warwick, who are generally supposed to have been incensed at the unequal and impolitic marriage, took the fair Elizabeth by the hand, and introduced her to the august assembly, by which she was welcomed as their good and right queen. In the month of December following, Edward summoned another great council at Westminster, which settled upon his wife 4000 marks a-year. Early in the following year he began to make preparations for her coronation; Jacquetta, who was come of a princely line, suggested or seconded an invitation which Edward sent to her brother James of Luxemburg; and James came over with a retinue of 100 knights and esquires to do honour to the coronation of his niece. On Saturday, the 25th of May, Elizabeth was paraded in a horse-litter through the streets of London, being most richly attired, and escorted by thirty-eight new-made knights of the Bath, four of whom were citizens of London; and on Sunday she was crowned at Westminster. The feasts, the tournaments, and public rejoicings which followed were unusually magnificent.

Up to this time Edward had left most of the offices and emoluments of government to the great family of the Nevils, to whom he indisputably owed his crown. Warwick, the eldest brother, was chief minister, general, and admiral; he held, besides, the post of warden of the West Marches, chamberlain, and governor of Calais— the last the most profitable of all. The second brother, the Lord Montague, after his victories at Hedgley Moor and Hexham, had received the title and forfeited estates of the Percies, Earls of Northumberland, and he had the wardenship of the East Marches besides. The youngest brother, whom Edward had found Bishop of Exeter, had received the seals as chancellor on the 10th of March, 1461, six days after Edward's accession; and he had very recently been raised to the archiepiscopal see of York. Other members of the family had found most liberal provisions in the spoil and estates of the Lancastrian families; and while Edward had employed himself in the pursuit of pleasure, the Nevils had had their own way in the council. But now the Woodvilles, the Grays, all the relations and connections of the new queen, rushed to the table with an enormous and undiscriminating appetite, every man, in right of consanguinity, seeking a title, an estate, a place, or a rich wife. The court had great influence in such matters; and as the fortunes of the family had taken a turn by an unexpected marriage, they seem to have determined to pursue the system, and actually contracted five or six profitable alliances in a very short time. In one of these matches they clashed with the Nevils. Warwick had solicited the hand of the heiress of the Duke of Exeter for his own nephew; but by the superior influence of Elizabeth, this young lady was contracted to Thomas Gray, her eldest son by her former marriage. The Nevils were incensed at this measure; and other things trenching on their monopoly soon followed. The queen's father, now created Earl Rivers, was made treasurer in the place of their friend Lord Mountjoy; and, shortly after, the hitherto insignificant husband of Jacquetta was made lord high constable, in lieu of the Earl of Worcester. Other great families were irritated by the queen absorbing five heirs of dukes or earls for her five unmarried sisters. For a time the history of this reign is nothing but a scandalous chronicle of match-making and match-breaking, and selfish family intrigues.

A.D. 1467. In this year a marriage was negotiated for Edward's sister, Margaret of York, whose hand was solicited by Charles, Count of Charolois, heir to Philip, Duke of Burgundy, and by Louis XI. of France, Charles' deadly enemy, for one of his sons. This Count of Charolois, who, in a very few months, succeeded to his father, and who obtained the name of Charles the Rash, had always been the declared friend of Henry VI. and the Lancastrians; but he changed, like other men, on seeing

Edward firmly established, and courted his alliance, in the hope that he would assist him against Louis. Edward inclined to these proposals, and was in this probably seconded by the nation, which considered the trade with Flanders as a primary object, and which never was well disposed to French marriages and alliances; but Warwick, who hated the Count of Charolois, insisted that it would be more honourable and advantageous to marry Margaret to the French prince. Edward yielded, or pretended to yield to his arguments, and commissioned the great earl himself to go over to France and negotiate the alliance. Warwick went with his usual magnificence; and the astute Louis, who beat all his contemporaries in king-craft, received him with the honours usually paid to a sovereign prince. The first interview took place at La Bouille, on the Seine, five leagues from Rouen, on the 7th of June. Warwick then proceeded to the capital of Normandy. "The queen and princesses came likewise to Rouen; and the king remained there with the Earl of Warwick the space of twelve days, when the earl returned to England."[1] During the whole or the greater part of the time that Warwick stayed at Rouen the King of France lodged in the next house, and he visited the earl at all hours, passing through a private door with a great air of mystery. This looks like one of the usual mischievous tricks of Louis, who must have known that the best way to weaken and distract the English government was to provoke suspicions and a rupture between Edward and Warwick. The earl arrived in London on the 5th of July, and he was soon followed by the French king's ambassadors, the Archbishop of Narbonne and the Bastard of Bourbon, who, it appears, were charged to put the finishing hand to the treaty of alliance. But another more prevailing bastard had been before them. Under pretence of performing a joust with Edward's wife's brother, Anthony Woodville, who, by marrying the heiress of the late lord, had become Lord Scales, Anthony, Bastard of Burgundy, had crossed over to England while Warwick was absent in France. According to the chronicler, this visitor performed his deeds of arms much to his credit; but the encounter did not last long — "for as it was done to pleasure the King of England, he would not suffer the combat to continue fierce any time, so that it seemed rather for pastime."[2] Indeed, Messire Anthony had come on another errand than to get his bones broken in Smithfield, where the joust was held. He was commissioned by the Count of Charolois to press the match with Margaret; and he had obtained the promise of Edward, who overlooked the commission he had given Warwick to treat with King Louis. If afterwards any obstacle arose, it was removed by the sudden death of Duke Philip, which happened at Bruges, on the 15th of July, and which left to the count, his heir, the succession of states and territories which exceeded in wealth, if not in extent, the whole kingdom of France as then possessed by Louis. Such a suitor was sure to prevail over a weak young French prince with nothing but a narrow and uncertain appanage. But weighty as were these considerations, they did not prevent the proud Earl of Warwick from considering himself juggled, insulted, and disgraced; and as the king, who had resigned himself to the counsels of the queen's relations, took no steps to soothe his irritation, he soon retired, in the worst of humours, to his castle of Middleham. Edward, upon this, pretended to be in danger from treasonable attempts: he no longer moved anywhere without a strong body-guard of archers, and he or his court circulated reports that Warwick had been won by Louis, and that that king considered him as secretly disposed to restore the line of Lancaster. The Nevils were now expelled from court; but the youngest of the brothers, George, Archbishop of York and chancellor, notwithstanding the family resentment, put himself forward as an arbitrator and peace-maker; and chiefly by his means a reconciliation was effected in the beginning of the following year.[3]

A.D. 1468. Warwick presented himself again at court and in the capital, where he was hailed by the people. He appeared with the king and queen in some public pageants; but he could not tolerate the abridgment of his influence. The Woodvilles and the Grays, on the other hand, thought that he was still too powerful; and Edward, who desired a life of ease and pleasure, was annoyed by the stern interference of the man who had made him a king. It was soon understood that all this was likely to end in another field of Towton.

The Duke of Clarence, second brother to King Edward, was considered as next male heir to the throne; for Edward, as yet, had only daughters by his marriage with Elizabeth. The duke's position probably made him an object of suspicion and dislike to the queen, and, at the same time, of ambitious speculation to Warwick, whose society he much affected. The earl had a daughter, the fair Isabella, who, it appears, inspired the young prince with a sincere, and, for a time, uncalculating passion. Edward and the queen's party endeavoured to prevent the union; but, in spite of all opposition, the Duke of Clarence married the Lady Isabella at Calais, in the month of

---

[1] Monstrelet, Comin.   [2] Ibid.   [3] Worcester; Rymer.

July, 1469. While the Earl of Warwick and his brother, the Archbishop of York, were engaged abroad with this ceremony, an insurrection of the farmers and peasants of Yorkshire broke out, and assumed a very alarming character; and it appears that Warwick's other brother, the Earl of Northumberland, who was on the spot, did little to crush it. The rallying words of the insurgents varied several times; but at last they fixed in a general cry for the removal of the queen's relations—the taxers and oppressors—from the council. Edward advanced as far as Newark; but his army was weak and unsteady, and he fled, rather than retreated, to Nottingham. From Nottingham Castle he wrote letters with his own hand to Calais, beseeching his brother Clarence, Warwick, and the archbishop to come immediately to his assistance. These personages did not appear for some weeks, and in the interval a royal army, under the command of the Earl of Pembroke, was defeated at Edgecote, on the 26th of July. Pembroke fell in the battle, and it is said that 5000 of his men perished with him. The insurgents, in a hot pursuit, overtook and captured in the forest of Dean the Earl Rivers, the father, and Sir John Woodville, one of the brothers of the queen; they carried these victims to Northampton, and there cut off both their heads. The Earl of Devon, whose folly and pride had been the real cause of the wretched defeat at Edgecote, was also taken and beheaded. The court believed that the insurgents in these executions acted under orders received from Clarence and his father-in-law Warwick.[1] These great personages, with the Archbishop of York, now arrived in England, and being joined by the Archbishop of Canterbury, they repaired in a very friendly manner to Olney, where they found Edward in a most unhappy condition; his friends were dead or scattered, fleeing for their lives or hiding themselves in remote places; the insurgents were almost upon him. A word from Warwick sent the rebels quietly back to the north; but the king was scarcely freed from that danger ere he found that he was a prisoner in the hands of his pretended liberators, who presently carried him to the strong castle of Middleham. Thus England had two kings, and both prisoners.

At this remarkable crisis the Lancastrians rose in arms in the marches of Scotland; and, after some trifling successes in those parts, meditated an advance into the south. Warwick had at this moment no notion of restoring Henry. In conjunction with the parliament, he summoned all loyal subjects to the standard of King Edward, and immediately marched northward to meet these new insurgents. The murmurs of the army compelled him to release his captive; and at York Edward was presented to the troops as a free and happy king. Warwick then went on and dispersed the Lancastrians: he took their leader prisoner, and brought him to Edward, who ordered his immediate execution. Soon after—but not before Warwick and his associates had exacted sundry grants and places—Edward was allowed to return to London, where, for the first time since his leaving Olney, he became really free. Then family treaties were signed, pledges given, and the most solemn oaths interchanged—each party binding itself to forgive and forget all that had passed. Edward was to love his brother Clarence as before; and even the insurgents of Yorkshire and other parts were included in an amnesty.[2]

A.D. 1470. In the month of February, when this family peace had lasted about twelve weeks, the Archbishop of York gave an entertainment to the king, the Duke of Clarence, and the Earl of Warwick, at his manor of the Moor, in Hertfordshire. As Edward was washing his hands previous to supper, an attendant whispered in his ear that an armed band was lurking near the house. Without his supper, and without any examination as to the correctness of this report, the king got secretly to horse, and, riding all night, reached Windsor Castle. The Duchess of York, the mother of the king, and the friend of Warwick, laboured to dispel these jealousies and animosities, and another hollow reconciliation was brought about. But then there broke out an insurrection among the commons of Lincolnshire, who complained of the extortions and oppressions of the purveyors and other officers of the royal household. Although he believed that this new disorder was their own work, the king was obliged to permit the Duke of Clarence and the Earl of Warwick to take the command of some forces destined for its suppression. Edward, however, marched from a different point with a more numerous army; and, after some faithless and savage deeds, he came up with the insurgents before Clarence and Warwick could reach them, and beat them in a sanguinary battle, which was fought on the 12th of March, at Erpingham, in Rutlandshire. The common insurgents were permitted to depart; but all the leaders who had not fallen in battle were sent to the block. The king then turned openly against his brother Clarence and Warwick, who, it was said, would have joined the insurgents on the following day. After some military manœuvres and long marches, the duke and the earl found

---

[1] It seems, however, probable that the unfortunate men were sacrificed by the spontaneous fury of the people. The Earl of Devon was beheaded at Bridgewater.

[2] *Cont. Hist. Croyl.*; *Rot. Parl.*; *Paston Letters*.

it necessary to disband their forces, and listen to conditions which the king offered by proclamation from the city of York. These terms were not very harsh, if they had been honourably meant; but they were not, and this was well known. Warwick, therefore, turned from the north, fled into Devonshire, and, with his wife, daughter, and several other ladies, his son-in-law Clarence, and a considerable number of friends, embarked at Dartmouth, and made sail for Calais. But when, after a tedious navigation, he reached his old place of refuge, he found the artillery of Calais pointed against his ships, and, on seeking an explanation, learned that a Gascon knight, whom he had left there as his lieutenant, was advised of all that had recently passed in England, and was resolved to keep the place for King Edward.

Warwick then sailed away for the coast of Normandy, to seek a temporary asylum with his cunning friend King Louis, who was right glad to see him as he was; for, in the preceding year, as soon as Warwick had made his peace with Edward, it had been resolved to join the Duke of Burgundy, who was at war with the French, and to send a great English army to the Continent. It was in the month of May that Warwick, Clarence, and their families landed at Harfleur, where the Lord-admiral of France received them all with great respect, showing much gallantry to the ladies. Their vessels were admitted into the harbour, though they were numerous enough to excite some suspicion. After a short time, the ladies with their retinues were honourably escorted to Valogne, where lodgings had been prepared for them by order of the French king. Though a truce had been concluded, Louis was exasperated against his nominal vassal Charles the Rash, who, since his marriage, had become wholly English and Yorkist; he wore on all occasions the blue garter on one of his legs, and the red cross on his mantle, which, adds the chronicler, plainly showed how fierce an enemy he was to his liege lord the King of France. When the Duke Charles heard of the honourable reception given to the fugitives, and of Warwick's men being allowed to sell the captured ships and goods of his subjects in Normandy, he became still more furious, and, by way of reprisal, seized upon all the French merchants who had gone to the fair of Antwerp. Louis, who was prepared for a war, cared little for all this, and gave frequent audience to the fugitives at Tours, Amboise, Vendôme, and other places. He was happy in his own way; for never did sovereign so delight in political manœuvre and intrigue, and never was intrigue more difficult than the one he had now upon his hands.

In the month of June, in the château of Amboise the fallen Lancastrian Queen Margaret

THE CHÂTEAU OF AMBOISE.—From France Monumentale et Pittoresque.

and her son the Prince of Wales met (at first by secret appointment) their old enemy the Earl of Warwick. It was a scene for Shakspeare. Warwick had accused the queen of an attempt to murder him, and he knew her to have been the person that had sent his own father, his friends and associates, to the block. Margaret had cursed the name of Warwick for fifteen long years of misfortune and humiliation. Through that nobleman's means her husband was a prisoner, and she and her son, after suffering the extremity of privation and peril, were exiles and wanderers, dependent on the stinted bounty of relations or political friends. But even the vengeance and hatred of Margaret of Anjou could give way to higher considerations, and, when Warwick joined in cursing Edward of York, and engaged to restore the Lancastrian line, either in the person of her husband or son, she took him to her heart as a friend and brother. The great earl, however, did not engage to do all this without driving another of his hard bargains. Margaret's son, Prince Edward, married the Lady Anne, Warwick's second daughter; and thus, though he destroyed the prospects of Isabella, Duchess of Clarence, he still provided, and in a more direct manner, that one of his children should be Queen of England. "An unaccountable match this," exclaims Comines, "to dethrone and imprison the father, and then marry his daughter to the son; but this was by King Louis' adroit management." "It was no less surprising," continues the chronicler, who wrote of state matters with the knowledge of a statesman and diplomatist, "that he should delude the Duke of Clarence, brother to the king whom he opposed, who ought, in reason, to have dreaded and endeavoured to prevent the restoration of the house of Lancaster; but affairs of this nice nature are to be managed with great craft and artifice, and not without." Up to this point it seems pretty evident that Warwick's scheme was to place his first son-in-law, the Duke of Clarence, upon the throne instead of his brother Edward; but this plan would never have found favour in the sight of King Louis, whose assistance was indispensable, and even the all-prevailing Warwick might have doubted whether the Yorkists, to whom he must have addressed himself in this case, would have been mad enough to divide against each other, and endanger a revolution which had been effected with such difficulty. The Lancastrian party, on the contrary, weakened though it was, was quite ready for another desperate plunge into the vortex; and Warwick, who was determined to recover his ascendency and vast property, and to be revenged on him whom he considered the ungrateful king of his own making, by whatsoever means that offered, did not despair, when allied with Margaret and her son, of making that party believe in the sincerity of his conversion, though he had slaughtered their relations and friends in the field and on the scaffold.

The Duke of Clarence was at this time not much more than twenty-one years old, and, judging from all that is recorded of him, he must have conjoined a weak bad head to a very indifferent heart. He was not, however, so far gone in fatuity as to be insensible to Warwick's startling alliance—perilous to the whole house of York—or to be blind to his own false position; and now an excellent negotiator came to him from his brother's court in the person of a fair lady. Comines, who was actively engaged in some of these transactions as friend, agent, and confidential minister of the Duke of Burgundy, and who had gone to Calais to keep the lieutenant-governor "true to his principles," tells us, that one day a lady of quality passed through that town into France to join the Duchess of Clarence. "But," he adds, "the secret business to be managed by this lady was to implore the Duke of Clarence not to contribute to the subversion of his own family, by going along with those who were endeavouring to restore the house of Lancaster—to remember their old insolences, and the hereditary hatred that was between them, and not to be so infatuated as to imagine that the Earl of Warwick, who had married his daughter to the Prince of Wales, and sworn allegiance already, would not endeavour to put that prince upon the throne to the exclusion of all the Yorkists. This lady managed the affair with so much cunning and dexterity, that she prevailed with the duke to go over to King Edward's party, the duke desiring first to be in England. This lady was no fool nor blabber; and being on her way to join her mistress the Duchess of Clarence, she, for that reason, was employed in this secret mission rather than a man." This mission appears to have been the sole precaution taken by Edward or his court at this crisis. "The king seemed never concerned at anything, but still followed his gallantries and his hunting; and nobody was so great with him as the Archbishop of York and the Marquis of Montague, both brothers to the Earl of Warwick: these swore to be true to him against all enemies whatsoever, and the thoughtless king put an entire confidence in them."[1] His brother-in-law, Charles the Rash, was both prudent and active on this occasion: he got ready a strong fleet to blockade Harfleur and the mouth of the Seine; he sent Edward word of the very port where Warwick designed to land; and, as the sea was an uncertain element, and the earl might break his blockade and escape his ships, he repeatedly warned him to take care of himself, and put his kingdom in a posture of defence. But Edward only laughed at these fears: he said he wished his adversary were landed; and only begged the duke to keep a good look-out at sea, so as to prevent the earl from again escaping into France, when he, Edward, should have beaten him in battle by land.

Warwick did not make him wait long. The Duke of Burgundy's fleet, which lay in battle array at Havre, was dispersed by a storm; as soon as the weather cleared Warwick set sail with a fair wind, and on the 13th of September landed safely on the Devonshire coast. Edward at the moment was in the north, whither, it appears, he had been drawn by a feigned revolt headed by some of the Nevils. The great earl had not been landed above five or six days before the whole country flocked to his standard. "Fully furnished on every side by his kindred and friends, he took his way towards London, where he expected to find more open friends than privy enemies."[2] The capital, indeed, had been greatly excited by one Doctor Godard, who had preached at St. Paul's Cross in favour of the king in the Tower; and, in the neighbourhood,

[1] Comines.   [2] Hall.

the men of Kent had taken up arms. As London seemed secure, and as news was brought that Edward had retraced his steps to Nottingham, Warwick soon changed his direction, and marched straight towards the Trent, summoning every man between the ages of sixteen and sixty to join him. Edward, in the mean time, found that the men he summoned did not come, and that those who were with him began to desert. One day, as he sat at dinner, news was brought him that the Marquis of Montague, Warwick's brother, and several other persons of quality, had mounted their horses and caused the soldiers to toss their bonnets in the air, and cry "God bless King Harry!" Edward was at this moment in Lincolnshire, near the river Welland: he instantly armed himself, and posted a battalion of his guards at a neighbouring bridge in order to prevent the passage of the enemy, for Warwick's van was within half a day's march of him. The Lord Hastings was with Edward with a body of 3000 horse; but Hastings had married a sister of the Earl of Warwick, and, while the king had probably no great confidence in him,[1] the soldiers possibly had no great affection for the queen's brother, Earl Rivers, who was also in attendance. Edward, at all events, determined to flee; and as his bravery was always conspicuous, we must conclude that resistance was hopeless.

It happened that his quarters were at no great distance from the sea, and a small ship that followed with provisions for his army lay at anchor with two Dutch vessels hard by, apparently in the Wash.[2] He had but just time to get on board these vessels, with a few lords and knights, and about 300 men. Before leaving the rest, they were exhorted to go and join the Earl of Warwick, pretending great friendship, but at the same time to retain secretly in their hearts their old affection and allegiance to King Edward. The three vessels presently weighed anchor: not one in twenty of Edward's followers knew where they were going, and they were all without any clothes except the warlike gear they had on their backs, and no money had they in their pockets.[3] Edward sailed directly for Holland. The Easterlings, who joined the calling of privateers to that of merchants, and who at times appear to have been pirates as lawless and cruel as the corsairs of Tunis or Algiers, were then at war both with the English and French: they had many ships in the narrow seas, and had done the English much prejudice this year already. Eight of these Easterlings gave chase to Edward's weak squadron. Edward ran his ships ashore on the coast of Friesland, near the small town of Alkmaar. Grutuse, the governor or stadtholder of Holland, Friesland, and Zealand, was at that time in Alkmaar, and he, by his prompt protection, saved the whole party from captivity—for the Easterlings had brought their ships close in shore, and only waited the turn of the tide to board the three vessels. "The king," says Comines, "having no money, was forced to give the master of his ship a gown lined with martens, and to promise to do more for him another time; and sure so poor a company was never seen before; yet the Lord de la Grutuse dealt very honourably by them, giving them clothes, and bearing all their expenses till they came to the Hague, to which place he safely conducted them." From the Hague the governor despatched news to the Duke of Burgundy, Edward's loving brother-in-law, "who," adds the chronicler, "was much surprised when he heard it, and would have been much better pleased if it had been news of Edward's death, for he was in great apprehension of the Earl of Warwick, who was his enemy, and now become absolute in England." On the other side, King Louis, whose many agents soon carried him the intelligence, was overjoyed, and, being a religious sovereign, he gave orders that the nobles, the clergy, and the good people of Paris should make processions in honour of God and the Virgin Mary, and continue them for three days, with praise and thanksgiving for the great victory which Henry of Lancaster, lawful King of England, had gained over the foul usurper, the Earl of March, as also in gratitude for the happy peace that would now subsist between the two countries. Processions were afterwards performed in all the principal towns in Louis' dominions.

Warwick was now possessed, in appearance, of all the power in England. From the neighbourhood of the Welland he turned back upon London, which he entered in triumph on the 6th of October, in company with Clarence—for as yet this son-in-law concealed his hostile projects. Warwick went directly to the Tower, and released King Henry, whom five years before he had himself committed to that prison. "When he imprisoned him he went before Henry, crying 'Treason! treason!' and 'Behold the traitor!'—but now he proclaimed him king, attended him to his palace at Westminster, and restored him to his royal title; and all this in the presence of the Duke of Clarence, who was not at all pleased with the sight."[4] A great number of persons of the first rank, who were in King Edward's interest, and who afterwards did him good service, took sanctuary in different religious houses. The

---

[1] Hastings, however, remained true to Edward, accompanied him in his flight, contributed to his return, and continued to serve him faithfully, with the exception of taking "bribes from France."

[2] Hall says that Edward embarked at Lynn on the Wash.
[3] Comines; Hall.

[4] Comines.

queen, with her mother Jacquetta and her three daughters, had fled to the sanctuary of Westminster, where, being in great want of all things necessary, Queen Elizabeth was shortly after delivered of her first son. Save that of the Earl of Worcester, who was hated for his severity by the people, no blood was shed in this rapid revolution. We are left in the dark as to the proceedings of the parliament which met in the month of November, for its acts were erased from the rolls at the subsequent counter-revolution. It is stated, however, on good authority, that an act of settlement entailed the crown on Henry's son Edward, Prince of Wales, and, in case of that prince's death, on the Duke of Clarence. Warwick, of course, would take care to attaint his enemies and reward his friends: this "king-maker," in fact, was in all essentials king, and the imbecile Henry was still a captive, and in all probability a more unhappy one than he had been in his undisturbed prison in the Tower.[2]

A.D. 1471. But if Edward had lost a crown like a game at cards, he regained it with equal rapidity. On the 12th of March, about five months after his flight from the Wash, he appeared with a fleet off the coast of Suffolk, having been assisted in secret by the Duke of Burgundy, who played as double a part in this business as might have been expected from his great rival Louis XI. He had issued a proclamation forbidding any of his subjects to join Edward, but, underhand, he sent him 50,000 florins, with St. Andrew's cross, furnished him with three or four great ships of his own, which he had equipped for him at Vere, in Walcheren, and hired secretly fourteen Easterling ships, all well armed—"which supply was very great, considering the times."[3] As Edward's troops, however, did not exceed 1200 men, he was deterred from landing in the Wash, on the shores of which was assembled a Lancastrian army, but, bearing to the north, he sailed into the Humber, and landed on the 16th of March at Ravenspur, the place where Henry of Bolingbroke had disembarked when he came to dethrone Richard II. Finding the people in the north not very favourable, he veiled his designs: and even at York he only engaged the citizens to assist him to recover his honour and estate as Duke of York, solemnly swearing not to attempt to recover the crown.[4]

A few oaths cost nothing in these times, and, in the present case, the necessity for dissimulating soon passed. At Pontefract, Warwick's brother, the Marquis of Montague, who already repented of the revolution he had helped to make, opened a correspondence instead of fighting, and permitted Edward's weak column to march within sight of his quarters, where a great force was collected. As soon as the Yorkists crossed the Trent they were on their own ground, and the people flocked from all sides to the standard of Edward, who then re-assumed the royal title. In the neighbourhood of Coventry he found himself in presence of a Lancastrian army, under the command of the Earls of Warwick and Oxford and the Duke of Clarence: now was the moment for the latter to act, and, making his men put the White Rose of York over their gorgets, he went over with colours flying to his brother Edward. Upon this sudden manœuvre of his son-in-law, Warwick found himself compelled to decline the battle which was offered to him, and then Edward threw himself fearlessly between his enemies and the capital, which had forgotten the sermons of Doctor Go-

REMAINS OF THE SANCTUARY, WESTMINSTER.[1]—Smith's Antiquities of Westminster.

---

[1] This noted sanctuary was one of those exempted from suppression by Henry VIII. The church belonging to it was supposed to have been of the time of Edward the Confessor. It was destroyed about a century ago; but some remains survived, and were discovered on the demolition of some buildings with which the vestiges had been incorporated.

[2] Cont. Hist. Croyl.; Fabyan; Hall; Comines.

[3] Comines.

[4] We are indebted to the Camden Society for the publication of a very curious Historie of the Arrivall of Edward IV. in England, which throws much light upon the short and extraordinary campaign that commenced at Ravenspur. This history is also valuable as confirmatory of the narrative of Hall and other old writers.

dard and the roast-meats[1] of the Earl of Warwick, and was once more all for King Edward. Cominos attributes the enthusiastic reception he met with in London to three things especially:—the first was, he says, the great number of his partizans in sanctuary within the walls, and the recent birth of a young prince; the next, the great debts which he owed to the richest of the merchants, who could only hope for payment through his restoration; and the third was, that the ladies of quality and rich citizens' wives, whom he had formerly delighted with his gallantries, forced their husbands and relations to declare themselves of his side. Whatever were their motives, it seems certain that the return of the White Rose of York was hailed with enthusiasm by the citizens. But Edward had short time to enjoy these demonstrations: the Lancastrian army had collected in one mass, and Warwick was advancing upon the capital by the high north road. After passing only two days in London, Edward took the field. He found Warwick's force drawn out in order of battle on Barnet Common, only twelve miles from London. About 40,000 Englishmen prepared to draw the sword and bend the bow against each other—the two armies, it appears, being nearly equal in number. But it was late in the day, and the eve of Easter Sunday, and so the battle was delayed till the morrow. Edward slept this Saturday night at Barnet; the Earl of Warwick lay to the northward of that town. The Duke of Clarence sent to make an offer of his mediation, but this was indignantly rejected by his father-in-law. "Go tell your master," cried the proud earl to the messenger, "that Warwick, true to his oath, is a better man than false perjured Clarence, and will settle this quarrel by the sword to which he has appealed." At an early hour on the following day, battle was joined. "Both sides fought on foot, and the king's vanguard suffered extremely in this action; the earl's main battle advanced against his, and so near, that the king himself was engaged in person. The Earl of Warwick's custom was never to fight on foot; but now, at the importunity of his brother the Marquis of Montague, he sent away his horses. The conclusion of all was, that the earl, the Marquis of Montague, and several other brave officers were killed."[2]

This battle of Barnet lasted from four o'clock in the morning till ten, during which time there was a thick mist, raised, as was once generally believed, by Friar Bungay, a great magician. There is a mist of another kind, and one which we cannot now clear, hanging over nearly the whole history of the battle, which, notwithstanding the time it lasted and the statement of Cominos, we are disposed to believe was much less fierce and murderous than most of the preceding conflicts.[3] The results, however, are well authenticated. Of all the great Lancastrian lords who had fought on the side of the king-maker, not one escaped except the Earl of Oxford, who joined Jasper Tudor, Earl of Pembroke, who was in arms for King Henry in Wales. Edward lost Lord Cromwell, Lord Say, and the son of Lord Berners, with Sir John Lisle, Thomas Parr, and John Milwater, who were esquires to his brother Richard, Duke of Gloucester. The common dead were buried on the same plain, half a mile from Barnet, where a chapel was erected for the good of their souls.[4] The body of the "king-maker,"

OBELISK NEAR BARNET TO MARK THE SPOT WHERE WARWICK FELL.—From a sketch by J. W. Archer.

with that of his brother Montague, was carried,

---

[1] One of the secrets of Warwick's popularity lay in his kitchen and buttery. His hospitality was as boundless as his wealth. "When he came to London," says old Stow, "he held such an house, that six oxen were eaten at a breakfast, and every tavern was full of his meat; for he who had any acquaintance in that house, he should have had as much boiled and roast as he might carry on a long dagger."

[2] Cominos.

[3] Sir John Paston, who, along with one of his brothers, fought in the battle on the Lancastrian side, says, in a letter to his mother, written on the Thursday following, that the killed of both parties amounted to more than 1000.—Paston Letters Some historians make the amount of the slain 10,000!

[4] Stow says that this chapel, which marked the field of battle, was standing in his time. Lysons (see Environs of London) gives it as his opinion that the battle was not fought on Barnet Heath, but rather to the south-east, about East Barnet; but he quotes no authority, and all tradition is strongly opposed to his opinion. The conflict seems really to have taken place on the elevated plateau to the north of the town of Barnet, and is probably marked with sufficient accuracy by the modern stone column at the end of the common, where the high road forks.

to London, and lay naked in the church of St. Paul's for the space of three or four days, that all men might see the end he had met with. King Henry, who had been taken in London, defenceless and helpless, was sent back to his old apartments in the Tower. But Margaret of Anjou, who was as active and resolute as ever, called the victorious Edward again into the field only five days after the battle of Barnet. Many circumstances had detained her on the Continent, and it was her fortune to land at Plymouth with her son Prince Edward and a body of auxiliaries, chiefly French, on the very day on which Warwick was defeated and slain. In part, probably, on account of their old antipathy to the French queen, who now came surrounded with Frenchmen, and in part because they were weary of this civil war, the people opposed her progress, and, by securing the bridges and fords of the river Severn, prevented her joining the forces under the Earl of Pembroke in Wales. On the 4th of May, King Edward, with his brothers Clarence and Gloucester, fell upon her on the left bank of the Severn, near Tewkesbury. Her troops had thrown up some intrenchments, from which they had repulsed the Yorkists; but the Duke of Somerset, who commanded her army, had the folly to quit this position, and, sallying forth, he ordered the mass of his troops to follow him, which some did, and others did not. Those who sallied were driven back with dreadful loss, and those who stayed behind were suspected of treachery, for no general was now sure of his officers. Somerset rode up to the Lord Wenlock, who had remained behind the intrenchments, and knocked out his brains with his battle-axe. The banner of the audacious Richard, Duke of Gloucester, was already within the Lancastrian lines; Edward and Clarence now followed, and the affair of Tewkesbury terminated in panic, confusion, and murder. Margaret of Anjou, who had survived so many catastrophes and escaped from so many battles, remained a prisoner at last, and with her was taken her son, the Prince of Wales, who was now in his eighteenth year. "What brought you to England?" cried the ungenerous Edward. "My father's crown and mine own inheritance!" replied the royal youth. Edward brutally struck him on the mouth with his gauntlet, and then Clarence and Gloucester, or their attendants (or, according to an earlier account which does not mention Clarence and Gloucester, Edward's servants) despatched him with their swords in the king's tent.[1] The Duke of Somerset, with the grand-prior of St. John's, Sir Humphrey Audely, Sir Gervis of Clifton, Sir William Gainsby, Sir William Cary, Sir Henry Rose, Sir Thomas Tresham, and seven esquires, escaped from the field, and took sanctuary in a church in Tewkesbury. This sacred kind of asylum had long been respected, and to this principle and feeling Edward had recently owed the preservation of his wife, his children, and his best friends, whom the Lancastrians had permitted to live undisturbed in the sanctuaries they had chosen in London and Westminster. But the king and his brothers were regardless of these circumstances, and Edward broke into the church at Tewkesbury sword in hand. A priest bearing the sacrament threw himself between the savages and their victims, and would not move till the king promised to pardon all who had taken sanctuary there. These men, who might have escaped, tarried in the church, trusting in the royal pardon, from Saturday the 4th of May till Monday the 6th, when they were dragged from the foot of the altar and beheaded.

Margaret of Anjou lived for five years the prisoner[2] of her conqueror, was then ransomed by Louis XI., and died in France about eleven years after the fight at Tewkesbury. The death of her husband, which immediately followed Edward's return to London, probably did not much affect her. The triumphant party had now evidently made up their minds to show no mercy; but that event was probably precipitated by a desperate attempt made on the 14th of May, by Thomas Nevil, the Bastard of Falconbridge, Warwick's vice-admiral, to release Henry from his confinement and proclaim him once more. On the 21st of May King Edward entered London in great pomp with 30,000 men, and on that evening, or the following morning, King Henry was found lifeless in the Tower. The best of the contemporary chroniclers, though he does not name the murderer, hints clearly that he *was murdered*, and that the deed was done or ordered by Edward, or by his brother Clarence, or Richard, Duke of Gloucester, or some other member of the royal house of York. "May God," he exclaims, "grant time for repentance to the person, whoever he was, who laid his sacrilegious hands on the Lord's anointed."[3] The dead body, surrounded by guards and torches, was exhibited to the people in St. Paul's, and afterwards quietly buried in the abbey of Chertsey. But this unhappy prince was not allowed rest even in the

---

[1] *Cont. Hist. Croyl.; Fabyan; Hall; Stow.*

[2] She was at first confined in the Tower of London, afterwards at Windsor, and then at Wallingford. All that Edward would allow for the support of herself and servants was a pittance of five marks per week.

[3] *Cont. Hist. Croyl.* Fabyan, who was living in London at the time, says, "Of the death of this prince Henry VI.), divers tales were told; but the most common fame went, that he was sticked with a dagger by the hands of the Duke of Gloucester, which, after Edward IV., usurped the crown, and was king, as after shall appear."

grave. A few years after, Gloucester, then Richard III., was made uneasy by the popular belief that miracles were wrought at his tomb, and he ordered his bones to be removed—some say to Windsor: then, on the fall of Richard, Henry VII. wished to bring them back to Westminster, but it appears that they could not be found.

The episodes to the lamentable history of the fall of the house of Lancaster are numerous, and, in some respects, exceedingly romantic. Some of the leaders, like the Duke of Exeter, appear to have been secretly assassinated; others, like the Earl of Oxford, were shut up in different castles; and others, like the Earl of Pembroke, the late king's half-brother, and uncle to Henry VII., escaped to the Continent, where, for the most part, they lived in extreme poverty. Some Lancastrians, whose learning and abilities were worth purchasing—as Dr. Morton, and Sir John Fortescue, lord chief-justice to Henry VI., and the greatest English lawyer of his time—obtained the reversal of their attainders, together with fresh employments from the Yorkists.

Now seemed the "glorious summer" of the house of York. The young Prince Edward, who had been born in the sanctuary of Westminster during his father's flight into Holland, was created Prince of Wales, and recognized as lawful heir to the crown—not in parliament—but in a great council of prelates and lay lords. The Lancastrians as a party were annihilated. There was nothing to disturb the tranquillity of the Yorkists but the base and selfish passions of the three royal and most legitimate brothers. The Duke of Clarence, the second brother, it will be remembered, had married the Earl of Warwick's eldest daughter, Isabella, and, in her right, he now demanded the entire property of his deceased father-in-law; but Richard, Duke of Gloucester, the youngest brother, was eager to divide the great prize with him, and therefore proposed to marry Anne, Warwick's younger daughter, and widow to Prince Edward, whom the brothers between them had murdered at Tewkesbury. Clarence, to defeat this project, concealed the young lady; but Gloucester had far too much activity and cunning to allow himself to be duped by so miserable a manœuvre—he soon found out the Lady Anne in London, where it is said she was disguised as a cook-maid, and, getting possession of her person, he lodged her, for present security, in the sanctuary of St. Martin's. Richard then appealed to Edward and the council, and was allowed to marry the Lady Anne; but Clarence swore that he would not "part the livelihood with him." The loving brothers pleaded each his cause in person before the king in council, and every man, says the monkish chronicler, admired the strength of their respective arguments. In the end, but not until the whole capital had been agitated as if by the approach of another civil war,[1] the king composed these differences, alloting a handsome portion to the Lady Anne, and leaving all the rest of the property to the elder sister, Isabella, the wife of Clarence. As it has been remarked,[2] the greatest sufferer in this adjustment was the widowed Countess of Warwick, who was mother to both the ladies, and who had brought the mass of the property into the family; for Clarence and Gloucester got the whole between them, and the countess was reduced to absolute want.

A.D. 1475. After some curious negotiations with the Duke of Brittany and his brother-in-law the Duke of Burgundy, who was finding himself overmatched by the policy and craft of Louis XI., Edward contracted an alliance offensive and defensive with the two dukes; and in order, we presume, to give a startling effect to his beginning, he sent a herald to demand from the French monarch the immediate surrender of his kingdom, which he claimed on the old grounds. Comines says, that this was only a letter of defiance,[3] and that it was written in such an elegant style, and such polite language, that he could scarcely believe any Englishman wrote it. When Louis had read the letter to himself, he withdrew into another room, and, sending for the herald that brought it, he told him that he had a wonderful respect and affection for his master, King Edward, whom he knew in this matter to be set on and deluded by the Duke of Burgundy, a weak and treacherous ally. "Besides which," continues Comines, who had changed sides, and was now in the service of Louis, "the king used several good arguments to induce the herald to persuade his master to a peaceful accommodation, secretly putting 300 crowns with his own hands into his pouch, and promising him 1000 more when the good peace should be

---

[1] Sir John Paston, writing to his brother on the 17th of February (1471), says:—"Yesterday, the king, the queen, my Lords of Clarence and Gloucester, went to Sheno to pardon; men say, not all in charity; what will fall men cannot say. The king entreateth my Lord of Clarence for my Lord of Gloucester; and, as it is said, he answereth, that he may well have my lady, his sister-in-law, but they shall part no livelihood, as he saith; so what will fall can I not say." On the 15th of April, 1473, he writes: "The world seemeth queasy (uneasy) here; for the most part that be about the king have sent hither for their harness, and it is said for certain that the Duke of Clarence maketh him big in that he can, showing as he would but (only) deal with the Duke of Gloucester; but the king intendeth, in eschewing all inconvenience, to be as big as they both, and to be a stiffler (stickler) between them; and some men think that under this there should be some other thing intended, and some treason conspired; so what shall fall can I not say."—Paston Letters.
[2] Walpole, Hist. Doubts.
[3] He states, however, that Edward demanded the French crown as "his inheritance."

concluded; and then, in public, his majesty ordered that a piece of crimson velvet, thirty ells long, should be presented to the said herald, who was gartered king-at-arms."[1] His chivalrous occupations did not render him insensible to a good bribe. Garter promised to do what he could, and advised Louis to open a correspondence with the Lord Howard or the Lord Stanley, two of Edward's favourites and ministers, whom he knew to be averse to the war.

Having prolonged a truce with Scotland, and concluded a matrimonial treaty with that court, and being most abundantly furnished with money by means of repeated grants voted by parliament, and of benevolences—an unheard-of species of imposition first introduced in the present period—Edward collected a fine army of 16,000 or 18,000 men. With this force he landed at Calais, on the 22d of June. The first check to this mighty enterprise proceeded from his brother-in-law of Burgundy, who had agreed to join him in force, but who, having wasted his resources in one of his rash expeditions in another direction, came to the rendezvous with a mere handful of troops. Edward, irritated at this circumstance, and still more at seeing that Duke Charles and his subjects entertained the greatest jealousy of the English, refusing them admittance into the towns of Artois and Picardy, soon inclined his ear to the skilful negotiators of Louis and to the lords of his own council, who, through conviction or bribery, recommended an immediate peace with the French king. The English army lay inactive for nearly two months at Peronne, where all the preliminaries were settled, and where the money of Louis was made to circulate freely among the corrupt ministers and courtiers of Edward. The French diplomatists promised whatever was asked, and agreed, among other things, to pay 50,000 crowns for the release of Margaret of Anjou. One day the King of France sent the King of England 300 cart-loads of the best wines of the kingdom; and a few days after, the two sovereigns agreed to a personal interview on a bridge thrown across the Somme at Picquigny, near Amiens, there being a strong barricade of wood between them—for Louis was very suspicious, and he knew the old story of the bridge of Montereau, in which his own father had figured. Comines and another agent were sent to survey the river and neighbourhood. "On the one side, by which our king was to come," says this historian, "was a fine open country; and on the other side, indeed, was the same, *only* the King of England, to come to the river, was obliged to pass a causeway about two bow-shots long, with marshes on both sides of it, which might have been of very dangerous consequence to the English, if our intentions had not been honourable. And certainly, as I have said before, the English do not manage these matters with so much cunning and policy as the French do, let people say of them what they will, but proceed more ingeniously, and with more frankness; but one must be patient with them, and take care not to quarrel." The barricade in the midst of the bridge is described as being made of strong grating or lattice-work, such as lions' cages are made of, the space between the bars being no wider than to admit a man's arm. On the 29th of August, in the morning, the two kings appeared on opposite sides of the river. Louis went first to the grating, attended by about twelve persons of the greatest quality in France, among whom were John, Duke of Bourbon, and the cardinal, his brother. "The King of England advanced along the causeway, very nobly attended, there being in his train his brother the Duke of Clarence, the Earl of Northumberland, Lord Hastings, his chamberlain, his chancellor, and other peers. He was dressed in cloth of gold, and he wore upon his head a black velvet cap with a large *fleur-de-lis* made of precious stones. In truth, he was a prince of a most noble, majestic presence; his person graceful and erect, but now a little inclining to fat. When he came within a short distance of the railing he pulled off his

BELFRY AND MARKET-PLACE, PERONNE.—From Voyages dans l'Ancienne France.

[1] Comines.

cap, and bowed to within a foot of the ground; and Louis, who was leaning against the barrier on the other side, bowed in the like manner. They embraced through the holes of the grating; and the King of England making another low bow, the King of France said, 'Cousin, you are right welcome; there is no person living I was so ambitious of seeing, and God be thanked that this interview is upon so good an occasion.'" The King of England returned the compliment in French; and Comines tells us that his French was very good. When the compliments and ceremonies were over, they proceeded to business, and, in the end, a missal and a crucifix, said to contain some of the wood of the true cross, were brought to the grate, and the two kings, putting one hand on the book and the other on the crucifix, swore religiously to observe the present treaty. When the two kings had sworn, "our king," continues Comines, " who had always words at command, told the English king, in a jocose way, that he should be right glad to see him at Paris; and that if he would come and divert himself with the gay ladies there, he would assign for his confessor the Cardinal of Bourbon, who he knew would grant him easy absolution for any peccadillos in the way of love and gallantry. The King of England was much pleased with this raillery, and made his majesty several smart repartees—for he knew that the cardinal was a gay man with the ladies, and a boon companion." After a few words spoken in secret to one another, the lords being sent to a distance, these gracious sovereigns shook hands through the grating, and departed, each his own way, Louis riding back to Amiens, and Edward to his army. The King of England was accommodated out of the King of France's stores with whatever he wanted, to the very torches and candles. The minute relater of these events expressly tells us that Richard, Duke of Gloucester, and some other Englishmen of high rank, were not present at the interview of Picquigny, as being averse to the whole treaty, and esteeming it dishonourable to their country; but he adds that they recollected themselves after the treaty was signed, and went into Amiens to King Louis, who splendidly entertained them, and generously presented them with plate and some fine horses. Louis, while thus buying and bribing, hated, feared, and despised Edward, all in a breath; and his caution, timidity, and contempt are hit off, as if involuntarily, by his confidential agent. During their ride back to Amiens he told Comines that he was rather uneasy at the readiness with which Edward had accepted his invitation to Paris. "Cortes," said he, " our brother of England is a very fine king, and a warm admirer of the ladies; he might chance to find some dame at Paris so much to his taste as to tempt him to return; his predecessors have been too often in Paris and Normandy already, and I have no great affection for his company on this side the Channel, though ready to hold him as good friend and brother on the other side of the water." " Nor," continues Comines, " ought any man to wonder, considering the mighty mischiefs which the English had brought upon France, and the freshness of their date, that the King of France should be anxious to send them home again, and to do all he could, by money or otherwise, to keep them in a good humour." That same evening, as they were going to supper, Lord Howard, who was to remain some time with the court, made Louis quake again, by telling him in his ear, with great glee, that it should go hard, but he would find a way to induce his master to go to Paris to be merry a while with him. " Though this proposition was not in the least agreeable to the king," adds Comines, " yet he dissembled pretty well, and fell a washing his hands, without giving a direct answer to the Lord Howard; but he whispered me, that he feared his forebodings were coming to pass. After supper, they fell upon the same subject again; but the king put them off with the greatest gentleness and wisdom imaginable, pretending that his expedition against the Duke of Burgundy would require his immediate presence in a different part of France." In private, Louis expressed his opinion of Edward in pretty strong terms; but if he perceived that his words were overheard by any save his most confidential friends, he fell into a tremor and trepidation, and took great pains to prevent his words from being repeated.[1] Some of his friends, and the chivalry of France generally, considered the treaty of Picquigny as very dishonourable to the nation; but he let them talk on, and felt himself a happy man when he saw Edward's back fairly turned, and heard that he and his army were on the other side of the Channel. If the French thought it disgraceful to buy, the English thought it disgraceful to be bought; and as they had given immense sums for carrying on the war, and had flattered themselves with recovering Normandy, Anjou, Maine, and Guienne, at the very least, they were greatly incensed at the transactions of Picquigny, though all the corruption of Edward's ministers and courtiers was not revealed to them, and but few understood the fact that both the king and his cabinet had become pensioners to France. The principal articles of the treaty of Picquigny were, that Louis should pay instantly (which he did) the sum of 75,000 crowns; that he should pay Edward an annuity of 50,000 crowns; that he

---

[1] For some very amusing instances, see *Comines.*

should marry his son, the dauphin, to Edward's eldest daughter Elizabeth, or, in case of her death, to her sister Mary—such marriage to be concluded when the parties were of proper age; and that a peace or truce for seven years, at least, should be secured, together with a free trade between the two countries. Following their master's example, the Lord Hastings and the chancellor got pensions of 2000 crowns each; and Louis agreed to distribute annually 12,000 crowns more among the Marquis of Dorset, the Lord Howard, Cheney, the master of the horse, Sir Thomas Montgomery, Thomas St. Leger, and some others of the profligate courtiers.

On the whole, the country seems to have been tranquil for some years, till the house of York became suddenly involved in one of the darkest tragedies. It was impossible for a nature like Edward's to forget conduct like that of his brother Clarence; and that weak-headed prince appears to have accelerated his fate by fresh imprudence, and the betrayal, on all occasions, both public and private, of a provoking suspicion and jealousy of his brothers, the king and the Duke of Gloucester. In 1476 Clarence's wife, Isabella, died after an illness of two or three months; and one of her female attendants was condemned and executed for poisoning her. About the same time the Burgundian duke, Charles the Rash, was killed at the battle of Nancy, and, leaving no heirs male, his immense estates fell to his daughter Mary. Taking advantage of his opportune widowhood, Clarence immediately proposed himself as a husband to this great heiress, whose step-mother (Clarence's sister) seconded his suit. But as soon as Edward heard of this negotiation, his jealousy took the alarm; he opposed it with all his might, and caused it to miscarry. Clarence, who had not been guarded in his expressions before, could now put no restraint upon his tongue. The court, probably well informed of all this incautious man did and said, soon made him feel its vengeance. At first they attacked him through the sides of his friends. One Stacey, a priest in his service, was accused of having recourse to damnable magic (much like that laid to the charge of Eleanor Cobham, the wife of the unfortunate Duke Humphrey) to hasten the death of the Lord Beauchamp, by the slow melting of certain images. Being put to torture, that he might be forced to confess who were his setters on and accomplices, he named Thomas Burdett, a gentleman of Clarence's household, and one to whom the duke was greatly attached. These unfortunate men, it appears, were tried in a hurried manner by the judges and some temporal peers, convicted, and executed. They both died protesting their innocence. Clarence, who was too late to save their lives, presented himself in the council, which for some time he had rarely attended, to prove that his servants had met with an unjust doom; and for this attempt, which was called an interference with justice, his brother, the king, in a public manner committed him to the Tower. Everything was conducted in a public manner except the execution. A parliament was summoned on the 16th of January, 1478, when the king appeared in person to prosecute his own brother Clarence, who was brought to the bar of the lords. The charges were monstrous, and for the greater part absurd; but Edward had witnesses to swear to them all, and the impossible part of the guilt was probably that which made the greatest impression. Clarence was accused of dealing with the devil by means of conjurors and necromancers; of having plotted to dethrone the king and disinherit the king's children; of having given to his servants large sums of money, venison, &c., that they might assemble and feast the king's subjects, in order to induce them to believe that Thomas Burdett had been wrongfully executed, and to spread a rumour that the king himself was notoriously guilty of the black art and dealing with the devil, and secret poisoning, and was, besides, a bastard, without right to the crown. After all this, it was charged that Clarence had induced divers of the king's subjects to be sworn upon the sacrament to be true to him and his heirs; that the duke had engaged to restore the confiscated estates of the Lancastrians; that he had gotten and preserved an act under the great seal of Henry VI., the latter king, whereby he, Clarence, was declared next heir to the crown in case of the death of Edward, Prince of Wales, and that the duke had ordered his retainers to keep themselves ready to take up arms for him and his rights at an hour's notice. None of the peers spoke in his behalf; but Clarence, it appears, vehemently denied every charge. His reply, however, has not been preserved; for, during the greater part of this tyrannical reign, nothing was inserted or allowed to remain on the rolls of parliament that was displeasing to the king. The duke was found guilty, and received sentence of death on the 7th of February. Soon after, the House of Commons were induced to appear in the lords, and petition for the immediate execution of this sentence.[1] But, notwithstanding these high sanctions, it was not thought proper to execute the sentence in an open manner, or, indeed, to allow that it had been executed in any way. On the 18th of February, or, according to some authorities, on the 11th of March, it

[1] About the same time an act was passed, reversing, as illegal, the judgment passed upon the female servant accused of poisoning the Duchess of Clarence.

was whispered that the duke had died in the Tower, upon which people speculated in their usual manner as to the mode of his death; the most popular belief — which there is nothing either to prove or disprove — being, that his brothers had secretly caused him to be drowned in a butt of Malmsey wine. Suspicion rested on Richard, Duke of Gloucester, on account of their old enmity, and because Richard kept fair with the queen, and profited by Clarence's forfeiture.

A.D. 1480. In this year the voluptuous life of the king was somewhat disturbed by a war with Scotland; but, though greatly irritated, Edward did not take the field: he intrusted the command to his brother Richard, who had an indefatigable activity, a good military reputation, and the favour of the army. At the northern court, brothers were intriguing against brothers, and the king, James III., whose tastes and habits were little suited either to overawe his boisterous nobles or to secure their willing obedience, was tottering on his throne; yet, notwithstanding these auspicious circumstances, the English made no impression upon Scotland. Richard of Gloucester failed in an attempt upon Berwick; and for two years the war was little more than an alternation of those raids on the borders of the two countries, which no truce or peace had ever yet prevented. But matters took a different turn when the Duke of Albany, the brother of King James, returned from a short exile in France, and laid claim to the crown, pretending that his brother was a bastard. On coming to the English court, Albany proposed that Edward should lend him a good army, and, in return for such assistance, he offered to surrender Berwick, to acknowledge himself the vassal of England, to renounce all alliance with Louis of France, and to marry one of Edward's daughters, if the church would permit — for he had two wives already. Without pausing at the consideration that Albany was pursuing that very line of conduct for which only four years before he had procured sentence of death against his own brother Clarence, Edward joyfully listened to the traitor Albany, and concluded a treaty with him in the month of June, 1482, at Fotheringay. The army was again intrusted to Gloucester, who marched to Berwick and invested that town. Richard had upwards of 20,000 men; and Albany, who co-operated, had a Scottish force, and a party within the walls of Berwick. The gates of the town were opened, but the castle defied the enemy; and King James, having assembled his barons, marched towards the Borders. As that sovereign lay at Lauder, his nobles, headed by Archibald Douglas, Earl of Angus, commonly called, after this event, "Archibald Bell-the-Cat," burst into the royal tent at an early hour between night and morning, carried off the chief favourite, Robert Cochran, together with five more of the king's habitual associates, and hanged them all over the bridge of Lauder. Upon this summary execution, James fled, or was carried a prisoner, to the castle of Edinburgh. The army disbanded, and the road to the capital was left open to the Duke of Gloucester and Albany, who appeared there in the month of July. The presence of an English army seems to have made some of the great lords sensible of the madness of their conduct: and the Archbishop of St. Andrews, the Bishop of Dunkeld, Lord Evandale, the chancellor, and the Earl of Argyle, collected a small army of patriots, and posted themselves at Haddington, between Edinburgh and the English borders. These noblemen summoned all true Scots to their standard, but, at the same time, opened negotiations with the Duke of Albany, who, on the 2d of August, concluded a treaty, the principal clauses of which were, that he, on his part, would be a true and faithful subject to his brother, and that the court should restore to him all his estates and honours, and grant to him and his adherents a pardon for all past offences. There was, however, a third party to conciliate: this was the King of England, who obtained the town and castle of Berwick, and the restitution of certain sums of money which he had paid to James on a now exploded treaty for a marriage between his daughter Cecily and the son of the Scottish king. The Duke of Gloucester returned into England; and his companion, the Duke of Albany, liberated his brother from the castle, rode with him to Holyrood House on the same horse, and slept with him in the same bed — for these things in Scotland, as in France, were considered the best proofs of a perfect reconciliation.

By the treaty of Picquigny, the dauphin was to marry Edward's eldest daughter as soon as she was of proper age. By the usage of the times, a princess was marriageable at the age of twelve; but Elizabeth was now sixteen, and yet the French court never sent to claim her. Edward had been told repeatedly that Louis would not keep to this family engagement; but he believed, or pretended to believe, that that sovereign would not dare to insult him in so tender a point. But the old fox of France was now in a very different position from that in which he stood when he was fain to bribe, and fawn, and flatter through the grating on the bridge at Picquigny: his consummate craft had reduced his factious nobles to obedience; his great rival the Duke of Burgundy was in his grave, and he had cut off the head of the Duke of Brittany, that other ally of the English. While princes were disputing for the hand of Mary, the daughter of Charles the Rash (whom

Clarence had wanted to marry), Louis had seized most of the territories which belonged to that orphan, and now he saw an opportunity of giving a colour to that appropriation, and of rounding his kingdom, by means of an union with the house of Burgundy. In the month of February, 1482, the Duchess Mary, who was holding her court in the rich city of Bruges, went out to fly her hawks at the herons which abounded in that neighbourhood. In following the sport, her palfrey, in taking a leap, burst the girths of the saddle, and she was thrown with great violence against the trunk of a tree. She died in consequence of the injury she sustained in the month of March. She was only twenty-five years old. She left three children by the Duke Maximilian of Austria: Philip, born in 1478; Margaret, called "Margot la gente demoiselle," born at the beginning of 1480; and Francis, born at the end of 1481. Her old persecutor King Louis was in a very languishing state of health at the time; but the joy he felt at the death of his fair neighbour and kinswoman revived him wonderfully, and he instantly prepared to take advantage of the event. With all their turbulence, the people of Flanders had entertained some respect and affection for the fair Mary of Burgundy; but they had none for Maximilian, whom they considered not as their prince, but only as the husband of their duchess, whose authority or influence was terminated by her death. Louis opened a secret correspondence with the people of Ghent, and then demanded the hand of the "gente demoiselle" for his son the dauphin, the affianced of the Princess Elizabeth of England. Maximilian, the father of the infant, was averse to the match; but Louis expected this, and had provided against it. The citizens of Ghent, who had all three children in their custody, forced a consent, and delivered up Margot to the agents of the French king, who settled upon her, as her marriage portion—which she was to convey to his son, the dauphin—all the broad and rich provinces which he, Louis, had gained from her mother Mary by fraud and by force of arms. The infant Margot, thus affianced at the age of three years, was carried into France to be "nourished and brought up." As long as it was necessary, Lord Howard, the English ambassador, was bribed, and Edward was amused with fine assurances; for, if the English had supported the Duke Maximilian at the proper time, they might have defeated the project—the last great achievement of the greatest politician of his day. But now the veil was dropped; the contract of marriage was confirmed publicly at Paris, and great rejoicings and feastings were held in that city. Edward felt himself duped, insulted, and disgraced, and he vowed that he would punish the old traitor Louis, and carry such a war into France as had not yet been seen in that country.[1] The excess of his rage is supposed to have hastened his death; but, from the dissolute life he had led for twenty years Edward was not likely, under any circumstances, to reach an old age. He died, after an illness of a few weeks, on the 9th of April, 1483, in the twenty-first year of his reign, and the forty-first or forty-second year of his age. He was exposed on a board, naked from the waist upwards, in order that people might see he had not been murdered. The body was buried with great pomp in the new chapel at Windsor.

---

[1] *Comines; Barante.*

CHAPTER VI.—CIVIL AND MILITARY HISTORY.

EDWARD V.—ACCESSION, A.D. 1483—DEATH OF RICHARD III., A.D. 1485.

Proceedings of the Duke of Gloucester on the death of his brother, Edward IV.—His plots against the queen's relatives—He denounces Lord Hastings, and causes him to be executed—The queen's relatives executed—Penance of Jane Shore—The children of Edward IV. declared illegitimate—Richard, Duke of Gloucester, appointed king—He commences his reign as Richard III.—He causes his nephews to be murdered in the Tower—The Earl of Richmond set up against Richard III.,—The Duke of Buckingham adopts Richmond's cause—Insurrection and execution of Buckingham—Richard III. seeks his niece Elizabeth in marriage for his son—On his son's death he endeavours to obtain her for himself—The Earl of Richmond prepares to invade England—Unpopularity of King Richard—The Stanleys league against him—Richmond lands in England—Battle of Bosworth—Richard III. defeated and slain—Henry, Earl of Richmond, proclaimed king—Affairs of Scotland—Reign of Robert III. of Scotland—Dissensions in his family—His son Robert starved to death—Duke of Albany becomes regent—James, Prince of Scotland, taken prisoner by Henry IV.—Duke of Albany's regency in Scotland—His alliance with France—James, Prince of Scotland, liberated—His reign in Scotland as James I.—His vigorous and strict administration—Conspiracy against him—He is assassinated—James II., his son, a minor, succeeds him—Troubles during the minority of James II.—Rebellion of the Douglasses—Sudden death of James II. at Roxburgh—He is succeeded by James III.—Feeble character of James III.—Factious among his family and courtiers—Execution of his favourites at Lauder Bridge.

WHEN Edward expired at London, Richard, Duke of Gloucester, was in the marches of Scotland at the head of an army devoted to his service; the Prince of Wales, a boy of thirteen, was at Ludlow Castle, with his maternal uncle, the Earl of Rivers; and Edward's second son, who was only eleven years old, was in London with his mother. It is apparent that all eyes were from the very beginning fixed with doubt upon the powerful uncle, whose first movements, however, were calculated to remove suspicion from the public mind. Upon receiving the news of his brother's death, he rode southward to York, which city he entered with a retinue of 600 knights and esquires, all clad, like himself, in deep mourning. His first care was to order a grand funeral service in the cathedral; his second to collect all the nobles and gentlemen of that neighbourhood, who swore fealty at York to his nephew, Edward V. Richard himself was the first to take this oath; he then wrote to the widowed Queen Elizabeth and to her brother the Earl Rivers, assuring them of his loyalty and affection. When he again put himself in motion, it was observed that the number of his followers was greatly increased; but, as he asserted that this force was only meant to give security and dignity to his nephew's coronation, the circumstance did not awaken any great suspicion. But though they had been sworn friends and confederates, the queen-mother had her misgivings, and the fear and imprudence of Elizabeth contributed not a little to the ruin of her children. She had written to her brother, Earl Rivers, to bring up the young king to London, with an escort of 2000 armed horsemen, and she had attempted to collect another army against the advice of the council. At this moment, the Marquis of Dorset, her son by her first marriage, had possession of the Tower, other Woodvilles and Grays had commands in different places, and the young princes were both in the hands of the queen's relations, who, unrestrained by the frightful executions made by Warwick on the insurgents, were ambitious and daring. On his death-bed, Edward, foreseeing evil consequences to his children, had patched up a reconciliation between his wife's relations and their rivals, the Lords Howard, Hastings, and Stanley, and they had all embraced, and sworn oaths of mutual forgiveness and future friendship. But we have seen the policy of such ceremonials: the Howards, the Stanleys, and the rest of the great lords hated the aspiring family as much as ever, and the instinct of self-preservation alone would have excited a lively alarm at seeing the whole power of the state divided among them. The queen-mother, too, disregarding the precedents which established as a principle of the constitution that the right of regulating regencies belonged to parliament alone, betrayed, or at least she was suspected of a design to assume the regal power during the minority of her son, and this the great lords knew would lead to an administration composed exclusively of her relations, who had most of them the passion of revenge to gratify, as well as the passion of ambition. Before Richard began his march from the Borders, the most violent altercations took place at the council-board. The Lord Hastings was so irritated that he threatened the queen. But the greatest of the malcontents was the Duke of Buckingham, a prince of the blood.[1] Richard, it appears, sent secret emissaries to Buckingham from York, and probably this adroit plotter did not forget Hastings and other lords. He so calculated time and distance that he arrived from the north at the town of Northampton on the same day (the 22d of April) that his nephew, young Edward, travelling from the north-west, reached Stony-Stratford, only ten miles distant. The Earl Rivers and the Lord Richard Gray rode back to Northampton to salute the Duke of Gloucester on the part of the king. Richard received them with much courtesy, and invited them to sup with him; but immediately after their arrival there came another visitor of higher rank, and whom he received with a more sincere welcome. This was the Duke of Buckingham, who brought with him a retinue of 300 horse. The two dukes, the earl, and the lord spent the evening together in a pleasant convivial manner, but after supper the two latter retired to quarters assigned to them in Northampton, and, while guards were placed over them, and all the outlets from the town secured, Gloucester and Buckingham remained in secret debate. On the following morning the Duke of Gloucester continued his progress to Stony-Stratford, riding a-head in company with the Duke of Buckingham, the Earl Rivers, and the Lord Gray, and still maintaining a friendly appearance with the two latter. As soon, however, as he was within the town, and found the young king within his grasp, he changed his tone, accused Rivers and Gray of estranging the affections of his nephew, and ordered them both under arrest. Then, accompanied by the Duke of Buckingham, he waited on the king. The two dukes bent their knees and saluted the poor boy as their sovereign, but in the next minute they arrested Sir Thomas Vaughan and Sir Richard Hawse, two of his favourite servants, and ordered all the rest of his attendants to disperse immediately. All this part of the story is somewhat obscure; it is not explained very clearly whether the 2000 horse that came from Ludlow retired at this order or joined the dukes; but it appears pretty certain that the Earl Rivers, Lord Richard Gray, Vaughan, and Hawse were immediately conveyed northward under a strong guard to Pontefract Castle, and that from this moment young Edward remained a prisoner in the hands of Gloucester and Buckingham.[2]

The news was soon carried to London: the queen-mother received the tidings "a little before the midnight following, and that in the sorest wise; that the king, her son, was taken, her brother, his son, and her other friends arrested, and sent, no man wist whither, to be done with God wot what," and in "great heaviness," at the dead of night, she fled to her old sanctuary at Westminster, taking with her second son, the Duke of York, and her five daughters. Meanwhile the Lord Hastings assured the people that the two dukes were loyal and acting for the public weal. From the fate he met with we must conclude that Hastings was a dupe, or that though he was ready to go to a certain length in order to displace the queen-mother and her relations, he was not prepared to abandon the cause of the children of his deceased master. He, however, obeyed the summons of the dukes, and went from London to meet them. Rotherham, Archbishop of York and chancellor, went to the queen-mother and endeavoured to comfort her and soothe her alarms; he delivered to her a friendly message which he had received from Hastings. Elizabeth suspected the faith of this nobleman, and she exclaimed—"A woe worth him, for he is one of them that goeth about to destroy me and my blood!" The archbishop replied—"Madam, be of good cheer, for I promise you if they crown any other king than your son whom they have now with them, we shall on the morrow crown his brother whom you have here with you." He then delivered the great seal to Elizabeth and departed home again, as day was dawning, by which time "he might in his chamber window see all the Thames full of boats of the Duke of Gloucester's servants, watching that no man should go to sanctuary, nor none should pass unsearched."[3] Then, continues the contemporary historian, "was great commotion and murmur as well in other places about, as specially in the city, the people diversely divining upon this dealing." The Archbishop of York, whose intellect seems to have been confounded, presently repented of so hastily delivering up the great seal to the queen-mother, "(to whom the custody thereof nothing pertained), and he sent secretly for the seal again, and carried it with him, after the customable, to a meeting of the nobility and gentry. The Lord Hastings, whose truth towards the king no man doubted nor needed to doubt, attended this meeting, and asserted again that the Duke of Gloucester was sure and fastly faithful to his prince, adding that the Earl Rivers and the Lord Richard, with the other knights, were, for matters attempted by them against the Duke of Gloucester and Buckingham, put under arrest for their surety, not for the king's jeopardy, and that they should soon be examined by all the other lords of the king's council

---

[1] This weak man was a lineal descendant of Thomas of Woodstock, the youngest son of Edward III.
[2] *Cont. Hist. Croyl.;* Sir Thomas More; Hall.

[3] Sir Thomas More.

indifferently." Hastings recommended peace and good order in the city, in order that the king's coronation might not be disturbed, for which ceremony he said the dukes were coming up. He admitted, however, "that matters were likely to come to a field, but that, if they did, though both parties were in all other things equal, yet should the authority be on that side where the king himself was." With these persuasions of the Lord Hastings, "whereof," says Sir Thomas More, "part himself believed, of part he wist the contrary," London was somewhat quieted. The adherents of Gloucester and Buckingham spread the report through the city that proofs had been obtained of the horrible plotting of the queen's relations to destroy the two dukes and others of noble blood, to the end that they might alone govern the young king at their pleasure; and they even exhibited to the populace barrels filled with arms, which they said the traitors had privily conveyed to destroy the noble lords withal. The common people were very well satisfied with this kind of proof, and said, "it were alms to hang the traitors."

It is quite evident that the queen-mother had no party in London, that her relations were most unpopular, and that the peaceful and wealthy citizens longed for the arrival of the two dukes in order that tranquillity might be restored. At the approach of the young king, Edmund Shaw, goldsmith, then mayor, with William White and John Matthew, sheriffs, and all the other aldermen, in scarlet, together with 500 of the citizens, clad in violet, and all gallantly mounted on horseback, rode out to meet him as far as Hornsey Wood, where they received him right reverently.[1]

There is a difficulty in fixing precise dates to these rapidly succeeding events, but it appears to have been on the 4th or 5th of May that Gloucester arrived in London, riding bare-headed before his nephew, who was shown to the people attired and attended as became a king. At first the royal boy was lodged in the palace of the bishop, but a great council was summoned, and, at the motion of the Duke of Buckingham, it was agreed to send the young king to the Tower, as the place of greatest safety. The lords in council then fixed the 22d of June for the coronation; summoned fifty lords and gentlemen to attend and receive the honours of knighthood, which were usually distributed before that ceremony; appointed the Bishop of Lincoln chancellor, in the place of the Archbishop of York; changed a few other officers of the crown, and gave the post of protector to the Duke of Gloucester, who thereupon styled himself "brother and uncle of the king, protector and defensor, great chamberlain, constable, and lord high admiral of England."[2]

Richard took up his residence in Crosby Place, Bishopsgate, where the majority of the council

GREAT HALL, CROSBY PLACE, BISHOPSGATE.—From a drawing by J. W. Archer.

attended him late and early. At the same time, a minority, composed of Lord Hastings and others, met in the Tower; but they seem to have had the garrison of that place against them. Hastings vainly thought that he was secure, and that he could outwit the cunning Gloucester. On the 12th of June he told Lord Stanley, who was uneasy at the proceedings at Crosby Place, that he kept his secret agent there, who was sure to inform him of all that was doing. On the following day the protector suddenly entered the Tower, and took his seat at the council-table.

---

[1] *Fabyan.*

[2] *Sir Thomas More; Cont. Hist. Croyl.; Fabyan; Rymer.*

[3] This fine specimen of the domestic architecture of the fifteenth century was built by Sir John Crosby, sheriff in 1470. The chief parts of the mansion surrounded three sides of a small deep quadrangle. The great hall, which still remains, is a magnificent apartment 54 ft. long, 27 ft. wide, and 40 ft. high. It has a beautiful bay window and a highly enriched timbered roof. Henry VIII. bestowed this mansion, in 1542, on Antonio Bonvica, a rich Italian merchant. In the reign of Elizabeth it was appropriated to foreign ambassadors. Here Sully lodged when on embassy to England, in the reign of James I.

Shakspeare has helped Sir Thomas More to make this scene immortal. More says that Richard presented himself on Friday the 13th of June, about nine in the morning, "in a very merry humour. After a little talking with them, he said unto the Bishop of Ely, 'My lord, you have very good strawberries in your garden in Holborn; I request you let us have a mess of them.' 'Gladly, my lord,' quoth he: 'would to God I had some better thing as ready to your pleasure as that!' and then, withal, in all haste, he sent his servant for a mess of strawberries. The protector set the lords fast in communing, and thereupon, praying them to spare him for a little while, departed thence, and soon after one hour, between ten and eleven, he returned into the chamber amongst them all, changed, with a wonderful sour angry countenance, knitting the brows, frowning and fretting, gnawing on his lips, and so set him down in his place." Soon after, he asked what those persons deserved who had compassed and imagined his destruction. Lord Hastings answered that they deserved death, whoever they might be; and then Richard affirmed that they were that sorceress his brother's wife (meaning the queen) and others with her. "And," said the protector, "we shall see in what wise that sorceress, and that other witch of her council, Shore's wife, with their affinity, have by their sorcery and witchcraft wasted my body." On saying this, he plucked up his doublet sleeve to his elbow upon his left arm, when the arm appeared to be withered and small, "as it was never other." The lords, of course, perceived that this matter was but a quarrel, and they were all silent except Hastings, who said, " Certainly, my lord, *if* they have so heinously done, they be worthy heinous punishment." "What!" quoth the protector, "thou servest me, I ween, with ifs and with ands! I tell thee they have so done, and that I will made good on thy body, traitor!" "And therewith," continues More, "as in a great anger, he clapped his fist upon the board, a great rap. At which token one cried 'Treason!' without the chamber. Therewith a door clapped, and in came there rushing men in harness as many as the chamber might hold. And anon, the protector said to the Lord Hastings, 'I arrest thee, traitor!' 'What! me, my lord!' quoth he. 'Yes, thee, traitor!' quoth the protector. Another let fly at the Lord Stanley, which shrunk at the stroke, and fell under the table, or else his head had been cleft to the teeth; for as shortly as he shrank, yet ran the blood about his ears. Then were they quickly bestowed in divers chambers, except the lord-chamberlain (Hastings), whom the protector bade speed, and shrive him apace, 'for by Saint Paul,' quoth he, 'I will not to dinner till I see thy head off.'"

Whatever were the charges brought forward by Richard, it seems certain that the Lord Hastings was instantly seized by a body of armed men, who, rushing into the council-chamber, crying "Treason! treason!" at a signal given by Richard, hurried him to the green by the side of the Tower chapel, stretched his neck over a log of wood which happened to lie there, and cut off his head; and that the Lord Stanley, the Archbishop of York, and the Bishop of Ely were arrested at the same time, and shut up in separate cells in the Tower. On the very day upon which these things happened in London, the Earl Rivers, the Lord Gray, Sir Thomas Vaughan, and Sir Richard Hawse were beheaded at Pontefract Castle, without any form of trial. The execution was public; but the victims were prevented from addressing the people by an armed band, that was directed in person by Sir Richard Ratcliffe, one of Richard's boldest adherents, who is described as "a man that had long been secret with him, having experience of the world and a shrewd wit, being short and rude in speech, and as far from pity as from all fear of God." The Earl Rivers, who thus perished, was an accomplished man; he was fond of literature—he encouraged literary men, and first introduced to the notice of Edward IV. William Caxton, the first English printer.

These executions, it should appear, produced no reaction. On the 16th of June, only three days after, the protector, with my lord-cardinal the Archbishop of Canterbury, and several other prelates and lay lords, proceeded to the sanctuary at Westminster, to demand the person of the Duke of York, whose presence at the coronation was said to be indispensable, and whose abiding in sanctuary was held to be dangerous and dishonourable, as causing slanderous rumours to be spread and suspicions to be cast on the protector. The cardinal undertook to persuade the queen-mother with gentle words, for Richard was quite ready to disregard the sacred rights of church and sanctuary. According to the best authority, Elizabeth at last yielded rather to the conviction of the uselessness of all resistance, than to the arguments of the cardinal-archbishop, and calling for her beautiful boy, she embraced him and delivered him over to them, and then burst into tears, as though she felt her child was lost. Richard carried the poor boy to the Tower, and secured him there with his brother.

The "pleasant vices" of the late king were now made scourges for his innocent progeny, and the dissoluteness of the whole court had disposed the minds of many people to look with a favourable eye upon any prince or minister that should present himself as a reformer of morals. Stories were circulated, both new and old! the late king was again said to be a bastard; and his children were made equally illegitimate in reports which stated, with much circumstantiality, that the marriage of Elizabeth Woodville was altogether illegal. Among the many mistresses of Edward was none so conspicuous as Jane Shore, whom he had seduced from her husband, a young and wealthy citizen, and to whom he continued attached to the time of his death. "Many," says More, "the king had, but her he loved: whose favour, to say the truth (for sin it were to belie the devil), she never abused to any man's hurt, but to many a man's comfort and relief; where the king took displeasure she would mitigate and appease his mind; where men were out of favour she would bring them in his grace; for many that had highly offended she obtained pardon; of great forfeitures she got men remission. . . . . A proper wit had she, and could both read well and write. As if it were in a virtuous anger, not for covetousness" (it appears, however, that Richard kept the goods or the money), "the protector sent into the house of Shore's wife (for she dwelt not with her husband) and seized all her plate and jewels, to the value of 2000 or 3000 marks, and then sent her to prison." She was delivered over to the ecclesiastical court to be punished according to canons which had long been a dead letter, at least about court. "Every man," says More, "was surprised to see the matter so suddenly and so highly taken; and for this cause, that Duke Richard, as a godly, continent prince, clean and faultless of himself, sent out of heaven into this vicious world for the amendment of men's manners, he made the Bishop of London put her to open penance." With no clothes on but her girdle, bare-footed, and carrying a lighted taper in her hand, Jane Shore was compelled to walk through the crowded streets of the city on a Sunday. The exhibition had the double effect of fixing the attention of the people on the immoralities of the late king, and of displaying in a striking light the moral rigour of the new protector.

This scene was followed by a sermon preached by Dr Shaw, the brother of the lord-mayor, upon the text—"The multiplying brood of the ungodly shall not thrive, nor take deep rooting from bastard slips."[1] The doctor proceeded boldly to show that the two young princes in the Tower were illegitimate, inasmuch as Edward their father, in the very beginning of his reign, before he knew Elizabeth, the widow of Sir Thomas Gray, had clandestinely married Eleanor, the widow of the Lord Boteler of Sudeley. He afterwards took up the scandal which had been propagated by the Duke of Clarence, and by the Duke of Burgundy before him, expressing his learned doubts whether Edward, the late king, were in reality the son of his reputed father Richard, Duke of York, seeing that there was no resemblance between them. But then he went on to tell the great crowd that attended him—for he was holding forth at Paul's Cross, and was a very popular

St. Paul's Cross.—From a print by Hollar.

preacher—that the lord-protector, that right noble prince, was the very image and plain express likeness of that royal duke. It had been previously arranged that Richard should appear in the sermon-ward just as Dr. Shaw drew this striking comparison, but either he came too slow or the preacher went on too fast: he appeared at length, and then the doctor repeated his similitude; but the words lost the air of an inspiration, and the people, instead of shouting "Long live King Richard!" as they ought to have done, stared at each other in silent astonishment. The protector then pretended to be displeased with the preacher, who sneaked away.

On the Tuesday following (the 24th of June) the Duke of Buckingham, who went hand-in-hand with the Duke of Gloucester, presented himself on the hustings at the Guildhall, and there, supported by a number of lords, knights, and citizens, he eloquently harangued the Londoners. He spoke of the tyranny, extortion, and lust of the late king—of the numbers he had reduced to beggary by benevolences—of the honest families he had disgraced by his illicit amours. He went over the whole sermon of Dr. Shaw, and told the people that Richard was the only true issue of the Duke of York, and that the lords and commons of the north had sworn never to submit to a bastard. It appears that the more respectable citizens, among whom, however, Richard had a very strong party, required time for deliberation; but many of the poorer sort now threw up their bonnets, and cried "Long live King Richard!"

---

[1] *Wisdom of Solomon*, iv. 3.   [2] This cross was erected about 1450, and remodelled in 1595.

On the next day a great deputation from the citizens, headed by Shaw the mayor, and accompanied by the Duke of Buckingham and many lords and gentlemen, waited upon the protector, who was lodging in Baynard's Castle. Richard, it is said, affected to be alarmed, and at first declined receiving them; but soon Buckingham was admitted to present an address, which was styled the "Consideration, election, and petition of the lords spiritual and temporal, and commons, of this realm of England." In this remarkable document, of which a copy has been preserved in the rolls of parliament, the former allusions to the illegitimacy of the late king and his brother Clarence were suppressed, but Edward's marriage with Eleanor Boteler was insisted upon; and "as Edward (the discourse proceeded) during his life and Elizabeth lived together sinfully and damnably in adultery, against the law of God and of his church, so it appeareth evidently and followeth that all the issuing children of the said King Edward be bastards." Then, to get rid of the children of the Duke of Clarence, Richard's elder brother, the attainder for treason against that prince was quoted; and, finally, Richard was invited and pressed to take the crown as his by right of birth, and by lawful election of the three estates of the land.

The protector hesitated; spoke of his want of ambition; his warm affection for the young princes, his nephews, for whom he yet trusted to preserve the crown. "Not so," said Buckingham; "the free people of England will never be ruled by a bastard; and if you, the lawful heir, refuse the crown, they know where to find another who will gladly accept it." Upon this, Richard modestly replied, that it was his duty to submit to the will of his people; and that, since they would have him for their king, he would take upon himself the royal estate of the two noble realms of England and France—the one to rule from that day forward, the other (meaning France), with their good help, to subdue and get again as soon as might be.[1] This is commonly reckoned the last day of the brief nominal reign of Edward V.

RICHARD III.

On the 26th of June, the day following the scene acted at Baynard's Castle, Richard proceeded to Westminster, where he seated himself between the great Lord Howard and the Duke of Suffolk upon the marble seat in the hall, telling the admiring people that he commenced his reign in that place, because it was his first duty as a king to attend to the laws and the doing of justice. He then rode back to the city, and was received at St. Paul's by a grand procession of the clergy and the joyful shouts of the people. Ten days after, on the 6th of July, he was crowned in Westminster Abbey with his wife Anne, the daughter of Warwick. Neither lords spiritual nor lords temporal started the least difficulty: the Archbishop of Canterbury, with his clergy, anointed the usurper. There was a very full attendance of peers and peeresses; and while the Duke of Buckingham bore the train of the king, the Countess of Richmond did the like office for the queen. The ceremony was followed by promotions, donations, and acts of mercy. The Lord Howard was made earl marshal, and received the title of Duke of Norfolk: his son was created Earl of Surrey. Of the prisoners made in the council-chamber in the Tower on the day of Lord Hastings' execution, Lord Stanley was received into favour, the Archbishop of York was set at liberty, and the Bishop of Ely was released from the Tower, to be more gently guarded by the Duke of Buckingham in his castle at Brecknock.

Richard did not call a parliament, but he held a long conference with the lords who had attended his coronation, and whom he charged to be strict in preserving the peace, and putting down all crimes and disorders in their several counties. In a few days he began a royal progress through the kingdom, and wherever he stopped, he listened to petitions and administered justice in person. His course lay through some of the pleasantest parts of England, and the fine summer season disposed the people to enjoy the splendour and parade of the court. Everywhere he was received with acclamations—in the north with enthusiasm. From Warwick he went by Coventry, Leicester, Nottingham, and Pontefract, to York, where he and his queen were again crowned to gratify his northern adherents.[2]

But while all was sunshine at York, a dark cloud arose in London, that threatened a tempest in the south. Meetings were held by the friends of the queen-mother in different parts, and it was resolved to make an attempt to liberate the princes from the Tower. Their healths were drunk in secret; but the poor boys were already dead, and their fate had probably been hastened by these friends—for nothing was likely to escape the quick and suspicious eye of their uncle and his numerous agents. We venture to repeat the old story as told by Sir Thomas More; for, in spite of the scepticism of a few modern writers, it has not only consistency and probability, but

---

[1] *Sir Thomas More.*

[2] Rotherham, Archbishop of York, here officiated, and set the crown upon his head. *Sir Thomas More: Cont. Hist. Croyl.;* Drake, *Eborac.; Rouse.* Rouse, who was living an eremitical life at Guy's Cliff at the time of this splendid royal progress, saw Richard at Warwick, and describes his personal appearance.

also some remarkable evidences in its favour. In the course of his progress, Richard despatched from the neighbourhood of the town of Gloucester one John Green, " whom he specially trusted," with a letter to Sir Robert Brackenbury, governor of the Tower, ordering that the said Sir Robert should, "in somewise, put the two children to death." Brackenbury refused the commission, as something too horrible and dangerous to himself. Green returned with this answer to Richard, who, being then at Warwick, despatched Sir James Tyrrel, his master of the horse, with a commission to get, and keep for twenty-four hours, all the keys and the command of the Tower. One night, apparently in the month of August, Tyrrel, accompanied by Miles Forest, "a fellow fleshed in murder before-time," and John Dighton, Tyrrel's own horsekeeper, "a big, broad, square, and strong knave," ascended the staircase which led

THE BLOODY TOWER, TOWER OF LONDON.[1]—From a sketch by H. G. Hine.

to the chamber where the young princes lay sleeping together. While Tyrrel waited at the door, Miles Forest and John Dighton entered the room, and smothered the children in the bed-clothes as they lay, keeping the pillows and feather-bed hard upon their mouth. When the deed was done, Tyrrel stepped into the chamber to take a hasty view of the dead bodies, which were then, by his orders, carried down and buried by the two murderers "at the stair-foot, meetly deep in the ground, under a great heap of stones.'[2] Honours and rewards were immediately bestowed upon Tyrrel, Forest, Dighton, Green, and Brackenbury.

It was not King Richard's intention to reveal that the children were dead; but when the insurgents were up in arms he permitted the fact to be divulged. The news disconcerted the conspirators; but these men had gone too far ever to expect mercy from such a king, and they resolved to raise up a new competitor for the crown in the person of one who was not a prisoner in the Tower, but an exile in France—who was not an innocent, helpless boy, but a man in the vigour of life,[3] and crafty, cool, and sagacious, as became one that had studied his politics in the school of Louis XI.

This was Henry, Earl of Richmond, the grandson of Owen Tudor and Catherine, the widow of Henry V. Richmond was considered as representing the line of Lancaster by right of his mother Margaret Beaufort, who was daughter of a Duke of Somerset, and a great-grand-daughter of John of Gaunt. Some princes or princesses might have been found in Spain or Portugal among the descendants of John of Gaunt, who were nearer representatives of that house; but the eyes of the legitimatists on this side did not reach so far; and the Yorkists could not very consistently recognize the rights of a line of princes whom they had voted usurpers. It was, therefore, proposed that Henry, Earl of Richmond, should marry the Princess Elizabeth (formerly affianced to the dauphin), eldest daughter of the late king, and now, by the death of her brothers, the representative of the more legitimate house of York. Elizabeth, the queen-mother, whose sanctuary was still respected, found means of corresponding with the managers for this new revolution; and she entered warmly into the project of the marriage. The Dowager-countess of Richmond, who had married Lord Stanley, became a party to the contract, as representative of her son, the exile Henry; and the Marquis of Dorset, with several members of the Gray and Woodville families, and many other noblemen who had hitherto pursued very different politics, united against Richard, and entered into the scheme. The best explanation of the conduct of the Duke of

---

[1] The Bloody Tower forms the gateway of the inner ward of the Tower of London. Tradition points out the room over the archway as the place where the children of Edward IV. were murdered, hence the name.

[2] *Sir Thomas More.* The continuator of the *History of Croyland*, another contemporary, says simply that the children were reported to have died in the Tower, though it was uncertain by what kind of violent death. A little more light will be thrown on this mysterious transaction in our narrative of the reign of Henry VII.

[3] Henry was nearly thirty years old when he ascended the throne.

Buckingham who had done more than any man to place Richard upon the throne, is, that he was a fool and something worse. The more detailed explanations usually given are, that though made constable of the kingdom, justiciary of Wales, governor of all the royal castles in Wales, and steward of the royal manors in Hereford and Shropshire, and though he had obtained from Richard what had constantly been refused to him by Richard's brother and predecessor,[1] the whole or the greater part of the immense inheritance of Humphrey de Bohun, which he claimed in right of descent, Buckingham was still dissatisfied, and was, therefore, induced to listen to the acute reasoning of his prisoner Morton, Bishop of Ely, who was an implacable enemy of King Richard, and (next to Richard) the most adroit statesman in the country, and to the earnest persuasions of his own wife, who was sister to Queen Elizabeth. It is certain that indignation and horror at the murder of his wife's nephews in the Tower had nothing to do with Buckingham's sudden change; for he engaged to put himself at the head of an insurrection before that event was known; and by letters rashly written, and imprudently delivered, he called upon his friends to join him in placing upon the throne the legitimate king, Edward V., whom he (Buckingham,) on the 24th of June last past, had proclaimed a bastard at Guildhall. When that plan fell to the ground, he entered eagerly into the other, and was among the first to invite the Earl of Richmond into England. The astucious Henry Tudor, Earl of Richmond, who had fled into France after the battle of Tewkesbury, had gone through many perilous adventures, and had occasionally suffered poverty and want. But now the French court and the Duke of Brittany, hoping much from his gratitude if he should become King of England, agreed to furnish him with some ships, men, and money.[2]

King Richard obtained the first hint of what was intended from the answer which Henry sent to the invitation of his friends in England. This was within a few days of the 18th of October, the time fixed for a general rising. He summoned all his loyal subjects to meet him at Leicester. The summons was readily attended to in the north, and a good army gathered round his standard. On the appointed day the insurrection broke out, and Henry Tudor was proclaimed at Exeter by the Marquis of Dorset; by the Bishop of Salisbury at Devizes; by the gentlemen of Kent at Maidstone; by the gentlemen of Berkshire at Newbury; and by the Duke of Buckingham at Brecknock.

Richard hit all the leaders at once by a remarkable proclamation, in which, maintaining his tone of morality, he called them all traitors, adulterers, and bawds, and said that their object was, the letting (hindrance) of virtue and the damnable maintenance of vice. At the same time, he set a price upon the heads of Buckingham, Dorset, and their confederates. Henry appeared with a fleet off the coast of Devonshire; but none of the confederates were there to meet him, and it did not accord with his prudence to attempt a landing with the small force he had brought. While he was sailing back to St. Malo, Buckingham, who moved from Wales too late, and who, when he did move, proceeded like an idiot, was blundering along the right bank of the Severn, seeking in vain for a passage across that river. The people of Herefordshire, Worcester, and Gloucestershire, who had no great affection for him and his Welsh army, broke down or defended all the bridges; and the fords, it is said, were rendered impassable by the autumnal rains. In a very short time the Welshmen, finding that the duke had made no arrangements for feeding them, and that they could not maintain themselves by plunder, deserted almost to a man, and returned to their mountains. Buckingham fled and concealed himself; and the news of his miserable failure induced the rest of the insurgents to disperse. Richard, without drawing a sword, marched all the way from Leicester to Salisbury, where Buckingham, his captive, having been betrayed by one of his own servants, a man named Banister, meanly implored to see him. Richard would not grant him an interview, but ordered his head to be struck off in the market-place, which was done immediately. The king then continued his march into Devonshire; but this was scarcely necessary, for the Marquis of Dorset and his friends had already taken flight for Brittany. He executed a few insurgents, the most conspicuous of whom was St. Leger, a knight, who had married Richard's own sister, the Duchess of Exeter; and then he returned to London to meet a parliament which had, at length, been summoned.[3]

This, which was Richard's only parliament, met on the 11th of November, and was so far from showing any dissatisfaction, that it proceeded at once to confirm the celebrated petition which had been presented by Buckingham and the citizens at Baynard's Castle the day before the protector changed himself into a king; and

---

[1] Edward IV. had kept the De Bohun inheritance to himself.

[2] "The Earl of Richmond," says Comines, "told me, not long before his departure from France, that from the time he was five years old, he had always been a fugitive or a prisoner. He had endured an imprisonment of fifteen years, or thereabouts, in Brittany, by command of the late Duke Francis, into whose hands he fell by extremity of weather, as he was escaping out of England with his uncle the Earl of Pembroke."

[3] *Rot. Parl.; Rymer; Cont. Hist. Croyl.; Drake, Eborac.; Hall; Stow.*

it declared him the lawful sovereign by birth, inheritance, free election, consecration, and coronation, and entailed the crown on the issue of his body, beginning with his son Edward, now declared Prince of Wales. It voted a bill of attainder, in the usual form, against the traitors who had attempted to disturb the lawful government. This bill was much less severe than might have been expected. The Countess of Richmond, Henry's mother, who had taken a most active part in the late attempt, was pardoned at the earnest entreaties of her second husband, the Lord Stanley—a man who seems to have been a match even for Richard in craft and duplicity, and who now, and indeed to the last moment, persuaded him that he had renounced all former notions, and had become his truest friend and servant. In the address or petition presented at Baynard's Castle, was the following strong passage, expressive of the feelings with which the rapacity and misgovernment of Edward IV. had filled the citizens: "For certainly, we be determined rather to adventure and commit us to the peril of our lives and jeopardy of death, than to live in such thraldom and bondage as we have lived long time heretofore, oppressed and injured by extortions and new impositions against the laws of God and man, and the liberty, old policy, and laws of this realm, whereof every Englishman is inherited." Parliament now passed an act, which, after reciting in equally strong terms the grievances lately suffered, abrogated and for ever annulled all exactions under the name of benevolences—that equivocal and odious term introduced in the late arbitrary times. This was a boon to the nation, whose liberties were not directly impaired by the usurpation[1] of Richard.[2] His tenure was too precarious, and his reign too brief to allow him to become despot.

A.D. 1484. Richard felt that in spite of acts of parliament and all other instruments, whereby the children of his brother had been declared illegitimate, the whole party of the Yorkists were still inclined to consider the Princess Elizabeth as heiress to the crown. He was aware of the project of uniting her to Henry, Earl of Richmond, whose title was otherwise most defective, and he resolved to get the young lady into his power. He was startled by a circumstance which took place during the festival of Christmas. The English exiles, with the Marquis of Dorset at their head, met Henry at an appointed place in Brittany, and after he had sworn to make Elizabeth his queen, they did homage to him as their legitimate sovereign. Richard opened an active and affectionate correspondence with his brother's widow, who was still with her daughters in the sanctuary at Westminster; and that vain, ambitious, heartless woman, tired of her long privations, and eager again for the pleasures of a court, listened to the proposals offered by the murderer of her children, brother, and nearest friends. Some precautions, however, she took; for Richard swore upon the host before some bishops and lords, and the lord-mayor and aldermen, that her life and the lives of her daughters should be in no peril; that they should all be treated as his kinswomen; and that he would grant an annuity to the mother, and marriage portions to the young ladies. After this, she left the sanctuary and went to court, where every possible attention was paid to her eldest daughter. Richard's design was, in this instance, transparent—it was to marry the Princess Elizabeth, whom he had called a bastard, but whom others called the lawful heiress, to his son, the Prince of Wales, a boy of eleven years. The plan, however, was defeated by the death of the young prince, who expired *suddenly* at Middleham Castle. For a time Richard was bowed to the earth by this unexpected calamity, but as soon as he recovered he evidently resolved to work out his scheme of ambition by marrying Elizabeth himself. Except for the poor boys who perished in the Tower, or in some other place, it is scarcely possible to feel the least sympathy for a single member of this abominable family. The Lady Elizabeth was kept constantly about the person of Richard's queen, and indulged in all the pleasures of the court, which did not always wear a puritanical gloom, for Richard found, that though his affectation of moral austerity might gain him friends in one direction, it made him lose friends in another. On a sudden Richard's wife Anne fell sick, and it seems to have been calculated that she should die. In the month of February (1485) Elizabeth, the mother, wrote to her son, the marquis, telling him to retire immediately from Henry, Earl of Richmond, as she had arranged a better plan for the family; and Elizabeth, the daughter (the worthy child of such a mother), wrote to Howard, now Duke of Norfolk, and in high favour with the king, to implore his good offices in forwarding her marriage with Richard, whom she called "her joy and maker in this world—the master of her heart and thoughts." She expressed her surprise that the queen should be so long in dying—the better part of February, she observed, was past, and

---

[1] Lord Campbell observes of the statute 1 Rich. III. c. 1, that "it is remarkable that this is the first statute in the English language, the statutes hitherto having been all in Latin or French, and it was taken as a precedent, for all statutes afterwards are in English. It is curious that in this reign, which we regard with so much horror, not only were laws given to the people of England for the first time since the Conquest, in their own language, but acts of parliament were for the first time printed."—Macpherson's *Annals of Commerce*, i. 704.

[2] *Rot. Parl.; Cont. Hist. Croyl.*

the queen still alive—would she never die? Anne died in March, and then the young Elizabeth, who had already worn robes similar to those of the queen, and who had appeared at court balls and festivals as the peculiar object of her uncle's attentions, expected to mount the throne. But when Richard opened his plan to his chief advisers, Ratcliffe and Catesby, they represented that such a marriage would be considered as incestuous by the clergy and the people; that it would confirm suspicions, already beginning to be entertained, that he had poisoned Queen Anne; and that such a conviction would assuredly deprive him of his friends in the north, whose attachment to him had mainly arisen out of their hereditary affection for the daughter of the great Earl of Warwick. Richard had counted on obtaining a dispensation for the marriage from the pope; but he was now made to feel that this, even if he had got it, would not be sufficient to screen him from popular indignation, and he resigned all thoughts of making the heiress his wife. His next step was to assert that he had never entertained any such project. He summoned a meeting in the great hall of the Temple, and there, before the commoners and the lord-mayor and aldermen, who had an unusually large share in state matters during this reign, he protested that he had never thought of such an event. In order to tranquillize the people of the north, he wrote a letter to the citizens of York, telling them how he had explained matters to the citizens of London, and requiring them to seize and send before the council all such persons as propagated false and malicious reports.

In the preceding summer Richard had adopted measures which drove Henry from Brittany, and well-nigh proved fatal to that rival. By means of money he converted Landois from a friend and ally into an enemy, and that Breton minister, with or without the consent of his master, the Duke Francis, engaged to seize the Earl of Richmond and send him a prisoner into England. Henry, being warned of this plot, fled with a few friends from Vannes, threw himself into a neighbouring forest, and, by pursuing unfrequented roads and using great speed, he gained the territories of the King of France.[1] There he was safe, for the French court considered Richard as an usurper. "This Richard," says Comines, "desired to live in the same friendship with our king as his brother Edward had done, and I believe would have had his pension continued; but our king looked upon him as an inhuman and cruel person, and would neither answer his letters nor give audience to his ambassadors." And though Louis XI., the king here alluded to, died seven weeks after Richard's coronation, his son, Charles VIII., entertained the same sentiments. Henry was kindly received at Paris, and Charles even supplied him with some money and about 3000 Normans, whom Comines describes as "the loosest and most profligate fellows of all that country." "And thus," says the same writer, "did God of a sudden raise up against Richard an enemy without power, without money, without hereditary right (according to my information), and without any reputation, save what his person and deportment had acquired for him."

The real descent of his rival, his alliance with the French king, and the complexion of the army he was bringing into England, were all made the most of in a proclamation which Richard issued with the intention of exciting the prejudices of the people. He called him "One Henry Tudor, descended of bastard blood both by father's and mother's side, and who, therefore, could never have any claim to the crown of England, but by conquest." He asserted that this Henry Tudor, that he might achieve his false intent by the aid of the ancient enemies of England, had covenanted to give up in perpetuity to the crown of France all right to Normandy, Anjou, Maine, Guienne, and even Calais, and to dissever the arms of France from the arms of England for ever; that he had promised and given away, to traitors and foreigners, archbishoprics, bishoprics, duchies, earldoms, baronies, and other inheritances of knights, esquires, and private gentlemen; that he intended to change and subvert the ancient laws and liberties; that he was coming with bands of robbers and murderers, and with rebels attainted by the high court of parliament, of whom many were known for open cut-throats, adulterers, and extortioners. He called upon his subjects, like true and good Englishmen, to arm for the defence of their wives, children, goods, and hereditaments, and he promised, like a diligent and courageous prince, to put his most royal person to all labour and peril necessary in their behalf. But he was without money, and he soon found that he could depend but little on his officers.

The last remnant of his popularity among the citizens of London appears to have been rent and destroyed by the exacting of some forced loans. As he and his parliament had for ever proscribed those practices of the late reign, he would not permit these extortions to be called "benevolences;" upon which the Londoners called them "malevolences."[2] The plan of his campaign was to intrust the defence of the sea-coasts to his friends, and to collect himself a great army in the centre of the kingdom. Most of these friends betrayed him; but, when he raised his own ban-

---

[1] Daru, *Hist. Bretagne.*
[2] *Cont. Hist. Croyl.*

ner at Nottingham, the people of the north hastened to it, under the Earl of Northumberland. On the 7th of August Henry landed at Milford Haven with about 5000 men, of whom not above 2000 were English.¹ Richard moved southward to Leicester, where he was joined by the Duke of Norfolk, the Lord Lovel, and Brackenbury, who brought up the levies from the eastern counties, from Hampshire, and from London. Many other lords and sheriffs of counties, who had been summoned, did not appear, and the Lord Stanley, the husband of Henry's mother, was among the missing. Keeping up his deception to the last, Stanley sent to say how much he regretted his non-attendance, which was caused solely by the sweating sickness that confined him to his bed. But Richard, who probably knew by this time that Henry had been allowed to march undisturbed through Wales, and through the whole country where the influence of the Stanleys was greatest, determined to look after the Lord Strange, the son of Lord Stanley, who was in his camp. Strange attempted flight; was seized, interrogated, and made to confess that the Stanleys were in league with the invader—all of them except his father, who, he said, he knew would soon join King Richard. He was allowed to write to Lord Stanley to hasten his coming, but he was kept a close prisoner as hostage for his father. It was then arranged by the Tudor party that the Stanleys should march a little in advance of the invading force, as though they were retreating before it, and that they should only join openly on the field of battle, when it was calculated Richard's mind would be too much occupied to attend to Lord Strange.

Henry, after crossing the Severn, was joined by the Talbots and a few other families, but his force was still very inconsiderable as compared with the army under his bold and experienced rival. But Henry knew that not one man in ten would fight for Richard, and he continued to press forward. On the 21st of August he moved from Tamworth town to Atherston, where he was joined by swarms of deserters from the enemy. On the same day Richard marched from Leicester and encamped near the town of Bosworth.

Early on the following morning Richard, with the crown on his head, mounted his horse, mar-

BLUE BOAR INN, LEICESTER.²—Antiquarian Repertory.

shalled his troops, and advanced. Henry at the same time moved from Atherston: and the two armies soon met in the midst of the fine and spacious plain, nearly surrounded by hills, which commences about a mile to the south of Bosworth. "There," in the quaint language of a contemporary, "was fought a sharp battle, and sharper should it have been if the king's party had been fast to him: but many, towards the field, refused him, and rode over to the other party, and some stood hovering afar off, till they saw to which party the victory should fall."³ In fact, of all the lords that followed Richard scarcely one was

---

¹ "On his landing he (Henry) displayed a red flag, the old banner of the Cambrians, as if his design had been to excite that nation to take up arms and to render it independent of the English. That enthusiastic nation, over which the power of signs was always very great, without examining whether the dispute between Henry Tudor and Richard III. was not foreign to itself, rallied, by a sort of instinct, round its old standard. The Red Dragon was planted on the mountain of Snowdon, which the pretender appointed as the rendezvous for such of the Welsh as had promised him to arm in his cause. Not one of them failed to keep the appointed day; the bards themselves, feeling their ancient spirit rekindled, sang and prophesied in the style of the olden time, the victory of the Kymrys over the Saxon and the Norman enemy. But it was never contemplated to free the Cambrians from the yoke of the foreigner; the single fruit of the victory was to place a man with a little Welsh blood in his veins upon the throne of the Norman conquerors of Wales. . . . Henry VII. placed the Cambrian dragon in his arms, by the side of the three lions of Normandy. He created a new office of pursuivant-at-arms, with the title of Rouge-Dragon, and by means of the archives of Wales, authentic or fabulous, traced his genealogy to Cadwallader, the last chief who bore the title of King of Britain; and from thence to Brutus, son of Æneas, the pretended progenitor of the Britons. But these frivolous acts of vanity, rather than of gratitude, were all that the new king did for the people whose devotion had given him victory and a kingdom."—Thierry, *The Norman Conquest*, conclusion, section ii.

² Tradition states that Richard lodged in this house on the night before the battle of Bosworth Field. ³ *Fabyan*.

true to him except the Duke of Norfolk and his son the Earl of Surrey. As he gazed along the enemy's lines he saw many a banner which, a few hours before, had been on his own side; and either immediately before the first attack, or very soon after, Lord Stanley appeared in the field with 3000 men, and joined his adversary. On looking back on his own lines he saw them wavering and broken by desertion, for whole bands at a time left their positions to fall into the rear or go over to Henry. Even the Earl of Northumberland, with the hardy men of the north, seemed inclined to keep aloof. Hesitation could only increase these evils: Richard gave the order, and the Duke of Norfolk, who led the van, began the attack by falling upon the advanced guard of the enemy, which was commanded by the old Earl of Oxford, who had recently been delivered from prison by Sir Walter Blount, once Richard's sworn friend, but who now, like so many other adherents, drew his sword for the Earl of Richmond. Norfolk's attack made a great impression, but no other leader seconded him. Of a sudden Richard put spurs to his horse, and, shouting "Treason!" galloped into the midst of the enemy. His quick eye had caught a glance of Henry, and, desperate as seemed his case, he hoped to retrieve it by his personal valour and his skill in the use of arms, if he could only engage his adversary hand-to-hand. He cut his way to Henry's standard; killed Sir William Brandon, the standard-bearer; made Sir John Cheney bite the dust; and was directing a deadly thrust at his rival, when a whole host closed upon him, threw him from his horse, and despatched him with many wounds. Then Lord Stanley picked up his crown, battered and blood-stained, and put it on the head of Henry. The Duke of Norfolk, the Lord Ferrers, Sir Richard Ratcliffe, Sir Robert Bracken-

bury, and a few other knights, shared the fate of their master. It is said that, in the battle and the flight, 3000 men perished; but, considering the way in which the affair was managed, and Henry's politic anxiety to reconcile parties, and to show himself a clement sovereign, it is probable that this number is somewhat exaggerated. The battle of Bosworth Field, which terminated the war of the Roses, and placed a new dynasty on the English throne, was altogether on a scale inferior to that of several preceding conflicts. Counting both armies, there were not 18,000 men on the field, and of these the greater part were never engaged. When the victorious party had finished shouting "Long live King Henry!" they picked up the body of King Richard, stripped it, and laid it across a horse behind a pursuivant-at-arms, who, thus mounted, rode a little in the rear of the new king into the town of Leicester. There the body was exposed for two or three days, "that all men might behold it;" after which it was buried with little reverence in the church of the Grey Friars.

Such was the fate of Richard III., who had reigned two years and two months. There is some uncertainty about his precise age, but it appears probable that he was only in his thirty-third year when he died.[1] The disputes which have been raised on every part of his history have been extended even to his personal appearance. It seems very certain that the portrait usually exhibited is an incorrect one: he was small of stature, had a sharp visage, and unequal shoulders—his right shoulder being a little higher than his left:[2] the other traits seem to have been put in by imagination. There is some evidence to show that, instead of being a monster of ugliness, he was almost as handsome in features as his brother[3] Edward IV.[4]

---

[1] *Cont. Hist. Croyl.; Fabyan; Hall; Buck, Life of Richard III.;* W. Hutton, *Battle of Bosworth Field.*

[2] So at least says Rouse, the hermit of Guy's Cliff, who saw Richard (whom he hated) at Warwick.

[3] Walpole, *Hist. Doubts.* This appears to us one of the particulars in which the ingenious writer has best made out his case; and yet he can scarcely be said to have got rid of Richard's hump.

[4] As we have now closed the reigns of the Plantagenets, which had continued so long and been so influential, this seems the proper place to introduce Mr. Hallam's remarks on the state of manners in England, as well as elsewhere, during the long period of their reign.

"All Europe was a scene of intestine anarchy during the middle ages, and though England was far less exposed to the scourge of private war than most nations on the Continent, we should find, could we recover the local annals of every country, such an accumulation of petty rapine and tumult, as would almost alienate us from the liberty which served to engender it. This was the common tenor of manners, sometimes so much aggravated as to find a place in general history, more often attested by records, during the three centuries that the house of Plantagenet sat on the throne." Mr. Hallam then quotes in a note this passage from Walsingham: "The same year 1332, certain evil-minded persons, enjoying the support of some of the magnates,

despising the youth of the king, and intending to disturb the kingdom, increased to such a multitude, and occupied the woods and defiles, so as to be a terror to the whole kingdom." Mr. Hallam proceeds: "Disseisin, or forcible dispossession of free-holds, makes one of the most considerable articles in our law-books. High-way robbery was from the earliest times a sort of national crime. Capital punishments, though very frequent, made little impression on a bold and licentious crew, who had not at least the sympathy of those who had nothing to lose on their side, and flattering prospects of impunity. We know how long the outlaws of Sherwood lived in tradition; men who, like some of their betters, have been permitted to redeem by a few acts of generosity, the just ignominy of extensive crimes. These indeed were the heroes of vulgar applause; but when such a judge as Sir John Fortescue could exult that more Englishmen were hanged for robbery in one year, than French in seven, and that if an Englishman be poor, and see another having riches, which may be taken from him by night, he will not spare to do so, it may be perceived how thoroughly these sentiments had pervaded the public mind."

Mr. Hallam ascribes the frequent impunity of these robbers to the general want of communication facilitating escape, and to the extensive forests that harboured evil-doers—to the frequent purchase of charters of pardon—nay, to the countenance of the nobility, for which he finds it difficult to account, but

The course of affairs in Scotland has been adverted to from time to time in the preceding pages; but it will be convenient to subjoin a brief summary of the history of that kingdom from the commencement to the close of the period, that the leading events may be seen at one view in their sequence and proper connection. The arrival of the fifteenth century found the throne of Bruce occupied by his great-grandson Robert III., who had ascended it in 1390;—a prince whom much amiability of nature, a genuine though a somewhat superstitious piety, and even intellectual tastes and accomplishments beyond the rude times upon which he was thrown, did not protect from the misfortunes and contempt that were the natural consequences of his extreme deficiency in all the more energetic and manly virtues. He had passed his fiftieth year before he obtained the crown; and for some years before his accession, the whole powers of the government, in the feeble old age of their father, had been left in the hands of his two younger brothers, the Earls of Fife and Buchan, whose very vices were fitted to win more admiration from their countrymen than his good qualities; for, although the one was a man of craft, the other of violence, both were equally unrestrained either by conscience or feeling, and in their respective ways of action equally unscrupulous and daring. The weakness of the new reign was sufficiently indicated from the first, by the Earl of Fife, afterwards created Duke of Albany, being permitted to continue, with the office of Custos or Guardian, ruler both of the kingdom and the king. From his timid brother, Albany never would have encountered any attempt to overthrow or limit his power: but Robert's eldest son, the Duke of Rothesay, showed himself, as he grew up to manhood, to be of a very opposite temper to his father. A strong party of the nobility as well as the national feeling rallied around the heir apparent; and in 1398, Albany found himself compelled to resign the post of regent to his nephew. The government was in the hands of Rothesay, when Henry IV. of England, in the close of the year 1400, made that inroad into the country as far as Edinburgh, which was attended with no results, but is memorable as the last expedition ever conducted by an English monarch in person against the northern kingdom. In bending, however, for the moment to the storm, and retiring from the head of affairs, the dark and ambitious Albany had only stepped aside to lie in wait for an opportunity of regaining his position. The thoughtless character of Rothesay made him an easy prey to his designing uncle. His wild pursuit of pleasure, and neglect first of his wife, and then of the mistress for whom he had abandoned her, had already involved him with several powerful enemies, when, by means of artful representations conveyed to the old king of the licentious conduct of his son, he was induced, about the beginning of the year 1402, to give an order, under the royal signet, to Albany, to arrest the prince, and place him in temporary confinement. He was seized at Strathtyrum, near St. Andrews, as he rode towards that city, and immediately lodged in the castle there, from which he was soon after transferred to a dungeon in the royal palace of Falkland, and there, it is believed, starved to death. The resumption by Albany of the office of regent immediately followed this horrid tragedy. Soon after, hostile operations against England were resumed: two Scottish armies were successively marched into that country, and were both defeated and dispersed—the first at the battle of Nesbit Moor, the second at that of Homildon Hill. In the latter, Lord Murdoch Stewart, Albany's eldest son, along with many other Scottish noblemen, fell into the hands of the victors. The following year, a numerous Scottish force again advanced towards the Border—this time under the command of Albany himself; but, although the regent gave out that his design was to avenge himself on the Percies for the disasters of the preceding campaign, there is every reason to believe that he was really in league with his former enemies, and was prepared to join their rebellion against King Henry IV., when the news of the result of the battle of Shrewsbury, which he received before he had entered England, at once induced him to return home and disband his army. The connection, however, that had been formed by the Scottish government with the disaffected party in England, was not broken off by the failure of the bold enterprise of Hotspur. Albany appears to have been again a party to the conspiracy of old Northumberland and Archbishop Scroop, in 1405; and to have, after its detection, actually raised another army for the invasion of England. At this moment, however, there was a truce between the two countries, and no hostile movement on the part of the Scottish regent had yet taken place when the remarkable event occurred of the capture, by an English vessel off Flamborough Head, of King Robert's second son, James, now the heir apparent, on his voyage to France. Robert III. survived the capture of his son rather more than a year, dying

---

which may have arisen from the necessity of keeping on good terms with such outlaws and desperadoes.

Three things, not mentioned by Mr. Hallam, had probably much to do with this frightful demoralization:—1st. The substitution of a foreign clergy and rites for the old native Anglo-Saxon pastors and their vernacular instructions; 2d. Easy absolution for crime by priests; and 3d. The traditional feeling of antipathy on the part of the Anglo-Saxon population to the Normans, transferred naturally enough to all wealthy persons.

at his castle of Rothesay, in Bute, on the 4th of April, 1406.

Immediately on the death of the king, a parliament met at Perth, and, after declaring James, now a captive in England, their lawful king, continued Albany in the regency. He was now in possession of whatever power belonged to the royal station, unlimited by even the form or shadow of participation. For some years after this, peace was preserved between the governments of England and Scotland. Meanwhile a formidable rebellion of the Lord of the Isles was suppressed by his defeat in the destructive battle of Harlaw, gained by the Earl of Mar, on the 24th of July, 1411, and by the treaty of Lochgillip, by which Albany soon after compelled the northern potentate to acknowledge himself a vassal of the Scottish crown, and to give hostages for his fidelity. On the 17th of May, in the following year, a new truce was concluded with England, to last for six years. In 1414, Albany at last succeeded in obtaining from Henry V. what he had long vainly endeavoured to extort from the more obdurate disposition or more cautious policy of the late king, the liberation of his son Murdoch. He was exchanged for the young Henry Percy, the son of Hotspur, who was not only re-admitted to his native country, but reinstated in all the forfeited honours of his family.

The Scottish regent made no such effort to procure the restoration of his captive sovereign as he had made to get back his son. It is supposed that it was an apprehension of not being able much longer to ward off the return of the king, if the two nations should remain at peace, that moved him suddenly, in September, 1417, to break the truce, and to commit what was long popularly remembered as the "Foul Raid," by marching towards the Border at the head of an army of 60,000 men, and, after beginning the siege of Roxburgh, immediately retreating in all haste on learning that an English force was on the way to meet him. The consequence was, that all the south of Scotland was laid waste by the avenging invaders.

It is possible that this unfortunate attempt of the Scottish government may have been made at the instigation of the French court, with which a close alliance had always been maintained by Albany, even while at peace, or at least in peaceful intercourse, with England. It was not until a short time after the "Foul Raid," however, that the Duke of Vendôme came to Scotland on an embassy from the dauphin; when it was agreed to send a body of Scottish troops to serve against the English in France. Seven thousand men were sent under the command of the Earl of Buchan (the regent's second son) and the Earl of Wigton. The services of these brave men in a succession of bloody fields, till they were nearly all, together with 5000 more that had been subsequently brought over by the Earl of Douglas, swept away at Crevant and Verneuil, have been already commemorated. Long before these disastrous days, however, the state of affairs in Scotland had undergone a great change. The Regent Albany died at the palace of Stirling on the 3d of September, 1419, having reached the age of eighty years, during thirty-four of which he is said to have held the supreme power, under the nominal reigns of his father, brother, and nephew. He is properly to be regarded as the chief or leader of the feudal nobility, by whom he was raised up and supported against both the crown and the people, and whom, in return, he protected in all their local despotism and oppression. In the accounts of the old historians the feudal tyranny under which the country groaned during the whole period of the government of Albany is drawn in the darkest colours. The strongest proof of the closeness of the union that bound the one party to the other was given on the death of the old duke, when his son and heir Murdoch was suffered, as a matter of course, to assume the regency at the same time with his hereditary estates and honours. But Murdoch had neither the capacity nor the ambition of his father; he continued indeed to occupy the elevation to which he had been lifted by circumstances and accident, but all real power gradually fell from his hands, and his government at length became a mere anarchy. Things were in this state when the captive King of Scots, after the death of Henry V., whom he had accompanied on his glorious expedition to France, was at last permitted by the English government to return to his own country. His liberation was the result of negotiations which his friends in Scotland had long been pursuing, and which terminated in an agreement concluded at York on the 10th of September, 1423, by which it was stipulated that 40,000 pounds should be paid to England within six years, by half-yearly payments, under the name of compensation for the expenses of the maintenance of James during the eighteen years of his captivity. On the 24th of February following, the Scottish king espoused, in the church of St. Mary Overy, in Southwark, the Lady Joanna Beaufort, the daughter of the Duchess of Clarence, by her first husband the Duke of Somerset, and the descendant of Edward III. by both her parents. Tradition makes him to have fallen in love with this lady some years before, on beholding her from his prison in the Round Tower of Windsor Castle, an incident which is believed to have suggested his plaintive and elegant poem entitled "The King's Quhair." He arrived in Scotland on the 5th of April,

1424, and on the 21st of May was solemnly crowned, with his queen, in the usual venerated sanctuary, the abbey church of Scone.

The first great work to which James found it necessary to address himself, in the state to which his kingdom had been brought, was the reduction of the power of the nobility. The overthrow of that many-headed domination was indispensable, both for the security of his own position, and for the restoration of the blessings of order and good government to his people. Nor did he proceed timidly or by half measures towards an object, his success or failure in the complete attainment of which was to be his salvation or his ruin. "Let God but grant me life," he is said to have indignantly exclaimed when made fully acquainted with the universal violence and rapine that prevailed, "and by his help I shall make the key keep the castle, and the furze-bush the cow, throughout my dominions, though I should lead the life of a dog to complete it." A truce for seven years had been concluded with England, and James lost no time in taking advantage of this season of security from foreign hostility, to proceed with his work of internal reform. In a parliament which met at Perth five days after his coronation, a complete review of the manifold disorders of the kingdom was gone into, and numerous regulations were enacted for their correction. But legislation could in such circumstances only lop and somewhat repress the growth of the evil; its root lay too deep to be so reached. Having sedulously employed the interval in gaining over the instruments of his scheme, and making the other necessary preparations, James assembled another parliament at Perth, on the 12th of March, 1428, and on the ninth day after, suddenly ordered the arrest of Murdoch, Duke of Albany, his youngest son Alexander, and twenty-six of the other principal barons, their partizans, whom he had thus got into his power. Walter Stewart, Albany's eldest son, had been seized and placed in custody some time before. He was the first of the prisoners brought to trial, in a court held in the palace of Stirling, and over which the king himself presided, on the 20th of May. It is needless to add that he was condemned to die. He, his father, his brother Alexander, and Albany's father-in-law, the Earl of Lennox, now in his eightieth year, were all executed on the Heading Hill, in front of Stirling Castle. All the estates of this once-powerful family being then declared forfeited to the crown, the other nobles who had

STIRLING CASTLE.¹—From an old view by Elphinstone.

been apprehended were set at liberty, and left to their reflections on the terrible example they had witnessed.

For several years after this, James continued to occupy himself, with the assistance of his parliament, which was usually summoned every year, in endeavouring to promote the improvement of his kingdom, and to remedy the mishaps of a long course of misgovernment, by means of a series of legislative enactments, still preserved, which comprehend the subjects of agriculture, commerce, foreign and domestic manufactures, the regulation of weights and measures, the police of the country, its defence against foreign hostility both by land and by sea, the administration of justice, and even the constitution of the supreme government, and which probably, taken altogether, furnish the most complete collection of materials that now exists for the illustration of the internal condition of any European country at this remote era. He also strengthened himself, and made provision for calling into activity

¹ Stirling Castle presents an assemblage of buildings erected at different periods, mostly altered and adapted to the uses of a modern garrison. The principal vestiges are a palace built by James V., a hall adjacent built by James III., and adjacent to this a royal chapel built by James III., and rebuilt by James VI. (I. of England). An area to the south-west of the castle, surrounded by an ancient wall, was formerly the royal park and gardens; a series of concentric polygonal mounds indicates a spot in the garden where some game now out of use and forgotten was played; a hollow called the valley was appropriated for jousts and tournaments, which were witnessed by the ladies from a pyramidal mound called the ladies' hill. The castle crowns a rocky eminence, which rises 220 ft. above the level of the plain, and terminates precipitously on the north-west side of the town.

the industry and resources of the country, by treaties of alliance or commerce with France, Flanders, and other foreign powers. The only part of his dominions in which the authority of the laws continued for some time to be set at nought, or imperfectly obeyed, was the Northern Highlands. Determined that the chiefs of that region should bow under the same sceptre which had already repressed the turbulence of the southern nobles, in the spring of 1427 he assembled a parliament at Inverness, and there ventured again upon the same bold expedient which he had adopted two years before at Perth. About fifty heads of clans, who had been summoned to give their attendance, were seized; of whom some were instantly condemned and executed, others were not put to death till after a more deliberate investigation, and others were only imprisoned for a time. Of the last-mentioned class was Alexander, Lord of the Isles. This potent chieftain, upon being set at large after a confinement of about two years, collected his followers, and rose in open revolt against the royal authority; but James instantly marched against him in person, and coming up with him near Lochaber, defeated and dispersed the rebel force. Alexander soon after threw himself on the royal mercy. Another Highland rebellion, which broke out in 1431, headed by Donald Balloch, a near relation of the Lord of the Isles, was met by the Scottish king with the same promptitude and spirit, and as successfully repressed. Balloch himself lost his life. About the same time another truce for five years was concluded with England.

If James had stopped at this point he might, perhaps, have succeeded in maintaining and consolidating the reforms which he had commenced with so much courage and ability. But his scheme for breaking the strength of the nobility, and re-establishing the royal supremacy, was yet far from being completed. The blood that had been shed had, after all, destroyed but one of the great families; many others still remained sufficiently powerful to be dangerous, even singly, and nearly irresistible if they should combine. On the other hand, the crown had been greatly impoverished and weakened during the regency, by many lavish alienations of the royal domains, that had helped to build up the greatness of the aristocracy. These grants James now determined to resume. By acts which did not perhaps in any case go beyond the letter of the law, but which were at the least very rigorous and harsh applications of it, several of the most eminent among the nobility were suddenly stripped of estates of which they or their predecessors had held undisturbed possession for many years. Meanwhile, having formed an intimate alliance with France, and sent his infant daughter Margaret, in 1435, to that country to be betrothed to the dauphin (afterwards Louis XI.), he became involved through this connection in a dispute with the English government, which led him, in the course of the following year, to break the truce, and, marching with an army to the Border, to lay siege to the castle of Roxburgh. While he lay before Roxburgh, however, the queen suddenly made her appearance in the camp, and, apparently in consequence of something she had communicated, the king immediately raised the siege, disbanded his army, and returned to the north. This was before the middle of August. The conspiracy against his life was probably already arranged; but it would appear that the king's suspicions, if they had really been awakened, were again lulled, and he resumed his usual mode of life. On the approach of Christmas he repaired to Perth, and there, taking up his lodging in the great monastery of the Black Friars, spent the holy season in the midst of a numerous and brilliant court. The gay succession of revels and festivities had been prolonged far into the new year before the conspirators determined to strike their blow. The chiefs of the plot were Sir Robert Graham, Walter Stewart, Earl of Athole, and his grandson Sir Robert Stewart, who held the office of chamberlain in the royal household, and whom, it appears, it was the intention to proclaim king, as being the descendant of Robert II., and, as was pretended, his rightful heir and representative—Robert III. having, it was affirmed, been born out of wedlock. Both Graham and the Stewarts had been adherents of Albany, and both had also more recent injuries of their own to avenge. Graham, a man of the darkest and most determined character, took the conduct of the bloody enterprise. On the night of the 20th of February he proceeded, with his armed accomplices, towards the royal bedchamber, where James, standing in his night-dress, was still conversing with the queen and her ladies before retiring to rest. The noise of their tumultuous approach instantly struck alarm to the hearts of the king and those with him. He flew to the windows, but found them secured by immoveable bars. When they rushed to fasten the door, it was found that the bolts had been removed; in his extremity of despair, James then tore up one of the planks of the floor; and in this way, after replacing the board, dropped into a dark vault below, while an heroic woman, Catherine Douglas, making her arm a bolt for the door, held it till the bone was snapped in two. At first, the mode of the king's escape was not detected; but, on hearing a noise, which was occasioned by his attempt to come up from the vault, the assassins returned again to the chamber, and soon discovered where he was concealed. Naked and unarmed as he was, he made a desperate defence when they sprung down upon him to despatch him; but Graham himself at last succeeded in giving him his death-stroke. His body, when examined, was found to be pierced with sixteen wounds.[1]

Thus perished James I., in the forty-fourth year of his age, and the thirteenth of his actual reign. The conspirators gained none of their ulterior objects; on the contrary, although they escaped in the first instance, they were all eventually taken and put to death, every complicated refinement of torture being applied to deepen and prolong their dying agonies. The only son of their murdered king, an infant of six years old, was immediately crowned as James II. The early part of this reign is a scene of the most perplexed intestine confusion, of which the records are so imperfect as to make the whole nearly unintelligible. The principal personages that figure in the dark and troubled drama are Sir William Crichton, Sir Alexander Livingston, and the several mighty barons who successively became the heads of the house of Douglas. Both the royal infant and his mother were for some time constantly prisoners in the hands of one or other of the fierce and restless factions. As the boy grew up towards manhood, however, notwithstanding all the disadvantages under which his early years had been passed, he evinced his inheritance of no small share of the spirit and ability of his great father, and also of all the determination of the late king to be king in reality as well as in name. William, the fifth Earl of Douglas, and also Duke of Touraine in France, a youth of seventeen, had already been cut off, along with his younger brother, in 1440; the two were seduced by Crichton and Livingston, at that time in confederacy, to the castle of Edinburgh, where the king was, and then seized as they sat at dinner, and, after the briefest form of a trial, hurried to execution—a deed of perfidy which shocked even that unscrupulous age, and was long a theme of popular horror and execration. After a few years, however, nearly all the old power of that great baronial house was revived in the person of William, the eighth Earl of Douglas; he was the most formidable subject of the crown at the time when the king began to take the management of affairs into his own hands. James, though still very young, proceeded from the first with wonderful prudence and dissimulation. From among the several competitors for the supreme power he selected Crichton, whom he made lord-chancellor, as his confidential adviser, along with the able and enlightened Kennedy, Bishop of St. Andrews, a prelate whose high birth, for he was first cousin to the king, added additional influence to his eminent rank in the church. The first blow was struck at the Livingstons; the principal heads of that faction, being assembled in 1449, in a sort of family convocation at the bridge of Inchbelly, near Kirkintilloch, were suddenly surrounded by the king's forces, seized, and thrown into prison. A few of them were afterwards executed, the rest made their submission, and the power of the faction was completely destroyed. The more united strength of the Earl of Douglas, whose great territorial possessions in the most important district of the kingdom made him almost a rival potentate, was not so easily thrown down: policy and force were alternately resorted to: at last the mighty earl was induced to visit the king in Stirling Castle. In a conversation between him and James warm words were uttered on both sides, till the king at last, giving way to his passion, drew his dagger and plunged it into the earl's throat. Some of the courtiers, rushing in from the adjoining apartment, soon despatched the defenceless man. This atrocity happened in February, 1452, when James was yet only in his sixteenth year. The consequences did not cease to be felt to the close of his reign. The open rebellion of the adherents of the house of Douglas that immediately followed was indeed speedily suppressed; but the new earl, James, the brother of him who had been murdered, never relinquished his vengeance while the murderer lived. By his intrigues with the faction of the Yorkists in England, after he had been driven from his own country, he was instrumental in fomenting those differences which eventually led James, soon after Margaret of Anjou and her son had taken refuge in his dominions, to raise an army, and set out at its head for the invasion of England. Marching directly upon Roxburgh, he proceeded to lay siege to that castle, which had now for more than a century been in the hands of the English. The siege had not lasted many days, when one of the cannons that were pointed against the fortress burst on being fired off as the king stood beside it, and killed him on the spot. This event happened about the end of July, 1460.

The death of James II. again placed the crown of his unfortunate country on the head of a minor, James, the eldest of his sons by his wife Mary of Guelders, whom he had married in 1449. The new king was only in his eighth year. The history of his reign is in great part a repetition of the same scene of turbulence and intrigue which

---

[1] Pinkerton, (*Hist. Scot.*, app. to vol. i. pp. 462-475), has published a contemporary narrative of this barbarous murder, and also of the execution of the regicides, which professes to be translated from a Latin original—probably the account published by authority at the time. Few stories, either in history or in fiction, can compete with the horrors of this grim chronicle.

filled the commencing years of the last. The families of the Boyds and the Hamiltons now enact nearly the same parts which had been before sustained by the Livingstons and the Douglases. James III., however, as he outgrew his boyhood, showed himself to be, in various respects, of a very different character from his father and grandfather. Without any of their energy and resolute qualities, he seems to have had some degree of the love of art and literature which distinguished the first James; but an indolent and unwarlike disposition, after all, had probably more to do with his fondness for privacy, than any strong devotedness to intellectual occupations. What little we know of his tastes and studies betrays the weakest and most frivolous character of mind. He early, also, manifested a baneful passion for favourites, no trace of which is to be found in the history of either of the two preceding kings. The Boyds first obtained possession of his person and his affections, in consequence of one of them having been employed to assist in his education. For some years their ascendency at court placed the whole government of the country in their hands. Means, however, having been found to alienate the versatile and suspicious mind of their royal protector, they were, in the year 1469, not only suddenly hurled from favour and power, but pursued with a rancour on the part of the king, which did not rest satisfied till it had slaked itself in their blood. After the Boyds were thus swept away, the most conspicuous figures that appear on the scene are James' two younger brothers, who bore the titles of the Duke of Albany and the Earl of Mar. These two princes were both of a character altogether the opposite of that of the king, and as much the favourites of the warlike nobility, whom they resembled in tastes and habits, as he was their aversion and scorn. It is not at all improbable that they had, one or both of them, early begun to cherish the design of getting the government into their own hands, and that their existence, therefore, was not without danger to the royal power. They were attacked, however, by the king before they appear to have committed themselves by any aggression against the throne. Mar was arrested in 1480, on the insane charge of seeking to destroy the king's life by witchcraft (in which James was a devout believer). According to one account, he was immediately put to death by the royal order; another version of the story is, that he was seized with fever, and occasioned his own death by tearing off, in his delirium, the bandages that had been tied round his temples after having been let blood by his medical attendant. Albany's career was much more protracted. After escaping to France, he returned from that country in 1482, and entered into a treaty with the English king, Edward IV., in which he boldly assumed the title of Alexander, King of Scotland, consenting to receive the crown from the gift of Edward as his lord superior. It was in consequence of this agreement that the Duke of Gloucester, afterwards Richard III., entered Scotland, as related in a preceding page, at the head of an army in the summer of the above-mentioned year. James also raised an army, and went forth to meet the invader. Meanwhile, however, the Boyds had been succeeded in the monopoly of the king's regards by a number of persons of the lowest rank, some of whom, indeed, are said to have been persons of talent and accomplishments, but whose ascendency did not on that account the less disgust both the nobility and the whole nation. The most notorious of these favourites was a person of the name of Cochran, upon whom the infatuated king had lavished wealth and honours with the most profuse and senseless prodigality. We have already related how, when the army, on its march southwards, had reached the town of Lauder, this person, and about half a dozen more of the royal minions, were suddenly seized by a party of the nobility, headed by Archibald, Earl of Angus, and, without even the form of trial, hanged over the parapet of the bridge. The king himself was then shut up in the castle of Edinburgh, and the army was disbanded. After a short time a reconciliation was effected between the king and Albany, on which the former was released from imprisonment, and the latter appointed lieutenant-general of the kingdom. But, before many months had passed, another revolution had taken place, and Albany, driven from office, was again in rebellion. His resistance, however, was speedily put down, on which he fled once more to England. By this time Edward IV. was dead; but Albany and Richard had hitherto been good friends, and the latter at first showed some inclination to aid the duke's pretensions. The necessities of his own position, however, soon made him anxious for a termination of the war with Scotland; and, negotiations having been opened, a peace between the two countries, to last for three years, was concluded at Nottingham in September, 1484. Thus stood Scottish affairs at the close of the present epoch: the short remainder of the reign of James III. belongs to the next period of our History.

CHAPTER VII.—HISTORY OF RELIGION.

A.D. 1399—1485.

Decay of the influence of Rome—Its causes—Succession of the popes—Rivalry of popes and councils—Alliance of the crown and the church in England—Lollardism—Its origin and tenets—Its prevalence in England—Laws against it during the reign of Henry IV.—Martyrdom of Sawtre—William Thorpe arraigned for heresy—His examination and trial—Martyrdom of Badby—Persecution of Lollardism in the reign of Henry V.—Execution of Lollards—Persecution of them continued during the reign of Henry VI.—Charge of heresy against Reginald Pocock, Bishop of Chichester—His recantation and severe treatment—Divisions of the nation in regard to ecclesiastical matters—Opposition of the church to reform or concession—Increased strictness of canonical rule—Profligate lives of the clergy—Statute against the proselytism of the mendicant friars—Mode of preaching at this period—Ecclesiastical affairs of Scotland—Culdees—Condition of the Scottish church in the fifteenth century—Entrance of the doctrines of Wycklife into Scotland—Martyrdom of John Resby—Of Paul Crawar—Increase of Lollardism in Scotland—St. Andrews erected into an archbishopric—Account of Patrick Graham and William Schevez, its first archbishops.

THE history of the Romish fabric of ecclesiastical polity during the fifteenth century exhibits the established authorities of the state still standing by the system as steadily as ever, but that hold on the affections and respect of the people, which was its real strength, manifestly loosened, and becoming weaker and weaker every day. The support it received from kings and their ministers was now, indeed, augmented in the direct ratio of the decline of that other and better strength, and of the growth of the popular alienation and hostility. Its pretensions as a rival power were no longer formidable, and at the same time its maintenance was felt to be the common cause of old establishments, all of which, whether of a spiritual or temporal character, seemed to be menaced by its danger.

One of the main causes which precipitated the decay of this once mighty dominion was undoubtedly the great schism which broke out on the death of Gregory XI., in 1378, and divided the Western church for half a century. The death of Gregory was followed in a few weeks by the election in the usual form, and by the unanimous votes of all the cardinals then in Rome, being sixteen of the twenty-two composing the sacred college, of the Archbishop of Bari, Bartholomew Pregnano, who took the name of Urban VI. It is alleged, however, and is probably true, that this choice was compelled by the threats of the populace. On this pretence, at least, the cardinals, five months after, stole away from Rome, and, assembling first at Anagni and then at Fundi, excommunicated Urban as an apostate and Antichrist, and announced as the pope of their free election Robert of Caneva, or Clement VII. The imperious and severe rule of Urban probably drove them to a bold and rash act from which they would otherwise have shrunk; but the primary motive with the majority of the college of cardinals, as with the people of Rome, was to obtain a pope of their own nation. Only the preceding year, after his predecessors, from Clement V. inclusive, had resided for seventy years at Avignon in France, Gregory XI. had restored the Papacy to its ancient seat. A pope of ultramontane birth, it was apprehended by the Romans, would again remove his court from Italy. A majority of the cardinals, on the other hand, were Frenchmen, and, as such, opposed to an Italian pope. The different nations of Europe were influenced by feelings of the same kind. Most of the Italian states adhered to Urban, and on the same side, actuated chiefly by enmity to France, were ranged England, Portugal, the Netherlands, Germany, Sweden, Denmark, and Norway; France, acknowledging the election of Clement, was supported by Scotland, Navarre, Castile, Aragon, Savoy, Sicily, and Cyprus.

The succession of the Roman (now generally held to be the true) popes was continued after Urban VI. by the elections in 1389, of Perrino Tomacella, or Boniface IX.; in 1404, of Cosmato Meliorato, or Innocent VII.; and in 1406, of Angelo Corrario, or Gregory XII. On the death of Clement VII., in 1394, the cardinals at Avignon chose as his successor Peter de Luna, who assumed the name of Benedict XIII. After many attempts had been made to effect an accommodation, both Gregory XII. and Benedict XIII. were deposed, in 1409, by the council of Pisa; and by an unanimous vote of the same assembly, Peter Philaret, a Greek, or Alexander V., was raised to the chair of St. Peter. On the death of Alexander, the following year, Balthazar Cossa, a Neapolitan, or John XXIII., was in the same manner chosen to succeed him. Meanwhile, however, notwithstanding these interferences of the council, Germany, Hungary, and Naples still adhered to Gregory; and Benedict, himself a native of Spain, commanded the obedience of that important country. In this state affairs remained till the assembling of the council of Constance, in 1414. That assembly deposed the monster John: Gregory, deserted by the powers that had at first supported him, and left without dominion or authority beyond the walls of Rimini, resigned; and in 1417 the Cardinal Otho de Colonna, who took the name of Martin V., was declared the head of the Christian world. The election was made by the college of twenty-three cardinals, assisted by thirty deputies from the council, six from each of the five great nations into which Christendom was held to be divided—the Italian, the German, the French, the Spanish, and the English. "I cannot," observes Gibbon, "overlook this great national cause, which was vigorously maintained by the English ambassadors against those of France. The latter contended that Christendom was essentially distributed into the four great nations and votes of Italy, Germany, France, and Spain; and that the lesser kingdoms (such as England, Denmark, Portugal, &c.) were comprehended under one or other of these great divisions. The English asserted that the British Islands, of which they were the head, should be considered as a fifth and co-ordinate nation, with an equal vote; and every argument of truth or fable was introduced to exalt the dignity of their country. Our countrymen prevailed in the council, but the victories of Henry V. added much weight to their arguments."

The election of Martin V., however, did not altogether put an end to the schism. Benedict XIII., who fixed his residence at Peniscola, in Valencia, continued to be acknowledged by the kingdom of Aragon till his death, in 1424. His cardinals then elected a successor, who took the name of Clement VIII. In 1429, however, this person made his submission to Martin V., who was thus at last acknowledged by the whole Latin church. But, as an eminent Catholic historian of our own day has remarked, "if the schism was thus terminated, it had previously given a shock to the temporal authority of the pontiffs, from which it never recovered."[1]

The absolute power of the popes also met with serious resistance during this period from the pretensions of the great body, or at least of the aristocracy of the clergy, as assembled or represented in general councils. The council of Constance, before its separation in 1418, enacted that such synods should henceforth be held regularly for the government and reformation of the church, each, before dissolving, appointing the time and place for the meeting of its successor. But the council of Basel, which, reluctantly convoked by Martin V., assembled in 1431, immediately after the accession of his successor Eugenius IV., and continued to sit till 1443, went a great deal further, assuming and maintaining, indeed, an attitude of open revolt against the supremacy of the pontiff. It not only solemnly asserted the superiority of a general council over the occupant of the chair of St. Peter, but proceeded to divest the pope of some of his most valuable and hitherto universally recognized rights; prohibiting him from creating new cardinals, and suppressing the annates, or tax of the first year's income upon benefices, which constituted a large portion of the Papal revenue. At length, in 1437, Eugenius, who had taken up his residence at Bologna, dissolved the council, and called together another, which met at Ferrara in 1438. All Christendom was now divided between the two councils, as it had lately been in the case of the rival popes. Nor was it long before there was again a rivalry of popes as well as of councils. Having deposed Eugenius, the council of Basel, in 1430, called to the pontifical dignity, from the hermitage of Ripaille, the retired Duke of Savoy, Amadeus VIII., who thereupon exchanged his temporal style for the spiritual title of Felix V. Eugenius and his council at Ferrara were adhered to by the governments of Venice and of the southern and middle states of Italy; Germany, France, Lombardy, Spain, England, and the rest of Europe generally, supported Felix V. and the council of Basel. In point of fact, however, everywhere the bishops and the rest of the ecclesiastical aristocracy were with Eugenius: the supremacy of general councils, as asserted by that of Basel, was favoured by the great body of the clergy. A short time before the deposition of Eugenius, indeed, the lower house of convocation of the province of Canterbury had, in answer to questions proposed by the archbishop, resolved, after some days' deliberation, that the pope had the power of dissolving a general council—that the council of Basel had no power to depose Pope Eugenius—and that, if that council should depose him, they would still obey him as lawful pope. But some years afterwards the same body, to all the appeals both of pope and archbishop, firmly refused any contribution to the expense of sending representatives to the meeting at Ferrara. Meanwhile the two popes and councils continued an active and bitter warfare of decrees and denouncements, each party treating the other as rebels against the fundamental constitution of the church. In a bill of excommunication which he launched against all the members of the council of Basel, Eugenius designated that synod

---

[1] Dr. Lingard, *Hist. England*.

an assembly of demons; they retaliated by charging him with simony, perjury, tyranny, heresy, and schism, and by declaring him to be incorrigible in his vices, unworthy of any title of honour, and incapable of holding any ecclesiastical office. This unseemly condition of the Christian world lasted till after the death of Eugenius, in 1447. By this time all parties were become weary of the contest; and when the cardinals at Rome had elected Nicholas V., it was proposed by Felix himself that he should resign the tiara, and thus terminate the scandal of the church. The abdicator of two sovereignties returned to his hermitage on the banks of the Lake of Geneva, in 1449. But the habitual respect of the people for the whole system was rudely and powerfully shaken; the violent recriminations of the contending pontiffs could not fail lastingly to impair the authority over the minds of the multitude both of pope and council; the noise of such a contention must have awakened many feelings that would otherwise have slumbered; and the suppression of the process of reform from within the church would really only tend to prepare and hasten its much more tempestuous reform from without.

In England throughout this period the crown continued to make common cause with the clergy; every successive king began his reign by courting their favours, and ever after relied upon them as his chief supporters. The part which the clergy took in the deposition of Richard II. has been characterized as "the only instance in English history wherein their conduct as a body was disloyal."[1] Even here, however, they took no part against the crown. Of two competitors they only sided with the one against the other; they still stood by their natural ally, the king. They probably espoused the cause of Henry, simply as being that of the party most likely to prevail in the struggle—in other words, of the competitor who was properly to be considered as most truly king of the two—thus substantially adhering to their principles even in the seeming violation of them. At all events, their accustomed loyalty was suspended only for a moment; their attachment, withdrawn from Richard, was immediately transferred to the house of Lancaster, and was never found wanting by the princes of that house so long as they maintained themselves on the throne. One of the first acts of Henry IV. after his accession, was to despatch the Earl of Northumberland with a gracious message to a convocation of the province of Canterbury, which met on the 6th of October, 1399, in the chapter-house of St. Paul's at London. While he begged the prayers of the church for himself and the kingdom, he declared, first, that he would never demand any money from the clergy except in cases of the most extreme necessity; secondly, that he would protect them in all their liberties and immunities; and, thirdly, that he would assist them with all his power in exterminating heretics. The first of these promises was but indifferently observed: Henry IV., indeed, throughout his reign, demanded subsidies from the clergy as regularly as from the laity; he even threatened on one or two occasions to take their money or goods from them by force; but still they acted as if they felt their interests to be bound up with his. Nay, not even his daring execution of Archbishop Scroop, after the insurrection of 1405,[2] made any permanent breach between him and the church: a vague and inoperative censure, retracted on the first explanation, was the only notice taken by Rome of an act that in other times would have shaken the strongest throne in Christendom. On the other hand, Henry gratified the clergy by steadily supporting them in the assertion of all such powers as could be conceded to them consistently with the maintenance of the integrity of the civil authority, and in particular of that upon which they set the highest value, the empire which they flattered themselves with exercising over opinion and belief. In the falling away of their old popular strength, they now had recourse to new expedients, in order to sustain this tyranny, exposed as it was, at the same time, to a more vigorous resistance than it had ever before encountered.

Till the present age, the offence of heresy had never greatly vexed the church in England. The old laws accordingly upon that subject were comparatively mild; a considerable degree of protection was thrown around the accused; and sanguinary punishments for the offence appear to have been nearly unknown. The zeal of the heads of the church, however, was not long satisfied with such moderate measures.

Among the small number of persons by whom Bolingbroke was accompanied on his return from exile, was Thomas Fitz-Alan, or Arundel, the Archbishop of Canterbury, who had been banished by Richard the year before. Arundel, who was the second son of Robert Fitz-Alan, Earl of Arundel and Warrenne, had, during the interval of his deprivation, been nominated by the pope, Boniface IX., to the see of St. Andrews, in Scotland. It appears that Richard assented to this nomination, though at first he objected that St. Andrews was too near England. Arundel, however, never took possession of his Scottish dignity, but remained on the Continent till his return home with Bolingbroke; when, on the

---

[1] Southey's *Book of the Church*, i. 319.

[2] See vol. i. p. 540.

latter obtaining the crown, he recovered his archbishopric—Roger Walden, dean of York, and treasurer of the royal household, who had been set by the deposed king in his place, being obliged to retire, after the example of his master. Arundel was a man of talent, as well as accomplished in the learning of the times. The latter circumstance probably did not tend to make him more indulgent to the innovators in religion, who, under the name of Lollards, now began to show themselves in great numbers.

The Lollards have been usually regarded as the disciples or followers of Wyckliffe; but they seem to have rather been a sect of foreign origin, whose opinions, in their general complexion, resembled those taught by the great English Reformer. It is said, indeed, that some of the writings of Wyckliffe had been carried into Bohemia, by one of the natives of that country, who had visited England, in consequence of the marriage of Richard II. with his first wife the Princess Anne, sister of the Emperor Wenceslaus, king of that country; and that from them the celebrated John Huss drew those opinions for which he was, in 1415, condemned to the stake by the council of Constance, and which were, through him, extensively propagated over Germany. One account of the name Lollards derives it from *lolium*, the Latin word for tares; as if it had been intended to designate the Reformers as tares among the wheat—not without an allusion to the expediency of consigning them to the flames. Another notion is that they were so called from the old German word *lollen* or *lullen* (the same with our English *lull*), signifying to sing, as a mother when she lulls her babe, in reference to their practice of singing hymns. But the true origin of the term is probably from the German Reformer, Walter Lollard, who was burned at Cologne in 1322, and was charged with holding opinions very similar, on the whole, to those that have been imputed to the English Lollards of the fifteenth century. Besides preaching against the mass, extreme unction, the efficacy of penances, and the authority assumed by the pope, he is alleged to have maintained that no obedience was due to magistrates—that there was no use either in baptism or repentance—with various other tenets of a similar character—all, however, most likely misrepresented in the accounts that have come down to us. It appears that the name of Lollards used to be given on the Continent to bodies of religionists marked by any peculiarity of creed or practice, long before it was known in England. The English Lollards were certainly declared opponents of the established church and of all the pretensions of the Romish hierarchy. They were as truly Reformers and Protestants as Luther and his followers in the next century, though their doctrines may not have been in all respects the same. The most distinct and authentic account which we have of their creed is that given by themselves in a petition which they presented to the House of Commons in 1395, and which may be considered as a protest against the whole system, doctrinal and institutional, of the established religion. In this document they maintain, in substance, that the possession of temporalities by the clergy is contrary to the law of Christianity, and destructive of faith, hope, and charity—that the Romish priesthood is not that established by Christ—that outward rites of worship have no warrant in Scripture, and are of little or no importance—that the celibacy of the clergy is the occasion of scandalous irregularities in the whole church—that the pretended miracle of transubstantiation tends to make people idolaters—that exorcisms and benedictions pronounced over wine, bread, water, oil, salt, &c., have more in them of necromancy than of religion—that the clergy, by accepting secular places under the government, become hermaphrodites, attempting at the same time to serve both God and Mammon—that prayers made for the dead are more likely to be displeasing than otherwise to the Almighty, inasmuch as, for one among other reasons, they are probably in most cases offered for persons (more especially the founders of monasteries and other such pernicious endowments) who have already been consigned to punishment for their evil lives and are beyond the reach of mercy—that pilgrimages and prayers made to images are nearly akin to idolatry—that auricular confession is a highly objectionable practice—that priests have no power of absolution for sin—that to take away the life of a man, either in war or by sentence of a court of justice, is expressly contrary to the spirit and the precepts of Christianity—and, lastly, that certain trades ought to be put down as both unnecessary and the occasion of a great deal of sin, especially those of the goldsmith and the sword-cutler, both of which, though they might be tolerated under the Mosaic dispensation, were not lawful under that of the New Testament.[1] All these positions the petitioners attempted to support by reasoning and by the authority of Scripture, professing to deliver their testimony by virtue of a Divine commission, and under the character of ambassadors of Christ. It may be remarked that these Wyckliffites, as they have been often styled, and avowed adversaries of the pretensions of the see of Rome as they unquestionably were, nevertheless, in this solemn declaration of their opinions and articles of faith, make no mention either of Wyckliffe, on the one

---

[1] Wilkins, *Concilia*, iii. 221.

hand, or of the pope on the other. The denial, however, of the Papal infallibility is involved in the whole tenor of their statements and arguments.

In these new heretics, therefore (as they were deemed), the church saw a hostile force, formidable from numbers and enthusiasm, openly arrayed against it, and avowing the desire to pull it down. The measures which the clergy and other friends of the existing order of things took for their own protection in these circumstances were neither morally justifiable nor even politic in any enlarged view. Very soon after the accession of Henry IV. they availed themselves of the circumstances of the time to obtain a new law for the punishment of heresy. In January, 1401, the commons joined the clergy in a petition upon the subject to the king, and the result was, the passing of the famous statute known as the 2 Henry IV. c. 15. The preamble of this statute sets forth, among other things, that, whereas the Catholic faith and holy church had been hitherto maintained in England without being "perturbed by any perverse doctrine, or wicked, heretical, or erroneous opinions, yet, nevertheless, divers false and perverse people of a certain new sect, of the faith, of the sacraments of the church, and the authority of the same, damnably thinking, and against the law of God and of the church openly preaching, do perversely and maliciously, in divers places within the said realm, under the colour of dissembled holiness, preach and teach these days, openly and privily, divers new doctrines, and wicked, heretical, and erroneous opinions; and of such sect and wicked doctrine and opinions they make unlawful conventicles and confederacies, they hold and exercise schools, they make and write books, they do wickedly instruct and inform people, and, as much as they may, incite and stir them to sedition and insurrection, and make great strife and division among the people, and other enormities horrible to be heard daily do perpetrate and commit." The unspecified enormities may be passed over as merely a flourish of legislative rhetoric; but from the rest of the description, making the requisite allowance for the misrepresentations of an adverse party, we may gather some information as to the ways which the Lollards took to diffuse their tenets. The act goes on to complain that "the diocesans of the said realm cannot by their jurisdiction spiritual, without aid of the said royal majesty, sufficiently correct the said false and perverse people, nor refrain their malice, because the said false and perverse people do go from diocese to diocese, and will not appear before the said diocesans, but the same diocesans and their jurisdiction spiritual, and the keys of the church, with the censures of the same, do utterly contemn and despise, and so their wicked preachings and doctrines do from day to day continue and exercise to the utter destruction of all order and rule of right and reason," In order that "this wicked sect, preachings, doctrines, and opinions, should from henceforth cease and be utterly destroyed," it is then ordained, "by the assent of the great lords and noble persons of the said realm," that no person presume to preach anywhere, openly or privily, without the license of the diocesan of the place; that none shall "anything preach, hold, teach, or instruct, openly or privily, or make or write any book, contrary to the Catholic faith or determination of the holy church," or hold schools or conventicles for the dissemination of the new doctrines, or in anywise favour the preachers or teachers of them; and that all persons having any heretical books or writings shall deliver the same to the diocesan within forty days from the time of the proclamation of this ordinance and statute. The diocesan is empowered to cause the arrest of all persons failing to render due obedience to these requirements, and to detain them in his prison until they clear themselves of the articles laid to their charge, or else abjure the new opinions, the diocesan being bound to proceed in the case and determine it within three months after the arrest. On the conviction of any prisoner, he is further empowered to keep him in custody–" as long as to his discretion shall seem expedient," and also to fine him in proportion to the manner and quality of his offence, the fine being paid to the king and levied by authority of the secular courts. And then follows the terrible enactment, to the effect that persons so convicted refusing to abjure, or relapsing after abjuration, shall be made over to the sheriff of the county, or mayor and bailiffs of the nearest town, "and they the same persons, and every of them, after such sentence promulgate, shall receive, and them before the people in an high place do to be burned, that such punishment may strike in fear to the minds of other, whereby no such wicked doctrine, and heretical and erroneous opinions, nor their authors and fautors in the said realm and dominions, against the Catholic faith, Christian law, and determination of the holy church, which God prohibit, be sustained, or in anywise suffered."

At this time the commons would seem to have been as zealously opposed to Lollardism as either the nobility or the clergy. At a date only a few years later, however, we find the sentiments of the lower house to have undergone a great change. In the famous lack-learning parliament which met at Coventry, in October, 1404, the commons, as we have seen, in answer to the king's demand of a grant to carry on the Welsh war, went the length of proposing that he should seize the revenues of the church and apply them to the public service.[1] The clergy, they represented, while engrossing a great part of the wealth of the kingdom, lived in idleness, and contributed very little in any way to the public advantage—a complaint which, so far as it went, was the very language of the Lollards, and one, no doubt, of the most offensive of their heresies. Afterwards, also, in a parliament which met at Westminster in 1409, when the king demanded another large grant, the commons, according to the historian Walsingham (although there is no notice of the affair on the rolls), again strongly advised him to have recourse to the revenues of the church. On this occasion the peers interfered, praying the king to protect the patrimony of the church, and to punish all such as taught the people that it was lawful to take it away; and Henry severely reprimanded the commons for their presumptuous proposition.

Meanwhile the statute against Lollardism had not been allowed to remain a dead letter. A case came before the same parliament in which it was passed, that put its sharpness of fang to the proof. William Sawtre had been rector of Lynn, in Norfolk, and had been deprived of that living on a charge of heresy in 1399. Having been prevailed upon, however, to abjure his alleged erroneous opinions, he had since been appointed priest of St. Osith's, London. Holding that situation, he now petitioned the parliament that he might be heard before them on the subject of religion—unhappy, apparently, under the feeling of having denied his convictions, and anxious to make up, by a public profession of what he deemed the truth, for the pusillanimity of his late recantation. "The enthusiast," says a reverend modern historian, who, in his contempt for the unfortunate man, has forgotten to characterize the conduct of any of the other parties in the affair—" the enthusiast aspired to the crown of martyrdom, and had the satisfaction to fall a victim to his own folly."[2] There are probably few persons at the present day capable of contemplating the transaction with the equanimity indicated by these remarkable words. Sawtre was, in fact, summoned to appear before the convocation to answer to various charges, of which the chief were his having affirmed that he would not worship the cross on which Christ suffered, and that the sacramental bread continued to be bread after it was consecrated. It is said that he admitted the truth of the charges, but denied that he had already abjured the same opinions. The probability must be held to be, that he endeavoured to show, by argument, that the opinions he had abjured the preceding year were not identical with those he now admitted. On this point, however, the court decided against him; he was adjudged to be a relapsed heretic, and as such, sentenced to be degraded, deposed, and then delivered over to the secular power, according to the awful doom of the new law. The primate

OLD ST. PAUL'S, LONDON.[3]—From a print by Hollar.

Arundel and six other bishops assembled in the cathedral of St. Paul's, arrayed in their ponti-

---

[1] See vol. i. p. 547.
[2] Lingard, *Hist. of England*, iv. 322.
[3] By Wren's discovery of a presbyterium, constructed in the Roman manner, on the site of St. Paul's, it is surmised that a Christian edifice had been erected there in the reign of Constantine. In 603, Sebert either built a church or repaired a former edifice. This church, which was ornamented by Erkenwald, the fourth in succession to Melitus, the first Bishop of London, was burned down in a fire which consumed the city in 1086.

Towards the close of the eleventh century, Bishop Mauritius laid the foundation of a new church, which took upwards of forty years in building, and the edifice is described by William of Malmesbury, as being "so stately and beautiful that it was worthily numbered among the most famous buildings." In 1221 a new steeple was added, and in 1240 a new choir. The crypt of St. Faith underneath was begun in 1257. This was the parish church, and contained several chantries and monuments. Henry Lacie, Earl of Lincoln, who died in 1312, made what was called the new work, at the east end, in which was the chapel of our Lady and that of St. Dunstan. The chapterhouse, adjoining the south transept, projected into a stately cloister two stories. The dimensions of this noble edifice, as taken in 1309, were as follows: the length 690 ft., the breadth 130 ft., the height of the roof of the west part from the floor, 102 ft., of the east part 188 ft., of the tower 260 ft., of the spire, which was constructed of wood and covered with lead, 274 ft. The whole space the church occupied was three acres and a half, one rood and a half, and six perches (Dugdale). This vast pile, with its shrines and monuments, the rich accumulation of six centuries, fell amid the havoc of the great fire of 1666.

fical robes, to perform the impressive preliminary ceremonial. Their victim was brought before them in his priestly attire, with the chalice for holding the host, and its paten or lid in his hands. The archbishop solemnly pronounced his degradation from the priestly order, and took from him all the sacred insignia. When he had been thus wholly divested of his clerical character, he was delivered over to the custody of the high constable and marshal of England, who were there present to receive him, the primate finishing his task by pronouncing the formal recommendation to mercy with which the church was accustomed to veil, but only with a deeper horror, its deeds of blood. Sawtre was burned in Smithfield in the beginning of March, 1401, a vast multitude of people crowding to witness, with various, doubtless, but all with strong emotions, a spectacle then new in England.

This terrifying example seems to have had the effect of putting down the open profession of Lollardism for some years. The new opinions, however, continued to spread in secret. The next recorded case in which we find the aid of the secular power called in by the church for their suppression is that of William Thorpe, a priest distinguished for his learning and ability, who was brought before Arundel, on a charge of heresy, on the 3d of July, 1407. We have his own account of the proceedings, drawn up at considerable length and with much particularity.[1] He was first called into the presence of the primate in his castle of Saltwood, after having lain for some time in prison in that stronghold. The archbishop told him that he knew well he had been for twenty winters and more travelling about busily in the north country teaching his false doctrines, but now at last he was taken, and should be suffered to spread his poison among the people no longer. Thorpe having obtained permission to declare what his opinions really were, recited them at great length; the archbishop seems to have heard him patiently, but at the end only replied, "I will shortly that now thou swear here to me that thou shalt forsake all the opinions which the sect of Lollards hold and is slandered with." He also required that Thorpe should not favour any man or woman holding the said opinions, but do his utmost to withstand all such disturbers of the holy church; "and them," he added, "that will not leave their false and damnable opin-

SALTWOOD CASTLE, Kent.[2]—From a view by Lambert.

ions, thou shalt put them up, publishing them and their names, and make them known to the bishop of the diocese." On the prisoner's refusal to assent to these conditions, "Thine heart," exclaimed the primate, "is full hard endured (indurated) as was the heart of Pharaoh, and the devil hath overcome thee and perverted thee. But I say to thee, lewd losel (low rascal), either thou quickly consent to mine ordinance, and submit thee to stand to my decrees, or by St. Thomas thou shalt be degraded, and follow thy fellow to Smithfield." To this Thorpe made no answer for some time; at last, after being repeatedly urged to speak, he addressed the primate in another long discourse, in which he related how his father and mother had "spent mickle money in divers places," in educating him for the priesthood—how, when he came to years of discretion, he had no will to be a priest—how he was at last persuaded to take holy orders by the vehement and incessant solicitations of his friends—and how he had then acquired his knowledge of the truth from the conversation and example of various pious and learned clergymen, of whom one of the chief, he declared, was Philip of Rampenton, since become Bishop of Lincoln, and now a zealous persecutor of the very opinions he had formerly held and taught. In the course of the conversation that ensued the archbishop said, "Thou

[1] In Foxe's *Acts and Monuments*, and also in the *State Trials*.

[2] This castle is situated near Hythe, on an eminence commanding a fine view of the sea. In the reign of John it became one of the palaces of the Archbishops of Canterbury, and was rebuilt by Archbishop Courtenay, in the reign of Richard II. It was exchanged by Cranmer to Henry VIII., who in turn gave it to the Clintons.

and such other losels of thy sect would shave your heads full near to have a benefice. For, by Jesu, I know none more courteous shrews than ye are when ye have a benefice. For, lo! I gave to John Purvay a benefice but a mile out of this castle, and I heard more complaints about his covetousness for tithes, and other misdoings, than I did of all men that were advanced within my diocese." After this, Thorpe proceeds to give an interesting account of the teachers from whom he had obtained his knowledge of the Reformed doctrines. At the head of the list he places "Master John Wyckliffe," who, he observes, "was holden of full many men the greatest clerk that they knew then living;"—"great men," it is added, "communed oft with him, and they loved so his learning that they writ it, and busily enforced them to rule themself thereafter." The rest are spoken of as all of them the disciples and imitators of Wyckliffe. We may transcribe the now little remembered names of these first English Reformers; they were, Master John Aiston—Philip of Rampenton, while he was a canon of Leicester—Nicholas Herford—Davy Gotray of Pakering, monk of Byland, and a master of divinity—John Purvay (or Purnay, as he is elsewhere called)—"and many others which were holden right wise men and prudent;" notwithstanding that, now, "some of these men," adds the speaker, "be contrary to the learning that they taught; for they feign, and hide, and contrary (contradict) the truth which before they taught out plenily (fully) and truly." "That learning," replied the archbishop, "that thou callest truth and soothfastness, is open slander to holy church, as it is proved of holy church. For albeit that Wyckliffe, your author, was a great clerk, and though that many men held him a perfect liver, yet his doctrine is not approved of holy church, but many sentences of his learning are damned, as they well worthy are." He soon, however, broke off the argument, recurring to his former demand—"Wherefore tarriest thou me thus here with such fables?—Wilt thou shortly, as I have said to thee, submit thee to me or not?" "I dare not, for the dread of God, submit me to thee," answered the prisoner; on which the archbishop, "as if he had been wroth," desired one of his clerks to fetch him quickly the certification that came from Shrewsbury, " witnessing the errors and heresies that this losel hath venomously sworn there."

The document, on being produced, was found to attest that Thorpe had asserted openly in a sermon preached shortly before in St. Chad's Church in Shrewsbury, that the sacrament of the altar, after consecration, still remained material bread—that images should in nowise be worshipped—that men should not go on pilgrimages—that priests have no title to tithes—and that it is not lawful to swear in anywise. He now, however, emphatically denied that this was a true account of what he had said. "I am," he exclaimed, "both ashamed on their behalf, and right sorrowful for them, that have certified you these things thus untruly; for I preached never nor taught thus privily nor apertly." After much further wrangling, it is at last suggested by one of the clerks that the prisoner should be questioned on the points certified against him one by one, that they might learn what his real opinions were out of his own mouth. The long debate that followed is of much interest and value in reference to the history of the Reformed doctrines; but we shall only notice one or two passages that curiously illustrate the notions or customs of the times in the matter of religion. Touching the sacrament of the altar, Thorpe denied that he had said a word at Shrewsbury. Only, he said, as he stood in the pulpit preaching, there knelled a sacring bell, when many of the people turned away hastily, and began with great noise to run forth from the church; on which he turned to them, and remarked that they would do better to stand still and hear God's Word—the virtue of the holy sacrament of the altar standing much more in the belief thereof that they ought to have in their souls, than in the outward sight thereof. The discussion upon the second point—the worship of images—is very curious. Thorpe begins by stating his belief as follows: "Wood, tin, gold, silver, or any other matter that images are made of, all these creatures are worshipful in their kind, and to the end that God made them for; but the carving, casting, nor painting of any imagery made with man's hand, albeit that this doing be accept of men of high estate and dignity, and ordained of them to be a calendar to lewd people, yet this imagery ought not to be worshipped in the form nor in the likeness of man's craft; nevertheless, every matter that painters paint with, since it is God's creature, ought to be worshipped in the kind and to the end that God made and ordained it to serve man." An image, the archbishop admits in reply, ought not, indeed, to be worshipped for itself; but still, he contends, it ought to be worshipped for the sake of the religious doctrine that is depicted therein, and "so brought there-through to man's mind." "It is a great moving of devotion," he goes on to argue, "to men to have and to behold the Trinity and other images of saints carved, cast, and painted; for beyond the sea are the best painters that ever I saw. And, sirs, I tell you this is their manner, and it is a good manner, when that an image-maker shall carve, cast in mould, or paint any images, he shall go to a priest, and shrive him as clean as if he should then die, and take penance, and make some certain vow of fasting or of praying, or of pilgrimages doing, praying the priest specially to pray for him that he may have grace to make a fair and devout image." Afterwards taking up another ground—"Ungracious losel!" he exclaimed, "thou favourest no more truth than an hound. Since, at the rood at the north door at London, at our Lady at Walsingham, and many other divers places in England, are many great and praisable miracles done, should not the images of such holy saints and places be more worshipped than other places and images where no such miracles are done?" The Virgin at Walsingham, in Norfolk, was the most famous image in England. In that invaluable record and picture of the social customs of the fifteenth century, the *Paston Letters*, this renowned object of superstitious devotion is repeatedly noticed. Thus, in one letter, we find Sir William Yelverton, one of the judges of the King's Bench, ascribing all the good fortune he had met with in the world, and all his escapes from danger, and from the malice of his enemies, to our Lady of Walsingham.[1] Our Lady of Walsingham was particularly resorted to by women in anticipation of the perils of child-bed.[2] Erasmus, who visited Walsingham in the reign of Henry VIII., informs us, in one of his letters, that the place was almost entirely maintained by the great numbers of persons who came to make their offerings to the Virgin. In the church, he tells us, in which the image stood, was a little chapel of wood, into which the pilgrims were admitted from each side by a narrow door. There was but little light—almost none, indeed, except that of the gratefully odorous wax-tapers; but a person looking in would say that it was an abode of the gods, so bright and resplendent it was all over with jewels, gold, and silver. It is said that Henry VIII., when a child, walked barefoot to Walsingham from the neighbouring town of Basham, and made an offering of a necklace of great value to the Virgin. The same king afterwards stripped the magnificent shrine of all its treasures, and dissolved the religious house of which it was the pride and the support. In September, 1538, the image of Walsingham, with those of Ipswich, Worcester, Welsdon, and many others, were all taken away at the instance of the Lord Cromwell; those of Walsingham and Ipswich were brought up to London, "with all the jewels that hung about them," and along with the rest were burned at Chelsea by Cromwell's order.[3]

We return to the Archbishop of Canterbury's examination of Thorpe. The question of pilgrimages is next debated. Thorpe is accused by the archbishop of having asserted that "those men and women that go on pilgrimages to Canterbury, to Beverley, to Karlington, to Walsingham, and to any other such places, are accursed and made foolish, spending their goods in waste." Thorpe, in effect, admits such to be his opinion, and in justifying himself, is led into a lively description of what the fashionable pilgrimages of the time really were. "Examine," he says, "whosoever will, twenty of these pilgrims, and he shall not find the men or women that know surely a commandment of God, nor can say their Pater-Noster and Ave-Maria, nor their Credo, readily in any manner of language." "The cause," he affirms, "why that many men and women go hither and thither now on pilgrimages is more for the health of their bodies than of their souls; more to have riches and prosperity of this world than to be enriched with virtues in their souls; more to have here worldly and fleshly friendship than for to have friendship of God and of his saints in heaven." Such persons as thus spend much money in seeking out and visiting the bones or images of this or that saint, do that, he contends, which is in direct disobedience to the commands of God, inasmuch as they waste their goods partly upon hostellers (or innkeepers), many of whom are women of profligate conduct, partly upon rich priests that already have much more than they need. "Also, sir," he concludes,

Remains of the Church of our Lady of Walsingham.—From *Vetusta Monumenta*.

---

[1] *Paston Letters*. [2] Ibid. ii. 96, and iv. 414. [3] *Holinshed*, p. 945.

"I know well that when divers men and women will go thus far after their own wills, and finding one pilgrimage, they will ordain with them (arrange with one another) before to have with them both men and women that can well sing wanton songs, and some other pilgrims will have with them bagpipes; so that every town they come through, what with the noise of their singing, and with the sound of their piping, and with the jangling of their Canterbury bells, and with the barking out of dogs after them, they make more noise than if the king came there away with all his clarions and many other minstrels. And if these men and women be a month in their pilgrimage, many of them shall be an half-year after great janglers, tale-tellers, and liars." The defence of all this merriment by the archbishop is too good to be omitted. "Lewd losel," he replies, "thou seest not far enough in this matter. I say to thee that it is right well done that pilgrims have with them both singers and also pipers, that when one of them that goeth barefoot striketh his toe upon a stone, and hurteth him sore, and maketh him to bleed, it is well done that he or his fellow begin then a song, or else take out of his bosom a bagpipe, for to drive away with such mirth the hurt of his fellow. For with such solace the travel and weariness of pilgrims is lightly and merrily brought forth." Arundel is quite of the mind of the host in Chaucer :—

"Ye gon to Canterbury: God you speed
The blissful martyr quitté you your meed;
And well I wot as ye gon by the way
Ye shapen you to talken and to play;
For tru-e-ly comfort no mirth is none
To riden by the way dumb as the stone."

There was no greater agreement between the two parties on the remaining points of tithes, oath-taking, confession, &c., than in regard to those previously discussed; but the rest of their debate contains nothing that is necessary to be adverted to for our present purpose. Neither persuasions nor threats would move the intrepid Lollard, though, in the end, some of the persons that were sent for to give their counsel advised the archbishop to burn him, and others proposed that he should be drowned in the sea, which was near at hand. He was at last led forth to what he calls "a foul, dishonest prison," where he had never been before. It is not certainly known what was the fate of Thorpe, but he was never again heard of, and most probably he died in his dungeon.

We can only notice very shortly the cases of the other Lollards that are recorded to have suffered in England during this period of persecution. The second victim known to have perished at the stake was John or Thomas Badby, called in some accounts a tailor, in others a smith, who, on the 1st of March, 1410, was, after an examination by Archbishop Arundel, conveyed to Smithfield, and there burned in a large tun surrounded with dry wood. "The king's eldest son, the Lord Henry, Prince of Wales (afterwards Henry V.), having been present," says the chronicler, "offered him his pardon, first before the fire was kindled, if he would have recanted his opinions; and after, when the fire was kindled, hearing him make a roaring noise very pitifully, the prince caused the fire to be plucked back, and exhorted him, being with pitiful pain almost dead, to remember himself, and renounce his opinions, promising him not only life, but also threepence a-day so long as he lived, to be paid out of the king's coffers; but he, having recovered his spirits again, refused the prince's offer, choosing eftsoons to taste the fire, and so to die, than to forsake his opinions; whereupon the prince commanded that he should be put into the tun again, from thenceforth not to have any favour or pardon at all; and so it was done, and the fire put to him again, and he consumed to ashes."[1]

The accession of Henry V., in 1413, did not put a stop to these scenes of horror. With all his generosity of disposition, the new monarch had a soldier's sternness of feeling in regard to human suffering; and, besides that considerations of policy made it expedient for him, as it had been for his father, to conciliate the clergy, he took pride in showing himself a dutiful son of the church, and a zealous defender of the faith. The history and fate of Cobham have been already related.[2] His apprehension and condemnation were among the last acts of Archbishop Arundel, who died in February, 1414; the sentence by which Cobham was made over as a heretic to the secular judgment being dated the 10th of October preceding. Arundel was succeeded in the primacy by Henry Chicheley, translated from the see of St. David's —a change which brought no relief to the Lollards. Chicheley, indeed, seems to have proceeded against the new sect in a more sweeping fashion than his predecessor, not, perhaps, as being of a more sanguinary or unscrupulous temper, but rather, probably, from being driven to more desperate and wholesale methods for the suppression of the obnoxious opinions, by their increasing diffusion. The Lollards were now apprehended in great numbers, and crowded the prisons of the church. It was Chicheley who built the addition to Lambeth Palace, still known as the Lollards' Tower, from the small apartment at its summit in which the unhappy persons accused of heresy were confined, tied, as it would appear, to iron rings, which remain fixed in the walls, the thick wainscot of which also yet exhibits the names of some of the sufferers rudely scratched upon it. In August, 1415, John Clay-

[1] Holinshed. [2] See vol. i. pp. 554, 506.

don, a furrier in London, in consequence of certain English books of Lollardism which were found in his possession, was condemned by the archbishop as a relapsed heretic (he had formerly been imprisoned on a similar charge), and was burned in Smithfield. Richard Turmin, a baker

PRISON CHAMBER IN THE LOLLARDS' TOWER, LAMBETH.[1]—From a drawing by J. W. Archer.

of London, underwent the same fate the same year. Cobham was put to death in St. Giles' Fields on the 25th of December, 1417, being hung by the middle in iron chains, from a new pair of gallows, over the fire, till both his body and the gallows were consumed to ashes.[2]

The early part of the reign of Henry VI. also witnessed many similar executions. It was impossible, however, to burn or otherwise put to death all the parties whom the spiritual courts were constantly finding guilty of heresy; and Chicheley soon found it necessary to substitute, in the greater number of cases, prolonged imprisonment, whipping, and various other punishments. The utmost rigour of the law appears to have been, for the most part, reserved for such of the clergy as were convicted of preaching or holding the new opinions. In 1423 four ecclesiastics were committed to the flames in Smithfield for the crime of Lollardism. Archbishop Chicheley died in 1443, and was succeeded by John Stafford, Bishop of Bath and Wells; Stafford was succeeded by John Kemp, Archbishop of York, in 1452; he lived only two years, and, on his death, Thomas Bourchier, Bishop of Ely, was promoted to the primacy. These three last-mentioned bishops were all cardinals, and each of them for a time held the office of lord high chancellor.

The most remarkable charge of heresy which occurs in the latter years of the present period, and the last we shall here notice, was that brought against Reginald Peacock or Pecock, Bishop of Chichester, who was cited on the 22d of October, 1457, to appear to answer for various false opinions that were imputed to him before Archbishop Bourchier, at Lambeth. Peacock was one of the most learned men of his age, and was as much distinguished for his moderate and conciliatory spirit as for his high talents and extensive acquirements. He had been one of the eminent scholars patronized by the Duke of Gloucester—" the good Duke Humphrey"—and this connection may have had some share in exciting a party against him; but his published opinions were quite sufficient to call down upon him the hatred and vengeance of the church, notwithstanding that they did not go the length of absolute Lollardism. Peacock, indeed, was decidedly opposed to some of the tenets of the Lollards, and gave only a qualified assent to others; he wished the church to yield at least so far to the spirit of the times as to tolerate a latitude of opinion upon some points that, if not indifferent, were so obscure as scarcely to be comprehensible by the human judgment; in a few other things he may have been more inclined towards the new than the old doctrines; but it was at most the reform of the church that he sought, not its overthrow; nor did he either join its adversaries or withdraw himself from its communion. The very moderation and reasonableness, however, of his dissent from his brethren made it only the more irritating to a body inflamed with suspicion and fear, and apt to regard everything as lukewarmness or concealed hostility that was not undiscriminating and reckless partizanship. Peacock's fate was that which, in all ages, has usually attended moderators and mediators between extreme opinions in the height and fury of their mutual opposition and resentment. In one material point, at least, Peacock had distinctly laid himself open to a charge of heresy. In admitting

[1] The prison chamber is situated at the summit of the tower, and is entirely covered—walls, ceiling, and floor—with thick oak planks, in which many names and devices are carved, but few of them are now legible. It is guarded by an inner and an outer door, 3½ inches thick, covered with bosses and plates of iron. The room is about 13 ft. by 12, and about 8 ft. high. Eight large rings, to which unfortunate inmates have been chained, are rivetted in the wall. On the river side is a small deep splayed window, and near it a very massive stone fireplace, over which a rude representation of the crucifixion is carved.

[2] Holinshed. Account, by Bishop Bale, in State Trials.

that a particular belief upon certain mysterious questions was not necessary to salvation, he had unavoidably denied, by implication if not in terms, the assumed infallibility of the church, which had declared such belief to be indispensable. This accordingly appears to have been the chief accusation laid against him. The other heresies with which he was charged amounted to a denial of the necessity of a belief in certain doctrines, not to a denial of the doctrines themselves; the only doctrine he was charged with denying was this of the church's infallibility. He was convicted upon all the articles exhibited against him, and would have been put to death, if, in the spirit of conciliation and aversion to extreme courses by which his life had been distinguished, he had not consented to a recantation of his obnoxious opinions. He read his abjuration at St. Paul's Cross before the archbishop and three other bishops, delivering at the same time fourteen of his books with his own hand to an attendant, who threw them into a fire lighted for the purpose, while many thousands of spectators filled all the space around. Such other copies as had been collected, were afterwards, in like manner, delivered to the flames. Their author, however, although he thus saved his life, did not obtain his liberty. "He was sent to Thorney Abbey (in the Isle of Ely), there to be confined in a secret, closed chamber, out of which he was not to be allowed to go. The person who made his bed and his fire was the only one who might enter and speak to him without the abbot's leave and in his presence. He was to have neither pen, ink, nor paper, and to be allowed no books except a mass-book, a psalter, a legendary, and a Bible. For the first quarter he was to have no better fare than the common rations of the convent; afterwards the pittance of a sick or aged brother, with such further indulgence as his health might require; for which, and for fitting up his close apartment, the prior was allowed eleven pounds."[1] Peacock died in his prison after a confinement of about three years. Notwithstanding all the efforts of the church to destroy them, some of his works still remain, especially an answer to certain of the more extravagant opinions of the Lollards, which, it has been remarked, "contains passages well worthy of Hooker, both for weight of matter and dignity of style."[2]

One effect of the distracting wars of the Roses was to interrupt for a time the persecution of the Lollards. As Fuller has finely said, "the very storm was their shelter." That tempest of blood put out, while it lasted, the fires of Smithfield.

The convulsion, also, which shook and unsettled everything ancient, was probably favourable to the growth of the new opinions in another way as well as by affording a breathing time to the hunted converts.

The nation appears to have been divided during this period, in regard to ecclesiastical matters, into three parties—the avowed enemies of the established church—the members of the church who desired its reform, but not its abolition—and the unswerving and unyielding adherents to the existing establishment. The mere reformers were perhaps more numerous than has been generally supposed. It is likely that more of the clergy had imbibed the sentiments of Bishop Peacock than those of Thorpe and the thorough Lollards, which would have gone almost to the complete extinction of their order. That portion of the community of which the House of Commons, as then constituted, is to be taken as a fair representative, may also be regarded as having been inclined rather to the correction of the abuses of the church than to its entire overthrow, or even to any great change either of the basis on which it stood, or of the general form and character of the edifice. In general, the House of Commons went with the lords and the clergy in calling for the execution of the laws against the followers of Wycliffe as disturbers of the public peace, and in denouncing their doctrines with regard to the revenues of the church as destructive of all the rights of property. The old subject of Papal provisions repeatedly engaged the attention of the legislature during the reigns of the Lancastrian princes. The former statutes were renewed and extended immediately after the accession of Henry IV., and both then and at various other times great solicitude was evinced to prevent any unconstitutional interference from the Roman See in regard either to this or other matters. The contest here, however, was mainly one between the pope and the heads of the national church—whatever was taken from the former was acquired by the latter. Whether the kingdom was any gainer by the prohibition of Papal provisions came, after some time, to be doubted. Complaints were very soon heard that the patronage of benefices was not exercised by the bishops with so much advantage to the interests of religion and learning as it had formerly been when it was to a considerable extent in the hands of the pope. A representation to this effect had been presented to the convocation in 1399 by the two universities; they stated that the popes, in dispensing livings by the mode of provision, had always been wont to give the preference to the most distinguished graduates; but that since provisions had been put down, this encouragement to talent and in-

---

[1] Southey's *Book of the Church*, i. 392.
[2] Hallam, *Mid. Ages*, iii. 476. The *Life of Bishop Peacock* has been written by the Rev. John Lewis. One of his works, entitled *A Treatise on Faith*, was printed, in 4to, in 1688.

dustry had been so entirely removed, that the schools were almost deserted. And at length the evil became so evident that, in 1416, we find the commons petitioning the king that, if no other adequate remedy could be provided, the statutes against provisors should be repealed. In consequence of this application the convocation passed a law the following year, that, for the next ten years, every spiritual patron should bestow the first vacant benefice of which he had the patronage, and after that term every second, on some member of either university, graduated in divinity, law, or physic. The parliament during this period steadily maintained the great principle which had been established by the act of præmunire and other statutes, of the supremacy of the civil over the ecclesiastical courts. In 1447 the bishops and clergy presented a petition, bitterly complaining of this encroachment, as they considered it, upon the rights of the church, and representing that the spiritual courts were much better qualified to be the interpreters of statutes and the tribunals of ultimate appeal, than the temporal; but to this remonstrance the parliament paid no respect.

The church (meaning by that term the body of the clergy) continued to set its face against all reform or concession to the spirit of the age. In a very few points of mere order and discipline some amendments of the ancient practice were attempted: on none of the doctrinal questions at issue between the adherents to the Papal system and their opponents was the slightest approximation made to the new opinions. The only deviations from the ancient standards of faith and worship were in the opposite direction. Archbishop Arundel endeavoured to put down the holding of fairs in church-yards on Sundays; and his successor, Chicheley, forbade the barber-surgeons to keep open their shops on that day, which, in the prohibition, still extant,¹ he somewhat strangely described as the *seventh* day of the week. On the other hand, the ritual observances were in various ways stretched to a greater height of rigour than ever. Arundel, in particular, affected a great zeal for the adoration of the Virgin. It is said that he was wont to ascribe to her intercession the fortunate revolution in the state which had restored him to his see; he accordingly amplified the ceremonial of her worship; he also made the day dedicated to the memory of her visitation, and other saints' days, double festivals. Several new saints were likewise added to the calendar during this period, for each of whom, of course, a festival day was set apart. The number of holidays thus received a considerable increase. The churches also became much more crowded than they ever had been before with images of the Virgin and of other saints. All the ancient popular superstitions, indeed, were still sanctioned by the church as much as in the earliest and darkest ages. Among others, the veneration for holy wells was still a favourite species of devotion among the people. It was during this period that the cup in the sacrament of the eucharist was gradually taken from the laity. In one of the ecclesiastical ordinances of the time the clergy are directed to begin by withholding the cup in small, obscure churches.² The people were at the same time to be taught that both the body and blood of the Saviour were given at once in the bread—that the wine was mere wine, which had been given to enable them to swallow the bread the more easily, but that it was better swallowed without the wine, and also without chewing, that none of it might stick in their teeth. The efficacy of indulgences, and the importance of confession, of processions, and of pilgrimages, were now exalted more than ever. Great pains were taken to denounce heresy as the chief of all possible sins. In certain constitutions of the province of Canterbury, published in 1409, all persons in any manner calling in question the determination of the church were declared to be excommunicated for the first offence, and subject to the punishment of heresy for the second; and it was declared at the same time to be heresy to dispute either the utility of pilgrimages, or the lawfulness of the adoration of images and of the cross. Pilgrimages to Rome were still frequent; a few individuals even continued to find their way to Jerusalem, and were glad, at the cost of submitting to many exactions and insults, to be allowed to pay their devotions at the holy sepulchre. Nor was even the old crusading mania altogether unknown in the fifteenth century. When Pope Martin V., in 1428, proclaimed a crusade against the famous Zisca and his followers, the insurgent Hussites of Bohemia, the great Cardinal Beaufort was appointed captain-general of the crusaders, and immediately raised an army of 2000 English archers and 250 lancers to act against the heretics. It has been already related how this force was intercepted before it reached Germany, and employed in France in another sort of contest.³ These were the last soldiers ever raised in England for a war against either heretics or infidels. When Pope Pius II. (better known as Æneas Sylvius) proclaimed his crusade against the Turks, a few years after the fall of Constantinople, he found little inclination in England, among the clergy or laity, either to take the cross or to contribute their money to the expedition: it was with great

---
¹ Wilkins, *Concilia*, iii. 308.   ² Wilkins, *Concilia*, iii. 662.   ³ See vol. i. p. 495.

difficulty that the clergy were induced by the king, Edward IV., to tax themselves on the occasion to the extent of sixpence in the pound. The countenance of the pope and of the church was at this time of considerable importance to Edward, in the circumstances in which he had just mounted the throne. While he exerted himself, therefore, to gratify the former by endeavouring to procure this assessment, he sought to secure the favour of the national clergy by the grant of a charter endowing them with the most extravagant privileges. In this stretch of prerogative he boldly dispensed with the statute of præmunire, and deprived the temporal courts of all right of interfering in the case of offences, of whatever nature, committed either by ecclesiastical persons, or even by persons pretending to possess the clerical character—thus again elevating the spiritual courts to that entire independence of the state which they had enjoyed in the first years after the Conquest, and which it had cost so long a struggle on the part of the parliament and the judges to destroy. The charter was never confirmed by parliament; but at that era of confusion, and the temporary restoration of arbitrary power in the government, it was not to be wondered at that the clergy should, under such a sanction, again put forth some of the most objectionable of their old pretensions.

The general conduct and character of the clergy of this age are not presented in a favourable light by such notices as the documents of the time afford. In 1415 the university of Oxford, being commanded by Henry V. to furnish a statement of such things in the church as needed reformation, drew up a catalogue of abuses in forty-six articles, most of which are, in fact, charges of rapacity and various descriptions of profligacy against the general body of the clergy. It is asserted, among other things, that the debaucheries of churchmen, however notorious, were never punished except by a small fine privately exacted, no public notice being taken, by suspension or otherwise, even of the most heinous cases. About half a century later we find Archbishop Bourchier, in a commission empowering his commissary-general to take measures for the establishment of an improved discipline, describing many of the clergy, both secular and regular, as persons wholly destitute both of literature and capacity; and adding that they were as profligate as they were ignorant, neglecting their cures, spending their time in strolling about the country in the company of loose women, and their incomes in feasting, drinking, and other excesses.[1] These accounts, it is to be observed, are not the inflamed invectives of the enemies of the church, but the admissions of its friends.

[1] Wilkins, *Concilia*, iii. 573.

We may here mention, though not strictly belonging to the period under review, a curious enactment of the reign of Richard II., touching the keeping of dogs by the clergy; from which we may gather that the custom was not confined to the opulent spiritual nobility, the bishops and abbots, but was followed, on such a scale as they could afford, by the humblest members of the ecclesiastical order. The act (the 13 Rich. II., st. 1, c. 13) sets forth that artificers, labourers, servants, and grooms kept greyhounds and other dogs, with which they were wont to go hunting on the holidays, when good Christian people were at church hearing Divine service. The clergy could hardly have been decently enumerated in this preamble; but the enacting part of the statute shows that some of their body were addicted to the same practices as the artificers and labourers. While it is ordained that no layman who is not possessed of lands or tenements of the yearly value of forty shillings shall in future keep any greyhound or other dog for hunting, the same prohibition is extended to all priests or clerks whose benefices are not of the yearly value of ten pounds; they shall not, it is added, use ferrets, hays, nets, hare-pipes, nor cords, nor other engines for taking or destroying deers, hares, coneys, or other game, under pain of a year's imprisonment.

A statute respecting the mendicant friars was passed in 1402 (the 4 Hen. IV. c. 17), which deserves to be here noticed. It ordained that no friar of any of the four orders—the Minorites, Augustines, Preachers, and Carmelites, should take into their order any infant under the age of fourteen without the consent of his nearest relations or guardians, nor should remove such infant, during the first year after his reception, away from the place where he had been received. To the intent, it is added, that this statute and ordinance should hold place for ever, the principals of the four orders (who are mentioned by name) "being in their proper persons before the king, and the lords spiritual and temporal, and the commons of the realm, in the full parliament, laying their right hands on their breasts, made an oath, and promised in the same parliament, to hold, keep, observe, and perform the statute and ordinance aforesaid, for them and their successors for ever." The unusual solemnity adopted on this occasion indicates how prevalent had been the evil which it was the object of the new law to put down. The friars, it was asserted, used especially to haunt the universities for the purpose of seducing into their ranks the most promising of the youthful members; and this practice had been carried so far that parents were thereby deterred from sending their sons to Oxford or Cambridge—a circumstance which was alleged as a principal cause of the decay of these national establishments. The universities accordingly had now come to look upon the friars with feelings of alienation and strong aversion. A keen jealousy also existed between the mendicants and the general body of the secular clergy, with whom they competed too successfully for the popular reverence and favour. In the reign of Edward IV., this antipathy broke out into a violent controversy, in which each party maintained its cause by the most unscrupulous abuse of its opponents. The great boast of the mendicants was, that Jesus Christ himself, while on earth, had belonged, as they said, to their class. This assertion the secular clergy, on the other hand, denounced as both false and daringly impious. At last Pope Calixtus II., by a bull published in 1475, declared the doctrine of the friars to be heretical.

Some notion of the mode of preaching commonly followed at this time may be gathered from the constitutions of a convocation of the province of York, held in 1466. These contain both directions as to the manner in which the clergy ought to conduct the religious instruction of the people, and a summary of the doctrines they were to inculcate. Every parish priest is commanded to preach, either by himself or by a substitute, to his flock four times in the year, and on these occasions to explain in English, with plainness of speech, and without any attempt at metaphysical refinements, the fourteen articles of faith, the ten commandments, the two precepts of the gospel, the seven works of mercy, the seven mortal sins, and the seven sacraments.

A few notices remain to be added respecting the history of ecclesiastical affairs in Scotland. The clergy of that kingdom, or some of them, are spoken of under their ancient name of Culdees down to so late a period as the close of the thirteenth century. The Culdees, indeed, whatever may have been peculiar in their original constitution, appear to have gradually become converted into a body of the same character with the clergy of England and of the other countries of Christendom. Till about the commencement of the eleventh century, they seem to have been derived chiefly or exclusively from Ireland and from the Irish seminary of Iona; after that date learned churchmen were often brought from England to fill the principal stations in the Scottish establishment. The earliest historical record of any interference with Scotland on the part of the Romish pontiffs is that of the appearance in the country of John of Cremna as Papal legate in 1126; but we are scarcely entitled thence to assume, as has sometimes been done, that the Papal supremacy over the Scottish church was then for the first time asserted or admitted. Little can be inferred from the silence of history upon a particular point, in a period of which scarcely anything that can be properly called history has come down to us. Some other circumstances, however, make it appear probable that, if any dependence upon Rome was so much as formally acknowledged by the early Scottish church, it was practically all but or altogether unfelt. The mere remoteness and barbarous condition of the country would secure its being left very much to itself. The most ancient bishopric in Scotland north of the Forth, that is, in ancient and proper Scotland, was undoubtedly St. Andrews. It was most probably founded towards the close of the ninth century. From this time St. Andrews was considered as holding the primatial rank, which had been held by Iona till the destruction of its monastery by the Danes in the ninth century, and had been then transferred to Dunkeld. Long before the commencement of the present period, the ecclesiastical establishment of Scotland had become completely assimilated, in the general outline of its constitution, to the other churches of the Latin world.

The history of the Scottish church in the fifteenth century, so far as it can now be recovered, consists principally of the enumeration of a series of provincial councils, whose acts, reported as they are, contain little or nothing of much interest. The most accurate notice of them is that given by Hailes, in his *Historical Memorials concerning the Provincial Councils of the Scottish Clergy, from the Earliest Accounts to the era of the Reformation.*¹ They appear to have been usually held at Perth.

The following passage gives, in brief compass, a comprehensive view of the state of the Scottish church at this period:—"The privileges of the church seem to have been an exemption from tribute and war, and from the sentence of a temporal judge; a judicial authority in the spiritual causes of tithes, testaments, matrimonial and heretical affairs; freedom to let lands and tithes; submission to no foreign church, but to the pope alone; a power of holding provincial councils for the regulation of the national church. In benefices the pontiff had only the right of confirmation and deprivation, and the purchase of any benefice at Rome was strictly prohibited. (By an act of parliament passed in 1471, the procurement of any benefices from the court of Rome, other than those anciently at the disposal of the pope, was declared to be a crime punishable with the pains of treason.) The bishops were elected by the chapter, and the royal recommendation seems seldom to have intervened. Abbots were chosen by the monks alone; the secular clergy

---

¹ See also the fourth volume of Wilkins' *Concilia*.

were named by the proprietors of the lands. These clergy were either parsons (rectors) or vicars. Many were in the appointment of the bishops, and of collegiate bodies, whose chapters they formed. Hence the lay patronage was much confined. Many sees and abbeys were opulent; but James III. seems to have been the first monarch who seized and made a traffic of the nomination."[1]

The religious zeal of the age expended itself upon the same objects in Scotland as in England. Whithern, in Galloway, appears to have been the most noted Scottish pilgrimage. St. Treignan, repeatedly mentioned by Itabelais as the name of a Scottish saint, is supposed to be a corruption of St. Ninian, the founder of the bishopric of Whithern.[2]

The new doctrines, however, penetrated to the northern part of the island very soon after they made their appearance in the south. The first propagators appear to have come from England —whether seeking a refuge from the active inquisition after heresy, which had begun in that kingdom, or, as is more likely, ambitious of exercising the apostleship of the truth in a new land. In the year 1408, John Resby, an English priest, was apprehended as a Wyckliffite, and brought before a council of the clergy, presided over by Laurence of Lindores, an eminent doctor of divinity—the same who, on the institution, a few years after, of the university of St. Andrews, was appointed reader of the canon law in the new seminary. Resby, it is said, was charged with maintaining no fewer than forty erroneous opinions, of which, however, only two are particularized—one, that the pope was not Christ's vicar; the other, that he was not to be esteemed pope if he was a man of wicked life. The unfortunate man was condemned on these and the other charges, and was burned at Perth along with his books and writings—being, as far as is known, the first person who thus suffered in Scotland. The example, like that of the similar execution of Sawtre in England a few years before, appears to have been considered sufficient to strike terror into the popular mind for some time. The second Scottish martyrdom did not take place till the year 1433, when Paul Crawar, a Bohemian physician, was burned at St. Andrews on the 23d of July. Crawar appears to have been sent by the Reformers of Bohemia to open a communication, partly, perhaps, of a political as well as of a religious nature, with those of the same creed in Scotland, and to propagate in that country the tenets of Wyckliffe, Huss, and Jerome of Prague. He is admitted by the ecclesiastical chroniclers to have been a person of great learning and of singular acuteness and dexterity in argument. All his knowledge of the Scriptures and logical powers, however, availed him nothing in the contest with his hostile judges, and with the remorseless inquisitor, Laurence of Lindores, who was again the president of the court. It is lamentable to have to add that both these executions also took place during the primacy of Bishop Henry Wardlaw, the venerated founder of the first Scottish university—a prelate to whose enlightened munificence history and tradition bear the same testimony with this and other still enduring works of public usefulness.

Although no person is recorded to have been brought to the stake for heresy in the space of nearly thirty years that elapsed between the executions of Resby and Crawar, it is certain, nevertheless, that the new opinions obtained an extensive diffusion in Scotland during that interval. This is evident from the accounts of the trial of the Bohemian, who is spoken of as an emissary to a numerous body sharing the sentiments of himself and his countrymen. The growth of Lollardism may also be inferred from a statute that had been passed for its suppression by the parliament that assembled immediately after the return of James I. from England in 1421. This statute directed that every bishop should make inquisition within his diocese for all Lollards and other heretics, in order that they might be punished according to the laws of holy church, the civil power being called in for that purpose, when necessary, in aid of the ecclesiastical. It is stated that the little treatises which Resby and his disciples had dispersed had spread the obnoxious doctrines; Bower, the continuator of Fordun, who wrote some years after the second of the two executions that have been mentioned, tells us that there were still in his day some unhappy persons, instigated by the devil, by whom these writings were secretly preserved, and their pernicious heresies cherished, in accordance with the scriptural text, that "stolen waters are sweet, and bread eaten in secret is pleasant."

The most important event that happened during the present period in the history of the Scottish ecclesiastical establishment was the erection of the see of St. Andrews into an archbishopric by Pope Sixtus IV., in 1471. This measure was resorted to in consequence of the renewal by Nevil, Archbishop of York, of the old claim of his see to supremacy over the kingdom of Scotland. The Papal bull declared it to be an unfitting thing that an English prelate should be Primate of Scotland, and ordained all the rest of the Scottish bishops, twelve in number, to be henceforth subject to St. Andrews. The occupant of the latter see at this time was Patrick Graham,

---
[1] Pinkerton, *Hist. of Scotland*, i. 174.
[2] See, among other passages, *Liv.* i. ch. 33, and *Liv.* ii. ch. 38, with the Notes of Le Duchat.

a nephew of the late King James I., but who had been driven by the ascendency of the Boyds, in the reign of James III., from his native country to Rome. He was resident at the pontifical court when the bull was granted; but he now thought that, with his increase of dignity, he might venture to return home, the rather as he was at the same time appointed Papal legate for three years, with a commission to reform all abuses in the national church. He found, however, that his new rank and authority only made him new enemies. He was soon after arrested at the suit of some Roman bankers, who had advanced the money to pay the dues on his bull of privileges, and whose claims he was now unable to satisfy in consequence of the arbitrary seizure of part of his revenues by the king, and his expenses in bribing the persons possessing influence at court, that he might be allowed to retain the rest. He was first shut up in his own castle at St. Andrews, and soon after committed to the custody of William Schevez, the archdeacon of his diocese, a young man who had insinuated himself into the favour of the court by his agreeable talents, and especially, it is affirmed, by his skill in astrology, a study which he had pursued under John Spernick at the university of Louvain. In no long time Schevez was appointed his coadjutor; and eventually a process was raised against the unfortunate archbishop, the result of which was, that he was found guilty of schism, simony, heresy, and other crimes, and sentenced to lose his dignity and to pass the rest of his life in confinement. This strange affair was terminated by Schevez being appointed archbishop. He held the primacy from 1478 till his death in 1494. Meanwhile his deposed predecessor had been transferred first to Inchcolm, thence to Dunfermline, and finally to the castle of Lochleven, where he died a few months after Schevez had obtained his place.

CHAPTER VIII.—HISTORY OF SOCIETY.

FROM THE ACCESSION OF HENRY IV. (A.D. 1399), TO THE DEATH OF RICHARD III. (A.D. 1485).

Progress of English liberty—The advantages it derived from Henry IV. and his successors—Classes who composed the parliament during this period—Emancipation of the villains—Improved condition of the peasantry—State of the mercantile classes—Their commodities of traffic—Mercantile shipping—Hinderances to the mercantile enterprise of the period—High estimation in which the mercantile profession was already held—Manners and customs—Decay of chivalry—Causes of the decay—English archery—Its origin—Laws enacted for its general practice—The old English bow—The string—The arrow—Mode of handling the bow—Sports and competitions of archery—Rules by which proficiency in archery was acquired—Public sports—Dramatic representations—Miracle and mystery plays—Morality plays—Private theatricals—Royal pageant plays of this period—Amusements of the aristocracy—Inclosure hunting—Tennis—Card-playing—Costume of the higher classes—Female costume—Domestic life of the higher classes—Mansions of the nobility—Halls of the mansions—Banquets—Materials and accompaniments of the banquet—Ordinary meals—Retinues of the nobility—Domestic life of the commons—Glutton masses—Poverty of food in certain districts—Active sports of the commons—The play of quarter-staff—Wrestling matches, &c.—Bowling—Various games of ball—Prisoners' bars—Blindman's buff—Boating—Prohibited games—Condition of London—Metropolitan sightseeing of the period—London riots—Literature and literary society of England—Falling off in the colleges—Futility as yet of learned pursuits—Depreciation of the study of medicine and theology—Preachers of the day—Specimens of their sermons—Higher estimation of the study of law—Causes of this preference—Education of students in law—Distinguished lawyers of the period—Decline in English poetry during this period—English poets of the day—John Lydgate. Architecture—Perpendicular style—Its peculiar distinctions—Buildings in which it is illustrated—Tudor style—Its characteristics. Condition of Scotland—State of government in Scotland—Restrictions upon the royal authority—Power of the Scottish nobles—Imperfections of Scottish agriculture—Moss-troopers of Scotland—Mendicants—Military customs and warlike sports of the Scots—Scottish weapons—Deficiency in the archery of Scotland—War laws of Scotland—Signal beacons—Modes of living in Scotland—Chiefs and their retainers—Insecure state of society—Rude condition of Scottish dwellings—Fruitless attempts of James I. and James III. to introduce civilization among the people—Learned Scotchmen of the period—Erection of the first Scottish universities—Scottish poets—James I.—Henry the Minstrel—Robert Henderson.

EW subjects in history are more interesting or more important than the growth and progress of English liberty. It was by no sudden outburst of popular energy, or rapid development of the national character, that so great a blessing was achieved. In this case, its existence would have been as precarious as its birth, and it might have been lost as rapidly as it had been won. On the contrary, whole centuries of struggle were necessary, and all the sufferings as well as changes of infancy, boyhood, and youth, had to be undergone before it could acquire a confirmed and permanent manhood. Such is the chief lesson of the epoch at which we have now arrived. The combination of the English nobility at Runnymede laid bounds to the power of royalty, while the wars with Scotland and France which succeeded, made each sovereign more dependent upon popular favour and support than had been the case with his predecessors; and thus, energetic though they were, and capable under other circumstances of establishing a complete despotic rule, Edward I. and Edward III. were obliged not only to confirm, but also to enlarge the concessions of the imbecile John. The next era in the history of English liberty was still more favourable for its progress. This was the accession of the house of Lancaster, and the wars of the Roses, events, indeed, whose immediate fruits were apparently little else than suffering and calamity, but whose substantial benefits were realized by the nation at large, long after the York and Lancaster contention had passed away.

No event could have been more seasonable to the liberties of England at this period than the accession of Henry IV. His predecessor having crushed both lords and commons, had created for himself a new parliament that was subservient to his wishes; he had placed the administration of the kingdom in the hands of his creatures; and being thus completely absolute, everything was to be apprehended from his weakness and extravagance. Had this state of things continued, the people, oppressed by tyranny and taxation, would probably have betaken themselves for remedy either to a new Wat Tyler insurrection, or even a French *jacquerie*, and only confirmed their bondage by a failure. It was then that Henry ascended the throne, and ascended it, not by legitimate right, but by usurpation. In this case, one such act of tyranny as those which Richard II. had perpetrated would have overthrown him; and of this he showed that he was conscious by the cautiousness with which he approached the royal seat, as well as the moderation with which he occupied it. The same rule was continued by his two successors under the same urgency: for still they were usurpers, and the elder line of the house of York might at any time reassert their claims to the throne. Under these circumstances, the parliament of England was now of higher account than hitherto, while the people were more fully and equitably represented. This last fact may be understood from the character of the classes of which the parliament was composed. It now consisted of the three estates — the nobility, the clergy, and the *commons*, while the last of these classes consisted of between two and three hundred members composed of knights, citizens, and burgesses. In this way, every grade of rank in the commonalty, and every trade and profession, could find its representative and advocate in the assembled parliament of England. These knights alone constituted a very important element in the popular representation. They were seventy-four in number, and from their birth, habits, and occupations, they were sufficiently conversant with public affairs to make their suggestions respected, as well as sufficiently high-spirited and formidable to check the aggressions of despotism. In this way, every great change during the reigns of the three Lancastrian Henries, advanced the cause of English liberty, by reducing the monarchical power to fixed and constitutional limits. Another formidable despotism, however, remained, that threatened to rise by the limitation of monarchy, and become the worse oppression of the two. This was feudalism, whose strength mainly lay in civil commotion, and which, on the removal of one sole tyrant, could at any time have produced a hundred in his room. But this portentous danger was removed by the wars of the Roses, in which the nobility, as the party most interested in the strife, perished by proscription and mutual extermination. The field and the scaffold did their utmost, and the high seignorial rights of the proud king-makers passed away with those who had held them. The battle of Bosworth was the last gleaning of that terrible harvest in which the feudalism of England was irrecoverably destroyed.

This progress of liberty is especially illustrated in the history of English villanage. During the preceding period, the better class of villains had been rising into copy-holders of land, while the inferior were becoming free labourers and artizans; and in either case they were freed from that degrading bondage by which they had hitherto been the absolute property of their masters, and even of the locality in which they were born. So great a change, however, could not be effected without a struggle on the part of the villains themselves; and the character of this struggle is fully explained by a statute enacted upon the subject in 1377. From this it appears, that landholders and masters had made grievous complaints of the losses they had sustained through the villains who "have now late withdrawn, and do daily withdraw their services and customs due to their said lords, by comfort and procurement of other their counsellors, maintainers, and abettors in the country." These counsellors, it is added, "by colour of certain exemplifications made out of the *Book of Doomsday*, and by their evil interpretations of the same, they affirm them to be quite and utterly discharged of all manner of servage due, as well of their bodies as of their said tenure, and will not suffer any distress or other justice to be made upon them; but do menace the ministers of their lords of life and member, and, which more is, gather themselves together in great routs, and agree by such confederacy that every one shall aid other to resist their lords with strong hand." Here we have the act of self-emancipation conducted according to form of law, and afterwards followed by combination to make it good by force, if need should be. In this way, the conflict so important, although unnoticed in history, seems to have gone on until the rebellion of Wat Tyler in 1381, when one of the demands of the insurgents was the complete abolition of villanage. The suppression of this rebellion was followed by severe enactments, through which the old state of serfage was attempted to be restored; but the opportunity had gone by, and a spirit of independence had been awakened that went onward in spite of statutes. The result of this was evident in the next rebellion of the people conducted by Jack Cade in 1450. Here, nothing was spoken about villanage, for the legality of villanage was no longer absolute. The demands of the people had assumed a higher tone, and were directed against the wasteful expenditure of the crown and the abuses of the government, of which immediate redress was required. And besides this, they demanded the full exercise of their right to elect their own representatives in parliament without the interference of the nobility. This insurrection, too, was not so easily quelled as the first had been, when the boy Richard II. rode up to the angry mutineers, and appeased them with a few empty words. Instead of this, they repeatedly defeated the king's troops that were sent against them, and were only quelled at last from want of sufficient leaders. Their principles, also, instead of being permanently arrested, sustained nothing worse than a temporary check, under which they gained additional vigour for a more successful renewal of the contest.

During the present period of our history, the peasantry of England, who were now becoming free to serve whom and where they pleased, must, with their liberty, have been acquiring a correspondent increase in the means and comforts of domestic life. This is evident from the rise in the wages of rural labourers between 1388 and 1444, and the sumptuary laws that were afterwards enacted to repress extravagance of dress among the working-classes. It was found necessary to decree, that no labourer should be dressed in broad-cloth costing more than two shillings a yard; that his nether habiliments, called hosen, consisting of breeches and stockings composed of one piece, should not cost more than fourteen pence, and that his wife shall no longer wear a girdle garnished with silver, or a kerchief of cloth costing more than twelve-pence per plight —that is, a yard and a quarter. Only nineteen years afterwards, the rise in the condition of the

HUSBANDMAN AND COUNTRY WOMAN OF 15TH CENTURY.
From Royal MSS. 18. D. VII. and 20. C. VII.

working-classes is curiously indicated by a fresh sumptuary law, in which this twelve-penny kerchief is superseded by one of twenty-pence, beyond which, for the present at least, the head attire of the labourer's wife was not allowed to trespass. From the same source we learn, that domestic servants, whether of lords, tradesmen, or artificers, were well and comfortably fed, having at least one substantial meal a-day of flesh or fish, while the other meals chiefly consisted of "milk, butter, cheese, and other such victuals."

In turning from the agricultural to the mercantile progress of England during this period, it is necessary in the first case to take into account the population of the towns by which the commerce of the country was represented. We find, then, that as yet, the increase in the number of the people had been small, compared with the time that had elapsed and the opportunities that had apparently been enjoyed; for while the whole population at the time of the Norman conquest appears to have been about 2,000,000, at the close of the reign of Edward III., after a lapse of 300 years, it only amounted to 2,500,000. The visitation of dearth to which England had been frequently subject, the wars with Scotland and France, and above all, the destructive pestilence of 1349 by which Europe at large was almost half depopulated, are the only causes to which we can trace this slowness of increase. Of this population, the town part of it is reckoned at not more than 170,000, or little more than a fifteenth. In these statistics, many of the chief cities of England present an astounding contrast to the greatness into which they afterwards expanded. Thus, the population of London is rated at about 35,000, that of Bristol 9500, that of New-castle-upon-Tyne 4000, that of Yarmouth 3000, that of Hull 2300. Scarcely, indeed, were there thirty towns in England containing a population of more than 2000 souls, according to the roll of the capitation tax in 1377. And yet, all this was much, according to the estimate of the day; and the Greek historian Laonicus Chalcondyles, in his description of the principal kingdoms of Europe in 1400, gives the following account of England:—" It is *full of towns and villages.* It has no vines, and but little fruit, but it abounds in corn, honey, and wool, from which the natives make great quantities of cloth. London, the capital, may be preferred to every city of the West for population, opulence, and luxury. It is seated on the river Thames, which, by the advantage of the tide, daily receives and despatches trading vessels from and to various countries."

In the above extract, the Byzantine mentions the principal article of English commerce, which still consisted of wool. This staple, by the fifteenth century, had become so excellent, that it was reckoned superior to the wool of Spain, and was used therefore even by the Spaniards themselves in the manufacture of their finest cloths. The Flemings also, who were still the principal manufacturers of Europe, found that they could not make such good cloth of the Spanish wool by itself, as when it was mixed with English. Besides wool, the trade of England with foreign countries at this time consisted of gunpowder and guns, and of tin; while the imports received in return, were articles of mercery and haberdashery, and wines, spices, and groceries. The chief countries with which the English traded were Flanders, Spain and Portugal, Venice, Genoa, and Florence, and the Hanseatic towns. With this increase of traffic, the tonnage of merchant ships and improvement in the art of shipbuilding had been making commensurate progress. Thus, Henry V. built several dromons or ships of war at Southampton, so large, we are told, that the world had never seen the like; and one of them, called the *King's Chamber,* of extraordinary splendour, carried a sail of purple silk, with the arms of England and France embroidered on it. With regard to the merchant vessels, an estimate may be formed of their size, when we are told that the largest carried 400, 500, and even 900 tons. As ship-building was now of such importance to the nation, it appears to have had a due share of royal encouragement, independently of the stimulus of mercantile gain. A proof of this we have in the history of John Taverner, the rich merchant of Hull. During the reign of Henry IV., he built " by the help of God and some of the king's subjects," as it is expressed in the royal license, a ship as large or even larger than a great Venetian carrack. In recompense of such a patriotic deed, the king directed that the ship should be called the *Carrack Grace Dieu,* and its owner permitted to take on board " wool, tin, lamb-skins, wool-fels, passelargos, and other hides, raw or tanned, and any other merchandise, in the ports of London, Hull, or Sandwich, and, on paying aliens' duty, to carry them direct to Italy, from which he might bring back bow-staves, wax, and other foreign produce necessary for the country, to the great benefit of the revenue and of the nation."

The development of mercantile enterprise during this period was impeded by many serious obstacles. Of these, the most obvious was the military spirit fostered by the war with France. The recent successes of Edward III. and the Black Prince, and the renewal of these under Henry V., gave such a bias to the spirit of the nation, that the peaceful occupations of merchandise were despised, and even wealth itself was cheaply estimated except as the prize of valour and conquest. It was no wonder, therefore, if the active adventurous spirits of the country were more eager to cut out for themselves a fair lordship in France, than to attain the envied rank of wealthy aldermen and worshipful sheriffs at home, by a dull unchivalrous life of buying and selling. Then came the cost of these worthless victories, and the loss occasioned by their abandonment, which acted as successive drains upon the profits of the mercantile community. All this was nothing more than natural to a people who, in adopting commercial pursuits, had abated nothing of their high military character, and were ready to alternate the chances of traffic with those of war and invasion. But even worse than the obstacles which arose from this source, and which were only of a temporary character, were those that accrued from legislative enactments devised with the view of furthering the mercantile interests of the nation. These consisted of such restrictions as, for the price of a present benefit, which after all was more apparent than real, destroyed that reciprocity of one nation with another in buying and selling, which forms the true basis of mercantile confidence and prosperity. A few specimens of these laws will suffice. No merchant was allowed to trade to Iceland and Finland, where the only commodity of traffic was salted fish, without a license both from the King of England and the King of Denmark. No Englishman was to sell goods to any foreign merchant except for ready money, or goods immediately delivered. No foreign merchant was to sell any goods in England to another foreigner without forfeiting the goods thus sold—and why?—that the .king should sustain no loss, and the national merchandise no damage, by under-selling. Another mischief arose from the privileged classes themselves entering into the gainful occupations of traffic, which they were enabled to pursue at greater advantage from their superior power and immunities, than could the commons. Thus, the kings and nobles were traders, so that Edward III. was nicknamed the wool-merchant by the sovereign of France. Even bishops, abbots, and other church dignitaries, were also traders, and fitted out ships under the protection of the church, which exempted the property of ecclesiastics from the usual custom-house duties. In all these obstacles we distinctly perceive that English commerce, like English liberty, had a long period of experiment and trial to undergo before it attained its complete maturity. But in either case, was it not a maturity worth whole centuries of waiting for? In the meantime, notwithstanding these difficulties, the mercantile enterprise of the country was indicating its future grandeur, in the merchant-princes with which the present period of the history of England was adorned. Of these, perpetuated a royal dynasty, but for the transitions in which the Plantagenets were exchanged for the Tudors, and afterwards for the Stuarts. Another distinguished English merchant, was William Cannyng. He founded St. Mary Church in Bristol, distinguished himself by other public benefactions, and was so eminent as a merchant, that the largest ships of England, and the farthest extent of its commerce, owned him for their enterpriser and master. Another was John Taverner of Hull, already mentioned as one of the chief merchant-favourites of Henry IV. But the most renowned, if not the richest, of all, was Sir Richard Whytington; for what man, woman, or child over England or even Scotland, is ignorant of the his-

WILLIAM CANNYNG'S BRAND OR MERCHANT'S MARK.—From stained glass in St. Mary Redcliffe, Bristol.

SIR RICHARD WHYTINGTON.—From the portrait engraved by R. Elstrack.

a considerable list might be given, but at present we can only allude to the principal names. Among these, the Poles stand conspicuous. The first of the race, William de la Pole, was nothing more than a merchant of Hull in the time of Edward III., who by his success in traffic became the chief moneyed man of the country, and, as such, was made a knight-banneret, and chief baron of the exchequer. His son Michael, who trod in the footsteps of his father, was made Earl of Suffolk; and his descendant, after many family mutations, was Duke of Suffolk in the reign of Henry VI., and first peer of the realm, whose son married the sister of Edward IV., on which account John, the eldest son of this union, was declared by Richard III. his presumptive heir. In this way the descendants of a Hull merchant would have occupied the throne of England, and tory of Whytington and his cat? Independently of the tale of his feline friend, which is a ridiculous blunder founded in after ages upon the figure of a cat, or panther, or tiger, stretched at the feet of his effigy on his tomb, he was famous as thrice lord-mayor of London, as a princely lender to Henry IV. and his son in their pecuniary difficulties, and as a founder of benevolent institutions, in one of which he is characterized as "that worthy and notable merchant, the which while he lived had right liberal and large hands to the poor people." The munificence of these early merchant-princes of England was still more remarkable than the large fortunes that rewarded their labours, and was nobly attested by the colleges, schools, hospitals, and alms-houses which they erected and endowed, not only in London, but throughout the kingdom. In this generous public-spirited fashion they expended their wealth, and secured for themselves a grateful remembrance, long after the names of their highborn chivalrous contemporaries had utterly passed away.

In turning our attention to the manners and customs that were prevalent during this period in England, we cannot fail to observe that the iron age of chivalry was rapidly passing away, and even its most solemn forms degenerating into idle pageantry.

ARMOUR FOR THE TOURNAMENT (1463).[1]

The first cannon sounded its death-knell. This was the inevitable consequence of the introduction of a new arm of warfare, against which the best tempered mail, as well as the most practised skill of the tourney, were to be equally unavailing. Knights and steel-clad nobles, indeed, were reluctant to doff the rich armour which had given them such superiority both in the display of a pageant and the shock of battle; and therefore they tried to arrest the inevitable departure by more gaudy crests and armorial cognizances — by a more complete as well as more cumbrous panoply—and by extending the code of rules and observances peculiar to combats and tournaments. To this, among other causes, may be attributed the slow progress that was made

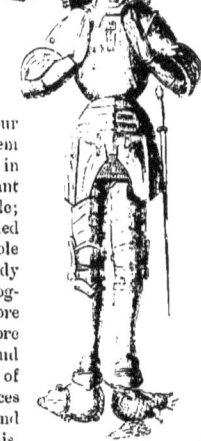

ARMOUR OF 15TH CENTURY.[2]

in the use of gunpowder, compared with its destructive powers, and its suitableness for every kind of warfare. The hand that had wielded a lance would have made a sorry figure in using a linstock. It was not, therefore, among the aristocracy of Europe that gunnery was first studied as a science; and artillery, which was originally used in the form of cannon, and that, too, of huge calibre and most unwieldy structure, was rather planted in battery against the walls of a town, than wheeled into the field of battle. Therefore it is that in the pictures and descriptions of the sieges of the period, we find such a curious blending of the new with the old mode of warfare—the cannon with the breaching-tower and battering-ram, and troops of long and crossbowmen intermingled with small parties who used hand-guns and arquebuses. But even nobility and royalty itself were at last obliged to acknowledge the superior powers of a cannonade; and Henry V., who took every town to which he laid siege, was perhaps the best artillery officer of his day.

Abandoning, therefore, any further mention of the chivalrous exercises and usages of this period, we pass onward to a consideration of the archery of England, and the arts by which it was improved and perfected. This is the more necessary, as it formed so essential a part in the occupations of the commons, was so distinguished in the military history of the nation, and was so soon to pass away among the things that had been. To its archery, even more than to its gallant knighthood, England was indebted for its most distinguished victories; and the history of the country itself would be imperfect, without a full understanding of the means by which such important advantages were gained.

The history of English archery dates in a great measure from the Norman conquest. Long before this period, the marauding Danes and Saxons were acquainted with the use of the longbow; but after their settlement in England they seem to have laid it aside for weapons adapted to a close standing fight—the sword and spear, but chiefly the heavy two-handed battle-axe which they wielded so gallantly at Hastings. On the other hand, the victory of William was chiefly owing to his archers, and the manner in which he ordered them to discharge their arrows upwards so that they should fall upon the defenceless heads of the English. It has been generally supposed that it was the crossbow which was solely used on this occasion; but that this is a mistake, and that the longbow must also have been employed by the Norman archery, is evident

---

[1] This specimen is from Meyrick. A man in this armour could not raise, lower, or turn his head, nor stir his left shoulder; he had only the movement of his bridle arm from the elbow, to enable him to stop his horse, but the lance arm was quite free, for obvious reasons.—*Meyrick*.

[2] This figure represents Richard Beauchamp, Earl of Warwick, from his monumental effigy in the Beauchamp Chapel, Warwick.

from the Bayeux Tapestry, where Harold is represented as falling dead with several shafts of the latter weapon sticking in his body, and one in his forehead. The general disarming of the English that followed, and the miseries that drove them into the forests, naturally made them archers. The materials for weapons were at hand; a longbow and sheaf of arrows could be constructed without the aid of the armourer; and with these they could bring down the game that formed their precarious subsistence, or the enemies that were sent to apprehend them. In this way, a stern necessity converted them by thousands into admirable bowmen; and when better days arrived, the instrument that had so befriended them, became their favourite and national weapon. They had thus acquired such means of independence as made them formidable to their Norman rulers; and perhaps it was this circumstance, and the clearance of Sherwood and other such forests of their numerous bands of outlaws, more than military considerations, that induced Richard I. to enact such laws as tended to banish the longbow out of England, and introduce the crossbow, which was of more difficult fabrication, in its stead. But his own death, which occurred at the siege of Chaluz from a crossbow bolt, was regarded as a righteous retribution, and the English soon made his successors aware how necessary their favourite weapon and matchless skill in using it were for the national defence. Hence the high encouragement that was given to the practice of archery, and the prominent figure it assumed among the rural sports and competitions of the yeomanry; and hence also the high wages that were given to the archers of an English army during the period of military service. To the same effect were the numerous laws enacted during different successive reigns, by which good bows and dexterous bowmen were to be abundant over the whole realm. A few specimens of these laws will suffice to show the importance of the subject. By two statutes, Edward III. encouraged and enjoined the use of the longbow among his English subjects. In the reign of Richard II., an act was passed to compel all servants to practise with it on Sundays and holidays. By the 7th of Henry IV., the heads of arrows were to be well boiled or brazed, and hardened at the points with steel, on pain of forfeiture of the arrows, and imprisonment of the maker, whose name was also to be stamped on every arrow head. Henry V. ordered the sheriffs of the several counties to procure feathers from geese to the number of six from each goose, for the purpose of winging the missiles—often poetically called the "gallant gray-goose shaft." And to close these examples, it was decreed in the reign of Richard III., that ten bow-staves were to be imported from abroad with every butt of Malmsey or Tyre wine, under a penalty of thirteen shillings and four pence for each butt that was not thus accompanied. This act was framed by parliament in consequence of the rise that had taken place in the price of bow-staves, so that those which had formerly cost only 40s. or 46s. 8d. a hundred at the utmost, had now, as the act declared, risen to the "outrageous price" of £8 the hundred, and all through the "seditions confederacy of the Lombards trading to this country." During the same reign, it was also enacted in 1482, that "from the feast of Easter next coming, no bowman should take from any of the king's liege people for a longbow of yew more than 3s. 4d." The fact that this reduction of the usual price was still equal to that of a good musket in the present day, the different value of money being considered, shows the difficulty that now existed of procuring good wood for the manufacture of a bow, as well as the labour with which it was prepared and fashioned.

This brings us to the consideration of the weapon itself, so terrible in the hands of an English archer, and so available in national conquest and defence. The stave was six feet in length, and of such proportionable strength, weight, and thickness, that only to bend it would have been beyond the archery of any other country. The wood itself was generally yew, as being the strongest and most elastic; but sometimes elm, ash, or Brazil wood was substituted, although not frequently. In selecting the stave, the nicest scrutiny was necessary to see that the wood was free from knot, warp, and every kind of blemish; and on being chosen, the utmost care was used in cutting and smoothing it, so that it should taper by just degrees from its centre to the extremities, and be thus fit to endure every strain that might be laid upon it. Being thus fashioned, the weapon was to be strung, and then came the question of cordage, upon which the efficiency of the bow so much depended. Too soft a cord would snap, and leave the archer defenceless; too hard or too fine a one, however strong, would cut the wood, and soon make the bow useless. The medium adopted was a string of silk, which was twisted with the utmost care, so that it might be sound and equal throughout. To save also both wood and string, and have them always ready for action, the weapon was usually carried in a sheath or case made of woollen or canvas. The importance of this precaution was well shown at Azincourt, where the Genoese archers armed with crossbows were rendered utterly useless by a shower of rain that relaxed their bow-strings, which were composed of gut and unprotected, while the English had only to uncase their bows that were as efficient as ever. Even when not engaged in active service, the English archer was obliged to tend his weapon with the care of a nurse; too damp or too dry a place was certain to injure it, and from want of rubbing, oiling, and polishing, it would become brittle, or lose its elasticity. Even the place, therefore, in which it was laid up within his cottage, as well as the regularity with which it was tended, were matters of vital consideration.

The manufacture of arrows, which comes next to be considered, was fully as important and difficult as that of bows. So various was the choice of material for this purpose, that Ascham, in his *Toxophilus*, has enumerated fifteen different kinds of wood with which arrows were made; but the asp and the ash were generally preferred, the first for target-shooting and archery competitions, and the second for warfare. On this account, asp-wood was of such importance, as in 1416 to claim the attention of parliament; and a decree was passed by which patten-makers were forbid to use this material for making clogs or pattens, as such wood was necessary for the making of arrows. It was not till nearly fifty years after that the unfortunate patten-makers, in consequence of their remonstrance, obtained permission to use such asp-wood in their craft as was unfitted for the purposes of the archer. In

ARROW HEADS, one-half the actual size.[1]

making an arrow, the utmost attention had to be bestowed upon the different parts of which it was composed, that all might duly correspond, and be fitted for their respective uses. The stele or shaft must be so straight and smooth as to pass correctly from the bow, and the feathered extremity be exactly proportioned in its buoyancy to the weight of the steel head. The head itself

[1] From specimens in the British Museum, &c.—(1, 2), Found at New Farm, Blenheim Park, Oxon; (3, 4), Found on the field of the battle of Barnet; (5), A quarrel with the shaft attached, found packed with others in a barrel in the arsenal of Mont Ferrand (Clermont-le-Ferraud); (6, 7), Found in Friday Street, London; (8), Cloth-yard arrow head, found near Salisbury.

VOL. I.

was made of fine steel, critically edged and pointed; the feather was generally from the goose, and gray in colour, so that its flight might give as little warning as possible, and sometimes from the second feather of the wing, which was esteemed the best by the most skilful connoisseurs in archery. These arrows were of various kinds: thus, we read of forked arrows, where the sharp steel barbs pointed towards the feathers; and broad arrows, of which the barbs pointed forwards; and sometimes, though not so frequently, they had sharp heads not barbed but rounded like a bodkin. Arrows, too, were of different weight and thickness, to suit the distance of the mark and the changes of the wind. Besides these missiles which were fashioned for deadly purposes, whistling arrows were sometimes used in war for giving signals in the night.

It is now full time, however, to see how these weapons were handled; but for this purpose, we would rather repair to the village green than to the field of battle. There, at set times, the whole village and its neighbourhood were assembled, and those who were to compete in archery wore not only the succinct picturesque dress which old tradition has so indelibly associated with the gay greenwood, but also a bracer laced on the left arm, and a shooting glove on the right hand. The bracer was made of hardened leather, and so stiff that the motion of the arm did not wrinkle it, and so smooth that it did not arrest the free motion of the string; while the glove, which protected the fingers from being chafed in drawing the cord, had the leather upon the forefinger thicker than the rest, as it was there that the pull of the string was most felt. The marks to be shot at in such trials were of three kinds—butts, pricks, and rovers. The first was a level mark, and required a strong arrow with a broad feather; the second was a mark of compass, but at a fixed distance, for which a shaft of middling-sized feather was necessary; and the third was a roving or shifting mark, carried to different places of the field, and requiring arrows of various kinds suited to the distances. The general range of distance for marks in the practice of archery was from eleven to twelve score yards; but some of the old English ballads describe tremendous shots, where the distance was 400 yards, and the mark nothing more than a slender white wand, that was to be cleft in two with a broad arrow.

Having now taken his stand and bent his bow, the archer selected from his quiver, or the sheaf in his belt, the arrow best suited for the mark. Having surveyed place and distance, he also calculated the force of whatever current of air might be in motion, and the precise bearing it would have upon his arrow in full flight. All

86

being in readiness, he took his station fairly and uprightly, his left foot at a convenient distance in advance of his right, holding the bow by the middle, with his left arm stretched out, and with

ARCHER OF 15TH CENTURY.—From Royal MSS. 14. E. IV.

the three first fingers and the thumb of the right hand upon the lower part of the arrow affixed to the bow-string. If the mark was a distant one, the arrow had to be drawn to the head; but the pull required to be steady and uniform, otherwise the string might snap, or the bow itself be broken. The arrow had then to be delivered smartly and at once, as further delay might have disturbed the hand or injured the aim. Thus the archers shot, and thus the mark was hit, while the onlookers let loose their suspended breath in an applauding huzza. In reading the exploits of English archery, we are not so much struck with its accuracy as its force, for seldom could plate

ARCHER OF 15TH CENTURY.—From Cotton MSS. Julius E. IV.

and mail resist the terrible dint of the clothyard shaft. But independently of the strength of the bow and the weight of the arrow, the string was pulled not to the breast, as among other nations, but to the right ear, while the shooter, instead of depending upon mere strength of arm, threw the whole weight of his body forward upon the bow while in the act of drawing the string, so that every muscle was brought into full play. As no other toxophilites had either strength to bend or skill to handle such a weapon, England remained unrivalled in the use of the bow, and hence the anxiety of parliament to enforce the practice and encourage the competitions of archery, as well as the care with which it legislated for the due manufacture of the weapons. But this was not all; for by other enactments, the male children of the yeomanry were to be furnished with bows proportioned to their size, and exercised in shooting until they had reached full-grown manhood. Acts of parliament, however, powerful though they may be in creating festivals, cannot furnish the joviality that is necessary to gladden them; and these oft-repeated laws that commanded people to assemble and be merry, only produced such a deadening effect as at last made the village meetings anything but grateful to the commons of England. This, too, was especially the case, when it was found that hagbut and arquebuse could disable an enemy as effectually as the longbow, without demanding the training of a lifetime to use them. Archery, therefore, declined with chivalry, and from the same cause; so that we hear little of it after the battle of Flodden, where the quiver of England was well nigh expended.

Among the public sports of the English of this period, dramatic representations held a distinguished place. There, which were at first of a religious character, commenced not in England but France, which took the lead of the former country not only in civilization, but in that inventiveness and love of excitement upon which the drama so essentially depends. As they were at first of a religious character, they naturally originated in those who were properly the officebearers of religion—palmers and pilgrims to the Holy Land and other consecrated places, who, on their return, recited "harsh-sounding rhymes" and ballads at the corners of streets, about the deeds of Christ, and the miracles of the apostles and saints. The crowds, who perhaps had no other means of acquiring such instruction, flocked as eagerly round these sacred troubadours, as Asiatics round a story-teller; and thus buildings were soon erected for the accommodation of the audience, and stages for the singers. At last, action was added to recitation, and the simple ballad was expanded into the miracle play, by the same natural transition that the cart of Thespis became a theatre. It was not long before the miracle play, which was rude and inartificial in its structure, assumed the more complex form of the mystery. In this kind of play, the stage, which was now a huge structure, was composed of several scaffoldings or stories, the highest of which represented heaven, the second earth, the third Pilate's house or Herod's palace, and the fourth hell, which was upon the forefront of the stage, and exhibited as the gaping mouth of a huge dragon, that opened and shut as the devils made their exits and entrances. From the mixture of so many characters, celestial, terrestrial, and infernal, and from the multitude of events, a single play often required several hundreds of actors; but these could be easily found for audiences that were not disposed to be over-critical.

These religious dramas appear to have been exhibited in London so early as A.D. 1180. This we ascertain from Fitz-Stephen, in his introduction to the life of Becket, where he commends them as a greatly superior kind of plays to those acted in ancient Rome, as they represented the miracles of holy confessors, or the sufferings in which the martyrs had displayed their constancy. Even playhouses also appear to have existed at this time in London; but in the want of such accommodation, the miracles and mysteries were often performed in churches. When they were exhibited in the open air, temporary scaffolds or stages were erected for the purpose, that sometimes moved upon wheels, so that each part of the town, in turn, might enjoy the benefit of the representation. These plays appear to have had neither regular dialogue nor plot, but were generally a collection of episodes, which were sometimes so numerous, that a single piece occupied several days in the performance. Thus, one acted in 1391 by the parish clerks, at the Skinner's Well, beside Smithfield, at which the king, queen, and nobility were present, lasted three days; while another in 1409, which commenced with the creation of the world and went onward through the whole gospel history, lasted eight days. In England, as in France, the actors were not far to seek; and sometimes they were the scholars of a particular school, at other times the craftsmen of a guild, who provided the play at their own proper expense. Even the clergy also, who soon esteemed these plays as cheap and popular gospels by which the people might be enlightened, and the cause of religion advanced, because not only the composers of miracles and mysteries, but also actors in their representation, while the sacred vestments and ornaments of their churches were freely lent to further the exhibition. It is not strange, however, that these dramas, in course of time, degenerated from the sacred character in which they had commenced, and that the full scope which they allowed to the fancy descended into buffoonery and profanity. Thus, in St. Paul's Church, where mysteries were frequently exhibited, the third Person of the Trinity was represented by a white pigeon let down through a hole in the roof, succeeded by a censer smoking with perfume. In the exhibitions of hell, also, in the lowest compartment of the stage, instead of the tragic warnings which the mouth of the dragon should have breathed forth, all was farce and merriment; and the harlequin devils who issued from it, kept the audience in a roar of laughter by their coarse jokes, and the ludicrous punishments which they inflicted upon condemned sinners. The earliest miracle play that exists in English, was written in the time of Edward III., and is to be found in the Harleian MSS.; and the subject is the descent of Christ into hell for the liberation of Adam and Eve, the prophets, and John the Baptist.

As these plays were little better than gaudy pageantries and a mere bustle of action, a more simple species of the drama succeeded in the form of morality plays, by which the miracle and mystery were superseded. By this plan, the unwieldy tiers of scaffolding were reduced to a single stage, that could not only be set up at the corners of streets, but moved into court-yards and halls; while the subject of the play was simplified, and the number of the actors diminished. The personages were now the representatives of good and evil qualities, while the moral consisted in the triumph of the former, and the discomfiture and punishment of the latter. It was not long, however, that this poetical, even-handed justice was strictly adhered to, or even thought of; and the taste of the many, as in every such attempt, at last predominated over that of the judicious few. The chief characters in the morality were the Devil and the Vice. The first of these was generally a hideous monster, invested with all the popular attributes of horns, hoofs, tail, and shaggy hide, and who usually made his entrance upon the scene with the startling cry of "Ho! ho! ho!" Sometimes, however, when he had a more seductive part to perform, his costume was that of a trim gallant according to the court fashion of the day, as the following inventory of a dress for Satan in one of the Coventry Plays will fully attest:—

"Of fine cordevan, a goodly pair of peaked shoon. Hosen enclosed of the most costious (costly) cloth of crimson, ... with two dozen points of cheverelle, the aglets of silver fine.
A shirt of fine Holland.
A stomacher of clear Reynes, the best that may be bought.
Cadice wool or flock, to stuff withal the doublet.
A gown of three yards.
A dagger for devotion
With side-locks to the collar hanging down.
A high small bonnet."

As for the Vice of the play, he was a merry but most iniquitous buffoon, similar to the harlequin of a modern pantomime, who encountered Satan with a sword or dagger of lath, and usually had the best of it through the performance, until the close, when he was worsted, and carried off to hell on the devil's back. We have already adverted to the deterioration of these moralities, which at length became anything but moral; while the religion they inculcated was often in full keeping with their practice. Sometimes this had to be apologized for; and in the Chester Plays, a proclamation was usually made, that though some things therein were introduced "not warranted by any writ," they were brought in "to make sport," and "to glad the hearers." Of those productions in writing that gradually were matured into the English drama, we have, 1st, the Towuley Collection, supposed to have been written about the time of Henry VI.; 2d, the Coventry Plays, which are as old as the reign of Henry VII.; and 3d, the Chester Plays, that were the immediate precursors of Shakspeare and the Elizabethan period. The usual seasons for acting them were Christmas and the Whitsun holidays. As from the extensive properties, and great number of actors which they required, they could only be exhibited in London and the largest cities, the smaller towns and villages were contented with occasional bands of strolling players, who already were reckoned vile in the eye of the law, and whose migrations were, like those of gipsies or outlaws, closely watched by the country justices. What might be called puppet plays were also exhibited, in which the most sacred events in the history of our Saviour and his apostles were acted by little wooden puppets.

It was not, however, within these limits that the struggling spirit of the English drama could now be confined; and private theatricals were in abundance at the festivals of the wealthy, usually in that allegorical form which so much pervaded the public theatrical representations. Besides these, there were mummings performed at court, and by persons of the highest rank, at Christmas, wherein the performers dressed and masked themselves to represent birds, beasts, mythic personages, and angels, according to their several fancies. It was through a fearful court mumming of this kind that Charles VI. of France lost his reason, by which such miseries were entailed upon his kingdom. Of a higher description still were those national pageants by which a public event was commemorated, and in which all the powers of the miracle, mystery, and morality plays were exhausted to the uttermost, as well as commingled in most admired disorder. Such was that with which Henry V. was welcomed on his arrival in London, after the victory of Azincourt, that had made the whole nation wild with triumph. On reaching Eltham, he was met by the mayor and aldermen of London dressed all in red, with white hoods; and on passing forward to Blackheath, he was received by 20,000 citizens who rode out to welcome him. On crossing London bridge at the head of this mighty cavalcade, he found at the drawbridge two temporary pageant turrets that had been set up for the occasion, and in front of them a large giant, who hailed him in well-conned verse. On the top of one turret was a lion and an antelope, and on the other, a host of angels, that saluted him with the anthem, "Blessed is he that cometh in the name of the Lord." He rode through the city, the streets in his route being canopied with rich cloths, and the windows hung with pieces of tapestry and silk; and at Cornhill there was a tower occupied by the patriarchs, who broke forth at his coming with, "Sing unto the Lord a new song; praise his name in the holy church;" and having ended, they let loose a shower of live birds that flew and fluttered round his victorious head. On reaching Cheapside, where the conduits ran wine, the chief conduit was surmounted by the twelve apostles, and their song was, "Have mercy on my soul, O Lord;" and when they finished it, twelve kings who accompanied them knelt and presented offerings to the victor of France, and welcomed his return. This part of the pageant was also rivalled by another that was near it; this was the cross of Cheapside, which was now turreted and bannered, and a host of angels upon it singing, "Nobel, nobel," and presenting basons, no doubt filled with costly offerings, to the hero. All this mummery, as modern taste would account it, but which is described both in poetry and prose with enthusiastic unction by Lydgate, Fabyan, and the old historians, was closed at St. Paul's Church, where Henry was received by fourteen bishops, richly attired and mitred, and with censers in their hands, who performed a triumphant *Te Deum*; after which he retired, no doubt right weary, to his palace at Westminster. How strangely do our thoughts pass from the hero of such a pageant, to the same hero impersonated by the glo-

A MUMMING.—Strutt's Sports and Pastimes.

rious genius of Shakspeare! What was all this compared with a single scene in the Boar tavern at Eastcheap?

In turning to the more common sports and amusements of this period, we begin, as we have done hitherto, with the aristocracy. In addition to the rough exercises and training of chivalry, now become more laborious than ever from the greater weight of armour which the changes of warfare had made necessary, they still continued the sports of hawking and hunting. In the latter, however, an innovation was introduced by inclosures being paled, into which the beasts of game were driven, while from sheds and sylvan booths erected at the entrance of these inclosures, the hunters coolly selected the animals, and brought them down with their arrows. In this way, kings, lords, and reverend bishops and abbots endeavoured to enjoy the sport of hunting, without the toil and risk that usually attended it. Was this significant of the fact that the commons were better protected in their property, and their grounds better cultivated than hitherto? A growing disinclination to rough exercises may also have had its weight in promoting this inclosure hunting, as the sports of running, wrestling, pitching the bar, and spear-throwing were going out of fashion among the higher classes, and descending to the lower. The game of tennis, afterwards so fashionable, appears by this time to have been introduced into England, as we may judge from the insolent message of the French dauphin to Henry V., who, according to our early historians, sent the English king by way of present a set of tennis balls. The game at first was played in the open air; but when it grew into favour, tennis-courts were erected in great inns and the mansions of the chief nobility. In sedentary games dicing still kept its place; but already a game had been introduced into England before whose seductions all the others were to yield. This was card-playing, which, as is well-known, was invented to amuse the melancholy hours of the insane Charles VI. From France the amusement quickly extended not only to Italy, Spain, and Germany, but also to England, where it became so prevalent, that in the reign of Edward IV. a law was passed in favour of the English card-makers, prohibiting the importation of cards from abroad. At first, the cards were rich paintings executed with artistic skill, in the highest departments of colouring and gilding, so that a single pack was a very costly purchase; but when the passion for this amusement increased, the wits of men were set to work in inventing cards of inferior price, and better fitted for daily handling. The result was, the application of the newly-invented art of printing; and accordingly cards were made in the first instance by stamping them with wooden blocks, and afterwards filling the outline with colouring, which was done by hand. In this way card-making soon became a regular craft. The games first used were Trump and Primero, but soon others of a more complex character were invented, by which money was more cleverly lost and won than ever it had been by dice, chess, and tables. The history of card-playing in England after this date is too well known to require further comment.

The fashionable costume of this period underwent few alterations; it had attained its climax of foppery during the reign of Richard II., and there it was suffered to remain. Accordingly, in the dresses of gentlemen during the reigns of Henry IV. and his son, as they are delineated in the illuminated MSS. of the period, we have the same flowing attire as formerly, and the same preposterous wideness and length of sleeves, that must have cost the wearer no little trouble to keep from trailing on the ground as he walked along. Happily, however, we miss the high muff-like bonnet which makes such a grotesque figure in the illuminations of the period of Richard II.; but instead of this, we have hats of every shape, and hoods twisted into every variety. Of course, we find in these every change from the graceful to the

MEN'S HEAD-DRESSES OF FIFTEENTH CENTURY.—Figs. 1, 2, 4, Royal MSS. 15. D. III.; Fig. 3, Cotton MSS. 20. C. VII.

ridiculous—from the elegant and regal-looking turban of the East, to the wide-brimmed uncouth hat of the modern dustman or coal-heaver. But the most becoming of these, as well as the best known of them all, from being the head-dress with which the pictures of Henry IV. are usually adorned, was the roundlet, a light turban surrounding a skull-cap, from which a graceful drapery descended on either side. From the same pictures we find the hair closely cropped and the faces shaven, with the exception of old men and grave government functionaries, who appear to have worn their beards either peaked or forked; and martialists, who retained their mustachios. During the earlier part of this period, the long pike disappeared from the shoe, but in the later part it returned in greater longitude than ever. So highly valued indeed was this singular piece of extravagance, and in consequence, even already "the toe of the peasant came so near the heel of the courtier," that by a sumptuary statute of 1463, none but lords were allowed to wear shoes or boots having pikes more than two inches long. Toward the close of the reign of Edward IV. the love of rich clothing had become so great, and the distinctions of rank so confounded, in consequence of inferiors vieing in dress and ornament with those above them; that parliament again interfered; and in 1482 the following restrictions were enacted, from which the spirit of the age, as manifested in its costume, will be best understood. None were to use cloth of gold and silk of purple, except the king and the royal family. No one under the rank of a duke was to wear cloth of gold of tissue. No one under the rank of lord was to wear plain cloth of gold. No one under the rank of knight might presume to wear any velvet in his doublet or gown, or any damask or satin in his gown; and no one under the rank of esquire or gentleman might have a doublet of damask or satin, or a gown of chamlet. No one, also, who was not of noble rank was to wear either foreign woollen or fur of sables; and (strangest of all!) no one was to wear garments which were characterized as being of indecent brevity, unless he had the high privilege of belonging to the peerage.

With regard to female costume, the greatest variations which it underwent were chiefly in regard to head attire. These variations, too, were by no means for the better; so that instead of the gold net-work, or flower-chaplets with which they had been so gracefully adorned, the heads of ladies were now attired in a fashion of which even the paintings of the day have failed to give a sufficiently intelligible idea. In the reign of Henry V. these head-dresses were forked or horned in such a preposterous fashion, and rose to such a height, as to outdo all former extravagances, and as such were vehemently denounced by the preachers, and ridiculed by the poets of the day. But besides these, there were the reticulated and the heart-shaped head-dresses, as they have been termed by modern antiquaries; and steeple head-dresses, similar in form to those still worn by the female peasantry in Normandy. But over all these the horned fashion bore the pre-eminence, and in some of the pictures of the Cotton and Harleian MSS. they appear with such an enormous altitude, as makes us wonder how female taste could at any period have become so depraved. At last, towards the close of the reign of Edward IV., these absurdities disappeared, and were succeeded by a more rational adornment.

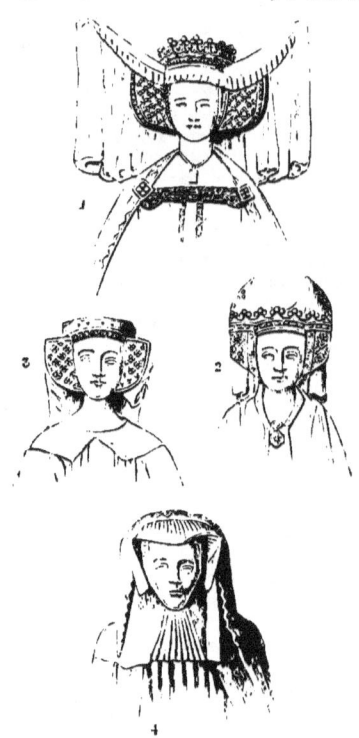

LADIES' HEAD-DRESSES.[1]—From Monuments.

This was a velvet cap or cowl turned back upon the brow, and hanging down to the shoulders behind in plaits; but such a simple fashion was not enough without wings made of some light gossamer stuff, and standing out, as if the wearer was prepared for instant flight. In other respects, the female costume consisted of the long gown, or the *cote hardie* of the period of Richard II., remarkable chiefly for the long trailing sleeves, and upon which all that superfluity of cloth was wasted that was soon

---

[1] (1), Beatrice, Countess of Arundel, died 1432; from her monument in the church at Arundel. (2), Joan, wife of William Phelip, Lord Bardolph; from her effigy in Hoveringham Church, Notts; died early in fifteenth century. (3), Catherine, Countess of Michael de la Pole, Earl of Suffolk; from their monument in Wingfield Church, Suffolk. (The earl died at the siege of Hexham, A.D. 1432). (4), Philippa, Duchess of York, died 1433; from the monumental effigy in the chapel of St. Nicholas, Westminster Abbey.

after transferred to the sweeping train. This last change occurred in the reign of Henry VI., when, in addition to the contraction of sleeves, the waist of the gown was reduced to extreme brevity, the gown seeming to consist of nothing but shoulders and train, with a high-girdled zone to mark their respective limits. Such is the general outline of the females as they are robed in the illuminated MSS. of this era; but the filling up of the picture we cannot otherwise describe, than that it presents the usual amount of fur, embroidery, and jewellery.

In proceeding to the domestic life and habits of the nobility and gentry of England, our first business is to inquire into the state of the dwellings which they now inhabited. And here we find that the strong, tyrannous-looking castle with which the noble had overawed his own district, was already becoming a mere relic of departed feudalism, and giving place to mansions of a less warlike, but more comfortable character. The towers and turrets of the new habitations were not so much the defences as the ornaments of the building, while what might be called the home part of it, instead of being a *keep* in the centre, extended over nearly the whole range; the moat, too, was either contracted or dispensed with, while the windows were greatly enlarged and multiplied. Like the state of the age itself, they were transitions from the feudal to the civilized life—the combination of castle and manor, in which the latter characteristic was fast predominating. While such were the homes of the nobility, those of the gentry of England were still more modernized and peaceful in their character, having now an amount of gracefulness, ornament, and comfort that were the best indications of peaceful security and advancing civilization. As yet, however, the walls of the apartments, whether of castle or manor, had frequently neither wainscotting on the walls, nor plaster on the ceiling; and this cold, discomfort, and nakedness were but clumsily concealed by the dust-laden and time-soiled arras and tapestry that still kept their wonted places. The great hall, too, was still the principal apartment in the building, and to its amplitude every other room in the mansion, whether for domestic privacy or comfort, was more or less obliged to give way.[1] This, however, mattered little with a people whose lives as yet were chiefly spent in the open air, and who required the shelter of a roof for little else than eating and sleeping. A hundred guests, and as many attendants, could find accommodation, and comfort to boot, within a compass in which a tithe of that number would in modern times be scarcely able to enjoy a sufficiently ample lodgment.

COSTUMES OF THE FIFTEENTH CENTURY.—Royal MSS. 15. D. III.

HADDON HALL, a Castellated Mansion of Fifteenth Century.—From Lysons' Derbyshire.

As this hall was so important a place, comprising, as it did, the chief amount of domestic life among the aristocracy of England, we shall do well to pause for a few minutes on its threshold, and mark the doings of its inmates. At the lower end of it was a passage concealed by a screen, which led

[1] The hall of Crosby Place, London, is a good example of a hall of this period. See cut, vol. i. p. 642.

into the kitchen; and by this vital communication, the smoking dishes were conveniently transferred from broach and caldron in hasty or in solemn procession, as its nature might require. At the upper part of the hall, which was lighted by a large bay window, was the raised place called the *dais*, on which stood a huge table, and near it an open cup-board, that gave to full view the grandeur and glitter of the family plate. This place, however, was only for the privileged; and below the dais, a still larger table stood, extending nearly the length of the hall, for the crowds of humbler guests and retainers who also had a full share in the hospitality of their noble landlord. The dinner hour was ten o'clock; and the noble, if he was one of the highest rank, appeared in his place like a king, with his splendid retinue of secretary, privy councillors, marshal, stewards, and master of the horse—his chaplain and choristers who officiated in cathedral state in the chapel of the steward knocking loudly on the huge oaken board, the blessing was said or sung, and the guests seated themselves upon or beneath the dais according to their rank and holding, while even at the lower table, the upper and lower classes were distinguished by a ponderous silver salt-cellar, above which no one beneath a certain rank might presume to take his seat. In this way, though all were assembled at one entertainment, and in the same apartment, lines of demarcation were drawn, and three grades distinctly specified. And now came the feast itself, borne in by trains of servants, and, for the most part, presenting courses distinguished more by their bulk and substantiality than by their elegance; for they consisted of platters of beef and mutton salted and fresh, of mountains of fowl and fish, of pasties and loaves of wastel and simnel bread, of dishes into which every variety of animal and vegetable food was curiously disguised, and compounded according to the freaks of a most artificial style of cookery. The dessert we shall not pretend to describe, as its strange names and stranger compounds are utterly beyond a modern understanding. As for the liquors, which consisted of wine, ale, beer, and hippocras, they circulated in plentiful abundance, being handed in silver cups to the higher guests by troops of ser-

ANCIENT SALT-CELLAR AT NEW COLLEGE, OXFORD.

A JESTER, 15TH CENTURY.—Harleian MSS. 2897.

castle, and chanted grace at the table—his constables, heralds, guards, pursuivants, pages, and trumpeters—and though last, not least, his jester. At the signal, which was given by the master-

¹ This salt-cellar was presented, in 1493, by Walter Hill, warden of the college. It is of silver gilt, exquisitely chased, and ornamented on the cover with blue enamel.

vants, and at the lower table in flagons of pewter, horn, and wood. But still, discomfort and grossness continue to look forth amidst all this plenty, and the dishes of the entertainment are in contrast to the splendid retinue of the entertainer: even when we look curiously into the bill of fare, we find that salt junk forms the chief part of it. And yet, such was the appetite, and more especially the thirst of the guests, that the dinner generally occupied three hours. The era of conversation, indeed, had not yet commenced, either to enliven the circulation or fill up the pauses of a feast; but this important office was supplied by the jester of the household, who, pranked in his cap, bells, and motley, and brandishing his bauble garnished with a pair of asses' ears, exercised his unlimited privilege by cracking jokes on all and sundry, and keeping the whole hall in a roar of merriment. There were also never-failing bands of minstrels, tumblers, jug-

A TUMBLER, FIFTEENTH CENTURY.—Strutt's Sports and Pastimes.

glers, and buffoons, whom the savour of a flesh-feast was certain to allure, and who were ready to appear and exercise their office at a moment's warning. In this way, the banquet-hall was graced with harping, juggling, rope-dancing, posturing, and harlequinading, and the feasters had both conversation and merriment brought to their hand without the trouble of creating it.

Such was the usual routine of a dinner in the princely halls of the nobility of England during the present period; and it will be seen from these statements, gathered as they have been from various accredited sources, that notwithstanding the pompous ceremonial with which it was invested, and the abundance of which it consisted, the most important part of the concern—the art of cooking and preparing it aright—was still very defective. Show, indeed, was not neglected, and many dishes upon the table glittered with gold leaf, as well as every variety of colouring, by which the eye might be feasted to the full; but still, that delicacy, neatness, artistic skill, and substantial comfort were wanting, with which modern cookery can invest the poor man's banquet, and give it a relish unknown in the feasts of the Plantagenets. No man in the present day, except under the urgency of a wager, would venture, for instance, upon fried porpoise or stewed seal; but these sometimes figure as choice dishes at the stately banquets of this period—showing what iron stomachs and matchless digestion our ancestors must have possessed. One really elegant preparation, however, which generally figured in the regal banquets of the day, must not be omitted. This was called a *soteltie* (subtlety), and was generally served up at the end of each course, when it was brought in with solemn procession and amidst the blare of trumpets. This soteltie appears to have been composed in a great measure of jellies, preserved fruits, and confectionaries, moulded into the figures of men, animals, buildings, and rural scenery, which were so grouped, as to embody some allegory, or represent an historical event. In this way, it was often a pleasing riddle, calculated to exercise the curiosity as well as regale the palates of the guests; and while it thus comprised the resources of the painter and statuary in its formation, poetry expended upon its moral her choicest verses, which were attached to it in a beautifully written and illuminated scroll. On the return of Henry V. from France, these dishes formed the most important part of the banquets with which he was welcomed, and as such, are commemorated at great length in the chronicles of the period. We have only room, however, to allude briefly to three subtleties served up at a banquet given by the hero of Azincourt to the Emperor of Germany on his visit to London. The first was "Our Lady arming St. George, and an angel doing on his spurs;" the second soteltie, was St. George riding in full career against the dragon with his lance couched; and the third, was a castle, into the gates of which the victorious saint was entering, accompanied by the king's daughter leading her snow-white lamb.

The other details of noble domestic life in England at this period may be briefly summed up. The two original Norman meals were now increased to four. Of these, the first was breakfast, which was taken at the hour of seven in the morning; but as four o'clock was the usual hour of rising, and as morning exercise generally consisted of hunting, hawking, and other such active sports, the appetites of the family were well prepared for a substantial meal, which, for the most part, consisted of bread, boiled chines of beef and mutton, and a large allowance of wine and beer. Then followed dinner, which, as we have already mentioned, was usually at ten o'clock. The third meal was supper, which was taken at four o'clock in the afternoon, and was similar to the breakfast. The fourth, called *liveries*, was taken between eight and nine in the evening, and in bed; but instead of being a light refection and preparative for sleep, according to the most approved modern rule, it was a substantial nightmare feast, as appears by the *Northumberland Family Book*, where we find Earl Percy and his countess having for their livery two manchetts (or loaves of the finest flour, each weighing six ounces), a loaf of household bread, a gallon of beer, and a quart of warmed and spiced wine. The retinues with which the mansions and castles of the chief nobility were filled, must have crowded every nook and corner of the building however large, and impeded rather than furthered every kind of work, if we may estimate them by the large trains with which the "brave peers of England" were accompanied upon important public occasions. Thus, when the chief nobility were called up to London in 1458, just previous to the outbreak of the wars of the Roses, the Earl of Salisbury came with 500 attendants on horseback, Richard, Duke of York, with 400, the Dukes of Exeter and Somerset with 800, and the Earl of Northumberland, Lord Egremont, and Lord Clifford with 1500. Pre-eminent among these, too, was Richard Nevil, Earl of Warwick, soon to become the "king-maker," who had for his retinue 600 riders, all clad in red jackets, embroidered before and behind with the cognizance of his family—the ragged staff. In those days, each nobleman, when he repaired to the metropolis, took up his temporary abode in an inn, which thus served him for a town-house, and was frequently called by his name.[1] This was sufficient for one whose usual residence all the year round was in the country, where he could enjoy an undivided pre-eminence among his thousands of tenants and retainers.

Of the in-door life of the common people we still know comparatively little. As we have seen, however, their condition was so materially improved, that the means of comfortable living were more completely within their reach than at any former period; and we may suppose, they were not slow in using the opportunity. The style of cookery probably continued the same as it had been in the days of Chaucer, with plenty of materials on which to exercise it; and the eminent lawyer Fortescue informs us, that while the commons of England in his day fared abundantly, they seldom drank water except for penance. It was no wonder, therefore, that in such a state of things, "glutton masses" were so easily established among them, and observed with such riotous devotion. These were the inventions of the clergy, who, to the full, were as inordinate lovers of good cheer as the laity, and who resolved to turn the well-filled larders of the people to their own account. It was easy, therefore, to persuade the parishioners to repair at set times to the village church laden with provisions, and there hold a feast in honour of the Virgin, preceded and consecrated by a mass. Tremendous gluttony and intemperance were the consequences of these meetings, where every excess was converted into a religious merit, and each village contended with its neighbour in the costliness and amount of eating and swilling in honour of the "Queen of Heaven." Five times a-year these glutton masses were usually held, during which the parish churches were converted into the most uproarious of taverns. But, as a contrast to this, we must take into account certain places in England where no such abundance prevailed. Such was the case of Northumberland, which Æneas Sylvius, afterwards Pope Pius II., visited in 1437, where at a populous village he astonished the natives with his wheaten bread and wine, of which they had never seen the like before. This was probably upon that part of the Border most exposed to the visits of the Scottish moss-troopers. But a similar destitution was too often general throughout the kingdom under those famine-visits, against which, as yet, the improvident habits of the people had not learned to make due provision. One of these many visitations occurred in 1438, and is thus described in the *Chronicle of London from* 1089 *to* 1483:—" Also this year was so great dearth of corn, that men were fain to eat rye bread and barley, the which *never ate none before;* and rather than fail, bread made of beans, pense, and vetches, and well were him that might have enough thereof; for a bushel of wheat was worth 3s. at London, and in some counties dearer; and that made bakers lords; but I pray God never let us see that day no more if his will be." In such famines, however, as may easily be imagined, there were many who could not procure even the beans, pense, and vetches, so that they were obliged to burrow for roots, and convert them into the likeness of bread, while many died of utter destitution.

In coming to the active sports in usual practice among the commons of England at this period, the first place is due to the truly national game of quarter-staff. This weapon was a strong heavy

---

[1] One of the finest existing examples of an inn of this period is the George, at Glastonbury, still used for the same purpose. It is of stone, and its details are remarkably good. The Blue Boar Inn, at Leicester, was of timber and plaster, but it is now entirely destroyed. See cut, vol. i. p. 650.

staff or pole about five or six feet in length, which was held firmly in the centre with one hand, while the other shifted its place from one side to the other, according to the necessity either for striking or guarding. In this way, the weapon was made to clear a wide circle round him who knew how to wield it, while either end could deal a stroke that was both heavy and unexpected. It was thus both sword and shield, and that, too, in such perfection, that a dexterous quarter-staff player could guard himself against very trying odds. Of this, a curious proof is given in a pamphlet written in the seventeenth century, under the title of *Three to One*, by a gentleman who records his exploit of having defeated three Spaniards armed with rapier and poniard, while his own weapon was nothing but a quarter-staff. Next to this was the game of wrestling, in which the people in general, but especially the Cornish and Devonshire peasantry, were distinguished for their strength and skill. Competitions in this athletic sport were frequent, in which not only a champion would challenge his own village, but one village defy another; and at these Olympic trials on a small scale, where the victor was rewarded with a ram or a cock, the greatest glory was for a man to hold possession of the public wrestling ring for years, against every competitor. In this manner, the practice itself, like fencing, was raised into a science, demanding the utmost skill as well as mere rude strength; and among the many dexterous sleights that were practised, by which the heels of Hercules himself might have been tripped up, what was called the "Cornish hug," was a favourite one that continued in use for centuries. Broken ribs and dislocated joints were of course not unusual in such trials, but they kindled less personal animosity, and do not seem to have produced the same brutality, which boxing matches afterwards occasioned, when wrestling was superseded by the more artistic science of bruising. Besides these competitions of a warlike and chivalrous character, bull-baiting and cock-fighting often drew the whole inhabitants of a village into the public green. A more gentle amusement, and one peculiar to England, was bowling, which seems to have been in use from a very early date. The game, however, as performed during this period, was with one ball for each player, instead of three, which are used in modern bowling. So high in favour did this sport become, not only among the commons but the upper classes, that bowling greens, fairly laid out, and sheltered from the weather, were attached to noblemen's houses and the principal inns of the metropolis. Ingenuity was also set to work to devise various modifications of bowling; and of these, closh was one, which was nothing more than our modern skittles, where pins are thrown down by a wooden ball: another was the game of half-bowl, where, as the name intimates, a wooden hemisphere was used, requiring more dexterity in its handling than a completely rounded ball.

From bowls, the transition is easy to the various games that were played at ball both with hand and foot. Of the former kind, the chief was the balloon-ball, a large leather skin inflated with air, and struck with all the strength of the arm, which was braced and bandaged to give vigour to the blow. Another game, called club-ball, consisted in striking a similar ball not with the hand, but a large club, which was wielded, it is probable, with both hands, and required the utmost both of dexterity and strength. These were games for men, and were pursued with such zeal, that towns and villages often turned out to practise them by mutual challenge, while the aristocracy of the district attended as spectators and judges. Other games, which were more appropriate for children, were trap-ball, where the trap itself, unlike the modern one, was nearly half the height of the striker; and shuttlecock, which was played in the same manner as it is at present. Another active sport, that could only be practised by children, was for two boys to hold up a hoop, and a third to pass through it with a flying leap, where he alighted upon his cloak that was spread out to receive him. A game frequently mentioned at this period under the names of bays, base, bars, and prisoner's bars, consisted, like many similar games, in a person overtaking and capturing as many of the players as he could, and who, unless he was swift of foot and strong of gripe, could be kept at arm's-length through a whole hour of fruitless exertion. Among these sports, too, that of hoodman-blind must not be omitted. This was nothing else than our modern game of blindman's buff, which was played by old and young, as appears from a picture in the Bodleian MSS., where, as in Wilkie's picture on the same subject, men, women, and children are mixed together. In playing this game, the person who was hood-winked, was done so literally, as he had his hood reversed and drawn down over his eyes, while those whom he was vainly endeavouring to catch thumped him well with their own hoods, which they pulled off for the occasion. Besides these games, there were several peculiar to London, the chief of which was boating, that at this period acquired additional *eclat* from the lord-mayor's annual water procession, which was first commenced in 1453. Another amusement was skating on the Thames, where the sheep-shanks formerly used for the purpose had now given place to regular skates.

As the English have ever been jealous of their

liberty, it was with no little suspicion as well as resentment, that they viewed the interference of government with those games which they most especially cherished. But the country needed good archers, which could not be obtained as long as the village archery trials were abandoned for more alluring amusements; and therefore, in the reign of Edward III., the games of quoits, hand-ball, foot-ball, stick-ball, canibuca, and cock-fighting were prohibited by name to the people on holidays, while they were commanded instead to repair to the archery ground, and practise with the longbow. The same prohibition was repeated in the reign of Edward IV., where, besides the games above-mentioned, kayles, closh, half-bowl, hand-in and hand-out were also specified, and magistrates were commissioned to seize and destroy whatever tennis-balls, closhes, tables, dice, cards, and bowls might fall in their way. This was hard measure—so hard, indeed, that it defeated its own purpose; and the prohibited games were practised with greater zest, and the archery trials more completely neglected than ever.

London being a city of such world-wide celebrity, and so influential upon the character and fortunes of the people at large, a few notices of its condition during the present period will assist us more fully in understanding the manners and customs by which the age was distinguished. In this, we are much aided by the short, humorous, sketchy poem called the *London Lyckpeny*, by John Lydgate, in which the poet, under the character of an unlucky visitor from the wolds of Kent, describes the streets of the principal districts of the metropolis, and the crowds that filled them. He has come to London in the prosecution of a law-suit, but having neglected "to put money in his purse," his applications at the Inns of Court and Westminster Hall, to which he repaired in the first instance, were useless, and nothing is left for him but a short trip of sight-seeing before he returns to the country. Even within the sacred court of Westminster, he found that there were thieves, as well as sordid lawyers and bribe-loving justiciaries, for his hood was stolen in the crowd. He hurries to the door—

"Where Flemynge began on me for to cry,
'Master, what will you copen or by,
Fyne felt hatts, or spectacles to reede?
Lay down your sylver, and here you may spede.'"

He has no money, however, and leaving the Flemish pedlar-merchants and their commodities of hats, spectacles, and other wares, he proceeds to Westminster gate, at mid-day, the hour of dinner among the commons of London; but there, still more tempting materials solicited his notice: these were cooks' shops, or perhaps stalls, where tables spread with a fair cloth were covered with ribs of beef "both fat and full fine," and abundance of bread, wine, and ale. We can easily imagine how the approaches to the courts of justice were favourable to such a traffic, and what crowds of hungry litigants must have repaired to such places of refreshment during the intervals of a long-protracted law-suit. Clearing Westminster, which was still a town by itself, the interval between it and London being ornamented by rural villas, the Lyckpeny enters the capital, where every street was alive and swarming with traffickers, each endeavouring to out-bawl his neighbour, by proclaiming his article of sale and recommending its excellence, while spice, cherries, strawberries, and hot pease-cods made a Babel that must have been stunning to the unsophisticated ears of every newly-arrived visitor from the country. He proceeds to "the Chepe," and here the Lyckpeny finds that he has only entered into a new element of traffic, where shops have taken the place of wandering huxtery, and costly articles of dress that of perishable fruits and vegetables. There, each dealer, standing at his own door, proclaims with untiring voice what articles he has within for sale—velvets, silks, lawns, fine Paris threads—and even takes the stranger by the hand, that he may tempt him to inspect the wares, and become a purchaser. But still, our poor friend of Kent is moneyless; and rebuffing these invitations as well as he can, he presses right onward, and enters Canwyke Street, afterwards called Candlewick, and sometimes Candlewright Street, in consequence of the number of wax and tallow chandlers who followed their craft in that quarter. Now, however, it was a street of miscellaneous commodities, where shops of cheap cloth and second-hand clothing were alternated with those that dealt in mackerel, hot sheep's feet, and green rushes for the fresh carpeting of rooms. As this street was crossed on the west by Eastcheap, here our pilgrim soon found himself, he, or rather the poet whom he impersonates, little guessing with what an imperishable name this locality would afterwards be invested. But even already, Eastcheap was a place of merriment and good cheer; for savoury pies and ribs of beef were lustily shouted by their venders, mixed with the clattering of pewter pots, the twanging of harps and pipes, the old songs of "Julian and Jenkin"—at that time the favourite ditties of street minstrelsy, and oaths of street controversy and contention. Here, indeed, the spirit of good eating seemed to have taken up its permanent abode; for Stow, in his *Survey of London*, written in 1598, thus speaks of it:—"This Eastcheap is now a flesh-market of butchers, there dwelling on both sides of the street; it had sometime also cooks mixed amongst the butchers, and such other as sold victuals ready dressed of all sorts. For of old time, when friends did meet, and were disposed to be merry, they went not to dine and sup in taverns, but to the cooks, where they called for meat, what they liked, which they always found ready dressed at a reasonable rate, as I have before showed." Eastcheap was also famed in ancient times for a riot, the chief actors in which were very near relations of "mad Hal" himself, and had probably used the Boar tavern as their favourite resort. It is thus related by Stow:—"In the year 1410, the 11th of Henry IV., upon the even of St. John Baptist, the king's sons, Thomas and John, being in Eastcheap at supper (or rather at breakfast, for it was after the watch was broken up, betwixt two and three of the clock after midnight), a great debate happened between their men and other of the court, which lasted one hour, till the mayor and sheriffs, with other citizens, appeased the same; for the which afterwards the said mayor, aldermen, and sheriffs were called to answer before the king, his sons and divers lords being highly moved against the city. At which time William Gascoyne, chief-justice, required the mayor and aldermen, for the citizens, to put them in the king's grace; whereunto they answered, that they had not offended, but (according to the law) had done their best in stinting debate and maintaining of the peace; upon which answer the king remitted all his ire, and dismissed them."

It will be seen from this account of the civic tour of Lydgate's hero, that the streets were well filled with pedlars who sold goods and edibles of every description; that the medley of sounds, called "London cries," were as loud, and almost as multifarious, as they were in after periods; and that the different trades had already chosen their favourite localities. But the Lyckpeny's ramble had not yet ended. He went into Cornhill; and that quarter, now so famed for its banks and rich merchandise, was then, it would appear, nothing better than a mart for stolen goods; and there, among other things, he saw his own hood, so lately stolen, hung out for sale, but had not wherewithal to buy it back. As he plodded along, a tavern-keeper took him by the sleeve, and courteously invited him to turn in and assay his wines, upon which our traveller, weary enough by this time, and having as yet a penny in his purse, spent it in purchasing a pint of wine, being unable to add to it the important concomitant of a dinner. He went to Billingsgate, at that time a place of wherries and barges, with watermen plying for customers to the cry of "Ho! we are a-going hence!" but to his piteous entreaty of being wafted across to the Southwark "for the love of God," he was told that he could not be carried thither without paying a fare of two-pence. At last he got safely back into Kent, leaving behind his parting benediction upon London, and praying that its lawyers might obtain their due reward.

In a city so rich and so full of merchandise, robberies and thefts appear to have been of frequent occurrence; but justice almost kept pace with crime, so that public executions of hanging, burning, and pressing to death, occur in the memorabilia of the period with alarming rapidity. In such a state of society, also, riots were of frequent occurrence, and these, too, not merely among the commons, but persons of high rank and grave occupation. We have noticed already the Eastcheap riot, in which princes and their retainers were actors, upon the eve of a public religious festival. The following summary of the "occurrents" of a twelvemonth during the reign of Henry VI., throws further light upon the subject of London rioting in general:—" It was a custom that upon St. Bartholomew's Day, the lord-mayor and sheriffs of London should go to the wrestling-place near Moorfields, where at this time the prior of St. John's likewise was to see the sport; and a servant of his being ashamed to be foiled before his master, desired to wrestle again, contrary to custom, which the lord-mayor denied; whereupon the prior fetched bowmen from Clerkenwell against the mayor, and some slaughter was made; the mayor's cap was shot through with an arrow, yet he would have the sport go on, but no wrestlers came, whereupon he said 'he would stay a while to make trial of the citizens' respect to him;' and presently after a great party of them came with banners displayed, and fetched him home in triumph. Soon after, another quarrel happened in Holborn between the gentlemen of the Inns of Chancery, and some citizens, in appeasing whereof, the queen's attorney and three more were slain. The year after, the apprentices of London, upon a very slight occasion, fell upon the foreign merchants, rifling and robbing their houses, but the lord-mayor, by his discretion, appeased the tumult, punishing some of the offenders with death, and others by fine, and all things are quieted and appeased."

When we direct our attention to the condition of learning and literary society in general, as they existed in England at this period, we cannot fail to be struck with the small progress that had been made, contrasted with the ample means of improvement that were now in operation. Caxton, so early as 1477, had set up his printing-press in the Almonry, near Westminster Abbey, and soon had such active imitators that, before the close of this period, English books were printed, not only for home use, but foreign exportation.

The erection and endowment of colleges were still going on both at Cambridge and Oxford, and public libraries were founded or enlarged. But in contrast to all this, there is scarcely a literary name or a scientific discovery to be found worth mentioning. Even the universities seem in a great measure to have lost their charm, and the crowds that had formerly resorted to them by the thousand, were now reduced to as many hundreds—and these, too, little better than paupers upon a public charity, and generally treated as such. But when we turn to the causes of this general depreciation of literature, we can easily discover them in those which had also a paralyzing effect, although in a far less degree, upon the gainful pursuits of merchandise. During nearly the whole of this season war was in its highest ascendency, and every active aspiring spirit found more congenial occupation in French conquests, and the civil commotions that followed, than could be obtained in the peaceful cloisters of a college. The facilities for study, therefore, which were now so abundantly multiplied, were still like seed cast into the earth: a long interval had to occur, and a better season to return, before the harvest shot up and ripened. And that harvest, too, was to be of a different character from those that had preceded, and demanded a long preparation. The taking of Constantinople, and the diffusion of ancient learning that followed—the means of that diffusion by the recent invention of printing—and the new impulse that was to be given to intellect at large by the Reformation—were now silently at work, and awaiting their enfranchisement. Another century was to show that this long interval of repose had not occurred in vain.

In taking into account the state of the different learned professions during this period, we find ample proof that the halls of Oxford and Cambridge, and the schools of learning which were still continuing to be multiplied, were as yet of little account, and no apparent efficacy. To read futurity in the stars, to discover the philosopher's stone, which, by a touch, could transmute all metals into gold, and to compound the *elixir vitæ* that could cure or prevent all diseases, was still the favourite pursuit of the scholar, but without the intellect or the learning which men like Roger Bacon, Michael Scott, or Raymond Lully had brought to such investigations. It was no wonder, therefore, if the knowledge of surgery and medicine was still neglected, and the art of healing in its infancy. It is a curious fact, that among all that army of heroes by which wounds and death were so plentifully inflicted at the battle of Azincourt, there was only *one* English surgeon; and that, although fifteen assistants were allowed him, these had to be seized by the "king's press," while their pay was nothing more than that of a common archer. We may guess what summary cures were attempted in the battle field, and what wild work was made in the hospital. In passing from the medical to the clerical profession, we expect, that among the priesthood, whatever learning exists in a country will be improved or at least preserved; but here we find, that while the clergy of England were not a whit behind their predecessors in the love of ease, field sports, wealth, and good living, they had even fallen behind their predecessors in literary acquirements and studious habits, and were neither able teachers, nor yet sound moral exemplars to the flocks who looked up to them for guidance. Such was generally the condition of the clergy of England, both lay and secular, at this period, and the bitter objurgations which Wyckliffe heaped upon them were but too well justified by the notices of contemporary chronicles. "It is a marvel," said Latimer somewhat later, "when mischief is in the land, if a priest be not at one end of it." As for preaching, this was a duty almost wholly dispensed with, or left in a great measure to the begging friars, whose discourses chiefly illustrated the necessity of purchasing heaven by liberal donations to the church, or the miracles wrought by the patron saints of the order to which they belonged. The preaching places, too, were various, being sometimes in the open air, in which case the town cross was a consecrated station; sometimes in a moveable pulpit, that might be set up in the corner of a street, or within the shelter of a building; and sometimes in the crowded cathedral, where the dignified ecclesiastic, in addition to enforcing some fresh impost, or reading a Papal bull, would vouchsafe a sermon under the shrine of a saint, the picture of a martyrdom, or some such painting as the "*duos cherumbinos cum hilari vultu et jocoso*," given in the directions of the day for church pictures and ornaments.

Of the kind of sermons preached at this period, we give the following extracts by way of specimen. They are from a sermon apparently of no mean pretensions, and written with much care, among the MSS. of the Harleian collection, upon the subject of the three days called *Tenebræ*, immediately preceding Easter. We have only taken the liberty of modernizing the spelling, to make it intelligible to the generality of our readers:—

"Worshipful friends, ye shall come to holy church on Wednesday, Thursday, and Friday, at even, for to hear Divine service, as commendable custom of holy church hath ordained. And holy church useth the three days, Wednesday, Thursday, and Friday, the service to be said in the eventide in darkness. And it is called, with diverse men, Tenables, but holy church calleth it Tenebras, as *Rationale Divinorum* saith; that is to say, thirus, or darkness, for then is the service said in darkness, for three causes; one is, for Christ that night before he was taken, he went thrice to the mount of Olivet, praying his Father in bliss for to take away his hard painful passion that he felt in his spirit; he sweat water and blood for anguish of his death. The second cause is this—for after midnight gathered fifty knights with great company of armed men, with swords, clubs, bats, weapons, and lanterns before them, for to take Christ, but it was that they could not know Christ from St. James the Minor, for they were like in person and stature. That false traitor Judas gave the Jews and men of arms a token, saying *Quicunque osculatus fuero*, &c.—Take him that I shall kiss, for he it is; hold him, and lead him slily and warily. And so they took Christ and put him on the cross. The third cause why the service chose three nights beside in darkness— for when our sovereign Saviour Christ Jesus was nailed unto the cross, foot and hand, hanging three hours of the day, from under unto noon the sun withdrew his light, and it was dark throughout all the world, tokening and showing that the matter of light, of sun and moon, was that time pained unto the death. For these three causes the service of these three nights is done in darkness. But unto the service of Thursday at eve and Friday is no bell rung, but a clapper the sound of a tree, tokening that every man and woman should come devoutly to the church without noise-making. And all that they should speak in going and coming should sound of the tree of Christ; that is to say, of the holy cross that Christ died upon for man's redemption, and of his precious passion; and remember how merciable Christ was when he granted the thief paradise that hung on his right side, when he axed mercy. So every man, and woman, and child should dispose them virtuously coming and going to this holy place, and leave talking of vanities, and speak God's worship of his holy passion and of his mercy. Also, in this service called Tenebras, before the altar is set a hearse, with twenty-four candles burning, for twelve apostles and twelve prophets, which candles be quenched one after another, in tokening that Christ's disciples went from him every one after another. But when all be quenched, yet one is kept light, which light is secretly, whiles the clerks sing the *kyries* and the verses, and that signifieth the holy woman that made lamentation at Christ's sepulture. Then afterwards that candle is brought again, which betokeneth Christ in his manhood dead and laid in sepulture. But soon after he rose from death to life, and gave light of mercy and grace to all that were quenched by despair. The strokes that the priest giveth upon the book betoken the thunder-claps when Christ brake hell-gates and destroyed the power of the devil in his resurrection."

This strange medley will give us a distinct idea, not only of the manner in which the puerilities of superstition were blended with the highest truths and most sacred mysteries of religion, but of the character of those auditories who listened and were edified by such instruction. And now comes the practical application of the discourse:—
"Now ye have heard what this service betokeneth, be not unkind to that merciful Lord that suffered his painful passion for you: for unkindness is a sin that stinketh in the sight of God. Wherefore, saith St. Ambrose, there may no man find a pain sufficient to punish an unkind man. Example I find of Alexander Nexam, as he writeth, how there was sometime a knight came from far countries would seek adventures. So it fortuned to a forest where he heard a great noise of a beast crying. So this knight drew nigh, and there he saw how an adder had accumbered and all to [altogether] clipped [folded] a lion, and venomed him, and bound the lion to a tree while he lay and slept. When the lion waked of his sleep, and perceived himself bound, and might not help himself, he made an horrible cry. Then the knight had compassion on the lion, and saw that the king of beasts was in distress: he drew out his sword, and slew the adder and loosed the lion. And when the lion found himself unbound he fell down to the knight's feet, and ever after he served the knight, and every night lay at his bed's feet; in tournaments and battles ever helped the knight, insomuch that all men spake of the knight and the lion. By this knight is understood Christ Jesus, second person in Trinity, that came from far country— that is to say, from heaven, into the vale of this wretched world, to unbind mankind that was bound with the old adder, the devil, that had bound mankind to the tree of inobedience. And so Christ loosed mankind out of the bond of the devil with the sword of his precious passion, and made him free. Wherefore must every man and woman show kindness to that good Lord, as the lion did unto the knight, to be obedient to him and thank him of his goodness, and of his unbinding from the bonds of the devil, and pursue and follow the true teaching of God, that so, when we shall pass the pain of bodily death, that we may have the perpetual joy of bliss bought by Christ's blessed blood. Amen."

After this specimen of the preaching of the age, need we wonder that mystery and miracle plays were in such high account, or that the clergy were so ready to give them their countenance and aid? While the plays were sermons, the sermons themselves appear to have been more plays, and these, too, of an inferior and less attractive stamp. It was a natural consequence that the theatre at last should empty the church, and the priesthood perceive their error when it was too late to amend it.

While the study of theology and medicine was thus in abeyance, that of law was in higher favour than ever. This, indeed, was absolutely necessary, when we recollect the change which society was undergoing, and the multiplication of statutes which was taking place to meet the new emergencies of that change. Rights and privileges were now possessed not by the powerful alone, but the people at large, and these were no longer to be maintained by an appeal to arms, but legislation. The law-court was the *champ clos* in which the questions of right and possession had to be maintained; and the appellant, instead of girding on his armour for the combat as in times past, had only to draw his purse-strings and fee his advocate. As was to be expected, a profession so profitable and so much in request, multiplied the practitioners to an undue amount, and attorneys became so numerous that it was thought necessary to diminish them by act of parliament. Accordingly, the king's courts in the city of Norwich, and the counties of Norfolk and Suffolk, where the attorneys had increased nearly tenfold, were selected for the prohibition; and in the reign of Henry VI, and A.D. 1455, an act was passed in which the eighty attorneys who practised in these counties were reduced to fourteen. The causes for this restriction, as they are stated in the preamble, show that the evils of litigation had fairly entered into England in the train of law and order. It was alleged that these attorneys, besides having nothing to live upon but the gains of their profession, were but little acquainted with law—that they had originated much trouble in the aforesaid city and counties, and that they were wont to "come to every market, fair, and other places where there is an assembly of people, exhorting, procuring, moving, and inciting the people to attempt untrue and foreign suits for small trespasses, little offences, and small sums of debt." These, however, appear to have been nothing better than mere pettifoggers, who either had undergone no training for the profession, or had broken down in the midst of it. This is evident from Sir John Fortescue's account of the education of lawyers, which he gives in his work *De Laudibus Legum Angliæ*. Speaking of the hostels or inns of court, he says: "In these great hostels no student can be maintained at less charge yearly than 80 scutes (£28), and if he has a servant with him, as many of them have, then is his charge the greater; so that by reason of this great expense, the sons of gentlemen do only study the law in these hostels, the vulgar sort of people not being able to undergo so great a charge; and merchants are seldom willing to lessen their traffic by undergoing such burdens." In this way the respectability of the legal profession was secured at the outset in England, by such an expensive probation that none but families of rank were willing or able to encounter it. The education itself was fully correspondent to such a demand; for he tells us further, that these residents of the hostels "did not only study the laws to serve the courts of justice and profit their country, but did further learn to dance, to sing, to play on instruments on the ferial days, and to study divinity on the festivals; using such exercises as they did who were brought up in the king's court."

As the practice of the legal profession was at this time in such high demand, and the study of law so diligently prosecuted in preference to other literary occupations, it would have been strange if this age had not at least produced some distinguished lawyer during the absence of every other kind of scholarship. Accordingly, two eminent names stand out at this period, in those of Sir John Fortescue and Sir Thomas Littleton. Fortescue, who was appointed chancellor by Henry VI., soon afterwards shared in the fate of the Lancastrian party by being driven into exile, whither he accompanied young Edward, Prince of Wales, afterwards assassinated at Tewkesbury. His chief productions were a work entitled *De Laudibus Legum Angliæ*, written in exile, in which he indoctrinates the prince upon the superiority of English law to that of other countries; and an English treatise, entitled *Of the Difference between an Absolute and Limited Monarchy*, in which he advocates the latter form of government as the best. Littleton, who was judge of Common Pleas in the reign of Edward IV., was author of the work on "Tenures," in three books written in Norman French, and addressed to his son, for whose use, in the first instance, it was composed. As he was one of the earliest, so he was also one of the best authors and authorities on English law; and the commentary upon his work has made his name at least familiar to general knowledge in the present day, under the title of "Coke upon Littleton."

The splendid dawn of English poetry which had commenced so auspiciously with Chaucer, was not followed by a correspondent sequel, so that after he and his follower Gower had passed away, nothing better was produced in the list of English poets than the very inferior names of Occleve and Lydgate. Of Thomas Occleve, we only know that he lived somewhere about the earlier part of the fifteenth century, and was the author of a considerable number of poems, most of which still remain in manuscript, while those that have been published make us scarcely regret that the rest have been consigned to obscurity. He appears, indeed, to have been a rhymer and nothing more. Considerably his superior, however, was John Lydgate, the monk of Bury, who after a course of education at the university of Oxford, travelled in France and Italy, and on returning to England, opened a school in the monastery to which he belonged, and instructed the sons of noble families in poetry and belles-lettres. He was so voluminous a writer, that Warton tells us, "to enumerate his pieces would be to write the catalogue of a little library." His chief poems, however, are three, under the titles of the "Fall of Princes," the "Siege of Troy," and the "Siege of Thebes." These were written by commission from his titled and courtly patrons; but he seems to have made verse-making a regular trade, and to have written upon any subject with equal facility. For nearly two centuries his works retained a popularity considerably beyond their merits; but afterwards, the reaction of modern taste was so much in the opposite direction, that it became a fashion with critical antiquaries to ridicule and decry them. Still, it must be confessed, that he was an accomplished scholar for the age; and that to his learning he added the experience of travel, as well as much natural shrewdness of observation, while his writings tended to amplify and refine his native tongue. Such is the testimony of Warton, who declares that he was the first of our writers whose style was clothed with that perspicuity in which the English phraseology appears at this day to an English reader.

Leaving the Literature, we now pass onward to the Architecture of England. During the present period, the Perpendicular style not only attained its highest state of perfection, but commenced its decay. In tracing the progress of this phase of Gothic architecture, it will be necessary to revert to the latter part of the reign of Edward III., at which period, as has been mentioned already (p. 524), Gothic architecture underwent its last great change. The tracery had then reached, apparently, its utmost limit, and nothing can be conceived more beautiful than some of the magnificent windows of that time. But the difficulty and costliness of executing, in the Decorated style, the large windows required for the exhibition of stained glass, occasioned a change, and led to the introduction of the Perpendicular style, which, from the predominance of straight lines, was much more easy of execution, and by this means brought about a great alteration in the appearance of churches. This change seems to have been originated by Edington, Bishop of Winchester, who rebuilt the church of his native village, Edington, in Wiltshire, between 1352 and 1361. In this church, though much of the Decorated is retained, there is an evident attempt at something different. Many of the curves are converted into straight lines, but the vertical principle is not fully carried out. This prelate shortly afterwards commenced some additions and alterations in his cathedral of Winchester in the same style, but dying before they were completed, the work was continued by his successor, William of Wykeham, who fully carried out the principles of the new style, and to whom its invention is usually attributed; although it appears to be rather due to his predecessor, for the west window of that cathedral, erected by Edington, is as decidedly Perpendicular as anything we possess. William of Wykeham proceeded with the work, and converted the Norman nave of Winchester into one of Perpendicular character, by incasing the Norman piers with Perpendicular shafts. He afterwards, in the reign of Richard II., between 1380 and 1386, built New College at Oxford, the first complete building in the style, and which, though of that early date, exhibits all its characteristics as clearly as any subsequent erection. But, though the style was thus fully developed in these instances, it did not for some time obtain a firm footing, for during the reign of Richard II., we find numerous examples of buildings which display a thorough mixture of the characters of the old and new styles, and it was not till the succeeding reign that it was fully established. It continued in use, without any material alteration, until the death of Henry VII., though in this reign a slight mixture of Italian detail may be perceived.

The broad distinction between this and the preceding styles, lies in the preponderance of upright lines, particularly observable in the tracery of windows, the panelling of flat surfaces within and without, and the multiplicity of small shafts with which the piers, &c., are overlaid. The vertical line everywhere predominates, catching the eye at first sight, so that when once this characteristic has been pointed out, it is impossible to mistake a building in this style. Another peculiarity is the increased width of the windows and the lowness of the roofs, which are frequently so low as not to rise above the parapet. This is owing to the use of the four-centred depressed arch, which gave an opportunity of employing greater width, without increasing the height of the windows. To such an extent is this peculiarity carried, that the chancel of a church of this period is almost as light as a conservatory, the whole space between the buttresses being occupied with the windows; and these, when filled with stained glass, for which they were designed, must have had a gorgeous effect, very different from their present cold appearance.

The upper tier of windows or clear-story, offers another peculiarity. In the preceding styles, these windows were generally small; but in the Perpendicular, when that style became fully developed, they are often so large and placed so closely together, that the whole clear-story almost becomes one large window, merely divided by the mullions; an arrangement which, though it adds light to the interior, detracts greatly from the appearance of the exterior of the edifice. In the earlier part of this period, the new principle was carried out, but with the feeling of the old; and the buildings exhibit the best features of the new style, without the flat, bald, and meaningless effect observable in later examples. The ante-chapel of Merton College, Oxford, is one of the best examples of this early date.

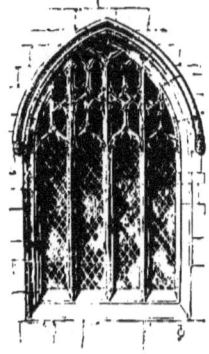

PERPENDICULAR WINDOW, St. Mary's, Taunton.

The distinctive characters of Perpendicular windows will be best understood by reference to the accompanying specimens, and comparison of them with the examples given of the preceding style (see p. 522). It will be seen that the principal mullions, instead of running into flowing tracery, are here carried straight through to the head of the window, and that the subordinate tracery is likewise converted into straight lines. In this consists the essential difference of the two styles. Beauchamp Chapel, one of the accompanying examples, exhibits not only the peculiarity in the windows just adverted to, but likewise characteristic panelling, parapets, buttresses, and turrets. The depressed arch was likewise used, particularly in the later period, for the pier arches, and thus by lowering them, gave greater space to the clear-story. It is in general used, also, for doors, but is then almost always included in a square moulding or label, the *spandrel* being filled with quatrefoils or other ornament.

PERPENDICULAR DOOR-HEAD, Westminster Abbey.

Its magnificent church-towers form a leading beauty of this style. These towers are seen in the greatest perfection in Somersetshire, and the neighbouring counties, where they form a remarkable feature in the appearance of the country.

EAST END OF THE BEAUCHAMP CHAPEL, WARWICK.

TOWER OF MAGDALEN COLLEGE, OXFORD.

They are usually divided into stages by bands of quatrefoils, each stage being filled with large windows, frequently double. The angles have large buttresses, ornamented with shafts and niches. The parapet is panelled and pierced, having lofty panelled and crocketed pinnacles at the angles, and lesser ones in the intermediate spaces. The towers of St. Mary's, Taunton, St. John's, Glastonbury, and St. Stephen's, Bristol, may be taken as the best types of this kind of tower. The effect of the Taunton tower is rich and magnificent, but it is overloaded with ornament, and cannot, for quiet grace and dignity, be compared to one of the same date, but of far less pretensions—that of Magdalen College, Oxford. In this tower the decoration is reserved entirely for the upper story, which, as it rises above the surrounding buildings, first catches the eye, the lower stages being only sufficiently relieved by windows to take away the appearance of flatness, and are thus with the truest taste subordinated to the upper. Many towers are finished with lofty spires, usually crocketed; and sometimes by an octagonal stage called a *lantern*, as at Boston, Fotheringay, and the celebrated example at Newcastle-upon-Tyne.

In the interior of the buildings, the predominance of the perpendicular line is even more striking than on the exterior. The small shafts and mouldings with which the piers are covered, the vaulting shafts, the panelling of the walls, and the mullions of the large clear-story windows give it the appearance of one mass of upright lines, while the vaulting ribs, which are now become very elaborate and intricate, form a complete network over the ceiling. That beautiful kind of vaulting called *fan-vaulting*, or *fan-tracery*, which belongs exclusively to this style, is much used in the later buildings of this period. It is peculiarly English, no examples of it being met with in foreign erections, and receives its distinctive appellation from the ribs, which rise from the shaft in the manner of a fan, curving equally in every direction, the spaces between the fans being filled with circles, quatrefoils, or frequently with pendants. Its peculiarities will be best understood by the specimen here given. The roofs of Henry VII.'s Chapel, Westminster, and King's College Chapel, Cambridge, are also of this kind; and it is much used on monuments and other minor constructions.

Many buildings of this period, instead of stone groined roofs, have open-work roofs of timber, of various design, but all having a rich and fine effect. Of these, Westminster Hall, Crosby Hall, and some of the churches in Norfolk, are choice examples.[1] A flat panelled ceiling, painted blue, with gold stars, is also frequently used. Great labour and cost were likewise bestowed on the roodlofts, stalls, screens, font-covers, and tabernacle work in churches, which were elaborately carved and richly painted and gilt. The panels were usually filled with figures of saints, and the cornices with foliage, and surmounted with a crest of flowers or *fleur-de-lis*, known as the Tudor flower, from its being

LANTERN, Boston Church, Lincolnshire.

FAN-TRACERY, Aisle, North St. George's Chapel, Windsor.

STALLS, WITH TUDOR FLOWER, Higham-Ferrers Church, Northamptonshire.

---

[1] See cut of Crosby Hall, vol. i. p. 642.

so much used in the Tudor period. The foliage, however, in this carving, and throughout the style, has in general a stiff and artificial appearance, and wants the freshness and reference to natural forms, which are found in the Decorated. The leaf chiefly imitated is the vine, but though very beautifully and delicately executed, it is converted into a quadrangular figure, and this form runs through every part of the style. The intersections of the mullions and transoms of the windows form squares, the door with its exterior label is a square, the panelling which everywhere prevails is nothing but a series of squares, and the foliage, whether it be used in cornices, on capitals, or in door-jambs, is little more than a repetition of square forms; but all this is relieved by such minute and delicate

CORNICE MOULDING, Perpendicular Style.

execution, that we overlook both the air of formality which pervades it, and the continual repetition and subdivision of the parts. For shrines and monumental chapels, this style is particularly adapted; and the multiplicity of small canopies and pinnacles, armorial and symbolical devices, of angel-brackets, and of saints in canopies, give an appearance of richness which we do not find elsewhere. Some fine specimens of this kind occur at St. Alban's.

It is in the later examples of the style, or that period which is usually designated as the *Tudor*, that we chiefly find this elaborate detail. The term *Tudor style*, though frequently used, has no very definite meaning, it being impossible to draw a line of demarcation between it and the Perpendicular style generally. A more correct term for it would be *late Perpendicular*. It differs chiefly in the more constant use of the depressed, four-centred arch, and the profuse use of panelling, of the fan-tracery vaulting, and of a peculiar dome-shaped turret instead of pinnacles. These characteristics are seen to advantage in Henry VII.'s Chapel, Westminster, St. George's Chapel, Windsor, and King's College Chapel, Cambridge; which may be taken as the true types of this variety of the Perpendicular style. In the first of these buildings the panelling is carried to such an excess that the exterior looks more like carving in wood than a stone building; and the interior is so delicately finished with its fan-vaulting and graceful pendants, and its lines of lace-like cusping, that one can scarcely reconcile its appearance to the fact of its being wrought in so brittle a material. The term *Tudor*, as applied to domestic architecture, has more meaning, since it describes a distinct class of buildings, which will be more fully treated of under the next period.

The Perpendicular style is much used for domestic buildings; and during the period when it prevailed, many of the colleges in Oxford and Cambridge were built. Some of the gateways,

GATEWAY OF TRINITY COLLEGE, CAMBRIDGE.—From Le Keux's Memorials of Cambridge.

in both universities, display great architectural beauty, as the one to the cloisters at Magdalen College, and that of Brazen-nose College, Oxford, and Trinity College, Cambridge. Beautiful examples of the graceful form of window known as the *oriel*, occur in domestic buildings of the period. The one here given displays many of the peculiar characters of the style.

There seems to have been a tendency, all through this style, to exaggerate its defects and to lose sight of its beauties. In the earlier examples, though the principal mullions are carried through to the head of the window, the eye is not offended, as by a judicious subdividing of

ORIEL WINDOW, Baliol College, Oxford.

the space, the straight lines are not perceived; but afterwards this was not attended to—in many cases all the mullions were carried through, and large spaces left in the window-head. Everything seems to have given way to the desire to provide openings for stained glass. This is painfully apparent in the Abbey Church at Bath, where the effect in the interior is flat

THE ABBEY CHURCH, BATH.

and poor in the extreme. Here strength and solidity are sacrificed to the craving for glass; and the clear-story, which, in the former styles, was merely intended for lighting the centre of the nave, and was consequently subordinate to the windows of the aisles, is made a principal feature, its windows much exceeding in size those of the lower tier, and giving the building a false and unnatural appearance. This edifice, which was erected immediately anterior to the Reformation, and was scarcely finished when that event took place, may be considered as almost the last example of Gothic. Italian features had already begun to be mixed with it, and these increased so much in the next reign that it ceased to be a distinctive style. Under the next period we shall endeavour to trace this mixture of ideas until at last it merged into the Renaissance, and the revival of classic architecture.

In turning our inquiries to the progress and improvement of the Scots during this period, we still find our materials both scanty and obscure. The Scottish kings were not absolute sovereigns, as in other countries of Europe, but of limited power and authority; and it depended upon their own individual energies whether that little might not be reduced to an absolute nonentity. Hence the difficulty of understanding the form of government that prevailed in Scotland, as compared with that of England. If the Scottish king was brave and active, he could only maintain his regal superiority by availing himself of the mutual jealousies of his nobles, and arming the one half against the other; but if, on the other hand, he was weak or facile, he generally sank into their tool, and reigned by their sufferance. All this is evident in the history of Robert Bruce, as contrasted with that of Robert III.; or of James I. and James II. with that of James III. In either case, it was a continual struggle for superiority between king and nobles, where the latter claimed an independence almost equal to his own. In the case of these sovereigns, also, we find nothing of that divinity that hedges a king, by which his person is invested with such sacredness as to exempt it from violence, and his authority with such abstract right that to resist it is sinful, as well as unconstitutional. On the contrary, when a vassal rebelled, he had only to send letters to his sovereign, renouncing all further allegiance, and bidding him defiance, in which case he was no longer a traitor but an open enemy, and might even slay the king should the opportunity be within his reach. Such was the argument of Sir Robert Graham, a man well versed in the laws of Scotland, when he was placed upon his trial for the assassination of James I. By letters under his hand he had disclaimed the king's authority and proclaimed himself the mortal enemy of James, upon whom he would inflict his worst; and after this, he thought himself justified in striking down the king, even within the sacred precincts of a monastery. His judges might therefore slay him in return, now that the opportunity was theirs; but to torture him as well as put him to death, was a stretch of tyranny which the law of Scotland could not justify.

These restrictions upon the regal authority, lead us to a consideration of that feudalism by which they were imposed. In England, the nobility established over the country by William, were Norman conquerors, whose lands and privileges were the rewards of violence and oppression; and the people, who continued to regard them as strangers and as enemies, thought themselves entitled to recover their own lost rights, as soon as they were strong enough for the purpose. Hence the jealousy with which the English nobility were watched by the commons, and the facility with which an English sovereign could pull these temporary tyrants down, when he adopted the wise policy of making himself strong in the affections of the people. But the character, as well as the origin of Scottish feudalism, was different. The founders of its noble families, although for the most part Normans also, had entered the country not as conquerors, but refugees or malcontents, and were received with that distinction which was due to their bravery, military skill, and superior civilization. They thus became Scotland's best counsellors in peace and leaders in war, and the lands and honours which they won in the new home of their adoption, were the willing awards of a grateful king and people. In this way, they became not the lordly oppressors, but the fathers and protectors of their Scottish vassals, and the feeling of devotedness towards their feudal superiors became in the hearts of the latter a downright national characteristic. Possessed of such power, and surrounded by such adherents, it was no wonder if, in process of time, these nobles became envious of the regal authority, and sought to repress it. This was all the more natural, as the Scottish kings, whether of the Bruce or Stuart line, had originally been nothing more than Norman nobles like themselves, and had been elevated to the throne by a lucky combination of chances. Hence the power of the Scottish nobility, and their readiness to turn it against the sovereign; so that while England had only one Leicester, and one Hotspur, and one Warwick, Scotland had a hundred.

In a country by nature so sterile, and among a people so incessantly occupied either with intestine wars or English invasions, the arts of agriculture were not likely to be well understood, or even greatly cared for. A feudal lord, who wished to increase his followers, had only to subdivide his barren acres into roods, and the families so located had neither the means nor the stimulus to turn such miserable strips into regular, well-cultivated farms. Besides, with even more ample means, the Scottish agriculturist had little inducement to plough or sow when he knew not by what hand the harvest might be gathered. When an English army crossed the Border it generally drove into the heart of the kingdom, eating whatever produce it could find, and destroying what it could not use; and when the peasants returned after the invasion was over, they found nothing but wasted fields and empty larders. Their only hope of present subsistence in this case arose from a counter-foray into England, with which they generally requited every inroad of the enemy, and thus they contrived to indemnify themselves for their losses among the rich corn-fields and fat pastures of Cumberland and Northumberland. Added to these evils by which agricultural industry was checked, may be mentioned the tenures upon which farms were generally held, where the leases only lasted from year to year, so that the occupant might be displaced upon a very short notice. The rent, too, was commonly paid by military service; and thus, while the farmer was almost continually in harness under the banner of his lord, his fields were left to the cultivation of women, children, and villains, as villanage was still continued in Scotland after it had ceased in England. All these causes not only serve to explain the very defective state of Scottish agriculture, but might make us wonder how such a numerous population could have been supported, did we not call to mind how heavily the whole English border was taxed by the hungry stomachs of their northern antagonists. Pasturage, rather than tillage, indeed, formed the main dependence of the Scots, as this required little labour, while the cattle, in the event of an inroad, could be driven to the hills and fastnesses. But if the miseries of famine were so destructive in England, with all its industry and abundance, we may conceive what such visitations were in Scotland, whose inhabitants, even at the best, were generally confined to scanty rations. Conscious of the prevalent national defect, and anxious to assimilate his native country to the improved state of England, James I. endeavoured to amend its agriculture, but this, too, was by act of parliament, for which his subjects little cared. By this act every farmer having a plough and eight oxen was required to sow annually a firlot of wheat, half a firlot of pease, and *forty* beans, under a penalty of ten shillings; and every baron to sow a like quantity upon his own ground, under a forfeiture of four times the sum.

Besides destroying peaceful industry by converting the peasantry into soldiers, the wars with England created more than one class of society, by which the progress of Scottish civilization was heavily retarded. And first of these, we should mention the moss-troopers, men who lived upon the Border, and were therefore exposed to the first brunt of every onset. As they were thus the outposts of a hostile encampment, they were, by birth, necessity, habit, and inclination, soldiers, and nothing else; men who lived by English plunder, and generally died upon an English gallows, if they were not so fortunate as to die in harness, and upon the battle-field. Sometimes, also, when English plunder was not so abundant, or so easily reached, they betook themselves to what they modestly called "a little shifting for their living," and robbed the pasturages or granaries of their own inland countrymen as readily as those of the Southrons, of whom they were the born and sworn enemies. Such men, notwithstanding their gallant services in a national campaign, were the very scourges of their country, not only by their dishonest modes of living, but their restless belligerent propensities, so that no peace could be formed with England which they were not ready to break, or internal feud commenced into which they were unwilling to throw themselves. But besides these moss-troopers, who were amenable to the Border laws and subject to the rule of the Border wardens, there were the broken clans, composed of communities settled upon those portions of the Border usually called Debateable land. These men, who had lost their feudal lords, as well as their native homes, and been driven hither and thither by the continual shifting of the boundary line between the two kingdoms, at length came to regard both as their natural enemies, and robbed either indiscriminately, while it was difficult to follow them into their fastnesses, or drive them from their strongholds. A less formidable, but equally pernicious class, whom the wars with England tended to create, were the sturdy beggars, otherwise called *sorners* or *gaberlunzies*, who multiplied in Scotland to an incredible extent. These, too, were not exclusively composed of the lowest of society; on the contrary, many of them either were, or pretended to be, men of gentle birth, although impoverished in their circumstances; and, upon the strength of their honourable descent, they pursued their humble vocation, not in rags, and with a piteous whine, but with horses, hawks, and attendants, so that where they could not obtain admission in virtue of their high-sounding names, they were able to enforce it by storm or onslaught. These jackdaws, however, were often detected, stripped of their borrowed plumes, and driven forth to herd with their own kind. But still, beggary continued to thrive, on account of that mistaken hospitality which would allow no one to pass the door, as well as that craving for news which is always strongest in a divided and thinly-peopled country, so that Scotland remained pre-eminently a land of sturdy beggars, until they dwindled into the Bluegowns and Edie Ochiltrees of the close of the eighteenth century.

While such were the consequences which the wars of the two rival countries entailed upon Scotland, on account of its being by far the weaker and the poorer, the war usages and customs of the Scots demand our consideration, as these constituted a large portion of the every-day life of the people. This subject, however, is so fully explained in the history of their military achievements, that it may be dismissed with a brief notice. The training and customs of chivalry among them, were of the same kind that prevailed not only in England, but over Europe; and the country produced such stalwart knights as England or Europe could seldom have overmatched. There was little, however, of tournament practice in Scotland, owing to the poverty of the people, and their constant occupation in the realities of war, although its knights, when summoned to the trial, could back a war-horse and couch a lance as skilfully as the best. One favourite weapon of these champions was the axe, which, notwithstanding its unwieldiness, they could handle, according to Froissart, with wonderful dexterity, and deal with it such strokes that, according to the great chronicler's favourite phrase, "it was a pleasure to behold them." Of this, indeed, the encounter of Bruce at Bannockburn with De Bohun was a sufficient testimony. While tournaments were seldom held in Scotland, single combats, either judicial or from private feud, were of almost constant occurrence, and were fought out on horseback with the lance, or on foot with the two-handed sword, or axe and dagger. A terrible display of this kind, happily unique in the history of chivalry, was given at Perth in the reign of Robert III., between the chosen champions of two rival Highland clans, thirty on each side, from which only one man escaped unwounded. As in the wars between the English and Scots the former were generally the assailants, their favourite weapon, the long-bow, was well fitted for such a purpose; while the Scots, who stood on the defensive, and generally fought on foot, preferred the spear eighteen feet in length, with which they stood shoulder to shoulder, presenting such a bristly array that neither cavalry could easily break through their ranks, nor infantry reach them. This was well when matters came to a close hand-to-hand engagement, in which the Scots were generally the victors; but when the English, on the other hand, depended upon their archery, and contented themselves with a distant fight, it was then

"Alas, alas for Scotland
When England's arrows fly!"

It was singular that the Scots profited so little by the lesson which Bruce gave them at Bannockburn, when he let loose among the English archers a small body of mounted men-at-arms, who quickly cut them down, or drove them back upon the main army; and thus their defeats were generally caused by those fatal shafts to which their serried ranks offered an easy and unresisting mark. But after the reign of Henry V., the lesson of Bruce would have come too late on account of the sharp-pointed stakes which the former caused his bowmen to carry, and with which they could effectually stockade their position on every part of the field. The Scots, indeed, were not wholly without archers; but these were generally Highlanders or Islesmen, whom the Lowlanders heartily hated; and their bows of four feet long, where the string was only drawn to the breast, could not send an arrow with the same distant range and deadly force that were given to the "cloth-yard shaft." The Scottish kings, especially James I. and James II., anxious to make their subjects a full match in every kind of conflict to their enemies, endeavoured to introduce among them the longbow, and the careful apprenticeship which it required; and accordingly the popular out-door sports were prohibited. Every male above the age of twelve was to practise archery, and butts were to be erected at every village church, at which every man was to shoot at least six arrows each holiday, while the defaulter was to forfeit twopence as drink-money to those who gave regular attendance. But the Scots, still more impatient of such coercion than their rivals had ever been, chose rather to be shot with English arrows than learn to requite them, and accordingly the spear of six ells long, which needed little beyond a stout heart and steady hand, continued to be the favourite and national weapon, until, like the English bow, it was superseded by hagbut, arquebuse, and matchlock, and, better still, by the bayonet.

As war was of necessity so much the occupation of the Scots, the war-laws were sufficiently numerous. These chiefly regarded Border inroads and the division of plunder—matters, as we have seen, of paramount importance in the military operations of the country. As invasions also from England were so frequent and sudden, the system of war-signals in Scotland was brought even at an early period to a considerable state of improvement. The laws of James II. in this respect were well suited to the requirement. All the fords and passages of the Tweed by which the English could cross, were to be carefully watched, and bale-fires or beacons to be established at each, to give notice of the coming enemy. The nature of the invasion was distinctly announced by the number of fires that were lighted. Thus, one beacon kindled, gave warning that an inroad from England was apprehended; two such signals announced that it was certain; and when four were lighted, it was a token that the invaders were coming in great numbers. From Hume Castle, the nearest point, these signals were taken up and transmitted to Edgerton; from Edgerton they passed to Soutra Edge, and thence to Dunbar, Haddington, Dalkeith, Edinburgh, and the Lothians, so that in a few hours the most populous districts could be warned and in readiness over the whole kingdom. The military muster, from a band to a numerous army, according to the nature of the warning, could be effected with almost equal promptitude, as every peasant was a trained soldier, bound to repair to the banner of his feudal landlord, and more or less completely armed, according to the amount of land he held in fee. All these points were minutely specified by laws, which were as familiar as household words, and every man knew his place and duty, however sudden might be the summons. The campaign, however, was necessarily a short one, as each soldier carried his own provisions, and these only for forty days at the utmost; and hence the impatience of the Scottish armies to decide the contest at once, and by a pitched battle, although against more numerous and better armed antagonists. The case, however, was different when the war was carried into England; for there, the Scottish soldier's little bag of oatmeal could be replaced from the well-stored girnels and abundant stalls of the south with richer fare, in which he revelled with a zest for which his previous short commons had fully prepared him. When the English viands were thus found, the ingenuity of military Scottish cookery was by no means wanting; for the bullock's hide supplied not only a regimental caldron for boiling the carcass, but shoes for the march, while the animal's horns sufficed for trumpets to cheer the invaders on the way, or sound to the onset.

In a society so diversified as that of Scotland, and amidst such a constant whirl of events and changes, it is difficult to describe within a narrow compass the every-day life of the people, and the manners and customs that prevailed among them. Not only every district, but every village had its palatial edifice, from the castle of the great noble, to the peel or single square tower of the baron; and in each of these was generally contained the right of pit and gallows, so that its master, however limited his territory, was absolute sovereign over it, and might hang or imprison his offending vassals according to his own good pleasure. To these strongholds also, on the approach of the enemy, the women and children repaired for shelter, while the chief's retainers from the age of sixteen to sixty manned the walls, or marched out to the open field. At the best, however, these castles were but sorry buildings when compared with the stately residences of the English nobility, and even the palaces of the Scottish kings, up to the close of this period, were roofed with thatch. The style of living within these castles was often as coarse as it was precarious, more especially when their victualling depended upon a successful inroad into England, or a foray in which cattle was to be lifted from friend and enemy indifferently—as was, for the most part, the case over the Border counties. As far, however, as attendants went, there was no lack of grandeur, for every tower was a crowded hive of jackmen, grooms, and gillies, while every chief when he rode forth had generally a whole regiment of retainers at his heels. A Douglas was usually accompanied by 1200 followers, practised in battle and armed to the teeth, while the trains of the chief nobility were scarcely inferior. This was all the more necessary, when each had a score of feuds on his hands, and might have as many encounters in a journey from Jedburgh to Holyrood. While the habitations and style of living among the noblest was so rude and uncomfortable, notwithstanding the external pomp and glitter of feudal authority with which they were surrounded, the condition of the commons corresponded with that of their lords. Such was the case especially in the reign of James I., when Æneas Sylvius, afterwards Pius II., made an adventurous visit into Scotland. Upon the Borders he found that most of the houses were not even huts, as they were generally a small breast-work composed of mud, or such materials as were at hand, and raised to a sufficient height by three or four poles meeting a-top, and covered with straw or turf; while those of the villages were little better, and had no door but a cow's hide suspended at the entrance. As for the towns, the houses were generally built of wood, but if of stone, then lime was omitted. This will sufficiently explain the cause of so little domestic architecture being indicated in Scotland previous to the sixteenth century, except in the ruins of strong castles that either defied every attack, or were thought not worth the trouble of demolition. From the Border to the metropolis, no one thought of building a costly edifice, which a single hour of foreign invasion or domestic feud might level to the ground. That neither the will nor the ability, however, was wanting, was sufficiently attested by the stately cathedrals and monasteries that towered above the huts of their builders, and upon which all the resources of architecture were expended, in the hope that their sacredness would be respected by a Christian foe. But the feeling of the Macedonian conqueror was awanting, and therefore, while temple and tower went to the ground, the "house of Pindarus" would not have been spared. The noble ruins of Kelso, Jedburgh, Melrose, and Dryburgh Abbeys, are melancholy monuments of what Scotland might have achieved in architecture, had not the battle for national independence occurred, to task all her energies, as well as exhaust all her resources.

While comfortable homes and the details of domestic life were thus so materially affected by these wars, the graces that impart a charm to them were not only unknown, but even their very entrance into Scotland was obstinately resisted. This, too, originated, in a great measure, in that intense national hatred which made them regard every refinement as English, and therefore hostile and abominable. Such was especially the case on the return of James I. to Scotland, when

he attempted to cure the barbarism of his subjects by those new arts of life which he had learned in his captivity, and the benefits of which none was better able to appreciate. But although comforts were multiplied by the change to a degree hitherto unknown in the country, the worst evils followed in their train—ease, luxury, and licentiousness—by which public tranquillity was destroyed, and individual sobriety corrupted. Hence arose sumptuous entertainments by day, and revellings by night, a love of attire of the most costly foreign materials, houses built not for use but for show, and a perversion of manners under the name of elegance, so that native customs came to be despised, and nothing was esteemed graceful or becoming that was not new. So says Buchanan, in the full rhetorical style of the ancients whom he loved to imitate; and unfortunately he was not alone in his judgment, for the grim nobles of the court of James were equally hostile to these innovations, so that while they denounced them as the fopperies of the queen and the English courtiers who had accompanied her to Scotland, they condemned them as subversive of that manly courage, hardihood, and simplicity which hitherto had formed the best distinctions of their countrymen. The king was compelled to yield to the storm, and the consequence was a sumptuary law enacted by the parliament at Perth in 1430. By this it was decreed, that none should wear pearls but ladies, and that, too, only in a small collar around the neck, while the use of furs and ermines, and gold and silver lace, was prohibited, as also banquetings, riotous feastings, and all such foreign luxuries. In this way the storm was quieted for the present, but only to break out in a new form, and with greater violence, under his grandson James III. This unfortunate king, imbued with a taste for the fine arts that was considerably in advance of his age, delighted chiefly in the society of architects, musicians, and connoisseurs in graceful attire and ornament. But here again the nobility interposed. Their self-love was wounded, and their ignorance and grossness rebuked, by his attachment to such favourites, whom they stigmatized as masons, fiddlers, and tailors; and their hostility never rested until these unfortunate men were hanged over Lauder bridge, and the king himself despatched by the dagger of an assassin.

Hitherto, the few learned men that Scotland produced, had been indebted for their acquirements to the universities of England or France, but at last, in the fifteenth century, the country was provided with colleges of its own. The first of these was the university of St. Andrews, erected by its bishop, Henry Wardlaw. This eminent individual, who was appointed to the

Scottish primacy in 1404, while he was residing in the Papal court at Avignon, found, on his return to his native country, everything in a confusion that was soon after deepened by the death of Robert III., the capture and imprisonment of the young prince, afterwards James I., and the usurpation of the Duke of Albany. Wardlaw, who was an accomplished scholar as well as able statesman and true-hearted patriot, was keenly alive to the chief source of this disorder and misrule, and addressed himself to cure it by the benefits of education, which the priesthood and nobility needed almost as much as the people at large. This was a formidable as well as hostile aggression, and needed to be cautiously commenced. He first formed an association at St. Andrews of such scholars as the country then possessed, who gave lectures upon the subjects that were usually taught at colleges—divinity, logic, physics, and the canon and civil laws. In this way, having established the reality of a university without the name, his next step was to invest it with a charter or grant of privileges, which he did in 1411; and two years afterwards, these privileges were confirmed by six Papal bulls sent by Benedict XIII., which were received in St. Andrews with the ringing of bells, the lighting of bonfires, and every demonstration of popular triumph. James I., on his return from captivity, fostered the rising institution, which at length comprised thirteen doctors of divinity, and eight doctors of laws, as its teachers, while the students amounted to several thousands. At first, the professors had no fixed salaries, and the students paid no fees, while the only building for the delivery of lectures was a large wooden edifice called the pedagogy. But in 1455, James Kennedy, the successor of Wardlaw, built and endowed the college of St. Salvator. The chief reason assigned for the founding of the university was, the consideration "of the many dangers and inconveniences to which the clergy of Scotland who desired to be instructed in theology, the canon and civil laws, medicine, and the liberal arts, were exposed, from wars and other impediments, in their journeys to foreign *studia generalia*, in consequence of there being no such institution to which they might repair in their own country." The injunctions laid upon these ecclesiastics while they attended college, give us a strange idea of the morals of the Scottish clergy of this period. They were to live decently according to their sacred calling, "so as not to keep concubines *publicly*, nor to be common night-walkers or robbers, or habitually guilty of other notorious crimes." Was it in consequence of these restrictions that so few of the clergy availed themselves of a university so expressly founded for their benefit? At all events, nothing is more certain than that, while the laity were eager to improve themselves by its instructions, the priesthood stood aloof, or opposed it. But Divine as well as poetical justice requited them in the following century for their criminal remissness, for it was chiefly from this university that the Reformation issued, before which they were swept away.

The next Scottish establishment of the kind was the university of Glasgow, founded by William Turnbull. This ecclesiastic having been appointed bishop of that see in 1448, addressed himself to the erection of a college in that city, and obtained a bull to that effect from Nicholas V. at the beginning of 1450. The grant was for the establishment of a university there in all time; and the reason given for the preference of that locality was, on account of its "being ane notable place, with gude air, and plenty of provisions for human life," while all the privileges, rights, honours, and exemptions were conferred upon it, that had been bestowed upon the university of Bononia. In order still further to aggrandize the institution, which commenced its labours in 1451, the bull granted a universal indulgence to all faithful Christians who should visit the cathedral of Glasgow during that year. At first the building was a humble tenement on the south side of the Rottenrow near the cathedral, but afterwards, the college was transferred to its present residence, in consequence of a rich bequest for that purpose from Lord Hamilton. Originally, as in the case of St. Andrews, no salaries were attached to the professorships ; no lands nor rents belonged to the institution, and the fees of the students were so small as to be scarcely worth taking into account. But the high privileges with which the university was endowed as a self-governing independent body, were a sufficient counterpoise to this lack of funds or emolument; so that rich ecclesiastics as well as poor scholars were glad to enrol themselves among its members. As in the case of St. Andrews, the course of study and form of government were modelled upon those of the university of Paris. Both of these Scottish colleges, instead of being monastic institutions, where the students were lodged within the walls and supported at a common table, were rather great academies, composed of class-rooms which the students attended daily during the prescribed hours. This was all in the way of education that so poor a country as Scotland was able in the first instance to accomplish.

While Scotland was not more distinguished than England had been during this period for men of high attainment in literature and science, the case was different in poetry; for in this respect Scotland has names to offer with which her more richly-endowed rival was unable to compete. The first as well as the most distinguished was James I., that minstrel king, whose poetical history was as romantic as his political career, but without the same stormy troubles or melancholy termination. His iniquitous capture and detention in England by Henry IV. have been already narrated. As if to quiet his conscience by softening the evils of this unjust captivity, Henry supplied the young prince with an education far beyond what he could have enjoyed in his own country, and by this James profited so highly, that he became an accomplished knight and statesman, as well as ripe and learned scholar. It was with poetry that he seems to have chiefly solaced his imprisonment in the castle of Windsor; and how could he have otherwise than succeeded, under the inspiration that so soon converted his prison into a palace?

"And therewith kest I down myn eye ageyne,
Quhare as I saw walkyng under the Toure,
Fall secretly, new comyn hir to pleyne
The fairest or the freschest young floure
That ever I sawe, methoght, before that houre;
For which sodayne abate, anon astert,
The blude of all my body to my heart."

This beautiful apparition was Lady Jane Beaufort, thenceforth his muse, and finally his queen. He became a poet scarcely inferior to Chaucer himself, who was his model; and his principal poem, entitled the *King's Quhair* (*quire* or book); is the only work in English worthy of being placed by the side of the *Canterbury Tales.* Several other poetical works have been attributed to him, but from their character and style, they were more likely to have been the productions of James V., his talented descendant.

Another distinguished Scottish poet of this period was Henry the Minstrel, better known among the people at large by the homely epithet of Blind Harry. Of his personal history there is little known, except that he belonged to that class now proscribed in Scotland among the "vagabondis, fuilis, and sic like idill peopill;" that he recited his ballads from house to house for a living, and that he was born blind. All this gave little promise of the celebrity he was afterwards to acquire among his countrymen. But happily he hit upon a popular theme, which was the life and adventures of Sir William Wallace, the almost worshipped national hero, which he must have composed between the years 1470 and 1480; and the materials of the work, he informs us, were chiefly derived from the *Life of Wallace*, written in Latin by John Blair, the chaplain of the hero, and amplified by Thomas Gray. In classical refinement, depth of reflection, and historical fidelity, the poem of *Wallace* cannot stand comparison with Barbour's *Bruce;* but as a spirit-stirring narrative, as well as descriptive epic, it is greatly superior to that of the philosophical archdeacon; so that while the latter work was chiefly confined to the reflective few, the former obtained a universal acceptance among the peasantry of Scotland, whom it roused and animated in the great struggle for national independence. In this way, the blind minstrel became the Homer of his country. Even, too, when his language had become all but a dead letter to common readers, and when Barbour was almost forgotten, the poetical fame of Henry suffered little diminution, as his *Wallace* was faithfully modernized by William Hamilton of Gilbertfield, the friend and correspondent of Allan Ramsay, and in this condition continues to be a favourite in almost every cottage of Scotland.

A third Scottish poet, but of a different character from the preceding, was Robert Henryson or Henderson, of whose life little is known, except that he was chief schoolmaster of Dunfermline during the fifteenth century. Classical and elegant in taste and refined in language, his poetry is a complete contrast to the rough trumpet-like strains of Blind Harry, as well as his favourite themes, which were chiefly recommendatory of peacefulness, purity, and religious contemplation. He wrote a collection of fables, thirteen in number, also the tale of *Orpheus* founded on the old classical story, and the *Bludy Serk*, an allegorical tale, in which the highest doctrines of Christianity are impersonated in the adventures of a young prince freeing a king's daughter from captivity. But the best known of his works are the *Testament of Cresseid*, written as a sequel to Chaucer's *Troylus and Cresseyde*, and *Robene and Makyne*, the earliest pastoral poem written in the English language. The poetical merits of Henryson are thus justly summed up by P. F. Tytler: "Of the works of this remarkable man it is difficult, when we consider the period in which they were written, to speak in terms of too warm encomium. In strength, and sometimes even in sublimity of painting, in pathos and sweetness, in the variety and beauty of his pictures of natural scenery, in the vein of quiet and playful humour, which runs through many of his pieces, and in that fine natural taste, which, rejecting the faults of his age, has dared to think for itself, he is altogether excellent."

BOOK VI.

PERIOD FROM THE ACCESSION OF HENRY VII. TO THE END OF THE REIGN OF ELIZABETH.—118 YEARS.

FROM A.D. 1485—1603.

CONTEMPORARY PRINCES.

England.	Spain.	Germany.	
1485 HENRY VII.	1474 ISAB. and FERDINAND.	1440 FREDERICK IV.	1522 ADRIAN VI.
1509 HENRY VIII.	1516 CHARLES I.	1493 MAXIMILIAN I.	1523 CLEMENT VII.
1547 EDWARD VI.	1556 PHILIP II.	1519 CHARLES V.	1534 PAUL III.
1553 MARY.	1598 PHILIP III.	1558 FERDINAND I.	1550 JULIUS III.
1558 ELIZABETH.	**France.**	1564 MAXIMILIAN II.	1555 MARCELLUS II.
	1483 CHARLES VIII.	1576 RODOLPH II.	1555 PAUL IV.
Scotland.	1498 LOUIS XII.		1559 PIUS IV.
1460 JAMES III.	1515 FRANCIS I.	**Popes.**	1566 PIUS V.
1488 JAMES IV.	1547 HENRY II.	1484 INNOCENT VIII.	1572 GREGORY XIII.
1513 JAMES V.	1559 FRANCIS II.	1492 ALEXANDER VI.	1585 SIXTUS V.
1542 MARY.	1560 CHARLES IX.	1503 PIUS III.	1590 URBAN VII.
1567 JAMES VI.	1574 HENRY III.	1503 JULIUS II.	1590 GREGORY XIV.
	1589 HENRY IV.	1513 LEO X.	1591 INNOCENT IX.
			1592 CLEMENT VIII.

CHAPTER I.—CIVIL AND MILITARY HISTORY.—A.D. 1485—1492.

HENRY VII.—ACCESSION, A.D. 1485—DEATH, A.D. 1509.

Accession of the Earl of Richmond to the crown as Henry VII.—Edward Plantagenet, son of the Duke of Clarence, imprisoned in the tower—Reception of Henry VII. in London after his victory at Bosworth—His coronation—Adjustment of his royal rights—Date established for the commencement of his reign—Act for the settlement of the crown—Henry unites the rival claims of York and Lancaster by marrying the Princess Elizabeth—Dispensation of the pope for the marriage—Royal progress of Henry through the kingdom—Appearance of a pretender to the throne as Earl of Warwick—He is crowned in Ireland—He invades England—Is defeated at Stoke—Henry's avaricious proceedings—His policy under the growing predominance of France—He receives bribes from France, and deserts the Bretons—Indignation of his subjects at his conduct—Events in Brittany in connection with England—Henry's coalition with foreign powers against France—France obtains possession of Brittany—Henry makes traffic of the popular discontent against France—His pretended invasion of France.

RICHARD being removed from the scene, the person that gave most uneasiness to the conqueror of Bosworth Field was Edward Plantagenet, Earl of Warwick, son and heir to the late Duke of Clarence, who for some time had been kept a prisoner in the manor-house of Sheriff-Hutton, in Yorkshire, by the jealous fears of his uncle Richard. This unfortunate boy was indisputably the next heir of the house of York after the Princess Elizabeth; he had even at one time been treated by his uncle Richard III. as heir-apparent; and as he was already in his fifteenth year, he was not likely to be overlooked by Henry, who had "the ingenious forecast of the subtle serpent." Before leaving Leicester, he sent Sir Robert Willoughby to remove the captive from Sheriff-Hutton to London, where the young prince, "born to perpetual calamity, was incontinent in the Tower of London put under safe and sure custody."[1] At Sheriff-Hutton[2] Edward Plantagenet had for a short time a fellow-prisoner, if not a companion, in the Princess Elizabeth, who had been sent thither by her uncle Richard soon after the failure of his scheme for marrying her. This lady, not long after Edward Plantagenet's removal to the Tower, was brought up to London, and was there lodged with her mother, the queen-dowager, Elizabeth Woodville.

---

[1] *Hall.*

[2] This edifice was erected in the time of Stephen (1140) by Bertram de Bulmer, from whose family it descended by marriage to the Nevils, who held it till the battle of Barnet, in 1471, when Richard Nevil, Earl of Warwick, was slain, and his

From Leicester, Henry travelled by easy journeys towards the capital; and when he approached the city on the 27th of August, five days after the battle of Bosworth Field, the mayor, aldermen, and companies, all clad in violet, met him at Hornsey Wood, and, with great pomp, conveyed him through the city to St. Paul's Church, where he offered his three standards on the high altar — one, an image of St. George; the second, a red dragon; the third, a dun-cow — and after prayers said and *Te Deum* sung, he departed to the bishop's palace, and there sojourned a season; during which time plays, pastimes, and pleasures were showed in every part of the city.[1] These profane amusements were interspersed with religious pageants: immense processions were ordered to express the hearty and humble thanks of *the people*, who, it was said (rather prematurely), had been restored to liberty and freedom. The concourse of people in the capital, and their constant meeting in great crowds, appears to have spread a disease which had been for some time raging with less violence in the provinces.[2] The "sweating sickness," as it was called from one of its symptoms, is not easy of description; but it was an epidemic that committed great ravages, and which, like the plague, generally proved fatal within a very short time. It began in London about the 21st of September, and continued till the end of October. We are not told that this visitation, so inauspicious at the beginning of a new reign and dynasty, was held to be a judgment, though it may have been so considered by some of the losing party, who had no historians. When the malady abated, Henry prepared for his coronation. On the eve of St. Simon and Jude, he rode from Kennington to Lambeth, and there dined with Thomas Bourchier, Cardinal-archbishop of Canterbury; and after dinner, with a goodly company of lords, both spiritual and temporal, he went by land towards London, his nobles riding, "after the guise of France, upon small hackneys, two and two upon a horse;" and, at London bridge end, he was met

MANOR-HOUSE OF SHERIFF-HUTTON.—From a drawing by Whittock.

CARRIAGE OF THE PERIOD.[3]—Archæologia.

and welcomed by John Warde, the new mayor, with his brethren and the crafts. The king took up his lodging in the Tower. There, on the following day, the 28th of October, he made a num-

---

estates confiscated. Edward IV. bestowed it upon his brother, subsequently Richard III., and it became the prison of Edward Plantagenet, son of the unfortunate Duke of Clarence, who was confined within its walls until the death of Richard on Bosworth Field: the Princess Elizabeth of York, afterwards consort of Henry VII., was also confined here. The castle and manor remained in the hands of the crown till 1625, when they were granted to the Ingrams.

[1] Hall; Stow.
[2] It will be remembered that Stanley excused his non-attendance on King Richard by saying that he was laid up with the sweating sickness. See vol. i. p. 650.
[3] Henry entered London in a clumsy, *close* carriage, carefully shut up so as to conceal his person. The Londoners, who had always been accustomed to see their kings ride on horseback, thought this a very bad sign.

ber of promotions. His uncle Jasper, Earl of Pembroke, was made Duke of Bedford; the Lord Stanley, who had put the crown upon his head on Bosworth Field, was made Earl of Derby; and Sir Edward Courtenay was raised to the rank of Earl of Devonshire. On the 30th of October, Henry was, with all ceremonies accustomed, anointed and crowned king, by Bourchier, the cardinal-archbishop, who, little more than two years before, had performed the same ceremonies for Richard.

On the 7th of November, he met his parliament at Westminster for the proper establishment of affairs.[1] It seems quite certain that Henry, from the battle of Bosworth Field to the last days of his life, considered himself indebted for the throne to his sword, and he always fixed that battle as the epoch of his accession.[2] Now, when the commons waited upon him to present their speaker, he told them that he had come to the throne " by just title of inheritance, and by the sure judgment of God, who had given him the victory over his enemy in the field." It was found immediately that a great many of the members of the new House of Commons were persons attainted and outlawed by Richard or his brother Edward, for their adherence to the house of Lancaster, or for other causes; and it was also remarked that Henry himself, who had called this parliament, had been attainted. The commons therefore questioned whether their house were lawfully constituted, and the king, to his great displeasure, was obliged to refer the case to all the judges, who assembled in the exchequer chamber. The judges determined that such members of the House of Commons, as were attainted by course of law must forbear taking their seats till an act should be passed for the reversal of their attainder: as for what regarded the king himself, they asserted it as a maxim, that the crown takes away all defects and stops in blood, and that, from the time the king took upon himself royal authority, the fountain was cleared, and all attainders and corruptions of blood discharged.[3] The elections had been made before the blood was well dried upon Bosworth Field; the spirit of the aristocracy (and the people were as yet too weak to oppose the royal power without it) was broken and degraded—evaporated with the noble blood shed in the score of battles fought during the wars of the Roses, or upon the scaffold; and men of all classes had acquired, by long practice, a wonderful facility in discovering and siding with the strongest party. No Yorkist opposition of a serious nature was therefore to be expected in the house which, not many months before, had rung with the unanimous praise of King Richard; and, by a single act, all the attainted members were restored to their rights and then took their seats.[4]

Henry in reason ought to have been satisfied with the declaration which effaced all former blemishes and deficiencies, and made him a good and lawful king from the time he assumed the crown, which was on the field of battle; but he resolved to be a king even before that time, in order to punish men for treason which had never been committed, unless he could antedate his royal existence. This antedating involved some very curious points: if he claimed the crown by right of his descent from the house of Lancaster, he might have been expected to date from his boyhood or from the murder of Henry VI.; if people looked to the rights he would derive from his marriage with the Princess Elizabeth of the house of York, though they could not help knowing that this marriage had not even yet been celebrated, they might have allowed him the latitude of dating from the murder of Elizabeth's brothers in the Tower; but Henry took a very different course, and with characteristic nicety, as if so small a theft from time were no

---

[1] As a new historical era had commenced with the new dynasty, it will be sufficient in this place to point out the principal circumstances in the polity of England, at the accession of Henry VII.

" The essential checks upon the royal authority were five in number:—1. The king could levy no sort of new tax on his people, except by the grant of his parliament, consisting as well of bishops and mitred abbots or lords spiritual, and of hereditary peers or temporal lords, who sat and voted promiscuously in the same chamber, as of representatives from the freeholders of each county, and from the burgesses of many towns and less considerable places, forming the lower or commons' house. 2. The previous assent and authority of the same assembly was necessary for every new law, whether of a general or temporary nature. 3. No man could be committed to prison, but by a legal warrant specifying his offence; and by an usage nearly tantamount to constitutional right, he must be speedily brought to trial, by means of regular sessions of jail delivery. 4. The fact of guilt or innocence on a criminal charge, was determined in a public court, and in the county where the offence was alleged to have occurred, by a jury of twelve men, from whose unanimous verdict no appeal could be made. Civil rights, so far as they depended on matters of fact, were subject to the same decision. 5. The officers and servants of the crown, violating the personal liberty or other right of the subject, might be sued in an action for damages, to be assessed by a jury, or, in some cases, were liable to a criminal process; nor could they plead any warrant or command in their justification, not even the direct order of the king.

" These securities, though it would be easy to prove that they were all recognized in law, differed much in the degree of their effective operation. It may be said of the first, that it was now completely established. After a long contention, the Kings of England had desisted for near 100 years from every attempt to impose taxes without consent of parliament; and their recent device of demanding benevolences, or half-compulsory gifts, though very oppressive, and on that account just abolished by an act of the late usurper, Richard, was in effect a recognition of the general principle which it sought to elude rather than transgress."—Hallam's *Const. Hist. of England*, chap. i.

[2] Sir Harris Nicolas, *Chron. of Hist.*

[3] Bacon. *Life of Henry VII.*; *Rot. Parl.*

[4] *Rot. Parl.*; Bacon; Marsolier, *Histoire de Henri VII., surnommé Le Sage, et le Salomon d'Angleterre.*

theft at all, he only antedated by a single day, making his reign begin on the 21st of August, the eve of the battle of Bosworth, when the crown was on the head of Richard, and he, Henry, was nothing but Earl of Richmond. In this manner the marches and counter-marches, and all the long preparations of the friends of Richard to meet the invader were overlooked, and they were accused of nothing treasonable before that day. In the preamble of the bill which he caused to be introduced in parliament, after a recital of the unnatural, mischievous, and great perjuries, treasons, homicides and murders *in shedding of infants' blood*, with many other wrongs, odious offences and abominations against God and man, committed by Richard late Duke of Gloucester, it was shown how John, late Duke of Norfolk, Thomas, Earl of Surrey, Francis, Viscount Lovel, John, Lord Zouch, Robert Middleton, Robert Brackenbury, Ratcliffe, Catesby, and others, had, "on the 21st day of August, the first year of the reign of our sovereign lord, assembled to them at Leicester, in the county of Leicester, a great host, traitorously intending, imagining, and conspiring the destruction of the king's royal person, our sovereign liege lord," &c.[1]

The absurdity of this antedating by a day was too manifest to escape observation, and the whole tendency was startling. It was asked how Richard, and Norfolk, and Surrey, and the other adherents of the late king, could have committed treason against Henry, then only Earl of Richmond, and at a time when he had never publicly laid claim to the crown. All constitutional and legal objections were, however, overruled, and, in spite of a faint opposition within doors and a louder outcry without the subservient parliament passed the bill as required, and attainted the late king, the Duke of Norfolk, his son the Earl of Surrey, Lord Lovel, Lord Ferrers, and twenty-five other noblemen and gentlemen. Henry thus obtained what he much wanted—an immediate supply of money:

[1] *Rot. Parl.*

some of the confiscated estates, the largest and finest in the kingdom, he kept to himself, and others he distributed among his needy followers. Of the thirty persons thus attainted, some had fallen with Richard and the Duke of Norfolk at Bosworth; some, like Lord Lovel, had taken sanctuary, and some had fled beyond sea. The new king was only fond of executions on great state occasions, and the only blood which was shed at this revolution, was that of Richard's confidential adviser, Catesby, and of two persons named Brecher, who were put to death immediately after the battle.

But the most important operation pursued during this session of parliament, and that in which Henry most forcibly displayed his wary, hesitating, and equivocating character, was the settlement of the crown by vote and enactment. The act was dictated by the king himself: all mention of the Princess Elizabeth, and of every branch of her family, was carefully avoided; no stress was laid on his descent from an excluded and illegitimate branch of the house of Lancaster; he satisfied himself with repealing in his own favour all such acts as treated Henry IV., Henry V., Henry VI., and Edward of Lancaster, Prince of Wales, as usurpers and traitors; and in favour of Elizabeth, he merely revoked the bastardy act passed against her and all the children of Edward IV. and Elizabeth Woodville at Richard's accession. He ordered that every record of parliament which contained any mention of his own attainder should be taken off the file, that the original of the bastardy act should be burned, and that all persons who kept copies of it, after a certain day, should be fined and imprisoned. Dropping the high tone of hereditary right and heavenly judgment "shown in issue of battle," he caused it merely to be written in the act of settlement, that "the inheritance of the crown should be, rest, remain, and abide, in the most royal person of the sovereign lord, King Henry VII., and the heirs of his body lawfully coming, perpetually

Henry VII.—From the family picture painted by Holbein for Henry VIII.

with the grace of God so to endure, and in none other." But this excess of caution excited suspicions and discontents which might have proved fatal, had Henry not been ready to fulfil a contract of a more private nature, through which only—gloze it as he would—he could pretend to any right to the crown. He was well aware of all the manœuvres of the queen-dowager and the Princess Elizabeth; he knew that the first had fallen in with the views of the late king, and that Elizabeth had consented to marry Richard and convey her rights to him. These circumstances were not likely to conciliate Henry; but affection and respect had no part in his political match; his great object in delaying the union was to avoid making the rights of the house of York too prominent—to disguise the fact that, in law at least, he owed the crown to a woman: and even at last he made it appear that he yielded to the prayer of parliament. The friends of the house of York—the parties who had contracted for the marriage in France a year before—were irritated at seeing no allusion made to the Princess Elizabeth; and the nation at large felt that if this new revolution were to have any value, it would only be inasmuch as it put an end to civil war, by uniting the White and Red Roses. When the commons presented to the king the grant of tonnage and poundage *for life* (now a usual grant), they saddled it with a plain and direct request that he would "take to wife and consort the Princess Elizabeth." When this petition was read, the lords, both spiritual and temporal, rose from their seats and joined in it, by bowing with proper solemnity to the throne, and then Henry graciously replied that he was ready and willing to satisfy them on this point.[1]

In the same parliament all grants made by the crown since the thirty-fourth year of Henry VI. were resumed; and thus Henry acquired the power to take from the partizans of the house of York, or to confirm to them the possession of whatever property they had obtained in this way. There was also passed a general amnesty in favour of all such adherents of Richard as would submit to the king's mercy and take the new oath of allegiance. But here, again, Henry showed his character: he would not allow the houses of parliament to have anything to do with this act of grace, which was published and proclaimed as originating in his own royal breast, and emanating solely from his own royal mercy. All these things were sufficient indications of the spirit of absolutism—a spirit which would not have been tolerated by the proud and bold aristocracy of former times, but which there was now little to oppose. Several of Richard's adroit agents were presently employed about the court; and among these were Sir John Tyrrel, the reputed murderer of the sons of Edward IV. in the Tower.[2]

A.D. 1486. On the 18th of January Henry married the Princess Elizabeth; and thus, at last, the long-desired blending of the rival Roses was accomplished. But her jealous husband allowed her the smallest possible share of authority or influence: her coronation was indefinitely postponed; and, until policy obliged her husband to adopt a different course, she was little more than a queen in name. Nor did her mother, Elizabeth Woodville, reap any great benefit from the revolution; she did not recover her dower, but lived, it should seem, on an allowance made by Henry, who was too fond of money to be liberal.

The Bishop of Imola, Papal legate, had given the dispensation considered necessary for the marriage, as Henry and Elizabeth were related; but the king was determined to make more of this opportunity. He thought that he might gain something over scrupulous minds, by obtaining the express sanction of the pope to his elevation to the throne: and for this he determined to apply in his usual indirect manner. Pretending scruples or apprehensions as to the lawfulness of the marriage he had contracted, he applied for a second dispensation, to be given by the pope himself. Innocent VIII. readily complied. In his document every clause was inserted that Henry required, and contradictory rights were heaped one upon another. It was recited that the crown of England belonged to the gracious Henry by right of conquest—by notorious and indisputable right of succession—by right of election made by all the prelates, lords, and commons of the realm—and by right of the act of settlement passed by the three estates in parliament assembled—but that, nevertheless, to put an end to the bloody wars which had risen out of the claims of the house of York, and at the urgent request of parliament, King Henry had consented to marry Elizabeth, the eldest daughter and true heir of Edward IV., of "immortal memory." The pope, therefore, at the prayer of the king, and to preserve peace in the kingdom, confirmed the dispensation. So far the dispensation did not very much exceed its proper office: but the pontiff proceeded to confirm the act of settlement passed by the parliament, and to define and fix irrevocably the meaning of that act. According to his interpretation, that act meant that, if Queen Elizabeth should die without issue before the king her husband, or if her issue should not outlive their

---

[1] *Rot. Parl.*

[2] *Rot. Parl.*; Bacon, *Life of Henry VII.*

father, then, and in that case, the crown should devolve to Henry's children by any subsequent marriage. Sentence of excommunication was pronounced against all who should call in question this interpretation, or who should hereafter attempt to disturb Henry in the present possession, or the heirs of his body in the future succession:—and so ended this extraordinary bull.[1]

When parliament was dissolved, Henry prepared to make a royal progress through the kingdom, with the more express object of staying some time in the north, in order to gain the goodwill of the people in those parts. "In the prime time of the year he began his journey towards York, and, because the feast of Easter approached, he turned aside to the city of Lincoln, where he tarried during the solemnity of that high feast." Here he was informed that Lord Lovel, with Humphrey and Thomas Stafford, "had fled from the sanctuary of Colchester, and had gone, with dangerous intentions, no man knew whither." On the 6th of April Henry left Lincoln for Nottingham, well attended; by the 17th he was at Pontefract, where he was stopped for awhile by the intelligence that Lord Lovel, with a considerable body of insurgents, had thrown himself between Middleham and York. To retreat might have proved more dangerous than to advance, even in face of an equal force; but the insurgents were greatly inferior, and, on seeing that the enterprise was hopeless, Lord Lovel disbanded them, and fled into Lancashire. After lying concealed there for a short time in the house of his friend Sir Thomas Broughton, he passed over to Flanders. A few of the men who had taken up arms with him were seized and executed. This failure wholly disconcerted the project of the Staffords, who had prepared an insurrection in Worcestershire. The two brothers fled for sanctuary to the church of Colnham, near Abingdon; but this time their sanctuary was not respected: they were dragged by force from the church, and had sentence passed upon them as traitors. Humphrey, the elder, was executed at Tyburn, but Thomas, the younger brother, was pardoned.[2]

On the 26th of April Henry entered York, in which city the memory of King Richard, his mortal enemy, was yet "recent and lively, and not all forgotten of his friends." But the visitor, on necessary occasions, could relax his avarice: he reduced the town-rent to the crown from £160 yearly to £18, 5s.—he dispensed favours and honours—held feasts—exhibited pageants and miracles—fed some poets who recited some bad verses in his honour—and distributed money among the people, who cried, lustily, "King Henry! King Henry! Our Lord preserve that sweet and well-favoured face!" Having spent nearly a month at York, he turned to the southwest, and visited Worcester, Hereford, Gloucester, and Bristol. In the course of his slow and stately progress he was very attentive to the public observance of religious worship; but he chose his own subject for the sermons that were preached. On every Sunday or saint's day one of the bishops read and expounded from the pulpit the bull which Henry had obtained on his marriage from Pope Innocent. On his return to London, in the month of June, he received an embassy from the King of Scotland, who joyfully consented to a treaty of truce and amity, to be followed in due season by a matrimonial alliance between their families.[3]

On the 20th of September, eight months and two days after her marriage, Elizabeth was delivered of a son, who was christened Arthur, after the hero of ancient romance, with whom Henry claimed relationship on the father's side through the Tudors and Cadwalladers.

We left the young Earl of Warwick, the son of the Duke of Clarence, safely lodged in the Tower. In the month of November a young priest of Oxford, and a beautiful boy, landed at Dublin. The priest gave out that the boy was Edward Plantagenet, Earl of Warwick, who had escaped in a marvellous manner from the Tower of London; and among a people of lively imagination and warm feelings, and enthusiastic in their attachment to the house of York, a ready belief was accorded to the story, and a generous sympathy spread from heart to heart for the young hero of it. What was credulity in the common people was design and craft in some, possibly in most of the Anglo-Irish nobles, who were averse to Henry, who had scarcely submitted to his government, and who were ready to adopt all such measures as chance might offer, provided they held out a prospect of overthrowing the new order of things in England. Thomas Fitzgerald, Earl of Kildare, and lord-lieutenant or deputy of Ireland, received the priest and his pupil with open arms, and presented the latter "to all his friends and lovers," declaring "the coming of the child, and afterwards affirming that the crown and sceptre of the realm of right belonged to this young prince." The boy was not only beautiful and graceful in person, but witty and ingenious: he told his touching story with great consistency, and, when questioned, he could give minute particulars relating to the royal family. The citizens of Dublin declared unanimously in his favour; and his fame was "shortly bruited throughout all Ireland, and

---

[1] *Rymer.*   [2] *Year Book.*   [3] *Herald's Journal,* MS. Lel Collect.; *Hall; Bacon; Rym.*

every man was willing to take his part, and submit to him, calling him, on all hands, king." When news of these doings reached King Henry, he summoned a great council to meet in the Charter House, near his royal manor of Richmond. His bad faith had made many men desperate; and, in the homely saying of the chronicler, "had set all things at sixes and sevens." The pardon which he had granted in the first parliament was not only hampered with exceptions and restrictions, but the parts that were free from such qualifications had not been observed; several persons who had submitted and claimed the benefit of the amnesty had been thrown into prison and cruelly treated; and in this number was the Earl of Surrey,[1] who was now a close prisoner in the Tower. Henry, trembling at the effect of all this, now resolved to proclaim another general pardon, free from all exceptions. The next resolution adopted in council was to arrest Elizabeth Woodville, the mother of the queen; and the third was to produce the real Earl of Warwick, and show him in the most public manner.

East Gate of Bermondsey Abbey.[2]—From an engraving dated 1794.

The council was held with great secrecy. The resolutions, however, were immediately carried into execution; and, first, the queen-dowager was arrested, deprived of all her property, and placed as a close prisoner in the monastery of Bermondsey. The motive set forth by Henry was certainly not the true one; it seemed altogether incredible to the historians of the following age, and it was not credited by Henry's contemporaries. It was that Elizabeth Woodville was punished for her intrigues with King Richard, and for delivering her daughter into the hands of the usurper, contrary to her pact and agreement with those that had arranged with her concerning the marriage of her said daughter Elizabeth with Henry himself, then an exile in France. Bacon, and Hall, whom he follows, plainly assign another reason. After observing that the priest of Oxford, who had never seen the real Earl of Warwick, must have had a prompter in a person conversant with the history of the court and family of York, Bacon says, "so it cannot be, but that some *great* person, that knew particularly and familiarly Edward Plantagenet, had a hand in the business, from whom the priest might take his aim. That which is most probable out of the precedent and subsequent acts is, that it was the queen-dowager from whom this action had the principal source and motion. For certain it is, she was a busy, negotiating woman, and in her withdrawing-chamber had the fortunate conspiracy for the king against King Richard III. been hatched, which the king knew and *remembered, perhaps, but too well;* and was at this time extremely discontent with the king, thinking her daughter (as the king handled the matter) not advanced, but depressed: and none could hold the book so well to prompt and instruct this stage-play as she could."[3]

Soon after, the Marquis of Dorset, Elizabeth's son by her first marriage, was arrested and thrown into the Tower. The amnesty was of course published immediately; but, not relying wholly on this measure, Henry sent trusty agents to the seaports to prevent fugitives, malcontents, and suspected persons from passing over to Ireland or to Flanders: on a Sunday he brought young Edward Plantagenet, Earl of Warwick, out of the Tower, and conducted him in the most public manner through all the principal streets of London, that he might be seen and recognized by the citizens, many of whom had known the boy up to his tenth year. This well-studied and most open exhibition had its effect in England. "Nevertheless, in Ireland, where it was too late

---

[1] Surrey had fought bravely for King Richard at the battle of Bosworth Field, where his father, the Duke of Norfolk, was slain.

[2] Bermondsey Priory was founded in 1081, by Ailwyn Childe, a citizen of London, for monks of the Cluniac order, first introduced into England by Archbishop Lanfranc. In the reign of Edward III. the priory was sequestrated, together with other alien priories, but re-established and erected into an abbey in the second year of the reign of Richard II. The abbey was finally surrendered in the year 1539, by Robert de Wharton, who received in compensation the large pension of £330, 6s. 8d., and also the bishopric of St. Asaph *in commendam.*

[3] Bacon, *Life: Hall.*

to go back, it wrought none; but contrariwise, there they turned the imposture upon the king, and gave out that *he*, to defeat the true inheritor, and to mock the world, and blind the eyes of simple men, had tricked up a boy in the likeness of Edward Plantagenet, and showed him to the people, not sparing to profane the ceremony of a solemn procession, the more to countenance the fable."[1]

But, for a time, the plot thickened even in England. John, Earl of Lincoln, son of John de la Pole, Duke of Suffolk, and of Elizabeth, second sister of Edward IV. and Richard III., had, like the Earl of Warwick, fallen into the power of Henry after the battle of Bosworth. It was known that his uncle, the late king, had at one time appointed this young earl to be his successor on the throne, and that many persons looked up to him as the most promising member of the house of York. The young earl is described as a person of great wit, courage, and enterprise, "with thoughts highly raised by hopes and expectations;" yet, if he had been of a different temper, it seems probable that, at a moment when Henry's suspicions and jealousies were so much excited, self-preservation might have induced him to flee, if not to embark in some desperate project. Immediately after the private sitting of the council at Richmond, Lincoln disappeared, and it was not known for some time whither he had betaken himself. The Irish lords had sent emissaries into Flanders. The high personage to whom they addressed themselves was the Dowager-duchess of Burgundy, the widow of Charles the Rash, and sister to Edward IV. and Richard III., who lived in good state in the Netherlands, having sovereign authority in the district which her husband had left as her dower. Good and amiable as she was in other respects, this princess hated King Henry and all his race with a most enduring and implacable hatred. Bacon says, rather ungallantly, that she had "the spirit of a man, and the malice of a woman;" and that, "abounding in treasure by the greatness of her dower and her provident government, and being childless and without any nearer care, she made it her design and enterprise to see the majesty royal of England once again replaced in her house, and had set up King Henry as a mark at whose overthrow all her actions should aim and shoot." It was to her that Lovel had fled on the failure of the insurrection in Yorkshire, and it was to her that her nephew, the Earl of Lincoln, now repaired. The duchess presently got together a body of 2000 Germans, under the command of Martin Swart, a valiant and experienced captain. With these foreign mercenaries, the Earl of Lincoln, the Lord Lovel, and some other English exiles, embarked for Ireland. In the month of May, a few days after their landing, the Earl of Warwick of that side of the water was crowned in the cathedral church of Dublin in the most solemn fashion, the Bishop of Meath performing the ceremony. This was done without any show of opposition, there being not a single sword drawn for King Henry, and, indeed, no displeasure testified in Ireland, except in the city of Waterford and among the people of the Butlers, who were old Lancastrians and hereditary enemies of the Earl of Kildare, the lordkeeper.[2] Edward VI., as the new king was styled, issued writs, convoked a parliament, and caused penalties to be enacted against the Butlers and the citizens of Waterford.

Henry, meanwhile, levied troops in different parts of the kingdom, put on a smiling, yet at the same time a devout face, and, with great policy, resorted to the best means for disconcerting the plots hatching in England, and for securing the good-will of the people. Shortly after the sudden flight of Lincoln, he travelled leisurely through Essex, Suffolk, and Norfolk, in which counties the young earl's influence was high. He was courteous to all the gentry, many of whom held themselves ready to do him service.[3] From Bury St. Edmunds he went to Norwich, and, to captivate the populace, he went from Norwich "in manner of a pilgrimage" to Walsingham, where he visited our Lady's Church, famous for miracles. He then proceeded by way of Northampton and Coventry, to Kenilworth Castle, within the strong walls of which he had placed his mother, his wife, and his infant son, Prince Arthur. While he lay at Kenilworth, the king, from Ireland, landed at the pile of Foudray, in the southern extremity of Furness. Immediately on their landing, the Earl of Lincoln and the Lord Lovel were joined by their sworn friend Sir Thomas Broughton, whose estates lay in Lancashire. From the coast they advanced boldly towards York, expecting to be joined on the road by many malcontents. "But their snowball did not gather as it went; for the people came not in to them, neither did any rise or declare themselves in other parts of the kingdom for them, which was caused partly by the good taste that the king had given his people of his government, joined with the reputation of his felicity (good luck), and partly for that it was an odious thing to the people of England to have a king brought in to them upon the shoulders of Irish and Dutch, of which their army was in substance com-

---

[1] Bacon.

[2] Three or four of the bishops, however, kept aloof.
[3] We learn, from one of the Paston letters, dated in the month of May, that the king and his lieutenant, the Earl of Oxford, were right well content at the conduct of the Norfolk gentry.

pounded."[1] Though cruelly disappointed, the young Earl of Lincoln boldly turned southward to meet Henry, who was advancing upon York by way of Coventry, Leicester, and Nottingham, at the head of a well-appointed and numerous army. On the 16th of June the Earl of Oxford, who led Henry's van, was brought into action at Stoke, then a little village upon the brow of a hill not far from Newark. Henry remained with the rear-guard, which never came into action. The battle was fierce and obstinate for about three hours; but the invaders had little or no cavalry, and the mass of them were ill provided with arms. "Martin Swart, with his Germans, performed bravely, and so did those few English that were on that side; neither did the Irish fail in courage or fierceness, but being almost naked men, only armed with darts and skeins, it was rather an execution than a fight upon them; insomuch as the furious slaughter of them was a great discouragement and appalment to the rest." The veteran Germans died in their ranks almost to a man; nor was the victory decided till one-half of the whole invading force and many hundreds of the Earl of Oxford's men had perished. His majesty Edward VI., now plain Lambert Simnel, the son of a baker, and the priest of Oxford, whose proper name was Simons, were taken prisoners; the Earl of Lincoln, the Lords Thomas and Maurice Fitzgerald, Sir Thomas Broughton, and Martin Swart, died fighting like brave men. The Lord Lovel was seen to escape from the field; his name was not included in the mournful list of the dead, made as usual by an herald, but, as he was never more seen, it was believed that he had been drowned in attempting to swim his horse across the river Trent. Long after, when the race of the Tudors had gone to their account, and when the dynasty of the Stuarts had been driven out of the kingdom—nearly 200 years from the time of this forgotten battle of Stoke—some workmen accidentally discovered a subterranean chamber at Minster Lovel, in Oxfordshire, the ancient seat of the adventurous lord. Within this chamber was a skeleton of a man seated in a chair with his head resting upon a table; and these sad relics were supposed, with some reason, to tell a tale of horror.[2]

Henry's conduct after the victory of Stoke was very characteristic. "For Lambert (Simnel)," says Bacon, "the king would not take his life, both out of magnanimity—taking him but as an image of wax, that others had tempered and moulded—and likewise out of wisdom, thinking that if he suffered death, he would be forgotten too soon, but being kept alive he would be a continual spectacle, and a kind of remedy against the like enchantments of people in time to come. For which cause he was taken into service in his court, to a base office in his kitchen; so that he turned a broach[3] that had worn a crown. . . . And afterwards he was preferred to be one of the king's falconers. As to the priest, he was committed closer prisoner, and heard of no more—the king loving to seal up his own dangers."[4]

One of the king's first cares after the battle of Stoke was to return a solemn thanksgiving, and to offer up his banner at the shrine of our Lady of Walsingham. He then travelled northward to punish such persons as had assisted or favoured the rebels. His proceedings were wholly independent of the ordinary courts of justice; but, as on many other occasions, his revenge was subservient to his avarice, so that the chief punishments he inflicted were by fine and ransom. But the pleasure Henry derived from a harvest of this kind, and from seeing that all immediate opposition had vanished, did not blind him to the facts, that his behaviour to his queen had created him many enemies, and that his jealousy of the whole house of York, instead of strengthening had weakened him, by alienating the affections of the people. Elizabeth, the rightful heir, was kept in obscurity: she had been his wife a year and a half, and had borne him a son, and still she was not crowned. Now, however, he was "willing to give some contentment of that kind, at least in ceremony." Elizabeth was crowned at Westminster, on the 20th of November, Henry witnessing the whole ceremony, and the feast which followed, from behind a screen or lattice that concealed his person.[5] He liberated the Marquis of Dorset from the Tower, but it appears that he still left Elizabeth Woodville, that nobleman's mother, and the mother of his queen, in the hands of the monks of Bermondsey. The chief business of the parliament when it met was to vote supplies and a bill of attainder, which, on slight evidence, included a great number of persons said to have been concerned in the late insurrection. It appears that no names were inserted except of persons who had property to forfeit.[6]

Ever since his accession Henry had been occu-

---

[1] Bacon.   [2] Bacon; Hall; Rot. Parl.; Carte, Hist. Eng.
[3] A spit; French, "broche."   [4] Bacon.
[5] A curious account of the coronation is given by Ives. See Select Papers, &c.
[6] "Next the king required their aid to put down the dangerous and unlawful practice of 'maintenance.' The reader will recollect that by maintenance was understood an association of individuals under a chief, whose livery they wore, and to whom they bound themselves by oaths and promises, for the purpose of maintaining by force the private quarrels of the chief and the members. Hence the course of justice was obstructed, jurors were intimidated, and offenders escaped with impunity. Hence also and this it was that chiefly provoked the hostility of the king: powerful noblemen were furnished with the means of raising forces at a short warning to oppose the reigning, or to assist a new claimant. In the preceding parliament an oath

pied exclusively in settling his affairs at home; but now, complicated intrigues and great political movements forced him to look abroad. The aspect of affairs in France, even before these demonstrations, was sufficiently alarming: the dissevered parts of that country were gradually uniting into a consistent whole, and forming a great and compact kingdom, while the much narrower extent of Britain was still divided into two rival kingdoms, frequently at war with one another. The rapid growth of the French power threatened to cast a dangerous shadow over all the neighbouring countries; and, both according to the principles of common policy, which seeks to check the too rapid aggrandizement of a rival, and to the juster and nobler policy which opposes itself to the conquest of small and weak states by strong ones, Henry seemed bound to take an active part in the affairs of the Continent. But Henry was no warrior, and his avidity for money, his juggling and double-dealing, prevented him from taking up the honourable position of an arbiter and peacemaker; for, with the means he had in his hands, he might have curbed the ambition of France without any war. At the time of the death of Louis XI., which happened on the 30th of August, 1483, about two months after the accession of Richard III., by craft and policy, by fortunate marriages, and by the sword, the French monarchy had swallowed up all the independent principalities, except Brittany, which still preserved its duke and its comparatively free institutions. Charles VIII., the son of Louis, was only fourteen years of age when he ascended the throne of France; and, according to arrangements made by his father, he was placed for a fixed time under the tutelage of Madame Anne, his elder sister, who had married Peter of Bourbon, Lord of Beaujeu. What followed was according to precedent:—the Duke of Orleans (afterwards Louis XII.), who hated Bourbon and his wife, flew to arms; but Orleans was unsuccessful and driven to seek refuge in Brittany. Duke Francis II. had always been a weak prince, and he was now growing old and infirm. His guest, notwithstanding he was already married to one of the daughters of Louis XI., conceived the idea of obtaining possession of the duchy by marrying Anne of Brittany, the elder daughter and heiress of Francis; and a party among the turbulent Breton nobles entered into his views. At the same time there was another faction that favoured the French court, and another that inclined to an alliance with England. The country was ravaged by a civil war. Encouraged by the prevailing disorders, the French regency precociously betrayed their design of seizing the duchy, upon the ground of some inexplicable right. Duke Francis thereupon summoned the three estates of the duchy, who took a most solemn oath of allegiance to the Princess Anne, and, in case of her dying without issue, to her younger sister Madame Isabeau. This act fixed the eyes of several princes upon the heiress of Brittany, and, besides the Duke of Orleans, who had many formidable difficulties to overcome, the Sire d'Albret, whose dominions lay in Gascony and at the foot of the Pyrenees, and Maximilian, son of the Emperor Frederick IV., aspired to her hand. The poor duke, who had engaged to consult the three estates on the choice of his son-in-law, neglected so to do, and encouraged the hopes of these three suitors, and even treated with others at one and the same time. The Duke of Orleans made his peace with the French court and returned to Paris, but he was soon detected in a fresh conspiracy, and was again obliged to flee to Nantes. He soon found that his party was losing ground in Brittany, where the nobles were disgusted at seeing that he did what he chose with their imbecile prince, and filled all the offices with French adventurers, his own adherents. The course they pursued to correct this evil was absurd enough: a great many of the Breton nobles opened a correspondence with the French court, and implored its aid. At this moment a

---

had been required from the lords, and was ordered to be taken by the commons in each county, that they would not keep in their service men openly cursed, or murderers, or felons, or outlaws; that they would not retain persons by indentures, or give liveries contrary to law; and that they would not make riots or maintenances, nor oppose the due execution of the king's writs."—*Lingard*, vol. iv. p. 139.

"From the time of Edward I., the feudal system and all the feelings connected with it declined very rapidly. But what the nobility lost in the number of their military tenants, was in some degree compensated by the state of manners. The higher class of them, who took the chief share in public affairs, were exceedingly opulent; and their mode of life gave wealth an incredibly greater efficacy than it possesses at present. Gentlemen of large estates and good families, who had attached themselves to those great peers, who bore offices which we should call menial in their households, and sent their children thither for education, were of course ready to follow their banner in a rising, without much inquiry into the cause. Still less would the vast body of tenants and their retainers, who were fed in the castle at time of peace, refuse to carry their pikes and staves into the field of battle. Many devices were used to preserve this aristocratic influence, which riches and ancestry of themselves rendered so formidable. Such was the maintenance of suits, or confederacies for the purpose of supporting each other's claims in litigation, which was the subject of frequent complaints in parliament, and gave rise to several prohibitory statutes. By help of such confederacies, parties were enabled to make violent entries upon the lands they claimed, which the law itself could hardly be said to discourage. Even proceedings in courts of justice were often liable to intimidation and influence. A practice much allied to confederacies of maintenance, though ostensibly more harmless, was that of giving liveries to all retainers of a noble family; but it had an obvious tendency to preserve that spirit of factious attachments and animosities which it is the general policy of a wise government to dissipate. From the first year of Richard II., we find continual mention of this custom, with many legal provisions against it; but it was never abolished till the reign of Henry VII."—*Hallam, Hist. of England during the Middle Ages*, vol. iii. p. 245.

French army was on their frontiers; for the Regent Anne had made up her mind to take advantage of the condition of affairs. The Bretons formed a confederacy at Châteaubriant, and stipulated that the king should not send more than 400 men-at-arms and 4000 foot into their country—that the liberties of the duchy and private property should be respected—and that, as soon as the Duke of Orleans should be expelled, the French should recross the frontier. Charles poured 16,000 men into the country, and, of course, broke all his engagements as soon as he was able. In the month of May, 1487, while Henry was expecting Lambert Simnel from Ireland, the French army advanced in three divisions; the first took Ploërmel, the second Vannes, and the third laid siege to Nantes, within the walls of which Duke Francis took refuge with his daughters. Maximilian, now titular King of the Romans, sent a body of 1500 German and Flemish soldiers to the assistance of Francis; and these, being joined by some Bretons, under the command of the Count of Dunois, cut their way through the French lines, and relieved Nantes in the beginning of August. Another of Madame Anne's suitors was less fortunate. As the Sire d'Albret was marching through the Limousin, with 3000 or 4000 Gascons, to succour Duke Francis and the ladies, he was attacked by a superior force of French, to which he capitulated. Though foiled before Nantes, La Tremoille, Charles' general, took Anray, Vitré, and St. Aubin-du-Cormier: at the same time fresh troops poured across the French frontier, while Maximilian could send no further reinforcements. At the approach of the storm Duke Francis applied to England for assistance. At that moment Henry was absorbed by his own troubles; but when those difficulties were over he was in no haste to accede to the prayer of the Bretons. We believe the fact to be, that he had already accepted of a *retainer* from the French court. If this were not the case, he must forfeit his reputation for cunning and quick-sightedness, and stand in this particular in the light of a dupe. "King Charles," says Bacon, "knew well he could not receive any opposition so potent as if King Henry should, either from policy of state, in preventing the growing greatness of France, or upon gratitude unto the Duke of Brittany[1] for his former favours in the time of his distress, espouse that quarrel, and declare himself in aid of the duke. Therefore, he no sooner heard that King Henry was settled by his victory (at Stoke), than he sent ambassadors unto him, to pray his assistance, or at the least that he would stand neutral: which ambassadors found the king at Leicester."[2]

Henry, to acquit himself, as he said, of his gratitude to the King of France and the Duke of Brittany, for whom he "was ready even to go a pilgrimage," and to "satisfy all obligations both to God and man," offered himself as mediator. Upon this the ambassadors departed well pleased, for they knew that his mediation would not stop the progress of their army. Charles' generals, indeed, proceeded with more vigour than ever; and, while they were fighting, Henry despatched Christopher Urswick, his chaplain—"a person by him much trusted and employed"—to talk to the French court. From Paris Urswick went to Rennes, the capital of the Duke of Brittany. When Francis saw the priest, he told him that, having been a benefactor and a kind of foster-father to Henry for many years, he looked, at this time, from the "renowned King of England" rather for succour in a brave army, than a vain treaty of peace. The chaplain then returned to Paris, and the court there sent him back to London, to tell his master of the obstinacy and disrespect of Duke Francis. And still the French troops continued their operations, and whenever they gained a battle or took a town they emphatically repeated that they had no wish to make conquests, but were most anxious for the success of Henry's mediation. Another embassy was sent over to England, and Henry could not do less than return the compliment. Urswick was despatched again to the French court, and with him were associated the abbot

THE CASTLE AND CATHEDRAL, NANTES.—From Touchard Lafosse, La Loire.

[1] "Britain" is the form of the name used by Bacon; to prevent confusion, we have substituted the more usual form in this and other places.   [2] *Bacon.*

of Abingdon and Sir Richard Tunstal, a layman. But by this time the people of England were beginning to lament that the French king should be allowed to aggrandize himself at the expense of an ancient ally of their country; and some gallant knights, in whom the spirit of chivalry and the recollections of Crecy and Azincourt were not yet extinct, were all on fire to hasten to the rescue of an unfortunate prince, and measure swords with the French. Sir Edward Woodville, one of the queen's uncles, collected a brave band of 400 men, and set sail from the Isle of Wight for St. Malo, on the coast of Brittany. When the news of this expedition reached the French court, the poor chaplain Urswick and his brother ambassadors there had a narrow escape from the fury of "divers young bloods." But " presently came an agent from King Henry to purge himself touching Lord Woodville's going over, using for a principal argument, to demonstrate that it was without his privity, for that the troops were so small, as neither had the face of a succour by authority, nor could much advance the Brittany affairs. To which message, although the French king gave no full credit, yet he made fair weather with the king, and seemed satisfied."²

This was, indeed, a business where everybody was seeking to deceive everybody. Henry, however, forbade other English adventurers to join Duke Francis; and, as the zeal of the nation blazed the more from repression, he determined to turn it to his advantage financially. "Wherein first he thought to make his vantage upon his parliament, knowing that they, being affectionate unto the quarrel of Brittany, would give treasure largely."³ The wily Morton, now Archbishop of Canterbury and chancellor, was instructed so to address parliament as to affect them towards the business, but without engaging the king in any express declaration of war; and the ambiguous speech of the right reverend minister fully answered these ends. Parliament eagerly caught at the bait, and recommended strong measures, "as well in respect of the emulation between the nations, and the envy at the late growth of the French monarchy, as in regard of the danger to suffer the French to make their approaches upon England, by obtaining so goodly a maritime province, full of sea-towns and havens that might do mischief to the English either by invasion or by interruption of traffic." They were also indignant at the injustice and oppression used in Brittany, for no one could be well deceived by the manifestoes of the French court; and they advised the king to embrace the cause of the Bretons openly and manfully, and then they, with " much alacrity and forwardness," voted an unusually large subsidy. When Henry got the money, he sent his chaplain to *warn* the French court, and to explain that, with all his friendly feelings, it would be *impossible* for him to resist the motion of his people. At the same time the priest was to hint that the English succour to be sent to Duke Francis would be limited, and that the troops would be instructed not to wage war against the French beyond the limits of Brittany. The French did what might be expected; they reinforced La Tremoille, who carried the towns of Châteaubriant, Ancenis, and Fougères. By this time the Breton nobles were fully aware of the folly they had committed in inviting them into the country: the factions united for common defence, and an army of the unfortunate duke, strengthened by the few English under Woodville, and by the 1500 Germans sent by Maximilian, and by a few companies of Gascons and of Basques, sent by the family of D'Albret, took the field under the supreme command of the Duke of Orleans. After some minor operations, the two armies engaged in a general battle on the 20th of July, 1488, between Andouillé and St. Aubin-du-Cormier. La Tremoille, by his superiority in numbers and in field artillery, gained a complete and sanguinary victory. Sir Edward Woodville was slain; and of his 400 men and 1700 Bretons who had assumed the white coats and red crosses of the English, to deceive the enemy, but very few escaped. The Duke of Orleans, who had fought bravely on foot, was taken prisoner, and

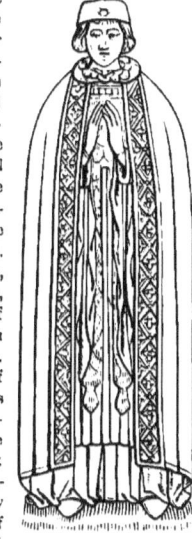

CHRISTOPHER URSWICK.¹—
From his monumental brass
in Hackney Church.

---

¹ The monument of Christopher Urswick is an erection resembling an altar tomb, surmounted by an obtuse arch ornamented with foliage and tracery. Beneath the arch is the following inscription—"Christophero Urswyk, Rectore, Aᵒ Dñi 1519." On each side are the contractious MIA (Misericordia). On the slab of the altar is the effigy in brass of Urswick, with the word "Misericordia" at length, and on the stone beneath the arch is, likewise, a brass plate inscribed with his epitaph in Latin—

"Christopher Urswick was a man of equal talent and piety. He was chaplain to Henry VII., and employed in promoting the union between that king and Elizabeth of York. Refusing an offered bishopric, and resigning several valuable preferments, he retired to his rectory at Hackney, where he passed the decline of life in the exercise of religious offices. He died in 1521, in the sixty-fourth year of his age."

² *Bacon; Daru, Hist. de la Bretagne; Lobineau.*   ³ *Bacon.*

Brittany lay helpless at the foot of the conqueror.¹

When the news of this disastrous battle, and of the slaughter of their countrymen, reached England, the people raised so loud an outcry that Henry was startled from his pleasant dream. Still, however, he was disposed to wait events, hoping that Maximilian would succour Brittany, and that he should be allowed to keep the money which parliament had voted for the war. But the course of events did not improve. La Tremoille took Dinant and St. Malo, and threatened to besiege the unfortunate Duke Francis in Rennes, his capital. Finding that no assistance arrived from England or from any other quarter, Francis at last accepted the hard terms offered by the French court; and in the middle of August (1488) he signed the treaty of Verger. Hereby the claims of the French crown to the duchy were submitted to the consideration of certain commissioners: the French were to retain the conquests they had made, and the duke was bound never more to call in troops from England or any other country, and not to marry either of his daughters without the full approbation of his suzerain lord, the King of France. The Bretons prepared for a fresh struggle, but their poor duke, who seemed heart-broken, sickened, and died on the 7th of September, about three weeks after he had signed the treaty.²

The Princess Anne was even now only in her twelfth year, and her little court was distracted by the intrigues of the rivals for her hand. D'Albret, one of her suitors, who had found his way into Brittany in a beggared state, attempted to carry her off and marry her by force, for Anne felt a very natural aversion to a man who was old, exceedingly ugly, and of a ferocious temper. The Count of Dunois rescued her, and carried her off, seated behind him on his war-horse, and she was subsequently protected by the people of Rennes. While men were disputing within Brittany who should be her husband, the French court claimed the right of being her guardian; and before the bishops and barons could get ready a proper answer, a French army took the field, and carried by assault Pontrieu, Guingamp, Concarneau, Brest, and other places of less importance. This most unequal war now excited fresh cries of indignation in England, and Henry was urged, as the sovereign of a generous people, as a father, to save the helpless orphan. The king conceived the notion of forming an extensive coalition. He despatched ambassadors to Maximilian, King of the Romans, to his son the Archduke Philip, to the King of Spain, and to the King of Portugal, calling upon them to act in concert with him, in order to check the lawless ambition of the French court. He then summoned another parliament, and asked for more money *to carry on the war.*

A.D. 1489. Parliament, which could not be ignorant of the use made of the sums already voted for the defence of Brittany, reduced Henry's demand from £100,000 to £75,000.³ But the levying even of this diminished amount, in the temper in which the nation was, occasioned alarming commotions. These we shall presently notice. Meanwhile Henry offered to the Breton government the services of 6000 archers, but he limited the time of their service to six months, and would not send them at all until two of the best seaport towns of Brittany were put into his hands as security for the repayment of the entire expense of the armament, and until the young duchess had taken an oath never to marry without his consent. In the spring the Lord Willoughby de Broke landed in Brittany with his small army; at the same time a Spanish force advanced through Roncesvalles, to make a diversion in the south of France; and Maximilian hoped, after subduing an insurrection of his Flemish subjects, to attack the French on their northern frontier. By this plan of operation the French were prevented from concentrating in full force in Brittany, and Lord Willoughby de Broke, with his small army, was enabled not only to keep them completely in check, but also, with the help of some Breton troops, to gain several advantages over them. Though nearly half a century had passed since the last *real* battle fought by the English on the Continent, the French had not forgotten the old campaigns, and they paid such a respect to the valour of the Islanders, and their conduct in the open field, that they cautiously avoided anything like a pitched battle. They kept themselves in fortified towns and entrenched camps, and limited their operations to skirmishes. The Lord de Broke, instead of being encouraged to risk his little army frankly, was constantly checked by the unwarlike and most cautious king, who, moreover, recalled him and his troops in *less* than six months. The French had been obliged to detach a great army towards Fuenterrabia to oppose the Spaniards; and Maximilian, aided by a small force of English, chiefly drawn from Calais, had gained some important advantages in the north, and taken the town of St. Omer. Not more for these reasons, than for others of a less apparent nature, resulting from a change of plan which was not made visible until a year and a half later, the French court offered to treat for peace, and soon after signed a treaty at Frank-

¹ Daru, *Hist. de la Bretagne;* Actes de Bretagne; Mezeral; Bacon; Hall.
² Original MSS. and *Actes de Bretagne,* quoted by Daru.
³ *Rot. Parl.*

fort with Maximilian. The chief clauses were—that the French troops should retire from Brittany; that the Duchess Anne should dismiss all her foreign auxiliaries; that the fortresses of St. Malo, Fougères, Dinant, and St. Aubin, should be put into the hands of the Duke of Bourbon and the Prince of Orange, to be by them held till all the differences between France and Brittany should be amicably settled; and, finally, that a congress should be held at Tournai for that settlement. Maximilian pretended to act merely as a friendly mediator, and the French had their eyes too constantly fixed on their own intrigues and deceptions to perceive his.[1]

Thus finished the war of 1489. The English had expected great glory, and they got none. The harshness used in levying the subsidy had driven the northern counties into insurrection, and had cost the life of the king's lieutenant, the Earl of Northumberland, who was murdered by the people. At one moment this insurrection threatened to shake the throne, but it was put down by an army commanded by the Earl of Surrey. John à Chambre, "a very *boute-feu* (fire-brand), who bore much sway amongst the vulgar and popular," was taken alive; and Sir John Egremont, who had joined the insurgents for higher objects, "fled into Flanders to the Duchess of Burgundy, whose palace was the sanctuary and receptacle of all traitors against the king."[2] John à Chambre was executed at York in great state, for he was hanged upon a gibbet raised a stage higher, as a traitor paramount, and a number of his men were hanged upon the lower story, round about him.

A.D. 1490. In the beginning of this year parliament made up the deficiency in the subsidy (which, instead of £75,000, had produced only £25,000) by passing a new grant of a tenth and fifteenth, in order that the war with France might be carried on with vigour; for Henry's interests were not taken into account by the treaty of Frankfort, and it was already evident that that treaty would not preserve the independence of Brittany. The English people again expected to be gratified by an active war, but Henry put their money into his coffers, and sent some priests to the Continent to negotiate with the various courts. A new coalition was now formed, the principal members being Henry, Ferdinand of Spain (a sovereign who was his match in craft), and Maximilian, King of the Romans,[3] wherein each sovereign, under the pretext of aiming at the benefit of Europe by checking French ambition, sought nothing but his own selfish aggrandizement.

Maximilian, whose suit had formerly been approved by Duke Francis, in spite of the treaty of Frankfort, and without consulting his new allies, whose treaty, as yet, remained a secret, proposed an immediate marriage with the young duchess, and Anne was induced to give her consent. But at the moment, Maximilian feared to make the journey into Brittany either by land or water, and sent the Prince of Orange in his stead. A marriage, by proxy, was performed at Rennes with so much mystery, that the servants of Anne were not aware of it until some time after, and the date of the ceremony has never been precisely ascertained. As soon as that disappointed suitor, the fierce D'Albret, ascertained the object of the Prince of Orange's mission, he gave information to the French court, and betrayed the important city of Nantes, which he had surprised, to a French army. As the treaty of Frankfort had been but indifferently observed by the French, and as they had kept possession of many of the fortresses in the heart of Brittany, they renewed the war with many advantages. The young duchess applied to her husband for aid; but he was again distressed by the revolt of his Flemish subjects, and could give her nothing but the empty title of "Queen of the Romans," which she now publicly assumed; and King Henry, in reply to her demands for English troops, increased her distresses by asking her for money at a time when her coffers were quite empty, and when the only money current in Brittany was stamped leather cut into pieces of different sizes.

About the same time an important revolution had taken place in the French court. King Charles, who was now in his twenty-first year, freed himself from the authority and guardianship of his sister, released the Duke of Orleans from his dungeon at Bourges, changed most of the ministers and officers, and took upon himself the business of government. This politic and crafty king, who, however, was excessively ignorant in other respects, saw that to obtain possession of Brittany by force of arms would, after all, be a work of great danger and difficulty, and he resolved to obtain his end in a very different manner. For more than seven years he had been solemnly affianced to Margot—the "gentle demoiselle," the daughter of the fair Mary of Burgundy and Maximilian. Margot had been "nourished and brought up" at the French court, and, as she was now in her eleventh year, it was expected that the marriage would be consummated in two or three years. But Charles, who had now firm possession of the rich provinces of France which had been constituted her dower, and who saw but a distant and uncertain prospect of deriving any further advantage from the contract, determined to break it, and marry the Duchess Anne, in spite of that princess'

[1] *Daru; Bacon.*   [2] *Bacon.*
[3] *Rymer; Rot. Parl.; Bacon; Daru.*

marriage by proxy to Maximilian, the *father* of Margot; for thus he confidently hoped to obtain quiet possession of Brittany. This sudden move took all parties by surprise. At the same time Charles bribed most of the ladies in the court of Brittany, and cajoled or terrified the ministers of that weak and distracted government. The Countess of Laval, the Countess of Dunois, the Marshal de Rieux, and Montauban, chancellor of the duchy, engaged to obtain Anne's assent; and the Duke of Orleans, who had formerly aspired to her hand, now pleaded and intrigued in favour of his sovereign. But they had a greater difficulty than they expected. The young duchess, or "Queen of the Romans," considered her marriage contract with Maximilian as binding, both by Divine and human law; and she was well aware of the contract which existed between the King of France and Margot of Burgundy. She was now in her fifteenth year, and her natural talents had been developed by an unusually careful education, and by an early experience in the affairs and troubles of the world. She saw that this new husband they wished to force upon her was the oppressor of her country—the despoiler of her family; it was sword in hand that he wooed her, and he was not a generous conqueror. Besides all this, he was rude, ugly, and illiterate, while she was learned, accomplished, and remarkably beautiful. Though constantly assailed by her ladies and her ministers, her repugnance did not yield until a French army advanced and threatened to besiege her in her capital. Then, seeing that she must be either the wife or the captive of Charles, she consented to a treaty, the principal article of which was, that she should marry the French king, and convey to him her rights over Brittany. Charles paid Anne a short visit in Rennes, and then retired into Touraine. His court maintained a specious farce to the last; they treated his affianced bride Margot as Queen of France, giving her splendid fêtes at the very moment that Charles was enforcing another marriage; and still farther to lull and delude Maximilian, they drew up and published an extraordinary passport or safe-conduct, permitting the Duchess Anne to travel through France to join her husband, the King of the Romans, in Flanders. But now the scene changed: instead of his bride, it was his rejected daughter that Charles sent to Maximilian; and the fair bride, the heiress of Brittany, was conducted to the castle of Langeais, in Touraine, and there married to Charles on the 6th of December, 1491.[1]

A.D. 1492. Maximilian, who had lost for himself a wife and a great terri-tory, for his daughter a husband and one of the first thrones in Europe, made every court in Europe resound with his complaints and imprecations; and he threatened France with an invasion from the co-operating armies of the house of Austria, of Spain, and of England. Henry, seeing that there was business to be done in the way of money-making, pretended to be greatly shocked (irritation was a state of mind he never felt or affected) at the double-dealing and overtopping ambition of his cousin of France: he addressed himself to the gathering up of the loosened threads of the European coalition, and he summoned a parliament to vote him fresh supplies—almost the sole duty which parliament had to perform in his reign. During the preceding summer he had levied a few troops, and as recently as the mouth of October he had obtained a grant of two tenths and two fifteenths.[2] He now, in the month of January, pressed for an accelerated rate of payment, and got a parliamentary sanction to measures by which the English gentry might ruin themselves in bearing personally the expenses of a campaign. An act was passed to allow the warlike spirits, who were eager for glory, to alienate their estates without payment of the ordinary fees or fines, and to enfeoff lands, to the end that their executors might have funds to fulfil their bequests.[3] Many persons of the best quality, knights and noblemen, thus encouraged, proceeded at once to sell their estates, or to raise money upon them. They hoped to indemnify themselves by conquests and possessions in France; but, in the event, they found that they had impoverished—in many instances utterly ruined — themselves and their families to no purpose. Henry had declared in parliament, with his own mouth, that Charles was a disturber of the Christian world, and that he was now determined to conquer the French crown, his rightful inheritance, for himself. The levies of troops proceeded with rapidity; and from one end of England to the other nothing was heard but the magical words of Crecy and Poictiers, Azincourt and Verneuil. "But, for all this," says Bacon, "and though the king showed great forwardness for a war, not only to his parliament and court, but to his privy council likewise (except the two bishops[4] and a few

---

[1] *Daru; Bacon; Archives de Nantes* and *Actes de Bretagne,* quoted by Daru.

[2] He had also issued a commission to extort money in the different counties and cities, under the illegal name of "Benevolence." The citizens of London were forced to pay £10,000. Archbishop Morton, now chancellor, put men between the horns of a cruel dilemma: if they lived frugally and without show, they were told that they must be rich from their parsimony, and therefore could well afford to pay; if they lived hospitably and splendidly, their rate of expenditure proved that they must be opulent, and therefore they could well afford to pay.

[3] *Rot. Parl.*

[4] Morton and Fox.

more); yet, nevertheless, in his secret intentions, he had no purpose to go through with any war upon France. But the truth was, that he did but traffic with that war to make his return in money." Some suspicion was excited by seeing that he let the spring, and the summer too, go by without taking the field. At last, in the month of October, a season in which commanders usually thought of retiring into winter quarters, and not of opening a campaign, he embarked, and sailed for Calais, where he safely landed with a magnificent army of 25,000 foot and 1600 horse. Some of his captains ventured to hint that, after all, this would prove a mere demonstration, and that the king would not have taken the field at such a time of the year if he were not sure of concluding a peace presently.[1] The fact was, Henry had arranged a treaty three months before this, and peace was in substance concluded with Charles before the army left England; but this he was anxious to conceal; and he silenced the captains by asserting that, as he had come over to make an entire conquest of France, which was not the work of one summer, it was of no consequence at what season he began the invasion, especially as he had Calais ready for winter quarters. To have an air of doing something, he marched from Calais to Boulogne, and sat down before that place as if he meant to besiege it. So completely was this campaign settled beforehand upon paper, that the French did not employ the useless and expensive ceremony of setting an army on foot to resist the invaders. There were scarcely any troops between the coast and the capital. This reliance upon a secret bargain might have proved dangerous, but King Charles had a secret security in his hands, as we shall see presently. Instead of pressing the siege, Henry caused letters from his ambassadors to be published in the camp, showing that no co-operation was to be expected from Ferdinand and Maximilian, and that no reliance was to be placed on either of those allies. On the 27th of October, eight days after his arrival before Boulogne, he summoned twenty-four of the principal officers of the English army to a solemn council, and submitted to their consideration the preliminaries of a treaty of peace with France. Those great captains did what they were required to do, and what they had been paid to do (for all Henry's favourites touched some French gold): they put their names to a report, and strenuously advised him to sign the treaty. Early in November two treaties were duly signed—one public, the other private. By the first,[2] Henry and Charles were to live in peace and alliance all the days of their lives; and the peace between the two countries was to last for one year after the death of the survivor of the two kings. By the second, Charles was to pay Henry, by instalments, the sum of £149,000 sterling; £124,000 to go in discharge of all claims upon Anne of Brittany, and £25,000 in payment of the pension (our kings called it tribute) due to Edward IV. It was thus that Henry, under the full sway of his money-making spirit, sold war, or the hopes of it, to the people, and peace to his enemies. "But the truth is, this peace was welcome to both kings: to Charles, for that it assured unto him the possession of Brittany, and freed the enterprise of Naples: to Henry, for that it filled his coffers, and that he foresaw, at that time, a storm of inward troubles coming upon him, which presently after broke forth."[3]

---

[1] Sismondi remarks that at this time, France had considerably outstripped England in the military art. "Henry VII.," he says, "was clear-sighted to be aware that no sooner should he be engaged in a war with France, than a rebellion would break out in England. He knew the Continent, where he had lived long, and that the time of Crecy, Poictiers, and Azincourt, perpetually recalled to the remembrance of the English, had passed away. The military art had undergone great improvements in France. Charles VIII. had at his disposition a superb artillery, superior to that of all Europe beside; a body of men-at-arms, as constantly exercised during peace as during war; *francs-archers*, whom his predecessors had for thirty years been training for the field; and brave bands of Swiss, ever ready to rally under the flag of France. The English, on the contrary, for two generations, had no military practice, beyond the sudden ebullitions of their civil wars, which lasted only for a few days; they had no troops of the line, and they had brought their artillery to no perfection. Besides, they were far from prodigal in their subsidies, and could not long maintain a war requiring enormous expense for the transport of troops and provisions by sea."

[2] This treaty went by the name of the peace of Etaples.

[3] *Bacon.*

CHAPTER II.—CIVIL AND MILITARY HISTORY.—A.D. 1492—1509.

HENRY VII.—ACCESSION, A.D. 1485—DEATH, A.D. 1509.

Perkin Warbeck, a new pretender to the crown—He is used as a tool by the courts of France and Burgundy—Contradictory reports of his real origin—Execution of Warbeck's abettors in England—Sir William Stanley executed as a traitor—Warbeck makes an unsuccessful landing in England—He repairs to Scotland—State of Scotland at this period—Rebellion against James III, its king—His defeat and assassination—Succeeded by James IV.—Plots of Henry VII. against James IV.—James adopts the cause of Warbeck—He invades England in Warbeck's behalf—Unsuccessful result of the invasion—Warbeck dismissed from Scotland—He again lands in England—He is defeated and taken prisoner—His attempts to escape from the Tower—He is executed—Execution of the Earl of Warwick—Attempts of Charles VIII. of France to obtain Naples—His death—Marriage of Margaret, daughter of Henry, to James IV. of Scotland—Death of Prince Arthur, son of Henry—His widow espoused to his younger brother—Henry's extortions—His agents, Dudley and Empson—Henry entraps the Earl of Suffolk—Inquiry about the murder of the sons of Edward IV. in the Tower—Henry dispenses with parliaments—The Archduke Philip lands in England—Ungenerous advantages taken of the event by Henry—He seeks in marriage the widow of Philip—His negociations with Ferdinand of Spain—Last sickness and death of Henry VII.—His character.

HE "storm of inward trouble," which Henry had foreseen, proceeded from a new pretender to the crown, in right of an assumed descent from the house of York. In the preceding year a stranger—a beautiful young man—landed in the Cove of Cork, and gave himself out to be Richard, Duke of York, the second son of Edward IV. The murder of the elder son by order of their uncle Richard was admitted, but this youth (so went the story) had escaped by some marvellous means from the Tower; and, after being a fugitive and a wanderer for seven long years, had come to claim his inheritance. Without caring for the recent case of the baker's boy, the citizens of Cork warmly declared in favour of the adventurer, whose name was soon spread over the greater part of Ireland. Many of the Anglo-Irish nobles were quite ready to draw the sword; but the powerful Earl of Kildare was rather more cautious than he had been on the previous occasion, and the young man was induced to accept a pressing invitation to the French court. King Charles, who was then expecting the invasion of Henry, and who had not as yet begun his secret negotiations, saw the use that might be made of him in disturbing and alarming the English government, and he therefore gave him a most courteous reception, and caused his whole court to treat him as the real Duke of York and heir to the crown of England. A royal body-guard was appointed to wait upon him; the story of his adventures, and the list of his accomplishments, were diligently circulated; and Sir George Nevil, Sir John Taylor, and about 100 English exiles, went to Paris and bound themselves to his service. The person of this claimant was the security which Charles had against Henry, and of which he made the most, threatening to espouse his cause and to let him loose in England, backed by a French army; and it was this consideration that hastened the conclusion of the peace of Etaples. When that treaty was concluded, Charles turned the adventurer out of France. Henry endeavoured to make the French court deliver him up; but Charles, probably thinking that he might be useful hereafter, said that such a measure would be inconsistent with his honour. The wanderer then retired for protection and assistance to the Duchess of Burgundy. This princess pretended many scruples, and submitted his whole story to a studied and imposing scrutiny, in order that the world might see that she did not take up his cause lightly. All this, and something more, may have been necessary to counteract the recollections left by her conduct in relation to Simnel. But in the end she embraced her guest as her dear nephew, the living image of her loving brother King Edward IV. She bestowed on him the poetical surname of "The White Rose of England," in allusion to his pure Yorkist descent. The people of Flanders, out of their love and respect for the duchess, showed a great alacrity in believing what she desired, and, by means of the active commercial intercourse between them and the English, the present condition of the young man was soon made known,[1] and a correspondence was opened in his behalf in England. Sir Robert Clifford was despatched as the confidential agent of these malcontents to the court of the Duchess Margaret, to ascertain whether this were a true prince or not. Sir Robert

---

[1] Bacon says, "The news came *blazing* and *thundering* over into England that the Duke of York was sure alive."

reported that he had seen "The White Rose," had conversed with him and his aunt, and that there could not be a shadow of doubt as to his birth and rights. But Henry also had sent *his* secret emissaries into the country, and *they* framed a report of a very different nature, stating, as the result of their diligent researches, that "The White Rose" was none other than one Peterkin or Perkin Warbeck, the son of a merchant—a converted Jew—of the city of Tournai; that he had lived much with the English merchants in Flanders, and that he had recently been travelling about Europe as a servant to Lady Brompton, the wife of one of the exiles. In the summer of 1493 Henry despatched an embassy to the Archduke Philip, son of Maximilian and Mary of Burgundy, grandson of Charles the Rash, and now sovereign prince. The ambassadors were charged to demand the surrender, or at least the expulsion of Warbeck; but the answer they received was, that, to have the love and favour of the King of England, the archduke from that time forward would neither aid nor assist Perkin or his accomplices, but that it was not in his power to interfere with the duchess-dowager, because she, in the lands assigned to her for her dower, might, as a sovereign princess, do and order all things at her own will and pleasure. Henry upon this withdrew the mart of English cloth from Antwerp to Calais, and prohibited all intercourse with Flanders. "After this the king, looking circumspectly to his matters, purposed to pacify the storms and blasts that he perceived to be growing rather by policy and council than by dubious war." The first thing he did was to bribe Sir Robert Clifford and William Barly, his associate; and these secret agents of the English malcontents, won by his money and promises, betrayed the names of all the gentlemen in England who had entered into Warbeck's scheme. On the same day Henry caused to be arrested, in different places, and brought before him in London, John Ratcliffe, Lord Fitzwalter, Sir Simon de Mountford, Sir Thomas Thwaites, William Daubeney, Robert Ratcliffe, Thomas Cressemer, Thomas Astwood, "as also certain priests and religious men," as Sir William Richeforde, doctor of divinity, and Sir Thomas Poynes, both friars of St. Dominic's order, Dr. William Sutton, Sir William Worsely, dean of St. Paul's, Robert Layborne, and Sir Richard Lessey. It was not possible to keep secret so many arrests of conspicuous persons, and many who had been sharers in the same treason fled and took sanctuary. Judgment of death was passed upon all the prisoners, and Sir Simon de Mountford, Sir Robert Ratcliffe, and William Daubeney, were beheaded immediately. The others were pardoned, and all the priests for their order's sake; "but," adds the chronicler, "few of them lived long after." Lord Fitzwalter was pardoned of his life; but afterwards, being sent to Calais and there laid in hold, he was beheaded, because he corrupted the keepers in order to escape out of prison, intending, as was thought, to have gone to Perkin.

These transactions passed towards the end of the year 1494, or nearly two years after the peace of Etaples.[1]

A.D. 1495. Henry's suspicions had fallen upon Sir William Stanley, brother to Lord Stanley, who had placed the crown upon his head at Bosworth Field. After the festival of Christmas the king and court went to lodge in the Tower of London. One day, as Henry sat there in council, the false Clifford was introduced suddenly to enact a part. Falling upon his knees, as if he who had sold his party were in fear of his life, he implored the royal pardon; and Henry, as good an actor as the traitor, granted it with much benignity of countenance. The traitor was then questioned concerning the full extent of the conspiracy, and Clifford named Sir William Stanley. Henry expressed both horror and incredulity, but he recommended his friend Stanley to keep his room in the Tower, where Sir William was residing with the court in discharge of his duties as chamberlain. Regard had no doubt been paid to the convenience of having the court and prison within the same walls. On the following morning, when he was brought before the council, Stanley "denied little of that wherewith he was charged, nor endeavoured much to excuse or extenuate his fault, so that (not very wisely), thinking to make his offence less by confession, he made it enough for condemnation."[2] The judges at Westminster considered his confession sufficient grounds for a sentence of death. People could scarcely believe that Henry would refuse the royal pardon in such a case. To the Stanleys he had been chiefly indebted for the crown; the criminal himself had saved his life at Bosworth Field, when he was near falling under the furious charge of Richard; and the Lord Stanley, Sir William's brother, in addition to his many important services, was husband to the king's mother, who was still living. But the prisoner was "the richest subject for value in the kingdom"—and, accordingly, he died the death of a traitor on the 15th of February. Other political reasons, such as a wish to inspire terror by striking down a great man, have been assigned; but nearly all the writers who lived near the time seemed to agree in thinking that Stanley would have had a much better chance for his life if he had not been so very rich.[3]

---

[1] *Hall; Stow; Bacon; Rot. Parl.*   [2] *Bacon.*
[3] *Bacon; Hall; P. Virgil; André (MS. in Brit. Mus.); Stow.*

The party of Perkin Warbeck, after all these executions, and the treachery of Sir Robert Clifford, were filled with despair and distrust. At the same time, the Flemings, who suffered severely from the interruption of the trade with England, began to murmur, and even to threaten the pretender. Warbeck, upon this, adopted the bold resolution of landing in England. On the 3d of July, while the king was in Lancashire on a visit to his mother, a few hundred desperate men —English exiles or foreign adventurers—landed near Deal, and attempted to raise the country in favour of "The White Rose." The people were easily moved, but it was fiercely to repel, not to join, the invaders, who, after a sharp conflict, were driven back to the sea-shore. One hundred and sixty-nine were taken prisoners; the rest, with Perkin among them, returned with a press of sail to Flanders.[1] All the captives were driven to London tied together like a great team of cattle, and they were executed to a man, some at London and Wapping, others at different places upon the coast of Kent, Sussex, Essex, and Norfolk, their bodies being gibbeted, "for sea-marks or light-houses to teach Perkin's people to avoid the coast."[2]

A.D. 1496. The interruption of the commercial intercourse with Flanders was of necessity almost as injurious to the English as to the Flemings, and Henry agreed to a reconciliation with the Archduke Philip. A "great treaty of commerce" between the two countries was signed in the month of February, bearing this important appendage—that Philip should prevent the Dowager-duchess of Burgundy from assisting or harbouring the king's rebels, and that each of the contracting parties should banish from his dominions the enemies of the other.[3] Upon this, Warbeck, who could no longer stay in Flanders, returned to Ireland, where he met with a cold reception. From Ireland he crossed over to Scotland, where the court, which was incensed against Henry, received him with open arms.[4]

To James III., who had so readily recognized his accession, and made treaties with him, Henry was never a warm friend, or an open enemy. He kept up a correspondence with the factions in Scotland even at a time when he had no ground whatever for a quarrel with the king. But in the summer of 1487, when he was preparing to take part in the war on the Continent, he despatched his favourite negotiator, Richard Fox, lord privy seal, who had recently been appointed to the bishopric of Exeter, to negotiate with James, who referred him to the Bishop of Aberdeen. The two bishops agreed that the truce subsisting should be prolonged till the 1st of September, 1489; and then, taking up a project which had already been entertained in the English court, they settled the following extraordinary marriages: 1. The King of Scots was to take to wife Elizabeth Woodville, widow of Edward IV.; 2. James, Prince of Scotland and Duke of Rothesay, was to marry one of the daughters of Elizabeth Woodville and Edward IV.; and, 3. The Marquis of Ormond, the second son of the Scottish king, was to marry another daughter.[5] This treaty, however, soon fell to the ground, because the Scottish monarch, as a preliminary, insisted upon the surrender of the town of Berwick, which, it appears, Henry had at one time promised. From this moment the English court gave a more decided countenance to the faction of the Scottish aristocracy. Although the turbulent Albany had been killed at a tournament in France, and the great Douglas had been confined like a monk to the monastery of Lindores, the barons were still powerful, and still bent on the destruction of the king, whom they had treated so harshly, that they could never believe in the sincerity of his reconciliation and forgiveness. When the unfortunate James began to display more activity and vigour than had been customary with him, and to adopt measures for curtailing their authority, they won over his eldest son, the Duke of Rothesay, a youth only in his sixteenth year, but who had some ability, and all that impatience which has so frequently distinguished the heirs of weak kings. At the same time they strengthened their party with some of the Scottish bishops and higher clergy, who were irritated by the king's denunciation of the practice of buying and selling church promotions. The King of England secretly sanctioned the unnatural conspiracy of the son against the father; but so adroitly did Henry manage this matter, that it could never be discovered to what extent he went. James was not very wise in his new energy: he set up his second son, the Marquis of Ormond, in opposition to his first; and he still further irritated the higher order of the clergy by insisting that the right of disposing of vacant benefices belonged solely to him, and not to the court of Rome. His parliament went along with him in this measure, and interdicted appeals to the pope in such cases. They also passed acts of great severity against the Earls of Argyle and Angus, the Lords Drummond, Hailes, and Lyle, the Bishop of Glasgow, and many others. As

---

[1] It appears that Warbeck never landed, but kept himself on board with sails bent, to make off in case of not finding the people favourable.
[2] Bacon; Fabyan; Hall; Stow; Rot. Parl.
[3] Rymer. This last clause Henry continued to insert in all his treaties with foreign powers.
[4] Hall; Polydore Virgil; Stow; Tytler, Hist. Scot.
[5] Rymer.

soon as this parliament adjourned, the barons collected their vassals in arms; and the Duke of Rothesay, who was now addressed as "King of Scotland," issued from Stirling Castle, and put himself at their head. Upon this, James sent the Earl of Buchan, the Lord Bothwell, and the Bishop of Murray, on an embassy to Henry, to solicit the assistance of a body of English troops—in every respect the worst step he could have taken. This application was soon known, and it was made one of the strongest grounds upon which the Scottish insurgents declared that he had forfeited the crown. His son was immediately proclaimed under the title of James IV.; and a new administration was formed, which acted in his name. Henry, hoping to profit by these troubles, and caring little in what manner, did not hesitate to recognize the son as king. The unfortunate father was soon driven from Edinburgh; his baggage and money were seized at Leith; and he escaped with difficulty into Fife, by throwing himself on board a ship belonging to the brave Sir Andrew Wood. As the whole of the south had risen in arms against him he fled to the north, where he was soon joined by the Earls of Athole, Huntly, and Crawford, the Lord Lindsay of the Byres, a veteran who had served the French in the wars on the Continent, and by many other noblemen of great name. Old Lindsay presented him with a gray charger remarkable for height, power, and spirit, and said, "Only keep a good seat, and his speed will outdo all I have ever seen, either to flee or follow." From the north James soon turned southward, with an army of 30,000 men. He found his enemies, with his own son at their head, at Blackness, near Linlithgow. His force was far superior; but by the advice of some of his friends he listened to terms of accommodation, and even signed a pacific treaty. But almost immediately after, either with or without his consent, the Earl of Buchan fell unawares on the prince's army, gained a decided advantage, and killed a great many men; though the affair did not break up the array, or even force the prince to retreat. Indeed, within a few days the king renewed the treaty with his enemies, who stood with arms in their hands, and who obtained very advantageous conditions. He then retired to Edinburgh Castle, and dismissed his northern forces. But the prince's party, or rather the faction which made that youth their instrument, either kept together their forces, or re-collected them immediately after the pacification of Blackness, and once more forced the king into the field. After some minor operations, this short but sanguinary civil war was terminated on the 18th of June, 1488, at Little Canglar, a moor upon the east of a brook called Sauchie Burn, about two miles from Stirling, and one mile from the memorable field of Bannockburn. The royalists were rather inferior in number, and the naked Highlanders were not a match for the hardy and well-armed Galwegians, and the yet better equipped Borderers of Liddesdale and Annandale. While his followers still maintained a desperate conflict, the king, who was no warrior, and apparently no horseman, stuck his spurs into his charger, and galloped from the field. The horse he rode was the gallant gray which had been presented to him by the Lord Lindsay of the Byres, and which probably proved too much for an unskilful or a timid rider. It is possible that James may really have been killed by a fall from this horse; but the following is the singular account given by all the Scottish chroniclers who lived nearest to the time, and also, we believe, universally adopted by later writers, as well as still attested by popular tradition. As the king crossed the brook of Bannock, close to a small hamlet called Miltoun, a poor woman who was drawing water from the brook, threw down her pitcher in alarm close before him; upon which his bounding steed took fright, swerved in his course, and threw him to the ground with such violence as to deprive him of his senses. The cotters ran to his assistance, and, wholly ignorant of his quality, carried him into the house of the miller, took off his heavy armour, and laid him upon a wretched flock bed, with a coarse rug thrown over him. As soon as he recovered his senses he asked for some priest or monk to whom he might confess before he died. The poor people then asked who he was; and James, as the story goes, said incautiously, "Alas! this morning I was your king." Then the woman of the house ran forth wringing her hands and crying out for a priest to shrive the king! Attracted by her clamour, a man, who was one of a party of stragglers from the victorious army of the prince, went into the house, and recognizing the king, stooped over him, as if he were a priest about to administer the last consolations of religion, and stabbed him to the heart with a dagger. James III. was only thirty-five years old when he perished. At the dismal news of his death his undutiful son was overwhelmed with remorse; but though this feeling embittered the remainder of his life, and cast a gloom upon his most festive hours, it did not prevent him from ascending the throne, nor from embarking most ardently in the pursuit of pleasure. He attended his father's funeral, and then proceeded to Perth, and was crowned at Scone Abbey, with the usual pomp and rejoicings, on the 26th of June. He had set an example highly dangerous to kings; but this did not seem to affect Henry, who granted passports to the ambassadors of his "dear cousin," James IV., taking care, however, at the same time, to send strong reinforcements to Berwick, which might be attacked with the vigour which generally characterizes a new revolution. Having agreed with the young king for a three years' truce, he then waited events; and the course they took, for some time, seemed likely to lay Scotland at his feet without his making war, which he disliked, and without his touching his treasures, which he disliked still more.

The late King of Scotland had not died unlamented, and there were some bold and desperate men who were quite ready to try another revolution. In the following year the Lord Forbes took up arms, and marched through the country with a bloody shirt, said to be the late king's, fixed upon a spear, as his banner; and this ghastly token had a wonderful effect upon the common people, who had always been rather attached to the deceased sovereign. At the same time the Lord Lyle occupied the strong castle of Dumbarton in defiance of the new government, and the Earl of Lennox, the Lord Darnley, and some others, armed their vassals and put their castles in a state of defence. But James, who was as active and warlike as his father had been sedentary and pacific, and who was surrounded by men of energy, rapidly collected an army, and, after a few sieges and a desperate nocturnal fight at Talla Moss, about sixteen miles from Stirling, he completely suppressed this revolt. His clemency in the hour of victory and triumph was still more effective than his arms, and the disaffected nobles were pretty generally reconciled, and even attached to his government.

In the following year (1490), at the very moment when the Scottish king was negotiating with Henry in the most friendly manner for the settlement of some Border differences, and for a prolongation of the truce, a dark plot was hatched at the English court for the seizing of his person, together with that of his brother, the Duke of Ross, the heir-apparent to the throne. Ramsay, Lord Bothwell, the favourite of the late king, who had fled into England, the Earl of Buchan, who had recently been received into James' favour, and one Sir Thomas Tod, of the realm of Scotland, entered into an agreement with Henry to seize the two princes and deliver them both into his hands. For present aid in this treasonable enterprise Henry advanced the sum of £260; but, with his accustomed parsimony, he stipulated that the money should be restored to him by a certain day. The bargain was drawn up at Greenwich, and Tod delivered his son as an hostage or security.[1] But although James had no suspicion, and had probably never learned that such a plan was on foot, the project came to nothing. In the following year Henry received with open arms the Earl of Angus, one of the most powerful of the Scottish nobles, and concluded another dark agreement with him; and though this conspiracy, which was known, at least in part, to James, failed, like that of Bothwell, Buchan, and Tod, he did not, for that, cease to maintain a secret intercourse with the disaffected portion of the Scottish nobility, nor neglect to keep spies in the court. James, though he was very imperfectly informed of these practices, still knew enough to excite his indignation; and his natural disposition alone made him hate the cold and crafty character of Henry. The young king, moreover, had, from the time of his accession, kept up a friendly correspondence with Henry's implacable enemy, the Duchess of Burgundy; and there are good reasons for believing not only that James knew of Warbeck's coming, but that he had negotiated with him several years before he came.

Whether James entered into these relations with his eyes open to the fact that Perkin was not what he gave himself out to be, or whether he, at this or at any later time, believed him to be an impostor, must remain matter of doubtful speculation. What is certain is, that he and his people had long entertained the notion of breaking with Henry, as with a man who could never be trusted, and who had the art of making peace more dangerous than war. When, therefore, the wanderer presented himself, he found the Scots in a humour which would not dispose them to be very critical in the examination of his proofs of royal birth; but such was the wonderful tact, such the winning manners of Perkin, that he soon convinced people through their feelings to himself personally, and most of them seem to have proceeded in the honest belief that their interesting guest was really the person that he reported himself to be. There was certainly no real prince at the time more beautiful, and graceful, and accomplished, than this extraordinary pretender. Immediately after his arrival in Scotland, James IV., who always addressed him as "cousin," entertained him with tournaments and other great festivals; and when these were over he took him with him on a royal progress through Scotland, by which means he was seen and enthusiastically admired by all classes. As if to prove the warmth of his attachment, and the sincerity of his conviction that Perkin was the real Duke of York, he married him in a short time to the Lady Catherine Gordon, the beautiful daughter of the Earl of Huntly, who, on the mother's side, was nearly related to the royal house of Stuart.

---

[1] The industrious Rymer first brought this transaction to light. The original agreement is published in his *Fœdera, Conventiones*, &c.

Henry was much disquieted by these transactions; nor were his apprehensions abated when he learned that James had summoned all his lieges to meet him in arms at Lauder. The first thing he did was to renew an old friendship with Ramsay, Lord Bothwell, the discontented favourite of the late king;[1] to send a present to the reigning king's brother; and to employ one Master Wyat, an Englishman, and an old servant in this kind of business, as a secret envoy in Scotland. Henry's bosom friend, Fox, now Bishop of Durham, was commissioned to negotiate in a more open manner; but he was less successful than Wyat. The English bishop was soon succeeded at the Scottish court by a French knight, a more welcome ambassador, from Charles VIII. This was the Sire de Concressault, who had been captain of the French guard of honour assigned to Perkin by King Charles in 1493. In public, the accomplished diplomatist showed himself as a mediator anxious to reconcile the differences existing between the French and English sovereigns; in private, he favoured Perkin and the war party, and pressed for the invasion of England; for his master Charles was irritated and alarmed by the conduct of Henry, who had now formed a league with the pope, the King of the Romans, the King of Spain, the Duke of Milan, and the Doge of Venice, in order to prevent the French from establishing themselves as conquerors beyond the Alps. In a short time Ramsay, Lord Bothwell, wrote secretly to Henry, informing him that the Earl of Buchan[2] took it upon himself to fulfil what was meant, and that he hoped to be able, "in the long nights," to surprise Warbeck in his tent, and take him prisoner. He went on to tell his employer that he had spoken to the king's brother, who engaged to do his grace service, and not to join the army against his grace for aught the king might do, and that the Bishop of Moray undertook to solicit the young prince to go over to his grace, in case his brother King James should persist, against the will of his baronry and his whole people, in making this war. This spy, who was trusted by King James all the time, certainly worked hard to earn Henry's money, and scrupled at no measures, however base. In other letters he mentions the names of the Dacres, Nevils, Lovels, and Herons, and some other gentlemen of the north of England, as being in correspondence, or having stolen interviews, with King James and Warbeck.[3]

The Dowager-duchess of Burgundy contrived to send to Scotland sixty picked men-at-arms, and a supply of crossbows, arms, armour, and other military stores; and Perkin soon found himself at the head of 1400 men of all manner of nations. James now concluded a treaty with Warbeck as with a sovereign prince. Many of the Scottish nobles besides Bothwell and Buchan were sold to Henry, and ready to betray the army; others, out of prudence and good policy, were against the war, for Scotland had been much weakened by the recent internal dissensions; but James, who was young and ardent, knew not the treachery of one party, and rejected the advice of the other. By some means not explained, Buchan failed in his plan of seizing Warbeck in his tent; and on the 8th of September Bothwell informed Henry that, on the 15th day of the same month, James would be at Ellam Kirk, within ten miles of the marches of England, with Perkin and his followers, and all the Scottish troops he could muster.[4] The spy made a trifling mistake in point of date; but early in the winter James crossed the Borders, being preceded by a declaration of war, and an address on the part of Perkin to his faithful subjects, the people of England. Had Perkin come alone, or with the few Englishmen who had joined his standard, his chance would have been better, though in no circumstances could that chance have been a good one. Warned in proper time by Bothwell, Henry had adopted measures to indispose men's minds to insurrection.

Instead of a general rising in his favour, Perkin saw that he, and the Border gentlemen who had joined him, were regarded with detestation, as being in close league with the natural enemies of England. At the same time, the French adventurers could not agree with the Germans and Flemings, and the Scots quarrelled with all the foreigners alike. Then, to convert Warbeck's last faint hope into despair, the ill-disciplined invaders, with or without James' consent, began to plunder the country, and thereby to convert every yeoman and every peasant into a determined enemy. Warbeck said (or at least it is reported, to his honour) that he would rather lose the throne than gain it by the sufferings of Englishmen. It should appear that the cattle and stores had been removed betimes from the open country, and that this marauding expedition was not very productive in the article of victuals; for the invaders soon felt the want of provisions, and thereupon retreated across the Borders without fighting a battle, or waiting for a sight of an English army, just as Bothwell had foretold.[5]

---

[1] At the memorable execution in 1482, when James III.'s favourites were hanged by the barons on the bridge of Lauder, this Ramsay was the only one that escaped. As the plot for seizing King James and his brother seems to have originated with him, he must have had a genius for this kind of undertaking.

[2] Buchan, it will be remembered, had also been concerned in the Greenwich plot for seizing James and his brother.

[3] *Original Letters illustrative of English History*, by Sir Henry Ellis. [4] Ibid.

[5] *Bacon; Hall; Stow; Tytler's Hist. Scot.; Sir Henry Ellis' Letters.*

This incursion, though little better than a foul raid, was productive of serious consequences; for the people of Cornwall, considering themselves over-taxed by Henry to meet the expenses of the war,[1] rose in open rebellion, and crying for the execution of the Archbishop Morton, chancellor and chief minister, and of Sir Reginald Grey, they poured into Devonshire to the number of 16,000 men. From Devonshire they advanced into Somersetshire, where they were joined by the Lord Audley, and many other persons of less note. They then marched through Wiltshire, Hampshire, and Surrey, into Kent, and encamped on Blackheath. Henry, whose great sagacity did not preserve him from superstition, believed that Saturday was his lucky day; and, accordingly, he ordered battle to be given on a Saturday. While the Lord Daubeney moved from London to attack in front, the Earl of Oxford made a circuit to attack in rear; and the king, with a great body of reserve and most of the artillery, kept his person out of danger at St. George's Fields, in the suburbs of London. Lord Daubeney, after a sharp conflict, in which the Cornish archers did great execution, drove in the advance post of the insurgents at Deptford-Strand, carried the bridge, ascended the hill, and established himself on the heath. At the same time, Oxford showed himself in their rear. Though without horse or artillery, or any good officers to command them, the Cornish men fought bravely, until 2000 of them were slain. Fifteen hundred were taken with arms in their hands; and among the prisoners were Lord Audley and Flammock, an attorney, and Joseph, a blacksmith. The Lord Audley was beheaded at Tower Hill; Flammock and Joseph were hanged, drawn, and quartered, at Tyburn. The blacksmith died like a hero. All the rest were pardoned by proclamation, and the prisoners were permitted to compound for their liberty with the men that had taken them.

The battle of Blackheath was fought on the 22d of June, 1497. A short time before it happened King James again crossed the Tweed, and swept the country as far as the Tees; but he retreated when the Earl of Surrey marched northward with a powerful army. The English then ravaged a part of the Scottish borders; but after gaining or losing a few insignificant conflicts they retired, and the war languished. Henry's correspondents were not slow in informing him that James wished for peace; whereupon the English king repented an offer he had already made of the hand of his eldest daughter, Margaret, to his cousin, the King of Scots. Some time elapsed before the treaty was signed, and the marriage was not concluded till more than five years after. James, though young, thoughtless, dissipated, and extravagant, was too honourable to think of selling Perkin Warbeck, for whom he had coined his plate, and even converted the great chain of gold which he was accustomed to wear into money. Before dismissing his army, or concluding anything with Henry, he permitted Perkin to depart; being no longer able to assist him, and seeing that, if he remained, his presence would only embarrass the negotiations. A ship was privately got ready at Ayr, and a delicate attention was paid to whatever might contribute to the comfort of the passengers. Warbeck was escorted to the sea-port by a guard of horse, and he embarked with a few followers who were much attached to him, and who would on no account leave him. Though he had nothing to offer her but a wandering and perilous life, his wife resolved to share his fortunes to the last—for, prince or impostor, he had won the heart of that beautiful woman. At the end of July the "Duke and Duchess of York"—as they were still called —left Scotland for ever.[2] They stood over to Ireland, and, landing at Cork, Warbeck tried once more to raise the Irish. Failing in this attempt, he acted on the bold resolution of trying his fortunes in Cornwall. At the beginning of September he arrived in Whitsand Bay, with four small barks and some six or seven score fighting men. From the coast he marched inland to Bodmin, the native place of Joseph the blacksmith, whose fate at Tyburn seemed to his townsmen to call for vengeance. In other parts of the country there were many thousands who had lost relations and friends in the fierce fight at Blackheath, and who were equally eager for revenge. Warbeck soon found himself at the head of a host. Having assumed the title of Richard IV., King of England and France, and Lord of Ireland, and having sent his wife, "for present safety," to Mount St. Michael, he advanced into Devonshire, and, being joined by many disaffected persons, appeared before the city of Exeter on Sunday, the 17th of September, with an irregular force, estimated by those within the walls at 10,000 men. The nobility and gentry of all the neighbouring country had flocked into that city, where, headed by the Earl of Devonshire, and seconded by the wealthier burghers, they bade defiance to the insurgents, who had no artillery, nor any kind of engines proper for a siege. The Cornish men, however, boldly as-

---

[1] On the 13th of February, 1497, soon after receiving news that James and Warbeck had crossed the Borders, parliament passed a grant of two-tenths and two-fifteenths. The Cornish men pretended that the men of the north alone ought to pay for the defence of their own provinces.

[2] Tytler's *History of Scotland*. Mr. Tytler's curious extracts from the "Treasurer's Books" establish several very interesting points.

saulted the east and north gates; but they failed, and lost about 300 or 400 men. On the following morning they repeated their assaults upon the same two gates, and "especially at the north gate, which was again well and truly defended, and put Perkin from his purpose there; . . . insomuch, as when Perkin and his company had well assayed and felt the guns, they were fain to desire to have license to gather their company together, and so to depart and leave the city."[1] This failure disheartened such of the men of Devonshire as had joined the insurgents, and they began to return to their homes as quietly as they could; but the hardy men of Cornwall advised Warbeck to continue his march eastward, vowing that they were ready to die for him to a man. Making rapid marches, they reached Taunton, in Somersetshire, on the 20th, but they found no accession of force, though the country people, who were still complaining of the king's tax-gatherers, wished success to their enterprise. At Taunton their farther progress was checked by the presence of a royal army, numerous, provided with artillery, and well appointed in all particulars. The half-naked Cornish men, thus confronted, neither fled nor spoke of retreat; and Warbeck, showing a good countenance, rode along their lines, and made his dispositions for a battle, to be fought on the morrow; for the quiet shades of evening were stealing along the beautiful valley of Taunton Dean, and the royalists had pitched their tents and tethered their horses for the night. But Warbeck, with all his princely qualities, was deficient in one, very essential to princes in those days—he wanted courage; he was appalled by the sight of the measureless superiority of Henry's forces, and during the night he mounted a swift horse and fled from his company at Taunton, taking no leave nor license of them.[2] When morning dawned, and his flight was discovered, the Cornish men, without head or leader—"without stroke stricken"—submitted to the mercy of Henry, who hanged the ringleaders, and dismissed the rest, naked and starving. Great numbers of well-mounted men were despatched in every quarter in pursuit of Perkin, but his steed carried him well, and he reached the sanctuary

THE REFECTORY, BEAULIEU.[3]—From an engraving by Sparrow, dated 1766.

of Beaulieu, in the New Forest. There was also sent, with all speed, a troop of horse to St. Michael's Mount, in Cornwall, to seize, at all hazards, the person of the Lady Catherine Gordon, who had been sent there by her husband, " whom in all fortunes she entirely loved." "The king," adds Bacon, "sent in great diligence, not knowing whether she might be with child; *whereby the business would not have ended in Perkin's person.*" The horsemen easily got possession of the fair Catherine, and brought her like a captive and bondwoman to the king, in whose presence she blushed and wept bitterly. Her beauty and amiable countenance touched even the cold, impassive heart of Henry; he treated her with respect, almost with tenderness, and sent her to his wife, the Queen Elizabeth, in whose court she was received with great kindness.[4]

The sanctuary of Beaulieu was soon surrounded by the king's troops, but Henry hesitated to force so holy a place, and he proceeded by artifice, in which he was not often unsuccessful. He sent some of his skilful agents to work upon the

---

[1] Letter from the Earl of Devonshire to the king, dated the 18th of September, the same day on which this second attack was made.—Ellis' *Letters*.

[2] Letter from the king, dated the 25th of Sept.—*Sir H. Ellis.*

[3] The Cistercian abbey of Beaulieu was founded A.D. 1204, by King John. The stone wall which surrounded the precincts of the abbey is in several places nearly entire. The abbot's apartments, after the dissolution converted into a family seat, a long building, supposed to have been the dormitory, the ancient kitchen, and the refectory, are still standing. The church is entirely gone. The refectory, a plain stone building, with strong buttresses, and a curiously raftered oak roof, forms the parish church of the village of Beaulieu.

[4] *Hall; André; Bacon; Sir Henry Ellis' Letters.*

fears of Perkin, who, finding himself without help or hope, accepted the royal pardon, and, of his own will, frankly and freely departed out of sanctuary. Henry would not admit him into his presence, but his curiosity induced him to take a secret view, from behind a screen, of the spirit which had so long tormented him. A part of the royal army, whose presence was necessary for the enforcement of taxes and fines, marched westward into Devonshire and Cornwall. The commissioners appointed to levy fines upon the wealthier insurgents, according to one old writer,[1] "like a whirlwind, tossed and pierced the coffers and substance of the people;" and Bacon says that "they proceeded with such strictness and severity, as did much obscure the king's mercy in sparing of blood, with the bleeding of so much treasure."

When Henry returned to London, Warbeck rode behind him at a little distance, but not in any ignominious fashion. In order that he might be seen by all the citizens, he was sent through Cheapside and Cornhill to the Tower, riding on horseback in slow procession. The people crowded to gaze upon the handsome prisoner, whose wonderful adventures had occupied their minds during so many years. Some hooted and scoffed, but the majority preserved a wondering and respectful silence. When they saw the dismal gates close upon him they thought never to see him again; but presently he came forth of the Tower, and he was conveyed in the same slow state back to the palace at Westminster. In appearance, he lived at liberty in the court; in reality, he was watched by certain keepers, who were ordered never to lose sight of him, nor permit him to move from them a nail's breadth. He was not converted into a menial, like Simnel, but was treated with an outward show of respect. He was repeatedly examined before a select commission ; but, except a few particulars, which in no way explained the most mysterious parts of his story, his confessions were kept secret.[2]

A.D. 1498. Without speculating on Henry's motives, which it is clear were not penetrated by any of the contemporary writers, we will proceed to relate the outward and visible facts which wound up the marvellous history of Perkin Warbeck. In June, when he had resided some six or seven months in Henry's court, he contrived, or, what seems more probable, he was permitted to escape. Being immediately pursued, he took refuge in the house of Bethlem, called the Priory of Shene, beside Richmond, in Surrey. This house was one of those which enjoyed the right of sanctuary; but the prior having, by earnest solicitations, procured a promise from the king that his life should be spared, delivered him up. A paper was now put into his hand, and he was fettered in a pair of stocks before the door of Westminster Hall, where he stood a whole day, not without coarse insults; and there he read the paper, which purported to be his full confession. The next day he stood in the stocks at Cheapside, and read the same paper. The confession, which was afterwards printed by Henry's orders, though we believe that no full and authentic copy is preserved, was a very unsatisfactory, and in part a contradictory document. Henry's cunning and caution injured the weight of the evidence by which he wished all men should be convinced. After the second reading Perkin was shut up in the Tower, where he became the companion and friend of the unfortunate Earl of Warwick, who, after his exhibition in the city and at court, for the purpose of exposing the imposture of Simnel, had been recommitted to his old lodging.[3]

A.D. 1499. Perkin Warbeck had not been more than six months in the Tower when a new attempt was made to dethrone Henry; and one Ralph Wilford or Wulford, the son of a cordwainer, undertook to play the part of the Earl of Warwick. Several plots had been set on foot to release the unfortunate earl, and proclaim him king; but, though aided on one occasion by Charles VIII., they had all failed. Now a report was spread that Warwick had perished, or was missing in the Tower ; but after a short interval there was a whisper that he had escaped. From the borders of Sussex, Ralph Wilford and an Augustine friar, named Patrick, who was the chief contriver of this farce, stole into Kent, where they seem to have found some encouragement. The cordwainer's son told the story of his royal birth, captivity, and escape; and the monk undertook to prove it to be all true, in a discourse which he publicly delivered from the pulpit. Both, however, were arrested almost immediately: Ralph the scholar was executed—Patrick the monk and master was condemned to perpetual imprisonment. There was a very general impression at the time that this whole business "was but the king's device," and that the friar was soon permitted to go to some monastery abroad. Wilford was executed in the month of March. In the month of July it was rumoured that Warbeck and the Earl of Warwick had conspired together to escape from the Tower and get up a new insurrection. Such was the fascination of Perkin's manners, that he not only won the entire friendship of Warwick, but also the favour and kindness of his keepers. Strangways, Blewett, Astwood, and Long Roger, undertook to murder their master, Sir John Dig-

---

[1] *Hall*.   [2] *Bacon*.   [3] *Bacon; Hall; Grafton; Fabyan; André; Stow; Rymer.*

by, the governor, to get possession of the keys of the Tower, and to conduct the two captives to some place of safety, where *Warbeck might be proclaimed by the title of Richard IV.*, and whither Warwick might summon the retainers of his father the late Duke of Clarence. Such at least was the account given by the law officers of the king, though here again people doubted whether Henry had not excited the natural desires of the two prisoners for liberty, led them into the plot, and invented some of its worst features: for he was so cunning that it was not believed he could ever act in a straight-forward manner. The plot being discovered before it could be executed—or this at least being stated—Warbeck and Warwick were closely confined in separate cells, and preparations were made for their separate trials, for, though the only charge brought against Warwick was his being an accomplice of Perkin, it was not deemed wise to try them together. Henry's judges seem to have been ready to twist and turn the law just as it suited the purpose of their master; but on the present occasion there were long deliberations. At length, on the 16th of November, Warbeck was arraigned in Westminster Hall, upon divers treasons committed and perpetrated after his coming on land within this kingdom (for so the judges advised, because he was a foreigner). He was convicted, of course, and on the 23d day of the same month, he and John O'Water, the mayor of Cork, one of his first adherents, were drawn to Tyburn; there, on the scaffold, his confession was again read, and he affirmed, on the word of a dying man, that it was all true. Then he and his fellow-sufferer "asked the king's forgiveness, and died patiently."[1] Such was the end of this strange, long drama.

Before the execution of Warbeck the Earl of Warwick was brought, not before the judges, but as a peer (though he had never taken the oaths, and the act of attainder passed against his father, the Duke of Clarence, had never been reversed), to the bar of the House of Lords, and accused, not for the attempt to escape simply, but for the conspiring with Perkin to raise sedition, and destroy the king. The poor prince, who, from his long confinement, was unaccustomed to the ways of the world, and helpless and ignorant in a piteous degree, confessed to the indictment; the Earl of Oxford, as lord-steward, pronounced the judgment of the house; and on the 24th of November, three days after his trial, he was beheaded on Tower Hill.[2] Thus did Henry remove the last descendant of the Planta-

genets from whom he had anything to fear, and from this moment he stood without a competitor. The hapless Warwick was in his twenty-ninth year when he died; but he had been a state-prisoner from his childhood, and seems to have been almost as innocent as a child, when he was judicially murdered by the king and the degraded peers of England. The people, however, long continued to murmur; nor were their doubts wholly removed that Warbeck, after all, might have been the real Duke of York, and lawful heir to the throne. The dying words of that mysterious character might have been uttered on some secret promise of pardon, or on the threats of some execrable tortures; and the confession itself was so full of contradictions and reservations, that it could scarcely impose even on simple minds.[3] If there was a tenderer sympathy for the inoffensive Earl of Warwick, the exciting adventures of Warbeck were the more frequent theme of conversation. And what became of Warbeck's fair wife? The Lady Catherine continued in the queen's court, apparently much respected, and, on account of her beauty, the people continued to call her "The White Rose." She was afterwards re-married to Sir Matthew Cradoc, of North Wales, ancestor of the Earls of Pembroke, and was buried with him in the old church of Swansea, where their tomb and epitaph are still to be seen.

A.D. 1500. A fierce plague having broke out in London, the people considered it as a judgment from Heaven. After several changes of residence, Henry, partly from a delicate regard to his own health, and partly because he had business to transact with the Archduke Philip, went over to Calais, and stayed there till the pestilence was over. He invited the archduke to Calais, but that prince prudently declined putting himself within his power, and their meeting took place at St. Peter's Church, between Calais and St. Omer. The subjects of their long conference were commerce, and cross-marriages between their children; but there were no visible effects, and it was thought that the king's anxiety to confer personally with the archduke proceeded from some other causes, in which the case of Warbeck was included. About this time died, "much hated of the people," Morton, the chancellor and primate; but men were disappointed in their hopes that the death of that grinding minister, and the tranquillity at home and abroad, would render the king less eager for money.

---

[1] *Hall.*
[2] Blewett and Astwood, two of the servants of the governor of the Tower, were hanged at Tyburn, a few days after the execution of "the noble and commiserable" Earl of Warwick.

[3] The reader will be amused, though probably not convinced, by Walpole, who, in his *Historic Doubts*, maintains that Perkin Warbeck was really the Duke of York. For ourselves, we believe that Perkin was an impostor, but that Henry overdid his part, and never proved him to be one. We have, however, stated the clearer facts without any bias, and from them the reader may draw his own conclusions.

Charles VIII., of France, had now been nearly two years in his grave. In 1494, about sixteen months after buying off Henry by the treaty of Etaples, that strange king, who claimed by purchase from the house of Anjou an absurd right to the throne of the Two Sicilies, crossed the Alps with an army of 3600 men-at-arms, 20,000 French infantry, 8000 Swiss mercenaries, and an immense train of artillery. The little princes of the numerous states into which Italy was divided had no force to oppose to such an army, and their jealousies prevented the formation of a general league. The invaders poured on, from the foot of the Alps to the Bay of Naples, without meeting with any resistance. But Charles soon found that the lily of France was not destined to take root in an Italian soil.[1] The Neapolitans, who, in their frivolity and " mad love of change," had at first welcomed the French, were presently disgusted with their insolence, and opened communications with their expelled sovereign, Ferdinand II. of Aragon, who had not retired further than the island of Sicily. At the same time a formidable league, consisting of the pope, the King of the Romans, the King of Castile, the Duke of Milan, the republic of Venice, and a few of the minor Italian states, was formed against the invaders; and Charles not only lost his conquest as rapidly as he had made it, but had extreme difficulty in fighting his way back to France.[2] While waiting till the state of his finances should enable him to renew the mad enterprise, he gave himself up to pleasure and debauchery, neglecting his beautiful wife, Anne of Brittany. In 1498, he resolved to engage 15,000 men-at-arms, natives of Italy, and win over the pope, who had quarrelled with the republic of Venice, and with some other members of the coalition. " He also resolved, within himself, to lead a more chaste and religious life, to regulate the laws, to reduce taxation, under which his people were groaning, and to reform the church. He got good preachers about him, and was a constant hearer of their discourses."[3] Being thus in great glory in relation to this world, and in good mind as to the next [*his health had been for some time declining*], on the 7th of April, being the eve of Palm Sunday, he took his queen by the hand, and led her out of her apartment in the château of Amboise, where the court was then residing, to a place in which she had never been before, to see them play at tennis-ball in the castle ditch.[4] The king and queen had to pass through a filthy corridor, which was so low at the entrance that Charles, notwithstanding his diminutive stature, struck his forehead against the archway. The accident seemed slight, and the king spent some time in looking on at the tennis-players, talking freely with everybody. But about two in the afternoon he fell down backwards, and lost his speech, and being laid down on an old straw mattress in the open corridor, he died about nine hours after, in the twenty-seventh year of his age.[5] The Duke of Orleans succeeded to the throne, and married the widow Anne, having obtained a divorce from his wife Jane, who was still living, by agreeing to pay 20,000 ducats to Pope Alexander VI., and to cede the Valentinois in Dauphiny, with a pension of 20,000 livres, to the pope's son, the execrable Cæsar Borgia. Louis XII. —such was the title of Orleans—was as eager as his predecessor for the conquest of the Two Sicilies. That England might not hinder him in the prosecution of those distant wars, he gladly renewed the treaty of Etaples, and bound himself by solemn oaths to pay up the pension, which had fallen into arrears. Henry got some money, and in the summer of 1499, Louis descended from the Alps into the fertile plains of Lombardy.

A.D. 1501–3. Some Border forays afforded Henry a pretext for sending Fox, Bishop of Durham, on an embassy to James of Scotland. This skilful negotiator found the young king in Melrose Abbey, and induced him to *ask* the hand of the Princess Margaret, his master's eldest daughter. This match had long been a favourite scheme with Henry; it had been proposed more or less openly on several occasions, but James had hitherto shown a strong aversion to it. After tedious negotiations this treaty, which led, after the lapse of a century, to a no less important result than the peaceful union of England and Scotland, was concluded and ratified. Henry's old friend and correspondent, the Earl of Bothwell, came to London to act as proxy for King James; and "the fiancels" were solemnly celebrated in the queen's chamber, the Princess Margaret, in giving her consent, being made to say that she did it "wittingly and of deliberate mind, *having twelve years complete in age* in the month of November last past."[6] This ceremony took place on the 29th of January, 1502, but the young lady did not arrive in Scotland until nearly twenty months later. On the Borders she was met by a selected party of Scottish nobility, and on the 7th of August she made her entry into Edinburgh, King James riding behind her on the same palfrey. The following day the marriage ceremony was performed by the Archbishop of Glasgow. This marriage was preceded by a treaty of perpetual peace, wherein Henry's

---

[1] . . . . "Che non lice
Che il giglio in quel terreno abbia radice."—*Ariosto.*
[2] Giannone, *Storia del Regno di Napoli;* Guicciardini, *Istoria d'Italia.*   [3] *Comines.*   [4] Ibid.   [5] *Comines.*   [6] *Ellis' Letters.*

favourite clause was not forgotten—that neither prince should give shelter or encouragement to the revolted subjects of the other.

Before the consummation of the marriage of his eldest daughter, Henry's eldest son, Arthur, had been married and had died. As early as 1496, Henry concluded a bargain with Ferdinand of Spain, who agreed to give Prince Arthur his fourth daughter, Catherine, with a portion of 200,000 crowns. Three years after, when Arthur was in his twelfth year, he was solemnly affianced, the Spanish ambassador acting as proxy for the princess, who did not arrive until two more years had passed. On the 6th of November, 1501, the marriage ceremony was performed in St. Paul's Cathedral. On this occasion Henry had the heart to spend a considerable sum of money in feasts and tournaments; but some of his nobles, in order to flatter him, spent so much that they were reduced to ruin. The chief man that took care of the marriage pageants was Bishop Fox, "who," says Bacon, "was not only a grave councillor for war or peace, but also a good surveyor of works, and a good master of ceremonies, and anything else that was fit for the active part belonging to the service of court, or state of a great king." The historian adds that there was a great deal of astrology and fortune-telling in the masques and fanciful pieces which were represented. "You may be sure that King Arthur the Briton [after whom the young prince was named], and the descent of the Lady Catherine from the house of Lancaster [through the daughter of John of Gaunt], was in nowise forgotten." Prince Arthur was compared to Arcturus, and the princess to Hesperus; and her ancestor, old King Alfonso, "the greatest astronomer of kings," was brought on the scene to predict the wonderful and brilliant fortunes, and the glorious progeny which should spring from the match. "But, as it should seem, it is not good to fetch fortunes from the stars; for this young prince, that drew upon him at that time not only the hopes and affections of his country, but the eyes and expectation of foreigners, after a few months, in the beginning of April [1502], died at Ludlow Castle, where he was sent to keep his residence and court as Prince of Wales." Arthur was little more than fifteen years and six months old; and his amiable temper and handsome person seem to have gained the affection of the people. Ferdinand, the father of the young widow, for political reasons, instantly proposed that she should be married to her brother-in-law, Prince Harry, now heir-apparent to the English throne—a marriage more in accordance with Jewish law than with the canons of the Catholic church. Henry suggested some difficulties; but, when Ferdinand asked back the young lady, and the money which had been paid with her, he agreed to the match, provided that the dispensation could be obtained from Rome, and that 100,000 crowns, the remaining half of Catherine's portion, should be immediately remitted to London. The dispensation was more easily obtained than the money; and though, in 1503, in the thirteenth year of his age, Henry was contracted to his brother's widow, the marriage, for various reasons, was delayed for six years, during which time it was more than once nearly broken off altogether.

At the same time Henry was looking through Europe for a rich wife for himself—his queen, the daughter of Edward IV., having died in childbed in the Tower, shortly after the birth of her son, Prince Henry. He lost no time; he commenced his search before the dust had time to gather on his wife's coffin; but he was a suitor difficult to please in point of money. Having no longer any fear of insurrection at home, and seeing the great powers of the Continent too much absorbed by other wars to molest him, he fleeced his subjects more unmercifully than ever, giving all his affections and thoughts to the gathering and heaping up of treasure. His ministers, his lawyers, and his priests, did their best to gratify this ruling passion, and to prove to the people that all was done legally, and that the duty of all loyal subjects was passive obedience and a ready paying of money. "And as kings," observes Bacon, "do more easily find instruments for their will and humour than for their service and honour, he had gotten for his purpose, or beyond his purpose, two instruments, Empson and Dudley, whom the people esteemed as his horse-leeches and shearers, bold men, and careless of fame, and that took toll of their master's grist. Dudley was of a good family, eloquent, and one that could put hateful business into good language. But Empson, that was the son of a sievemaker, triumphed always upon the deed done, putting off all other respects whatsoever." These men, who, according to the forcible expression of the same great writer, "turned law and justice into wormwood and rapine," were both lawyers. Their modes of proceeding were very simple, but such as could hardly have succeeded had not the spirit of the aristocracy been annihilated, and the House of Commons reduced to a cipher. They charged the owners of estates, which had long been held on a different tenure, with the obsolete burdens of wardship, liveries, premier seisins, and the whole array of feudal obligations, for which they would only give quittances for payments in money: they not only converted nearly every offence into a case of fine and forfeiture, but they also invented new offences, that they might get the fines. To hunt up their game they kept up packs of spies and informers in every part of the kingdom; and to strike it down with the legal forms, they kept a rabble to sit on juries. In the end they did not "observe so much as the half face of justice."[1]

A.D. 1504. At the very moment that this system was in full vigour, a parliament met (in the month of January), and the commons chose Dudley, the leech, for their speaker, and passed all such bills as the king thought fit to propose. But though parliament had become the obedient tool of the court, there were loud murmurs out of doors; and there was a desperate man, a son of a sister of Edward IV. and Richard III., who appears to have been disposed to take advantage of the prevailing discontent. This was Edmund de la Pole, son of the Duke of Suffolk, and younger brother of the Earl of Lincoln, who came over with Simnel, and was killed at the battle of Stoke. When the Duke of Suffolk died Edmund claimed his titles and estates; but the king, who had a law and a logic of his own, maintained that he did not inherit from his father, but from his brother Lincoln, who had died before the father, and had never had possession; and that, as his said brother Lincoln had been attainted by parliament, he, Edmund, could have no claim to the honours or lands. Strange as was this course of argument, it received the sanction of the obsequious parliament; and Edmund was obliged to content himself with a fragment of his patrimony, which was given, not as of right, but as an act of kindness and liberality on the part of the king, and with the inferior title of Earl of Suffolk. This harsh usage had a great effect on a temper which seems to have been naturally irritable. The young earl, in a broil, had the misfortune to kill a man. The case, if properly tried, would not probably have gone beyond a modern case of manslaughter; but Henry, glad of the opportunity to reduce one connected with the house of York, had him arraigned as a murderer, and then, instead of permitting the trial to take place, commanded him to plead the royal pardon. Suffolk fled to the Continent, and took refuge in the court of his aunt, the Duchess of Burgundy. Henry, by means with which we are unacquainted, induced him to return to England, where he lived at large for some time without any talk of his offence. At the marriage of Prince Arthur and the Infanta Catherine, he attended with the rest of the nobility, and, being "too gay," sunk himself deep in debt. Almost immediately after he was again missing, as was also his youngest brother, Richard de la Pole. Henry soon learned that both the young men were with their aunt of Burgundy, and, resorting "to his wonted and tried arts," he caused Sir Robert Curson, who was employed at the time at Calais, to quit his post as if he had fled from it in disgust or in fear of the king, and to present himself to the Earl of Suffolk as a discontented man. This knight soon insinuated himself into the secrets of the earl, and found out the names of the persons upon whom "he had either hope or hold." To increase Suffolk's confidence in the spy, Henry, at one stage of the business, ordered the pope's bull of excommunication and curse against rebels to be read at Paul's Cross against the Earl of Suffolk and Sir Robert Curson. Curson communicated with Henry in great secrecy, and still maintained his own credit and inward trust with the earl. In consequence of the information given by this base agent, Henry arrested William de la Pole, another brother of Suffolk; the Lord Courtenay, who had married the Lady Catherine, one of the sisters of Henry's queen; Sir James Tyrrel, Sir William Windham, and some other meaner persons. Lord Abergavenny and Sir Thomas Green were apprehended at the same time, but they were not closely confined, and were liberated soon after. It was not easy, even in Henry's courts of law, to convict William de la Pole and the Lord Courtenay of any other crimes than their relationship to the fugitive, and their connection with the house of York; yet Courtenay, Henry's brother-in-law, remained a prisoner in the Tower during the king's life, and De la Pole "was also long restrained, though not so strictly. But for Sir James Tyrrel, against whom the blood of the innocent princes, Edward V. and his brother, did still cry from under the altar, and Sir John Windham, and the other meaner ones, they were attainted and executed; the two knights beheaded."[2] This sentence is another curious specimen of Henry's indirect dealing. Tyrrel and Windham were condemned, not for any conspiracy, but for having assisted the king's enemy, the Earl of Suffolk, in his first escape out of England in 1499, or nearly three years before this trial. If suspicions had rested upon Tyrrel as the murderer of the innocent sons of Edward IV., Henry had not thought it expedient to proceed against him for that horrible and mysterious business; on the contrary, he had employed Tyrrel, and seems even to have honoured this master of the horse of his predecessor. It appears to have been while Tyrrel was lying in the Tower, under sentence of death for having favoured the escape of Suffolk, that he confessed, or at least it was reported by Henry that he confessed, to his having employed Miles Forest and John Dighton to murder the princes, and that they had been murdered in their bed.

---

[1] *Bacon.* [2] *Bacon.*

and buried at the stair foot. From the manner in which this confession was obtained or reported, and from other circumstances, the mystery did not seem cleared up in an entirely satisfactory manner. As the story went, there were but four persons that could speak upon their own knowledge as to the murder—Sir James Tyrrel, Miles Forest, John Dighton, and the priest of the Tower, who, it was said, had buried the bodies. Sir Robert Brackenbury, who was removed from the custody of the Tower for twenty-four hours, must have known that the two children were either killed or carried off, but Brackenbury had died at Bosworth Field fighting for King Richard; and his servant, one Black Will, who guarded the princes, if alive, was never questioned or mentioned, any more than John Green, who had carried, or was said to have carried, Richard's order to Brackenbury. Of the four witnesses mentioned, Miles Forest and the priest of the Tower were dead; and from this showing there remained only Tyrrel and Dighton to speak to the facts. Dighton was a prisoner as well as Tyrrel, and, whatever the master may have done or said, it is quite certain that the servant confessed the murder, and that he repeated the particulars of the story to many men and in many places. But here, again, the course pursued darkened and deepened the shades of doubt in the popular mind. The confessions in the Tower were taken privately. Tyrrel, as we have seen, was got rid of on another charge; but, according to the remarkable words of Bacon, "John Dighton, who, it seemeth, *spake best for the king, was forthwith set at liberty*, and was the principal means of divulging this tradition."[1] Several years later (about 1513), when More wrote, Dighton was still not only alive, but at large; and though the same writer tells us that he was likely to come to the gallows at last,[2] he does not inform us for what crimes, or whether he ever really met the fate predicated for him.

As for the fugitive Earl of Suffolk, if, in fleeing the second time, he had arranged a conspiracy, there was certainly no proof of it made public by this inscrutable government. Sir Robert Curson, "when he saw the time, returned into England, and withal into wonted favour with the king, but worse fame with the people." Suffolk, dismayed, retired from the court of his aunt, and became a needy and neglected wanderer through the Netherlands, Germany, and France.

A.D. 1506. In the last years of his reign Henry dispensed with parliament, not caring for their votes, but levying money by the arbitrary and illegal method of benevolences. Dudley and Empson continued their profitable labours all the while. In 1504, when Prince Henry was knighted, the king called a parliament, and demanded, by the feudal customs, a payment for that occasion, and another for the marriage of his eldest daughter. They were instructed to offer £40,000; and then the king, to show his moderation, took £30,000. After this there was no more talk of parliaments. Henry's coffers were brimful; his wealth in ready money was enormous; yet he still earnestly endeavoured to increase it by marriage, and an accident occurred which seemed to offer him, not only the means of obtaining a wife, but also of getting possession of the person of an enemy whom he dreaded even in his helplessness and beggary. In the month of January a storm drove some foreign vessels to seek shelter in the harbour of Weymouth. Distressed by their sufferings at sea, and being in want of fresh provisions, a small party came on shore. Among them were the Archduke Philip, and his wife Joanna, now, by the death of her mother Isabella, Queen of Castile, of which country they were going to take possession when the tempest interrupted their progress. Their departure from Flanders had been watched, and, as if he had foreseen what would happen, or had been alarmed by the passage of a fleet through the Channel, where the vessels beat about for many days, Henry had stationed guards along the coast, and had issued his orders as to the treatment of the royal couple if they should land. They had scarcely set foot on shore when Sir Thomas Trenchard and Sir John Carew went with an armed force into Weymouth, where, with much humbleness and humanity, they invited the party to their houses—giving them, however, to understand that they would not be allowed to re-embark without the notice and leave of their king and master. Philip had no confidence in Henry's good faith: he knew him to be in close alliance and constant correspondence with his father-in-law, Ferdinand the Catholic, who, at the moment, was endeavouring to keep the kingdom of Castile for himself: he must have bitterly regretted not being guided by his council, who advised him to brave the storm rather than

---

[1] Bacon's account of this affair is unaccountably perplexed, and indeed contradictory—in singular opposition to his usual philosophic clearness. His narrative of the confessions of Tyrrel and Dighton distinctly makes these persons to have been committed to the Tower, and examined upon the subject of the murder of the princes, on the first rumour of Warbeck's attempt, and for the express purpose of putting down his pretensions. Yet he concludes the statement by informing us that Tyrrel was "soon after beheaded in the Tower-yard," leaving us to suppose that he had never been liberated between his said examination and his execution. His own *History* shows that it was, in fact, ten or eleven years after, that Tyrrel was put to death on another charge, and that in the meantime he had been long at large. We have followed the account of More, who speaks of Tyrrel's confession as having been made after his committal on the charge for which he suffered.

[2] "Dighton, indeed, yet walketh on alive, in good possibility to be hanged ere he die."

trust himself on any part of Henry's dominions; but, making a virtue of necessity, he put on a cheerful countenance, as if he considered himself a guest, and not a prisoner. Henry presently despatched the Earl of Arundel to tell his loving cousin how glad he was that he had escaped the dangers of the seas, that he was to consider himself as in his own land, and that he, the king, would make all haste to embrace him. Arundel went to the coast in great magnificence, with a brave troop of 300 horse. When Philip had heard the earl's message, "seeing how the world went, the sooner to get away, he went upon speed to the king at Windsor; and his queen followed by easy journeys." At three o'clock, on the 17th of January, the cunning host and the unwilling guest met upon Elworth Green, two miles from Windsor. The two princes saluted each other with all loving demonstrations. Philip said that he was now punished for not having gone within the walled town of Calais when they last met. Henry replied (did the by-standers keep their countenances?) that walls and seas were nothing where hearts were open. When they went from Elworth Green towards Windsor, Henry rode on the right hand of Philip, and when they reached the castle, the host, instead of being at the stirrup of his royal guest, permitted him to dismount, and to stand some time before he alighted from his own saddle. Within the castle Philip found a splendid apartment prepared for him. But the guest soon found that he had to pay a dear price for his entertainment. Henry drew up a new treaty of commerce wholly in his own favour; and while they were discussing this subject, choosing a fitting time, he drew Philip into a private room, and asked from him the immediate surrender of the Earl of Suffolk, who, after long sufferings and wanderings, had retired in penury to Flanders, where he was then enjoying Philip's protection. The King of Castile "herewith was a little confused and in a study;" he said that such a measure would reflect dishonour, not only on himself, but also on the King of England, who would be believed to have treated him as a prisoner if he exacted such a thing from him; but Henry told him to make his mind easy in this respect, for, as for the dishonour, he would take it all upon himself, and so the honour of Philip would be saved. "The King of Castile, who had the king in great estimation, and besides remembered where he was," consented reluctantly to oblige the king, from whom, however, he obtained the most solemn assurances that the life of Suffolk should be respected. Philip, in consequence, adopted such measures as induced the earl to believe that his sovereign pardoned him, and to come over of his own good-will. Henry next proceeded to exact a wife. Margaret, Duchess of Savoy, was sister to Philip, and a widow, and very rich. Henry had cast his eyes upon her as a suitable match, and now he forced her brother to agree to the marriage, and to fix her portion at 300,000 crowns. But Philip had a son as well as a sister; and this remorseless driver of hard bargains made him agree that his infant son Charles[1] (afterwards the Emperor Charles V.) should be married to the Princess Mary of England, his youngest daughter.

To draw out the time, Henry gave great feastings and entertainments; he made Philip a knight of the Garter; and Philip made him and Prince Harry knights of the Golden Fleece. At the proper season he conducted Philip and Queen Joanna to London, where they were entertained with the greatest magnificence; but as soon as the Earl of Suffolk had been conveyed to the Tower the festivities had an end, and the kings took leave. Philip and Joanna sailed instantly for Spain, having been detained nearly three months in England. The life of the unfortunate Earl of Suffolk was spared for two or three years; but in his last moments Henry left an order for his execution.

Before the negotiations could be finished for the marriage of Margaret, Duchess of Savoy, Philip died in Spain, and thereupon, thinking that his widow would be a better match than his sister, Henry dropped the treaty for the duchess, and proposed for Joanna the queen. At the very time, Joanna was bereft of her reason by the sudden loss of her young and handsome husband Philip—was sunk in the most hopeless insanity, from which she never recovered. But the bronze which fifty years of successful craft and assurance had put upon the face of Henry was not to be affected, and, in reply to her father, King Ferdinand, who had taken upon himself the government of Castile, he asserted that her malady had been brought on by the harsh treatment which she had received from her former husband; that it was only temporary, and by no means of a nature to prevent her from contracting a proper marriage. Ferdinand, not less from a desire of continuing to rule the whole Spanish monarchy, and to keep so great a master of intrigue from having any part of it, than out of tenderness for his unhappy child, renewed his representations of Joanna's condition. Upon this, Henry gave his old friend to understand, that if he were not permitted to marry one of his daughters (Joanna), his son Prince Harry should never marry his other daughter (Catherine). He had several advantages in this controversy: he knew that his alliance or neutrality in the great game that was playing between the French and Spaniards for supremacy in Italy was indispensable

---

[1] Charles at this time was just six years old.

to Ferdinand; he had the Infanta Catherine in his hands, and 100,000 of Ferdinand's dollars in his coffers. But at the same time he also knew the subtlety and power of the Spanish monarch; and even Henry's genius may have been overawed by the sublime craft and state policy of Cardinal Ximenes, who conducted the administration of affairs in Castile for Ferdinand. Three such minds have not often been brought in contact! In the end, seeing that he would never be allowed to marry Joanna, Henry gave up that suit, and concluded a new treaty, in which Ferdinand agreed, on the one hand, to remit 100,000 more crowns in completion of his daughter's portion; and Henry agreed, on the other, that his son should complete his marriage with the infanta as soon as all this money was received, but not before.

A.D. 1508. The king's health had long been in a wretched state; he was subject to violent fits of the gout, but an elder enemy was a periodical cough, "that wasted his lungs, so that thrice in a year, in a kind of return, and especially in the spring, he had great fits and labours of the phthisic." Henry was a religious prince; his declining strength and sufferings made him think "more seriously of the world to come"—and the world to come made him think of the sufferings of his people. In the spring of 1507 he distributed alms among the poor, and discharged all prisoners in London that were confined for fees or debts under forty shillings. The following year, being still worse, he opened his ears to the bitter cries raised against Dudley and Empson, and their accomplices. Formerly, many persons had been set in the pillory and had their ears cut off for uttering these complaints, or defaming the king's council; but now he was touched with great remorse for the oppressions and exactions he had permitted his two finance ministers to exercise. He even ordered justice to be done to all persons who had suffered wrong; but as his bad season passed these good resolutions departed, and his greediness for money returned. For, "nevertheless, Empson and Dudley, though they could not but hear of these scruples in the king's conscience, yet, as if the king's soul and his money were in several offices, that the one was not to intermeddle with the other, went on with as great rage as ever."

A.D. 1509. Thus, in spite of his repentance, did Henry continue to the last to grind his wealthier subjects in order to add to his immense treasures, which he kept for the most part under his own key at his manor of Richmond. But his last spring had now arrived; his cough was worse than ever, his thoughts were again turned to repentance, and he drew up a will, which strongly shows his remorse and anxiety, enjoining his young successor to do what he had never the heart to perform himself—to repair the injuries he had committed, and make restitution to the victims he had plundered. He died on the night of the 21st of April, 1509, at his new palace of Richmond, and was buried in the magnificent chapel which he had built, and which bears his name, in Westminster Abbey.

GATEWAY OF RICHMOND PALACE.[1]—From a drawing on the spot by J. W. Archer.

He was in his fifty-third year, and had reigned twenty-three years and eight months, wanting one day.

Henry, as a sovereign, was a man of the age; and *his* was an age of subtlety, as the preceding ones had been ages of rude force and violence. There was one great struggle going on in every part of Europe, the objects of which were to overthrow the feudal system, to depress the aristocracy, and to elevate the authority of kings. In other countries this led to the establishment of despotic monarchies, from which England herself had a narrow escape; for, if hardy and an-

---

[1] The name of this royal residence was originally Shene Palace. It was inhabited by the Edwards I., II., and III. The latter died in it, and likewise Anne, queen of Richard II. After her death, Richard, having demolished the apartments in which his beloved queen died, deserted the place. It was afterwards repaired by Henry V. In 1497 it was destroyed by fire, and rebuilt by Henry VII., who named it Richmond, from his earldom of Richmond, and died in it. Queen Elizabeth was for some time a prisoner here, and it was her favourite residence after her accession to the throne. The chamber in which she died was over the gateway. The palace was in part pulled down in the middle of the seventeenth century, and still further demolished in the eighteenth. The principal existing vestige is the gateway, but some of the offices remain among residences built on the crown lands.

cient seed remained in the ground, which craft could not detect, or of which it could not appreciate the importance, and if sturdy plants continued to thrive which no force or tyranny could ever uproot, yet the liberties of the country were, in a great measure, held in abeyance during the sway of the Tudors. The authority of the nobles had passed over to the king. The people were not yet strong enough to put in their claim for a portion of the power which had been wielded by the feudal lords, and which for a time fell almost entirely to the sovereign.[1]

CHAPTER III.—CIVIL AND MILITARY HISTORY.—A.D. 1509—1520.

HENRY VIII.—ACCESSION, A.D. 1509—DEATH, A.D. 1547.

Accession of Henry VIII.—His marriage with Catherine, his brother's widow—Trial and punishment of Empson and Dudley—Henry joins a league against France—France invaded—Failure of the invasion through the selfishness of Ferdinand of Spain—Naval encounters between the English and French—Death of Sir Edward Howard, Lord-admiral of England—Henry invades France—Indecisive military operations—Henry besieges Terouenne—Defeats the French at the "Battle of the Spurs"—He is duped by the Emperor Maximilian—England invaded by the Scots during Henry's absence—Unwise operations of James IV.—His total defeat and death at Flodden—Doubts entertained of the death of James IV.—The league against France dissolved—Peace between France and England cemented by a royal marriage—Death of the King of France—The Duke of Suffolk marries his widow—Wolsey made a cardinal—Previous history of Wolsey—His promotions—His style of living—Henry forms a new alliance with France—Becomes a candidate for the imperial crown—Is unsuccessful—Visit of Charles V. to England—Henry visits France—The "Field of the Cloth of Gold"—Sports and pageantries of this meeting.

ENRY, Prince of Wales, the only surviving son of his father, was in his eighteenth year when he ascended the throne, without opposition, and to the universal joy of the nation. His handsome person, his frank manners, his cheerful disposition, and even his ardent love of pleasure, were all made subjects of applause and endearment; and the people seemed to like him the more from his differing in all things from his father, whose death they openly rejoiced in. He had been prevented by the jealousy of the late king from taking any part in public business, but, in retirement, he had contracted a taste for literature and the arts, and his natural abilities were fancied to be of a high order. He was proclaimed on the 22d of April, and was crowned, with his Queen Catherine, on the 24th of June.

His marriage with the Spanish infanta, the widow of his own brother, had not been concluded without serious deliberation; but it appears that Henry himself offered no objection, and that Catherine was admired and beloved both by the court and the people. A bull from the pope did away with the restrictions of canonical law, and was considered sufficient to settle all scruples of delicacy. They were married at Greenwich on the 3d of June, twenty-one days before the coronation, Catherine being about eight years older than Henry. With the single exception of Warham the primate, every member of the council had forwarded the match, which, moreover, was strongly recommended by Henry's grandmother, the Countess of Richmond, who was still living, and much consulted by the ministers.[2]

The council of government, which was ap-

[1] ". . . Every one who takes a retrospective view of the wars of York and Lancaster, and attends to the regulations effected by the policy of that prince (Henry VII.), must see they would necessarily lead to great and important changes in the government; but what the tendencies of such changes would be, and much more in what manner they would be produced, might be a question of great difficulty. It is now the generally received opinion, and I think a probable opinion, that to the provisions of that reign we are to refer the origin, both of the unlimited power of the Tudors, and of the liberties wrested from our ancestors by the Stuarts; that tyranny was their immediate and liberty their remote consequence; but he must have great confidence in his own sagacity, who can satisfy himself, that, unaided by the knowledge of subsequent events, he could, from a consideration of the causes, have foreseen the succession of effects so different."—Charles James Fox, History of the Early Part of the Reign of James II.

"In the reign of Henry VII. all the political differences which had agitated England since the Norman conquest, seemed to be set at rest. The long and fierce struggle between the crown and the barons had terminated. The grievances which had produced the rebellions of Wat Tyler and Cade had disappeared. Villanage was scarcely known. The two royal houses, whose conflicting claims had long convulsed the kingdom, were at length united. The claimants, whose pretensions, just or unjust, had disturbed the new settlement, were overthrown. In religion there was no open dissent, and probably very little secret heresy. The old subjects of contention, in short, had vanished; those which were to succeed had not yet appeared."—Macaulay, Review of Hallam's Constitutional History of England.

[2] This lady, the mother of Henry VII., died in the same month of June in which her grandson was married and crowned. She believed 'and so it was generally believed both in England and Spain' that there had been no consummation of Catherine's first

pointed under the advice and influence of the old countess, consisted of Warham, Archbishop of Canterbury and chancellor; Fox, Bishop of Winchester, secretary and privy seal; the Earl of Surrey, treasurer; the Earl of Shrewsbury, steward; Lord Herbert, chamberlain; Sir Thomas Lovel, master of the wards and constable of the Tower; Sir Edward Poynings, comptroller; Sir Henry Marney, Sir Thomas Darcy, Thomas Ruthal, doctor of laws, and Sir Henry Wyat. Most of these were men of experience and ability: they had all served the late king, and had taken part in his most obnoxious acts: but this consideration did not prevent them from joining heartily in a measure of vengeance against their old colleagues in office, Empson and Dudley, who had been arrested immediately after the death of their master.[1]

When brought before the council these two learned lawyers made a skilful defence, but this did not save them from being committed to the Tower. Soon after, a proclamation was issued to encourage complaints against them, and the long-restrained fury of the people was purposely let loose against their spies and informers. Many of the "lesser rogues in country places" were torn to pieces; some were paraded through the streets of London, mounted on wretched horses, with their faces turned to the tail. Some were set in the pillory at Cornhill, and then conveyed to Newgate, where they soon died in consequence of the harsh treatment received from the mob

HENRY VIII. AND HIS QUEEN, CATHERINE OF ARAGON.—From portraits by Holbein.

and from their jailers. The gratifying of their spite seems to have been the only gratification the people received, for, though there was a talk of "restitution," the courts of law took such an alarm at the immense number of persons who presented themselves as victims, that their doors were soon closed in the faces of the applicants, and no more was said about refunding. Henry, who was no exception to the general rule, that the son of a miser must be a spendthrift, and who had dipped deeply into his father's coffers for his splendid coronation, and the jousts, tournaments, and expensive feasts and masques he was constantly giving, probably fancied that the heads of Empson and Dudley ought to serve as a receipt in full. It may be that he was also tempted by the great wealth those rapacious men had accumulated. Few pitied their fate, and law had no delicacies in those days. They were indicted, not for offences of which they were notoriously guilty, as in this case the character of the late king would have been awkwardly involved, and the question of restitution revived, but for the almost impossible crime of forming a conspiracy to deprive the present king of his succession and rights. The judges, the law officers of the crown, and two juries,[2] concurred in finding them guilty of treason, and they were condemned to death and forfeiture, not as robbers of the people, but as traitors to the king.[3]

---

marriage. Catherine was married to Henry, not with the ceremonies prescribed for widows, but with those appropriated to maids. She was dressed in white, and wore her hair loose.

[1] Peter Martyr; Herbert, Life of Henry VIII.; Stow.
[2] Dudley was tried at London; Empson at Northampton. The heirs of both were restored in blood, some two or three years after. John Dudley, the son of the first, became Viscount Lisle under Henry VIII., Earl of Warwick under Edward VI., then Duke of Northumberland, and was beheaded on the accession of Mary. It was the grandson of the rapacious minister of Henry VII. that was married to Lady Jane Grey.
[3] Herbert; Stow; Bishop Godwin.

Secure in his insular position, and for a long time in the hearty affection of his subjects, rich, and powerful, the English king might have defied the sovereigns of the Continent, and avoided taking any part in their wars. Even at this time he might have occupied the honourable position of an arbiter or friendly umpire, and given increase of wealth and strength to his country by commerce, while his contemporaries were exhausting their kingdoms by incessant hostilities. But Henry was anxious for military glory; his council were cajoled by his father-in-law, Ferdinand of Aragon, and by Pope Julius II.; Louis XII. of France was not inclined to continue the pension paid to his father, and thus, in the third year of his reign, the young and fortunate king was induced to join a coalition against France, and to take part as a principal in the continental war.

A.D. 1512. A herald was despatched to command Louis not to make war upon the pope, "the father of all Christians." As Julius II. was, at the least, as much a soldier as priest, and as he had formed the present league against France, it was not to be expected that Louis would submit to this injunction. He was soon visited by a second herald from Henry, who demanded the instant cession of Anjou, Maine, Normandy, and Guienne. This was equivalent to a declaration of war; and Henry summoned his first parliament to ask for money to enable him to fit out a proper army. Supplies were voted with the greatest alacrity; and though parliament no longer expressed the free voice of the nation, yet on this occasion the people applauded their votes, and began to dream once more of the glories of Crecy and Azincourt. A fine army was raised and equipped, and Henry thought of passing into France by way of Calais, when his father-in-law Ferdinand represented how much more advantageous it would be to make his attack in the south, and to begin operations by making sure of the rich province of Guienne, where the English rule was still regretted. His arguments seemed convincing, and when he sent a fleet to convey the English forces to the foot of the Pyrenees, whence they could march in a few days to the banks of the Garonne, his son-in-law consented to adopt his plan of operation. Ten thousand men were immediately embarked under the command of the Marquis of Dorset. Crossing the Bay of Biscay, they landed in Guipuzcoa, and were quartered, by Ferdinand's orders, at Fuenterrabia, near the mouth of the Bidassoa. Dorset immediately proposed passing the river into France, but he had little or no artillery, and found that he could not move except in concert with a Spanish force. Ferdinand promised everything that was necessary, and collected troops in the Biscayan provinces, as if for the invasion of the south of France. When all was ready, the English expected to be led to the siege of Bayonne, but Ferdinand pretended that it would be dangerous for the allied army to advance until they had made sure of Navarre, which that movement would leave in their rear. Navarre was then a separate kingdom, governed by Catherine and John d'Albret, who, to defend themselves against the encroachments of the King of Aragon, had contracted a close alliance with the King of France. As Dorset could not help himself, he consented to remain in force upon the Bidassoa, while his ally negotiated with the terrified court of Navarre. D'Albret readily consented to remain neutral during the present war, but Ferdinand demanded a free passage for his troops, the surrender of some of the most important fortresses, and the person of the Prince of Viana, the heir to the crown, as an hostage. The latter terms were indignantly rejected, and thereupon Ferdinand threw the army he had collected under pretext of joining the English into Navarre. This army was commanded by the Duke of Alva, who, after taking several of the towns, invited the English to join him in the siege of Pampeluna, the capital of Navarre. Dorset refused to make war anywhere but in France, and called for the artillery, and a supply of horses, which had been promised to him ever since his landing. With the greatest courtesy he was told that, since he scrupled to join the Spanish arms in Navarre, he must wait until that business was settled, and that then he would have all that he wanted, together with an auxiliary force to enable him to take Bayonne and Bordeaux, and the whole of Guienne. As the marquis could do nothing else, he again consented to wait. The presence of an English army on the Bidassoa obliged the French to concentrate their forces between that river and Bayonne, and prevented Louis from sending any succour to his unfortunate ally the King of Navarre, who was soon reduced to extremities, and obliged to flee with his wife and children across the Pyrenees into his little principality of Béarn. Pampeluna capitulated to Alva, and Upper Navarre was thenceforward joined to the Spanish monarchy—an important scheme long in contemplation, and for the happy execution of which Ferdinand had been so anxious for the presence of an English army in the south. When Dorset again made his impatient voice heard, he was told that the Duke of Alva was quite ready to march, but that it must be in the direction of Béarn, not of Bayonne and Bordeaux. Upon this the English commander refused to move at all, and Ferdinand sent an ambassador to Henry. It is little to the credit of the sagacity of the English council that they did not perceive how they were duped, but, on the contrary, sent Dorset orders to conform to the instructions of the Spanish court. But before these orders arrived the English troops, who during their inactivity had suffered severely from sickness and also from famine (for Ferdinand did not even supply them with proper provisions), took the decision of the case into their own hands, and insisted upon returning home. When the crafty Spaniard saw that their violence was becoming dangerous, he prepared some ships for them, well satisfied with the success of his past manœuvre. At this moment the order that they were to remain arrived from England; but the men mutinied, and, cursing the Spaniards and the Biscayans, forced their commanders to set sail. Greatly reduced in numbers, humiliated, and in tatters, this expedition, from which so much had been expected, reached England about Christmas.[1]

A.D. 1513. Having made up his mind to lead an army in person into France, Henry, in the preceding autumn, had summoned a parliament to ask for more money. Besides imposing a poll-tax and a sort of property-tax, the houses voted him two-fifteenths and fourtenths. With the money thus raised, and with the remnant of his father's hoards, the young king began to fit out ships and to levy a great army. By this time the French were not only driven out of Italy, where the Spaniards succeeded them, but were harassed on their own frontiers by the "Holy League," as the sovereigns continued to call a coalition which acted in the most base and worldly manner. In these difficulties Louis opened negotiations with the King of Scotland, in order to find Henry occupation in his own country. The Scots at the moment had several grounds of complaint against the English court. Henry had appropriated to himself certain jewels which his father had bequeathed to the Queen of Scotland, and his fleet had come into hostile collision with ships bearing the Scottish flag. Fully anticipating what followed, Henry put his towns near the Scottish borders in a good state of defence—collected troops in the marches, and gave the command of them to the Earl of Surrey, the best of his generals, who was instructed to watch James, while his royal master proceeded against Louis.[2]

The French king, though much exhausted in finances by his Italian wars, and though oppressed both with ill-fortune and ill-health, was no contemptible opponent. He determined, if possible, to obtain the command of the Channel, to meet the English at sea, which was already considered in a manner as their element, and to prevent their landing on his coasts. In the preceding year several naval encounters had taken place; and in one great battle, fought off Brest, the French had the advantage, though it was dearly bought with the death of their brave Admiral Primauget, who was blown up in his ship with 900 men. At the same time, however, the *Regent*, Henry's finest ship, perished in the like manner with 700 Englishmen. Louis reinforced his fleet and collected a great number of mariners, who were conveyed from the shores of the Mediterranean to the Channel, and there embarked under experienced commanders of various nations, but chiefly Genoese. This "great navy," says Hall, "which the French had prepared, and which was well furnished in all things, was, no doubt, a wonder to see!" To disperse or destroy it, Henry despatched "ships royal and others meet for war, to the number of forty-two, besides ballengers," under the command of the lord-admiral, Sir Edward Howard, one of the gallant sons of the Earl of Surrey. Howard sailed from Portsmouth in the month of March, 1513. Early in April he presented himself at the mouth of the harbour of Brest, within which the French ships were anchored, and defended by batteries and other works. He secured the mouth of the haven, and then wrote to the young king his master to come over in person to have the glory of a great and sure victory. Henry, it appears, had no taste for naval engagements, and his council, considering it very improper in Howard to send such an invitation, "for putting the king in jeopardy upon the chance of the sea," wrote sharply to him, and commanded him to do his duty as admiral. Howard was stung by this letter. On St. Mark's Day, despising the tremendous fire kept up both on sea and shore, he sailed right into the harbour of Brest, followed by a number of small row-galleys, and attempted to carry the whole fleet by boarding, or, failing in that, to cut out some of their best ships. He lashed himself alongside the French admiral and leaped on board, sword in hand; but only seventeen men had followed him when the French admiral cast himself loose, and the English galley slid away. The row-galleys, under the command of Sir Thomas Cheney, Sir John Wallop, and Sir William Sidney, pressed forward to his rescue, but they were engaged by the light vessels in the harbour, and before they could get alongside, Howard and his handful of men were all killed and thrown overboard. The death of their gallant admiral completely disheartened the fleet, which returned to England, being followed shortly after by the French, who sailed out of Brest and made some descents on the coast of Sussex.

At this moment King Ferdinand, who had

---

[1] *Herbert; Wolsey's Letters*, quoted by *Fiddes; Godwin*.
[2] *Sir Henry Ellis; Lord Herbert*.

led Henry into this absurd war, made a separate truce for himself with France, which, among other things, recognized his seizure of Navarre. Some of the English ministers thought that, as the strength of the league had thus received a mortal wound, it would be better to postpone the invasion of France; but Henry, the willing dupe of those who flattered him as the most warlike monarch and most perfect knight in Christendom, would not forego his purpose, and pretended that a new alliance which he had formed with Maximilian "the Moneyless," who was now emperor, would more than compensate for the secession of his father-in-law Ferdinand. His army was ready; his people, from one end of the land to the other, were singing beforehand the glory which should attend "the red rose," "the royal rose," in France. To desist at this stage would have been a marvellous effort, but Henry soon showed that he had not a particle of the military genius of his predecessors, and that he loved war for its pomp and parade rather than for its grand operations in the field. In the month of May he despatched his vanguard to Calais, under the command of Gilbert Talbot, Earl of Shrewsbury and Lord Herbert: he cut off the head of the Earl of Suffolk in the Tower (a cowardly mode of beginning a campaign); and then, "when all things were prest, accompanied with many noblemen and 600 archers of his guard, all in white haberdines and caps, he departed from his manor royal of Greenwich the 15th day of June."[1] Instead of steering straight for Calais, Henry ran down the Channel as far as Boulogne, to regale the French coast with a mighty firing of great guns. Having thus announced to France that the majesty of England was coming, he put about his fleet and landed at Calais on the last day of June, amidst such a roar of artillery from ships and batteries as had never been heard in the memory of man.[2] Lord Herbert had already taken the field and begun the siege of Terouenne, but Henry was in no great hurry to join him, passing his time very pleasantly at Calais with his courtiers and favourites, among whom Thomas Wolsey, his almoner, was already the most prevalent.[3]

The news that a French army, under the command of the Duke de Longueville and the far-famed Bayard—*Le Chevalier sans peur et sans reproche*—was moving to the relief of Terouenne, caused the young king to mount his war-horse; and on the 21st of July he marched out of Calais with a magnificent army amounting to about 15,000 horse and foot. They had scarcely got beyond Ardres when they saw a strong detachment of French cavalry manœuvring in their front. Expecting a battle, Henry dismounted, and threw himself into the centre of his busquenets, to fight on foot like the Henries and Edwards of former times. The brilliant Bayard, who was with the French horse, would have charged, but his superiors in command reminded him that King Louis had given orders that they should most carefully avoid fighting the English in open battle; and, after reconnoitring the invaders, the French withdrew, having already succeeded in another part of their commission, which was to throw provisions and gunpowder into the besieged town. The English, "without let or hindrance," joined the divisions under Lord Herbert, and the siege was then pressed with some vigour. The besieged garrison was numerous, brave, and skilful: they countermined a mine attempted by Baynam, the English engineer; and their artillery, though it made less noise, did more mischief than that of the besiegers. At the same time the Count of Angoulême (soon after Francis I.) advanced with a considerable army from Amiens, and threw out detachments of stradiotes (an active description of light cavalry), which scoured the whole country, frequently cutting off the convoys and foraging parties of the English. In this state of affairs the Emperor Maximilian, who had received an advance of 120,000 crowns from the English treasury to enable him to raise troops, came to Terouenne with nothing but a small escort. Henry put on all his magnificence for this reception; for, nominally, the emperor was the first of Christian princes. The two potentates met in a tremendous storm of wind and rain (which must have deranged the white silk jackets of the English courtiers) in the midst of a plain between Aire and the camp. The broad way to Henry's heart had been discovered by all his royal brothers, and, his vanity being once satisfied—for Maximilian assured him that he, the Emperor of the West, was come to serve under him in quality of volunteer—he seems to have overlooked the omission of which he had been guilty in not bringing an army with him. The emperor had scarcely arrived at head-quarters when Henry received a much less flattering visitor. This was Lyon king-at-arms, bringing him the defiance and declaration of war of the King of Scotland, who had already taken the field and sent his fleet to co-operate with his ally the King of France. Henry, however, knew that the brave Surrey was in the marches, and he told the messenger that that earl would know how to deal with his master.

Nearly six weeks had now been wasted in the

---
[1] *Hall.*
[2] *Tytler, Life of Henry VIII.; Herbert; Holinshed.*
[3] At this time we find Queen Catherine writing very humbly and affectionately to the rising Wolsey, and entreating him to send her frequent news of her husband, his grace the king.—See Sir Henry Ellis' *Collection of Letters*.

siege of the insignificant town of Terouenne; and so absurdly had the siege been conducted, that the garrison still continued to receive supplies from the army of the Count of Angoulême. When these communications were interrupted, the main body of the French army, consisting of about 12,000 men, advanced from Plangy, with a view of throwing in provisions under cover of a feigned battle. Upon this Henry and Maximilian crossed the river, and formed in order of battle between it and the town and the French army. The emperor, who had won a victory over the French on that very ground thirty-four years before, directed the operations of the English, wearing the red cross of England above his armour, and the red rose of Lancaster, Henry's favourite cognizance, in his helmet. All this, according to an old historian, deserves to be recorded to the eternal honour of our nation, as also the fact of the emperor's taking for pay 100 crowns a-day, besides what was disbursed among his attendants.[1] The French horse charged in a brilliant manner, but, after throwing some powder within reach of the besieged, they wheeled round to fall back upon their main body. Being hotly followed by the mounted English archers and a few squadrons of German horse, they quickened their pace to a downright flight, galloped into the lines of their main body, and threw the whole into uproar and confusion. As the English charged with tremendous shouts of "St. George! St. George!" the panic became complete; and every Frenchman that was mounted struck spurs into his horse and galloped from the field. In vain the bravest of their officers tried to rally them; the attempts, indeed, were worse than vain, for, owing to their not making the same use of their spurs and fleeing with the rest, the Duke de Longueville, the illustrious Bayard, La Fayette, and many other captains of high rank, were taken prisoners by the English. Henry could not help congratulating his captives on the great speed their men had put into their horses: the light-hearted Frenchmen joined in his laugh, and said that it had been nothing but a "Battle of Spurs." By this name, accordingly, the affair came afterwards to be popularly known. The panic, however, was both real and lasting; and if Henry had taken advantage of it, and of other circumstances, he might have inflicted a much more serious blow. The Swiss, to whom he had sent some money, had crossed the Jura Mountains in great force, and had penetrated into France as far as Dijon, the capital of Burgundy. With a Swiss army of 20,000 men on one side, and an English army on the other, Paris began to betray symptoms of alarm. But, to the great joy of Louis, Henry, instead of advancing, permitted himself to be amused another whole week by the siege of Terouenne. At the end of August the French garrison capitulated, and were allowed to march out with all the honours of war: the town, by the advice of Maximilian, who had an interested and evident motive for this advice, was dismantled and burned. That the destruction might be complete, without any labour to the English, the Flemings in the neighbourhood, the subjects of the emperor's grandson the Archduke Charles, were let loose upon the devoted place, and, being animated with the old enmities usual to bordering nations, razed the walls, filled up the ditches, set fire to the houses, and scarcely left one stone standing upon another. The weather continued to be very rainy, and Henry, by this time, "had so much of war that he began to be weary of the toil thereof, and to cast his mind on the pleasures of the court."[2] But still it was only the beginning of the month of September, and military etiquette required that something more should be done before going into winter quarters. What Henry *did* was a military absurdity; but he continued to be guided by Maximilian, who was still working for the profit of the Flemings and his grandson Charles. Instead of advancing into France, he turned back to lay siege to Tournai, which belonged to France, though it was *enclavé* in the territory of Flanders, over the trade of which it exercised a bad influence, while it gave a passage to the French into the heart of the country. As far as the Flemings were concerned it was altogether an unpleasant neighbour; and the emperor was wise in getting possession of it without cost or risk. But what interest Henry could have in such an enterprise was not very apparent. His favourite, Wolsey, however, had an interest, and a great one—Maximilian had promised him the rich bishopric of Tournai, and this prevailing favourite no doubt recommended the siege. The French citizens of Tournai refused the assistance of a garrison of the royal troops, and sacrificed themselves to a bad pun.[3] Upon being summoned they made a bold show of resistance, but, as soon as the English artillery got into play, they changed their tone, and in a few days capitulated. On the 22d of September Henry rode into Tournai with as much pomp and triumph as if he had taken the capital of France. Ten days before this inglorious conquest the Swiss, who saw what sort of an ally they had in the English king, concluded a treaty highly advantageous to themselves with the King of France, and marched back to their own mountains. Louis was thus enabled to concentrate his forces in the north, and the grand plan of the

[1] *Bishop Godwin.*
[2] *Bishop Godwin.*
[3] They said—" Que Tournai n'avoit jamais tourné, ni encore ne tournerait."—*Mémoires de Fleuranges.*

allies vanished in air. Wolsey got the rich bishopric, Henry spent some money in jousts and tournaments, and then returned well satisfied to England, where he arrived safe and sound on the 22d of October. Although he did not gain quite so much by it, Maximilian had duped the vainglorious king almost as much as Ferdinand had done before.

The money which Henry had expended on the Continent amounted to an enormous sum. But his confidence in the Earl of Surrey had not been misplaced; and during his absence that nobleman had gained one of the most remarkable victories on record. Following up his defiance, the Scottish king put himself at the head of a numerous and gallant, but somewhat undisciplined army, and, contrary to the advice of most of his ministers, crossed the Tweed and began hostilities.

The version most received of the fatal field of Flodden is so striking and romantic, that we scarcely hope to rectify what is incorrect in the impressions it has made; but the following appear to have been the real circumstances which preceded and attended that battle.

Although undertaken against the advice of the majority of the nobility, the war was very popular with the Scottish people, who flocked in such numbers to the royal standard that James was enabled, on the 22d of August, to cross the Borders with one of the most formidable armies that had ever invaded England. His artillery and appointments were also superior to what had hitherto been seen in Scottish armies. Instead of advancing, however, he lingered on the right bank of the Tweed, besieging Norham Castle, which did not surrender till the 29th of August. He then marched up the Tweed to Wark Castle, which detained him a day or two. From Wark he went to Etal, and thence to Ford, another Border fortress of no great consequence, but which he attacked out of spite to the family of the Herons (to whom it belonged), a member of which, John Heron, was suspected of having murdered his favourite, Sir Robert Kerr, the warden of the Scottish marches. William Heron, the head of the family and real owner of the castle, was a prisoner in Scotland, and Elizabeth, his wife, had passed southward to the Earl of Surrey, at York, in order to make arrangements by which the castle might be spared from the fury of the Scots, and her husband liberated from his captivity. James, however, took the castle by storm and razed it to the ground.

From York the Earl of Surrey, who was allowed time to reinforce his army, marched to Newcastle, and from Newcastle he advanced to Alnwick, whence, on the 4th of September, he despatched Rouge Croix, the pursuivant-at-arms, to reproach James with his breach of faith, and to offer him battle on the following Friday, if he had courage to remain so long on English ground. The same herald bore another message from Surrey's son, the Lord Thomas Howard, now Admiral

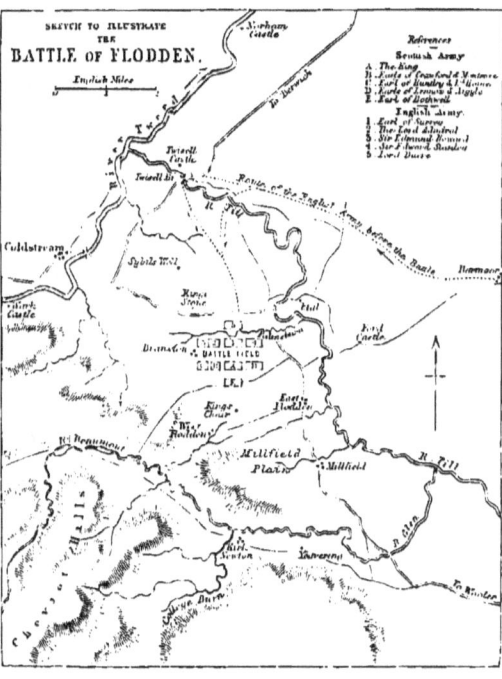

SKETCH TO ILLUSTRATE THE BATTLE OF FLODDEN.

of England, who, in very rude terms, told the Scottish monarch that he would come to justify the death of that pirate, Barton, which had been charged upon him as a foul murder by James, and that he neither expected to receive nor would give quarter. To Surrey James replied in a chivalrous tone, accepting his challenge; but he left the brutal message of his son unanswered. Though his army was already somewhat thinned by desertion, James was resolved to abide the battle, and chose his ground with some skill on Flodden Hill, an off-shoot of the Cheviot, steep on both flanks, and defended in front by the deep Till, a tributary of the Tweed. When the English came in sight of this position they did not like it; and Surrey, on the 7th of September, sent James a second letter, reproaching him with having "put himself into a ground more like a fortress or a camp, than any indifferent ground for battle to be tried." As this taunting message had not the desired effect, Surrey sought to obtain his end by manoeuvring round the position, by advancing towards Scotland, and then turning sharply round the rear of Flodden. On the morning of the 8th he crossed the Till, near Weetwood, without meeting any opposition, and marched over some rugged ground to the village of Barmoor, on the right bank of the river. Early on Friday morning, instead of pursuing his march towards Berwick, he faced the north-west, proceeded to Twisell bridge, re-crossed the Till, and advanced towards Branxton, as if it was his intention to occupy a hill to the westward of Flodden. James, who had thrown away an admirable opportunity of attacking the English while they were crossing at Twisell-bridge, and at a dangerous ford a little higher up, now put himself in motion, in order to prevent them from taking up a formidable position between him and his own country. Setting fire to their huts and litter, the Scots descended their hill, and, under cover of the great smoke they had raised, hurried forward to seize the heights of Branxton, towards which the English vanguard was hastening in another direction. Between Twisell-bridge and Flodden, but nearer to the latter than the former, runs the small stream of Palinsburn, which the English had crossed before the wind drove away the smoke, and discovered the Scottish army within a quarter of a mile of them, in perfect order, "marching like the Germans, without talking or making any noise."[1] Several of the Scottish nobles had advised a retreat: among these was the same Lord Lindsay of the Byres that made James III. the fatal present of the gray charger, a rough old soldier, who had a turn for parables, and who had represented to the council that the stakes between the combatants were not equal. For this advice James, it is said, threatened to hang Lindsay at his own castle gate; nor were the remonstrances of the Earl of Huntly and the Earl of Angus (the once terrible Bell-the-Cat) heard with more calmness. It is added, that the king told the latter that, if he were afraid of the English, he might go home. The taunt touched the old man to the quick, and he burst into tears. He turned, however, to depart, saying mournfully, "My age renders my body of no use in battle, and my counsel is despised: but I leave my two sons and the vassals of Douglas in the field: may old Angus' foreboding prove unfounded!"

To decline the battle was now impossible; and the Scottish nobles, with a very few exceptions, made up their minds to conquer or die with their sovereign. The two armies were about equal in number, each counting about 30,000 men. On the side of the English were 5000 whom Henry had sent back from France to meet this storm on the Borders—one, not altogether unimportant, consequence of the diversion of the Scots in favour of Louis. The disposition of both armies was also much the same, and very simple. The line of each was formed into a centre and two wings, and on each side a strong body of reserve was posted behind the centre. The battle began about four in the afternoon of Friday, the 9th of September, with cannonading on both sides. The English were superior in artillery, and their guns seemed to have been better served. "Then out burst the ordnance on both sides with fire, flame, and hideous noise; and the master gunner of the English slew the master gunner of Scotland, and beat all his men from their guns, so that the Scottish ordnance did no harm to the Englishmen, but the Englishmen's artillery shot into the midst of the king's battail, and slew many persons—which seeing, the King of Scots and his brave men made the more haste to come to joining." The Earl of Huntly and Lord Home, with part of the left wing of the Scots, who fought on foot with "long spears like Moorish pikes," fell upon part of the English right wing under Sir Edmund Howard, with a fury that was irresistible. Sir Edmund was beaten down; his banner was brought to the dust; his lines were completely broken, and part of his men fled in the greatest disorder. Sir Edmund, after being saved by the remainder of the right wing under the lord-admiral, fell back towards the English centre, which extended its line to receive him, while Lord Dacre, who was in reserve behind the centre, came up and charged with all the English cavalry. Though the Borderers under Lord Home, fancying they had already gained the victory, had begun to disperse over the field in search of plunder, that Scottish wing kept its ground with wonderful obstinacy, throwing off but charge after charge told upon them, and, after a long conflict, and a terrible slaughter on both sides, Huntly and Home retreated before Sir Edmund, the Lord-admiral Howard, and Lord Dacre. The Earls of Crawford and Montrose, who were not able to prevent this retrograde movement, were charged in their turn by

[1] Official account written to Henry VIII. in French.—The good order and striking silence of the Scots are noticed by nearly every contemporary writer. "Little or no noise did they make," says a black-letter account, printed by Richard Faques in 1513, and reprinted by Mr. Haslewood in 1809.

horse and foot, whom they received in line without wavering upon the points of their spears; and when they were reinforced from the centre, they not only became the assailants, but also threw the whole right wing of the English, with the cavalry from their reserve, into confusion. At this critical moment the lord-admiral sent the Agnus Dei which he wore at his breast to his father, who was with the English centre, requesting him to bring up the whole of that division with all possible speed. Surrey advanced; but King James, who watched his movements, fell upon him with the entire centre of the Scots, fighting himself most gallantly in their front. The battle was now tremendous; and when the Earl of Bothwell came up with the reserve to the support of the king, the victory for a while inclined to the Scots. But there were two circumstances—the shyness of Lord Home, and the rashness of the Highlanders who formed James' right wing—which proved fatal to the high hopes of the imprudent but gallant sovereign. When the Earl of Huntly urged Home to renew the fight and advance with his portion of the left wing, which had suffered cruelly, to the assistance of the king, he is said to have replied, "He does well that does for himself. We have foughten our vanguards, and have won the same; therefore let the lave [the rest] do their part as well as we." When the right wing, under the Earls of Lennox and Argyle, with the Campbells, the Macleans, the Macleods, and the other clans from the Highlands and the Isles, who obeyed no orders save those of their chiefs, descended a hill to join the main body, they were met by the extreme left of the English—hardy bowmen and stout pikemen from Cheshire and from Lancashire—under Sir Edward Stanley, who galled them sorely with their arrows. In a frenzy, the half-naked clansmen threw away shield and target, and with their broadswords and axes, and without any order, rushed among the English. In vain La Motte, a commissioner from the French king, and other experienced French officers, endeavoured to keep them in their ranks—on they rushed, as if every Highlandman thought of deciding that great engagement with his own right arm. At first the English were astonished at this fierce onslaught, but they stood firm, closed their ranks and squares, and opposed as wonderful a coolness to the wonderful impetuosity of their enemies, who, at length, were driven back, and, being unable to re-form, were slaughtered in detail, or put to downright flight. Their chief commanders, the Earls of Lennox and Argyle, both perished on the field. Stanley now charged the king's centre on its right flank and rear; and, at the same time, James had to sustain the shock of Surrey in front, and the attack of the Admiral Howard and Lord Dacre, who, after repulsing the Earls of Crawford and Montrose, who were both slain, had fallen upon his left flank. In fact, he was now surrounded—hemmed in within a gradually contracting circle of foes, who, by this time, seem to have adopted, to a man, the savage resolution of the lord-admiral, Thomas Howard —of giving no quarter. Now was the time that the nobles and the meanest subjects of the doomed prince showed their valour and their attachment to his person:—

"The English shafts in volleys hail'd,
In headlong charge their horse assail'd;
Front, flank, and rear, the squadrons sweep
To break the Scottish circle deep,
That fought around their king.
But yet, though thick the shafts as snow,
Though charging knights like whirlwinds go,
Though billmen ply the ghastly blow,
Unbroken was the ring;
"The stubborn spearmen still made good
Their dark impenetrable wood,
Each stepping where his comrade stood,
The instant that he fell.
No thought was there of dastard flight;
Link'd in the serried phalanx tight,
Groom fought like noble, squire like knight,
As fearlessly and well." [1]

Nor did they cease fighting when James bit the dust with an English arrow sticking in his body, and with a mortal wound from an English bill on his head: they closed round the body, which fell within a spear's length of Surrey, defending it dead as obstinately as they had defended it when living. Night closed upon the carnage, and separated the combatants. Surrey was for a while uncertain of the victory; but during the night his scouts brought him intelligence that the Scots were in full retreat towards their own country, and that none remained on the field; "upon which the earl thanked God with humble heart." But the intelligence of the scouts was not quite correct: during the night the Borderers, who had fought under the standard of Lord Home, being joined by marauders from Tynedale and from Teviotdale, stripped the slain, and pillaged part of the baggage of *both* armies; and when day dawned, Home's banner was seen hovering near the left flank of the English, while another body of Scots—apparently the remnant of the centre, which had fought under the king —appeared in front, occupying a hill, as if determined to renew the contest. Surrey brought his artillery to bear upon them, and they were dislodged; but even then they seem to have retreated very deliberately, and Lord Home's people carried a rich booty and a considerable number of prisoners across the Tweed. Lord Dacre found seventeen pieces of cannon deserted on the hill-side; and it appears to have been in the morning, and not in the preceding evening, that

---

[1] *Marmion.*

the English horse followed a portion of the retiring Scots for about four miles, and not further. It is quite certain that Surrey had suffered dreadfully in this stern conflict, and that he had no inclination whatever to try the fords of the Tweed, and the moors and morasses beyond it. The loss of the Scots, according to the most moderate calculation, amounted to 8000 or 9000 men; but in this number were included the very prime of their nobility, gentry, and even clergy. Besides the king and his natural son, Alexander Stuart, Archbishop of St. Andrews, who had studied abroad, and received instruction from Erasmus, there were slain twelve earls—Crawford, Montrose, Lennox, Argyle, Errol, Athole, Morton, Cassilis, Bothwell, Rothes, Caithness, and Glencairn: to these must be added fifteen lords and chiefs of clans; amongst whom were Sir Duncan Campbell of Glenorchy, Loughlan Maclean of Dowart, and Campbell of Lawers; and conspicuous in the sad list are the names of George Hepburn, Bishop of the Isles; William Bunch, abbot of Kilwinning; Lawrence Oliphant, abbot of Inchaffray; the dean of Glasgow; La Motte, the French agent, and most of his countrymen. Some families of the gentle blood of Scotland lost all their male members that were of an age capable of bearing arms. The body of the king was found by Lord Dacre among a heap of dead. Dacre, who had known him well, recognized it, though it was disfigured by many wounds, and it was afterwards identified by James' chancellor, Sir William Scott, by Sir John Forman, and some other prisoners. The body was conveyed to Berwick, where it was embalmed and wrapped in sheets of lead, and it was then sent secretly, among other packages, to Newcastle. From Newcastle the Earl of Surrey took it with him to London, and then placed it in the monastery of Shene, near Richmond. Meanwhile, in Scotland, the people were loath to believe that their king was dead; and those who believed it attributed his death, not to the English in the field, but to certain traitors in the retreat. It was said that James, after escaping across the Tweed, was murdered by some of the retainers of the Earl of Home; and the classical, but credulous and imaginative Buchanan tells us that he himself had heard one Lawrence Telfer say that he saw the king on the north of the Tweed after the battle. Lesley, again, informs us that it was asserted by many, that it could not be the king's body which Surrey had conveyed to London, as James was seen alive by many, and safe at Kelso, after the flight of Flodden; and he adds, that some of the Scots continued to believe that the king had gone on a pilgrimage to the Holy Land to pray for the souls of his slaughtered nobles, and to pass the rest of his life in devotion and penitence. By these romantic believers it was particularly objected to the English, that they could never show the token of the iron belt which James constantly wore round his body, in penance for his youthful rebellion and the death of his father; but the English produced the unfortunate monarch's sword and dagger, and a turquoise ring (supposed to have been sent him by the Queen of France), which are still preserved in the Heralds' College, London; and no rational doubt can be entertained that James perished at Flodden Field.[1]

Queen Catherine instantly announced this victory to her husband in a very spirited and very

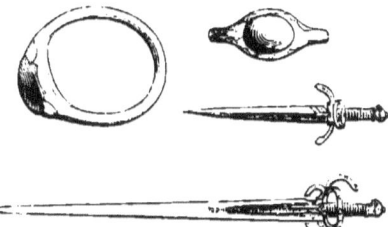

SWORD, DAGGER, AND RING OF JAMES IV.[2]—From the originals in Heralds' College, London.

English letter. Being on the winning side, she said, "All that God sendeth is for the best;" and she sent Henry the coat-armour of the unfortunate James.[3] The affectionate tone of the letter is remarkable. She calls the king "my Henry;" and concludes with praying God to send him home shortly, as without his no joy can be complete. The king received this conjugal despatch while he lay before Tournai. Soon after his return to England he rewarded Surrey, by restoring to him the title of Duke of Norfolk, which had been forfeited by his father, who fell in the battle of Bosworth Field.

The victory at Flodden had been so dearly bought, and money and provisions were so scarce in his camp, that Surrey was in no condition to follow up his advantages. Instead of invading

---

[1] Original despatch in French, attributed to the Lord-admiral Howard, preserved in the Heralds' College, and printed by Pinkerton.—*The Trewe Encountre or Batayle lately don betwene Englande and Scotlande*, &c., first printed in 1513, and reprinted by Haslewood, in 1809; Hall's *Chronicle*; Pitscottie; Lesley, *De Rebus Gestis Scotorum*; Walter Scott, *Notes to Marmion*; Ellis' *Letters*; Tytler, *Hist. Scot.*; *Rambles in Northumberland and on the Scottish Border*, by Stephen Oliver the Younger.

[2] The length of the sword blade is 3 feet ¾ inch, and of the hilt 6¼ inches. On one side of the blade is inscribed "*Maestro Dominge;*" on the other apparently the words, "ESPOIR CONFORTE LE GYEVAL." The blade of the dagger is 13¾ inches, and the hilt 5½ in length.—*Archaeologia*, xxxii. 335.

[3] The whole of the letter, which is preserved among the Cotton MSS. in the British Museum, and printed in Sir Henry Ellis' *Collection*, is exceedingly interesting.

Scotland he stopped at Berwick, and having put some troops in garrison, he disbanded the rest of his army. The Scots prepared manfully for the defence of their country; and the queen, at the same time, wrote an affectionate letter to her brother Henry, requesting his forbearance for a widowed sister and an infant orphan. Henry was, perhaps, not incapable of generous sentiments; but it is not uncharitable to suppose that the determined attitude of the Scots, and the old recollections of the unprofitable nature of Scottish wars, had their weight in his council, which agreed to a peace.

A.D. 1514. Louis XII. pursued a course of diplomacy which broke up the coalition against him, and which would have left the English to make war by themselves, had Henry's military ardour tempted him to a renewal of the struggle. He completely reconciled himself with the court of Rome, and he not only prolonged his truce with Ferdinand, but won over the Emperor Maximilian—the volunteer of England—by proposing a treaty of marriage. Louis offered the hand of Renée, his second daughter, with her claim to the duchy of Milan, to Prince Charles, who was grandson both to Maximilian and to Ferdinand. Charles, it will be remembered, had been affianced during the lifetime of the late king to the Princess Mary of England, Henry's youngest sister. The bargain had been arranged with Charles' father, Philip, during his detention in Windsor Castle; but Henry did not consider it the less binding from the force and treachery which had been used on that occasion, and, as Charles was now approaching the age of puberty, he expected shortly to see the completion of the marriage. The first person to inform Henry of these negotiations was the French king himself, through the medium of the Duke of Longueville, who had been taken prisoner in the battle of the Spurs and conveyed into England. That accomplished courtier soon won the favour of the English king; and when Henry was almost frantic at the treachery of his allies, the duke adroitly proposed a family alliance with his master. Louis' wife, Anne of Brittany, had died in the month of January, just in time for the furthering of this sudden scheme. She had left no son, and her widower, notwithstanding his declining health, hoped that a new marriage might bless him with an heir. Negotiations in other quarters had been opened before Anne was buried; but the friendship of England was worth purchasing, even at the price of taking a disagreeable wife—and the Princess Mary, on the contrary, was a beautiful and charming person. Henry, whose mind was seldom startled by sudden changes, caught at the proposal. Louis anxiously urged the treaty, and the private feelings of the princess were disregarded, as in all such cases. Louis was fifty-three years old, Mary was sixteen, and passionately enamoured of Charles Brandon, Viscount Lisle, one of her brother's favourites, and the handsomest and most accomplished nobleman in the English court. The treaty, which was to secure lasting peace and amity between the two nations, was concluded with the usual forms: Louis agreed to pay Henry a million of crowns, in ten yearly instalments, in discharge of arrears due on the old treaty of Etaples, and Henry agreed to give his sister, Mary, a dower of 400,000 crowns. On the 7th of August a marriage ceremony was performed at Greenwich, the Duke of Longueville acting as proxy for his master. If Mary was in no haste to leave England, Louis was very impatient for her society, and he wrote more than once to hurry her departure. On the 2d of September he addressed Wolsey, now Bishop of Lincoln and the manager of all Henry's affairs, desiring that his queen might be sent over without delay. A month after this Henry and his court accompanied the young Queen of France to Dover, where she embarked for Boulogne, accompanied by a splendid retinue, among whom were Surrey, now Duke of Norfolk, her lover, the Viscount Lisle, who had been created Duke of Suffolk, and *Anne Boleyne*, then a pretty little girl and maid of honour.[1] On the 8th of October she made her public entrance into Abbeville. On the following day the marriage was re-solemnized by a French cardinal, Louis suffering grievously from the gout during the ceremony; and the day after, to the great vexation of the young queen, he dismissed the Lady Guildford, her governess, Sir Richard Blount, her chamberlain, with all the rest of her English attendants, except Anne Boleyne, and two or three mere menials. The accomplished Charles Brandon, however, remained with the Duke of Norfolk in quality of ambassador. On the 12th of October Mary addressed her brother, complaining bitterly of this treatment. "Would to God," she exclaims, "that my Lord of York had come with me in the room of Norfolk! for then I am sure I should have been left much more at my heart's ease than I am now!"[2] My Lord of York was none other than Wolsey, who ran through all the grades of church preferment with unprecedented rapidity, and who had been translated from Lincoln to the archbishopric of York on the preceding 5th of August. The gallant Brandon excited a great jealousy among the French courtiers; and, if we are to believe the majority of the French writers of the time,

[1] In the original list signed by King Louis, which is preserved among the Cottonian MSS., this personage is merely named as *Madamoyselle Boleyn*. [2] Sir Henry Ellis' *Collection*.

the attachment between him and Queen Mary was apparent from the moment of their arrival in France, and excited suspicion, notwithstanding their great prudence and irreproachable conduct. In the month of December Louis wrote to his "good brother, cousin, and gossip," the King of England, to express his happiness in this marriage; and on the 1st of January following he expired at Paris, worn out with sickness and debility. Mary was not an inconsolable widow. It was generally rumoured that Francis I., who now ascended the throne of France in the twenty-first year of his age, was not insensible to her beauty and accomplishments; but he was provided with a queen, having recently married the Princess Claude, daughter of the late King Louis and Anne of Brittany. Henry sent the Duke of Suffolk, Sir Richard Wingfield, and Dr. West, with a "goodly band of yeomen, all in black," to bring the princess home again. Mary, who had been not quite three months a wife, and scarcely two months a widow, gave heart and hand to her lover, and was privately married at Paris to the captivating Brandon, almost as soon as he arrived at that capital. It had not been unusual for princesses of the blood to marry subjects, but the notion of the royal dignity was now wonderfully on the increase; and it had been set down as law, at least as far back as Henry VI., that no such marriages should be allowed without the express permission of the king; and for this it appears Mary did not ask. She wrote to implore pardon for the step she had taken to secure her own happiness, and then travelled with her husband to Calais, where a more public marriage was solemnized shortly after. Henry for a time was, or appeared to be, exceedingly wroth at the unequal match; and on their return to England, in the month of August, the duke and duchess went to their manor in Suffolk instead of joining the court. The king, however, had a warm affection both for his sister Mary and for the accomplished Brandon, who had been brought up with him from his childhood, and who delighted Henry by his cheerful humour, his gallant deportment, and his great address in tournaments and all martial exercises; and a perfect reconciliation soon took place, aided by the good-will of my "Lord-cardinal"—for Wolsey, still rising, got the cardinal's hat in the course of this summer.[1]

It is time to say a word touching the history of this gorgeous churchman, who for nearly twenty years was more King of England than Henry himself. Thomas Wolsey was the son of a substantial butcher, or more probably grazier, of Ipswich. His father, who was rather wealthy for the time, procured him a good education,

[1] Ellis' *Letters*; Hall; Bishop Godwin; *Hist. de Bayard*; *Lettre de' Principi*; Original Letters quoted by Fiddes.

and brought him up for the church. He studied at Oxford, where, on account of his precocity and early attainments, he was honoured with the name of the Boy Bachelor. For some time he taught the grammar-school adjoining to Magdalen College. Among other pupils, the sons of the Marquis of Dorset were committed to his care, and, by means of the marquis, the parsonage of Limington, in Somersetshire—"no very mean one"—was bestowed upon him. He was not distinguished at any period of his life by temperance and sobriety, and a command of his passions: in the hot season of youth he appears to have been guilty of sundry indiscretions. It is quite certain that the young parson soon grew weary of the obscurity of a country life; "bearing a mind that looked beyond this poor benefice," which he soon left to become domestic chaplain to the treasurer of Calais. The treasurer

CARDINAL WOLSEY.—From a picture by Holbein.

introduced him to the notice of Bishop Fox, the cunning minister and diplomatist—"a man that knew rightly how to judge of good wits." Fox warmly recommended him to his master Henry VII., whose particular talent it was to discover the abilities of other men, and who never employed a dull one. Henry presently employed Wolsey in certain secret affairs of great moment, and Wolsey justified the warm recommendation of his patron the bishop. "What need many words!" exclaims an episcopal historian; "he so far pleased the king, that in short time he became a great man, and was first preferred to the deanery of Lincoln, and then made the king's almoner."[2]

Upon the death of the old king there was a struggle for supremacy in the council between

[2] Bishop Godwin.

Bishop Fox and the Duke of Norfolk, then Earl of Surrey. The bishop was not slow in perceiving that the earl, whose military character and tastes pleased the young king, was getting the upper hand, and to counteract this influence, he introduced Wolsey to Henry VIII. It was the old story—the tool was too sharp for the hand that would have worked with it for its own purposes. Instead of propping the bishop against the weight of the earl, the chaplain supplanted them both, and soon acquired more power and influence at court than they had ever possessed between them. Though nearly twenty years his senior, Wolsey glided into all the tastes and habits of the young king, some of which, however, seem to have been natural to him; and though a churchman, he became a sort of model and a bosom friend to Henry, whose chief but not only ambition it was to figure as a warlike monarch and perfect knight. We have noticed his love of literature. Of the books he had read many were of the school divinity;[1] and his favourite author was the subtilizing St. Thomas Aquinas. Wolsey could entertain him on this subject, which he had studied professionally; and, with a happy facility, he could pass from St. Thomas to the ladies and affairs of gallantry. Henry, according to an old writer, had "as little inclination to trouble himself with business as a wild ox has to be yoked to the plough;" and it quite suited Wolsey's views to encourage this feeling, and to take the whole business of government upon himself.

A few months after the return of the Princess Mary from France, Archbishop Warham, finding his authority reduced to nothing, resigned the seals, upon which Wolsey became chancellor of the kingdom. This high promotion was soon followed by another of an ecclesiastical description: in consequence of services rendered or promised, Leo X. appointed him to the important and lucrative post of Papal legate. He now became most gorgeous in his dress, retinue, housekeeping, and all other things; carrying pomp, and ceremony, and expense to a higher pitch than men had ever before seen in a subject. It was calculated at one time that his income, with the pensions and presents he received from foreign princes, equalled the revenue of the crown. But his taste was rather for spending than accumulating. He maintained a train of 800 persons, amongst whom were nine or ten lords, the beggared descendants of proud barons. He had fifteen knights, and forty squires. All his domestics were splendidly attired : his cook wore a satin or velvet jerkin, and a chain of gold round his neck. Henry seems to have taken a pride in the splendour of his favourite, and jealousy was probably avoided by his considering all this glory as a mere reflection of his own. Even the nation was less jealous of the low-born minister than might have been expected; for Wolsey was an excellent paymaster, and constantly gave largesses to the people and alms to the poor. At the same time he encouraged men of learning, exerted himself for the revival of classical literature, and endowed colleges. Indeed, Wolsey, though the most absolute minister of an absolute king, was rather popular than otherwise, until Henry's wants obliged him to overtax the people. As chancellor he dispensed strict justice, though his severity too often savoured of the system of Empson and Dudley; for he set round fines on the heads of rich offenders, without any very scrupulous attention to legal forms or the positive amount of their guilt. On the whole, and with reference to that age, his home-government was not a bad one. His faults and vices were of a gigantic growth; but Wolsey was no vulgar upstart—no sordid mind.[2]

Francis I., the new King of France, whose views were all directed beyond the Alps, gladly renewed the treaty which his predecessor Louis had concluded with Henry. Having secured peace with England, and resumed alliances with Venice, with Genoa, and some other states, Francis poured 60,000 men into the plains of Lombardy. The splendid victory of Marignano and the acquisition of Milan were the fruits of this invasion.

The military glory which the young French king acquired beyond the Alps excited the jealousy of Henry, and an outcry was raised in the English court against French ambition and encroachment. As Francis had given great offence to Wolsey, that powerful favourite encouraged the hostile feelings of his master, and recommended him to form a fresh alliance with the Emperor Maximilian, in order to expel the French from Italy. If there had been money in hand war would have been immediately declared against Francis, but Henry by this time had completely exhausted the treasures left to him by his father; and Maximilian, on his side, was still the "moneyless," and could do nothing without English subsidies. He soon adopted an expedient which, by a very correct estimate of Henry's character, he calculated would induce him to make greater exertions for the raising of money than the mere prospect of a doubtful war. Gradually he hinted that he was weary of the weight of the imperial crown, and might be easily persuaded to resign it, for a proper consideration in money, to the English king. Duped

---

[1] According to several accounts Henry's father had at one time destined him for the church. Hence his knowledge of divinity, church music, &c.

[2] Cavendish; Fiddes; Hall; Bishop Godwin.

as he had been by Maximilian already, Henry's greedy vanity took the bait; and the Earl of Worcester and Dr. Cuthbert Tunstall, afterwards Bishop of Durham, were sent as ambassadors to the emperor's court to negotiate for this cession of a title. Tunstall, who was one of the most accomplished scholars in Europe, and a man of business besides, presently discovered the specious cheat. After begging his short-sighted master to pardon his frankness, he explained the trick in some admirable letters.[1] Henry was convinced; and he not only gave up his dream of being an emperor, but also his projected alliance with Maximilian, for the purpose of driving the French out of Italy. Nor did he stop at negatives. When once turned from a line of policy, it was his general custom to run for a time in a directly contrary direction. Francis, after securing himself in possession of the Milanese, went on to Bologna, where he held a long conference with the pope, whom he won over by his liberal treatment and the fascination of his manners. In the following spring the French monarch recrossed the Alps, leaving the Constable Bourbon to govern the duchy of Milan. He soon applied himself to arrange a reconciliation with Wolsey, and by means which are not explained, but at which it is not difficult to guess, my lord-cardinal was converted from an enemy into a zealous friend. A treaty of alliance, offensive and defensive, was then set on foot, and at length, on the 4th of October, 1518, it was solemnly ratified. Henry's biographer, Lord Herbert, holds up this treaty as a model for princes; but we see little in it that is new, either in matter or manner, and all its clauses were broken more rapidly even than usual. It was agreed, as a basis, that the infant dauphin, the son of Francis, should be contracted to Henry's *daughter*, the Princess Mary, who was then about a year and a half old; and that Henry should restore Tournai to Francis upon payment of 600,000 crowns, and under charge of an annual pension of 12,000 livres, which Wolsey was to receive in lieu of the revenues of the bishopric of that city. The cardinal, in the course of the negotiations, had not neglected his own interests, and he had a confidential agent attached to the embassy in France who received the presents of the French commissioners.

A.D. 1519. Henry's jealousy of Francis seemed now converted into a vehement admiration; and he proposed a personal interview, to take place in the month of July, 1519, between Calais and Boulogne. But this scene of parade was postponed in consequence of the occurrence of a great political crisis, which wholly occupied the attention of Europe for many months.

The Emperor Maximilian died suddenly in the month of January, 1519, and Francis proposed himself as candidate for the vacant dignity. Henry, in the month of March, when his head was full of the pageantry to be gotten up for their meeting, promised the French king his countenance and support; a little later (in the month of May) he sent the learned Richard Pace to the German electors, to announce himself as a candidate. But a greater than Henry or than Francis was now in the arena. This was the Archduke Charles, who had once been betrothed to the Princess Mary, Henry's sister. By the death of his maternal grandfather, old Ferdinand of Aragon, which happened in 1516, Charles had become possessor of the whole Spanish monarchy; and now, on the death of Maximilian, his paternal grandfather, he proposed himself as his successor in the empire. The claims of Charles were in all essentials preferable to those of Francis; he was of a German house (of the imperial house of Austria); he was born at Ghent, and was, by right of inheritance, sovereign of the Low Countries, which were held to be a subject part of the empire. The German electors had often been most corrupt, and Francis flattered himself that he could set aside all these advantages by intrigue and bribery.[2] But the Lord of the Netherlands, of Naples and Sicily, of Spain and the Indies, was a much richer sovereign than the French king; and as for political intrigue, Francis, though his senior in years, was a mere child to Charles, whose councils were directed by the most cunning diplomatists in Europe—men who had studied their craft in the school of his grandfather Ferdinand and Cardinal Ximenes. Henry soon found that, between two such competitors, there was no chance for him; and, either from that common desire men feel for being on the winning side, or from some new disgust against Francis, or in a lame attempt at manœuvre, he wrote to assure Charles of his earnest wishes that he might prove the successful candidate.[3] This young king went from Spain to the Netherlands; and while the electors were debating in the diet of Frankfort, he raised an army, which he kept sufficiently near to overawe the diet, and yet sufficiently distant to save appearances. After long deliberations, and a rapid circulation both of French and Spanish money, Charles was elected emperor on the 28th of June. Francis bore his disappointment and his heavy

---

[2] Francis told Sir Thomas Boleyn, who was one of Henry's ambassadors, that he would spend three millions of gold but he would succeed.

[3] At the same time, however, Sir Thomas Boleyn conveyed to Francis the most solemn assurances of Henry's support, and also (at the same time, or very nearly so) Pace recommended his master to the electors. (*State Papers*, reign of Henry VIII., published by his Majesty's Record Commission, A.D. 1830.)

---

[1] Ellis' *Letters*. The originals are in the British Museum.

pecuniary losses with seeming lightness of heart, saying to the Spanish ambassadors that, in ambition as in love, a discarded suitor ought never to cherish resentment. But notwithstanding this *bon mot*, he was deeply mortified, and he felt that he and Charles must be rivals for life. This, however, in all probability would have happened even if there had been no imperial crown to contend for. Ever since Charles VIII. had carried his lances through the defiles of the Alps—for more than twenty years—there had been a struggle between the French and the Spaniards for the dominion of Italy; and it was not likely that this would be given up under two young, active, and warlike princes, at a moment when Charles held the whole of the south of that beautiful peninsula, and when Francis had obtained a firm footing on the north of it.

The eagerness with which each of these rivals attempted to secure to himself the friendship of the King of England, was flattering to the power and importance of the nation; but Henry was utterly incapable of benefiting either himself or his people, or the cause of humanity, by the advantages afforded him by his enviable position. On the 6th of July he ordered Wolsey to draw up, "as his politic wisdom should think best," letters of congratulation to Charles;[1] and on the 8th of the same month we find Wolsey stating, in a letter to his master, that De Hesdin, Charles' ambassador, complained that proper respect had not been paid in London to this grand occasion. It is quite clear that both king and minister wished to play a double game, and to keep on the best of terms, for the present, with both Charles and Francis. What advantages Henry proposed to himself are not so obvious; but Wolsey had recently touched the French king's money, and was probably expecting more, while, with the emperor, he was engaging for a still higher prize. When Francis requested the king to fulfil his former purpose, and pass over to the Continent to a personal interview, it was agreed to give him this great sign of friendship and confidence; and the meeting was fixed for the following summer. Upon learning this appointment, Charles was greatly alarmed, and his ambassadors in England did all that they could to break it. But Henry, who longed to display his magnificence, was firm to his purpose, and, as the time approached (towards the end of May), he removed, with his queen and court, from Greenwich to Canterbury. He had scarcely collected his finery for embarkation at Dover, when he received news that the emperor was in the Channel. According to the commonly received account, Henry was taken by surprise, but not so was his minister. Wolsey had opened a secret negotiation with Spain, where the emperor was then residing, and had concerted this opportune visit; and Charles had granted his "most dear friend," the cardinal, a pension of 7000 ducats, secured upon two Spanish bishoprics. Wolsey was now detached from Canterbury with a splendid train to meet the imperial guest, who anchored at Hythe, on the 26th of May. The illustrious strangers were lodged in Dover Castle, whither Henry repaired to pay his respects. He arrived by torch-light, and saluted and embraced the emperor very tenderly. They conferred together in private during a great part of the night; and on the morrow, being Whit Sunday, they rode together in great state to Canterbury, the emperor always keeping the right hand, and the Earl of Derby bearing the sword of state before them.[2] As they approached the cathedral they were met by Wolsey at the head of a procession of the clergy, and conducted into the church. The cathedral, the adjoining

CANTERBURY CATHEDRAL, West Front.

monastery, and the different buildings thereto attached, and which formed a little town in themselves, were then at the height of their glory, enriched by the accumulated donations of nearly 1000 years. The sovereigns, according to precedent, laid their offerings on the tomb of St. Thomas à Becket, and some time was spent there in devotions, not only by the emperor, but even by him who shortly after defaced the monument and seized upon that infinite treasure. From the church they proceeded to the palace of the Arch-

---

[1] This letter to Wolsey, in the hand-writing of Sir Thomas More, is preserved in the British Museum, and is printed in Sir Henry Ellis' *Collection*, and in the *State Papers* published by government.

[2] Derby, it appears, was one of Wolsey's retinue.

bishop of Canterbury, where the emperor was joyfully welcomed by Queen Catherine, who was his aunt. Here, too, Charles saw, for the first time, Henry's sister, Mary, late Queen-dowager of France, and now Duchess of Suffolk. He gazed with unconcealed admiration on her exquisitely beautiful person; and it is said that, remembering how she had been affianced to him, he bitterly regretted the political views by which he had lost such a wife, and that these thoughts marred all the splendid festivities which were got up to do him honour. But if those tender feelings ever existed at all, they must have been of transient duration in such a mind; and Charles spent a good part of the time of his short visit in arranging fresh schemes of ambition, or in securing Wolsey to his interests. The cardinal, who considered every advancement but as a step to something higher, sighed for the triple crown of Rome; and the adroit emperor engaged to give him all the weight of his influence whenever the present pope should die. He also made Wolsey some magnificent presents, and conciliated his pride by treating him with great reverence, and affecting to submit to his superior judgment in state affairs. Three days were spent in this manner, and, on the fourth, Charles re-embarked at Sandwich, and set sail for his Netherland dominions, well satisfied that, by anticipating and by winning Wolsey, he had prevented any evil consequences that might otherwise have arisen out of the more formal interview with Francis. On the same day Henry, with the cardinal, the queen, and the whole court, sailed for Calais to keep that appointment. The place fixed upon, after deliberations of an interminable length, was within the English pale, between Guines and Ardres.[1]

On the 4th of June (1520) the king's grace, with all the lords, and the queen with her train of ladies, removed from Calais to the lordship royal of Guines, where a temporary palace of wood had been built, and most gorgeously decorated by 1100 workmen, most of them cunning artificers from Flanders or from Holland. The outside was covered with sail-cloth, which was so painted as to look like squared stone; the inside was hung with the richest arras. The furniture and decorations of the temporary chapel and apartments of state were gorgeous in the extreme. The walls glittered with embroidery and jewels; the altar and the tables groaned under the weight of massive plate.[2] Francis, that he might not be outdone, had prepared an immense pavilion, which was chiefly sustained by a mighty mast, with ropes and tackle strained to steady it. But there arose a most impetuous and tempestuous wind, which broke asunder the ropes and laid all this bravery in the dirt; and Francis was obliged to take up his lodging in an old castle near the town of Ardres. As soon as the two kings were settled in their respective residences, "the Reverend Father Lord Thomas Wolsey, cardinal and legate à Latere, as the king's high embassador, rode with noble repair of lords, gentlemen, and prelates, to the French court at Ardres, where the same lord cardinal was highly entertained of the French king." The Frenchmen were so struck with Wolsey's pomp and splendour, that they afterwards "*made books*, showing the triumphant doings of the cardinal's *royalty*." At the same moment that Wolsey visited Francis, a deputation of French nobles waited upon Henry. The cardinal, who had "full power and authority to affirm and confirm, bind and unbind, whatsoever should be in question," even as if the king his master were there present, spent two whole days in arranging an additional treaty with the French sovereign. Francis, whose heart was beyond the Alps, readily agreed to pay a high price for the neutrality of England in the war which he saw was inevitable: he renewed the recent marriage treaty, and, in addition to the money there promised, bound himself and his successors to pay to Henry and his successors the yearly sum of 100,000 crowns, in the event of the said marriage between their children being solemnized, and the issue of that marriage seated on the English throne. To do away with the jealousy which had long existed between France and England on the subject of Scotland, he consented that the affairs of that country should be referred to the friendly arbitration of Cardinal Wolsey and his own mother, Louisa of Savoy.

When the business was over, Henry, apparelled in a garment of cloth of silver of damask, ribbed with cloth of gold, and with all his nobles gaudily dressed and mounted, went forth to meet his brother of France. They met at last (on the 7th of June) in the valley of Andren, where a gorgeous tent had been pitched for the occasion. As had been previously arranged, in order to get over a delicate point of precedency, the two kings saluted and embraced on horseback. Francis spoke first, saying, "My dear brother and cousin, thus far to my pain have I travelled to see you personally. I think, verily, that you esteem me as I am, and that I am not unworthy to be your aid. The realms and seigniories in my possession demonstrate the extent of my power." To this Henry graciously replied, "Neither your realms nor other the places of your power are a matter of my regard, but the steadfastness and loyal keeping of promises comprised in charters between you and me. I never saw prince with

---

[1] *Herbert; Hall; Stow; Godwin.*   [2] *Hall.*

my eyes that might of my heart be more beloved; and for your love have I passed the seas into the farthest frontier of my kingdoms to see you." The two monarchs dismounted together, and walked arm-in-arm into the tent, where they partook of a costly banquet. After they had ended, and spice and wine had been served up in the tent, "ipocras was chief drink, of plenty to all that would drink outside." The kings then came out of the tent, when Henry's favoured historian ob-

MEETING OF HENRY VIII. AND FRANCIS I. ON THE FIELD OF THE CLOTH OF GOLD.—From a bas-relief in the Hôtel de Bourgtheroulde, Rouen.

tained a near view of the person and the clothes (which seemed to him of more importance) of the French monarch. "The said Francis," says he, "is a goodly prince, stately of countenance and merry of cheer; brown coloured, great eyes, high-nosed, big-lipped, fair-breasted and shouldered, with small legs and long feet."[1]

Several months before this meeting it had been proclaimed, in all the principal cities of Europe, that the Kings of France and England, as brothers-in-arms, would hold solemn jousts and tourneys, and defend the field against all knights. On the 11th June the jousts were opened, the queens having taken their places. Catherine was most brilliantly equipped, her very foot-cloth being powdered with pearls. The kings rode together to the mound, Henry having for his aids Charles Brandon, Duke of Suffolk, the Marquis of Dorset, Sir William Kingston, Sir Richard Jerningham, Sir Giles Capell, Mr. Nicholas Carew, and Mr. Anthony Knevitt; and Francis having for his aids the Lords of St. Pol, Montmorency, Biron, and other noble gentlemen. Many illustrious knights, from different countries, entered the lists as challengers; and then the mock combats began. Such was the address of the two monarchs, or such the practical flattery of their opponents, that they fought five battles each day, and invariably came off victorious. Six days were spent in tilting with lances, two in tourneys with the broadsword on horseback, and the two last in fighting on foot at the barriers. The feats of the combatants were registered in a book, wherein the heralds were not likely to permit the exploits of kings to lose by their modesty of expression.

No pageantry or outward show of friendship could reconcile the ancient jealousies of the two nations, or even remove their mutual suspicions. The English, as Comines has told us, had usually been very confiding in matters of conference; but the court of Henry was certainly not so on the present occasion. Francis, on the contrary, who had a certain generosity and nobleness of disposition, grew weary of these cautions, and made an effort to put an end to them, and break through the barriers of etiquette. This he did by a well-devised practical jest, through which mutual confidence was established. After this the intercourse between the two courts was more familiar. There were banquets and balls, masking and mumming, in which the ladies and the two kings played their parts, Henry being especially fond of masquerades and fantastic disguisings. "But," says an old historian, who moralizes his theme, "pleasures must have their intermission, and kings, if not by their greatness, are by their affairs severed." After consuming a fortnight, Henry returned to Calais, and Francis went towards Paris. The most lasting effect produced by the "Field of the Cloth of Gold," as the interview and the place where it was held were afterwards called, was the ruin of many of the nobility, both English and French, who, in their insane rivalry, contracted enormous debts.[2]

---

[1] Hall. Those who remember the spirited, intellectual-looking portrait of Francis, painted by Titian, will be inclined to think that this annalist has scarcely done the French king justice. But beyond pageants, and dresses, and feasts, Hall was wholly out of his depth. He was, notwithstanding, a proper historian for such a king as Henry VIII.; and there is no having a correct notion of the solemn trifles which filled up so large a part of this reign without referring to his ponderous sentences and elaborate descriptions.

[2] Hall; Du Bellay; Polydore Virgil; Godwin.

CHAPTER IV.—CIVIL AND MILITARY HISTORY.—A.D. 1520—1526.

HENRY VIII.—ACCESSION, A.D. 1509—DEATH, A.D. 1547.

Mutual visits between Henry VIII. and Charles V.—Duke of Buckingham suspected—Accused of treason—Tried and executed—Henry becomes champion of the Romish church against the Reformation—His negotiations with Charles V. against France—Wolsey's intrigues for the popedom—League against the French king—Wolsey disappointed of the popedom—Charles V. visits England—Wolsey's oppressive measures to raise money—France unsuccessfully invaded—Ireland and Scotland stirred up by France against England—Regency of Margaret, Henry's sister, in Scotland—She is succeeded in the regency by the Duke of Albany—Margaret's flight into England—Henry espouses her cause—Insurrections in Scotland—The Duke of Albany leaves Scotland—Margaret returns thither—Tumults in Scotland—Albany returns, and resumes the regency—Intrigues of Henry VIII. and Wolsey to embroil Scottish affairs—Albany invades England—The invasion followed by a truce—Albany again leaves Scotland—Henry re-assembles his parliament to raise money—Independent conduct of parliament—The demanded supplies withheld—France invaded—Troubles in that country—The Duke of Bourbon driven to revolt—His treaty with Henry VIII. and Charles V.—He escapes from France—Unsuccessful campaign of the English in France—Wolsey's intrigues for the popedom—His failure—Wars in France—Francis I. besieges Pavia—He is defeated and taken prisoner—Intrigues of the English court on that event—Wolsey's unpopular proceedings—Henry concludes a peace with France—Francis I. liberated from captivity—Fruitless attempt of Luther to conciliate Henry VIII.

WHEN the gaudy play was over, the first thing Henry did was to go to Gravelines, and pay a visit to the more sober-minded emperor, who had prevented his noble subjects from attending the meeting, and ruining themselves in shows and tournaments. Charles accompanied him back to Calais, to pay, as was given out, his respects to his dear aunt Catherine, but, in reality, to concert measures with those who had so recently pledged themselves to his rival, Francis. After spending three days at Calais, the emperor rode back to his Flemish dominions "mounted on a brave horse covered with a cloth of gold, richly beset with stones, which the king had given him." Before he departed he flattered the vanity of his dear uncle by appointing him umpire to settle every difference that might arise between himself and Francis. After spending a few more days at Calais, Henry and his court embarked for Dover, and then returned "all safe in body, but empty in purse," to London.[1]

Although, in these despotic times, it was dangerous to oppose or criticize the tastes of the king, there were not wanting men who expressed their disapprobation of the ruinous and useless expense into which the nobility of the kingdom had been led for the getting up of the Field of the Cloth of Gold. Among these murmurers one of the loudest was Edward Stafford, Duke of Buckingham, the son of that weak and vacillating duke who, after helping Richard III. to seize the crown, raised an insurrection against him, in which he lost his head, like a fool and coward.[2]

But, though Buckingham was marked out for destruction immediately after Henry's return from the Continent, it was not solely on account of his criticism, for he had long been an object of jealousy and suspicion, though the king pretended a great affection for him, and had appointed him to several high offices about the court. The origin of the duke's misfortunes was his connection with royalty, and his descent from the ancient line of the Plantagenets.[3] His next misfortune was his wealth, for he was one of the richest subjects in England. He kept a splendid and hospitable house,[4] and was exceedingly popular, not only with his servants and retainers, but with the nation at large. He had several of those virtues which it was customary to consider as peculiarly English: he was open-handed and open-hearted; frank and free spoken, almost to bluntness; and, unlike his father, he was bold and firm, and not destitute of talent. His credulity in matters of prophecy was a folly common to his age. About eight years before, when the king was preparing that expedition which was to conquer France, and which ended in the taking of two useless towns, the duke became acquainted with one Hopkins, a Carthusian friar, who had gained reputation as a fortune-teller. The friar, it is said, predicted to him (which, considering the selfish caution of Henry, and the

---

[1] Hall; Godwin; Du Bellay. [2] See vol. i. p. 647.

[3] Buckingham sprang from Anne Plantagenet, daughter of Thomas of Woodstock, Duke of Gloucester, a son of Edward III., and also traced through John of Gaunt, Duke of Lancaster. He was hereditary High-constable of England.

[4] Henry, it appears, was at times his guest at his splendid seat of Penshurst. Richard Pace, in a letter to Wolsey, written from that place in 1519, says, "The Duke of Buckingham maketh unto the king, here, excellent cheer."—*State Papers*.

rashness of James, he might have done without consulting the stars) that the King of England would return home safe from France, and that the King of Scots would surely perish if he crossed the Borders. The fulfilment of both prophecies raised the monk's fame, and with it the credulity of Buckingham, who, thereafter, had frequent and familiar intercourse with the prophet. The monk, seeing that the duke was mindful of his royal descent, and of the fact that the king had no sons, began to foresee that there was something wonderfully high in the destinies of young Stafford, the duke's heir. In other words, it seems he hinted that the duke's son would be Henry's successor on the throne. For so great an effect as the judicial murder of this popular nobleman, people naturally sought a variety of causes. "Being yet a child," says the Bishop of Hereford, "I have heard ancient men say that by his bravery of apparel and sumptuous feasts, he exasperated the king, with whom, in these things, he seemed to contend." Another cause assigned was the enmity of Wolsey, without whose advice, it was believed, the king never undertook anything; and, though the cardinal was not a man of blood, he *may* have contributed to the present execution, his dislike of the duke being notorious.

A.D. 1521. Buckingham, who was living quietly on his estate of Thornbury, in Gloucestershire, was now suddenly invited to court. The duke, suspecting no mischief, obeyed the summons, and started on his journey, not observing for some time that he was closely followed by three knights of the king's body-guard, "and a secret power of servants-at-arms." His suspicions were first awakened at Windsor, where he lodged for the night, and where he saw the "same three knights lying close by." He was also treated with marked disrespect by a creature of the court, one Thomas Ward, "who was gentleman harbinger to the king;" and the next morning, at breakfast, "his meat would not down." The whole management of the arrest is marked with a detestable treachery worthy of the worst of times. Before inveigling the duke to court, Henry had thrown one Perk, that nobleman's chancellor, into the Tower, in the view of extorting from him confessions injurious to his master. From Windsor Buckingham rode slowly on to Westminster, and there took his barge, in order to row down to Greenwich, where the court then was. He stopped on his way at my lord-cardinal's bridge,[1] where he landed with four or five of his servants, and desired to speak with Wolsey; 'but he was answered how my lord was diseased (indisposed).' "Well," said the duke,

"yet will I drink of my lord's wine as I pass;" and then a gentleman of my lord-cardinal's brought the duke with much reverence into the cellar, where the duke drank. But when he saw and perceived no cheer to him was made, he changed colour, and so departed."[2]

As he descended the Thames, and drew near the city, his barge was hailed and boarded by Sir Henry Marney, captain of the body-guard, who attached him as a traitor in the king's name. The duke was carried on shore, and conveyed through Thames Street to the Tower, to the great astonishment and regret of the people. This was on the 16th of April. On the 13th of May he was put upon his trial as a peer, but not before a full house assembled in a parliamentary manner. Seventeen peers chosen by the king, and the Duke of Norfolk, as high-steward, constituted the tribunal. He was charged with tempting Friar Hopkins to make traitorous prophecies, by means of messages and personal conferences; with having tampered with the king's servants and yeomen of the guard, by means of presents and promises; with having declared his determination, in the event of the king's death, to cut off the heads of the lord-cardinal and some others, and then to seize the government, &c., &c. At first Buckingham pleaded that nothing in the indictment amounted to an overt act, and that, therefore, even in the showing of the prosecution, there was no guilt of treason; but Fineux, the chief-justice, laid it down as good law, that there was treason in *imagining* the death of the king, and that words spoken without any overt act were evidence enough. The duke, then, with great force and eloquence, replied to the indictment, charge by charge, denied his guilt in every particular, and boldly demanded to be confronted with the witnesses. Hopkins the prophet, De la Court his confessor, Perk his chancellor, and Sir Charles Knevitt, *his own cousin, and formerly his steward,* were brought into court. All these individuals had been thrown into the Tower, where, according to the dark practices of those days, they may have been tortured, or threatened with torture, or corrupted by money and promises. They all persisted in their story; but the most determined evidence against him was that of his cousin Knevitt. The Duke of Norfolk rose to pronounce sentence, for the seventeen peers (as might have been expected) unanimously found him guilty; and the hardy soldier, the victor of Flodden Field, though he had not virtue enough to oppose a jealous tyrant, wept like a child as he spoke. Buckingham replied, with a manly voice, "My Lord of Norfolk, you have said to me as a traitor should be said unto; but I was never none. Still, my

---

[1] The quay, or jetty, at York House. The quays on the river side were called bridges.

[2] Hall, *Chron.*

lords, I nothing malign you for that you have done unto me. May the eternal God forgive you my death, as I do! I shall never sue to the king for life, howbeit he is a gracious prince, and more grace may come from him than I desire. I desire you, my lords, and all my fellows, to pray for me." The edge of the axe was then turned towards him, and he was led to his barge. He persisted in his resolution not to implore the king's mercy, and on the 17th of May the sheriffs led him from his dungeon to the scaffold on Tower-hill. He was as undaunted in sight of the block as he had been before his judges; and he died as brave men die—firmly and meekly, without bravado. As his head fell on the scaffold, the people groaned and lamented, for they were not yet brutalized by the frequent spectacle of such executions. "God have mercy on his soul!" exclaims one who reported his trial; "for he was a most wise and noble prince, and the mirror of all courtesy."[1]

It was while the blood of Buckingham was fresh upon him that Henry set himself up as the defender and champion of the holy (Roman) mother church. The Reformation was begun by Luther in earnest in the year 1517. The doctrines of the great Reformer had been eagerly received by many minds in England, where a respect for the Catholic clergy had long been on the decline, and where the seed scattered by Wyckliffe had never been entirely extirpated. On the 14th of May, 1521, Wolsey issued orders to all the bishops of England to seize all heretical books, or books containing Martin Luther's errors. On the 20th of the same month, three days after Buckingham's execution, Henry wrote, with his own hand, a fiery letter to Louis of Bavaria, denouncing "this fire which hath been kindled by Luther, and fanned by the arts of the devil;" and calling upon Louis, as a good Christian, to exterminate Luther, and burn both him and his books.[2]

But, as Henry had not the power to burn the Reformer, he took up the pen of controversy, being led thereto by a wish of showing his scholastic learning, and of pleasing the court of Rome, which, on a former occasion, when Louis XII. was lying under ban, had threatened to deprive the French kings of their title of "Most Christian," and to give it to Henry and his successors, the Kings of England. Another incentive was found in the fact that Luther had spoken disrespectfully of St. Thomas Aquinas, Henry's favourite author. Thus animated, and with plenty of priests and able scholars to supply fuel to his zeal, and give polemical point to his pen, Henry wrote his celebrated defence of the Seven Sacraments, which, as he fondly conceived, smashed Luther and all his doctrines. In the month of October, Clark, the English ambassador at Rome, presented this book to the pope in full consistory; and Leo X., after giving himself leisure to read the treatise, was pleased to declare, in an express bull, that he found it sprinkled with the dew of ecclesiastical grace, and that he rendered thanks to God for having inspired the king to write it for the defence of the blessed faith. In the same bull he formally conferred upon Henry the title of "Defender of the Faith," as a glorious and christianly addition to his other styles.[3]

While Henry was thus seeking distinction by the pen, Francis I. and Charles V. were fighting for worldly dominion. The French king was the first to draw the sword. Encouraged by a formidable revolt of the Spaniards against the despotic government of Charles, he marched an army to the crest of the Pyrenees, and, in fifteen days, overran the kingdom of Navarre. Thus far the insurgents of Spain looked on with indifference; but when the French rashly crossed the frontiers of Castile the Spaniards of all parties flew to arms, and not only drove them back, but also recovered Navarre in less than a fortnight. At the same time Francis and his auxiliaries threatened the emperor with an invasion of the Netherlands. But the French king was not more successful in the north than in the south; and, to increase his embarrassments, Leo X. threw up his alliance, and contracted a new one with the emperor. At this crisis Francis applied for the friendly mediation of Henry, who immediately engaged to act as a most impartial umpire, and then sent Wolsey, not to negotiate a peaceful and honourable arrangement, but to concert measures with Charles for the dismemberment of the French monarchy. The cardinal arbitrator—for the whole business was intrusted to him—embarked at Dover on the 30th of July, and landed on the same day at Calais with a magnificent train, including lords, bishops, doctors learned in the law, and knights and squires out of number. At Calais he was met by ambassadors from Charles and by ambassadors from Francis, and of course he found the pretensions of these diplomatists irreconcilable. Upon this, with the alleged design of disposing the emperor to more pacific measures, but with the real intention of completing the hostile league against France, he repaired in all his pomp to the city of Bruges, where Charles received him with wonderful respect.[4] "He spent a huge mass of money in that ambassage, not against his will; for he by all means sought the emperor's favour, hoping that Leo X., although much younger than he, either

---

[1] *State Trials;* Herbert; Hall; Stow; Holinshed.
[2] Geddes, *Hist. Reform.*
[3] Wilkins, *Concilia;* Fiddes, *Life of Wolsey;* Capefigue, *Hist. de la Reforme.*
[4] Tytler.

cut off by treachery or his own intemperance, might leave the world before him; and then were it no hard matter for him, being underpropped by the emperor and our king, to be advanced to the Papacy."[1]

On the 19th of August this impartial arbitrator wrote from Bruges to his master Henry, telling him that the emperor earnestly required his grace forthwith to declare war against France, and that he, Wolsey, had finally convinced the emperor, upon good reasons and grounds, that it would be better to defer the declaration of hostilities against France till Charles should pay Henry a visit in England.[2] In the same letter Wolsey told his master that he had discussed and debated with the emperor the articles devised at Calais with the emperor's ambassadors for the marriage of the Princess Mary (Henry's infant daughter) with Charles, and that he and Charles had finally concluded upon that marriage, and settled the date and all other particulars, all which treaties were to be kept strictly secret till such time as the emperor should speak with his grace in his realm of England.[3]

BRUGES, THE PRINCIPAL SQUARE AND TOUR DES HALLES.
From Delepierre, Album Pittoresque de Bruges.

[1] Bishop Godwin.   [2] State Papers.
[3] One of Henry's reasons for wishing to keep this treaty secret was, that he might continue to draw his pension from Francis till the last moment. Even so late as the 25th of September, we find Wolsey advising the king to send his ships and subjects to Bordeaux to load with wine as usual, "in order to exclude such suspicions and jealousies from the French king's mind as he might take by your keeping your subjects at home more this year than at any other vintage heretofore, whereby not *only the payment of your pension might be stopped*, but an inclination towards the wars might be in appearance on your part, whereof many inconveniences might ensue."—Letter from Wolsey to Henry in the British Museum, and printed in State Papers.

Towards the end of August the lord-cardinal returned to Calais and resumed the farce of the pacification with the French ministers. It would be doing great injustice to the diplomatic abilities of the French to suppose that they could be wholly blind to what was passing, or ignorant of the blandishments of Charles at Bruges. They, however, kept their countenances, and even received with respect a plan of pacification, which Wolsey drew up in a manner that he knew the pride of Francis would never accept. The cardinal affected to lament his obstinacy, and then, taking advantage of a good opportunity, he pronounced, as his award, that Francis had been the aggressor in the war, and that Henry was bound by treaty to assist his ally the emperor. The mask was now dropped, and the result of Wolsey's negotiations was disclosed in a league, signed at Calais in the month of October, between the pope, the emperor, and the King of England. It was agreed that, in order to check the wicked ambition of France, and to expedite an European crusade against the Turks, who were gaining ground beyond the Danube, each of these contracting powers should fall upon Francis from different quarters at the same time; and that, "for the common good of Christendom," the marriage between the dauphin and the Princess Mary should be set aside, and that princess be married to the emperor.[4]

Hostilities had not been interrupted during Wolsey's negotiations, and the results of the campaign were most adverse to Francis. Beyond the Alps the Italian league, headed by the pope, and assisted by the emperor, had driven the French out of Milan, and taken possession of nearly all their conquests. In the north of France the Imperialists had taken Tournai, for which Francis had recently paid so great a price to Henry; and all that the French had to set off against these losses was the capture of Hesdin and Fuenterrabia. The brilliant success of Leo X. was, however, closely followed by his death. This illustrious member of the great Medici family was only forty-six years old. He died at the height of glory and felicity, having freed himself, as was thought, by the victory of Milan, from all danger, and from those incalculable expenses which had exhausted his treasury, and forced him to adopt all sorts of measures to get money. "He was a prince," says the great Italian historian, who knew him intimately, "in whom there was much to praise and much to blame."[5]

Nobody was more interested in the death of

[4] State Papers; Lord Herbert; Hall; Guicciardini.
[5] Guicciardini.

Leo than Cardinal Wolsey, who was informed of the event in a wonderfully short space of time, and who instantly sent messengers to remind the emperor of his promises, and despatched Secretary Pace to Rome to manage his interests with the conclave. As the conclave began its close sittings on the 27th of December, there was not much time for intrigue. Thirty-nine[1] cardinals deliberated for twenty-three days on the choice of the head of the Catholic world, and their deliberations were as stormy as if they had met to elect the captain of a band of robbers. The candidate that started with the most advantages was Cardinal Giulio de' Medici, who had recently distinguished himself in the war in Lombardy. Giulio, indeed, obtained more than a third part of the votes, and as nobody could be elected without having two-thirds of the suffrages, it was clear that he could exclude any rival if he could not secure his own election. He and his partizans tried hard to weary out the old cardinals, whose infirmities made them feel sensibly the close imprisonment and other privations attendant on a conclave; but the old men were not easily beaten, and, as they were resolved not to elect him, and as they could not agree among themselves in proposing another candidate—nearly every one of them hoping that he might be chosen himself— the affair was drawn out to such a length that Giulio became uneasy as to business out of doors, well knowing that the interests of his family required his presence with an army in Tuscany. One morning at the scrutiny, which, according to form, was made every day, the Medici party most unexpectedly proposed Adrian, Cardinal of Tortosa, a Fleming by birth, who had been tutor to the emperor, and who was now Charles' confidential minister, and Viceroy of Spain. He was named without any notion of his being elected, and merely to consume time, but a vote or two were tendered for him, and then Cajetano, Cardinal of San Sisto, made what seemed an interminable oration in his favour, lauding his great learning and his many virtues, upon which a few of the cardinals began to yield, and then the rest, with extraordinary rapidity, as if rather from impulse than from deliberation, voted on the same side; and, in fine, that same morning Adrian was unanimously elected supreme pontiff. Those who elected him seemed themselves astonished at what they had done, and not being able to give any other reason to the Italians, who murmured at this election of an unknown foreigner, they attributed the event to the sudden inspiration of the Holy Ghost, who, as they said, always acted directly upon the hearts of the cardinals in their elections of popes—"as if that pure Spirit would deign to occupy souls full of ambition and incredible cupidity, and almost all the slaves of luxurious, not to say dishonest pleasures."[2] The Italian historians do not intimate that the emperor had influenced this election of his preceptor; but when the thoughts of the conclave were once turned in that direction, there were no doubt many who paid respect to the growing power of the Imperialists in Italy and in the rest of Europe; and as the name of Wolsey seems never to have been mentioned as that of a candidate, it is quite certain that Charles had not kept his promises with the English favourite. Wolsey, however, showed no ill-humour at the time; and he, in common with several of his scarlet brothers, probably consoled himself for his present disappointment by the thought that Adrian was an infirm old man, not likely to wear the tiara long. At his order Secretary Pace remained at Rome, to await the arrival of the new pope, to congratulate the holy father in his name, and to solicit from him the necessary confirmation or renewal of his high authority as Legate of England.

Francis, who knew the volatile temper of the English cabinet, did not despair of making Henry turn once more. He administered the most copious doses to his vanity—he humbled himself in a painful manner—he spoke of paying more money; but, finding that all this had no effect, he stopped the payment of Henry's pension, laid an embargo on the English shipping in his ports, and seized the goods of the English merchants.[3] This brought on a declaration of hostilities at an awkward time, and some two months sooner than Wolsey had calculated. As soon as Henry learned the seizure of his wine-ships he flew into a paroxysm of rage, as if Francis had betrayed him: he confined the French ambassador to his house, ordered the instant arrest of all Frenchmen in London, and sent his defiance to Francis by Clarencieux king-at-arms. Henry was now in the humour which the emperor wished for; and on the 26th of May Charles V. landed at Dover, to pay his promised visit. Wolsey met him at the landing-place, and, after a loving embrace, conducted him by the arm to Dover Castle, where the king, in his usual state, soon waited upon him. In the war they were to make together the emperor counted much upon the naval forces of England; and Henry now took great pride in showing him over the fleet which lay in the Downs. On the following day the emperor proceeded to the palace of Greenwich, where he reverently asked a blessing of his

---

[1] The deceased pope (Leo X.) had greatly augmented the Sacred College. At his own election only twenty-four cardinals had voted.

[2] *Guicciardini.*

[3] All the ships which Henry, by Wolsey's advice, had sent or allowed to go to Bordeaux, were seized.

aunt Catherine, and where he saw her infant daughter, his destined wife. "Henry, being a noble prince, and one that scorned money as much as any one breathing, was glad of the emperor's coming; yet was his treasury very bare, and so great a guest could not be entertained without a great expense." But not even the prospect of empty coffers and embarrassment could cure this gorgeous king of his passion for display, and finery, and feasting. By his orders the most expensive preparations were made in London, and he conducted the emperor into the city in triumph. Amidst the pomps and pageantries of this entrance, it is only worthy of notice that Sir Thomas More welcomed the emperor in a choice oration, in which he congratulated the two mighty monarchs upon the love and amity which was between them. From London Henry conducted his guest to Windsor Castle, where Charles, with great pomp, was installed knight of the Garter; and upon Corpus Christi Day these two princes, having on the robes of the order, heard mass in their stalls, and then, after receiving the sacrament, solemnly swore, at the foot of the altar, to observe the conditions of their new league. Eight days were spent, more in pleasure than in business, at Windsor, and then the sovereigns went to Winchester, and from Winchester to Southampton, where the emperor's fleet of 180 sail, of all sizes, had come to anchor. In every town which the emperor visited some costly pageant was exhibited, and for every day of the six weeks he spent in England some feast or other entertainment was devised. The business transacted lies in a very small compass; Charles still further pledged himself to marry the Lady Mary, the king's only child, and agreed to indemnify Henry for the loss of the pension from the French king; but, while he made this promise, he managed to procure a present payment or loan in hard cash from his impoverished and thoughtless ally—for Charles, with all his dominions, was poor at this time. It was mutually agreed that each power should begin a war with an army of 40,000 men: and that, while the English invaded the north of France, the emperor should fall upon the devoted kingdom both on the east and the south, where he promised to conquer the old English province of Guienne for his ally. On the 6th of July Charles embarked, and sailed for Spain.[1]

The Earl of Surrey had been for some time in Ireland, where his government was very popular among the Anglo-Irish. He was now recalled, and put in command of all the king's navy, as High-admiral of England. Surrey escorted Charles to the coast of Spain,[2] and on his return

[1] Hall; Lord Herbert; Godwin; Rymer; State Papers.
[2] In compliment to his uncle Henry, the emperor had given Surrey the nominal command of his own fleet.

ravaged the French coast, and burned the town of Morlaix, in Brittany, together with "some right fair castles, goodly houses, and proper piles."[3] This was a paltry way of commencing what was intended to be such a great war; but, owing to the state of his treasury, Henry encountered many difficulties in raising an army, and at last, instead of sending 40,000 men to France, he only sent 15,000 or 16,000. Now was Wolsey thrown upon those rocks which made a wreck of his remaining popularity. He raised a forced loan of £20,000 from the merchants of London, and after very short respite, in order to get more money, he called the citizens before him. On the 20th day of August the mayor, aldermen, and the most substantial commoners of the city of London, stood trembling before the lord-cardinal, who declared to them that the king had appointed commissioners through the whole realm to make inquest into the state of men's private property, and "to swear every man of what value he was in moveables, the more to be in readiness *for the defence of this realm*." "Wherefore, in convenient time," continued Wolsey to the Londoners, "certify to me the number of all such as be worth £100 and upwards, to the intent I may swear them of their values: for, first, the king asketh of you your loving hearts and due obedience, and, when the value is taken, he desireth *only* the tenth part of goods and lands, which is the least reasonable thing that you can aid your prince with. I think every one of you will offer no less." The aldermen returned to their wards, and named such as were esteemed merchants and dealers of substance, who thereupon waited on the lord-cardinal, and humbly besought him not to exact an oath as to the amount of their property—"because the true valuation to them was unknown, as many an honest man's credit was better than his substance," and therefore they dreaded the peril of perjury. "Well," said the cardinal, "since you dread the crime of perjury, it is a sign of grace; and therefore I will, for you, borrow of the king a little. Make you your bills of your own value, according to what you esteem your credit, and then more business needeth not; for you see what two costly armies the king hath already both against France and Scotland; therefore, now show yourselves like loving subjects, for you be able enough. I dare swear the substance of London is no less worth than two millions of gold." "Then," said the citizens, "we would to God that it were so; and the city is sore afflicted by the great occupying of strangers." "Well," said the cardinal, "it shall be redressed if I live; but, on Saturday next, I shall appoint one to receive your bills, and he that is of credit more than substance, let him come to me, and I

[3] *State Papers* published by government.

will be secret and good to him." "Thus," concludes the chronicler, "the citizens departed in great agony, saying that, at the last loan, some lent the fifth part, and now, to have the tenth part taken, was too much. Great was the mourning of the common people, as it is ever in such cases of payments. But, in the end, one Dr. Tonnys, a secretary to the cardinal, came to the chapter-house of St. Paul's, and to him the citizens brought in their bills, and on their honesty they were received, which values afterwards turned them to displeasure. The spirituality made suit to my lord-cardinal, that no temporal man should sit to examine them, or be privy to their possessions and goods. Wherefore, bishops and abbots were appointed to take the value of their substance."[1] Wolsey, however, promised that the lenders of money should be paid soon, out of the first subsidy voted by parliament, which it was intended to summon.

At the end of August, Surrey put himself at the head of the army of invasion, which had been collected at Calais, and which consisted of about 11,000 men paid by the king, 3000 volunteers, and 1000 horse, composed of Germans, Flemings, Walloons, and Spaniards. The season was far advanced, and the army was none of the best. They marched through Artois to the banks of the Somme, carefully avoiding the fortified towns, and burning all the defenceless places, villages, farm-houses, and cottages. The French, commanded by the Duke of Vendôme, would not hazard a battle, but they harassed the English incessantly, and frequently cut off their supplies. The weather fought for the French; incessant rains fell; and these, with cold and bad provisions, brought a dysentery into Surrey's camp. Hereupon the foreign horse took their leave, and retired to Bethune; and about the middle of October the earl was compelled to retreat to Calais, having done worse than nothing.[2]

In the meantime Francis had exerted himself to keep the English at home. He opened a correspondence in Ireland with the members of the powerful house of Desmond, who were still, in a great measure, independent of the English, and induced the earl to sign a treaty and to take up arms, under a promise of an annual pension and the assistance of a French army.[3] The earl kept his part of the engagement, and greatly embarrassed Henry's Irish government, but Francis failed in his, and, in the end, the Desmonds were left to the tender mercies of the English court. At the same time Francis negotiated with his old allies the Scots, whose last truce with England had recently expired, and who were incensed at the intermeddling in their affairs and the treacherous policy of Henry's ministers. Margaret, the queen-dowager and regent, had some good qualities, but she too closely resembled her brother Henry to make a wise ruler. Being, like him, of a very amorous disposition, she cast her eyes about her for a second husband immediately after the tragedy of Flodden Field; and as soon as she recovered from giving birth to a child, of which James had left her enceinte, she married the Earl of Angus, who was now the head of the powerful house of Douglas, but who was young, inexperienced, and weak-headed, with little to recommend him beyond a handsome, showy person, and a few courtly accomplishments. By the will of her late husband James—which provided for the case of her remarrying—Margaret now forfeited the post of regent; and a party of the nobility and clergy, opposed to her and the Earl of Angus, had the keeping of the young King James, and his infant brother, who was named Alexander, and created Duke of Ross. From this moment Scotland was split into two furious factions—the English party, at the head of which were Margaret and Angus; and the French party, which embraced the mass of the nobility, and was supported by the sympathies of the people.[4] An irregular kind of civil war broke out, in which the queen-mother and her new husband Angus were hard pressed; and thus Margaret was compelled more than ever to consult with her brother, who, apparently caring very little for what befel her, made use of the favourable opportunity in acquiring, by the most crooked means, an influence over the whole kingdom of Scotland. Henry's principal agent in these dark transactions was Lord Dacre, one of the English heroes of Flodden, and a man of, at least, as much craft and cunning as bravery.

At this crisis the Scottish nobility pressed for the immediate return from France of the Duke of Albany; and in the month of May, 1515, the duke arrived in the Clyde, to the great joy of the people, who looked up to him as the only person likely to tranquillize the country, and preserve its threatened independence.

Shortly after his arrival Albany, with the consent of a large majority of the nobility and clergy, took upon himself the trying office of regent. He soon showed that he was ready to carry his devotion to France to an excess almost as dangerous as that with which the opposite faction prostrated themselves to England. Nor was he long in showing that he was deficient in talents for

---
[1] *Hall.* [2] *Lord Herbert; Hall; State Papers; Villaret.*
[3] According to this wild treaty Ireland was to be divided between the Desmonds and Richard de la Pole, brother to the unfortunate duke beheaded in the Tower in 1513, and male representative of the house of York. This Richard de la Pole was in the French service. In 1525, about three years after the Irish treaty, he was killed in Italy, fighting gallantly in the battle of Pavia, where Francis was taken prisoner.

[4] *Pinkerton; Tytler.*

government—if not actually wanting in courage. At the same time, every corner of the kingdom was filled with spies and agents in the pay of England, who penetrated, by means of money, all the secrets of the council-table; and the faction in the scale of which the Douglases and the Homes threw their entire weight was heavy enough to crush a king. Notwithstanding the decisions of the parliament, who knew in what dangerous keeping they were likely to be, Margaret had got possession of the young king and his brother; and one of Albany's first measures was to make sure of their not being carried off to England. He summoned a parliament, which met at Edinburgh, and named eight lords, out of which number four were to be chosen by lot; and from these four the queen-mother was to select three to have charge of the princes. It was quite certain that Margaret was not to be trusted, but it seemed an odious thing to separate the mother from her children; and though this was not, in strictness, the intention of the government, it was easy for the queen to assert that it was, and to take up a position where she was pretty sure to be backed, at least for a time, by the sympathy of the people.

The queen-dowager, however, thinking it impossible to hold Edinburgh Castle, suddenly removed with her children to Stirling, where her party was strong. After some fruitless negotiations, the Regent Albany ordered Ruthven and Borthwick to blockade Stirling Castle. The powerful Lord Home now fled from the capital to Newark Castle, upon the Borders; and the Earl of Angus, Margaret's husband, retired within his estates and armed his vassals. Albany, accompanied by all the Scottish peers, with three or four exceptions, and by an army, proceeded in person to Stirling, where the queen was soon obliged to surrender; for none of her adherents seemed disposed to stand a siege for her sake. The regent was respectful and moderate; but he declared that Angus and Home were proved traitors, who had opened a correspondence with the enemies of the country, and were then actually in arms. Home presently threw himself openly into the arms of England, and concerted measures with Lord Dacre. Having committed the two princes to the safe keeping of the earl-marshal and the Lords Fleming and Borthwick, Albany proceeded against the insurgents, and took the castle of Home. Margaret applied to Lord Dacre; and Home requested the assistance of an English army, telling the lord-warden that Scotland lay open to invasion, and that King Henry might easily destroy his enemies there, and remodel the government according to his own interests and wishes. Assured of speedy assistance, Home seized the strong tower of Blac- ater, situated a little within the Scottish frontier, at the distance of about five miles from Berwick, where the English had a strong garrison. The object of this move was presently seen—for Margaret absconded from Edinburgh, and threw herself into the Border tower. The regent soon followed her with a considerable army, offering, however, liberal terms of accommodation, which Margaret arrogantly rejected. Meanwhile, though Dacre had strongly recommended an invasion, no English army made its appearance, and, after a few vicissitudes, the queen and her husband Angus, and her prime ally Home, were obliged to flee across the frontiers to seek refuge in the court of Henry. The king, for honour of his sister, on the 19th and 20th of May, kept solemn jousts, wherein he himself, the Duke of Suffolk, the Earl of Essex, and Nicholas Carew, answered all comers. But Margaret, at the time, was sadly in want of money, and for this she applied to my lord-cardinal in a very humble tone indeed.[1] Before her public reception in the English court, Angus, her husband, to whom she had recently borne a daughter,[2] deserted her, and returned into Scotland; and Home either accompanied him or followed soon after. They both made their peace with the Regent Albany, who restored them to all their estates and honours. Margaret now inveighed as bitterly against Angus as against Albany, whom, however, a short time before, she had accused of poisoning her second son, the Duke of Ross, who appears to have died of one of the many diseases incident to childhood. Henry and Wolsey had been prevented from proceeding to extremities by the startling successes of Francis in Italy. But things were now somewhat changed in this most changeable of cabinets; and Henry dictated an insolent letter to the three estates of Scotland, commanding rather than recommending them to drive the Regent Albany out of the kingdom, as one, by nearness of blood, suspicious and dangerous to the young king, his very dear nephew. The Scottish parliament told the arrogant dictator that they would do nothing of the sort, and that they were resolved manfully to resist any attempt to disturb the peace of their country, or to overthrow their existing government.[3] This passed in the month of July, 1516. But the English warden was at his dirty work, and his intrigues were but too successful in re-animating the spirit of faction. On the 23d of August, Dacre wrote from Kirkoswald to my lord-cardinal, telling Wolsey of his great doings. "I labour and

---

[1] See her letter in Sir Henry Ellis' *Collection*.
[2] She was delivered only seven days after her flight from Blacater into England, and was lying dangerously ill at Morpeth when Angus forsook her to return to Scotland. The child was the Lady Margaret Douglas, afterwards mother of Darnley, the hapless husband of Mary Queen of Scots. [3] *Rymer*.

studies," says this noble lord, "all that I can, to make division and debate; . . . . and, for that intended purpose, in that behalf I have the master of Kilmaurs kept in my house secretly, which is one of the greatest parties in Scotland, as the queen can declare unto your grace; . . . . and also I have secret messages from the Earl of Angus and others, which I trust shall be to the pleasure of the king's grace if the said duke submit not himself; and also I hath 400 outlaws (and giveth them rewards) that burneth and destroyeth daily in Scotland—all being Scotsmen, which should be under the obedience of Scotland."[1]

A new insurrection soon broke out, headed by the Earl of Arran, who was closely connected with the royal family, and by Lennox, Glencairn, and Mure of Caldwell; and Home, whom no kindness could conciliate, renewed his correspondence with Dacre, whose hired traitors—many of them Home's retainers—made continual forays across the Border, committing unusual excesses. The Regent Albany put down the rising of Arran, Lennox, and Glencairn, and pardoned those turbulent barons; but when he got possession of the persons of Home and his brother, he immediately brought them to trial as manifold traitors, and sent them to execution. On the 8th of October their heads were stuck above the toll-booth of Edinburgh, and the regent then succeeded in tranquillizing the Borders. But seeing that Dacre continued his system, and that Henry was inclined to raise an army, Albany thought his case hopeless unless he could procure assistance from France; and being at the same time anxious to revisit his foreign estates, he requested the permission of parliament to go over to the French court for four months. This permission was reluctantly granted, and in the month of June, 1517, Albany embarked at Dumbarton, intrusting the government to a council, consisting of the Archbishops of St. Andrews and Glasgow, the Earls of Huntly, Argyle, Angus, and Arran, and taking with him as hostages the eldest sons of many of the great barons. Previously to his departure, it had been settled in parliament that the queen-mother should be allowed to return to Scotland, upon the condition of submitting and enjoying her dower in tranquillity. As soon as Margaret heard of Albany's arrival in France, and not before, she set out for Edinburgh, where she arrived in a very poor condition. She had not been long in Scotland when she was suspected of a fresh attempt to carry off the young king; and when the Borderers, the vassals of the late Earl of Home, surprised and murdered De la Bastie, a brave and accomplished French officer, to whom Albany had intrusted the command of the marches, Home of Wedderburn (whose wife was the sister of Margaret's husband, Angus) galloped into the town of Dunse with the head of the unfortunate Frenchman tied to his saddlebow. In this universal confusion the council of regency, divided among themselves, pursued no imposing or consistent course; and Albany, despairing, wrote to his old enemy Margaret, recommending her, if she could unite the factions, to take the regency once more into her own hands. But Margaret, who had been reconciled to her handsome husband, insisted that Angus should be regent; and, as this was resolutely opposed by a large majority of the nobles, the government continued in the hands of the council. Angus, disappointed and irritated, soon quarrelled with his wife: he forsook the court, retiring with a mistress into Douglasdale. Margaret set no bounds to her wrath; she added the high tone of a queen to the bitterness of a betrayed wife; she heaped reproach upon reproach, reminding him that she had pawned her jewels to support him in his misfortunes, and expressing her determination to sue for a divorce. Her brother Henry at this time had no taste for such proceedings, and knowing the great power possessed by the house of Douglas, and that Angus was a tool most likely to work for his purpose, he despatched a learned friar to bring Margaret to a more orthodox way of thinking, and to threaten her with the serious effects of his displeasure. The monk threatened her with punishment in the next world as well as in this; telling her that she, was labouring under some damnable delusion, and hinting very broadly that her own conjugal behaviour had not been irreproachable, and that Angus might retort her charge of adultery. Margaret trembled, and, at the command of her brother, submitted to a hollow reconciliation with her husband in the summer of 1518. Angus, not satisfied with his share in the council of regency, soon attempted to monopolize the entire power, and hence arose a fierce contest between him and the Earl of Arran, in which blood was spilt, and nearly every kind of injustice committed. Archibald Douglas, one of the uncles of Angus, expelled Arran from his post of provost of Edinburgh, which was then considered a very important addition to the earl's other employments. When Arran attempted to enter Edinburgh he was set upon by an armed mob, who killed and wounded some of his attendants; and then Sir James Hamilton, commonly called the Bastard of Arran, slew one Gawin, a carpenter, a friend of Angus and a leader of the mob. About the same time Home of Wedderburn, who had recently killed De la Bastie, cut off the prior of Coldingham with six of his family; upon which his brother-in-law, William Douglas, the brother of Angus, took possession of the said priory. There was nothing

[1] Ellis.

in Scotland deserving of the name of a government; but in 1520 the Earl of Arran, and Beaton, the Archbishop of Glasgow, made a bold attempt to restore the authority of the council of regency. At a moment when they fancied that Angus had not many of his partizans with him in Edinburgh, they assembled their friends in the church of the Blackfriars. Gavin Douglas, the celebrated Bishop of Dunkeld, an uncle of Angus, presented himself at this meeting as a peace-maker, and remonstrated against their intention of arresting Angus—for this, he soon saw, was the real object of the meeting. Beaton struck his breast with his right hand, declaring, on his conscience, that they had no evil intentions against the earl; but the archbishop wore armour under his rochet, and the steel plates rattled as he struck his breast. "Ha! my lord!" cried the Bishop of Dunkeld, "your conscience is not sound; did you not hear it clatter?" While the meeting in the church of the Blackfriars were deliberating, Angus appeared upon the causeway with a formidable body of 400 spearmen, and a band of Borderers led by his brother-in-law, the fierce Home of Wedderburn. At this sight Sir Patrick Hamilton, the brother of the Earl of Arran, rushed into the street, and, with an inconsiderable number of retainers, fell like a madman upon the Douglases. Angus pressed forward and slew Sir Patrick on the causeway with his own hand, intending also to have killed his brother the earl. The party of Arran collected to the rescue, and, after many lives had been sacrificed, the earl was driven out of the city, and his friend, Archbishop Beaton, was fain to seek refuge behind the high altar of St. Giles' Church.[1]

Angus and his party now remained for a time absolute masters of the capital, where they speedily removed the heads of Lord Home and his brother from the toll-booth. Arran and his friends, with the young king and the queen-mother, occupied Stirling Castle. In the following year (1521) Margaret, incensed almost as much against her overbearing brother Henry, as against her husband Angus, wrote with her own hand to entreat Albany to return to Scotland, and to take upon himself the whole government. Albany, who was probably urged by the French court, which was most anxious to embarrass Henry, sailed from France, and landed in the Gareloch on the 19th of November. He proceeded forthwith to Stirling, where Margaret, very changeful in her affections, received him with transports of joy, and with such familiarity as excited scandalous rumours. The busy Lord Dacre told the king, his master, that, not satisfied with the day, she was closeted the greater part of the night with Albany, taking no heed of appearances.[2]

The restored regent summoned a parliament, and cited Angus and the Douglases before it; but the now discarded husband of Margaret, with several of his adherents, fled for refuge to the Kirk of Steyle, near the Borders, whence they opened a negotiation with Henry by means of Angus' uncle, Bishop Gavin Douglas, who was a better poet than politician, and who had more genius than morality or patriotism. At the same time they raised a loud outcry against Margaret's immoralities, accusing her, among other things, of a design to put aside her son, to marry her lover Albany, and to make him king. A great deal of this was the raving of a desperate faction, or the artful misrepresentations of the English agent; but there can be little doubt as to the nature of the intimacy between the regent and the queen-mother. In other respects the conduct of Albany was neither immoral nor imprudent: he tried to reconcile the factions, and to stop the dangerous venality of the nobles; and his feelings for France did not prevent him from seeking to secure peace with England. But the restoration of good order in Scotland would have been fatal to the projects of the English court; and Wolsey and Henry persisted in their plan of treachery and disorganization, encouraging the Homes and all other rebels, and, by means of the indefatigable Lord Dacre, distributing money among the factions.[3] In fact, Dacre soon saw matters in such a state that he earnestly recommended Henry to invade Scotland. The king, however, was not prepared for this open hostility; and Angus, with the Homes and other rebels, was glad to flee into England from the growing power and vigour of Albany's government. Margaret wrote to her brother. But Henry did not wish that there should be peace: he openly accused his sister of living in shameful adultery[4] with the regent; and he offered to the Scottish estates the alternative of the immediate dismissal of Albany, or an immediate rupture with England. Many traitors as there were among the nobles, and base and bought as were many of its members, the Scottish parliament replied with proper spirit.[5] Upon this Henry, with his usual moderation, ordered

---

[1] *Lesley; Pinkerton; Tytler;* Letter from Wolsey to the Duke of Norfolk, quoted by Mr. Tytler.
[2] Letter in the British Museum, quoted by Mr. Tytler.
[3] *State Papers.*
[4] Henry, who did not as yet foresee how he was shortly to vex the ear of Rome with a suit of that kind, felt or pretended great horror at his sister's applying for a divorce. The following passage from a letter of Wolsey's was meant to comfort him on this head:—" I signify unto your grace that I have not only written unto your orator ambassador at the court of Rome to impeche [oppose] and let stop the suit made in that court by the Queen of Scots, for a divorce betwixt her and her husband, the Earl of Anguishe [Angus], but also have caused the pope's orator, here being, to write in most effectual manner to his holiness, for stopping of the same."—*State Papers.*
[5] *Rymer.*

that all Scottish subjects found in England should be driven ignominiously across the Borders on foot, with a white cross marked on their backs; and shortly after (in the spring of 1522), without declaring war, he sent the Earl of Shrewsbury, with the forces of the northern counties, across the Tweed. Shrewsbury, whose movement was sudden and unexpected, penetrated as far as Kelso, and gave that beautiful district to the flames; but he was presently driven back into England with considerable loss, by the Borderers of Merse and Teviotdale.

The Duke of Albany, with consent of parliament, now declared war. Eighty thousand men joined his standard at Annan, and he was flattered with the hopes of assistance from France; but the fickle and unscrupulous Margaret had already grown tired of the regent, and she not only intrigued with a party of the Scottish nobles, but also betrayed his secrets and plans to Lord Dacre. There are doubts and contradictions in all the narratives of these transactions; but it appears that, without being fully aware of the double-dealing of the queen-mother, or of the determination of a large portion of the Scottish leaders (of whom some had Dacre's money in their pockets) not to prosecute the war with vigour, the regent, with his large army and forty-five pieces of brass ordnance, crossed the Borders and advanced upon Carlisle.[1] Henry's attention had been wholly drawn to the side of France, and Dacre, who was in the marches, had but few troops, and an exhausted money-chest; but this lord-warden well knew the slackness and want of preparation in the Scottish camp, and he always had wit and cunning at command. When the invaders were within five miles of the city of Carlisle, he opened communications with Albany. We can only guess at some of the arguments and arts employed, but the result was correctly and frankly told by Wolsey in a letter to the king, wherein, after mentioning the defenceless state of the northern counties, he says, that "by the great wisdom and policy of my Lord Dacre, and by means of the safe-conduct lately sent at the desire and contemplation of the Queen of Scots," the Duke of Albany had consented to "an abstinence of war for one month," in order that ambassadors might treat for peace. "And the said Duke of Albany," continues the cardinal, "hath not only, our Lord be thanked, forborne his invasion, but also dissolved his army; which being dispersed, neither shall, nor can, for this year, be gathered or assembled again."[2] The singular truce which put an end to this grand expedition was concluded on the 11th of September; and in the month of October Albany again went to France, leaving the Earls of Huntly, Arran, and Argyle to manage affairs during his absence.

Henry had now governed eight years without a parliament, following the precedent of his father; and, notwithstanding the obsequiousness displayed when they last met, it seems pretty certain that he would never have summoned the representatives of the people again had he not been forced to it by his poverty. But Henry had exhausted all other means of raising money, and so he met his parliament once more on the 15th of April, with Wolsey sitting as chancellor at his feet.[3] The commons chose for their speaker the celebrated Sir Thomas More, who, against

Sir Thomas More.—From a rare print after Holbein.

his inclination, had been drawn into the service of the court about four years before, and who was now thought to be devoted to the interests of the king, who courted his society, and took singular delight in his wit and humour. But More, though a somewhat timid, was an honest man. The commons presently showed infinitely more spirit than was expected; and, finding a ready echo out of doors, particularly among the merchants and citizens of London, their sayings and doings became the great subject of conversation. Henry testified his royal disdain "that people should talk about *his* affairs;" and Wolsey was heard to complain, that no sooner was anything said or done in the House of Commons, than it was blown abroad in every alehouse. The lord-cardinal thought that he could overawe the members by presenting himself in

[1] Cardinal Wolsey says that Albany was also furnished with "one thousand hagbuschis carted upon tressels, with a marvellous great number of hand-guns, and was plenteously stored with victuals."—*State Papers*. [2] *State Papers*.

[3] This parliament was not held at Westminster, the usual place, but at the Blackfriars, London.

person; and though this was a breach of privilege, he sent to tell the house that they must receive him, and hear from his lips what were the wishes of the king. His business was to tell them how necessary the war was, and what a fair opportunity was offered for the recovery of all the English had once held in France; provided only that the house had regard to the weakness of the sinews of war, and would instantly raise £800,000, by passing a property-tax, at the moderate rate of twenty per cent. The house, in agreeing to receive the cardinal, had also agreed among themselves not to commit their privileges by entering upon any debate in his presence; and this extraordinary demand was not likely to change their purpose. Every man remained as still and motionless as a statue, gazing on the glowing cardinal. Soon tired of this dramatic scene, Wolsey addressed one of the members by name: this gentleman, after rising from his seat, sat down again without speaking: he then turned to another member, but his authoritative tone elicited no answer. He then lost his temper, and exclaimed, "Masters, as I am sent here immediately from the king, it is not unreasonable to expect an answer; yet here is, without doubt, a surprising and most obstinate silence, unless, indeed, it may be the manner of your house to express your mind by your speaker only." More, upon whom the angry eyes of the cardinal were fixed, rose, and, after bending the knee, said that the members were abashed at the sight of so great a personage, whose presence was sufficient to overwhelm the wisest and most learned men in the realm; but *that* presence, he observed, was neither expedient, nor in accordance with the ancient liberties of that house. More added, that they were not bound to return any answer; and that, as to requiring a reply from him individually, the thing was simply impossible; for he, as speaker, could only act upon the instructions received from the house. The lord-cardinal retired sorely disconcerted; and the debate on the supplies was adjourned day after day. At length the commons agreed to send a deputation to solicit a diminution of the tax. The cardinal, notwithstanding More's courteous reproof, again went to the house, and endeavoured to draw them into debate. But the commons, as firm as ever, said that they would reason only among themselves, and not in his presence. He went away as he had come; but, soon after, the house agreed to a property-tax of about ten per cent., or half what Wolsey had asked. He had boasted of the readiness of the spirituality, but he now found the clergy almost as refractory as the commons; and, after being defeated in rather a humiliating manner in several of his manoeuvres, and high assumptions of authority over the church, as pope's legate, instead of succeeding in his enormous demand of fifty per cent., at once, he only obtained a grant of ten per cent. each year for five years. During the debates the Londoners frequently caught the members of the commons by the sleeve as they passed through the streets, and cried out to them, "Sirs, will ye grant four shillings in the pound? Do it, and take our threats and curses home with you to your households." But in many parts of the kingdom the people were dissatisfied even at the ten per cent.; and Wolsey, urged on by his master, who was now almost penniless, made matters still worse by attempting to accelerate the mode of payment. In many places the poorer people, driven to desperation, refused to pay the tax-gatherers anything. The blame of all fell upon the cardinal; and Henry did not scruple at condemning the proceedings of his ministers, in order to recover his own popularity.

The money that was wrung from the people was immediately spent in reinforcing the garrisons near the Scottish borders, in assistance lent to the allies in Italy, and in a new expedition into France. On the 24th of August (1523) the Duke of Suffolk took the command of the army at Calais; and on the 4th of September he commenced the campaign with about 12,000 English troops, and nearly an equal number of Flemings and Germans. The season again was late; the combined movements contemplated by the allies were difficult to execute with precision in point of time; and Charles Brandon was expert in all military exercises, without having any of the qualities of a great general. This time, however, as plainly appears from a letter of the lord-cardinal,[1] and from the dark conspiracy which broke out in France, the commencement of the campaign had been purposely delayed. Francis, intent on the recovery of the duchy of Milan, had collected an army at Lyons, and was actually on the point of crossing the Alps, when he learned that his enemies had intrigued with the most powerful of his subjects, who had engaged to declare himself as soon as the king should be in Italy. The story of Prince Charles, Duke of Bourbon and Constable of France, is one of the most remarkable episodes in the history of the sixteenth century. By birth, wealth, connections, ability, and bravery, he was the most distinguished subject in the kingdom; and his loyalty and affection to the king had never been doubted. But, in an evil season, Louisa of Savoy, the king's mother, became enamoured of his beautiful person, and proposed that he should marry her. The gallant constable was not disposed to unite himself to a woman who was old enough to be his mother, and who, on former occasions, had

---

[1] *State Papers.*

been the declared enemy of his house; and in rejecting or evading the suit of the amorous matron, he made use of some personal reflections, which a woman, and one who *had been* a beauty, was not likely to forgive. Louisa's revenge was as ample as were her means of gratifying it: and her influence over her affectionate son was almost boundless. Urged on by his mother, Francis insulted the fiery Bourbon, refused to pay him large sums which he had advanced for the war in Italy, stopped his salaries, and took from him the baton of constable, which he had wielded with great glory. These, and the indignities put upon him by the whole court, drove Bourbon almost to madness; and when the slavish parliament of Paris pronounced an iniquitous sentence, which virtually sequestrated all his fiefs and estates, he vowed revenge, and turned to the enemies of his country. Both the emperor and the King of England received his overtures with infinite satisfaction, and sent the Lord of Beaurain and Sir John Russell, as secret emissaries, to treat with him. A private treaty was soon concluded; the principal articles were—that Provence and Dauphiny should be united with his appanage, the Bourbonnais and Auvergne, and erected into a separate kingdom for the constable; that the constable should marry Eleanora, a sister of the emperor; that the emperor should occupy Languedoc, Burgundy, Champaigne, and Picardy, while the King of England overran the rest of France; and that the constable should hold himself ready, with 1000 horse and 6000 foot, to co-operate with the allies as soon as the French king should be on the other side of the Alps.[1]

Either Bourbon betrayed himself by too open preparations, or the secret was betrayed by some of the agents engaged in the business. Of a sudden Francis presented himself at his castle, and commanded him to join the army of Italy. The constable pretended to be dangerously ill; but Francis, who understood this feint, left spies to watch him. This strange interview took place about the time that the Duke of Suffolk landed in France. The French king, instead of marching into Italy, stopped at Lyons for the defence of his own dominions; but so confident was he, that he sent the army he had raised across the Alps, under the command of the Admiral de Bonnivet, and then applied himself to the raising of fresh forces for the defence of his kingdom, which was threatened on three of its frontiers. The constable eluded the vigilance of the spies, and, by pursuing by-roads and travelling in disguise, he traversed Auvergne and Dauphiny, and, after many dangers, got safely out of France and joined the emperor's army in Italy. Many of his friends were arrested, and no insurrection, such as the allies counted upon, broke out in the centre of France.

Instead of advancing at once, when the country was comparatively open, to form a junction with the German army of the emperor which invaded Burgundy, the Duke of Suffolk and the Imperialist general De Bure lost nearly a whole month under the walls of St. Omer, debating what they should do. Then, giving up the notion of besieging Boulogne, they marched in the direction of Burgundy. But they had thrown away their chance, and even now they stopped to besiege Bray, Montdidier, and one or two other insignificant places. Having crossed the Somme and the Oise, they pitched their tents within twenty miles of Paris, expecting, as it appears, that the Germans would join them there. But by this time these Germans were in full retreat before the Duke of Guise: and now the Duke of Vendôme advanced in front of the English, while Tremoille manœuvred on their flank, and threatened their rear by drawing out troops from the garrisons in Picardy. At length the position of the Duke of Suffolk became most critical, for the French kept constantly gathering round him. The weather, also, was dreadful, and this, with scanty or bad provisions, brought sickness into the army. Thus situated he ordered a retreat. The French even now respected the valour of the English troops, and would not risk an engagement; but the men perished of sickness daily, and in great numbers; the Flemish auxiliaries, as they drew near their own country, deserted in troops, and Suffolk had but the shadow of an army when he reached Calais. This failure nearly cost Brandon his head. In the south the Spanish army, commanded by the emperor in person, instead of conquering Guienne, merely recovered from the French their own town of Fuenterrabia.

On the 14th of September, while Suffolk was advancing towards Paris, an event occurred in Italy which revived the former high hopes of Wolsey: this was the death of Pope Adrian, whose severe economy was so distasteful to the Romans, that they styled the physician who had attended him in his last sickness—"The Saviour of his country." His pontificate had lasted only twenty months and six days. As soon as the English cardinal got the news he wrote a curious letter to Henry, telling him how reluctant he was to quit the service of so good a master— how unfit to assume the high responsibility of head of the Christian world. The king, who knew what this meant, applied to the Emperor Charles for the fulfilment of the promises which he had made to his favourite, and instructed his ministers at Rome to spare no money and no exertion to secure the election of Wolsey. This time Wolsey

[1] *Du Bellay; Henault; Guicciardini; State Papers.*

was not only named among the candidates, but he even obtained a considerable number of votes; but the turbulent people of Rome, and the Italians generally, were furious at the notion of having any more ultramontane (they called them *barbarian*) popes; the French interest in the conclave was considerable, and wholly opposed to Wolsey; and the interest of the emperor—if exercised at all—was not for him, but against him, notwithstanding the long promises of Charles. When the conclave had debated and voted for many days, and some of the ancients were worn out with the long confinement, it was seen that the chance lay between Jacovaccio Romano and Giulio de' Medici, who had so nearly obtained the tiara at the death of Leo X., and who had decided the last election in favour of Adrian. The hand that trimmed the scales was that of the Cardinal Pompeo Colonna, who was a most bitter enemy of the Medici, and who was inclined to give his whole weight to Cardinal Jacovaccio. But, irritated at the opposition he encountered from some members of the Sacred College, he set aside his old animosities, and suddenly engaged to support the Cardinal de' Medici, upon condition of receiving the lucrative post of vice-chancellor, and the sumptuous palace of San Giorgio at Rome. That very night Giulio de' Medici was unanimously saluted and adored as pontiff, and, on the following morning, the 19th of November, his election was publicly announced, to the great joy of the Italians. He took the name and style of Clement VII.[1]

Again, to all appearance, Wolsey bore his disappointment with equanimity, though this time he could hardly flatter himself with another chance, for the successful candidate was both young and vigorous. Henry's agents at Rome were instructed to press for the election of Giulio in case that of Wolsey should be found impracticable; and now while they felicitated him on his elevation, they bespoke his active co-operation with the emperor and the King of England, and requested that he would renew Wolsey's legatine commission. The new pope immediately appointed the cardinal his legate for life, enlarged his authority, and gave him a commission to reform and suppress certain religious houses in England. The latter was an unusual concession, tending to establish a dangerous precedent with a needy sovereign. Wolsey, however, is said to have acted conscientiously in this matter, for when he suppressed certain monasteries (which he did early in the year 1525) he employed the money thus gained for ecclesiastical purposes, particularly for the foundation of colleges, in which—as both he and his master Henry asserted—learned divines were to be reared and fostered for the better combating of the pernicious and fast-spreading heresies of that "monster" Martin Luther.

A.D. 1524. Bonnivet, who took the command of the Italian war in lieu of his master Francis, was at first very successful. But he lost time manœuvring on the river Ticino, and when he made his approach Milan had been put into so good a state of defence by Prospero Colonna that he durst not assault it, and, after making a vain attempt to reduce it by famine, he was obliged to seek winter-quarters, where he and his troops were half starved. Towards the close of the year the Emperor Charles appointed the Constable Bourbon his lieutenant in Italy. It was soon found that Bonnivet was no match for this bold and skilful general, who took the field early in the spring, and, by the month of May, drove his countrymen the French across the Alps, and recovered all the places they had taken. Bourbon, still inflamed with vengeance, and bent on the acquisition of the kingdom which had been promised him by the allies, out of the dismemberment of his native country, now prevailed upon Charles to invade France with his army of Italy. Henry was applied to in the hope that he would make a diversion by invading the north of France from Calais; but the English king excused himself, and merely promised to assist with some money. In the month of July the constable descended from the Alps into France, but the command of the imperial army was divided between him and the Marquis of Pescara, who had different views, and who had received conflicting instructions from the emperor. Bourbon would have pushed forward at once to Lyons, but the marquis insisted upon turning into Provence, and laying siege to Marseilles. Accordingly, on the 19th of August, this army of invasion, amounting to little more than 16,000 men, sat down before the city. After spending forty days in mining and bombarding, Pescara and Bourbon were obliged to beat a rapid retreat, for Francis had collected an army at Avignon, and Henry, instead of sending money, betrayed an inclination to abandon the league altogether. In an unlucky hour Francis determined to carry the war once more into Italy, and, while Bourbon retreated by the Maritime Alps, he made a dash across the Graian Alps. For three entire months Francis lay before the well-defended walls of Pavia, and in the interval he detached the Duke of Albany, the late Regent of Scotland, with 6000 men, to march through nearly the whole of Italy, in order to threaten the kingdom of Naples.[2]

---

[1] *Guicciardini.*

[2] *Guicciardini; Giannone; Du Bellay.*

A.D. 1525. Early in February Francis was roused by news that the Imperialists were concentrating in great force; but even then, out of a ridiculous point of honour, he would not relinquish the siege which he had begun. On the 24th of February he was attacked in his intrenchments by Pescara, Bourbon, and Lannoy, the Viceroy of Naples, and thoroughly defeated. After fighting most valiantly, Francis attempted to save himself by making a rush across the Ticino, but he found the bridge broken down, and the Spaniards closed upon him on the steep bank. His horse was killed under him; his bravest captains and dearest friends had fallen around him; he himself had received three wounds, but still he would not surrender to the Spaniards, who would have killed him had he not been recognized by Pomperant, a French gentleman in the service of the Constable Bourbon. This Frenchman rode up to the Viceroy of Naples, and told him what was passing. Lannoy calmed the fury of the Spanish soldiery, threw himself upon his knees before Francis, kissed his royal hand, and at last received his sword in token of surrender. To his mother, Louisa, whom he had left Regent of France in his absence, he wrote that he had lost everything except his honour.[1] The day after the battle of Pavia he was conveyed to the strong fortress of Pizzichitone, where he was most vigilantly guarded, but otherwise treated with kindness and respect.[2]

The news of this great victory, which, at first sight, seemed to lay France as well as Italy at the feet of the emperor, was received in the English court with demonstrations of joy. The king ordered a day of public thanksgiving; and Wolsey officiated at St. Paul's in the presence of the court, and the ambassadors of the emperor and of the other allies. Some months before, both the king and the cardinal had thought seriously of a reconciliation with France, and had treated secretly with Giovanni Giovachino Passano, a Genoese merchant, who had undertaken a mission from Louisa, the mother of Francis, in the view of making Henry break altogether with the emperor. But now turning again—hoping to be allowed a present share of the victor's spoils, and careless of the future—he despatched Tonstal, Bishop of London, and Wyngfield, chancellor of the duchy of Lancaster, to the emperor's court, to propose that he and Charles should invade France instantly, from different points, and that they should meet in Paris, there amicably to divide the French kingdom between them. Henry forthwith set his ministers to work to raise money. As he was determined not to assemble a parliament, ministers could only proceed by stretching the royal prerogative; and, with Wolsey still at their head, they demanded a fourth from the clergy, and a sixth from the laity. To levy this money, they appointed commissioners in the different counties of England, and resorted to all the means which seemed likely to win or terrify people into a ready parting with their cash without authority of parliament. But clergy and laity—people of all classes and conditions —most firmly opposed this most illegal attempt. "How the great men took it, was marvel; the poor cursed; the rich repugned; the lighter sort railed; and, in conclusion, all men execrated the cardinal as subverter of the laws and liberty of England. For, they said, if men should give their goods by a commission, then were it worse than the taxes of France; and so England would be bond, and not free."[3] Archbishop Warham, the old minister of Henry VII., and formerly chancellor to his son, addressed a striking, warning letter to Wolsey in this crisis. At the same time handbills, containing bitter reflections on the king and his government, were printed and circulated in London and other places; the churchmen protested that they would only pay money when voted by the convocation; and the people began to take up arms against the commissioners. The priests even encouraged the people in their discourses from the pulpit. The king took the alarm, recalled the commissioners, and declared, by proclamation, that he wanted nothing from his subjects but "by way of benevolence." But the people, who abhorred the name of benevolence, in this sense, said the thing was as illegal as the arbitrary commission; and a lawyer in the city quoted the statute passed under Richard III., by which benevolences were for ever abolished. Upon this Henry consulted the judges, who did not blush to affirm that the king might tax his people by commission, or by any other way which seemed to him best; and they agreed with the privy council in holding that, as Richard III. was an usurper, and his parliament a factious assembly, the laws passed by them were not binding on a legitimate and *absolute* king, who held the crown by hereditary right, and needed not to court the favour of a licentious populace. It was in vain, however, that Wolsey endeavoured to impress these maxims on the mayor and aldermen of London; and in the country the odious doctrine encountered a still sterner opposition. In Kent the people expelled all the tax-gatherers and fiscal agents of the court; and in Suffolk 4000 men flew to arms, and threatened Charles Brandon, their duke, who was on the commission, with death. The insurrection was checked by the wise moderation of Surrey, son of the Duke

---

[1] The well-known words were, "Tout est perdu hors l'honneur."
[2] Guicciardini; La Guerra di Pavia; Du Bellay.
[3] Hall.

of Norfolk; but Henry, who was always bolder in words than in deeds, was so much alarmed, that he issued a fresh proclamation to set aside and annul all the demands he had made.

We do not believe that so wild a scheme of conquest and partition, and one in which such volatile characters as Henry and Wolsey were to be principal actors, could, under any circumstances, have been successful; but still it was fortunate for France, at this crisis, that the emperor was as poor as the King of England, and that the seeds of discord were sown between the two unscrupulous sovereigns. Such, indeed, was the state of Charles' finances, that he could not pay the long arrears due to his army in Italy; and the victorious troops mutinied, seized and kept the city of Pavia, and even threatened to take forcible possession of the person of the French king, to hold as security for the money due to them. As the emperor had counted upon Henry for large subsidies, he seems to have considered him as the principal cause of these troubles, which at one moment were most alarming. We believe that it was from this consideration, and from irritation at the secret negotiations with France, and not from any feeling of conceit and inflation, that Charles changed his tone with Henry after the battle of Pavia. He no longer wrote to his loving uncle with his own hand, nor lavished his expressions of reverence and submission; and his letters to the English king were thenceforth merely signed "Charles,"[1]—a trifle that was likely to produce a great effect on the vain-glorious king. Before the arrival of the English ambassadors, the council of Charles had decided (or rather poverty decided for them) that the invasion of France was not to be thought of. They had even consented to a truce for six months, hoping to turn the captive Francis to good account, and to make their profits by negotiation. There was a great deal of diplomatizing, which deceived neither party; and Henry presently adopted the course which was most likely to bring him in an immediate supply of money. He renewed his separate negotiation with France, concluded a truce for four months, and then an alliance offensive and defensive. The price paid by France was high: Henry got for himself the sum of 2,000,000 crowns, to be paid by half-yearly instalments of 50,000 crowns each; and, after liquidation of this, an annual pension of 100,000 crowns. The cardinal got 30,000 crowns on account of his former resignation of the bishopric of Tournai, and 100,000 more for his kind services to the royal family of France; the whole to be paid by instalments in the course of seven years and a half. The French court also agreed to allow to Mary, their queen-dowager, Henry's sister, and now Duchess of Suffolk, the enjoyment of her dower, with the discharge of all arrears thereon. The only clause which was not a money one was an engagement that they would never permit Henry's enemy, the Duke of Albany, to return into Scotland during the minority of the present king, James V. The English court was not more suspicious than were the French unscrupulous as to the means by which they lulled its suspicions. Louisa, the regent, swore to the articles; Francis ratified them; and the principal of the French nobility, with the great cities of Toulouse, Lyons, Amiens, Rheims, Paris, Bordeaux, Tours, and Rouen, bound themselves, under the penalty of forfeiting all their property, to observe the treaty themselves, and compel their king to observe it. At the same time, however, the attorney-general and solicitor-general of the parliament of Paris secretly entered a solemn protest against the whole treaty, in order that Francis, who was rather delicate on the point of honour, might find thereon a reason for not fulfilling these onerous engagements.[2] But, notwithstanding the treaty with England, Francis encountered great difficulties in freeing himself from the hands of the emperor, and was obliged himself to plunge deep in perjury. At his own earnest request he was transferred from the castle of Pizzighitone to the Alcazar of Madrid; but, as the ministers insisted that Charles ought not to trust his feelings in a personal interview with the gallant and engaging prisoner, he never obtained the advantages he had counted upon from a personal interview with the young emperor. Negotiations were opened by cool-headed and cunning diplomatists. Francis offered to give up all his pretensions to Milan, Naples, and Flanders—to restore the Constable Bourbon—and to pay a large sum of money for the possession of Burgundy, which he said he could not dissever from his kingdom without ruining the monarchy for ever. It was replied, for Charles, that Burgundy had been robbed from his family, and that Francis must either restore it or remain a prisoner for life. At last, on the 14th of January, 1526, the treaty, or, as it was called, the concord of Madrid, was concluded and signed. As the price of his liberty Francis agreed to surrender Burgundy to Charles within six weeks after his return to France—to place his two eldest sons as hostages in the hands of Charles—to resign all claims to the Italian states, and to the suzerainty of Flan-

---

[1] *Guicciardini*. This great writer adds that Charles was already averse to the marriage with the Princess Mary of England, and was in treaty for the hand of the Princess Isabella of Portugal, whom he married in March, 1526. It appears, however, that even in this matter Henry's sincerity was equal to that of Charles', and that he had secretly offered his daughter Mary in marriage both to the King of Scotland and the King of France!

[2] *Rymer; Père d'Orléans.*

ders—to marry Eleanora, the sister of Charles, who had been promised by treaty to the Constable Bourbon—to replace the said constable in all his honours and states in France—and to guarantee the emperor against certain pecuniary demands of the king. An article was inserted binding Francis to place himself again as a captive if he should find himself unable to fulfil his agreements. On the very morning on which he made up his mind to sign these hard conditions, he caused a secret protest against the validity of the act to be prepared, and then he swore and signed. He set foot in France a little more than a year after the battle of Pavia.

Henry immediately despatched Sir Thomas Cheney and Dr. Taylor, a jurist of high repute, to congratulate the French king on his delivery, and to urge him to break every article of his treaty with the emperor—the latter being a most unnecessary precaution, for Francis never intended to do otherwise. The French king received the two ambassadors at Bayonne with the most flattering speeches, telling them that, after God, he thanked his kind brother of England for his liberty. Francis very soon told Charles that the surrender of Burgundy was impossible, it being contrary to the solemn oaths administered to him at his coronation and equally contrary to the will of the people of Burgundy, which was quite true; and he offered money in compensation, which he knew Charles would refuse. He then prepared for war; and he and his new ally Henry pledged their honour never to make peace with Charles except by mutual consent. The pope was soon induced to absolve Francis from the oaths he had taken at Madrid; and Clement, Sforza, the Duke of Milan, the Florentines, the Venetians, and some minor Italian states, entered into the league with the Kings of France and England.[1]

In the preceding year, 1525, the first misunderstanding occurred between Henry and Wolsey. According to the cardinal's showing, the subject of this difference was a mere trifle, "consisting in two things—the one concerning the office of clerk of the market within the liberties of the monastery of St. Alban's; and the other touching certain misorder supposed to be used by Dr. Allen, and other his (the cardinal's) officers," in the suppression of certain small monasteries, "wherein neither God was served nor religion kept;" which he intended, "with the gracious aid and assistance of the king," to convert to a far better use, by annexing their revenues to the new college intended to be founded at Oxford "for the increase of good letters and virtue." Martin Luther chose this moment for addressing Henry, whom he fancied to be wholly estranged from Wolsey—"the monster"—"the nuisance to God and man."—"the pest of the kingdom and caterpillar of England." He said he understood that his grace had now begun to loathe that wicked sort of men, and in his mind to favour the true doctrine. The Reformer, in excuse for the violence of the language he had used in replying to the king's book in defence of the Romish church, averred that he had believed the said book was not in reality the production of the royal pen. In his present attempt, however, Luther was premature; the quarrel between king and cardinal was made up; and Henry told the Reformer that "that reverend father," Wolsey, was the best, the most faithful, the most religious of men; that, whereas he loved him very well before, he would now, in consequence of Luther's impious railing, favour him more than ever; that he would never cease to reckon it amongst his good deeds that none that were infected with German leprosy, contagion, and heresies, could cleave to his kingdom or take root in it.[2]

---

[1] It is natural for Romanist historians to trace the great English schism which ended in the English Reformation, to Henry's disappointment in not obtaining his divorce so soon as he expected from the pope, and this has long been the common popular view of the case. Such, however, is not the view of Ranké, in his admirable *History of the Popes.* Speaking of the early Reformation period, he says:—"The Popedom was in a false and untenable position throughout. Its secular tendencies had brought upon it a decline, from which there had arisen innumerable opponents and deserters; but the continuance of the same symptoms, the still farther complication of spiritual and secular interests, completed its downfall. *The schism in England may in reality be traced to the same cause.* It is well worth noting that Henry VIII., with all his declared hostility to Luther, and intimately, too, as he was united with the Roman See, yet at the time of the first difference, in matters purely political, as early as the year 1525, threatened the Roman See with ecclesiastical innovations." The historian refers in a note to a letter addressed to Rome, in a threatening way, by Wolsey, as indicating the first movement in the English civil government's secession from Rome.

[2] *Bishop Godwin; Herbert.*

CHAPTER V.—CIVIL AND MILITARY HISTORY.—A.D. 1526—1533.

HENRY VIII.—ACCESSION, A.D. 1509—DEATH, A.D. 1547.

Difficulties of Pope Clement—Rome assailed by an army of mercenaries—Is stormed and plundered—Indifference of Henry VIII. to the fate of Rome—Commencement of his love for Anne Boleyn—Her early history—Her reception of the king's addresses—Henry's scruples about his marriage to Catherine—Wolsey's conduct on the occasion—His mission to France to negotiate a royal union—Terms of the treaty with France—Henry resolves to divorce Catherine and marry Anne—His negotiation with the pope to that effect—The pope's cautious and equivocal dealing—The sweating sickness visits London—Arrival of Cardinal Campeggio—Proceedings of Wolsey and Campeggio in the divorce of Catherine—They bring it to a trial—Catherine's defence—The trial adjourned by Campeggio—Wolsey declines in the royal favour—Is visited with confiscation and bereavement of office—Persecuted by Anne Boleyn and her party—He is arrested on a charge of high treason—Wolsey's last illness and death—Thomas Cranmer's first appearance—He is sent to collect the opinions of the universities on Henry's divorce—Their sentiments on the subject—Thomas Cromwell—His previous career—His rise after the fall of Wolsey—He advises Henry to renounce the Papal authority—The clergy of England accused as abettors of Wolsey—Henry's demand to be recognized as head of the church in England—Commencement of Henry's persecution of the Reformers—His secret marriage with Anne Boleyn.

ALTHOUGH flattered by the pope with the offer of the title of "Protector" of the new Italian league against the emperor, the main object of which was to preserve the independence of Italy, Henry made no exertion in his favour, nor did Francis keep any of his liberal promises to the pope. Beset on all sides—by the Spaniards from the kingdom of Naples, and by the Germans and Spaniards from Lombardy, Parma, and Piacenza—Clement was obliged to throw himself on the emperor's mercy, and implore for peace. Moncada, the Spanish Governor of Naples, signed a treaty, and a month after, in alliance with the great Roman family of Colonna, advanced secretly to the Eternal City, surprised one of the gates, plundered the rich palace of the Vatican, and obliged the pope to take refuge in the castle of St. Angelo. A day or two after this exploit (on the 21st of September, 1526) Clement obtained a new treaty of peace, and the Colonnesi left Rome, and Moncada returned to Naples. As soon as the pope was freed from these foes, he resolved not to observe any of the articles which had been extorted from him; and the more effectually to disturb the emperor's possession of Naples, he invited from France the Count of Vaudemont, who, as heir of the house of Anjou, advanced claims to that kingdom, in which there was a powerful faction quite ready to take up arms against the Spaniards. The Viceroy Lannoy heard of this invitation, and, in the month of December, marched out of the kingdom of Naples and fell upon the Roman states. But Clement was not unprovided with troops: his Italian allies had sent him reinforcements; and the Romans, the Florentines, and the Venetians not only kept in check the veteran forces of Lannoy, but gained some brilliant advantages over them. But this was only a gleam of success for Italy, and the year 1527 came on,—a year full of most atrocious, and, for many centuries, unheard-of incidents—a year marked with the imprisonment of the pontiff, the sack of Rome, famine, and the plague, which ravaged that beautiful peninsula from the foot of the Alps to the Faro of Messina.[1]

In the still wretched state of his finances, the Emperor Charles could raise no regular army, and, in order to keep his grasp on Italy, he employed all sorts of mercenaries and partizan leaders, who undertook the war with the tacit understanding that they were to make the invaded country pay its expenses, or, in other words, that they were to live and enrich themselves on the plunder of the poor Italians, whether friends or enemies, or neutrals in the pending contest. Their ranks were swelled by the vagabonds and marauders of nearly every country in Europe, but the more numerous divisions were Spaniards, Germans, and Swiss. Freundsberg, a German partizan, and thorough-paced soldier of fortune, was at the head of 14,000 of these adventurers; and the Constable Bourbon, who had been ill-used by all parties, until he was utterly reckless and ferocious, led another body of 10,000. The two desperate hordes formed a junction at Fiorenzuola, whence they marched to plunder the rich and beautiful city of Florence. The Italian Athens was saved by the rapid advance of the confederate army; but this movement exposed Rome, and the robbers precipitated their march in that direction. At the same time Lannoy, the viceroy, hemmed in the capital of the Christian world on the south.

---

[1] *Guicciardini; Summonte, Giannone.*

Reduced to despair, Pope Clement, in the end of March, submitted to a fresh peace, the articles of which were dictated by the viceroy, who, on his side, however, bound himself to stop the march of Bourbon and Freundsberg. Clement dismissed his troops, and Lannoy went northward to meet the invaders. Freundsberg had fallen sick, and lay with the rear at Ferrara; and Bourbon could not be prevailed upon to return, telling the viceroy that it was out of his power to control the troops, as he owed them money, and had no means of paying them except by sacking Rome.

On the 5th of May Bourbon encamped in the meadows on the north of Rome, and sent a trumpeter to the pope to demand a free passage. On the following morning, at early dawn, he led his ferocious rabble to the assault, and he was among the first to mount the walls. While his foot was still on the scaling-ladder he was struck by a ball from an arquebuse, and fell dead at the foot of the wall. The loss of their daring leader only increased the fury of the soldiery, who,

THE BRIDGE AND CASTLE OF ST. ANGELO, ROME.—From a drawing by Parke.

after two hours' hard fighting, hand-to-hand (for they had no artillery), carried the borgo or suburb, having lost about 1000 men in the attack. In the afternoon they crossed the Sistine bridge and entered the city, which, for the five following days, was abandoned to pillage, massacre, and all the atrocious excesses of which human nature is capable. Nothing was heard in the streets of the Christian city but the cries of "Blood! blood!" "Bourbon! Bourbon!" The pope escaped in time into the castle of St. Angelo; but some of the cardinals were not so fortunate, and these, with a number of bishops, were treated with infamous barbarity. In spite of the manifold corruptions of Rome, and the long-standing vices and debaucheries of the Roman hierarchy, a thrill of horror and indignation was felt from one extremity of Europe to the other. The news reached England at the end of May. On the 2d of June, Wolsey wrote a letter to Henry to inform him of the "most detestable, cruel, and maudlict tyranny of the Imperials, committed at Rome," and calling upon him, as "Defender of the Faith," to relieve and succour the pope and the cardinals who were pressed by siege in the castle of St. Angelo.[1] But Henry, being engaged in certain amorous matters which were soon to work an entire change in his devotion to Rome, did not respond to the zeal of the cardinal.

Although Henry had long been a most inconstant husband, setting no bounds to his intrigues, he had hitherto treated Queen Catherine with that respect to which she appears to have been entitled by her many excellent qualities. But at last he encountered—what seems to have been a rarity in his court—a beauty so moral or so proud, that she would not listen to the illicit suit even of a great sovereign. This was Anne Boleyn. The father of this important beauty was Thomas Boleyn, or Bullen, descended from a lord-mayor of London; but the family of traders had been aggrandized by intermarriages with the high nobility; and the wife of this Thomas, and the mother of Anne, was Elizabeth, daughter of Thomas Howard, Duke of Norfolk. Sir Thomas Boleyn had long been employed about Henry's court, and had executed several important missions and embassies to foreign powers, greatly to the satisfaction of the king and the lord-cardinal. Anne was born in or about the year 1507; and in 1514, when only seven years old, she was appointed maid of honour to the king's sister, who had just been married to Louis XII. We have seen her appearing in France with the Princess Mary, who was allowed to retain her when the other English attendants were so unceremoniously sent out of the country. Mary, on the occasion of her second marriage with Charles Brandon, was glad to leave the young Anne under the powerful protection of the new Queen of France—Claude, wife of Francis I. Anne was brought up in the French court—then, as at later periods, a good place for acquiring certain accomplishments and

[1] *State Papers.*

graces of manner, and which had not yet sunk to the extreme profligacy by which it was corrupted, during the closing years of the reign of Francis I. After the second marriage of her royal mistress to the Duke of Suffolk, she was installed in an honourable office in the court of Claude, queen of Francis I., and, in that school, was unlikely to acquire those indecorous habits which Popish writers have endeavoured to fasten upon her early history. The time of her return to England is rather doubtful; but it is probable that those historians are correct who fix it in 1522, when war was proclaimed against France, on which occasion she was brought home by her father, who was ambassador at the French court. Young, beautiful, and accomplished, Anne Boleyn, soon after her arrival in England, was appointed one of Queen Catherine's maids of honour, and, when little more than sixteen years old, a romantic attachment sprung up between her and Lord Percy, son and heir of the Earl of Northumberland, who made her an offer of marriage. But Henry had already turned his admiring eyes in the same direction, and, jealous of the rivalry of a subject, he caused the lovers to be parted through the agency of Cardinal Wolsey, in whose household Percy had been educated, and that young nobleman, probably under the same compulsion, married a daughter of the Earl of Shrewsbury,

ANNE BOLEYN, after Holbein.

soon after in 1523. Anne, on being separated from her lover, was conveyed to Hever Castle, in Kent, the seat of her father, and thither the king, at a later period, repaired on a visit; but probably suspecting the cause of his arrival, she kept her chamber under the pretext of sickness, and did not leave it till his departure. But this reserve was more likely to animate than daunt a royal lover and Henry, for the purpose of restoring the reluctant lady to court, and bringing her within the sphere of his solicitations, created Sir Thomas Boleyn Viscount Rochford on the 18th of June, 1525, and made him treasurer of the royal household. Even yet, however, his suit was unprosperous when it was made in due form; and she is said, by an old writer inclined to the side of her enemies, to have thus repelled it—" Your wife I cannot be, both in respect of my own unworthiness, and also because you have a queen already; and your mistress I will not be."

The king now began to talk of religious scruples regarding his marriage with Catherine, the widow of his own brother. Nor were there wanting other grounds of complaint. Though she had been his wife seventeen years, Catherine had only one child living, and this was a daughter—the Princess Mary. Besides, she was now in the forty-third year of her age, and retained little of her former beauty. There was still something of a political prejudice against female reigns, and many men regretted, upon public grounds, that there should be no male heir to the crown. There were other circumstances strongly tending to encourage the king in a plan wherein his own main, if not sole object, was

HEVER CASTLE, Kent.[1]

the gratification of his passions: notwithstanding

[1] This castle was erected in the time of Edward III. It is surrounded by a moat, and the inner buildings form a quadrangle inclosing a court.

Henry's recent boast that the Lutheran doctrine could not cleave to his kingdom of England, that doctrine had already struck its roots deep into the soil; and while those who secretly favoured its growth knew that Catherine was a devout Catholic, they had reasons for believing that Anne Boleyn inclined to the Reformation. At the same time Wolsey, upon very different motives, was ready to promote the divorce from Catherine, for he was now incensed against her nephew the emperor, and he ardently wished to strengthen the new alliance with France, by marrying his master to Renée, daughter of the late king Louis XII. It is said, indeed, that the cardinal, who during many years had professed the greatest friendship and devotion to Catherine, first suggested the divorce; but this point, though probable, is not proved, and Wolsey sometimes denied it, and at others admitted it, as best suited the purposes he had in hand at the time. It appears certain, however, that the cardinal never for a moment contemplated the possibility of the king's marrying Anne Boleyn. The usage of such marriages—though once common enough—between sovereign and subject, was now generally exploded, and the cardinal promised many advantages to himself from the French alliance. The Bishop of Tarbes, who was in England settling the other marriage proposed in the late treaty, between Henry's daughter Mary and Francis, or the Duke of Orleans, the son of Francis (a delicate specimen of royal matrimonial negotiation!) suddenly asked whether the legitimacy of the Princess Mary, as daughter of Catherine, was beyond the reach of all legal and canonical doubt. It was generally believed that this question was put at the suggestion of Wolsey, as a pretext for the king, as something likely to make a great impression on the public mind.[1] In the course of the summer Wolsey went over to France to negotiate in person. The cardinal was received as if he had been a king. Upon reaching Boulogne the artillery fired a royal salute; but hereby an accident well nigh befell the gorgeous churchman, "through the obstinacy of his mule," which took fright at the noise of the great guns. By the French king's orders he was permitted, in all such places as he passed through on his journey, "to release, pardon, and put at liberty all such transgressors as be detained in prison, of whatsoever quality their offence." On the 4th of August Francis himself welcomed the cardinal, having advanced a mile and a half from the city of Amiens to meet him on the road.[2]

The great ostensible object of Wolsey's splendid embassy was, to concert measures with Francis for the rescue of the pope, who was still besieged in the castle of St. Angelo by the Germans and Spaniards. This object, indeed, was loudly proclaimed on the journey; and wherever the cardinal stopped for Divine worship the litany which was chanted included a "Santa Maria, ora pro Papa nostro Clemente." On one of these occasions Cavendish, the attached servant and minute biographer of Wolsey, says—" I saw the lord-cardinal weep very tenderly, which was, as we supposed, for heaviness that the pope was at that present time in such calamity and great danger of the lance-knights." But, in the consultations which now took place, the pope and the interests of the Catholic church were secondary subjects, the primary ones being the treaties of close alliance and intermarriages between the courts of England and France, and the establishing of Wolsey as a sort of pro-pope during the restraint of Clement. The emperor, by means of his ambassador, remonstrated with Wolsey on his master's divorce from Queen Catherine, whispers of which had already got abroad, and which was considered by Charles as a grievous family insult, to obviate which he was ready to make many concessions. The emperor was also alarmed at the prospect of the close alliance between Henry and Francis; and he did his best to outbid the French king, offering, among other things, to give the hand of the Princess of Portugal, his wife's sister, to the Duke of Richmond, Henry's natural son, now a boy about eight or nine years old. Wolsey, by his master's orders, listened to all these proposals, and even treated the report of the divorce as an idle rumour. The cardinal, however, concluded four separate treaties with Francis. The first confirmed the recent engagement of perpetual alliance between England and France; the second stipulated that Henry's daughter should be married to the Duke of Orleans, the son, if she were not married to Francis, the father; the third fixed the subsidies to be furnished by England for the war in Italy, that was to be conducted by Francis in aid of the pope; and the last declared that, till the pope should resume the government of the church, whatever should be determined in France by the clergy of the Gallican church, and in England by the cardinal-legate (Wolsey) and the principal members of the English church, called together by the king's authority, should be held good and valid, even as if the pope had decreed and spoken it. It has been plausibly supposed—and

---

[1] Cardinal Pole, *Apologia; Hist. Divorce de Henri VIII.* par Le Grand, who quotes original letters.

[2] Letters from Wolsey to the king, in *State Papers*, published by order of government. The learned and accurate editor of this invaluable collection of historical materials remarks, that this appears to be the first occasion of Wolsey's adopting the style of "majesty," in addressing Henry VIII. Our kings had, till now, been satisfied with "your highness," or "your grace."

the supposition is in much seeming accordance with extracts from letters written by Wolsey at the time, to his master that the object of the last clause was to invest the cardinal with full power to manage "the great and secret affair," or the divorce of Catherine. But this throwing open of ecclesiastical authority had another effect, which Wolsey probably did not foresee; "for here," says a noble contemporary, "*began the relish our king took of governing the church himself!*"[1]

When the treaties were signed, Henry expressed his entire satisfaction at them; and Wolsey told Louisa, the mother of Francis, that within a year she would see a princess of her own blood Queen of England, and wife of his master, in lieu of the emperor's aunt Catherine. The cardinal returned to England rejoicing in his success; but, while he had been engaged for a French princess, Henry had been assiduously courting his fair English subject—Mistress Anne Boleyn.

As soon as Wolsey returned from France, Henry announced to him his fixed determination of making Anne Boleyn his wife and Queen of England. The astounded cardinal fell upon his knees and implored the king to renounce this project; but soon seeing, in Henry's wrath, that opposition and remonstrance would only be dangerous to himself, he adroitly changed his tack, fell in with the hard-set current, and soon engaged to perform whatever service the king might require of him in this matter. By Henry's orders his treatise on the divorce was submitted to the consideration of the learned Sir Thomas More, who, feeling the danger of acting as a reviewer in such a case, tried to excuse himself by saying that he was not a theologian. But Henry urged him to confer with some of the bishops, and so get up an approval of his writing. Sir Thomas, who was himself against the divorce, found but few ready to embrace the royal doctrines, and, in an ingenious speech, he recommended Henry to see what St. Jerome, St. Augustine, and the other fathers of the church, had said upon such subjects. When Wolsey attempted to win over the bishops and great divines, they said they thought it a matter to be referred to the supreme arbitrament of the pope.

After long hesitation, Henry's agents in Italy were instructed to refer the cause to the pontiff. But this application was provided against by the emperor. Long before it was definitively made, or any succour sent to his Holiness, Clement had been obliged by famine to capitulate and deliver up the castle of St. Angelo to the Imperialists, who continued to keep him and some thirteen of the cardinals in a kind of imprisonment at Rome; and in settling a treaty with the pontiff, who was made to pay 400,000 ducats, Charles did not neglect to bind him to oppose the divorce of his aunt Catherine. Clement, however, escaped from Rome, disguised as a gardener, and took refuge in the strong town of Orvieto; and a French army, under the command of Lautrec, which at last crossed the Alps, advanced through Lombardy to his relief. But Lautrec loitered at Piacenza, and, instead of his army, the first who waited upon the pope were Henry's matrimonial agents, who had been recently reinforced by the arrival of Dr. Knight, the king's secretary. The pope was in a distressing dilemma. If he refused to grant what Henry required he had to apprehend that the French army, partly supported by English money, would do nothing for him, and if he complied he drew down upon himself the vengeance of the Imperialists, who were still masters of Rome, and likely for some time to remain so, seeing the dilatory movements of Lautrec. He seems naturally to have wished to gain time, but the envoys, knowing the amorous impatience of their master, induced him to sign two papers which had been drawn up in England, empowering Wolsey to decide the divorce, and granting Henry a dispensation to marry any other woman whatsoever, without regard to certain canonical restrictions. He hoped that these papers might be kept secret, at least till the French army was near enough to support him, and this, it should appear, was promised to him by the English diplomatists; but scarcely had Clement signed the two authorizations when Gregorio Cassali, a friend of Wolsey, who seems to have dreaded the responsibility of acting alone, "presented himself, and requested that an Italian cardinal, a legate from Rome, should be sent into England, and joined in the delicate commission with the English cardinal." Clement remarked that this was likely to lengthen and embarrass the proceedings; but he complied with this request also, and offered Henry his choice of any one out of six cardinals whom he named. These transactions with the pope took place at the end of the year 1527.

A.D. 1528. As yet neither Henry nor Francis had openly declared war against Charles, but now, in the month of January, Clarenceux and Guienne, kings-at-arms, defied him, in the forms of chivalry, upon the same day. To the Frenchman Charles merely said that his defiance was uncalled for, as he and Francis had long been engaged in hostilities; but to Clarenceux he justified his conduct, protested he had done nothing to merit the resentment of his master, and delivered a long and well-written paper, which cast the whole blame upon Henry. The

---

[1] *Lord Herbert, letters quoted in Burnet's History of the Reformation; Le Grand; Guicciardini; Dr Lingard.*

affair of Queen Catherine was made very prominent. "Can I," said the emperor, "overlook the indignity with which he threatens my aunt, by applying for a divorce, or the insult which he has offered to me, by soliciting me to marry his daughter Mary, whom he now pronounces a bastard? .... But I well know who has suggested all this. I would not gratify the rapacity of the Cardinal of York, nor employ my armies to make him pope; and he has sworn vengeance against me, and now seeks to work out his purposes."[1] But, in reality, there was no war at all, except what was carried on by the French in Italy, Henry having neither money nor time to spare from his other grand pursuit. He had not thought it wise to make his selection of a second legate, and he doubted whether the pope might not consider himself at liberty to revise any sentence of divorce pronounced by Wolsey, or by any other delegate; and he now despatched Dr. Gardiner and Dr. Edward Fox to demand a fresh and more ample dispensation, and a new instrument, called a decretal bull, in which the pope was not only to promise an entire confirmation of the judgment which Wolsey and his other legate might pronounce, but also to declare that the prohibition in Leviticus, notwithstanding the permission in Deuteronomy, was imperative, and a fundamental law of the Christian church, and consequently that Henry's treatise upon the divorce was a correct piece of polemical reasoning. The two learned English doctors were instructed not to rely wholly upon their own eloquence, but to promise the pope possession of Ravenna and Cervia, which, by some means or other, he (Henry) was to obtain from the Venetians, a people by no means remarkable for a lack of tenacity in keeping what they had got. Clement readily enough signed the dispensation in the form prescribed; but he was more scrupulous as to granting the decretal bull, which went to destroy the dogma of infallibility, as his predecessor, Julius II., had fully sanctioned the marriage of Catherine, notwithstanding the fact of her previous union with Henry's own brother, Prince Arthur. But the doctor's reasoning, and the flattering promises made to him, shook the resolution of Clement, who consented to refer the original dispensation of Julius, which allowed the marriage, to a commission, and to authorize Wolsey, with the aid of any one of the English bishops, to pronounce thereon, and to dissolve the marriage, *if* the instrument had been obtained unfairly. In consideration to the Princess Mary, a clause was added to legitimatize her in case of her mother being divorced. The compliance of the pope filled Henry with joy and Wolsey with misgiving, for the cardinal saw that Clement was throwing the responsibility upon him. He sent to implore that Cardinal Campeggio should be joined with him in the commission, and he explained to the king some doubts and difficulties which he had encountered among the English canonists. Henry answered him with "terrible terms," forgetting the long services of his minister in his absorbing passion. He probably saw that since Wolsey had been disappointed in his expectations of marrying him to the French princess, he was not over eager for the divorce; and there was already a feud between the cardinal and the family and friends of Anne Boleyn. But the fury of Henry now made Wolsey tremble, and in great haste he supplicated the pope to sign the decretal bull, which he considered as the only security that his judgment would never be revoked, and that the court of Rome would never listen to any appeal on the part of the divorced queen. Clement at last signed the instrument, and appointed Campeggio to act with the English cardinal, instructing him not to let the said bull out of his hands, but merely to show it in the English court, if absolutely obliged thereto.[2]

In the month of May, the city of London and the court were thrown into great consternation by the sudden appearance of the sweating sickness. The disease soon showed itself among the female servants of Anne Boleyn. By the orders of the anxious lover, Anne was instantly conducted into Kent, to Hever Castle, the seat of her father, Lord Rochford; but she carried the infection with her, and communicated it to her parent. Both father and daughter, however, were soon out of danger. Some noble retainers of the lord-cardinal died in his palace, and several gentlemen of the privy chamber were in great danger. Upon this, the king fled, and sought to escape the contagion by locking himself up and frequently changing his place of residence.[3] His love was all forgotten, and he thought very seriously about his soul, confessing himself every day, and taking the sacrament, in company with his wife Catherine, every Sunday and every saint's day. People began to think that he would give up the project of the divorce, and lead a chaste and religious life; but, as soon as the sweating sickness was over, he recalled Anne to court, and ordered the degraded nobles to attend her levees as if she were their queen. Soon after this Cardinal Campeggio, who had loitered as long as he could on his journey, arrived at the English court, where he was received by Henry with exceeding great joy, and with tempting offers of bishoprics for himself, and lay honours for his son—by the un-

---

[1] Le Grand.

[2] Letters of the Bishop of Bayonne, quoted by Le Grand; Lord Herbert; Burnet.

[3] Wolsey was not more courageous than the king—he fled from his own sumptuous palace, and for some days concealed himself from everybody in the country.

fortunate Queen Catherine with tears and remonstrances. Campeggio exhorted her, in the name of the pope, and for the sake of peace, to retire into a convent. The queen replied that it was not for herself, but for her child, that she would struggle; and protested that she would never do anything to prejudice the rights of the Princess Mary, the presumptive heir to the throne of England. The king now expected that the legates would proceed with their commission, but such was not the intention of Campeggio, who consulted the interests of his superior, the pope, and who saw that the Emperor Charles was again acquiring that ascendency in Italy which would enable him to wreak his vengeance on the pontiff, if he should concur in degrading his aunt. We may believe that Clement would in no circumstances have been anxious for despatch in this unpleasant business; but it is certain that the unmarrying and remarrying of the English king were made to depend upon the chances of war beyond the Alps. When Pope Clement signed the decretal bull, and commissioned Campeggio to go to England, the Imperialists seemed defeated at all points; and Lautrec, the French general, after victoriously traversing nearly the whole of Italy, was laying siege to the city of Naples, with the good hope that the people within the walls would soon rise upon the Spaniards, and open the gates to the French. Nor could Lautrec have failed in this enterprise, even by force of arms, had he been properly seconded by his master; but Francis was as busily engaged with many mistresses as his brother Henry was with one, and he sent neither money nor reinforcements into Italy. He had also the lamentable imprudence to quarrel with the great family of the Dorias, upon which Andrea joined the Emperor Charles with the whole power of Genoa; and Filippino Doria, who was co-operating in the siege by sea, sailed away with all the Genoese galleys, leaving Lautrec to take Naples by himself. But Doria had scarcely sailed out of the gulf when a malaria fever broke out in the French camp, and this was soon accompanied by that more fearful scourge the plague. Men and officers died by heaps; and from besiegers the French became besieged in their intrenchments between Mount Vesuvius and Naples. Lautrec fell a victim to disease and grief on the 15th of August; and having fought their way with great loss as far as the town of Aversa, only six miles off, the wretched remnant of his army capitulated to the Imperialists in the beginning of September.[1] From this moment the pope, finding himself at the mercy of Charles, began to negotiate for a peace without informing Francis or Henry, who had both proved themselves bad allies.

---

[1] Giannone; Guicciardini.

A.D. 1529. A bright gleam of hope now broke both upon the king and Wolsey, for, in the month of February, Clement was not only dangerously ill, but reported to be dead. Francis engaged to make Wolsey pope in his stead; and in this elevation Henry saw the removal of all difficulties. But Clement recovered; and shortly after Henry learned, to his unspeakable wrath, that Francis himself was negotiating for peace with the emperor. As his imprecations could have no effect in changing the policy, either of the French or of the Papal court, he determined to hurry on the process as best he could, without waiting for any further concessions from Rome, whence he had recalled his learned ambassador Gardiner, to be his leading counsel; and, on the 30th of May, Henry issued a license under the broad seal to the two cardinal-legates, who were requested to proceed with all despatch. But Campeggio, though he had been already nearly eight months in England, was in no hurry; and not being able to prevent the assembling of the court, he resolved to prolong its deliberations as much as possible, and then, in the end (unless the affairs of Italy took a very different turn), to render them nugatory.

The court met on the 31st of May in the great hall of the Blackfriars, where Wolsey and Campeggio took their seats with much solemnity, and summoned the king and queen to appear before them. Henry appeared by proxy, the queen in person; and, protesting at once against the judgment of the two cardinals, appealed to the pope. Campeggio then adjourned the court, nor did they meet again till the 21st of June. On that day Henry sat in state on the right hand of the cardinals, and, when his name was called, he answered "Here!" Catherine, who sat on the left hand of the cardinals, attended by four friendly bishops, would not answer to her name or plead in any way. On the citation being repeated, she rose from her chair, crossed herself very devoutly, and then, throwing herself at the king's feet, thus addressed him:—"Sir, I beseech you, for all the loves that hath been between us, and for the love of God, let me have justice and right; take of me some pity and compassion, for I am a poor woman and a stranger, born out of your dominions. I have here no assured friend, much less impartial counsel, and I flee to you as to the head of justice within this realm. Alas, sir! wherein have I offended you, or on what occasion given you displeasure? Have I ever designed against your will and pleasure, that you should put me from you? I take God and all the world to witness that I have been to you a true, humble, and obedient wife; ever conformable to your will and pleasure. Never have I said or done aught contrary thereto, being always well-pleased and contented with all things wherein you had delight or dalliance, whether it were in little or much; neither did I ever grudge in word or countenance, or show a visage or spark of discontent. I loved all those whom you loved, only for your sake, whether I had cause or no, whether they were my friends or mine enemies." After reminding him that she had been his true wife these twenty years, and had borne him divers children, although it had pleased God to call them out of the world; denying that her previous marriage with his brother had been more than a form, on which point she appealed to his own conscience whether she spoke true or no; and declaring that, if there were any just cause why their marriage should be dissolved, she was contented to depart, "albeit in great shame and dishonour;" she continued—"The king, your father, was, in the time of his reign, of such estimation through the world for his excellent wisdom, that he was accounted and called of all men the second Solomon; and my father Ferdinand, King of Spain, was esteemed one of the wisest princes: both, indeed, were excellent princes, full of wisdom, and princely behaviour. . . . Also, as me seemeth, there were in those days as wise, as learned, and as judicious men as be at the present, who thought then the marriage good and lawful; therefore it is a wonder to hear what new inventions are brought up against me. . . . . Ye cause me to stand to the order and judgment of this new court, wherein ye may do me much wrong; for ye may condemn me for lack of sufficient answer, having no impartial advisers, but only such as ye assign me. . . . Ye must consider that they who be your subjects cannot be impartial counsellors for me: they have been chosen out of your own council, and they dare not, for fear of you, disobey your will, or frustrate your intentions. Therefore, most humbly do I require you, in the way of charity, and for the love of God, who is the just Judge, to spare me the extremity of this new court until I be advertised what way my friends in Spain may advise me to take; and if ye will not extend to me so much impartial favour, your will then be fulfilled—unto God I commit my cause."[1]

She then rose; and after a low obeisance to the king, and when every one expected she would return to her seat, she walked hastily out of the court, in which she would never again be persuaded to make her appearance, either personally or by proxy. To counteract the effect of her eloquent appeal, Henry made a most hypocritical speech, telling all present that, in truth, she had always been a dutiful and loving wife, and that his present proceedings arose solely from the delicacy of his own conscience and his Christian fear of God's wrath.

As Catherine would not appear in court, she was pronounced contumacious, and the trial was carried on without her. The king's counsel, who had it all their own way, maintained the three following points as justifying and imperiously calling for the divorce:—1st. That the marriage between her and Prince Arthur had been consummated, which fact made her subsequent marriage with Henry unlawful and unnatural; 2d. That the dispensatory bull of Pope Julius II. had been obtained under false pretences, and a concealment of facts; and 3d. That a Papal breve which had been procured to prop the bull was a manifest forgery. Holding all this to be proved, Henry urged Wolsey, and Wolsey urged Campeggio, to pronounce judgment. But the Italian legate had no such intention: his master, the pope, had concluded his favourable treaty with the Emperor Charles on the 29th of June, and no longer stood in dread of the wrath of Henry. On the 23d of July, Henry's counsel called for judgment in peremptory language. Campeggio said, "I have not come so far to please any man for fear, meed, or favour, be he king or any other potentate. I am an old man, sick, decayed, and looking daily for death. What should it, then, avail me to put my soul in the danger of God's displeasure, to my utter damnation, for the favour of any prince or high estate in this world? Forasmuch, then, that I understand the truth in this case is very difficult to be known, that the defendant will make no answer thereunto, but hath appealed from our judgment; therefore, to avoid all injustice and obscure doubts, I intend to proceed no further in this matter until I have the opinion of the pope, and such others of his council as have more experience and learning. For this purpose (he concluded, rising from his chair), I adjourn the cause till the commencement of the next term, in the beginning of October."[2]

As Campeggio finished speaking, Henry's brother-in-law, the Duke of Suffolk, struck the table with his fist, and exclaimed, in real or affected rage, that the old proverb was verified—"Never did cardinal bring good to England." The remark was especially meant for Wolsey. The court did not meet again; and in a few days after, it was known in London that the pope had revoked the legatine commission on the 15th of July, or eight days before this scene took place, and had entertained the appeal of Queen Catherine. Campeggio, who had skilfully drawn out the business to the proper moment, now took his leave of the English court. Henry, who could check the violence of his temper when he thought it expe-

---

[1] Cavendish. [2] Cavendish.

dient, behaved decently with the Italian cardinal, and even gave him some presents, as usual on such occasions; but as Campeggio lay at Dover, previous to his embarkation, his chamber was broken open by armed men, who searched his trunks, pretending that he was carrying out of the kingdom a great treasure belonging to Wolsey. The real object of this rough usage seems to have been to get possession of the decretal bull: though others think that the men were in search of Henry's letters to Anne Boleyn, which the cardinal had cautiously despatched beforehand to Rome.

But the English cardinal was more at the mercy of a vindictive court; and Wolsey soon found that "Mistress Anne," who had often expressed her gratitude and affection, and in the preceding year had vowed an eternal friendship to him, was bent heart and soul on his destruction. Suffolk, whom Wolsey had stung at the trial, and the great Duke of Norfolk, and others of the highest nobility, made common cause with her who was plainly about to become their queen. They represented that the cardinal had never wished for the divorce, except in favour of his French scheme; that he had constantly been bribed and bought by France. Henry turned a ready ear to all this, and to more, and already, in conceit, devoured Wolsey's immense wealth; and his courtiers began to talk at dinner-time, that, when once the cardinal was dead or ruined, they would relieve the church of its superfluous treasure.[1] The amorous king set out on a progress: Anne Boleyn was with him, and Wolsey was not. The cardinal, however, soon rode after the court, and joined it at Grafton, in Northamptonshire, where, to the great dismay of Anne and her party, the king received him with his old familiarity and affection. But either Henry was acting a part, or had changed his mind very speedily, for on the morrow Wolsey was ordered back to London, and he never saw his master's face again.[2]

A few weeks after the commencement of the Michaelmas term, when Wolsey proceeded to the Court of Chancery, it was observed that none of the king's servants paid him any honour; and on the same day Hales, the attorney-general, filed two bills against him in the Court of King's Bench, charging him with having transgressed the law of the land in exercising the functions of pope's legate. Wolsey's long courtier life seems to have deprived him of the spirit of a man, and the sudden loss of the royal favour was to him like the removal of the bright sun from the heavens. The gorgeous creature fell prostrate at once, and crawled in the dirt like a vile worm. Without an effort he submitted himself to the scourge, and, ordering his counsel to admit his guilt, where he was innocent, he threw himself on the king's mercy, whining and saying he knew not how he had offended. On condition of being allowed to retain his rank and property in the church, he drew up a deed, transferring his entire personal estate to his gracious master. The property thus surrendered was valued at 500,000 crowns—an immense sum; but Henry had need of it all, and of more, and the cardinal's promptitude could not disarm persecution. Shortly afterwards the Dukes of Suffolk and Norfolk waited upon him at York Palace, to tell him, from the king, who meant to live there himself, that he must quit that splendid palace, and confine himself to his house at Esher. Wolsey submissively prepared to depart. But he showed some little spirit when his sworn enemies, with an air of triumph, requested him to deliver up the great seal. "My lords," said he, "the great seal of England was delivered to me by the hands of my sovereign; I hold it by his majesty's letters-patent, which, along with it, have conferred on me the office of chancellor, to be enjoyed during my life; and I may not deliver it at the simple word of any lord, unless you can show me your commission." The *great* lords were mean enough to taunt and insult the fallen minister; and the next day, when Wolsey was ready for a short journey to Esher, they returned to him with an order under the sign-manual. The cardinal read the paper, immediately resigned the seal, and gave an inventory of his jewels, plate, cloth of gold, silks, satins, velvets, tapestries, and all other precious commodities. He then issued from his most sumptuous palace, and entered his barge. The news had got wing, and the Thames was covered with boats full of men and women, who hooted and shouted, and told him how happy they were to see him sent to the Tower. They were fools for their pains; for the words of Wolsey's faithful attendant were fully verified, and there came "another hungry and lean officer in his place, that bit nearer the bone than the old one." They were also disappointed as to the lord-cardinal's present journey, for, instead of descending the river to the Tower, he ascended it to Putney.

As he was travelling by land from Putney to Esher, one of the royal chamberlains (Sir John Norris) spurred after him, and overtaking him on the rise of a hill, presented him with a ring which the king, who had taken it from his own finger, sent him, with a very comfortable message. "Therefore," added Sir John, "take patience, for I trust to see you yet in better estate than ever." Hereupon the lord-cardinal alighted from his

---

[1] Letters written at the moment from the English court by the French ambassador, the Bishop of Bayonne.
[2] *Cavendish; Bishop of Bayonne; Hall.*

mule, fell upon his knees, pulled off his cap, and humbly thanked God for such happy intelligence from his lord the king. He told the chamberlain that his tidings were worth half a kingdom; but,

ESHER—GATEWAY OF WOLSEY'S PALACE.¹—From a view by Havell.

as he had nothing left except the clothes on his back, he could make him no suitable reward. He, however, gave Sir John a small gold chain and crucifix. "As for my sovereign," he added, "sorry am I that I have no worthy token to send him; but stay, here is my fool that rides beside me. I beseech thee take him to court, and give him to his majesty. I assure you, for any nobleman's pleasure, he is worth a thousand pound."²

But the beautiful solitudes of Esher were gloomy and horrid without the smiles of the king, and Wolsey soon sank in despondency and sickness. He wrote the most abject letters to his "most gracious, and merciful, and most pious sovereign lord," calling himself a poor, heavy, and wretched priest, that was dying for want of the light of his countenance; but Henry gave him no further comfort till he heard that a slow fever had fixed upon him, and that it was generally believed that he was dying. Then the king somewhat relented towards the man who had been his dearest friend for almost twenty years;

¹ Esher Palace belonged to the see of Winchester, and is supposed to have been erected by Archbishop Waindleet, who proceeded Wolsey in that see about eighty years. It was a stately mansion, built of brick. The only part now remaining is an elegant gatehouse. The interior of the tower comprises three stories, the apartments in which are small and greatly dilapidated.

² Cavendish. The fool, it appears, was so much attached to his old master, the cardinal, that he would not leave him until forcibly carried off by six stout yeomen, who delivered him to the king. But other men, besides his poor buffoon, loved Wolsey dearly.

and he not only said that he would lose £20,000 rather than he should die, but he also sent his physicians, and some presents and tokens of friendship, to the cardinal. This seems to have had a wonderful effect upon Wolsey. And when the Court of King's Bench pronounced sentence against him, the king took him into his protection.

At this crisis the king had thought fit once more to summon a parliament. On the 1st of December a bill of impeachment against the cardinal, containing forty-four articles, mostly of a vague and ridiculous description, and signed by fourteen peers and all the law officers, was presented to the commons, who, after an eloquent speech from Thomas Cromwell, formerly secretary to Wolsey, but now in the king's service, threw it out. The cardinal now mended rapidly. If he had been allowed to retain his numerous church preferments he would still have been a very rich man; but he soon found that Henry had no intention of keeping this promise. In the beginning of the following year he was deprived of everything except the bishoprics of York and Winchester, and the far greater part of the revenue of the latter was appropriated by the king, who divided it among the Viscount Rochford, Anne Boleyn's father, the Duke of Norfolk, the Lord Sandis, Sir John Russell, and other laymen. In return, however, Wolsey received a free pardon and some plate, furniture, and a little money for present expenses. He was now permitted to come nearer to the court, and he removed from Esher to Richmond. But the party of Anne took the alarm, and he was presently ordered to reside in the north of England, within his archbishopric. Lingering at every stage, in the fond hope of being recalled to court, Wolsey travelled to York. Yet, when once there, his mind seemed reconciled to the change, and he devoted himself with wonderful zeal to his ecclesiastical duties. At the same time, casting off his courtly pride and arrogance, he became meek and mild as a primitive apostle—courteous and affable to all men. The gentlemen of Yorkshire he entertained at a plain but hospitable table; to the poor he gave liberal alms and (what was better) abundant employment to 300 of them in repairing the churches and houses of the see. His popularity in the course of a few months waxed great all over that county. But this winning of men's hearts did not suit the party who now ruled at court, and who were alarmed, not only at the cardinal's popularity, but also at a correspondence he was carrying on with the French king and with the pope.

The clergy of York, delighted with their metropolitan, waited upon Wolsey in a body, and begged that he would be installed in his cathedral according to the custom of his predecessors. Wolsey consented, on condition that the thing should be done with as little pomp as possible; and the first Monday after All-Saints was fixed for the ceremony. On the 4th of November, three days before that fixed for the ceremony, as the lord-cardinal was sitting at dinner in his house at Cawood, near York, he was told that the Earl of Northumberland had arrived from court, and was dismounting in the yard. He expressed regret that he had not arrived before dinner began, for the earl had been brought up in his household, and he did not doubt that he had been chosen as the bearer of good news from the king. He arose with a cheerful countenance to welcome him as he came into the hall. Northumberland, according to an eye-witness, was

GATEWAY OF CAWOOD PALACE.[1]—From a view by Whittock.

much affected, and hesitated for awhile, but at length he laid a trembling hand on the old man's shoulder, and said, in a faltering voice, "My lord, I arrest you of high treason." For a season Wolsey stood rooted to the ground, mute as well as motionless; and when he recovered speech, it was only to utter unmanly and unavailing lamentations, accompanied by wretched tears. Passive as a doomed victim of an Eastern sultan, he followed Northumberland. When he reached Sheffield Park, the seat of the Earl of Shrewsbury, steward of the king's household, he was sick and faint, and soon after his arrival he was seized with a dysentery, which confined him to his bed for a fortnight. On resuming his slow journey he was so weak as scarcely to be able to sit on his mule. On the third evening he reached Leicester Abbey, where he was received at the gate by the monks, holding lighted torches, the hour being late. "Father," said he to the abbot, as he dismounted, "I am come to lay my bones among you." The monks carried him to his bed, from which he never rose again. In the course of the following day and night he swooned repeatedly; and on the second morning his servants, whose warm affection proves that there must have been good and amiable qualities in him, saw that he was dying. He called to him Kingston, the lieutenant of the Tower, who had been sent down to take charge of his person, and said, "Master Kingston, I pray you have me commended most humbly to his majesty, and beseech him, on my behalf, to call to his gracious remembrance all matters that have passed between us from the beginning, especially respecting Queen Catherine and himself, and then shall his conscience know whether I have offended him or not. He is a prince of most royal courage, and hath a princely heart—for, rather than miss or want any part of his will, he will endanger one half of his kingdom. And I do assure you, I have often kneeled before him in his privy chamber, sometimes for three hours together, to persuade him from his appetite, and could not prevail. And, Master Kingston, this I will say—had I but served God as diligently as I have served the king, he would not have given me over in my gray hairs." The cardinal expired as the clock was striking eight, on the morning of the 29th of November, in the sixtieth year of his age; and was at midnight, without any solemnity, buried in our Lady's Chapel, in the church of the monastery.[2]

The faithful Cavendish, his chamberlain, who witnessed his last moments, went on from Leicester to announce the event at court. He found the king amusing himself with archery in the park of Hampton, that stately pile which Wol-

---

[1] Cawood is a small town ten miles south of York, where the Archbishops of York had a palace or castle as early as the tenth century. The castle was dismantled and in great part demolished at the conclusion of the war between Charles I. and the parliament. The gateway, the only part now remaining, was built by Archbishop Kemp.   [2] Cavendish; Godwin; Fiddes.

sey had built and richly furnished, and had presented as a free gift to his sovereign. When his sport was done Henry listened to the mournful messenger. At first he showed some feeling, but this lasted a very little while, and then, with great eagerness, he questioned Cavendish touching a sum of £1500, which, as he had been told, the cardinal had concealed in some secret place. This was all the solicitude he showed about the death of so devoted a servant.

Nearly a year before the cardinal's death, and immediately after his surrender of the great seal, Henry had formed a new cabinet, from which churchmen were carefully excluded. The Duke of Norfolk, Anne Boleyn's uncle, became president of the council; but a still greater share of power fell to Charles Brandon, Duke of Suffolk and lord-marshal, and to the father of Anne Boleyn, Viscount Rochford, who soon afterwards was created Earl of Wiltshire. But a chancellor was still wanting, and this honour was thrust upon the unwilling shoulders of Sir Thomas More. More was a conscientious and zealous Catholic, who showed that he could face the scaffold for his religious opinions; but, a little before this time, chance had introduced into the councils of the king one who was equally zealous for the doctrines of the Reformation.[2] It chanced that Dr. Gardiner, then secretary to Henry, and Dr. Fox, supped with a gentleman of good family, named Cressy, at a time when the grand topic of conversation was the divorce of Queen Catherine. During supper a grave and learned man, who was tutor in the family, ventured to say, that the proper way of settling that tedious matter would be to have it discussed and determined by learned and holy doctors, upon the sole authority of the Word of God, without any further reference to the pope. When this conversation was reported to Henry, he said, "that the man who spoke thus had the right sow by the ear."[3] This man was Thomas Cranmer, who was immediately summoned to court, and ordered to draw up his opinions in writing. He was soon named chaplain to the king, and sent to reside in the house of the Earl of Wiltshire, Anne Boleyn's father, where a stimulus to exertion could hardly be wanting. But Cranmer had already a higher incentive; and there can be little doubt that many of his friends and associates, as well as he himself, saw the vantage-ground they might gain for the new doctrines. His main argument was sufficiently simple—it was, that the laws of God, as laid down in the Bible, and confirmed by the

RUINS OF LEICESTER ABBEY.[1]—From a view by Sargent.

---

[1] Leicester possessed several religious establishments, the principal of which was the Abbey of St. Mary Pré or de Pratis, founded for Black or Augustinian canons, by Robert Bossu, Earl of Leicester, A.D. 1143. Its revenue at the dissolution was £1062, 0s. 4d. gross, or £951, 14s. 5d. clear. Masses of its ruins still remain.

[2] Mr. Froude has no doubt of Sir Thomas More's having been a bitter persecutor, and of his presenting in this respect a very unfavourable contrast to Wolsey. "The Protestants," he says, "although from the date of the meeting of the parliament and Wolsey's fall, their ultimate triumph was certain, gained nothing in its immediate consequences. They suffered rather from the eagerness of the political reformers to clear themselves from complicity with heterodoxy; and the bishops were even taunted with the spiritual dissensions of the realm, as an evidence of their indolence and misconduct. Language of this kind boded ill for the 'Christian brethren;' and the choice of Wolsey's successor for the office of chancellor soon confirmed their apprehensions. Wolsey had chastised them with whips; Sir Thomas More would chastise them with scorpions. And the philosopher of the *Utopia*, the friend of Erasmus, whose life was of blameless beauty, whose genius was cultivated to the holiest attainable perfection, was to prove to the world that the spirit of persecution is no peculiar attribute of the pedant, the bigot, or the fanatic, but may co-exist with the fairest graces of the human character. The lives of remarkable men usually illustrate some emphatic truth. Sir Thomas More may be said to have lived to illustrate the necessary tendencies of Romanism in an honest mind convinced of its truth; to show that the test of sincerity in a man who professes to regard orthodoxy as an essential of salvation, is not the readiness to endure persecution, but the courage that will venture to inflict it." (By orthodoxy the author must mean Roman Catholic orthodoxy, not what is held to be orthodoxy by religious communions which hold all persecution for conscience sake to be the veriest heterodoxy.)—See Froude's *History of England*, vol. ii. p. 73.

[3] Todd's *Life of Cranmer*; Le Bas; *Biography Brit.* article "Cranmer."

ancient fathers, did not permit a man to marry his brother's widow; and his treatise was soon finished and committed to the press—that mighty engine whose infant activity was stimulated by this controversy. By the advice of Wolsey, Henry had already sent agents to consult some of the foreign universities, but without any notion of making their decision final, or subversive of the pope's authority. He now consulted Oxford and Cambridge, judging that his own universities would not dare to offer any opposition to his absolute will; but he was mistaken. At Oxford the subject was debated with the utmost violence, and a convocation dissolved in confusion and uproar, without coming to any conclusion. The doctors and seniors, "in hopes of reward, or out of fear, gave their opinions concerning the matter such as they thought would please the king; but the juniors disputed it very eagerly, and could not be drawn to their minds." Upon this the king addressed a remonstrance to Oxford, recommending the more discreet and aged men to bring their juniors to greater order and conformity; and admonishing the young gentlemen,

THOMAS CRANMER, Archbishop of Canterbury.—After Holbein.

that if they went on to play the masters as they were beginning to do, they would find that it is not good to provoke hornets.¹

John Longland, Bishop of Lincoln and master of All-Souls College, the principal champion for the divorce in this Oxford controversy, was a prelate after the king's own heart. He manœuvred and threatened, and carried his point. But his letter to the king,² which was unknown to earlier historians, completely upsets the assertion that the university of Oxford was allowed

¹ *Irritare crabones* is the royal expression, borrowed from the Amphitruo of Plautus, act ii. sc. 2, v. 77.   ² *State Papers.*

to manage the question in their own way, and to decide impartially. Lord Herbert and the minute Anthony à Wood both stated the facts correctly, but their evidence has been overlooked by our historians. At Cambridge the same kind of opposition was overcome by the same arts and threats, and the seal of each university was, at last, affixed to a long paper declaring the marriage of Queen Catherine to be illegal.

The foreign universities, which could not be threatened, were bribed; and Henry's active agents, who were now numerous, scattered money in all directions. In Italy the faculties of Bologna, Padua, and Ferrara, and some hundreds of learned men, declared for Henry. In Germany the power of the emperor was more prevalent than English money, and not a single university would justify the divorce. Whether Protestants or Catholics, all the German doctors, with a few exceptions, loudly condemned the project. Luther himself told Barnes, one of the agents in those parts, that it would be more lawful for Henry to have two wives at the same time, than to divorce Catherine for the purpose of marrying another woman; and the mild Melancthon seems to have entertained the same opinion. In France it was determined by the court to make a good bargain. Francis represented how dangerous it would be at that moment to irritate Charles, who still held his two sons as hostages; but, upon Henry munificently giving up a claim of 500,000 crowns and the lily of diamonds, and advancing the sum of 50,000 crowns, he consented that his universities should entertain the great subject. But still the learned of France were very dilatory in the cause, and the leading churchmen kept their eyes fixed upon the proceedings of the pope.

In the month of March, Clement, yielding to the personal application of Charles, who was then in Italy, published a breve forbidding Henry to contract a new marriage, under pain of excommunication. A few days after this the Earl of Wiltshire arrived at the head of a new embassy, which was instructed to use all kinds of means to prevail upon both pope and emperor to consent to the divorce. Clement received them in a mild, conciliating manner, but Charles was disgusted and irritated at the sight of the father of Anne Boleyn, whose employment in this mission showed a want both of tact and of delicacy. "Stop, sir," said the emperor to the Earl of Wiltshire, "let your colleagues speak—you are a party in this cause." The earl replied, smartly, that he was there as the representative of his sovereign, not as father of Anne Boleyn: but neither his self-possession, nor his liberal promises of money, produced any favourable effect upon Charles, who said that he would never sell the honour of his good aunt Catherine. Cranmer remained at Rome to convince the pope; the Earl of Wiltshire and the rest returned homeward through France, where the earl remained some time to urge on the unwilling universities. After many intrigues, the universities of Paris, Orleans, Toulouse, Angers, and Bourges, voted that the marriage of Catherine was contrary to the laws of God: the other French universities were not consulted, or, if they were, their answers were suppressed as unfavourable to Henry. But all these opinions rested upon the supposition that the marriage between Prince Arthur and Catherine had been consummated. The queen persisted in her solemn assertion that it had not, and the king could not prove the contrary.[1]

Cranmer, finding that he could do no good at Rome, went into Germany, where, some time after, he committed himself to the Reformed doctrines, by the decided step of marrying the niece of his friend Osiander, the Protestant pastor of Nürnberg. He kept the match a secret, however, for the time was not yet come in which he could advantageously break with the Church of Rome. There was wanting, to carry forward in England the important changes that had already begun on the Continent, a spirit more resolute than that of Cranmer, and this spirit had been already found in Thomas Cromwell.

Cromwell was the son of a blacksmith at Putney. As his father rose in wealth or condition, and became a brewer or a fuller, he was enabled

THOMAS CROMWELL, Earl of Essex.—After Holbein.

to give his son a tolerable education, including a little Latin. In his youth Thomas went to the Continent, where he learned several foreign languages. His first occupation seems to have been that of a clerk in the English factory at Antwerp: he afterwards served as a trooper under the Constable Bourbon, and followed that desperate leader to the sack of Rome. When peace was restored to Italy he returned to his commercial pursuits, and worked in the counting-house of a merchant at Venice. After this strange career, in which he acquired a deep knowledge of the world, he bent his steps towards England, where he took up the study and profession of the law. He soon attracted the notice of the great Wolsey, who took him into his household, appointed him his solicitor, and employed him in the dissolution of the monasteries, and as chief agent in the foundation of his colleges. In these offices he acquired wealth, and the hatred of the monastic bodies. He was soon returned as a member to the House of Commons, where his ready address and talent for business were conspicuous. As far as comported with an ambitious nature, he seems to have been attached to his old master, and when Wolsey was disgraced he followed him to Esher. This retirement was ill suited to such a mind; and he soon rode back to London and to court, saying that there he would "either make or mar." It is quite certain, however, that Wolsey, who had a great reliance upon his talents and his fidelity, and who, a few days after, wrote to implore him to "employ all his wit, good-will, and policy, in all places where he should think good might be done for his unfortunate friend,"[2] did not consider that Cromwell was deserting him, but saw his departure for court with pleasure and with hope. Indeed, it was at this juncture, and a very few days after his leaving his patron, that Cromwell made the eloquent speech in parliament in his defence. It is assumed, and very reasonably, that both Cromwell and the parliament, in rejecting the bill of impeachment, had received orders from the king to that effect, but it is not quite so fair to assume that Cromwell, who showed a grateful heart in other respects, did not use his newly-acquired influence over Henry's mind to the advantage of his old master. Cromwell played his part so well at court, that he was confirmed in the stewardship of the lands of the monasteries which had been dissolved under Wolsey, and was admitted frequently to personal conference with the king. At the critical moment when the weaker minds of Henry and his courtiers were wavering and half alarmed at the firm opposition of the pope, he asked for an audience, in which, after some necessary circumlocution, he said that the chief embarrassment was owing to the timidity of the king's ministers, who stood too much in awe of vulgar opinion, and that the best way to decide the question of the divorce was, to deny the

---

[1] Le Grand; Herbert; Hall; Godwin.

[2] Letter from Wolsey to Cromwell, dated Esher, 18th December, 1529, published in State Papers. The original holograph is in the Cottonian Collection of MSS., British Museum.

authority of the pope altogether—to rest upon the opinions already received from the universities, and the confirmation of the English parliament, which it was easy to obtain. Going further than this, Cromwell even recommended the king to follow the example of the German princes who had received the new religion, and declare himself the supreme head of his own church. He demonstrated that, by the present division of the spiritual and temporal powers, Henry was only half a king; and that, to have the full exercise of authority, the bishops and clergy ought to be made wholly dependent upon the crown, and not allowed to hold anything from the pope. No doctrine could be more palatable to the king, whose greedy imagination already fattened on the wealth of the ecclesiastical estate; and, without pretending to turn Protestant (which he never did), he resolved to follow the advice of Cromwell, who was forthwith sworn of his privy council.

It was not likely that the great churchmen would concur in this grand project, but it was presently seen that the clergy of England were now powerless.[1] By the advice of Cromwell the whole body were involved in a præmunire, or accused as fautors and abettors of Wolsey, in having acknowledged his authority as legate, which authority, as we have mentioned, had been confirmed by the king himself. At the same time, Henry and Cromwell took care to let the clergy, who, in great alarm, had assembled in convocation, that the royal wrath might be assuaged by a round sum of money. The convocation offered a present of £100,000. The king did not complain of the amount, but he refused to accept it or give any pardon unless, in the preamble to their grant, they formally acknowledged him to be "the protector and only supreme head of the church and clergy of England." For three whole days the clergy debated on this unexpected proposition. Many were averse to any such clause, but the majority, dreading the king's violence of temper, inclined to admit it, with the limitation, *quantum per legem Christi licoat* (as far as may be by the law of Christ). "Mother of God!" roared Henry to Cromwell, and the others whom he had appointed to manage this matter, "you have played me a shrewd turn. I thought to have made fools of those prelates, and now you have so ordered the business that they are likely to make a fool of me, as they have done of you already. Go to them again, and let me have the business passed without any quantums or tantums: I will have no quantum nor no tantum in the matter, but let it be done out of hand."[2] In the end, however, Henry yielded, pocketed the £100,000, and let the limitation stand. Shortly after Sir Thomas More, as chancellor, attended by twelve peers, spiritual and temporal, went down to the House of Commons, where the chancellor declared all that the king had done touching his marriage with Catherine, "who before time had been wedded and bedded to his own brother;" and showed how the king, like a virtuous prince, for the safety of his conscience and for the peace of his kingdom, had consulted divers universities, not only at home but also abroad, even in the pope's dominions. Then Sir Bryan Tuke took out of a box twelve writings sealed (the answers of the universities), and read them to the house word by word. He also produced many other papers, and divers books written by doctors of foreign nations, but, as they were long, and the day was already spent, they were not read; and, after a severe trial of patience, the members were dismissed, with strict orders to tell all their neighbours in the country how just and righteous was the king's cause.[3]

---

[1] This was largely owing to their loss of moral influence. Speaking of the ecclesiastical courts in 1529, Mr. Froude says:— "The people might have endured better to submit to so enormous a tyranny, if the conduct of the clergy themselves had given them a title to respect, or if equal justice had been distributed to lay and spiritual offenders. 'Benefit of clergy,' unhappily, as at this time interpreted, was little else than a privilege to commit sins with impunity. The grossest moral profligacy in a priest was passed over with indifference; and so far from exacting obedience in her ministers to a higher standard than she required of ordinary persons, the church extended her limits under fictitious pretexts as a sanctuary for lettered villainy. Every person who could read was claimed by prescriptive usage as a clerk, and shielded under her protecting mantle; nor was any clerk amenable for the worst crimes to the secular jurisdiction, until he had been first tried and degraded by the ecclesiastical judges. So far was this preposterous exemption carried, that previous to the first of the 23d of Henry VIII., those who were within the degrees, might commit murder with impunity, the forms which it was necessary to observe in degrading a priest or deacon being so complicated as to amount to absolute protection.

"Among the clergy, properly so called, however, the prevailing offence was not crime, but licentiousness. A doubt has recently crept in amongst our historians, as to the credibility of the extreme language in which the contemporary writers spoke upon this painful topic. It will scarcely be supposed that the picture has been overdrawn in the act books of the consistory courts; and, as we see it there, it is almost too deplorable for belief, as well in its own intrinsic hideousness, and in the unconscious connivance of the authorities. Brothels were kept in London for the especial use of priests; the 'confessional' was abused in the most open and profligate manner. Cases occurred of the same frightful profanity, in the service of the mass, which at Rome startled Luther into Protestantism; and acts of incest between nuns and monks were too frequently exposed, to allow us to regard the detected instances. It may be said that the proceedings upon these charges prove, at least, that efforts were made to repress them." The author then relates cases showing that such priestly offenders compounded for absolution by payment of trifling fines.—See Froude, vol. i. p. 177.

[2] Bailey, *Life of Bishop Fisher*.

[3] *Herbert; Hall; Stow*. During this session of parliament one Richard Rose, cook to Fisher, Bishop of Rochester, put poison into the soup, with the intent of killing his master. The bishop escaped, but no fewer than sixteen of his servants were poisoned. The cook was thrown into a cauldron of hot water, and boiled alive at Smithfield!

Soon after prorogation of parliament, the king sent several lords of his council to Queen Catherine at Greenwich, to terrify her into submission, and to make her agree to abide by the decision of four of the bishops and four of the lay peers of England. The high-minded Spaniard was still firm, upon which she was removed to Windsor. In the month of July she was ordered to quit that royal residence. "I go," said she: "but, go where I may, I shall still be his lawful wife." She went to the Moor in Hertfordshire, a beautiful manor with a park, which had belonged to the see of York. From the Moor she soon went to Easthampstead, and thence to Ampthill, where she finally fixed her residence.

About the same time, to prove the orthodoxy of the king and court, Thomas Bilney, a learned and amiable man, was burned at Smithfield as an accursed heretic, for having attempted to expose the errors of Popery. This was a beginning to the atrocious system pursued during the rest of this reign, in which the Catholic clergy were plundered and hanged on the one side, and the professors of the Reformed religion were burned on the other, in pretty equal proportions. Sir Thomas More, whose great learning and wit did not exempt him from the persecuting spirit of the times,[1] took a melancholy part in some of the prosecutions against Protestants, but he had no taste for those instituted against his own church: he disapproved of the plan pursued with regard to the unfortunate queen; and, in other respects, seeing nothing but danger and disgrace in the retaining of office, he represented to the king that he was growing old, and had need of repose. After making many efforts to retain him, Henry accepted his resignation; and More withdrew to solitude and poverty on the 16th of May, 1532. On the 4th of June following, the seals were given to Sir Thomas Audley.[2]

Notwithstanding all that had passed, the pope made overtures for a reconciliation; but Henry, acting upon the grand plan of Cromwell, who was now the most influential person in his council, rejected the proposals with wrath and disgust, for an indispensable condition was that he should take back his wife and put away "a certain Lady Anne." Under the absolute guidance of Cromwell, the parliament—which was now frequently assembled, because in all matters, except money-bills, it did precisely what the court wished—passed an act for the abolition of the annates or first-fruits, which formed a very considerable item in the fees or taxes paid yearly to the pope; and at the same time they abrogated the authority of the clergy in convocation, and annexed that authority to the crown. On the 15th of November Clement signed a breve, declaring both Henry and Anne Boleyn excommunicated, unless they should separate; but this deed was laid by for some time.[3]

Henry was now exceedingly anxious to strengthen his alliance with the French king, and, in the course of the summer, he had induced Francis to agree to a meeting. His grace of England, who could move nowhere without Lady Anne, whom he had recently created Marchioness of Pembroke, proposed as an equable arrangement, that his grace of France should also bring his favourite lady to the meeting; but Francis, though no great moralist, declined the proposal. But this circumstance did not make the Marchioness of Pembroke stay at home, and she went with the king and a most splendid retinue to Calais. On the 21st of October Henry went to Boulogne, where Francis received him, and entertained him for four days. The two kings then repaired lovingly together to Calais, and there Henry requited the hospitality of his royal brother with balls and masks, in which the marchioness was the principal personage. There was an idle talk of a coalition to oppose the victorious Turks on the frontiers of Christendom; but the only business done was, the making of an agreement by which Francis bound himself to invite the pope to a conference at Marseilles, and to take part with Henry in case Clement should not cease his opposition.

It was altogether improbable that Francis should carry his point with the pope; but Henry did not wait the result of his application. "Much about St. Paul's Day," that is, either the 4th, or more probably the 25th, of January, 1533, between night and morning, Dr. Lee, one of the royal chaplains, was summoned to celebrate mass in a remote garret of the palace of Whitehall. On going there the astounded priest found the king attended only by Norris and Heneage, two of the grooms of his bed-chamber, and Anne Boleyn, with her train-bearer, Mrs. Savage, afterwards the Lady Berkeley,[4] from which he understood that more was meant than a mass. A court chaplain—and in such a court—was not likely to have many scruples, or the courage necessary to face the wrath of such a king; but it is said that Lee did not perform the marriage ceremony until Henry told him that the Church of Rome had at length decided in his favour, and that he had the pope's instrument under lock and key in his closet. This strange marriage party separated in silence and secrecy before it was daylight; and some of Henry's most confidential advisers knew not what had passed until several

---

[1] More, however, denied that he had ever been cruel to the heretics. We believe that *willingly* he never was. [2] Roper.

[3] Herbert; Le Grand; Burnet, *Hist. Reform.*
[4] Another account makes her father and mother, and her uncle the Duke of Norfolk, to have been present.

weeks after. Feeling, however, that this clandestine measure would embarrass the French, who had sent ambassadors to the pope, he despatched Anne's father to explain matters to Francis, and to request the immediate presence in England of a confidential French agent. To this agent Henry promised that he would keep the marriage a secret till the month of May, by which time it was calculated the interview between Francis and Clement would be over.[1]

CHAPTER VI.—CIVIL AND MILITARY HISTORY.—A.D. 1533—1537.

HENRY VIII.—ACCESSION, A.D. 1509—DEATH, A.D. 1547.

Cranmer appointed Archbishop of Canterbury—The divorce of Queen Catherine effected—Henry's attempts to be reconciled to the pope—Birth of Elizabeth, afterwards queen—Injurious treatment of Catherine—Power of the Popedom abolished in England—Henry declared head of the church—The "Holy Maid of Kent"—Her visions and prophecies—She and her adherents executed—Sir Thomas More and Bishop Fisher tried and imprisoned—Henry persecutes Papists and Protestants—Cruel execution of certain monks—Execution of Bishop Fisher—Sir Thomas More refuses the oath of supremacy—His cruel treatment in prison—His execution—Cromwell appointed the king's vice-gerent in ecclesiastical matters—His severe proceedings against those who denied the king's supremacy—Death of Queen Catherine—Anne Boleyn arrested on a charge of adultery—Imprisoned in the Tower—Her conduct in prison—Her trial before the council—Her execution—Cranmer's conduct and letter on the occasion—Henry marries Jane Seymour—His treatment of his daughter Mary—Dissolution of the monasteries—Hardships of the monks and nuns—Henry's tyrannical proceedings as head of the English church—They occasion discontent and revolt—Insurrections in several counties—Rebellion called the "Pilgrimage of Grace"—Demands of the rebels—Henry's answer—The rebellion suppressed—Cardinal Pole—His birth and early history—His writings against Henry—Death of Jane Seymour.

IN the meantime Cranmer had returned from Germany, and again taken up his residence with the family of Anne Boleyn. The see of Canterbury had been vacant several months by the death of Archbishop Warham, and the king now offered it to Cranmer, who, notwithstanding his being privately a married man, and now an entire convert to the doctrines of Luther, agreed to accept it as a Catholic. As Henry had still a lurking respect for the Church of Rome in spiritual matters, he insisted, notwithstanding his assumption of supremacy, that Cranmer should obtain the bull and pallium from the pope, and take the usual oaths. How Clement agreed to ratify the election is difficult to understand; but, taking less than the ordinary fees, he signed the bull on the 22d of February, and Cranmer was consecrated in the usual manner on the 30th of March, taking the oaths of canonical obedience to the pope, whom he was resolved to disobey, and having been named to the vacant see by his master upon the express understanding that he should so act. Before swearing, Cranmer *protested* that he did not intend by these oaths to the pope to restrain himself from anything that he was bound to, either by his duty to God or his king.[2] His obedience to the king was soon put to the test—he was immediately ordered to proceed with "the great cause of matrimony." On the 11th of April he wrote a letter to the king containing a formal request that, for the good of the realm and the security of the succession, that matter might be proceeded with. This letter, which was intended by them both to be submitted to the privy council, was not quite to Henry's taste; it was therefore sent back, and the archbishop wrote a second letter, on the same day, in which he styled himself "a poor wretch and much unworthy," and pressed on the royal mind the

---

[1] "Fallen on evil times, which greater wisdom and greater courage than had for many a century been found in the successors of St. Peter, would have failed to encounter successfully, Clement VII. remained, with all his cowardice, a true Italian; his errors were the errors of his age and nation, and were softened by the presence, in more than usual measure, of Italian genius and grace. Benevuto Cellini, who describes his character with much minuteness, has left us a picture of a hot-tempered but genuine and kind-hearted man, whose taste was elegant, and whose wit, from the playful spirit with which it was pervaded, and from a certain tendency to innocent levity, approached to humour. He was liable to violent bursts of feeling; and his inability to control himself, his gesticulations, his exclamations, and his tears, all represent to us a person who was an indifferent master of the tricks of dissimulation to which he was reduced, and whose weakness entitles him to pity, if not to respect. The Papacy had fallen to him at the crisis of its deepest degradation. It existed as a politically organized institution, which it was convenient to maintain, but from which the private hearts of all men had fallen away; and it depended for its very life on the support which the courts of Europe would condescend to extend to it. Among these governments, therefore, distracted as they were by mutual hostility, the pope was compelled to make his choice; and the fatality of his position condemned him to quarrel with the only prince on whom, at the outset of these complications, he had a right to depend."—*Froude*.

[2] There was, besides, the vow of chastity, and Cranmer was a married man!

necessity of stopping the tongues of the rude and ignorant people, and of licensing him, the archbishop, to proceed to the examination, final determination, and judgment of the great cause. This second letter, which fully admitted the king's rightful superiority to all law, whether ecclesiastical or civil, gave entire satisfaction to Henry, who forthwith submitted it to the council, and wrote a loving answer to the archbishop, authorizing him to proceed—always in due subordination and submission.[1]

The said cause now proceeded roundly. Parliament, receiving their impulse from Cromwell, passed an act prohibiting for ever all appeals to the court of Rome; and another, declaring that Queen Catherine should no longer be called queen, but Princess dowager of Wales, as widow to Prince Arthur, her first and only lawful husband. Thus backed by the authority of parliament, and by a fresh decision of the intimidated clergy assembled in convocation, who voted, by a large majority, that there was canonical proof of the consummation of Catherine's first marriage, Cranmer, on the 8th of May, travelled to Dunstable, about four miles from Ampthill, where the discarded queen was then residing. Having constituted a court, in which the Bishop of Lincoln acted as assessor, and Gardiner, Bishop of Winchester, the Bishops of London, Bath, and Lincoln, and three others, as counsel for the king, Cranmer sent Dr. Lee, who had so recently married Henry to Anne, to cite Catherine to appear. The queen refused; but great pains were taken to conceal from her the fact that this court intended to proceed to a final judgment. Cranmer and the rest wrote every day to the king or to Cromwell, to report progress. The citation having been repeated fifteen times in as many days, and Catherine not appearing, judgment was given against her on the 23d of May, by Cranmer, who pronounced her marriage to be null and invalid; and on the same day the archbishop announced his sentence to the king, asking for further instructions concerning the "second matrimony;" adding, "for the time of the coronation is so near at hand, that the matter requireth good expedition."[3] Having received the royal orders to that effect, Cranmer hurried from Dunstable back to Lambeth, where he held another ecclesiastical court; and on the 28th of May, to complete his job, he declared that his master had already been lawfully married to the Lady Anne; that their marriage was and had been public and manifest; and that he now confirmed it by his judicial and pastoral authority. On the 1st of June, 1533, only four days after the confirmation of her marriage at Lambeth, Anne, "being somewhat big with child," was crowned and anointed at Westminster, "with as great pomp and solemnity as ever was queen," Cranmer officiating and setting the crown upon her head.[4]

These doings were soon noised all over Europe, and on the 11th of July the pope annulled the judgment given by Cranmer, and published his bull of excommunication against Henry and Anne. A few days before this was done at Rome, Lord Mountjoy made a report to Henry's council of a conference he had had on the 3d of July, with the princess-dowager (Catherine) in her residence at Ampthill. He had found her grace there, "lying upon her pallet because she had pricked her foot with a spyne (thorn), so that she might not well stand nor go, and also sore annoyed with a cough." But her spirit was as resolute as ever; she would not submit to be called princess-dowager, saying that she was still a

DUNSTABLE PRIORY CHURCH.[2] Britton's Architectural Antiquities.

---

[1] *State Papers.* The original letters are preserved in the British Museum, and in the State Paper Office.

[2] The most interesting architectural remains in Dunstable is the priory church, founded by Henry I. in 1131. It is a good specimen of a mixed Norman and Early English structure, and is still used as the parish church. Several parts of it have been renewed.

[3] *State Papers.*

[4] *State Papers;* Sir Henry Ellis' *Collection of Original Letters;* Burnet, *Hist. Reform.,* Le Grand, Herbert, Stow, Godwin.

queen, and the king's true wife; that she came to the king "a clean maid, and thereupon was crowned and anointed queen, and had by the king lawful issue, and no bastard; wherefore the name of queen she would vindicate, challenge, and so call herself during her life." When Mountjoy told her that she had been separated and divorced, and that, by consent of all the lords spiritual and temporal, and of all the commons of the realm, the Lady Anne was anointed and crowned Queen of England, she replied that bribery and unfair means had been used; that universities, and convocations, and parliaments had no faculty to divorce; and that she still appealed to the court of Rome."[1]

Popular opinion (whatever was its worth) set full on the side of Catherine, and nothing was heard from one end of the kingdom to the other, but virulent abuse of "Nan Bullen." The monastic orders, who were smarting under past grievances, and who foresaw more serious ones, set no limits to their clamour, and some of them were bold enough to reprehend the king to his face.

In the meantime, Henry, at intervals, showed an earnest desire to be reconciled to the pope; and Francis, who had his own views of political advantage[2] therein, more constantly laboured to bring this about. He sent the French fleet to convey his holiness, and, after many delays, Clement kept his appointment, and arrived in the city of Marseilles in the month of October. When the meeting took place, Henry regretted his having promoted it, and did what he could to render it of no effect. The Duke of Norfolk, who was a zealous Catholic, and seems to have hoped for a reconciliation with the church, was suddenly recalled from France, and the Bishop of Winchester and Bryan were left to attend the conference at Marseilles. Francis refused to proceed with any other business until the pope had promised him to stretch his authority to the utmost in order to satisfy the King of England: but the surprise and displeasure of both were great, upon learning that the two English ambassadors had no authority from their court to treat or to enter into any definitive arrangement. Apparently at the suggestion of Francis, they spoke of referring the matter to a consistory, from which all the cardinals holding preferments under the emperor, were to be excluded as partial judges; but early in November, before Clement could give an answer to this proposition, Bonner arrived from England, and appealed, in the name of his master, from the pope to a general council of the church. This was rudely putting an end to the solemn conference at Marseilles, and the pope returned into Italy; but, before he went, he arranged a marriage (which afterwards proved a great curse to France) between his niece, Catherine of Medici, and the Duke of Orleans, the second son of the French monarch. The young lady had no money, and the unlucky match was otherwise considered very unequal. Francis told Henry that he had consented to it *solely* on his account, and to make up his quarrel with Rome: but this was not quite true, though such considerations may have had some weight. Such, however, was the power of England, that the French king and the pope were alike eager to overlook the insults they had received from Henry, and to renew negotiations with him. The witty Bishop of Bayonne, now Bishop of Paris, who had resided so long at the English court, was sent from Paris to London, from London to Paris, whence, in the middle of winter, he was hurried to Rome with letters and verbal messages to the pope from Henry, who appears to have been once more disposed to return to the obedience of the Apostolic See, upon condition that Clement should approve of, and solemnly sanction all that he had done. The vivacious bishop wrote to England to say that all was going on well, and to implore Henry to stop all proceedings in parliament of a religious nature. But Henry was vacillating and impatient, and Cromwell and others of his council had fully made up their minds to prevent any reconciliation with Rome; some of them acting from a sincere conviction of a spiritual kind, and some, it must be admitted, from a mere longing after the property and power of the church.[3]

On the 7th of September, while the pope was preparing for his voyage to Marseilles, Anne Boleyn was brought to bed. Whether it was that the king pretended to some knowledge in these occult matters, or whether it was that he had consulted the astrologers, he had made quite certain that the child would be a son and heir; and not only his disappointment, but also his wrath, was great when it proved to be a girl. Yet this ill-received child—the lion-hearted Eli-

---

[1] *State Papers.* There are two other very long letters on the same harrowing subject, written within a few weeks by the same Lord Mountjoy, who was or had been chamberlain to Catherine. In his first report, which is preserved in the British Museum, the words *princess-dowager* are scratched out with pen and ink. This was done by Catherine's own hand. In his second letter Mountjoy says, "on showing her the report, she called for pen and ink, and carefully struck out the words *princess-dowager* wherever they occurred." Every part of Mountjoy's letters is full of interest. In one of them he says that Catherine rested on the unfairness of pretending to try her cause "within the king's own realm, *before a man of his own making*, the Bishop of Canterbury, *whom she thinketh to be no person indifferent* (impartial) *in that behalf*."

[2] The French king had a project of forming a grand coalition against the emperor. Henry was to be a principal member, and the pope was to give it his sanction, and to co-operate *vi et armis* in Italy.

[3] Du Bellay's *Letters and Instructions*, given by Lo Grand; Herbert; Burnet.

zabeth—showed herself to be worth many men. Soon after this event the persecution of Queen Catherine was carried on more keenly than ever, that unfortunate woman (to use the language of the courtiers) "still persisting in her great stomach and obstinacy." The highest in rank, the most martial and chivalrous in reputation, durst not refuse themselves to the vile office of insulting a helpless woman. The Duke of Suffolk, the gentle Charles Brandon, waited upon her at Ampthill to explain her grievous misconduct in calling herself queen, and to tell her that she must instantly remove from that manor to Somersham, there to live with a reduced establishment, and with such servants alone as the king should be pleased to appoint.[1] The queen said that they might hew her in pieces, but she would still style herself wife and queen until the court of Rome should decide to the contrary; that they might bind her with ropes, and violently enforce her thereunto, but that, of her own will, she would never go from Ampthill, or take upon herself the state and condition of Princess-dowager of Wales. After a violent scene the Duke of Suffolk and his noble and worshipful mates (for he was accompanied by the Earl of Sussex, Sir William Poulet, and Dean Sampson) locked up the queen's chaplains, who maintained that she was right both in law and in religion, and then wrote to the king for further instructions, "trusting, by God's help," to make a comfortable end of the matter.[2] Two days after, the duke and the earl, and the doctors, were followed by Archbishop Lee and Bishop Tonstal, who told her that his highness, after being discharged of the marriage made with her, had contracted a new marriage with his dearest wife Queen Anne; and that for so much as, thanked be God, fair issue had already sprung, and more was likely to follow, by God's grace, the whole body of the realm, gathered together in parliament, had, for the establishment of this issue, made acts and ordinances to which she and all others must submit. The two prelates, however, reported to their master that her obstinacy was undiminished. It appears that some money was sent down to pay her debts, that she was removed by force, and that all persons who persisted in calling her queen were thrown into prison or otherwise punished with great severity.[3]

It was a very awkward time for absent-minded parsons, and for old men who could not easily get out of the routine of praying for Queen Catherine, which they had been in the habit of doing for twenty-five years. A mere slip of the tongue was considered of sufficient moment to be circumstantially reported by a bishop to a minister of state.

A.D. 1534. Soon after the Christmas holidays parliament met for the despatch of very important business; and being it rose (on the 30th of March) it wholly broke the ties which for so many centuries had united England with Rome. Acting on the impulse already received, the parliament prohibited every kind of payment and every kind of appeal to the pope, confirmed Henry's title of supreme head of the English church, and vested in the king alone the right of appointing to all bishoprics, and of deciding in all ecclesiastical causes. The royal assent to the bills which abolished the Papal power in England was given on the 30th of March; and as the definitive sentence of the Roman consistory was not pronounced until the 23d of March, it seems certain that the bills were not produced by that decision. They had been drawn up by Cromwell some months before; they had been passed through the commons and the lords before the 20th of March (the reader will attend to dates); and when Henry gave the finishing stroke to them it was not possible that the news of the proceedings at Rome could have reached London. These last proceedings, in a business which had seemed to be interminable, were very simple. Notwithstanding the expectations of the Bishop of Paris, the pope, awed by the still growing power of the emperor in Italy, found himself obliged to entertain the appeal of the emperor's aunt, and to refer the whole matter to a consistory; and on the 23d of March, nineteen out of twenty-two cardinals pronounced Catherine's marriage valid and indissoluble, and hereupon the pope gave sentence. In the same parliament which proclaimed the spiritual independence of England, the marriage between Henry and Anne Boleyn was fully established as lawful; the Princess Mary, the daughter of Catherine, was set aside as illegitimate, and the succession was[4] vested in the children of Queen

---

[1] For some time she was left almost in utter solitude, without any attendants. Her servants were commanded to swear that they would never call her queen, but only princess-dowager: those who refused the oath were dismissed or imprisoned—those who took it she would not retain.

[2] Original letter in the Museum, and published in *State Papers*. The letter, which is addressed to the king, is signed by all four.

[3] *State Papers*; letter of Lee (Archbishop of York) and Tonstal (Bishop of Durham) to the king's highness.

[4] "There is no known instance in family history, in which a brother and his two sisters appeared to be doomed to be each other's enemies by a destiny inseparable from their birth. so

Vol. I.

extraordinary as that of Edward and the two princesses Mary and Elizabeth. The legitimacy of Mary necessarily rendered Elizabeth illegitimate. The innocence of Anne Boleyn threw a deep shade over the nuptials of which Edward was the sole offspring. One statute had declared Mary to be illegitimate, for the sake of settling the crown on Elizabeth. The latter princess was condemned to the same brand to open the door for the nuptials with Edward's mother. Both were afterwards illegitimated, as it might seem, to exalt the lawful superiority of their brother Edward. At his accession Mary was in the thirty-second year of her age, Elizabeth in her fourteenth, and Edward in his ninth year. Mary was of an age to remember

Anne. It was also enacted that anything written, printed, or done, to the slander of the second marriage, or of the children therefrom proceeding, should be high treason, and that all persons of age should swear obedience to this same act of succession.[1]

During the same session, parliament and that tyrannical tribunal, the Star Chamber, between them, sent the Holy Maid of Kent and six of her abettors to the gallows. This Elizabeth Barton, a young woman of Aldington, in Kent, had been subject to fits and a strange kind of disease, which not only afflicted her inwardly, but, as often as her fit took her, so wonderfully distorted her mouth and other parts of her body, that most people were of opinion it could not proceed from any natural causes. As among the Turks of the present day, so was it with the English and other Christian nations in these ignorant times—idiocy was looked upon as a proof of God's favour, and epilepsy was considered as the best medium of heavenly revelations. The incoherent sentences which the Maid uttered were caught up as prophecies, and she herself was induced to believe that she was a prophetess. This was at a moment when the monks were irritated at Wolsey's suppression of a few monasteries, and when the nation was excited by the question of Henry's divorce. Richard Maister, the rector of the parish, advised her to retire into a nunnery, and he appears to have conceived the notion of turning her to some political account; but Bocking, a monk of Christ Church, Canterbury, who became her confessor, was her chief prompter. It is possible, however, that accomplices and principal were alike, in part, the dupes of their own deception, as frequently happened in cases of similar imposture. From Kent the fame of her prophecies soon spread to London and other parts of the kingdom. The king, whose curiosity was excited, showed a collection of her sybilline leaves to Sir Thomas More, who told him that he found nothing in her words worth notice. As long as the Holy Maid limited her prophecies to obscure people she was safe enough, but as soon as she meddled with state matters her neck was in danger. She announced that she had, in a vision, seen God and Cardinal Wolsey together, and had heard the Almighty declare that, unless the lord-cardinal used his authority properly, it should be sorely laid to his charge. She, however, was not seriously molested during Wolsey's time. Her doom was precipitated by her venturing to prophesy, that if Henry put away Catherine, he would die some infamous death within seven months, and be succeeded on the throne by Catherine's daughter. The party that had chosen her for their instrument, not only took down her revelations in writing, but caused them to be printed and circulated. The jealous eye of the government was upon them; and, of a sudden, Elizabeth Barton and a number of her accomplices were apprehended.[2] Instead of being tried in the usual courts, they were brought up to the Star Chamber, which, in the month of November, 1533, sentenced them to confess their imposture on a Sunday, at St. Paul's Cross. After they had done this they were all conveyed back to prison. The imposition was thus laid bare; and Henry further proved that the Holy Maid was no prophetess, by outliving the term she had fixed. Thus she and her companions might have been safely dismissed with contempt, while the exposure and the long imprisonment they had undergone might have been deemed punishment sufficient for such an offence; but the majesty of Henry was not to be so easily satisfied, and he submitted their case to the slavish and brutalized parliament, who passed a bill of attainder of treason against the Maid; Bocking, the monk of Canterbury; Maister, the rector of Aldington;

---

with bitterness the wrongs done to an innocent mother. Her few though faithful followers were adherents of the ancient religion, to which honour and affection, as well as their instruction and example, bound her. The friends, the teachers, the companions of Edward, were, in many instances, bound to the Reformation by conscience. Many others had built their character and their greatness upon its establishment. The pretensions of young Elizabeth were somewhat more remote."—Sir James Mackintosh, *History of England.*

[1] Of the act 20th Henry VIII. cap. 13, whereby, for the better security of the realm, it was enacted—"That any person who, by words, writing, or otherwise, deprives the king or queen of any one of their just titles, shall be held guilty of high treason," Mr. Froude says:—"The terrible powers which were thus committed to the government, lie on the surface of this language; but comprehensive as the statute appears, it was still further extended by the lawyers. In order to fall under its penalties, it was held not to be necessary that positive guilt should be proved in any one of the offences specified; it was enough if a man refused to give satisfactory answers when subjected to official examination. At the discretion of the king or his ministers, the active consent to the supremacy might be required of any person on whom they pleased to call, under penalty to the recusant of the dreadful death of a traitor. So extreme a measure can only be regarded as a remedy for an evil which was also extreme; and, as on the return of quiet times, the parliament made haste to repeal a law which was no longer required; so in the enactment of that law, we are bound to believe that they were not betraying English liberties in a spirit of careless complacency; but that they believed truly that the security of the state required unusual precautions. The nation was standing with its sword half-drawn in the face of an armed Europe, and it was no time to permit dissensions in the camp. Toleration is good, but even the best things must abide their opportunity; and although we may regret that in this grand struggle for freedom, success could only be won by the aid of measures which bordered upon tyranny; yet here also the even hand of justice was but commending the chalice to the lips of those who had made others drink it to the dregs. They only were likely to fall under the treason act, who for centuries had fed the rack and the stake with sufferers for opinions."—Froude's *History of England*, vol. ii. p. 351.

[2] According to Hall, the matter was investigated by the "great labour, diligence, and painstaking of the Archbishop of Canterbury and the Lord Cromwell, and one called Hugh Latimer, a priest, which, shortly after, was made Bishop of Worcester."

Dering, a monk; Gold, bachelor of divinity; Rich, a friar of the order of the Observants; and Risby, a gentleman; and of misprision of treason against several other persons who had had communications with her, and had concealed her treasonable predictions. On the 21st of April, 1534, while parliament was sitting, all the seven victims attainted of treason were drawn to Tyburn.[1]

Among those accused of holding correspondence with the Holy Maid of Kent were Edward Thwaites, gentleman; Thomas Laurence, registrar to the archdeacon of Canterbury; John Fisher, Bishop of Rochester; and Sir Thomas More, late lord-chancellor. The venerable Fisher, the admired of Erasmus, was one of the most learned prelates of that age: he had been the friend of Henry from his youth and first accession—the friend of his father and of his grandmother, the Countess of Richmond, who, on her death-bed, recommended him as a good and wise counsellor for her inexperienced grandson. But Fisher was attached to his threatened church, and averse to the new marriage. The old bishop was told by Cromwell that he would be pardoned this offence if he would plead guilty, and throw himself upon the king's mercy; but he preferred justifying his conduct, and, being confined to his chamber by sickness, he sent a spirited letter to the House of Lords. He acknowledged that he had conversed with the Maid of Kent, and had even heard her utter her prophecies touching the king's death. It was also true, he said, that he had not mentioned these discourses to his sovereign; but his silence could not be criminal, because the prophetess had not spoken of any violent attempts against the king's life, but merely of a visitation of Providence; and because she had told him that she had communicated the revelation or vision to the king herself, and *he well knew that she had been admitted to a private audience by the king*. The lords, however, pronounced him guilty of misprision, or concealment, of treason; and he was forced to compound with the crown. The name of Sir Thomas More was erased from the bill (though his innocence was not more clearly established than that of his friend Fisher); and it is supposed to have been introduced into it for the sole purpose of terrifying him into an approval of the new marriage, and other changes which he was known in his heart to condemn. About a fortnight after, More and Fisher were called upon to take the new oath of allegiance, as recently voted by parliament, to the heirs of the king's body begotten, or to be begotten, of his beloved lawful wife, Queen Anne. Neither of them objected to swear to the succession, excluding the Princess Mary, as it had been established by the estates of the kingdom; but both scrupled to swear to certain doctrinal points which were involved in the oath. For example, they were called upon fully to approve the marriage with Anne Boleyn; and to swear that the former marriage had always been unlawful, and that the Church of Rome had no power to grant dispensations in such cases. Bishop Fisher declared that he could not take the whole of the oath with a safe conscience; upon which, against the wishes of Archbishop Cranmer, who would have been satisfied with his swearing to the succession without the theological part, he was committed to the Tower. Sir Thomas More expressed his objections in discreet and qualified terms; but he was, nevertheless, taken into the custody of the abbot of Westminster; and, upon a second refusal, was also sent to the Tower. Both bishop and chancellor were attainted of misprision of treason for refusing the oaths, and were condemned to imprisonment for life with forfeiture of their property, and both were treated with infamous severity in their prison. Fisher, in his seventy-sixth year, was left in sickness and pain, without clothes to cover him, and without proper food to eat; and More was only relieved from a similar condition by the charity of his relations and friends, and the filial heroism of his favourite daughter, Margaret Roper. While these two conscientious men lay in the Tower, " being not to be drawn by any persuasions to be conformable to the new law," all classes of people swore, as rapidly as Henry could wish them, being terrified out of their senses. As the oath had not been very nicely defined by parliament, and as Henry was not likely to pay much respect to any limitations prescribed by that subservient body, he altered it, and stretched it just as he thought fit—forcing, for example, the whole body of the clergy to declare, upon oath, whatever he chose to dictate, including several things wholly incompatible with their profession and existence as a Romish priesthood. If he had really made up his mind to change the religion of his country, and to adopt the Reformed faith, all this might have been intelligible and consistent enough; but, at the very same moment, he was actually burning people in Smithfield for differing from the Church of Rome—making no distinction as to sects, but consuming in the same flames Lollards, Lutherans, and Anabaptists. To free himself from all suspicion of favouring either Luther or any of the authors of the new opinions, he began to prosecute indiscriminately "all that sort of men whom the vulgar called heretics." On the 22d of July, during the prorogation of

---

[1] *Hall.* The annalist probably witnessed the execution of these seven persons. He says, very coolly, "They had most justly deserved it."

parliament, John Frith, "a very learned young man, of an excellent and godly wit," who had been long in trouble for the making of a book against purgatory, and for expressing certain opinions about transubstantiation and consubstantiation, and one Andrew Hewet, "a very simple and utterly unlearned young man, and a tailor," who told the bishops that he believed as his friend John Frith believed, were burned at one stake in Smithfield, as accursed heretics.[1]

In the month of November parliament re-assembled, and, under the guidance of Cromwell, passed a variety of acts, which had all for their object the erecting of Henry into a sort of lay-pope, with full power to define and punish heresies, and to support whatever he might deem the true belief or the proper system of church government. The first-fruits and tenths were now annexed to the crown for ever, and a new oath of supremacy was devised and taken by the bishops.

A.D. 1535. Some of the monks—the poorest orders were the boldest—refused either to take the oath, or to proclaim in their churches and chapels that the pope was Antichrist. The system pursued in regard to them was very simple and expeditious; they were condemned of high treason and hanged, their fate in the latter respect being sometimes, but not always, milder than that allotted to the Lutherans and other Protestants, who were burned. Cromwell had no bowels for the poor monks; and the gentler and more virtuous Cranmer seems to have done little or nothing to stop these atrocious butcheries. A jury now and then hesitated to return a verdict, but they were always bullied into compliance by Cromwell and his agents, who sometimes threatened to hang them instead of the prisoners. On the 5th of May John Houghton, prior of the Charter-house in London; Augustine Webster, prior of the Charter-house of Belval; Thomas Lawrence, prior of the Charter-house of Exham; Richard Reynolds, a doctor of divinity and a monk of Sion; and John Hailes, vicar of Thistleworth, were drawn, hanged, and quartered at Tyburn, their heads being afterwards set over the city gates. On the 18th of June, Exmew, Middlemore, and Nudigate, three other Carthusian monks, suffered for the same cause. On all these conscientious men, who preferred death to what they considered a breach of their duty as Catholic priests, the horrible sentence of the law was executed in all its particulars. They were cut down alive, had their bowels torn out, and were then beheaded and dismembered. They suffered on account of the oath of supremacy; but between the executions there was an atrocious interlude of a more doctrinal

[1] Herbert; Hall; Stow; Godwin.

nature. On the 25th of May there were examined in St. Paul's nineteen men and five women, natives of Holland, who had openly professed the doctrines of the Anabaptists, and denied the

INNER GATE OF THE CHARTER-HOUSE, LONDON.[2]—From a drawing by J. W. Archer.

real presence of the body and blood of Christ in the bread and wine of the sacrament. Fourteen of them were condemned to the flames: two, a man and woman, suffered in Smithfield; the remaining twelve were sent to other towns, there to be burned for example's sake, and for the vivid manifestation of the king's orthodoxy.

But greater victims were now stricken; for, casting aside all feelings except those of vengeance, Henry had resolved to shed the blood of Fisher and of More. The aged bishop was put upon his trial for having maliciously and traitorously said that the king, in spiritual matters, could not be the head of the church; and he was sentenced in the usual manner to die the death of a traitor. While he lay in the Tower, in respect for his sufferings in the cause of the church, his great age, learning, and unquestionable virtue, a cardinal's hat was sent to him from Rome. "Ha!" cried the savage Henry, "Paul may send him the hat; I will take care that he have never a head to wear it on." Accordingly, on the 22d day of June, of this same year of blood, the old prelate was dragged out of the Tower and beheaded. His gray head was stuck upon London bridge,

[2] Over this gate the head of John Houghton was exposed. Within the gate are the initials I H, according to the tradition of the place, a memorial of John Houghton. They are figured in the brickwork of one of the old buildings, together with a cross.

turned towards the Kentish hills, among which he had passed so many happy and respected years. His body, by the king's orders, was exposed naked to the gaze of the populace, and then thrown into an humble grave in Barking church-yard, without coffin or shroud.[1] Such was the end of Henry's oldest friend—of an amiable and most accomplished man - of one of the most indefatigable restorers of ancient learning.

Without losing time, the ruthless king proceeded against Sir Thomas More. Archbishop Cranmer, Cromwell, and others, had waited upon him several times in the Tower, with the object of winning him over, or inducing him to take the oath of supremacy, in order to save his life: but More, though he had sometimes shown a timidity of disposition, had now fully made up his mind to die rather than to act contrary to his conscience. Sharp interrogatories were ministered to him in his dungeon for the purpose of entrapping him. After many other questions, he was asked whether he would obey the king's highness as supreme head on earth of the Church of England, immediately under Christ; to this he said that he could make no answer. He was next asked whether he would consent and approve the king's highness' marriage with the most noble Queen Anne to be good and lawful, and affirm that the marriage with the Lady Catherine, princess-dowager, was, and is, unjust and unlawful; he replied, that he never did speak nor meddle against the same, but that he would make no further answer. Finally, they demanded whether he, being one of the king's subjects, was not bound to recognize the supremacy, as all other subjects were bound thereto by the statute; he replied again that he could make no answer.[2]

Before this he had said, in an affecting letter, "I am the king's true faithful subject and daily beadsman. I pray for his highness, and all his, and all the realm. I do nothing harm; I say no harm; I think none harm; and wish everybody good: and if this be not enough to keep a man alive, in good faith I long not to live. I am dying already; and since I came here have been divers times in the case that I thought to die within one hour. And, I thank our Lord, I was never sorry for it, but rather sorry when I saw the pang past; and, therefore, my poor body is at the king's pleasure. Would to God my death might do him good!"[3] But this mixture of an almost heavenly meekness with an heroic firmness made no impression on the king, who was now drunk and mad with the heady spirit of absolutism. By his orders they had deprived that glorious wit and scholar of the sweet solace of his books—Rich, the king's solicitor, having been sent to the Tower to take them all from him. Nay, they had even deprived him of pen, and ink, and paper. Some commiserating soul, however, put some scraps of paper in his way; and on such materials, and with a piece of charcoal, he wrote his last letter to his beloved child. At length, after a year's most trying imprisonment, he was brought out of the Tower, led on foot through the crowded streets to Westminster Hall, and there arraigned of high treason. He appeared in that court, where he had once presided as an upright judge, in a coarse woollen gown, bearing about him frightful evidences of a rigorous confinement. His hair had become white, his face was pallid and emaciated, and he was obliged to support himself on a staff. But the mind was much less bowed and bent, and some of his old wit and vivacity soon lighted up his sunken eye; and his vile judges—the slavish instruments of a despot—dreaded his eloquence, and the sympathy which the mere sight of him excited. They attempted to overpower and confound him with the length and wordiness of the indictment; but, after declining an offer of pardon upon condition of doing the king's will, he entered upon a clear and eloquent defence, stripping the clauses of their false coverings, and exposing them in their nakedness and nothingness. But his doom was fixed by those who had put themselves above all law or scruples of conscience. The infamous Rich, the solicitor-general, who was afterwards created Lord Rich, deposed that, in a private conversation he had had with the prisoner in the Tower, More said, "The parliament cannot make the king head of the church, because it is a civil tribunal without authority in spiritual matters." More denied that he had spoken these words; and he remarked upon the character which Rich had borne in the world, and which was so bad as to render even his oath unworthy of belief. Two witnesses were produced to support the charge made by Rich; but, in their case, conscience got the better of authority, and they declared that, though they were in the room, they did not pay attention to what was said. The judges, who were assisted by the Duke of Norfolk and other great men appointed by the king, laid it down as law that silence *was* treason, and the jury, without any hesitation, returned a verdict of guilty. When sentence had been pronounced, More rose to address the court: he was coarsely interrupted. He tried again, and was again interrupted; but on a third attempt he was allowed to proceed. He told them that what he had hitherto concealed he would now openly declare, and he boldly proclaimed that the oath of supremacy was utterly unlawful. He regretted to differ from the noble lords whom he saw on the bench, but his con-

---

[1] *Cardinal Pole; Hall; Stow; Fuller.*
[2] *State Papers, published by government.*
[3] *Roper's Life of More, by Singer.*

science would not permit him to do otherwise. He declared that he had no animosity against them, and that he hoped that, even as St. Paul was present and consented to the death of Stephen, and yet was afterwards a companion saint in heaven, so they and he should all meet together hereafter. "And so," he concluded, "may God preserve you all, and especially my lord the king, and send him good counsel!" As he moved from the bar his son rushed through the hall, fell upon his knees, and begged his blessing. With the axe turned towards him he walked back to the Tower, amid the great wonderment and commiseration of the citizens. On reaching the Tower-wharf his dear daughter, Margaret Roper, forced her way through the officers and halbardiers that surrounded him, clasped him round the neck, and sobbed aloud. Sir Thomas consoled her, and she collected sufficient power to bid him farewell for ever; but, as her father moved on, she again rushed through the crowd and threw herself upon his neck. Here the weakness of nature overcame him, and he wept as he repeated his blessing and his Christian consolation. The people wept too; and his guards were so much affected that they could hardly summon up resolution to separate the father and daughter. After this trial the bitterness of death was past. The old man's wit flashed brightly in his last moments. When told that the king had mercifully commuted the hanging, drawing, and quartering into simple decapitation, he said, "God preserve all my friends from such royal favours!" This happy vein accompanied him to the very scaffold. The frame-work was weak, and some fears were expressed lest the scaffold might break down. "Mr. Lieutenant," said More, " see me safe up, and for my coming down let me shift for myself." The executioner, as usual, asked forgiveness. "Friend," said More, " thou wilt render me to-day the greatest service in the power of man; but my neck is very short; take heed, therefore, that thou strike not awry, for the sake of the credit of thy profession." He was not permitted to address the spectators, but he ventured to declare that he died a faithful subject and a true Catholic. After prayers said he placed his head upon the block, but he bade the headsman hold his hand until he removed his beard, saying, with a smile, " My beard has never committed any treason." Then the blow fell, and the neck was severed at once. His head was picked up, and fixed upon London bridge.[1]

More was executed on the 6th of July, the eve of St. Thomas, in the year 1535, fourteen days after the death of his friend Fisher. These detestable murders spread a panic through the nation; and the expression of the popular opinion, however timid and meek, went, with the workings of his own conscience, to increase the tyrant's jealousy and apprehension. In the month of August, Erasmus wrote to a friend that the English were now living in such a state of terror that they durst not write to foreigners or receive letters from them. In fact, in all foreign countries where civilization had made progress, the fate of Fisher, and still more of that admirable wit and scholar, the author of the *Eutopia*, excited universal execration; and *there*, at least, men could speak their minds loudly. The lofty eloquence of Cardinal Pole, and the classical point of Erasmus, recorded the crime, and their striking accounts were afterwards circulated throughout Europe, awakening everywhere a hatred of its brutal author.

We are told that Henry himself was disposed to throw the blame upon his wife Anne. When an account of More's execution was brought to him he was playing at tables with the queen; and (as this probable story goes) he looked sternly at her, and, after saying, " Thou art the cause of this man's death," withdrew, in evident perturbation, to the solitude of his chamber. At Rome both Fisher and More were considered as martyrs in the cause of the church; and as Henry had shown by many other measures that he was determined to keep no terms with the Papacy, on the 30th of August Paul III. put his hand to a bull which allowed him ninety days to repent and appear at Rome in person, or by proxy; and in case of default, pronounced him and all his fautors and abettors excommunicated—declared him to have forfeited his crown, and his children by Anne Boleyn, and *their* children, to be incapable of inheriting it. Going still further, the pope enjoined all Christian priests and monks whatsoever to quit Henry's dominions; absolved his subjects from their oaths of allegiance; and commanded them to take up arms against him. He also dissolved all Henry's treaties and alliances with Christian princes; prohibited all Christian nations from trading with England; and exhorted them to make war upon him until he should cease his schism and rebellion against the church. But it was deemed expedient to keep this thunder in reserve for the present, and so the pope suppressed the bull for a season. It was, however, known in England that the instrument had been drawn up; and this circumstance only exasperated the court and a large portion of the country. Henry was apprehensive of the power of the emperor; and he now opened negotiations with the Protestants of Germany, whose doctrines he had pronounced to be damnable.

---

[1] According to Stow, the body of Fisher was then "taken up and buried with Sir Thomas More, both in the Tower."—*Annals; More's Works; Erasmus; Epist. Pole; Stapleton; State Papers; State Trials.*

Henry soon found that his new quality of "supreme head" of the English church overburdened him with business; he, therefore, established a separate department or ministry for the conduct of church matters; and at the head of this he placed the bold and vigorous Cromwell, as "royal vice-gerent," "vicar-general," and "chief commissary," with all the spiritual authority belonging to the king. This was a strange office to be held by a layman; but Cromwell, without hesitation, attended convocations of the clergy, discussed questions of schism and heresy, and took precedence of the Archbishop of Canterbury among his own bishops. The clergy hated Cromwell, and Cromwell hated the clergy. At the same time many members of the monastic body, undeterred by the gallows at Tyburn, refused the oath of supremacy, and even ventured to attack the king from the pulpit. The exchequer also was very bare; and when the vicar-general proposed the abolition of certain monasteries, convents, and abbeys in England, and the seizure of all their property, he found a willing listener in the needy king. "Now it was that Cromwell invented an engine to batter the monks more forcibly than the former course of torture and hanging had done. He sent abroad subtle-headed fellows, who, warranted by the king's authority, should, throughout England, search into the lives and manners of religious persons;"[1] for it was assumed, as a principle, that the vices of the monastic bodies not only justified, but imperiously called for their suppression. These commissioners were let loose in pairs to hunt every part of England wherein were monasteries, cells, priories, or any other religious houses. Their mission was called a visitation for the advancement of religion, and for the reformation of discipline and manners; but where those who had to pass judgment were the very men to profit by finding the monks guilty, it was not likely that they would declare many of them innocent. From this sole consideration we must decide that the vices and irregularities of the monks and nuns were grossly exaggerated, and in some cases altogether invented, by the greedy agents of Cromwell. But at the same time every impartial mind will feel that there were certain vices, the inevitable consequence of a monastic system; and there are pretty good proofs to show that in some cases there existed irregularities and delinquencies at which humanity shudders. But still there were certain clauses in the instructions of the visitors, and in the inquiries they were ordered to make, which compel us to regard their reports with considerable doubt and suspicion. They were commanded, for example, to make all the monks and nuns renounce the authority of the pope, to take the oath of supremacy, and to swear to the succession of the king's children by Anne Boleyn; and we may be sure, that when a monastery or a convent showed scruples of conscience on these heads, their morals were not spared in the report[2] of the commissioners.[3]

A.D. 1536. Queen Catherine, "whom extremity of grief cast into disease," died at Kimbolton on the 8th of January, her last moments being most wretched. At the approach of death she repeated an earnest request —made many times before—that she might be permitted to see her daughter Mary once, at least, before she died; but her heartless husband refused even this favour.

It is said that Anne Boleyn exulted in the death of Catherine, proclaiming to her friends

---

[1] Godwin. [2] Lord Herbert; Godwin; Collier; Strype; Stow. [3] "We must reject, in the excess of our candour, all testimonies that the middle ages present, from the solemn declarations of councils and reports of judicial inquiry, to the casual evidence of common fame in the ballad or romance, if we would extenuate the general corruption of those institutions. In vain new rules of discipline were devised, or the old corrected by reforms. Many of their worst vices grew so naturally out of their mode of life, that a stricter discipline could have no tendency to extirpate them. Such were the frauds I have already noticed, and the whole scheme of hypocritical austerities. Their extreme licentiousness was sometimes hardly concealed by the cowl of sanctity. I know not by what right we should disbelieve the reports of the visitation under Henry VIII., entering as they do into a multitude of specific charges, both probable in their nature, and consonant to the unanimous opinion of the world. Doubtless, there were many communities as well as individuals to whom none of these reproaches would apply. In the very best view, however, that can be taken of monasteries, their existence is deeply injurious to the morals of a nation. They withdraw men of pure conduct and conscientious principles from the exercise of social duties, and leave the common mass of human vice more unmixed. Such men are always inclined to form schemes of ascetic perfection which can only be fulfilled in retirement; but, in the strict rules of monastic life, and under the influence of a grovelling superstition, their virtue lost all its usefulness. They fell implicitly into the snares of crafty priests, who made submission to the church not only the condition, but the measure of all praise."—Hallam, iii. 382. After adducing some palpable proofs of the corruption of the monasteries, from among a mass of evidence, of which much is unfit to appear in print, Mr. Froude proceeds as follows:—"In reply to these and similar evidences of the state of the monasteries, it will be easy to say, that in the best ages there were monks impatient of their vows, and abbots negligent of their duties; that human weakness and human wickedness may throw a stain over the noblest institutions; that nothing is proved by collecting instances which may be merely exceptions, and that no evidence is more fallacious than that which rests upon isolated facts.

"It is true; and the difficulty is felt as keenly by the accuser who brings forward charges which it is discreditable to have urged, if they cannot be substantiated, as by those who would avail themselves of the easy opening to evade the weight of the indictment. I have to say only, that if the extracts which I have made lend persons, disposed to differ with me, to examine the documents which are extant upon the subject, they will learn what I have concealed as well as what I have alleged; and I believe that, if they begin the inquiry (as I began it myself) with believing that the poor monks have been over hardly judged, they will close it with but one desire—that the subject shall never more be mentioned."—Froude, Hist. Eng. ii. 428.

that she was now indeed a queen. But she herself was already doomed; for the king had cast his eyes on one of *her* maids of honour. It has been stated, that she accidentally discovered this secret by surprising Henry with the object of his new passion seated on his knee, and that her agitation brought on a premature accouchement. On the 29th of January, twenty-one days after the death of Queen Catherine, Anne was delivered of a son—an event which Henry had so long and so impatiently desired; but the child was still-born. Upon May Day following there was a great entertainment in Greenwich Park, the king and queen being present, and the Viscount Rochford, Anne's brother, and Henry Norris, one of the grooms of the stole, being principal challengers in a tilting match which was going on very gaily. Suddenly the king rose and departed for London, having not above six persons with him. "Of this sudden departing many men mused, but most chiefly the queen, who, the next day, was apprehended at Greenwich."[1] She was met upon the river by the Duke of Norfolk, Audley, the chancellor, and Cromwell, who informed her that she was accused of adultery. She fell on her knees, and exclaimed,

AN INTERIOR IN THE MARTEN TOWER.[2]— From a drawing by J. W. Archer.

wildly, "O Lord, help me, as I am guiltless of that whereof I am charged." She was presently

[1] Hall.
[2] Anne Boleyn was confined in the Marten Tower. On the wall of a part of that tower now used as a lobby, and represented in the engraving, the autograph of her name is still to be seen. This autograph is represented separately.

locked up in the Tower—though she knew it not, her brother, Viscount Rochford, and Henry Norris, were there before her—and she was soon followed to that dismal state-prison by Mark Smeaton, a musician, and William Brereton and Francis Weston, both gentlemen of the king's privy chamber. As if to finish the complete overthrow of her heart and intellect that had been sinking and wavering ever since her unfortunate accouchement, and the discovery which preceded it, they gave her for her

ANNE BOLEYN'S AUTOGRAPH.

prison the very chamber in which she had slept the night before her coronation, when the king and the nation seemed to be at her feet studying and striving how most they should honour her. On finding herself in this place she fell upon her knees, exclaiming, "Jesus have mercy on me!" and then she fell into a convulsive fit of weeping and laughing. As soon as she recovered some use of her reason, she began to ask a number of questions with great rapidity. "Wherefore am I here, Mr. Kingston?" she said to the lieutenant of the Tower;— "When saw you the king?—Where is my sweet brother?—Oh, my mother, thou wilt die of sorrow!" At last she said, "I shall die without justice!" Kingston assured her that there was justice for the meanest subject in England; upon which she burst into loud laughter. This was the effect of insanity; but if she had been perfectly in her senses, a laugh would have been no improper reply to the lieutenant's assertion.

By orders of the king, Mrs. Cosen, Mrs. Boleyn, her own aunt, but her enemy, and one or two other female attendants, were left with her in the Tower, with instructions to note down all that she might say in her moments of agitation or despair; and to entrap her into confessions or admissions by putting leading questions to her. Mrs. Cosen asked her why Norris had said to her almoner on Saturday last, that he could swear to her being a good woman. She replied, "Marry, I bade him do so; for I asked him why he did not go through with his marriage; and he made answer that he would tarry a time. Then, said I, you look for dead men's shoes; for, if aught but good should come to the king, you would look to have me. He denied it; and I told him that I could undo him if I would." It is said that she appeared to be greatly alarmed as to Weston, because he had spoken to her about Norris' excessive admiration of her person. Mrs. Stoner, another of the female attendants or spies, told her that Smeaton was treated with greater severity than the other prisoners, being put in irons: but to this she replied, that he was so treated *because he was not a gentleman born;* and she added, that Smeaton had never been in her chamber save once, when he went to play as a musician, and that she had never spoken to him since, until last Saturday, when she asked him why he looked so sad; and he replied that a look from her sufficed him. All this, with much more, was communicated to the king and the court lawyers. The habitual frankness of her disposition, and the distracted state to which she was now reduced, make it not improbable that she may have said some things which admitted of being turned against her; but, on the other hand, we must always suspect the subtle exaggerations of the court lawyers, and must remember that, even according to their showing, none of her words necessarily bore a more serious construction than that of imprudence, or over-familiarity with some of the courtiers—a result, in all probability, of her education in France, where such matters were not considered even indecorous. On the 6th of May Anne wrote to the king; but Henry paid as little attention to her touching appeal as he had formerly done to those made by Catherine—his whole soul was bent upon marrying another woman! Anne was sent back to Greenwich to be examined by the privy council, where she found her most determined enemy in her own uncle, the Duke of Norfolk. On her return to the Tower she told Kingston that she had been cruelly handled by the council. She was, however, very merry, and made a great dinner. She asked the lieutenant where he had been all the day, and Kingston replied that he had been with prisoners. This hard-hearted and stern man had been, no doubt, engaged with the Viscount Rochford, Norris, Brereton, and Smeaton; and there was much to do with them, in order to intimidate them, or otherwise prepare them for examination.

When brought before the council, they all maintained their innocence and the innocence of the queen, and were recommitted; but upon being brought up a second time, Mark Smeaton, the musician, who had been loaded with irons, and in all probability put to the torture, confessed his guilt. Edward Baynton wrote from Greenwich to tell the treasurer "that no man will confess anything against her, but only Mark, of any actual thing." "Wherefore," he continues, "in my foolish conceit, it should much touch the king's honour if it should no farther appear: and I cannot believe but that the other two be as culpable as ever was he; and I think assuredly the one keepeth the other's counsel." On the 10th of May a bill of indictment of high treason against the Lady Anne, Queen of England, Henry Norris, Weston, Brereton, and Smeaton, was laid before the grand juries of Kent and Middlesex, because, as it was stated, the acts of adultery had been committed in both counties; *and because* it was the usual character of this court to invest the most illegal proceedings with all the forms and niceties of law. The indictment charged the queen with treason and adultery of three years' standing, stating that, inflamed with pride and the lusts of the flesh, she had confederated with her brother the Viscount Rochford, and with Norris, Brereton, Weston, and Smeaton, to perpetrate divers abominable treasons; that she had lain with each of the five, not excepting her own brother, several times; that she had told each of them that she loved him better than the king or than any other man, which was slander of the issue begotten between her and the king; and finally—to end with the most improbable clause of all—that she and her paramours had been engaged in various plots for murdering the king. On the 12th of May, Norris, Weston, Brereton, and Smeaton, as commoners, were arraigned in the Court of King's Bench. As before the council, all pleaded not guilty, except Mark Smeaton, the musician; all, however, were convicted, and were sentenced as traitors to be hanged, drawn, and quartered. Bishop Godwin relates that the king greatly favoured Norris, and was reported to be much grieved that he should die with the rest. "Whereupon he offered pardon to him, conditionally that he would confess that whereof he was accused. But he answered resolutely, and as it became the progenitor of so many valiant heroes,[1] that in his conscience he thought her guiltless of the objected crime; but whether she were or no, he could not accuse her of anything; and that he had rather undergo a thousand deaths than betray the innocent: upon relation whereof the king cried out, 'Hang him up, then; hang him up, then!'"

There was no precedent for the trial of a queen, and Rochford, her brother, could claim the privilege, as a peer, of a trial before the House of Lords; but these impediments were trifles in the eyes of the absolute king, and it was determined that they should both be arraigned before a commission of lords chosen by himself, as had been practised with the late Duke of Buckingham. The Duke of Norfolk, Anne's uncle and enemy, was named high-steward, and there were twenty-

---

[1] The son of Norris was ennobled in the reign of Elizabeth by the title of Baron Norris, which is still borne by his descendant the present Earl of Abingdon. Sir John Norris, a grandson of the first Baron Norris, greatly distinguished himself in the wars of Elizabeth's reign in Ireland, the Low Countries, and elsewhere.

six other noble peers equally ready to do the king's pleasure. On the 15th of May the unhappy queen was led by the constable and lieutenant to the king's hall in the Tower, where a scaffolding was erected, upon which, under a cloth of state, as High-steward of England, sat the Duke of Norfolk, with the lord-chancellor on his right hand, and the Duke of Suffolk on his left, with other marquises and lords about him—the highest-sounding names of the English aristocracy! As all records of the trial were carefully destroyed soon after, we have no sure guide as to what passed; nor, indeed, were those records preserved and entire, could we consider them in the light of fair and impartial evidence. It is the curse of all such men and measures, and properly so, that they are suspected even when they have truth and right on their side. On an impartial consideration of such facts as are before us, we cannot, however, believe that Anne Boleyn was guilty of any part of the crimes laid to her charge by the depraved imagination of Henry; and the plot to murder him seems too absurd to arrest attention for a single moment. In regard to the most revolting charge of all, it appears that Lord Rochford had been seen lolling over his sister's bed. But Henry had not a monopoly of vice and malignancy—the nobility were becoming worthy of the king; and Rochford's own wife, a woman of infamous character, bore witness against her husband and the queen. There was also a death-bed deposition made by the Lady Wingfield, but we have no means of judging how it was procured, or whether it was not a forgery; and the document itself has been destroyed with the exception of the first lines.

But the peers, among whom the Duke of Suffolk, the king's brother-in-law, was chief—as one wholly applying himself to the king's humour—pronounced her guilty. Whereupon the Duke of Norfolk, bound to proceed according to the verdict of the peers, condemned her to death, either by being burned on the green in the Tower, or beheaded, as his majesty in his pleasure should think fit.[1] When she was removed from the bar, her brother, Lord Rochford, was put in her place —was convicted on the same evidence—and sentenced to lose his head, and to be quartered as a traitor. On the following day (the 16th of May) Kingston, the lieutenant of the Tower, wrote impatiently to Secretary Cromwell to know the king's pleasure touching the queen, as well for her comfort as for the preparation of scaffolds and other necessaries, adding, "I pray you have good remembrance in all this for us to do, for we shall be ready to do always to our knowledge." He also informs Cromwell that the king's grace had showed him that my lord of Canterbury should be her confessor, and that he, Cranmer, had been with the queen in the Tower that day. The mind of the wretched woman was evidently upset from the moment of her first committal; fits of anguish and despair were mixed with bright hopes and with bursts of levity—the most melancholy proof of her derangement. One hour she would say that she was ready to die—the next she would talk confidently of being allowed to live. If, in her sane moments, she really entertained any such hopes, they were soon put an end to; and as the crisis approached she looked on death without terror. On the 18th of May Kingston again addressed Cromwell, telling him that she had sent for him early in the morning, to speak touching her innocence (apparently in the presence of Cranmer), and that she had again sent for him while he was writing the same letter, and at his coming had exclaimed, "Mr. Kingston, I hear say I shall not die before noon, and I am very sorry therefor, for I thought to be dead by this time and past my pain." "I told her," continues the lieutenant of the Tower, "that it should be no pain, it was so subtle; and then, she said, 'I heard say the executioner was very good, and I have a little neck;' and she put her hands about it, laughing heartily. Truly this lady has much joy and pleasure in death." But she did not die that day. On the morrow, the 19th of May, a little before the hour of noon, she was brought to the place of execution, on the green within the Tower, some of the nobility and companies of the city being admitted, rather to be witnesses than spectators of her death. From the scaffold Anne addressed a few words to the "Good Christian people," and afterwards baring her beautiful neck, and kneeling down, kept repeating—"Christ have mercy on my soul! —Lord Jesus receive my soul!" until the executioner of Calais, at one blow, struck off her head. Thus perished Anne Boleyn within four months of Catherine, and in little more than three years after her marriage, for which the passionate Henry had moved heaven and earth.[2] An old tradition strongly depicts the impatience with which he now expected her death. On the fatal morning he went to hunt in Epping Forest, and while he was at breakfast his attendants observed that he was anxious and thoughtful. But at length they heard the report of a distant gun —a preconcerted signal. "Ah! it is done!" cried he, starting up—"the business is done! Uncouple the dogs and let us follow the sport."[3] In the evening he returned gaily from the chase, and on the following morning he married Anne's maid of honour, Jane Seymour, who on Whit-

---

[1] *Godwin.*

[2] *Original Letters* (printed by Sir Henry Ellis) as written at the moment by Kingston, the lieutenant of the Tower, Baynton, &c. *Hall; Stow; Godwin.* [3] Dr. Nott's *Life of Surrey.*

sunday, the 29th of May, clad in royal habiliments, appeared in public as queen, without any coronation, however, for Henry never indulged any of his wives with that expensive ceremony after Anne Boleyn.[1]

QUEEN JANE SEYMOUR.—After Holbein.

Smeaton, the musician, who is supposed to have been bribed and tortured into his confession, seems to have expected that his life would be spared, and so much, no doubt, was promised to him; but, "as it was thought not fit to let him live to tell tales," he was hanged. Rochford and the rest were beheaded.

Archbishop Cranmer, who had made Anne Boleyn queen, and who had lived in the most perfect friendship with her and her family, both before and after, had not heroic courage sufficient to resist the will of the king; and he certainly made no bold and generous effort to save her or her honour. To avoid his interference, Henry, on the day after her arrest at Greenwich, ordered Cranmer to keep to his palace at Lambeth, and on no account to venture to court. The archbishop evidently fancied that he was to be involved in her ruin. His fears, however, did not wholly overcome his gratitude and affection, and he wrote a curious letter to the king. He began by exhorting his grace to bear this bitter affliction with resignation. As for himself, his "mind was clean amazed;" the good opinion he had formerly entertained of the queen, who had been the best of his benefactors, prompted him to believe her innocent; but, as this was a dangerous assertion, he subjoined immediately, that his knowledge of the king's *justice* and prudence induced him to believe her *guilty;* and he went on to say that he hoped that it might be permitted him to pray that she might prove her innocence; but, still cautious, he here again added, that if she could not do so, he would deem that man a traitor who did not call for the severest punishment. He had loved her formerly, because he had thought that she loved the gospel; but if found guilty, men ought to hate her in proportion to their love of the gospel. He ventured, however, to hope that no misconduct on her part would arrest the important work of church reformation which (he did not blush to write) the king had begun, not through his affection for her, but solely out of his love for the truth. On the very day on which he wrote this letter Cranmer was summoned to the Star Chamber, where the king's commissioners declared unto him "such things as his grace's pleasure was they should make him privy to," and acquainted him with certain other things which the king expected him to do forthwith. A *brave* good man would have laid his head on the block rather than consent to this new duty, which was nothing less than to declare the marriage which he had pronounced good and valid to be illegal, and to dissolve it, as he had done the marriage with Catherine. Though she had not yet been brought to any trial, Cranmer may have been convinced of the queen's delinquency by depositions shown to him in the Star Chamber; and if he believed her guilty he might consider himself justified in declaring that the marriage was dissolved by her adultery; but this was not enough for the king, who exacted from him that he should declare that the marriage had been unlawful from the beginning, and consequently that the Princess Elizabeth was as illegitimate as her half-sister the Princess Mary. No doubt it was to save his head that the archbishop set to work vigorously, for Henry was not likely to be pleased unless he did the business in a solemn manner. He sent copies of articles of objection to the validity of

---

[1] "Before the discovery of this proceeding Lord Thomas Howard's contract of marriage with Lady Margaret Douglas), but in anticipation of inevitable intrigues of the kind, the privy council and the peers, on the same grounds which had before led them to favour the divorce from Catherine, petitioned the king to save the country from the perils which menaced it, and to take a fresh wife without an hour's delay. Henry's experience of matrimony had been so discouraging that they feared he might be reluctant to venture upon it again. Nevertheless, for his country's sake, they trusted that he would not refuse.

"Henry, professedly in obedience to this request, was married, immediately after the execution, to Jane, daughter of Sir John Seymour. The indecent haste is usually considered a proof entirely conclusive of the cause of Anne Boleyn's ruin. To myself, the haste is an evidence of something very different. Henry, who waited seven years for Anne Boleyn, was not without some control over his passions; and, if appetite had been the moving influence with him, he would scarcely, with the eyes of all the world fixed upon his conduct, have passed so gross an insult upon the nation of which he was the sovereign. The precipitancy with which he acted is to me a proof that he looked on matrimony as an indifferent official act which his duty required at the moment; and if this be thought a novel interpretation of his motives, I have merely to say that I find it on the statute book."—Froude's *History of England,* vol. ii. p. 502.

the marriage to the king in his palace, and to the queen in the Tower, "that it might be for the salvation of their souls;" and he summoned each to appear in his ecclesiastical court at Lambeth, to show cause why a sentence of divorce should not be passed. Dr. Sampson appeared for the king, and Drs. Wotton and Barbour for the queen —of course all three were appointed by the king. The objections were read in the court, and the doctors and divines soon joined in opinion. On the 17th of May, the day on which her brother and friends were executed, and two days after she herself had received sentence of death, Cranmer, having "God alone before his eyes," pronounced that the marriage of Anne Boleyn was, and always had been, utterly null and void, in consequence of certain just and lawful impediments which, it was said, were unknown at the time of the union, but had lately been confessed to the archbishop (Cranmer) by the lady herself. The process, after Anne's death, was submitted to the members of the convocation and the two houses of parliament; and the church, commons, and lords fully confirmed it, thus cutting Elizabeth off from the succession.[1]

In the month of June the king caused parliament to agree to a new act of succession, entailing the crown on such issue as he might have by Jane Seymour. Having some doubt or misgiving as to these children to be begotten, he proposed that he should be allowed to bequeath the crown by letters-patent, or by his last will, to any person whom he might think proper; and the obsequious parliament passed a bill accordingly! It was understood that the king hereby contemplated the appointing of his natural son, the Duke of Richmond, to be his successor; but at this very moment the duke died, in the eighteenth year of his age, to the great grief of Henry, who, like a very Turk, had no affection for his daughters, but a great deal for his son. The Lady Mary, who had been living in seclusion at Hunsden, under the displeasure of her father for her attachment to her mother, and to the discipline of the Romish church, made her peace with the court a few weeks before the Duke of Richmond's death, being obliged by Cromwell to subscribe to certain most humiliating articles of submission and acknowledgment.[2] She received a suitable establishment, but was not restored in blood—still remaining by law a bastard.

The parliament, which by successive prorogations had sat for the unprecedented term of six years, was now dissolved; and Henry, after all their passive obedience, seems to have been disgusted at some feeble effort at opposition.[3] He

[1] Lord. Herbert, Journals; Godwin; Wilkins; Burnet. Burnet gives the whole of Cranmer's strange letter to the king.

[2] After imploring the king's merciful heart and fatherly pity, Mary acknowledged that she had most unkindly and most unnaturally offended his most excellent highness, in that she had not been sufficiently obedient to his just, wise, and most virtuous laws. Then followed the confession "of me, the Lady Mary." First she confessed and acknowledged the king's majesty to be her sovereign lord and king, to whose laws, statutes, &c., she was bound to yield implicit obedience. In the second place she agreed to recognize, accept, take, repute, and acknowledge the king's highness to be supreme head of the Church of England; and she utterly renounced all manner of remedy which she by any means might claim of the Bishop of Rome, &c. But the last clause is by far the most striking of all:—"Item, I do freely, frankly, and for the discharge of my duty towards God, the king's highness, and his laws, without other respect recognize and acknowledge that the marriage heretofore had between his majesty and my mother, the late princess-dowager, was, by God's law and man's law, incestuous and unlawful."—Letter with Deed, from the Princess Mary to the king, in State Papers.

[3] This parliament is remarkable for the act incorporating Wales with England.

"As Henry was descended from the Tudors, a Welsh family, he naturally directed his attention to the native country of his paternal ancestors. It might be divided into two portions—that which had been originally conquered by the arms of his predecessors; and that which had been won by the courage and perseverance of the individuals afterwards called the lords-marchers. The former had been apportioned into shires, and was governed by the laws of England; the latter comprised 141 districts or lordships, which had been granted to the first conquerors, and formed so many distinct and independent jurisdictions. From them the king's writs and the king's officers were excluded. They acknowledged no other laws or customs than their own. The lords, like so many counts-palatine, had their own courts, civil and criminal, appointed their own officers and judges, punished or pardoned offences according to their pleasure, and received all the emoluments arising from the administration of justice within their respective domains. But the great evil was that this multitude of petty and separate jurisdictions, by holding out the prospect of impunity, proved an incitement to crime. The most atrocious offender, if he could only flee from the scene of his transgression, and purchase the protection of a neighbouring lord, was sheltered from the pursuit of justice.

"The king, however, put an end to this mischievous and anomalous state of things. In 1536, it was enacted that the whole of Wales should thenceforth be united and incorporated with the realm of England; that all the natives should enjoy and inherit the same rights, liberties, and laws which were enjoyed and inherited by others the king's subjects; that the custom of gavel-kind should cease; that the several lordships-marchers should be annexed to the neighbouring counties; that all judges and justices of the peace should be appointed by the king's letters-patent; that no lord should have the power to pardon any treason, murder, or felony, committed within his lordship; and that the different shires in Wales, with one borough in each, should return members to parliament. Most of these regulations were extended to the county-palatine of Chester."—Lingard.

Sir James Mackintosh, it will be seen, viewed this as a general benefit to the English constitution.

"Some direct benefits the constitution owes to this reign. The act which established parliamentary representation in so considerable a territory as Wales, may be regarded as the principal reformation in the House of Commons since its legal maturity in the time of Edward I. That principality had been divided into twelve shires, of which eight were ancient, and four owed their origin to a statute in Henry's reign. Knights, citizens, and burgesses were now directed to be chosen, and sent to parliament, from the shires, cities, and boroughs of Wales. A short time before, the same privileges were granted to the county-palatine of Chester, of which the preamble contains a memorable recognition and establishment of the principles which are the basis of the elective part of our constitution. Nearly thirty members were thus added to the house on the principle of the Chester bill—that it is disadvantageous to a province to be unrepresented; that representation is essential to good government; and that those who are bound by the laws ought to have a reasonable share of direct influence on the passing of laws. As the

now named commissioners to take possession of the suppressed monasteries, and to prepare measures for the seizure of others. If these men, mostly the friends of Cromwell or of Cranmer, had a better religion before their eyes, they certainly were not blind to the charms of lucre, and the temptations of fair houses and fat glebes; and most of them made a very rich harvest for themselves out of the spoils of the monks and nuns. The superiors of the suppressed houses were promised small pensions for life, which were very irregularly paid.[1] All the monks, not twenty-four years of age, were absolved from their vows, and turned loose on the world without any kind of provision: the rest, if they wished to continue in the profession, were divided among the greater houses that were still left standing. The poor nuns were turned adrift to beg or starve, having nothing given to them save one common gown for each. At the same time the crowds of poor who, by a defective but ancient system, had derived their support from the monastic establishments, became furious at finding their resources cut off, and at seeing the monks who had fed them now begging like themselves by the road-side. In the midst of these general discontents, Cranmer and Cromwell issued certain doctrinal injunctions to the clergy, which were too novel to find immediate favour with the multitude; and certain Protestant reformers, who had more courage than they, ventured to print books against image-worship, auricular confession, transubstantiation, and other fundamental tenets and practices of the Roman church. The king, who assumed all the authority in matters of dogmas that had ever been claimed by the popes, and much more than they had ever put in practice in England, pronounced awards and sentences which irritated both parties alike, and all these questions were referred to him—thus occupying a good deal of his time, and keeping in dangerous activity his old polemical bile.

Henry was by no means backward in issuing his final orders and decrees spiritual; and (the Reformers herein concealing their ulterior views) he was led to reduce the number of sacraments from seven to three—baptism, the Lord's Supper, and penance; to forbid the direct adoration of images; to abrogate a number of saints' days or holidays, especially such as fell in harvest-time; to declare the Scriptures, with the Apostolic, Nicene, and Athanasian creeds, the sole standards of faith; to order every parish priest to expound these to his parishioners in plain English, and to direct the printing and distribution of an English translation of the Bible, one copy of which was to be kept in every parish church. The king, in his wisdom, insisted on the necessity of auricular confession, and denounced any questioning of the real presence in the eucharist as a damnable heresy to be punished with fire and fagot. Purgatory, he confessed, puzzled him, and steering a middle course, he declared himself to be uncertain on this head, and kindly permitted his subjects to pray for the souls of their departed friends, provided only that they fell into none of the old abuses of enriching religious houses and shrines for this object.

Most of these changes were far too sudden; but the people seem to have more particularly regretted the curtailing of their holidays. Many of the nobility and gentry fanned the flames of discontent, though, for the most part, they afterwards found means of convincing the king that they had acted under compulsion of the people. The hereditary patrons of the suppressed monasteries pretended that those ho ses and lands ought by no means to fall to the crown, but that, if it was suitable and necessary to take them from the religious orders, they ought to revert to the descendants or representatives of the original founders and benefactors. In the month of October the commons of Lincolnshire, being assembled touching certain subsidies to be paid to the king, suddenly, as if animated by one spirit, took up arms to the number of 20,000 men, forcing certain lords and gentlemen to be their leaders, and to swear to their articles. Such as refused they threw into prison, and a few they killed. The king sent a great force against these rebels, under the command of the Earls of Shrewsbury, Kent, Rutland, and Huntingdon, and the Duke of Suffolk—the last having the highest authority. Suffolk found the insurrection so formidable, that, instead of fighting, he was glad to negotiate; and even the king himself, furious as

---

practical advantages are only generally alleged, and could scarcely have been proved, they must have been inferred from the nature of a House of Commons. The British constitution was not thought to be enjoyed by a district till a popular representation was bestowed upon it. Election by the people was regarded, not as a source of tumult, but as the principle most capable of composing disorder in territories not represented."—Sir James Mackintosh, *History of England*.

[1] "The pensions to the superiors of the dissolved greater monasteries, says a writer not likely to spare Henry's government, appear to have varied from £266 to £6 per annum. The priors of cells received generally £13. A few, whose services merited the distinction, obtained £20. To the other monks were allotted pensions of £6, £4, or £2, with a small sum to each at his departure, to provide for his immediate wants. The pensions to nuns averaged about £4.—*Lingard*, vi. 341. He admits that these were ten times their present value in money; and surely they were not unreasonably small. Compare them with those generally and justly thought munificent, which this country bestows on her veterans of Chelsea and Greenwich. The monks had no right to expect more than the means of that hard fare to which they ought, by their rules, to have been confined in their convents. The whole revenues were not to be shared among them as private property. It cannot of course be denied that the compulsory change of life, was to many a severe and unmerited hardship; but no great revolution—and the Reformation as little as any—could be achieved without much private suffering."—Hallam's *Const. Hist. Eng.*, note, p. 72.

he was, seems to have been more willing to rely on his pen than on his sword. By entertaining the proposal of a redress of grievances; by forwarding their petition to court; and by giving them fair promises, Suffolk stayed the first dangerous fury of the insurgents, gained time, and promoted dissensions among them; so that when Henry answered them, he was enabled to do so in a high tone. "The king," says an historian, who lived in servile times, "had a spirit befitting his greatness; and, perceiving them to shrink, could not dissemble the rage he had conceived at the presumption of this rascally rout, that durst capitulate with their sovereign, and seek to curb the unlimited power of kings."[1] Henry's answer "to the petitions of the traitors and rebels in Lincolnshire" has been preserved; and a most characteristic document it is! It ended by requiring them to deliver up into the hands of his lieutenants no fewer than 100 persons, to be punished according to their demerits, at his will and pleasure.[2] The insurgents, however, did not disperse till the 30th of October; and before they retired to their homes a fierce rebellion broke out beyond the Trent. Of the men of Lincolnshire, fifteen victims were given up to satisfy the royal vengeance. Among these were holy Dr. Makerel, the prior of Barlings, or Oxley, and Captain Cobbler, the chief leader, who is said by some historians to have been the prior himself, though it is conjectured, from a contemporary paper, that the real name of this Captain Cobbler was Melton.[3] These men were respited for a season, but they were afterwards executed as traitors with the usual barbarity. But Henry's thirst of blood grew with his years. On the 9th of October a priest and a butcher were hanged at Windsor by martial law, "for words spoken" about the insurgents. At the same time, Dr. Mallet, who had been chaplain to the late Queen Catherine, was summarily executed at Chelmsford, in Essex, for some words spoken to the like effect.[4] Meanwhile the insurrection north of the Trent spread from Yorkshire into Durham, Northumberland, Westmoreland, and Lancashire; and nothing seemed wanting but a proper leader to overthrow this most tyrannical government. Henry was greatly alarmed; but he told Wriothesley that he would rather sell all his plate than fail to subdue these traitors "in such sort that all others should take warning by their example."

Some money was sent to the Earl of Suffolk, who was now at Newark, and who made a good use of it in buying over some of the ringleaders, and in exciting jealousies and dissensions among the ignorant insurgents. The Earl of Shrewsbury was constituted the king's lieutenant north of the Trent; and the Duke of Norfolk was despatched into Yorkshire, with the Marquis of Exeter, and an army of 5000 men. Including all the forces, there was a regular army of about 10,000 men in the field; but the rebels at one time were estimated at 40,000, being under the nominal command of Robert Aske, a gentleman of Yorkshire, who was not destitute either of talent or of energy. These men of the north had given a religious character to their rising, and had bound themselves by oath to stand by each other "for the love which they bore to Almighty God, his faith, the holy church, the king's person, and the persons of the nobility, to expel all villain blood and evil counsellors from the privy council, not for any private profit, nor to do displeasure to any private person, nor to slay or murder through envy, but for the restitution of the church, and the suppression of heretics and their opinions." They painted on their banners the figure of Christ in his agony; they wore upon their sleeves the emblem of the

EMBLEM OF THE FIVE WOUNDS OF CHRIST.—From a boss in the Lady Chapel, Tynemouth Priory.

five wounds of the Saviour, with the name of Jesus; and they called their march the "Pilgrimage of Grace." Wherever they advanced they restored the monks and nuns to their houses; and by tremendous threats they compelled the people to take their oaths and join their ranks. Every man was summoned to be at a place of rendezvous at a fixed hour, and in his best array, as he would answer for it before the High Judge at the day of doom, as he would avoid the pulling down of his house, the loss of his goods, and the destruction of his body. The cities of Hull, York, and Pontefract admitted the "Pilgrims

---

[1] Bishop Godwin.
[2] State Papers. This remarkable paper is alluded to by Lord Herbert, and given at length by Hall. It is printed in the volume of the State Papers from the minute, corrected by Lord Cromwell, which remains among the miscellaneous papers in the Chapter-house. The hand and style of the king are most visible in the composition.
[3] Note by the editor of State Papers.
[4] Stow.

of Grace," and took the vows. The Lords Darcy, Lumley, Latimer, and Nevil, together with Edward Lee, Archbishop of York, with a vast number of the knights and gentlemen of the northern counties, joined the insurgents; but the tremendous threats favoured their pleading afterwards that they had done so upon compulsion. The undisciplined host was amenable to no authority, and there arose many conflicting opinions as to the proper mode of conducting their campaign. It is also very evident that some of their chiefs were already bought by Suffolk, for there was much difference of opinion and contention in the camp. When they moved upon Doncaster they were checked by the Earl of Shrewsbury and the Duke of Norfolk. The royal army, however, readily agreed to an armistice, during which the insurgents named delegates, who laid their demands before the king, who, in the meantime, had sent more money to the Duke of Suffolk.[1] The king also despatched the Lord-admiral Howard, and other soldiers and statesmen, to the north, with most elaborate instructions as to the way in which they were to proceed with the rebels. They were particularly charged to withdraw all fear of punishment from the Lord Darcy and the rest of the nobility that had joined the people; to offer them safe-conducts for the present, and a free pardon for the future.[2]

The paper presented by the northern delegates was longer than that which had been sent up by the men of Lincolnshire, but the chief grounds of complaint were the same in both. The most striking of the additional clauses (to some of which Henry deigned not to reply) were that the heresies of Wyckliffe, Huss, Luther, Melancthon, and others, should be rooted out, and that all heretical books whatsoever should be utterly destroyed; that the supremacy of the church, inasmuch as related to the care of souls, should be restored to the pope, who should have the consecration of bishops, with the first-fruits and tenths, as formerly; that the Lady Mary should be declared legitimate, and the statutes to the contrary annulled; that the pains and penalties against such as kept hand-guns and crossbows should be repealed, unless used in the king's parks and forests upon his royal deer; that parliament should be restored to its ancient privileges, and that the manner of conducting the elections of knights of the shire and members for boroughs should be reformed; that the cruel statute of treason for words spoken should be abrogated, and that the common law should be used as it was in the beginning of his grace's reign. Henry himself dictated the answer. Touching the maintenance of the faith, he says, he marvels not a little that ignorant people like them should go about, or take upon them to instruct him, "who something had been noted to be learned." As for the maintenance of the church, this was so general a proposition that, without distinctions made as to which was the real and true church, no man could answer it; but he told them that, mean what church they might, it pertained not to them, the commons, to meddle in the matter, and that he could not but reckon it a great unkindness and unnaturalness in them to prefer that a churl or two should enjoy the property of the monasteries in support of vicious and abominable lives, rather than that he, their prince, should have the profits, for the support of his extreme charges incurred in their defence. In the end, he told them that the greatest concession he could make was, to pardon them their rebellion upon their delivering up to him "ten of their ringleaders and provokers, such as he should name and appoint."[3] The insurgents rejected these terms, and kept the field; nor did the royal army consider itself strong enough to hazard a battle. Henry was put to his straits in order to send £6000 more to the north; and the Duke of Norfolk and the lord-admiral were ordered to look after and fortify the fords of the Don, the works at Nottingham, and the bridges and fords there. By this time it was the 21st of November; the weather was cold and stormy, and the rebels began to feel an anxiety to return to their agricultural labours. The Duke of Norfolk, however, was again glad to negotiate, and he made more promises than the king would ratify. The insurgents now became furious, and the royal army was compelled to retreat to the south of the Don and the Trent. At last Norfolk was authorized to give such assurances to the rebels as induced them to separate; and the king wrote gracious letters to his "trusty and well-beloved" Captain Aske, Lord Darcy, and others, expressing his earnest desire to see and converse with them, trusting that they were in heart repentant, and that he should have cause to reward them for their fidelity. They were both wise enough to decline the invitation; but Aske, it should seem, really undertook to oppose, if not to betray his party.[4]

A.D. 1537. As early as the 23d of January, bills and scrolls were stuck up, by night, upon the church doors, containing these words:—"Commons, be ye true among yourselves, and stick one to another, for the gentlemen have deceived you; but yet, if need be, ye

---

[1] The sum sent at this time amounted to about £10,000, and Wriothesley, in the name of the king, thanked Cromwell for the "great labours and travails" he had taken in the getting of this together.—*State Papers*.

[2] Letter of the king.—*State Papers*.

[3] *State Papers*: from a fair copy preserved in the Chapterhouse. The letter is supposed to be in the handwriting of Sir Ralph Sadler, but there are a few minute corrections in the king's hand.

[4] *State Papers*.

shall lack no captains." In spite of all the efforts made to produce a lukewarmness or desire of division among the people, they met in arms in the beginning of February. But most of their leaders had bargained to betray them; the royal army was reinforced, and admitted into the heart of the country, and, after failing in three or four sieges of towns or castles, the insurgents were disheartened and again dispersed — every man doubting of the good faith of his captain, and looking only to the preservation of his own life. The Lord Darcy, Robert Aske, and most of the original leaders, not excepting those who had betrayed the cause, were taken, sent to London, and there ordered for execution as traitors in the month of June.[1] The king's banner was unfolded; martial law was proclaimed in all the northern counties; and Henry wrote minute instructions to the Duke of Norfolk, fearing that that nobleman might be too lenient. "Our pleasure is," saith the king, "that before you shall close up our said banner again, you shall in anywise cause such dreadful execution to be done upon a good number of the inhabitants of every town, village, and hamlet, as have offended in this rebellion as well by the hanging them up in trees as by the quartering of them, and the setting of their heads and quarters in every town, great and small, and in all such other places, as they may be a fearful spectacle to all other hereafter that would practise any like matter, which we require you to do, without pity or respect, according to our former letters."[2] The monks had stood too conspicuously in the van to escape his vengeance; and after naming some of them whom he wishes to be sent up to him with all speed, he adds:— "And forasmuch as all these troubles have ensued by the solicitations and traitorous conspiracies of the monks and canons of those parties (parts), we desire and pray you, at your repair to Sawley, Hexham, Newminster, Lannercost, St. Agatha, and all such other places as have made any manner of resistance, or in anywise conspired, or kept their houses with any force since the appointment at Doncaster, you shall, without pity or circumstance, now that our banner is displayed, cause all the monks and canons that be in anywise faulty to be tied up without further delay or ceremony, to the terrible example of others, wherein we think you shall do unto us high service."[3] When the north had been converted into a shambles, and the pleasant banks of the Tweed, the Tyne, the Tees, the Don, and the Trent, were loathsome with the number of ghastly heads and reeking members, a pardon was proclaimed; and the king felicitated himself and his ministers on the wholesome vigour of government.

It is now time to allude to Cardinal Pole, the man that threw the greatest bitterness into the cup of the absolute Henry, and that recorded his infamy in strains of eloquence which the world could not forget. Reginald Pole was the son of Sir Richard Pole, by Margaret, Countess of Salisbury, daughter to George, Duke of Clarence, the unfortunate brother of Edward IV. He was thus second cousin to the king, and Henry, allowing the claim of consanguinity, and being charmed with the abilities of his young relative, patronized and protected him, allowing him a handsome pension, upon which he studied and lived

CARDINAL POLE.—After Sebastian del Piombo.

a considerable number of years in the universities of France and Italy. The king had been disposed to confer upon him the richest promotion in his dominions, but he exacted in return that the eloquent churchman should defend his divorce from Catherine, his assumption of supremacy, and all his other extreme measures; and this Pole was too high-minded to undertake. After several negotiations they quarrelled out-

---

[1] They were attainted in the court of the lord high-steward. Lord Darcy was not sent back from London, but was executed at Tower-hill; Aske was sent down to York, and executed there; Constable suffered at Hull; Lord Hussey at Lincoln; and other leaders of less name at other places.

[2] State Papers.

[3] State Papers. The pleasing prospect of blood did not blind the king to the charms of confiscation and forfeiture. In the same letter to Norfolk, he says:—"We desire and pray you to have good respect to the conservation of the lands and goods of all such as shall be now attainted, that we may have them in safety, to be given, if we shall be so disposed, to such persons as have truly served us; for we be informed that there were amongst them divers freeholders and rich men, whose lands and goods well looked unto will reward others well, that, with their truths, have deserved the same."

right, and, on Henry's rupture with the church, Pole declined all preferment in England, and, retiring to the north of Italy, he assailed the king both with argument and most stinging invective. He spread the infamy of the murder of Sir Thomas More through all Europe: his great work, entitled *De Unione Ecclesiastica* (On Ecclesiastical Union), was the best defence of the rights of the Romish church; and, even where it failed in argument, it touched the king to the quick, by exposing the baseness and the selfishness of his motives. Paul III. invited this noble English champion to Rome. For awhile Reginald Pole hesitated, for he feared what might befall his friends and relatives in England; but at last, in the end of 1536, he repaired to the Vatican, entered into the pope's service, and received a cardinal's hat. This was at the very moment that the insurrection was raging in the northern counties. The pope, it appears, thought that this demonstration would terrify Henry into a reconciliation with the church; but, if it failed to do this, the occasion would be most favourable for extending his protection to the monks and their party, and for shaking the king on his throne. He named Cardinal Pole legate beyond the Alps, and intrusted him with extraordinary powers. Intimidated by the threats of his loving cousin of England, who had requested him to arrest the cardinal and deliver him up, Francis refused to see Pole on his passage through France, and on reaching Cambrai he was denied permission to enter the territory of the Emperor Charles. The cardinal had been supplied with money to remit to the insurgents, and he was instructed to treat with some of the neighbouring princes, who were supposed by the court of Rome to be likely to exert themselves in the cause of the Catholic faith, and to support the rebels in England, notwithstanding the dangerous precedent that would be thereby established; but the insurrection was suppressed before Pole reached the frontiers of Flanders, and he soon found that his own person was in danger from the far-reaching hands of Henry, who proclaimed him a traitor, and offered 50,000 crowns to any man that should bring him his head; while his minister, the indefatigable Cromwell, vowed that he would make the cardinal eat his own heart through vexation! Pole was thus reduced to study how he should save his own life; and, being unable to hold any communication with England, or to do anything in behalf of the church, he returned to Rome in the month of August, being followed across the Alps by the loud curses of the king."[1]

On the 12th of October, Jane Seymour gave birth, at Hampton Court, to a son, and died twelve days after.[2] The king's joy at having an heir-male seems to have been greater than his grief for the loss of his wife; and the infant Edward, who succeeded him on the throne, was immediately created Prince of Wales,[3] Duke of Cornwall, and Earl of Chester—his maternal uncle, Edward Seymour, being made Lord Beauchamp and Earl of Hereford. "Then also William Paulet and John Russell began their races in the lists of honour, Paulet being made treasurer, and Russell comptroller of the king's household, and both being sworn of the privy council : neither was here their *non ultra*, the one being afterwards raised to Lord-treasurer of England and Marquis of Winchester, the other, Russell, to be Earl of Bedford." These latter promotions, however, did not take place till the next reign.[4]

---

[1] Pole, *Epist.*; Burnet.
[2] The story, so long told in all histories, of Prince Edward's being brought into the world by means of the Cæsarean operation, and by the sacrifice of his mother's life, is a complete fable, that seems to have first proceeded from the fertile imagination of Sanders, the Jesuit. Jane Seymour's death was owing to her having been suffered to take cold and eat improper food.— See *State Papers*, Despatch to the Ambassador in France.
[3] Such is the common account (see Nicolas, *Synopsis of the Peerage*, i. 7). Edward, however, tells us himself, in his journal, that he was only about to be created Prince of Wales, Duke of Cornwall, and Count-palatine of Chester, when his father died. Burnet (*Hist. Reformation*) says that Henry, towards the end of his life, designed to create his son Prince of Wales; for though he was called so, as the heirs of this crown are, yet he was not by a formal creation invested with that dignity. The formal creation designed by Henry seems to have been a solemn coronation of his son, somewhat similar to what took place in the case of Prince Henry, the eldest son of Henry II.
[4] *Bishop Godwin.*

CHAPTER VII.—CIVIL AND MILITARY HISTORY.—A.D. 1537—1543.

HENRY VIII.—ACCESSION, A.D. 1509—DEATH, A.D. 1547.

Selfish zeal of Henry VIII. for reformation in religion—Trial and sentence on the bones of Thomas à Becket—Spoliation of monasteries—Effects of this havoc on religion and learning—Effects on national industry and comfort—Henry's indiscriminate persecutions—The pope endeavours to promote a crusade against Henry—The relations of Cardinal Pole persecuted—Execution of the Countess of Salisbury—Henry's attempts to reconcile and rule Papists and Protestants—He holds a disputation for the purpose—He enacts the Six Articles—Cromwell negotiates the marriage of Henry with Anne of Cleves—Henry's aversion to his new bride—He falls in love with Lady Catherine Howard—Cromwell arrested and imprisoned—Henry marries Catherine Howard—His repudiation of Anne of Cleves—Cromwell executed—Executions of Papists and Protestants—Catherine Howard accused of adultery—Cranmer's account of her examination in prison—Attempts made to extort a confession of her guilt—Her trial, and the charges brought against her—Declarations of witnesses—Mean conduct of the Duke of Norfolk during her trial—Catherine Howard executed—Absurd law enacted after her execution—Henry's arbitrary proceedings in religion—His regulations for the government of Wales—Condition of Ireland at this period—Rebellion of the Fitzgeralds—Its treacherous suppression—It is succeeded by that of Cromer, Archbishop of Armagh—Disquietude of Henry's government by Irish insurrections—He resolves to elevate Ireland from a lordship into a kingdom.

MEANWHILE "the king continued much prone to reformation, especially if anything might be gotten by it."[1] Nothing was more easy than to prove that all the monastic orders had been engaged in the late insurrection; and, as many of the richest abbeys and priories remained as yet untouched, there was no want of wise counsellors, anxious to share in the spoils, to recommend the suppression of all of them. In some cases, out of a dread of martial law, or what was equally bad, a prosecution for high treason, the abbots surrendered, gave, and granted their abbeys unto the king, his heirs and assigns for ever; but still many replied, like the prior of Henton, in Somersetshire, "that they would not be light and hasty in giving up those things which were not theirs to give, being dedicated to Almighty God, for service to be done to his honour continually, with other many good deeds of charity which were daily done in their houses to their Christian neighbours."[2] These recusants were treated with great severity. The prisons were crowded with priors and monks, who died so rapidly in their places of confinement as to excite a dreadful suspicion.

Without waiting for a needless act of parliament, the king suppressed many other houses, and soon after, with the full consent of lords and commons, finished this business by seizing all the abbeys without exception, and all the rest of the religious houses, except a very few, which were spared at the earnest petition of the people, or given up to the representatives of their original founders. Before proceeding to the final suppression, under pretext of checking the superstitious worshipping of images, he had laid bare their altars and stripped their shrines of everything that was valuable; nor did he spare the rich coffins and the crumbling bones of the dead. At the distance of 400 years, exasperated at that extraordinary man's opposition to the royal prerogative, he determined to have vengeance upon the bones and relics of Thomas à Becket. The martyr's tomb was broken open, and, by an insane process, worthy of a Nero or a Caligula, a criminal information was filed against him as "Thomas Becket, sometime Archbishop of Canterbury," and he was formally cited to appear in court and answer to the charges. Thirty days were allowed the saint, but we need scarcely inform our readers that his dishonoured bones rested quietly at Canterbury, and did not appear to plead in Westminster Hall. We have repeatedly noticed Henry's nice attention to the forms of law and justice: on the present occasion, when Becket might have been declared contumacious, and have had judgment passed against him for default of appearance, the king, by his special grace, assigned him counsel to plead for him. With due solemnity the court opened its proceedings on the 11th of June, 1539. The attorney-general eloquently exposed the case for the prosecution; and the advocates of the saint, who no doubt spoke less boldly, were heard in defence: and that being over, sentence was pronounced that Becket had been guilty of rebellion, treason, and contumacy; that his bones should be burned as a lesson to the living not to oppose the royal will; and that the rich offerings with which many generations of men, native and foreign, had enriched his shrine should be forfeited to the crown

[1] *Bishop Godwin.* [2] *Ellis' Original Letters.*

as the personal property of the traitor. In the month of August, Cromwell, who must have smiled at the course pursued, sent down some of his commissioners to Canterbury, who executed their task so well that they filled two immense coffers with gold and jewels, each of them so heavy that it required eight strong men to lift it. A few months after the king, by proclamation, stated to his people that, forasmuch as it now clearly appears Thomas Becket had been killed in a riot provoked by his own obstinacy and insolence, and had been canonized by the Bishop of Rome merely because he was a champion of that usurped authority, he now deemed it proper to declare that he was no saint whatever, but a rebel and traitor to his prince, and that therefore he, the king, strictly commanded that he should not be any longer esteemed or called a saint—that all images and pictures of him should be destroyed—and that his name and remembrance should be erased out of all books, under pain of his majesty's indignation, and imprisonment at his grace's[1] pleasure.[2]

Other shrines had been plundered before, and certain miraculous images and relics of saints had been broken in pieces at St. Paul's Cross, and the machinery exposed by which some of the monks had deluded the superstitious people; but now every shrine was laid bare, or, if any escaped, it was owing to the poverty of their decorations and offerings. Hitherto Henry had burned the Reformers, and hanged the Catholics; but, on the 22d of May (1539), a monk was hanged up by the arm-pits, and underneath him a fire was made, "wherewith he was slowly burned." There was a pulpit erected near the stake, from which Hugh Latimer, now Bishop of Worcester, preached a sermon; and there was also a scaffold in the centre, for the accommodation of the Dukes of Norfolk and Suffolk, the Lord-admiral Howard, the lord privy-seal (Cromwell), and divers others of the council, together with Sir Richard Gresham, lord-mayor, and many citizens. By frequent spectacles like these was the mind of England brutalized to a degree scarcely ever seen before![3]

In the final seizures of the abbeys and monasteries the richest fell first. After Canterbury, Battle Abbey; Merton, in Surrey; Stratford, in Essex; Lewes, in Sussex; the Charterhouse, the Blackfriars, the Grayfriars, and the Whitefriars, in London, felt the fury of the san whirlwind, which gradually blew over the whole land, until, in the spring of the year 1540, all the monastic establishments of the kingdom were suppressed, and the mass of their landed property was divided among courtiers and parasites. The gold and silver and costly jewels of shrines had partly gone in that direction, and had partly been kept for the king's use. Between the ignorant zealots of the new doctrines, and the rudeness of the men employed in the suppression, who were all most anxious for spoil, and who probably cared little for any form of religion, or any decency of worship, innumerable works of art were destroyed, and magnificent specimens of architecture were defaced and left roofless; statues and pictures, many of them the productions of Italian masters, and which had in the eye of taste a sort of holiness independent of saints and Madonnas, were broken to pieces or burned. The mosaic pavements of the chapels were torn up, and the same brutal hands smashed the painted windows, which almost more than anything gave beauty and glory to our old abbeys and cathedrals. The church-bells were gambled for, and sold into Russia and other countries. The libraries—of which all the great houses contained one, numerously, if not well stocked, but wherein, no doubt, existed many a book in manuscript which we would now willingly possess—were treated with the greatest contempt. "Some books were reserved to scour their candlesticks, some to rub their boots, some sold to the grocers and soap-boilers, and some sent over sea to book-binders, not in small numbers, but at times whole shipsful, to the wondering of foreign nations—a single merchant purchasing, at forty shillings a-piece, two noble libraries to be used as gray paper."[4]

All the abbeys were totally dismantled except in the cases where they happened to be the parish churches also; as was the case at St. Alban's, Tewkesbury, Malvern, and elsewhere, where they were rescued, in part, by the petitions and pecuniary contributions of the pious inhabitants, who were averse to the worshipping of God in a stable. Cranmer and Latimer petitioned the king in some cases; but, as is proved by their existing letters, they were too dependent on the court, and too fearful of its wrath, to do very much.

The men who had recommended the wholesale spoliation of the church had represented it as a never-failing fund, which would enable the king to carry on his government with none, or but

---

[1] Wilkins' *Concilia*.
[2] "The part that Erasmus had in precipitating the downfall of the conventual establishments in England, by arming public opinion against them, must not be forgotten. 'Erasmus, the prince of European scholars, was in the fiftieth year of his age, and in the full maturity of his fame, when Luther began to preach the Reformation at Wittemberg. No man had more severely lashed the superstitions which were miscalled acts of piety, or scourged the frauds and debaucheries of the priesthood with a more vigorous arm. The ridicule which he so plentifully poured on the monks during his residence in England, doubtless contributed to their easy overthrow in this country.'"—Sir James Mackintosh, *History of England*.
[3] Hall; Stow; Godwin.
[4] Spelman, *History and Fate of Sacrilege*.

the slightest taxes, and would furnish him with the means of creating and supporting earls, barons, and knights, and of forming excellent institutions for the promotion of industry, education, and religion. But, in the event, the property was squandered in a manner which is scarcely accountable; and the king had the conscience to demand from parliament *a compensation for the expenses he had incurred in reforming the religion of the state;* and within a year after the completion of his measures, the slavish parliament voted him a subsidy of two-tenths and two-fifteenths for this express purpose. None of the objects spoken of were promoted by the money of the religious houses, always excepting the making and supporting certain noblemen. Pauperism increased, as the whole body of the poor, which had been supported by the monks, who had funds for that purpose, were thrown, clamorous and desperate, and unprepared for and unprovided with employment, upon the wondering nation, which had not before been aware of the extent of the evil. Education declined rapidly; the schools kept in the monasteries were at an end; and other schools and even the universities were comparatively deserted. Religion was not promoted—for nothing but miserable stipends were given to the preachers, and none but poor and unlettered men would accept the office. To preach at St. Paul's Cross had been a great object of clerical ambition; but now there was a difficulty of finding a sufficient number of preachers for that duty; and about four years after the final suppression, Bonner, Bishop of London, wrote to Parker, then master of Corpus, importuning him to send him some help from Cambridge; and, not long after that, during the short reign of Edward VI., Latimer said, "I think there be at this day 10,000 students less than were within these twenty years." The rural parishes were served by priests who had scarcely the rudiments of education. Following an example set them by the king, who required Cromwell to give a benefit to a priest who was kept in the royal service, because he had trained two hawks for his majesty's pastime, which flew and killed their game very well,[1] the patrons of livings gave them to their menials as wages or rewards, to their gardeners, to the keepers of their hawks and hounds.[2] So completely were the funds absorbed, and so greedy were the courtiers in keeping what they got, that no proper recompense was reserved for Miles Coverdale and his associates, who translated and printed the first complete English Bible—the greatest achievement of the age, and the measure that most effectually promoted the Reformation. Coverdale himself was left in great poverty; and the printers, in order to cover their expenses, were obliged to put a high price upon their copies, thus impeding the circulation of the book, and thwarting the wishes expressed by the king himself.[3]

The destruction of the monasteries left important gaps even in the physical accommodations of the people, which not a pound sterling of the spoil was devoted to fill up. They had been hospitals, infirmaries, and dispensaries for the poor—caravansaries to the wayfarer—and, in the absence of inns, the badness of roads, and the thinness of the population, their value had been felt in this respect both by rich and poor. In many of the wilder districts they had served as a nucleus of civilization, and sociality and hospitality were nowhere to be found but within these walls. The Chancellor Audley, who was seldom anxious to stop the hand of the spoiler, and who partook largely in the spoil, ventured, in a letter to Cromwell, to beg that two of the abbeys in Essex might be left standing on this account. The Archbishop Cranmer, however, did what he could with safety to himself; and Henry, startled perhaps by a popular outcry, resolved to appropriate a part of the spoil to the advancement of religion. Parliament passed an act for establishing new bishoprics, deaneries, and colleges, which were to be endowed with revenues raised on the lands of the monasteries; but it was too late: the money and lands were gone, or the king and his ministers needed all that remained. The number of new bishoprics was reduced from eighteen to six—those of Westminster, Oxford, Peterborough, Bristol, Chester, and Gloucester; and these were so scantily endowed that they scarcely afforded the new bishops the means of living.[4] At the same time, fourteen abbeys and priories were converted into cathedrals and collegiate churches, with deans and prebendaries; but the king kept to himself a part of the lands which had been attached to them, and charged the chapters with the obligation of contributing annually to the support of the poor and the repairs of the highways.

In order to bring this interesting subject—which, notwithstanding its connection with the history of religion, cannot be separated from the political history of the time—under one point of view, we have outrun several contemporary events which we must now take up.

Although the king had overthrown so many

---

[1] Letter from Fitzwilliam to Cromwell, dated at Hampton Court, the 12th September, 1537.—*State Papers.*
[2] Latimer's *Sermons;* Strype; Spelman, *Hist. and Fate of Sacrilege,* with letters quoted therein, and by Leland; Blunt's *Sketch of the Reformation.*
[3] Letters addressed by Coverdale and Grafton the printer to Cromwell, from Paris, in the year 1538, in *State Papers.*
[4] *Journals;* Strype; *Rymer;* Godwin. Westminster was erected into a bishopric on the 17th of December, 1510; Oxford in 1541; Peterborough in 1541; Bristol in 1542; Chester in 1542; and Gloucester in 1541.

of the fundamental doctrines and practices of the Roman church, he would allow no man in his dominions the right of questioning such as, in his wisdom, he had thought fit to retain; and in the month of November, 1538, only a few days after his proclaiming Thomas à Becket a rebel and traitor, the fires of Smithfield again blazed, and a man and a woman were consumed in them as Anabaptists. But in the same month, one John Lambert, formerly in priest's orders, but now a schoolmaster in London, who had adopted the views of the German Reformers respecting the sacrament of the Lord's Supper, was condemned, as an obstinate heretic and opponent of the truth, to be burned alive. The sentence was executed in Smithfield with some circumstances of unusual atrocity. Cranmer and the bishops concurred in the abominable proceeding, although some of them besides Cranmer were more than suspected of going the whole length of the German Reformers, and of entertaining precisely the same notions as to the sacrament for which Lambert was burned alive.[1]

Before this time the pope had not only published his bull of excommunication, but had laboured to reconcile the great Catholic princes of the Continent, in order that they might make a crusade against Henry, whose cruelties excited universal disgust. His great effort was to make up all quarrels between the King of France and the emperor; and by his mediation, a truce for ten years was concluded at Nice, on the 18th of June, 1538. During the whole of the years 1538 and 1539, Henry, who was unprepared for war, and who, by this time, had become suspicious of all his subjects, was kept in a constant state of alarm by reports that Francis and Charles were about to head a league against him; and great was the labour of his more courageous minister Cromwell to remove these apprehensions and jealousies.[2] On one occasion Cromwell assures his majesty that there is no need of being so hot and cold, seeing that there are no ships preparing in Spain for invasion: on another, he comforts him with the prospect of a new and extended alliance among the Protestant princes of Germany, which will be sure to find the emperor employment; and in another he thinks that the finger of God is visible in the stirring up of the Great Turk, who is resolved to make a fresh invasion of Christendom. Shortly after, however, the minister was obliged to allude to some practices of the Cardinal Pole, and to tell the king that he had learned from Rome a rumour that the emperor, the French king, and the pope were carrying on an active correspondence, but that it was thought that the two sovereigns were only giving the pope "fair words to feed him with."

At the end of the year 1538, the Lord Montacute and Sir Geoffrey Pole, brothers to the cardinal; Henry Courtney, Marquis of Exeter, grandson to King Edward IV. by his daughter Catherine; Sir Edward Nevil; two priests named Croft and Collins; and one Holland, a mariner, were suddenly apprehended and conveyed to the Tower. In the beginning of the year 1539, the Marquis of Exeter and the Lord Montacute were arraigned before some peers,[1] and the commoners were tried before a jury, on a vague charge of having devised to maintain, promote, and advance one Reginald Pole, late dean of Exeter, the king's enemy beyond the seas, and to deprive the king of his royal state and dignity. We have no particulars of these trials; but Geoffrey Pole, the youngest of the brothers, upon a promise of pardon, pleaded guilty, and made a confession involving all the rest, who thereupon were condemned to death as traitors.

Lord Herbert says that he "could never discover the particular offences of these great persons. . . . Only I find among our records that Thomas Wriothesley, secretary, then at Brussels, writing of their apprehension to Sir Thomas Wyatt, his highness' ambassador in Spain, said that the accusations were great, and duly proved;" and he adds that another writer said they had sent the cardinal (Pole) money. Cromwell might have had better proofs of their correspondence with the cardinal, through means of his spies and agents, but we have no letter of his that touches upon this prosecution. The Marquis of Exeter and Lord Montacute had remained steady and loyal during the insurrection in the north, where, on account of their descent from the White Rose, they might have exercised a dangerous influence. There was certainly no overt act of treason; and the main cause of their death seems to have been Henry's dread and jealousy of their royal descent, and his anxiety to be revenged upon the cardinal, whose own person was out of his reach, and whose abilities and energies were at the moment actively employed in raising him up enemies. Sir Geoffrey Pole was allowed a dishonoured life. His brother, Lord Montacute, the Marquis of

---

[1] *Hall; Godwin; Fox; Collier.*
[2] The king's dread, and Cromwell's labour to remove it, are both well proved by original letters still in existence. At this moment Cromwell maintained spies and secret agents at Rome, Naples, Milan, Genoa, Venice, Madrid, Paris, Brussels, Frankfort, and in almost every corner of Europe. One of the chief objects of these agents was to watch the movements of Cardinal Pole, and otherwise to pick up information as to the treaties between the Catholic princes, and their preparations or non-preparations for war.—*State Papers.*
[3] They were certainly not tried in a regular manner before the peers in parliament, for parliament did not meet for more than two months after their execution. It appears that the Chancellor Audley acted as high-steward on this occasion. On the 3d of March Sir Nicholas Carew was beheaded for being of counsel with the Marquis of Exeter and Lord Montacute.

Exeter, and Sir Edward Nevil, were beheaded on Tower-hill on the 9th of January, 1539; the two priests and the mariner were hanged and quartered at Tyburn. But Henry's hatred was not yet satisfied, nor his jealous fears set at rest. In the month of February, Cromwell "learned out of Scotland," that there was a French ship, with sundry passengers, about to set sail from Leith; and on the 14th of March, he wrote joyfully to inform the king "that a certain French ship, laden with Scottish goods, had been driven by stress of weather into South Shields;" and that the Earl of Westmoreland, "being advised by certain persons from Scotland," had seized and searched the ship, and had found "under the baggage, in the bottom thereof, a nest of traitors; that is to say, one Robert Moore, a priest of Chichester, who had lately escaped from Hexham prison, and two Irishmen, a monk and a friar, who had with them seditious and traitorous letters directed to the Bishop of Rome and to the traitor Pole." The poor Irish monk was carried up to London; and, a few days after, Cromwell wrote to the king: "We cannot as yet get the pith of the credence, whereby I am advised tomorrow to go to the Tower, and see him set in the brakes,[1] and, by torment, compelled to confess the truth."[2] We are not informed as to the full result of this visit to the Tower; but when parliament met on the 28th of April, they were instructed to pass bills of attainder against Margaret, Countess of Salisbury, the mother of Cardinal Pole; Gertrude, the widow of the Marquis of Exeter; the son of Lord Montacute, a boy of tender years; Sir Adrian Fortescue; and Sir Thomas Dingley. The cardinal's venerable mother (the Countess of Salisbury was seventy years old) was privately examined at her first arrest by the Earl of Southampton, and Goodrich, the Bishop of Ely, before whom she behaved with so much firmness of character, that they wrote to their employer Cromwell, that she was more like a strong and constant man than a woman—that she denied everything laid to her charge, and that it seemed to them either that her sons had not made her "privy or participant of the bottom and pit of their stomach, or that she must be the most arrant traitress that ever lived."[3] Cromwell himself examined the Marchioness of Exeter, but, as it should appear, without success.[4] Although Cromwell had got possession of the persons of some of the Countess of Salisbury's servants, he could not extract sufficient materials for a criminal information. Upon this he called up the judges, and asked them whether parliament might condemn persons accused of treason without any previous trial or confession; and the servile judges replied, that, though it was a nice question, and one that no inferior tribunal could entertain, there was no doubt that the court of parliament was supreme, and that any attainder by parliament would be good in law. Such a bill, accordingly, the parliament passed, condemning to death all the accused, without any form of trial whatever. The two knights were beheaded on the 10th of July: the Marchioness of Exeter, after being further questioned by Cromwell in the Tower, was pardoned some six months after. The old Countess of Salisbury was kept in prison, but what became of her grandson, the child of Lord Montacute, who was included in the attainder, does not appear. Nearly two years after the passing of the iniquitous act of attainder, on the 27th of May, 1541, the aged countess, the nearest to the king in blood of all his relations, on some new provocation, real or fancied, of her son Cardinal Pole, was dragged from her dungeon in the Tower to the scaffold.[5]

But before this happened the minister Cromwell had gone to his account. If the Catholic or Papist party were not the sole cause of the ruin of this man, they seem to have contributed to that event quite as much as his bad luck in match-making for the king. Each of the two great religious parties was animated with the most deadly animosity against the other, neither of them conceiving for a moment the expediency of a mutual toleration and an agreement among themselves as a means of resisting the still-growing tyranny of the crown; and both ministered in turn to the king's insatiable thirst for blood. Cromwell, with Cranmer, had all along proposed a close alliance with the Protestant states of Germany; and when Henry was alarmed about the coalition of the Catholic powers, he thought seriously of this alliance, and sent several ambassadors into Germany. But as religion was to be the basis of the alliance, the German Protestants wished to see a uniformity of faith and practice established in England, and insisted that, at the least, Henry should permit priests to have wives, and should command private masses to be abolished. The king, who, according to Cromwell,

---

[1] The brake was an instrument of torture: it was also called the "Duke of Exeter's Daughter."
[2] In this same letter Cromwell speaks of the new parliament which was to meet in April. "Amongst other, for your grace's parliament, I have appointed your majesty's servant, Mr. Morrison, to be one of them; no doubt he shall be ready to answer, and take up such as would crack or face with literature of learning, or by indirected waver, if any such shall be, as I think there shall be few or none; forasmuch as I, and other your delicate counsellors, be about to bring all things so to pass that your majesty had never more tractable parliament."—*State Papers.*
[3] *Ellis.* Letter from Lord Southampton and the Bishop of Ely to Cromwell.
[4] *State Papers.* Letter from Cromwell to the king.
[5] Pole, *Epist.*; Hall; Godwin.

"knew himself to be the learnedest prince in Europe," thought it became not him to submit to them, but expected that they should submit to him, and take his ecclesiastical ordinances as their model and guide. The Germans, who considered him as a slave to the very worst of the dogmas of the Roman church, would not listen to such conditions. Henry now evinced a sudden anxiety to reconcile himself with the Catholic party, by showing them that, though he had cast off the authority of the pope, he was as far as ever from entertaining the leading tenets of Luther. The Duke of Norfolk, who favoured the old learning, was unexpectedly sent for, commissioned to manage the affairs of the crown in the House of Peers, and placed, in many matters, over the head of Cromwell: Gardiner, Bishop of Winchester, the most zealous of all the Papists, was also recalled to court, and ordered to preach a course of sermons at St. Paul's Cross. The king must have known the diversity of sentiment which prevailed among the bench of bishops, and he was now resolved that this should cease, probably feeling that it was hard to expect unanimity among the people, when their spiritual teachers, the prelates appointed by himself, differed widely in opinion. In the parliament which attainted the mother of Cardinal Pole, and the rest of those victims, he ordered the appointment of a committee of spiritual lords, among whom Cromwell was included in virtue of his office of vicar-general; and this committee was charged to examine the diversity of opinions in matters of faith, with the view of producing a final agreement. In the absence of the king, Cromwell, and Cranmer, Shaxton, Bishop of Salisbury, and Goodrich, Bishop of Ely, ventured to oppose the more Catholic notions of Lee, Archbishop of York, Tonstal, Bishop of Durham, Aldrich, Bishop of Carlisle, Clarke, Bishop of Bath, and Salcot, *alias* Capon, Bishop of Bangor. Eleven days of disputation wore out the patience of Henry, who was not present to take part in it; and the Duke of Norfolk, seeing that the committee would never agree, suggested another course, which was adopted by the king's wisdom in concurrence with Bishop Gardiner. On the 18th of May, 1539, the duke proposed to the consideration of the whole House of Lords six questions respecting the eucharist, communion under one kind, private masses, the celibacy of the priesthood, auricular confession, and vows of chastity. On this occasion none but the spiritual peers spoke, and of them only such as were in favour of the Roman practices: the rest, who, no doubt, knew what was coming, remained silent in their seats. On the second day the king went down to the house and joined in the debate. It was perilous work to oppose a controversialist who was accustomed to back his arguments with the axe, the gallows, and the stake. The temporal lords, not excepting the Lord-chancellor Audley and the Lord Privy-seal Cromwell, were presently all of one opinion; and among the bishops, only those of Canterbury, Ely, Salisbury, Worcester, Rochester, and St. David's, defended the contrary side, which they did for a long time, "but yet they were finally confounded with his highness' goodly learning." There is a dispute between writers of opposite parties as to the extent of the opposition of the Archbishop of Canterbury, but it appears that Cranmer really resisted the bill as far as was consistent with the safety of his life, and that he never gave a very formal consent to it. Shaxton, Bishop of Salisbury, had more courage, and openly resisted to the last; or, in the words of one of the lords who was present, "he yet continued a lewd fool." A few days after, Henry proposed that the severest penalties should be enacted by parliament against all such persons as should dare to teach contrary doctrines, or question the sacred institutions of private masses, confession, and the rest. At the king's order the lords formed a committee, which, after some changes, was headed and wholly directed by the most violent partizans of the old learning—the Archbishop of York, the Bishop of Durham, and the Bishop of Winchester, the fiery but accomplished Gardiner. This committee readily adopted the Six Articles, or the Bloody Statute, as it was afterwards called, and which was evidently the joint production of Bishop Gardiner and the king.[1] It was submitted in a hurry to the clergy assembled in convocation; and being approved of there, was introduced by the Protestant Chancellor Audley, and passed through both lords and commons with infinite ease. These notorious articles were—1. That the eucharist was really the present natural body and blood of Christ, under the forms, but without the substance, of bread and wine, which were transmuted by the act of consecration. 2. That the communion under both kinds was not necessary to salvation. 3. That priests could not, by the law of God, marry. 4. That vows of chastity, whether in man or woman, priest, monk, or nun, must be observed. 5. That private masses must be retained as essential. 6. That the use of auricular confession is expedient and necessary. To these Six Articles were attached the following penalties: 1. If any person wrote, preached, or disputed against the first article—which settled the question of the real presence in the eucharist —he should not be allowed to abjure or recant, but should at once be burned as a heretic, and forfeit his property to the king—a worse penalty than ever was enacted by the Inquisition, which

---

[1] A draft of the act with many corrections, in the king's own hand, is preserved in the British Museum.

allowed the benefit of one recantation. 2. If any man preached, or spoke openly before the judges, against any one of the other five articles, he should incur the penalties of felony; but if he only held contrary opinions, and published them, he should, for the first offence, be imprisoned at the king's pleasure, forfeiting his lands during life, his goods for ever; and for the second offence he should die. 3. All marriages of priests or nuns already contracted were to be of no effect; the parties so marrying were to separate immediately, and if they cohabited afterwards it would be punished as felony; priests and nuns found guilty of fornication were to suffer imprisonment and forfeiture on the first conviction, and death on the second.[1]

As soon as this barbarous statute was passed, Shaxton, Bishop of Salisbury, and Latimer, Bishop of Worcester, resigned their sees, or they were deprived of them by the king, for refusing to subscribe the edict;[2] but Cranmer, Fox, and Goodrich did not follow their example. Cranmer, more than all, was in a critical situation; he had brought his German wife, the niece of the Protestant pastor Osiander, into England, and by this time she had borne him several children. He had kept his family in retirement, out of sight of the world; but it is difficult to conceive that such a connection could be wholly a secret. He had evidently hoped to prevail upon the king to adopt the Lutheran notion with respect to the celibacy of the clergy; but this hope must have failed him even before the passing of the Six Articles; and he, a married churchman, and the father of a family, had been compelled, on more than one occasion, to denounce severe pains and penalties against all churchmen in the same predicament. Now, however, in all haste he sent his wife and children into Germany, and made himself conformable to the bloody statute. But Cranmer, Latimer, and others, relied with a happy hope on the effect of the Bible, which was now circulated in the language of the people.[3]

The same dastardly parliament which passed the Six Articles voted also that the king's proclamations had, and ought to have, the full effect of acts of parliament; that all transgressions against such proclamations should be punished with fines and imprisonment, or otherwise, at the king's pleasure; and that for a person to quit the kingdom, in order to escape these penalties incurred by disobedience to proclamation, was high treason. (Are we speaking of England, or of an Oriental despotism?) Base, however, as were lords and commons, this bill encountered some opposition; but still the two religious parties were too intent upon other matters to coalesce and make a bold stand against this horrid tyranny.[4]

As if he feared he had gone too far in the direction of the Church of Rome, the king ordered a silly pageant on the river Thames, where two galleys, the one bearing the royal arms of England, the other the arms of the pope, met and fought in fierce guise. The royal galley was of course victorious, and effigies of the pope and cardinals were thrown overboard amidst the shouts of the king, the court, and the citizens.[5] On the 8th of July, the vicar of Wandsworth, with his curate, a man-servant, and one Friar Ware, were all hanged and quartered, apparently for questioning the king's supremacy. In the month of November, Richard Whiting, abbot of Glastonbury, was hanged and quartered; and two of his monks, John Thorne, the treasurer, and Roger James, the under-treasurer, were hanged and quartered with him.[6] In the same month, Hugh Farringdon, abbot of Reading, and two of his monks, were hanged and quartered near their abbey; and John Beche, abbot of Colchester, was drawn and quartered near his abbey. All these butcheries of men whom they must have considered as faithful sons of the Roman church, could not but have been distasteful to Gardiner and the other leaders of the old learning; but we do not see that they ever ran the risk of incurring destruction by opposing the king's will, or by protesting against his measures. They, indeed, stood by, and saw men hanged and quartered for questioning the supremacy or resisting the seizure of their abbeys and houses, just as the converts of the new doctrine saw men burned for entertaining the Protestant notions as to the sacrament and other points; and each party seems to have consoled itself for the sufferings of its own friends by the recollection and the prospect of the sufferings of the other.

Cromwell had identified himself with the Protestant party, and had gone to such lengths against the Papists, that it was impossible he could ever hope for a safe reconciliation with them. He saw also that the Duke of Suffolk and Bishop Gardiner were gaining ground at court; and to check their progress, he laboured hard to procure Henry a Protestant wife. "The king," says an old writer, "considering his wooing disposition, had long continued a widower."[7] He had, indeed, been a widower about two years; but this was not owing to a want of alacrity on

---

[1] *Journal; Statutes; Wilkins; Fox; Godwin; Strype; Le Grand.* Fragment of a letter preserved in the Museum.
[2] Latimer resigned on the 1st of July, 1539. He was soon afterwards in prison for speaking against the Six Articles, and remained in confinement till the king's death.
[3] A new and improved edition of the Scriptures, generally called Cranmer's Bible, was published just at this time.
[4] *Statutes; Fox; Le Grand.*
[5] Letter of Marillac, the French ambassador, quoted by Le Grand.   [6] Letter from Lord Russell to Cromwell.
[7] *Bishop Godwin.*

his part in seeking for another wife. Shortly after the death of Jane Seymour he proposed to the Duchess-dowager of Milan, who is said to have replied, facetiously, that if she had two heads she might think of the match; but that, as she had but one, she would rather decline the honour. He then addressed himself to the Princess Mary of Guise; but this princess was already affianced to his nephew, the King of Scots. A daughter of the house of Vendome was then recommended by the French court; but he refused her because she had been previously rejected by his nephew, the said King of Scots. After this, he had the delicacy to propose that the French king should carry the two sisters of Mary of Guise to Calais, in order that he might go over and choose one of them; but the gallantry of Francis revolted at this idea, and Henry remained wifeless. In the month of March, 1539, we find Cromwell extolling to the king the reported beauty of Anne of Cleves, the sister of the reigning Duke of Cleves, one of the princes of the Protestant confederacy; but he speaks as if the marriage had been already settled.[1]

Putting, we suppose, more faith in Hans Holbein, his own painter, than in Lucas the court painter of Cleves, Henry despatched Hans to take the young lady's likeness; and in the month of August, one of his ambassadors in Germany wrote a fuller account of her person and accomplishments, assuring his majesty, moreover, that my Lady Anne was not bound by any previous covenant or contract, but was at her free will to marry wherever she would. As for her education, *sobriety*, and morals, the diplomatist said that they were excellent.[2] The picture—a miniature, in Holbein's best manner—was brought over in an ivory box, which represented a rose, so delicately carved as to be said to be worthy of the jewel it contained. The king fancied himself in love as he contemplated this nice performance of his favourite artist; and the match proceeded. Hoping, no doubt, that a Protestant wife would finish his conversion, many of the German princes gave it their support; and in the month of September, the count-palatine and ambassadors from Cleves arrived in London, where Cromwell, who was in ecstasies at the success of the scheme, was instructed by his royal master to bid them as hearty a welcome as he could devise.[3] The king joyfully finished this treaty; but the marriage, instead of making, marred Cromwell. All things being prepared as was fitting, and her lover brooking no delay, Anne set forward on her journey in the dreary month of December. Though now unwieldy, Henry rode hastily to Rochester to meet her. He went in disguise, and his first view of her was a secret one; but it was enough: he shrunk back, tottering under the weight of disappointment and dismay; and it was some time before he composed himself sufficiently to wait upon her as her husband and king. It seems to have been with sensations like those with which one swallows a dose of noisome medicine that he embraced her, and gave her his conjugal kiss. The whole interview did not last above the speaking of twenty words: he then hurried from his bride without giving her the presents he had brought with him; and the next morning he sent Sir Anthony Brown, his master of the horse, "with a partlet of sable skins to wear round the neck, and a muffler furred, with as cold a message as might be, and rode himself back to Greenwich, marvellously heavy in heart." His fiercest wrath was kindled against all those who had promoted the match; and he considered that the deception practised upon him was a proof that all faith and loyalty had departed the world, and that no mortal man could be trusted. Cromwell was evidently less culpable than the ambassadors and the painters; but notwithstanding this circumstance, and his great boldness and ability, he must have trembled upon receiving the king's summons. A full council met at Greenwich, and there, after abusing him for marrying him to "a great Flanders mare," coarse, clumsy, and "unfit to nourish love," he commanded Cromwell to devise some pretext or plausible cause for preventing the conclusion of the hateful marriage.[4] In the very doubtful state of his relation with the Catholic powers, it was humbly but forcibly represented that it might prove very dangerous to give such an affront to the princes of the Protestant confederacy; and Cromwell seems to have made the most of the king's fears. "Is there, then, no remedy?—must I needs, against my will, put my neck into this noose?"—were the affectionate expressions of Henry as he agreed that the marriage should go on. The Lady Anne was met at Blackheath, and, with great state, brought to Greenwich on the 3d of January, and she was married on the 5th day of the same month. But Henry's aversion did not abate on a closer ac-

---

[1] State Papers.
[2] Ellis' Collection; letter of Nich. Wotton to Henry VIII. The original not perfect, but injured by fire is in the Brit. Mus.
[3] State Papers; letter from the king to Cromwell.
[4] After all, it does not appear that Anne of Cleves was an ugly woman; and much of Henry's distaste may have proceeded from the mere caprice of the jaded voluptuary. He was certainly himself no very loveable object at the time. As he grew fat he wished for a fat wife, and his agents had been expressly commanded to look out for a fine, large woman. But Anne, it appears, was on too large a scale. According to Holbein's picture, her complexion was wonderfully fair and beautiful, and her countenance very agreeable. Marillac, the French ambassador, no prejudiced observer, says that she was tolerably handsome—*de beauté moyenne*. Like a true Frenchman he criticises her German dress.

quaintance; and, without going into the disgusting details with which he, without hesitation, entertained his court, and the noble matrons thereof, we need merely state that he lamented his fate in the most pathetic terms, and declared that life would be a burden to him if he were forced to pass it with such a wife.[1] The Catholic party were greatly rejoiced at this manifest failure of a great Protestant experiment; and other religious feelings came in to hasten the destruction of Cromwell. We will not attempt to explain what perplexed those who were acting on the scene; but, while the Papists made sure that Cromwell's high offices of vicar-general and keeper of the privy seal would immediately fall to Tonstal, and Clarke, Bishop of Bath, he was not only left in possession, but received from the king's hands the order of the Garter, and was created Earl of Essex and lord-chamberlain, ostensibly as a reward for his exertions in obtaining an enormous grant from parliament.[2] It should appear, however, that Henry was making provision for the despatch of the enormous quantity of business which had hitherto been transacted by Cromwell, who must have been a man of iron. He made two secretaries of state, Wriothesley and Ralph Sadler, and divided many important functions of government between them.

We are not told how long the king had bemoaned his fate with Anne of Cleves when he saw the pretty little Lady Catherine Howard;[3] but it seems to have been some four or five months. The Lady Catherine was niece to the Duke of Norfolk, and as entire a Papist as Anne was a Protestant. Henry first met her at a dinner given by Gardiner, Bishop of Winchester. It is supposed that that prelate and his party had calculated upon the impression her charms would make upon him; and it was natural enough for them to suppose that the next step a man like Henry would take, after espousing a Protestant, would be to choose a wife from the opposite sect. By a "notable appearance of honour, cleanness, and maidenly behaviour," Catherine quite captivated the king, who, it appears, frequently met her afterwards at the house of Bishop Gardiner, or of some other person equally anxious for the interests of the Romish church. In this society, composed of the mortal enemies of Cromwell, the king was not likely to hear much good of his minister. Every glance of the bright eyes of Catherine Howard was dangerous to the Protestant interest. At the same time Cromwell, strangely blind to what was passing, continued to deal his sharp blows at the scrupulous Papists who refused the oaths of supremacy; and he was in the high exercise of despotic power, when, suddenly, on the 10th of June, he was arrested at the council-board on a charge of high treason, and forthwith carried to the Tower. In his days of favour he had encouraged the prostration of all law, and the establishment of the most arbitrary modes of proceeding in judicial cases. He had held up the king as being authorized to make and change statutes as he pleased; and he now felt the whole weight of the monstrous tyranny which he had helped to erect and inflate. His papers were seized—his servants were questioned—and out of their evidence, which was never produced in court, or submitted to any public examination, his enemies fabricated a series of charges, the greatest of which amounted to treason. In his fall Cromwell scarcely showed more fortitude than Wolsey: he wrote imploring letters to his most gracious prince, crying, "Mercy! mercy!" Once Henry's heart seemed touched by these appeals, but it was only for a moment. Archbishop Cranmer summoned courage to write a letter in his behalf, but the epistle was not calculated to produce any great effect; and he afterwards gave his vote against his friend. On the 14th of June, Cromwell, deserted by all the world, asked for a trial before his peers, but the court preferred to proceed by bill of attainder, without trial—a practice which he himself had helped the king to establish, with consent of the slavish parliament. The bill of attainder was hurried through the House of Lords; and on the 19th of June, nine days after his arrest, Cromwell received his doom as a manifold traitor and detestable heretic.[4]

But before he was executed, Anne of Cleves was divorced, and the king was united in the holy bands of matrimony with Catherine Howard. On the 25th of June, Anne was ordered to remove to Richmond, being told that that place would be more suitable to her health and pleasure than London. Then the king gave directions to his bishops and ministers to legalize his separation from Anne of Cleves; and the bishops and ministers acted accordingly. It was instantly discovered that there had once been a formal contract of marriage between Anne and the son of the Duke of Lorraine; and this, with Henry's assertion that the marriage had never been consummated, was deemed quite sufficient ground. Parliament met and humbly implored his majesty to investigate the subject. The case was submitted to a convocation of the clergy, and on the 9th of July, it was unanimously decided by the churchmen of all colours that the marriage was null and void, inasmuch as the king had married the princess

---

[1] Depositions of the king and Cromwell, in *Strype; Burnet; Holl; Stow*.
[2] During this session the Knights Hospitallers were dissolved, and their property was vested in the crown.
[3] This unfortunate young creature was below the usual stature of English women.

[4] *Le Grand; Strype; Burnet; Herbert, Journals*.

"without the inward consent of his own mind," and as there had been a pre-contract between her and another person. Poor Anne, who had the dread of the block before her eyes, and who was a person of more discretion than pride or passion, most quietly submitted to her fate,' and two days after, being properly prompted and assisted (for she could write no English), she addressed a letter to his most excellent majesty, wherein she declared that she was not and never had been his wife. "Yet it will please you," she continued, "to take me for one of your most humble servants, and so to determine of me, as I may sometimes have the fruition of your most noble presence, which as I shall esteem for a great benefit, so my lords, and others of your majesty's council, now being with me, *have put me in comfort thereof, and that your highness will take me for your sister*, for the which I most humbly thank you accordingly. Thus, most gracious prince, I beseech our Lord God to send your majesty long life and good health, to God's glory, your own honour, and the wealth of this noble realm."[2]

On the very next day Henry commissioned the Duke of Suffolk to go to the Lady Anne at Richmond, and "considering she be now come to her strength, and in good temper of body," to press her further to write to her brother the Duke of Cleves, in order to express her perfect concurrence in all that had been done.[3] Anne, too wise to resist, and in all probability but too happy to escape out of the lion's jaws, did everything that was required of her. On the 16th of July, she wrote the most submissive of letters to the most excellent and noble prince, her most benign and good *brother* Henry, subscribing herself, as had been agreed, his majesty's humble sister and servant.[4] The obsequious parliament finished its part of the work[5] by voting that it would be very lawful for the king to take another wife. A private marriage was performed, and some days after, on the 8th of August, Catherine Howard was publicly shown as queen.[6] On the same day, or nearly on the same day, that Henry took to himself his fifth wife, he sent his minister Cromwell to the block. On the 28th of July, Cromwell was beheaded on Tower-hill; and it is said that he died professing the Catholic faith, by which he might mean that kind of faith which had been established by the last act of parliament. When he was dead many of his virtues were remembered; and the people particularly called to mind that, twice a-day, 200 poor persons had been fed at his gate. Dr. Barnes, a great preacher and leader of the Protestant party,

QUEEN CATHERINE HOWARD.—After Holbein.

survived his patron Cromwell only three days, "being committed to the torments of the merciless fire," and burned alive, with Garret and Jerome, as an heretic. But, that the scales might be nicely trimmed, Powell, Abel, and Featherston were hanged and quartered at the same time for denying the king's supremacy. On this occasion, as on some others, they were coupled together, a Catholic with a Protestant, on the same hurdle, and so drawn to Smithfield to the horror of both sects. A Frenchman is said to have exclaimed, "Good God, how do people make a shift to live here, where Papists are hanged and anti-Papists are burned!" In the next month the prior of Doncaster and six others were hanged for defending the institution of the monastic life, a crime now become as capital as the greatest.[7]

A.D. 1541. There was a feeble attempt made in Yorkshire to revive the "Pilgrimage of Grace;" but it was easily suppressed, and cost the lives of fourteen gentlemen. In the month of August, the king made a progress into the northern counties, taking with him his young wife, whom he "entirely loved," after more than a year of matrimony. He had, indeed, repeatedly declared that he had never been

---

[1] In his despatches of the 31st of July, 11th of August, and 3d of September, Marillac writes:—"Anne makes no opposition whatever to the divorce, at which the king is the more pleased, because, as it is said, his new favourite ,amourette, is already with child. The former is now called merely Madame Anne of Cleves. She is anything but low-spirited—amuses herself in all possible ways, and dresses every day in new clothes, made in a strange fashion." The reported pregnancy of Catherine seems to have been merely a bit of court or city scandal.

[2] *State Papers.*
[3] From some expressions in this letter and elsewhere, it might appear that Anne had taken the matter more seriously to heart than is generally stated, and that she was or had been ill. Perhaps it was considered decorous that she should feign a sickness!
[4] *State Papers.*
[5] The lords implored him, out of his love of his people, to marry again! [6] *State Papers; Herbert; Stow; Godwin.*
[7] *Stow; Strype; Godwin.*

happy in love or marriage till now, and that the Lady Catherine was the most perfect of women, and most affectionate of wives. Nay, he had even gone so far in his gratitude as to make one of his bishops unite with him in praising the Lord for the great contentment he had found. But, on his return from his progress, Cranmer had a tale for his ear which struck him dumb, and it is said even drew tears in torrents from his eyes. The archbishop declared that the queen before her marriage, had led an abandoned life with Francis Dereham or Deram, a relation of her own, who had associated with her when she lived with her great aunt, the Dowager-duchess of Norfolk. Cranmer, who had consulted with the Chancellor Audley, the Earl of Hertford, and others of the Protestant party, had not undertaken to present this dangerous accusation without proof; *and his witness was a servant of the old Duchess of Norfolk.* The king's faith in the virtue of his wife was annihilated in a moment; but, wishing to proceed cautiously, he arrested all the persons who had been named as the queen's confidants and accomplices, and made them undergo, *in secret,* "a keen examination." Their servants, both men and women, were arrested also, and put to the torture.[1] Under these circumstances it was impossible to fail in procuring confessions against the queen; but it appears that these torture-compelled confessions merely went to show that Catherine had been incontinent before marriage; and this did not amount to treason. Francis Dereham is generally said to have confessed that he had been guilty with her; but the queen denied the charge altogether, and, from the best evidence[2] we possess, it seems doubtful whether Dereham confessed anything of the kind. That same night, however, she is said to have signed a written confession of her youthful irregularities, but of nothing farther. Cranmer undertook the office of making her disclose more, and admit that there had been a precontract of marriage between her and her kinsman and alleged seducer Francis Dereham, which, in itself, according to Henry's jurisprudence, would annul the marriage, while it might also be considered as a saving of the king's honour—seeing that, by such precontract, and such law, there could have been no marriage at any time, and Catherine must sink into the condition of a concubine, not having ever had the character of the king's wife. We have before us a letter to the king, which will not raise Cranmer in the estimation of the world. The archbishop begins by describing Catherine's wretched condition. He then tells the king that he had delivered to her his grace's *promise of mercy;* upon which she held up her hands and gave most humble thanks; and, for a time, she recovered from the frenzy in which he had found her, and began to be more temperate and quiet, saving that she still sobbed and wept; but, after a little pausing, she suddenly fell into a new frenzy worse than before. "Now," continues the prelate, "I do use her thus: when I do see her in any such extreme frights, I do travail with her to know the cause, and then, as much as I can, I do labour to take away, or, at the least, to mitigate the cause; and so I did at that time. I told her there was some new phantasy come into her head, which I desired her to open unto me. 'Alas! my lord,' she cried, 'that I am alive! The fear of death grieved me not so much before, as doth now the remembrance of the king's goodness—for when I remember how gracious and loving a prince I had, I cannot but sorrow; but this sudden mercy showed unto me at this time maketh mine offences to appear before mine eyes much more heinous than they did before.'" After this, Cranmer goes on to tell the king, that, by degrees, the distracted woman had come to herself; that she was meetly well unto night, and that he had had "very good communication with her," and, as he thought, had brought her into "a great quietness." He discloses all that he had been able to get out of her concerning any contract of matrimony with Dereham, which, he says, *although it did not go so far as he thought it would have done,* yet appeared to him sufficient to establish the contract.[3] After Cranmer had thus worked upon the unfortunate young woman in her frenzy, and, on the promise of the king's mercy, had induced her to confess improper conduct with Dereham before her marriage (and nothing more), the king changed his plan. A few days after, the council, consisting of the Duke of Norfolk, the Earl of Southampton, the Duke of Suffolk, Lord Russell, Sir Anthony Brown, Wingfield, and Sadler, addressed a long letter to the Archbishop of Canterbury, who had taken upon himself the principal conduct of this wretched business. The minuteness of detail—the petty and innumerable regulations that appear in every part of the transaction—fill the mind with a disgust against all engaged in it, accessories as well as principal. In the king's name they tell Cranmer that he must, with convenient diligence, remove the queen to the house of Sion, there to remain, "till the matter be further ordered, in the state of a queen, but furnished moderately, as her life and condition hath deserved—that is to say, with the fur-

---

[1] We derive this fact, which is not mentioned by historians, from a passage in a letter to Sir Ralph Sadler, signed by Cranmer, Audley, the Duke of Suffolk, the Earl of Hertford, and others:— "And because Damport confesseth this now, which he would not do for any torture that he could before be put to," &c.

[2] *State Papers.*

[3] *State Papers.*

niture of three chambers, hanged with mean stuff, without any cloth of estate." Mr. Baynton, her jailer, is to sleep in one of the three rooms; they are to dine in another; and the queen and her attendants are to sleep in a third. They send a book or list of servants to wait upon the queen; but the king's highness trusts to the archbishop's discretion in not exceeding a necessary number. It is also the king's highness' pleasure that my Lady Baynton,[1] the wife of her jailer, shall be one of those to attend upon the queen, and shall have the rule and government of the whole house. My Lady Mary, the king's daughter, who had led a most stormy life with her father's wives, was to be removed. But after these and other minutiæ, the council proceed to the pith of the business. "And where the king's highness, weighing deeply all circumstances of the matter, hath, by mature consideration, been determined, that to-morrow (12th November) my lord-chancellor, assembling his majesty's councillors of all sorts, spiritual and temporal, with the judges and learned men, should declare unto them the abominable demeanour of the queen, without calling Dereham,[2] as was before thought good, and *without speaking or mentioning any precontract of marriage, which might serve for her defence,* but only to open and make manifest the king's highness' just cause of indignation and displeasure, so as the world may know and see that which is hitherto done to have a just ground and foundation; .... the king's majesty also willeth, that those among you that know the whole matter, and how it was first detected, as also the king's majesty's sorrowful behaviour, and careful proceeding in it, should, upon Sunday next, assemble all the ladies, gentlewomen, and gentlemen, and declare unto them the whole process of the matter; foreseeing always that you *make not mention of any precontract;* but, omitting that, to set forth such matter as might impair and confound their misdemeanour, and as truth doth, indeed, truly bear, declare, and set forth the king's majesty's goodness, most unworthy to be troubled with any such mischance."[3]

The accusations against Catherine Howard were now brought to bear upon misconduct after marriage, in order that her guilt might amount to treason; for Henry seems no longer to have cared about that partial saving of his honour, which might have resulted from the contrary course. It was alleged that not only had Dereham been recalled from Ireland to court, since her marriage, but that Culpepper, one night when the court was at Lincoln, had stayed in the same room with her and the Lady Rochford for three hours. This Lady Rochford was the infamous woman that had borne testimony against her own husband and her husband's sister, Anne Boleyn. Culpepper was a gentleman of the privy chamber, and probably a near relation of Catherine Howard, whose mother's name was Culpepper. A day or two after, Sadler informs his grace of Canterbury and Mr. Comptroller, that the queen has been examined on the matter now come forth concerning Culpepper; but he adds, that she hath not, as appeareth by her confession, so fully declared the circumstances of what passed betwixt her and Culpepper as his majesty could wish; "and so his majesty would have his grace (Cranmer) once again essay and test to get something of her." Mr. Secretary Sadler next tells the Archbishop of Canterbury that my Lord-chancellor Audley has declared the case in the Star Chamber, *omitting and leaving out as much as in anywise toucheth the precontract;* and that he also has read divers of the depositions of such persons as had been examined, as well men as women, *always omitting as much as touched the precontract:* "and, in the end of his tale," saith Sadler, "he added, that there was an appearance of great abomination in her, which he (the chancellor) *left so in a cloud as it should seem doubtful to the hearers whether all were come out or not:* and the king's majesty would have you (Cranmer) follow this order without your mentioning anything of Culpepper or the precontract."[1] When this business had been in progress about a month, the king ordered that the old Duchess-dowager of Norfolk, her daughter Lady Bridgewater, one of her sons (the Lord William Howard), and other persons of rank, should be arrested upon suspicion of being privy to the queen's irregularities, and that their houses should be taken possession of and diligently searched. The Earl of Southampton took the old duchess into custody, and conveyed her to the house of the lord-chancellor. Here, according to the earl's letter, "she began to be very sick, even at the heart, as she said; which was the sickness of mistrust." The noble lord also reports that he has got one Pewson, a servant of the duchess, with whom he has "somewhat travailed this day, in order to make him confess; but, marry, he is yet stiff."[2]

The government was now divided into two councils, one of which removed with the king wherever he went; the other, with the Archbishop of Canterbury at their head, remained in London, in search of evidence. The attention of both councils seems to have been entirely absorbed by this one business. The champion of the Catholic faith moved about with the champion of the Reformation. Stephen Gardiner was associ-

---
[1] Both Baynton and his wife had done duty for the king, in the case of Anne Boleyn. They were practised hands in queen killing.
[2] This seems to prove that, up to this moment at least, Dereham had not confessed.   [3] *State Papers.*   [4] *State Papers.*   [5] Ibid.

ated with Thomas Cranmer, and his name appears to nearly all the letters inculpating his former friend and protégé Catherine Howard. On the 6th of December they reported to the king that they had met with some success in the questioning of Ashby, another man-servant of the Duchess-dowager of Norfolk, who, being in the custody of Sir Richard Rich, the chancellor of the augmentation,[1] had written, by commandment, three or four leaves of paper. Among many long tales of small importance, Ashby had confessed that, upon hearing what had happened at court, the duchess had broken open Dereham's coffers and a portmanteau, and had taken out of them all the letters and writings, and had carried them to her chamber, saying that she would peruse them herself at leisure, without suffering anybody to see them with her. Ashby said, also, that the duchess had been in great fear about one Alice Wilkes, a serving-woman, who was supposed to know something of a familiarity between the young Catherine Howard and Dereham. This Alice Wilkes they had safe, and would examine her closely, trusting to find out some pithy matter. They reported, also, that they had learned that Damport's, or Dammock's, coffers had been broken open in the Duchess of Norfolk's house, and the papers removed; that this Damport, who had hitherto been "very stiff, confessing nothing for any torture they had used," had at last become pliable and communicative, saying, that he once heard Dereham say at the time when the king's majesty was beginning to court Catherine Howard, "I could be sure of Mistress Catherine an I would, but I dare not. The king beginneth to love her; but, an he were dead, I am sure I might marry her."—[To be extracted by torture, this was a small revelation.] Afterwards, according to the same letter, Damport confessed that Dereham told him that the Duchess of Norfolk once said to a gentlewoman in the queen's chamber, when he, Dereham, was present, pointing to him —"This is he that came out of Ireland for the queen's sake." The council with the king, in reply, state to the council in London, that the king thinks the duchess' breaking open of the coffers of Dereham a very clear proof of an intention to conceal treason; and that if the judges do impartially weigh this act, and the concealment of the papers by the duchess, they must be led to conclude that she knew of the former naughty life betwixt the queen and Dereham; and that his coming again to the queen's service from Ireland was to an ill intent of the renovation of his former naughty life; and that all this was clear treason. His highness would have the judges answer this, his opinion, and satisfy him with reason. The judges, it appears, had already condemned Dereham; for, in continuation, the council state that his highness thinketh it expedient that they spare the execution of Dereham for a time, till the bottom of this matter shall appear, it being likely that new matter will arise daily upon which they might have cause to examine him. In the same letter, Mr. Pollard, that expert investigator, is commanded to examine the duchess' women, in order to find out whether she did of late burn any letters or writings. The council in London presently rejoined that they had "travailed another whole day in the examination of the duchess," who made herself so clear from all knowledge of the abomination between the queen and Dereham, that she would confess no mistrust or suspicion of their love or unseemly familiarity; and as to the coffers, she said she intended only to see what was in them, and finding anything material (which she said she did not), to send the same to the king's majesty. They go on to say that, having with them the Lord Chief-justice, Mr. Attorney, and Mr. Pollard, they had all come to the conclusion that the things proved against my Lady Norfolk and her son Lord William, "with all presumptions and circumstances," will extend to misprision of treason; and also that the Lady William Howard, the Lady Bridgewater, Alice Wilkes, Catherine Tilney, Damport, Walgrave, Malin Tilney, Mary Lascelles, Bulmer, Ashby, Anne Howard, and Margaret Burnet, be in the same case, "if it shall please his majesty to proceed against them."[2]

At a very early stage of these proceedings there was an anxiety betrayed as to the goods and chattels of the accused. Cranmer and his friends, in the same letter, desire to know how his grace would have my Lady of Norfolk and the rest used, and also whether they should commit the Lord William and his wife; "and how their things shall be used, which shall, by this offence, be all confiscate to his majesty, as in case of treason, and also the profit of their lands for the term of their lives, their bodies being sentenced to perpetual imprisonment; *the example whereof would be very notable if his majesty would proceed against them all.*" On the morrow they proposed to meet at the house of the lord privy-seal, the Earl of Southampton, there to examine the duchess' daughter, Lady Bridgewater, who would be brought thither secretly; and they hoped, "with travail and labour, to find out the bottom of the plot, according to their bounden duties." In a frightful postscript they say that they think they have already all that can be got out of Dereham, who, by no force, can be made to confess more; and, therefore, they would be glad to know his majesty's pleasure touching the

---

[1] Most of the witnesses and prisoners were thus kept locked up in the houses of the king's slavish and unscrupulous ministers.

[2] State Papers.

execution of him and Culpepper. They were not kept long waiting for their instructions. They were ordered to commit the Duchess of Norfolk, the Lord William Howard and his wife, the Lady Bridgewater, and all others noted in their letters, to the Tower, and to send forthwith "some substantial personages" to take charge of their houses, and to see their goods put into safe custody for his majesty's behoof; in which particular part, his majesty joining with their opinions, *thinketh that the example will be very notable.* Nevertheless, as this matter came first to light by Mary Lascelles, the servant-girl, and as Mary Lascelles had refused the queen's service,[1] and had seemed to be sorry and lament that the king had married Catherine Howard, his majesty thought it best to spare the said Mary without troubling or committing her; *thinking, also, that this may be a means to give courage and boldness to others to reveal things in like cases.*" Touching Culpepper and Dereham, they were commanded to proceed to their execution, after convenient warning, that they might prepare for the salvation of their souls. On the 10th of December Dereham and Culpepper were drawn to Tyburn, where Dereham was hanged and quartered, and Culpepper beheaded. By the 13th of the same month, the Duchess of Norfolk, Lord William Howard, her son, and the rest of her relations and servants, were shut up in the Tower, which was so full already that there was great difficulty in finding room for them.[2] By his majesty's orders, *Mary Lascelles was clearly left out of the indictment, his majesty considering if she should be indicted with the rest how slanderous it should be to her!* The council in London "travailed" very diligently in forcing confessions from the Lady Bridgewater, Alice Wilkes, and Bulmer; "but as for Bridgewater," they write, "she showeth herself her mother's daughter—that is, one that will by no means confess anything."

The council in London were startled at this moment by the loud expressions of public opinion in France, and proposed that his majesty should permit some explanation in order to stop men's tongues. At the same moment, while the fate of Catherine Howard was undecided, the Duke of Cleves, losing no time, proposed to Henry that he should take back to wife his sister Anne! Ambassadors arrived in England with letters from Oslynger, the vice-chancellor of Cleves, to Cranmer and to the Earl of Southampton.[3] Cranmer, who was in an agony of alarm lest he should be suspected of the heinous offence of aiding in giving the king back an unpleasant helpmate, wrote a base, flattering letter to his royal master, and refused to have any communication with the Cleves ambassadors, "unless it please the king's majesty to command him." Of course nothing came of this delicate embassy, and the Duke of Cleves was again obliged to consent that Anne should be called the sister, not the wife of his majesty of England.[4]

The affair of Catherine Howard, which had brought the ambassador of Cleves into England, now proceeded rapidly, and with a baseness on the part of all concerned which almost staggers belief.[5] No man had the spirit to recommend a more legal way of proceeding; none durst open their lips in favour of any of the accused; the nearest of blood to them sought favour with the court by crying for their condemnation. No humiliation was too vile for the loftiest aristocracy of the land. A day or two after their committal to the Tower, the Duke of Norfolk wrote to the king, telling him that he had learned that his ungracious mother-in-law, his unhappy brother and wife, and his *lewd* sister of Bridgewater, are in the Tower, which, he says, from his long experience of his majesty's equity and justice, he feels sure is not done but for false and traitorous proceedings. This mighty lord had urged on the ruin of his niece Anne Boleyn, and had presided at her trial; but Anne and he were enemies, and opposed in matters of religion; whereas, in the present case, there was no enmity and no conflicting views as to dogmas of faith. He, however, condemned his other niece, Catherine Howard, just as he had condemned Anne; and he lamented very pathetically, "the most abominable deeds done by two of his nieces against his highness," which, he adds, hath brought him into the greatest perplexity that ever poor wretch was in; fearing that his majesty, having so often and by so many of his kin, been thus falsely and traitorously handled, might not only conceive a displeasure in his heart against him, and all others of that kin, but also, in manner, abhor to hear speak of any of the name. "Wherefore," continues this noble Howard, "my most gracious sovereign lord! prostrate at your feet, most humbly I beseech your majesty to call to your remembrance that a great part of this matter is come to light *by my declaration to your majesty,*

---

[1] Query—Had not this Mary Lascelles been refused a service by the queen?

[2] On the 11th of December, two days after her committal to the Tower, Cranmer, Audley, Suffolk, Gardiner, and the rest of the council in London, inform the king that they have again been, "travailing" with the duchess, "both to make her confess the things testified against her, and also to cough out the rest, not yet discovered, if any such dregs remain among them."

They seem scarcely to have allowed the infirm old woman a moment's rest. Such was the treatment that Henry reserved for the widow of the hero of Flodden Field!

[3] *State Papers.* [4] Ibid.

[5] There are sundry points which we would not venture to assert on any authority less positive than the *State Papers*, where we find the king's own letters and orders, Cranmer's letters, Norfolk's letters, the letters of the council, written at the moment, &c.

according to my bounden duty, of the words spoken to me by my mother-in-law, when your highness sent me to Lambeth to search Dereham's coffers, without the which, I think, she had not been further examined, nor, consequently, her ungracious children."

Meanwhile they still " travailed" to force confessions from the prisoners in the Tower, and *to make them reveal their hidden treasures*. On the 21st of December, Southampton and Wriothesley informed their assured, loving friend, Sir Ralph Sadler, that they had been with the Duchess of Norfolk, whom they found " on her bed, as it appeared very sickly." They had pressed her hard, and had also promised her pardon of her life if she would make them " her ghostly fathers," and confess the intimacy before marriage between the queen and Dereham; but still this high-minded woman, sick and worn as she was, resisted alike their threats and their promises. Taking God to witness, she protested " that she had never thought them (Catherine and Dereham) to be of that abominable sort; nevertheless she would not deny that she had perceived a light love and favour to be between them, more than between indifferent persons; and that she had heard that Dereham would sundry times give Catherine money, which she thought proceeded upon the affection that groweth of kindred, the same Dereham being her kinsman." According to her examiners, she avowed that it was very sinful in her not to tell his majesty this before his marriage. " After we had done this degree," they continue, with all the coolness of practised hands, " we went to the second, that is, for her hidden money, plate, or jewels; and, without any denial, she confessed that she had hidden, in another place in her house, £700 or £800, giving us such tokens as we might easily find it, which I, Thomas Wriothesley, with Mr. Attorney, Mr. Pollard, and Mr. Bristow, this morning found, being £800, and have safe bestowed it at Westminster."[1] In the end these active agents told the old lady that her life would be spared; upon which she hoped that his majesty would give her something to live upon, and not take away her house at Lambeth, for she had not long to live. Lord William Howard was also " wonderfully troubled and out of all quiet;" and not without reason, for they had been travailing with his menial servants, and were about separating him from his wife, not considering it expedient to arraign them together, so as to bring man and wife to the bar in company. Two days after, the Lord William Howard, his wife, Malin Tilney, Elizabeth Tilney, and three other women, among whom was Margaret Burnet, a butter wife, and Bulmer, Ashby, and Damport, men-servants to the old Duchess of Norfolk, were tried separately,[2] on a charge of misprision of treason, before a trembling jury, the duchess herself being omitted, for good reasons. According to the report of the council in London,[3] Lord William pleaded not guilty; but seeing that this course would not serve him, he confessed to the indictment, or threw himself upon the king's mercy. The result of what they, the council, called their "day's work," was to condemn all the prisoners to perpetual imprisonment, forfeiture of goods, and sequestration of their estates during their lives; and yet nothing was even pretended to be proved against them except that they had been privy to the loves of Catherine Howard and Dereham previous to the marriage.

A.D. 1542. We here lose the sure guides which we have been for some time following through obscure paths that were closed to former historians.[4] It appears that men had been long aware that nothing but the blood of Catherine Howard would satisfy the king, and that the promise of life, conveyed to her by Cranmer from his majesty, would not be allowed the weight of a feather. A new parliament was summoned; and on the 16th of January the lords and commons, by petition, implored his gracious majesty that he would not vex himself with the queen's misconduct, but allow the two houses to pass a bill of attainder, to which he might give his assent by letters-patent, without suffering the pain of hearing them rehearse the offences of his wife. The king was pleased to grant this, their humble petition, and to thank them for their making his griefs their own. The bill was carried through the lords in three, and through the commons in two days; and on Saturday, the 11th of February, the Chancellor Audley produced the bill in the lords, signed by the king, and with the great seal appended to it; and then, all the lords being in their robes, and the commons being summoned, the act was read, and, at the same time, a paper, purporting to be the queen's confession. In this paper, which ap-

---

[1] It is quite clear that the court was greatly in need of these gleanings of violence and iniquity. In the same letter is the following passage:—" Furthermore there is now at Westminster, 5000 marks in money, and £1000 worth of plate, which came from Lambeth ,the Duchess of Norfolk's house'. I, Thomas Wriothesley, would beseech the king's majesty that it might be delivered to some such hands as his majesty will appoint, or I rought unto him to Greenwich. *Methinks I should sleep the better an it were once delivered*."—*State Papers*.

[2] They seem to have been tried in separate parties of twos or threes. Lord William, for example, was brought to the bar with Damport, and not with his own wife.

[3] This letter relating the trial is signed by Suffolk, Southampton, Sussex, Hertford, Gage, Wriothesley, and Rich, but bears the signature neither of Cranmer nor of Gardiner.

[4] In the volume of the *State Papers*, from which the preceding particulars are derived, there is a great gap from the 22d of December, 1541, to the 1st of May, 1542.

pears to have been studiously withheld till the last moment, the unfortunate Catherine was made to acknowledge that she had offended against God, the king, and the nation; to express a hope that her sins would not be visited on the head of her brothers and her family; and to implore as a last grace, permission to divide part of her clothes among her faithful female servants. A confession like this was very vague; and, supposing it to have been really and sincerely made by the victim, it might, after all, only refer to offences before the marriage. Lady Rochford was attainted by parliament at the same time; and two days after, both ladies were beheaded within the walls of the Tower. Upon the scaffold Catherine confessed that she had once led a sinful life, but protested, by her hope of salvation, that she had never been untrue to the king since she had been his wife. The Lady Rochford also died very penitent and meek, and was supposed to have made a blessed end.

The Protestants were as ready to believe in the guilt of the Papist Catherine Howard, as the Papists had been to believe in the guilt of the Protestant Anne Boleyn. Since the triumph and firm establishment of the Reformed doctrines, sympathy and admiration have been incessantly demanded for the unfortunate mother of Queen Elizabeth, but no Protestant tears have been shed for the still more hapless Catherine Howard. Yet an attentive examination of documents, contemporary histories, and traditions, will convince every impartial mind that the frailties and guilt of Catherine were no more substantiated and proved than were the guilt and frailties of Anne, and that, in the case of both ladies, Henry and his judges bade defiance to all law and justice. A living and distinguished Roman Catholic historian turns Anne Boleyn into a wanton, and Catherine into an innocent martyr. Alas! for the slow progress of truth and impartiality! Are these, and other historical subjects of still greater weight, always to be treated of with the same angry passions and the same wilful blindness to evidence? Is prejudice to hold for ever the scales? Must every history continue to be one-sided?

It was enacted in the bill of attainder against Catherine Howard, that every woman about to be married to the king, or to any of his successors, should, if she were not a virgin, disclose that fact beforehand, under penalty of treason; that all other persons cognizant of it, and not divulging it in the proper quarter, should be subject to the penalty of misprision of treason; and that the queen that should move any person to commit adultery with her should suffer as a traitor.

As Henry might deny the virtue of the chastest maid, if he became tired of her, and as he had provided a law to put her to death, people, who could joke in the midst of these deeds of blood, said that nobody ought to marry him but a widow. But for nearly eighteen months the king seemed to think of marrying no one—devoting his time and attention to divinity and politics. Although he adhered with wonderful firmness to transubstantiation, auricular confession, and the celibacy of the clergy, his mind was not made up as to various fractional parts which he had actually adopted of the Reformation; and while he vehemently condemned the vacillation of his subjects in matters of faith, he was himself wavering on these particular points.

As early as 1536, certain articles were set forth by the convocation of the clergy, which had for their title, "Articles devised by the King's Highness' Majesty to stablish Christian Quietness." In 1537, just after the publication of the whole Bible in English, there appeared the "Institution of a Christian Man," or the "Bishops' Book," as it was called, after its authors, who had worked under the eye of his majesty. In 1543, Henry ordered the publication of another work, entitled "A necessary Doctrine and Erudition for any Christian Man." This book, which was called the "King's Book," differed materially from the "Bishop's Book," which only six years before had been given to the world as an unchangeable standard of faith and practice: thus affording a glaring proof that the king's own mind was not settled. The "King's Book" did not lean so much towards the doctrines of the Reformation as the "Bishops' Book." It established that, for those "whose office it was to teach others, the reading and studying of Holy Scripture was not only convenient, but also necessary; but for the other part of the church, ordained to be taught, it ought to be deemed, certainly, that the reading of the Old and New Testament was not so necessary for all those."[1] And soon after, it was enacted in parliament, that the Bible should not be read in public; that it should not be read aloud in any private families except such as were of noble or gentle degree; that it should not be read privately to one's self except by men who were householders, and by females who were well born. By any other women, or any artificer, apprentice, journeyman, servant, or labourer, the opening of the book was unlawful, and an offence to be punished by one month's imprisonment! Cranmer and *all* the bishops, whether Papists or Protestants, or half-and-half, concurred in these regulations, and parliament authorized the king to make whatever alterations he might deem proper. The fury of persecution was, however, now somewhat allayed. Probably from

[1] Preface to the book itself.

seeing the indiscriminate executions done upon the two sects, the Papists thought it unwise to inform against the Protestants, the Protestants deemed it prudent to be silent as to the Papists with their breaches of the oath of supremacy; and, during the four years which closed this reign, it is said that *only* twenty-four persons were put to death for religion—fourteen of them being Protestants, who were burned; ten Papists, and recusants on the subject of the supremacy, who were hanged.[1]

In politics Henry was scarcely more moderate than in religion. The wisest of his measures had been adopted as early as 1536, when it was enacted that the whole of Wales should be united with the realm of England, and be governed by the same laws. Up to this period the principality had been in an anomalous state, from which, without any particular benefits to the Welsh people, there flowed many serious evils to the English. It had been divided into two parts, one of which was governed by English laws, and the other subdivided into feuds or independent lordships, which acknowledged no laws or customs save their own, and were amenable only to their several feudal chiefs. Hence it happened that all criminals who could escape across the English lines, might procure, by favour or purchase, the protection of some petty sovereignty, and bid defiance to English law. The little lordships— 141 in number—were frequently engaged in hostilities with one another, like the baronies of the middle ages. It was now, of course, provided that no lord should have the power of protecting or pardoning any criminal; and it was also established that the Welsh shires, with one borough in each, should return members to the English parliament. The most important of the regulations made for Wales were extended to the independent county-palatine of Chester, which had, up to this time, been another anomaly in the political system.

The transactions in Ireland, which have been recently illustrated by a mass of the most curious and minute information,[2] would form a large chapter of themselves, but we can only touch briefly on the chief events. Soon after the recall of the Earl of Surrey (in 1522), the Earl of Kildare was invested, for the third time, with the high office of lord-deputy. The factions of her great lords were the curse of Ireland, keeping her disunited, weak, and poor. The Butlers, under their chief, the Earl of Ormond or Ossory, had entertained for ages an inveterate feud with the Fitzgeralds, of whom the Earl of Kildare was chief. Their complaints induced the suspicious Henry to recall the lord-deputy to England, and commit him to the Tower on the usual charge of treason. The Earl of Kildare had been in the Tower before, and had then had a narrow escape from the block. On his present departure from Ireland (in 1533), the chief power fell into the hands of his son, the Lord Thomas Fitzgerald, a brave and generous young man in his twenty-first year, who was soon deceived by a report, purposely circulated, that his father had now been beheaded in reality. He flew to arms, and bade defiance to the King of England. He had then five uncles, brothers to his father, three of whom, at first, dissuaded him from these extreme proceedings; but the passion of vengeance excluded reason, and at length they associated themselves with their nephew Thomas, and were all involved in the same ruin. At first many of the Irish flocked to their standard, and the minstrels, in wild strains, sang the sacred duty of revenge, and inflamed them to fury. They surprised Alleu, the Archbishop of Dublin, who was supposed to be one of the accusers of the Earl of Kildare, and they murdered him in presence of the earl's son and brothers. They sent an agent to the Emperor Charles, then irritated by the recent divorcing of his aunt Catherine; and they opened communications with Rome, offering, upon conditions, to prevent Henry, or any of the English, from carrying their church reforms into Ireland. But they were repulsed by the citizens of Dublin, who entertained different notions; they were assailed by the whole power of the rival faction of the Butlers, and were compelled to retreat, in want and disorder, into the wilds of Munster and Connaught. "The poor earl (the prisoner in the Tower), already afflicted with a palsy, was so stricken to the heart with the news of this tumult, that he survived but a few days the knowledge of his unhappiness."[3] Sir William Skeffington, the newly-appointed lord-deputy, took the field with a numerous army of regular troops; and in the month of August, 1535, Lord Leonard Gray, son of the Marquis of Dorset, arrived in Ireland, and put himself at the head of other forces, which went in pursuit of Lord Thomas. This Lord Leonard bribed some of the rebels, who agreed to betray their leader. As Henry sent little or no money to his troops, they lived at large upon the unhappy country, plundering first, and burning and destroying afterwards, wherever they went. Lord Thomas Fitzgerald was soon reduced to such straits that he offered to surrender upon terms. It appears pretty certain that Gray promised him a full pardon, for he voluntarily surrendered, and was not taken in arms: but Skeffington gave a different

---
[1] Strype, *Memoir of Cranmer*; Blunt, *Hist Reform.*
[2] Published by the Record Commission. It fills vols. ii. and iii. of the important *State Papers*, to which we have so frequently referred, and which, indeed, have been our most valuable guides through this reign.

[3] Godwin.

account of the matter. He told the king that O'Connor "came in and yielded himself;" and that the "traitor Thomas Fitzgerald, with divers others his accomplices, considering that he could not be succoured by the said O'Connor, and that his band and strength were by policy allured from him, had in like manner submitted and yielded himself to his highness' mercy and pity, without condition either of pardon, life, lands, or goods, but wholly submitting himself to his grace; so that his desire was, now that he was brought to uttermost extremity, to be conducted to his highness by the Lord Leonard Gray."[1] O'Connor had been too wise to surrender in person—he only delivered certain hostages as security for his good behaviour; but Fitzgerald was forthwith carried over to England by the Lord Leonard Gray, and committed to the Tower. Gray soon returned to Ireland, where he was named marshal, and appointed to the command of the whole army. One of his main objects was to secure the persons of the five uncles of Thomas Fitzgerald, who were still at large. On the 14th of February, of the following year (1536), the council of Ireland, with great glee, informed Cromwell that "the five brethren" had been apprehended by the Lord Leonard, the chief-justice, and others. They did well to avoid particulars; for, by what they termed, "the politic and secret managing of this matter," was to be understood, that Lord Leonard Gray and the others had treacherously seized the five Fitzgeralds at a banquet! After a long imprisonment in the Tower, they were all beheaded, with their nephew, the young earl, in the month of February, 1537. Their betrayer, Gray, though, as a reward, he was promoted to be lord-lieutenant or deputy, did not long survive them: on charges and suspicions he was committed to one of the cells they had occupied, and on the 28th of June, 1541, he was beheaded as a traitor on Tower-hill.[2]

Of the ancient and powerful family of the Fitzgeralds there remained but one, a boy twelve years old, named Gerald, the younger brother of the Lord Thomas. According to one account, he was seized and conveyed to the Tower, and afterwards escaped from that state prison. There is, however, a better ground for believing that the young Fitzgerald was never brought to the Tower at all, but was secretly carried out of Ireland into France by a sea-captain or merchant who chanced "to be with his ship on merchandise in Ireland,"[3] where certain monks entreated him to take charge of the noble boy.[3] The remainder of his history is as authentic as it is romantic. Driven from France at the desire of Henry, who claimed the fulfilment of the old treaty, by which neither power should give refuge to the enemies of the other, the boy sought an asylum in Flanders. There he soon found himself in no less danger than before; upon which he fled into Italy, and implored the protection of his kinsman, Reginald Pole, who received and maintained him very nobly. At length, in the reign of Mary, by means of the same protector, he was restored to his country, and to the honours and estates of his ancestors the Earls of Kildare.

The Fitzgeralds had derived a large portion of that power with which they made themselves formidable to the English government by declaring themselves the champions of the old religion. Upon their arrest, Cromer, Archbishop of Armagh, prolonged the opposition to Henry on the same grounds, being generally supported by the native Irish, who had no hope whatever of sharing in the spoils of the abbeys and monasteries, and as generally opposed by the Anglo-Irish nobility, who had good expectations of enriching themselves by the processes of suppression and confiscation. If matters had been carried with a high hand in England, we may be sure that the government was not very observant of constitutional right in Ireland. The whole body of the Irish clergy was excluded from the Irish parliament, in which they had hitherto voted by their proctors; and then statutes were passed, abolishing the authority of the pope for ever, declaring Henry supreme head of the Irish church, and giving to him the first-fruits and tenths and all the estates of the suppressed monasteries. Fierce personal quarrels raged incessantly among the men intrusted with the government; all the functionaries had their feuds and differences, arising out of conflicting religious beliefs, and still more out of jealousy as to the apportioning of the confiscated lands; and it seems to have been the practice of nearly every one of them to play the informer at the English court for the destruction of his associates. They could never agree as to the proper mode of treating the native Irish, though the notion more generally adopted was, that they were to be treated without mercy; for we find continual complaints of there being overmuch favour shown to the Irishry. O'Connor was soon again in arms; and a still more formidable enemy to the English, or to the new system of church government, rose up in the person of O'Neil, the great chieftain of the north. The royal troops, and the Irish kerns acting with them, fell upon O'Neil's country, and plundered and burned it for six whole days. The *plundering* evidently retarded the operations of the war, which was allowed to linger on for nearly three years; nor was the pacification of the country promoted by a constant breach of faith on the part of the government.

---

[1] *State Papers.* [2] *State Papers; Stow; Godwin.*
[3] *State Papers*

The foreign enemies of Henry were not slow in perceiving his weak point. The Scots occasionally succoured the Irish insurgents; and the king was kept in a constant state of alarm by reports of armaments from Spain or France being in Bantry Bay. It was not to be expected that the English would have all the plundering and burning to themselves; in the vicissitudes of war they were often the victims of the same practices. In 1540, soon after the recall of Lord Leonard Gray, O'Connor invaded Kildare, burning every village and town that he could take; O'Neil fell upon Dundalk; M'Mordo and the O'Tholes moved on another line; and the English pale was visited in its whole length by fire and sword. But in the end of the year O'Connor submitted, upon promise of being made a baron, and after a sanguinary victory gained over the kerns, a certain degree of tranquillity was restored.

Hitherto Ireland had been but a lordship; in 1541, Henry resolved to elevate it to the rank of a kingdom. At the same time he adopted the policy of attaching some of the most powerful of the native chiefs, and also such of the great Anglo-Irish proprietors as had not already been ennobled, by admitting them to the honours of the peerage. The allurement thus held out was run after with wonderful eagerness by both. The De Burghs, the O'Briens, the O'Neils, the O'Tholes, the Cavanahs, and the rest, were all ready to make a sacrifice of independence for the title and privileges of peers. They consented to hold their lands of the crown by the tenure of military service; they swore fealty to Henry, and they accepted from him houses in Dublin, which they were to inhabit when summoned as peers to the Irish parliament. Thus Ulliac de Burgh became Earl of Clanricarde, Murrock O'Brien, Earl of Thomond, and the formidable O'Neil, Earl of Tyrone. In all these and other measures there was considerable prudence and ability, and the effect of Henry's general policy was greatly to extend the English power in Ireland.[1]

CHAPTER VIII.—CIVIL AND MILITARY HISTORY.—A.D. 1523—1547.

HENRY VIII.—ACCESSION, A.D. 1509—DEATH, A.D. 1547.

Affairs of Scotland—Earl of Surrey's invasion of Scotland—Return of the Duke of Albany—He unsuccessfully invades England—James V., a minor, proclaimed king—Rash proceedings of his mother Margaret—She is deprived of her authority—James V. escapes from the control of the Douglases—He defends the cause of the Romish church—His marriages—His severe proceedings against the Reformers—Henry VIII. seeks an interview with James V.—A Scottish army mustered to invade England—Its shameful rout at Solway Moss—Death of James V.—Design of Henry VIII. to reduce Scotland and England into one monarchy—He liberates the Scottish nobles his prisoners—Cardinal Beaton's attempts to obtain the regency of Scotland—Henry's rash proceedings alarm the Scots—Marriage resolved between Prince Edward of England and the Princess Mary of Scotland—Beaton recovers his ascendency—He is reconciled with the Regent Arran—They unite against Henry and the Reformation—Aid arrives to the Scots from France—Fresh rupture between England and Scotland—Henry's reconciliation with Charles V.—He marries Catherine Parr—Invades France—Besieges and takes Boulogne—Abortive close of the invasion—Invasion of Scotland by sea—The English land at Leith—They burn Edinburgh—Defeat of the English at Ancrum Moor—The French attempt to gain the mastery at sea—Their naval proceedings—Their unsuccessful effort to obtain the Isle of Wight—Henry's poverty—His illegal acts to obtain money—His intrigues with Scottish traitors—He attempts to procure the assassination of Cardinal Beaton—Singular correspondence for that purpose—Scotland again invaded—Havoc wrought by the invaders—Account of George Wishart—His labours in Scotland as a Reformer—His martyrdom—Beaton fortifies his castle of St. Andrews—He is assassinated—Growing infirmities of Henry—His theological debates with his queen—Rivalry between the houses of Hertford and Norfolk—The Duke of Norfolk arrested—His son, the Earl of Surrey, tried for treason—Tampering with the witnesses against him—Surrey executed—The Duke of Norfolk tried and condemned—Last illness of Henry VIII.—His death—Fortunate escape of Norfolk from execution.

E left the affairs of Scotland in a most embarrassed state, at the second departure of the Regent Albany for France, in October, 1522. Henry, who had pretended that the sole cause of his hostility was the presence of that prince, on the retirement of Albany, sent Clarencieux to declare, in a solemn manner, that he held the war to be unnatural, and that he was most desirous of living in peace with his dear nephew James. Nearly at the same moment his troops, collected in the east marches, ravaged and burned the greater part of Teviotdale; and the Earl of Surrey (the Duke of Norfolk of later times), with

[1] State Papers.

10,000 men, burst into the Merse, burning and destroying all before him, without even respecting the beautiful old abbey of Jedburgh, which he left a heap of ruins. Lord Dacre continued his ancient practices; and whenever there was a traitor in Scotland he was ready to bribe him. In 1523 Albany returned with a fleet of eighty-seven small vessels, 4000 foot soldiers, 500 men-at-arms, 1000 hackbutters, 600 horse, and a decent train of artillery, which had been furnished to him by the French. He found his former close and dear ally Margaret, the queen-dowager, who had taken to herself another lover, deep in negotiations with Dacre and Surrey, and sold to promote the English interests at the expense of the independence of the Scottish nation and her son's crown. His position was more than ever difficult; the Scots were jealous of the foreign army with which he was surrounded, and, being well informed of what was passing on the Continent, they maintained that Albany wished to urge them into a war with England for the sole object of obliging France. The Scottish parliament, however, assembled, and a proclamation was issued for a muster of the whole military force of the kingdom on the 20th of October, that the defeat of Flodden might be avenged, and reprisals made for the incursions of Shrewsbury, Surrey, and the other leaders, who had committed such havoc on the Borders. By means of money Albany won over some of the most venal of the nobles, and even shook the English politics of the queen-dowager, who, with great delicacy, informed the Earl of Surrey, that, unless her brother Henry remitted her more cash, she might possibly join the French interest, and co-operate with Albany. On the appointed day the Scottish army appeared in array near Edinburgh; but Argyle, the Lord Forbes, the Earl of Huntly, and other great lords, were absent—some openly condemning the invasion of England, some pretending sickness. Albany, however, marched to the Tweed with about 40,000 men: but the season was far advanced—the roads were almost impassable for his artillery—the Scots quarrelled with the foreign auxiliaries, and many of their chiefs had engaged with Surrey and Dacre to check the regent's progress. When they reached the wooden bridge of Melrose, a large body of troops refused to cross the Tweed; and, soon after, the divisions which had passed halted, wavered, and then, in spite of Albany's entreaties and reproaches, re-crossed the bridge to the Scottish side. The regent then attempted to keep them close on the left bank of the Tweed, and he laid siege to Wark Castle with his foreign troops and artillery. But he was foiled even in this paltry enterprise; and on the 4th of November, after losing some 300 Frenchmen in an assault, he was compelled to beat a retreat.[1] On his return to the capital, some of the Scottish peers accused him of being the cause of the disgrace they themselves had brought about; and, notwithstanding the presence of Surrey on the Borders, and the inclemency of the season, they insisted on his instantly dismissing the foreign auxiliaries. Soon after, in the spring of 1524, Albany, in disgust and despair, returned once more to France, whence he marched with the French king into Italy. The defeat and capture of Francis at the battle of Pavia completed the ruin of his party in Scotland, where the queen-dowager once more mismanaged affairs for a short time. Henry had opened a correspondence with her husband, the Earl of Angus, who had been living in exile on the Continent, and who, upon certain conditions, engaged to forward the views of the English in his native country. But before this project could be carried into execution, Margaret, assisted by the Earls of Arran, Lennox, Crawford, and others of the great nobles, got possession of the person of her son, carried him to Edinburgh, and there caused him to be declared of age, and to be proclaimed king. James was twelve years old when he received the oaths of allegiance of such of the spiritual and temporal peers as had espoused his mother's party. The whole plan was transparent, and all patriotic minds dreaded to see the government of the kingdom again in the hands of so capricious, unwise, and anti-national a person as Margaret. James Beaton, Archbishop of St. Andrews, and Dunbar, Bishop of Aberdeen, resisted and threw ridicule on the notion of a boy of twelve years being king; for which they were committed to prison. Wolsey flattered Beaton with the hope of a cardinal's hat if he would renounce his engagement to support the regency established by the Scottish parliament, and become the tool of England; but Beaton, with all his faults, had a high and patriotic spirit, and he rejected these proposals. Henry cared not by what means he obtained the ascendency: giving up Angus, who was now residing at his court, he determined to support this precious revolution, by which Margaret might reign in her son's name, and he might rule in hers. He sent her and the Earl of Arran some money, and 200 men-at-arms, as a body-guard for the young king; but Margaret was as wilful as her brother: she soon found fault with him for permitting the return of her now odious husband, and she threatened to throw herself into the arms of the enemies of England unless Angus were kept away from Scotland. At the same time she clamoured for more money, and demanded the order of the Garter for her friend the Earl of Arran. But, very soon after, she disgusted the

---
[1] *Buchanan; Tytler.*

powerful Arran by taking to herself another paramour, in the person of Henry Stuart, second son of Lord Evandale, a very handsome but inexperienced youth, whom she instantly raised to the important office of lord-treasurer. Upon this, her party fell from her rapidly, and she did not mend matters by making her young lover chancellor soon after. She continued, at the same time, to excite the suspicions of Wolsey and her brother Henry, who thereupon renewed negotiations with her husband Angus, who was still at the English court. After many shameful intrigues, Angus, having agreed to do the will of Henry, was sent into Scotland; and, with English assistance, he was enabled to obtain possession of the young king, and, with that, the exercise of the royal authority. After a bold but unsuccessful attempt at resistance, Margaret consented to a treaty, by which she was removed from any dependence as a wife upon Angus, and permitted to enjoy a voice in the council and the disposal of a portion of the patronage of the church. She would not have obtained such mild terms had it not been for the mediation of the English court, and the manœuvres of its skilful agents; yet the treaty was scarcely signed when she opened a secret negotiation with Albany and the French court, professing a readiness to go to all extremities against England, provided only they would assist her in expelling her husband Angus, and getting a divorce from Rome. But by this time Francis was a prisoner and Albany powerless; and, to complete her misfortunes, her brother's agents intercepted her letters, and laid them before the enraged majesty of England. She was now deprived of the very limited share of authority she had possessed; and her husband Angus, with the rest of the Douglases, governed the country. Angus consented, at last (in 1526), to a divorce, and Margaret married her paramour, and fell into deserved contempt with all parties.¹

The young King James soon felt a desire to free himself from the thraldom of the Douglases; and in July, 1528, when he was in his seventeenth year, with the assistance of Archbishop Beaton, he escaped from the confinement in which he was held, and threw himself into Stirling Castle, where he was soon joined by the Earls of Arran, Argyle, Eglinton, and Moray, and by many other powerful noblemen, who saluted him as their free and uncontrolled monarch—and, for the first time in his life, James *was* free. He instantly issued a proclamation, forbidding Angus, or any lord or retainer of the house of Douglas, to approach within six miles of his court, under pain of treason, and he presently levied an army,

¹ She died in 1539, having with great difficulty been prevailed upon *not* to divorce her third husband.

which enabled him to drive his enemies across the Borders. Angus became the pensioner of Henry, and remained for some years an exile in England. The young James soon proved that he was very capable of the duties of government; and his frank, generous disposition, and easy popular manners, gained him the hearts of his subjects. He resolved to free his country from foreign dictation and the interference of England; and to that end he sought the alliance of the emperor and the French king. In 1532 the intrigues of the Earl of Bothwell, who had traitorously allied himself with England, and the desperation of Angus and the banished Douglases, brought on a war between the two countries; but hostilities were confined to the Borders, where, properly speaking, peace never reigned; and a treaty was soon concluded under the mediation of the French king. The treaty, on terms very honourable to Scotland, was signed on the 12th of May, 1534. James was now in his twenty-second year. He publicly deplored his uncle, the King of England's conduct, and expressed his own determination of supporting in Scotland the religion of his ancestors. His counsellors were chiefly priests, whose intolerance was heightened by the notorious fact that many of the Scottish nobles who inclined to a reform of the church were bad patriots, and in the pay of England. The more Henry attacked the Roman church, the more James seemed determined to defend it. The English court was much distressed by this diversity of opinion; and, to win over his nephew, Henry made him an offer of the hand of his own daughter Mary, and sent him one of his own priests, Dr. Barlow, to preach to him. This Barlow found slight encouragement at the Scottish court, and the Scottish clergy shut up all the pulpits against him; upon which he described the clerical counsellors of James as being "the pope's pestilent preachers, and very limbs of the devil." The matrimonial negotiation fell to the ground, and so did a proposal made by Henry for a meeting with his nephew at York; and James soon after married the Princess Magdalen, daughter of the French king, a beautiful girl of sixteen. The ceremony took place in January, 1537, in the church of Nôtre Dame, at Paris; and on the 19th of May the royal couple landed safely at Leith. But Magdalen, who was in a delicate state of health when she married, died of a rapid decline on the 7th of July, leaving her husband in great affliction, from which, however, he was soon sufficiently roused to send David Beaton, afterwards the celebrated cardinal, to look out for another wife in France. Beaton, who was accompanied by Lord Maxwell and the Master of Glencairn, presently concluded a match with Mary of Guise, the widow of the Duke of Longueville, a lady who had refused the hand of his uncle of England. Mary of Guise arrived in Scotland, and the king's second marriage was celebrated in the cathedral church of St. Andrews, within a year after the death of his first wife. "The Pilgrimage of Grace," and other events in England, the Catholic feelings of his wife Mary, and other circumstances, confirmed James in his opposition to religious reform; and the affairs of the Scottish church, and in good part those of the nation, were chiefly intrusted to David Beaton, who, in

CARDINAL BEATON.—From the picture at Holyrood.

the autumn of 1539, succeeded his uncle, James Beaton, in the primacy. The pope had addressed flattering messages to the king, and David Beaton had received a cardinal's hat—a melancholy effect of which high honours was soon exhibited in the burning of more heretics. These detestable executions drove all those who favoured the new doctrine into an alliance with the banished Douglases, who could only work by English means, and by modes perilous to the national independence. And this course again exasperated the king more than ever against the Protestants. For a long time patriotism was allied with the old religion, and the new religion was banded with disaffection and anti-nationality. James, indeed, continued to support the church with all his might, not hesitating to adopt from his priestly counsellors a fierce spirit of intolerance and persecution.[1] Early in the following year his parliament passed more severe statutes against heresy; it was declared to be a capital offence to question the supreme authority or the spiritual infallibility of the pope; no person, with the least taint of heresy, was to enjoy any office under government; no private meetings, or conventicles, or societies for the discussion of religious subjects were allowed, and informers against them were invited by high rewards; no good Catholic was to hold intercourse with any man or woman that had *at any time* entertained heretical notions, were it his own brother or sister; the casting down of images of saints and the Virgin was declared to be a damnable offence; and a reference was made in the act to that rage for destroying the sacred edifices, which was now in its infancy, but which gathered strength under persecution, and which, in a few years, left the beautiful abbeys and churches of Scotland heaps of sightless ruins. At the same time, however, the parliament exhorted all churchmen, high or low, to reform their lives and conversation, in order to remove a great ground of scandal and reproach.[2]

Soon after this, Cardinal Beaton, and Panter, the king's secretary, proceeded on an embassy to Rome, *with secret instructions*. Alarmed at this mission, and at some new demonstrations on the Continent, Henry again pressed his nephew to meet him at York; and James, it appears, either consented, or deceived the English envoys with vague and ambiguous language. The English king, in the month of August, took the northern road (it was the fatal journey which preceded the arrest of Catherine Howard), travelled on to York, and waited there six days for the coming of the Scottish king. But James came not; and Henry, furious at what he considered a flaming insult, retraced his steps to London, whence he soon issued orders to Sir Robert Bowes to levy troops near the Borders, and to the Archbishop of York to make search into the records and muniments, so as to ascertain and establish the just title of the Kings of England to the kingdom of Scotland —which absurd claim he was resolved to revive.[3] James sent an embassy to deprecate his uncle's wrath; but Beaton and the Catholic party generally were not averse to an open war, fearing greatly that their needy king might not always resist the tempting proposals of the English suppressionists. But, in good truth, peace had never been established on the Borders; on the one side of which were the banished Douglases, eager to recover their estates with their swords; and on the other, English exiles, the victims of the "Pilgrimage of Grace," who were animated with the same desire. The first great movement, however, proceeded from the English lines: in August, 1542, Sir James Bowes, the warden of the east marches, with the Earl of Angus, Sir George Douglas, and other Scottish exiles, with a body of 3000 horse, rushed into Teviotdale. The invading force was met at Haddenrig by the Earl of Huntly and Lord Home, who gained a complete victory, taking no fewer than 600 prisoners of note. Henry, after proclaiming by manifestoes that the Scots were the aggressors,

---

[1] Sadler's State Papers.   [2] Acts of Parl. of Scotland.   [3] State Papers; Sadler; Tytler.

ordered a levy of 40,000 men, and sent the Duke of Norfolk, the Earls of Southampton, Shrewsbury, Derby, Rutland, and Hertford, to take the command of this army, which was joined by Angus and all the banished Douglases that had survived the fight at Haddenrig. At last, in the end of October, preceded by a fresh manifesto, in which Henry claimed the sovereignty of Scotland, Norfolk crossed the Border, and burned two towns and twenty villages on the left bank of the Tweed. There he continued ransacking the country without any opposition, and without venturing to advance, as James was gathering an army in his front, while Huntly, Home, and Seton were watching him on the flank. Thirty thousand men gathered round the standard of James on the Borough Muir, near Edinburgh; but there was disaffection in his camp: many of the nobles favoured the doctrines of the Reformation, either from a conviction of their truth, or from an earnest desire to possess themselves of the lands and houses of the monks; others were led wholly by their hereditary attachment to the banished Douglases, whose standard floated on the side of the English; others, again, felt the unprofitableness of a war with England, and were of opinion that they should only act on the defensive. The provocation was great, but the latter would have been the wisest course; for, before James reached the Lammermuir Hills, Norfolk, in want of provisions, and distressed by the inclemency of the weather, was in full retreat. Having halted on Fala Muir, and reviewed his troops, which were exceedingly well appointed, though, like the enemy, somewhat short of provisions, James proposed that they should follow Norfolk, and make retaliation for his raid in England; but, to his great dismay, nearly every chief refused to cross the Borders, alleging the lateness of the season, the difficulty of obtaining provisions, and the imprudence of exposing the person of their sovereign, who, like his father, might find a Flodden Field. It was in vain that the gallant James called them cowards and traitors, and attempted to excite their revenge by pointing out the still smoking towns and villages, and Scottish farms, that marked the line of Norfolk's destructive march: they would not move forward—they began to disband—and the king was obliged to ride back, with a bursting heart, to Edinburgh. The clergy, with a few of the peers, resolved to make an effort to retrieve the disgrace under which the king was sinking; and Lord Maxwell contrived to get together a force of 10,000 men, with which he proposed to burst suddenly into England by the western marches, and to remain there as many days as Norfolk had remained in Scotland, burning and destroying in the like manner. James rode with this little army to the castle of Caerlaverock, where, by agreement with his council, he halted: Maxwell dashed across the Border; but, no sooner were the Scots on English ground, on Solway Moss, than Oliver Sinclair, the king's minion, as he is termed, produced a commission appointing him to the supreme command of the army. Upon this many of the proud chiefs swore they would not serve under any such leader; and the clans and most of the troops broke out into open mutiny. In the midst of this scene of hopeless confusion a body of 300 English horse came up to reconnoitre. The Scots took them for the van of Norfolk's army, and, without attempting to ascertain the fact, fled in the greatest disorder. The English horse, charging the fugitives, took nearly 1000 prisoners—among whom were included the Earls of Cassillis and Glencairn, the Lords Somerville, Maxwell, Gray, Oliphant, and Fleming, the Masters of Erskine and Rothes, and Home of Ayton—and then marched back towards merry Car-

FALKLAND PALACE.—From an old drawing in the British Museum.

lisle.[1] This disgraceful and unparalleled defeat was a death-blow to James: he rode slowly back to Edinburgh, and from Edinburgh he proceeded to his palace at Falkland, where he shut himself

---

[1] *State Papers;* Hall; Herbert. Some accounts make the English horse 500 or 600, instead of 300; but no increase of

up, brooding over his disgrace, and sitting for hours without speaking a word to any living being. There are few such authenticated cases of dying of what is called a broken heart. He was in the flower and prime of life, being only in his thirty-first year, and, up to this last calamity, his constitution was vigorous, and he had scarcely known sickness; but now a slow fever fixed upon him, and he sank most rapidly. His wife, Mary of Guise, had borne him two sons, but they had both died in their infancy; she was now a third time *enceinte*, and near her time, and it was hoped that a seasonable turn might be given to his consuming thoughts by the birth of a son and heir; but the queen was delivered, at the palace of Linlithgow, of a daughter, the unfortunate Mary; and James died on the 14th of December, seven days after her birth, foreseeing the dismal fate of his child and his country, and muttering in his last moments, "It came with a girl, and it will go with a girl."[1]

A.D. 1543. The news of his nephew's death possessed Henry with new hopes of uniting Great Britain under one head. England had a young prince, and Scotland a queen, and he determined to marry his son Edward to the infant Mary. If he had been content with an arrangement for the future he might have succeeded, and had Edward lived, a great blessing for both countries would have been achieved; but Henry was anxious for an *immediate* enjoyment of the united sovereignty, and resolved to demand, as the natural guardian of the young princess, the entire government of the Scottish kingdom; and this selfishness and precipitancy defeated his scheme. He, however, proceeded at first with considerable craft, and found noble and powerful Scots, who, from anxiety to establish the Reformed religion in Scotland, and, still more, from motives of self-interest, were ready to throw their country in fetters at his feet. Foremost among these were the Earl of Angus and his brother Sir George Douglas, who had both long been in his confidence, and bound to his service. But the Earls of Cassillis and Glencairn, the Lords Somerville, Maxwell, Gray, and the other nobles who had been taken prisoners in the disgraceful rout at Solway Moss, and had been at first (at least in outward appearance) very harshly treated by Henry, who shut them up for a few days in the Tower like rebels and traitors, were also ready to second his views. As soon as they showed this disposition Henry treated them with great honour and kindness, and under these blandishments their last faint feelings of patriotism departed. They concluded a formal and a solemn treaty, agreeing to acknowledge Henry as the sovereign lord of Scotland, to exert their influence to procure for him the government of the kingdom, with the possession of all the fortresses and the person of the infant queen Mary, who was to be delivered into his hands, to be kept in England. They swore to this treaty; they delivered hostages for its execution, promising that, if they failed, they would return into England to the same state of captivity in which they were before the treaty was made. Sir George Douglas, the brother of Angus, was intrusted with the chief management of the business; and all these unpatriotic lords were bound to proceed with great caution, and to feel their way, at first, by merely speaking of the benefits of the marriage, without alluding to any of its immediate consequences.[2]

As soon as James was dead, Cardinal Beaton produced a will, by which *he* was appointed guardian to the infant queen, and regent or "governor" of the realm, with the assistance of a council composed of the Earls of Argyle, Huntly, and Moray. The Earl of Arran, now presumptive heir to the throne, and as much wedded to the reforming party as Beaton was to the Papists, declared that this will was a forgery, and he had sufficient power to drive the cardinal from his office, and to acquire possession of it himself in the course of a very few days. Arran became regent or governor on the 22d of December, 1542, upon which the current set wholly in favour of the Protestant party. It was determined that Angus and the Douglases should be recalled from their long exile of fifteen years. It was not then known that they had agreed to sacrifice the independence of the kingdom; and they did not leave England until after the 10th of January, 1543, when they received a safe-conduct from the Earl of Arran, permitting them freely to return to their homes. In order to ruin Cardinal Beaton and his party, a scroll was produced, which was said to have been found upon the king's person at his death, and which contained a list of above 360 of the Scottish nobility and gentry, who were marked out as heretics, and, as such, recommended as proper objects for confiscation and other penalties. At the very head of the list stood the name of the Earl of Arran, now regent! The cardinal despatched agents to France to represent to the house of Guise the danger of the queen-dowager and her

---

numbers can explain what happened to the honour of the Scots. We are justified in suspecting that many of them who had been traitors before, and who agreed to sell their country afterwards, were taken willing prisoners. Others, according to Bishop Godwin, were taken by *Scottish* freebooters, and *sold* to the *English*—"We charge them furiously; the Scots unazzedly fly; many are slain, many taken; more plunged into the neighbouring fens, and, taken by Scottish freebooters, sold to us."—*Godwin*.

[1] *Lesly; Drummond; Maitland; Sir W. Scott; Tytler.* The crown of Scotland was brought into the family of the Stuarts by a daughter of the Bruce.

[2] *State Papers.*

infant, and to beg for a supply of money and troops to resist the encroachments of the King of England and the manœuvres of the Scottish party sold to that monarch. As soon as the marriage was whispered, he saw all that Henry intended thereby, and he everywhere denounced the project, as tending to nothing less than the enslaving of Scotland. To quiet his dangerous eloquence, Arran, who found it necessary to seek the support of the men who had engaged to sacrifice their country, ordered his instant arrest; and the cardinal was seized on a charge of high treason, and carried off to the castle of Blackness, before he could get his own party together. Beaton had been recently appointed legate *a latere* for Scotland; and his influence with the clergy was as boundless as was their conviction that his talent and energy alone could prevent their ruin. They now shut up their churches; they refused to administer the sacraments or to bury the dead; and, as the great mass of the people were as yet Catholics, this conduct produced a deep impression; while, being relieved from other duties, the priests and monks had more time to devote to politics. Henry, in the meantime, was far too impatient. As if to proclaim his intentions, he demanded that Cardinal Beaton should be delivered into his hands; and he pressed Angus and the Scottish prisoners to begin by putting him in possession of the Scottish fortresses at once. The traitors told him that, if he would wait patiently, all would go well, and they would fulfil all that had been stipulated between them: but patience was a virtue unknown to Henry; he would only allow them a given time—he would only consent to prolong the truce till the month of June; and he at once collected what troops he could in the northern provinces. The heart of Wallace and the Bruce still beat in the general bosom of the brave Scottish people, though the proudest of the aristocracy—the barons of "the broken faith and the bloody hand"—were Baliols and Comyns. The traitor Sir George Douglas soon told Henry that to demand the government for him would be a perilous and fatal step,[1]—that even the boys of Scotland would resist it with stones, and the old women with their distaffs. With all this patriotism, however, the Papist party seemed resolved to allow of no liberty of conscience in religious matters. The Earls of Huntly, Bothwell, and Moray had demanded that Cardinal Beaton should be set at liberty, offering themselves in bail for his appearance, to answer the charges brought against him. Arran, the regent, refused. They then called to their assistance the Earl of Argyle, and repaired to Perth, where they were soon joined by a great number of bishops and abbots, and many barons and knights. They then drew up certain articles, which were presented to Arran and the council of regency by the Bishop of Orkney and Sir John Campbell of Caldour, uncle to the Earl of Argyle. One of the principal of these articles was, that the New Testament should not go abroad: by which was meant, that it should not be published in the vulgar tongue, or circulated among the people: another was, that the cardinal should be set at liberty. By the third article they demanded a share in the council: and by the fourth, they insisted that the ambassadors appointed to go to England should be changed for men of less questionable integrity and patriotism. Arran replied that he would grant them no such unreasonable desires; and the bishop and knight were presently followed to Perth by his herald-at-arms, who charged them, under pain of treason, to break up their meeting, and repair to the capital. The assembled lords, both lay and spiritual, readily obeyed, and, with a very few exceptions, went to attend the parliament, which was summoned for the 12th of March, 1543; but they had come to a good understanding among themselves—they were on their guard, and it was scarcely possible that any measure dangerous to the independence of Scotland should be carried, or even proposed in their presence, and in the state to which *they* had brought the popular mind.[2] The Archbishop of Glasgow, as chancellor, introduced the English proposals of peace and marriage; all voices were in favour of the union, but not one dared to propose the other demands which the King of England had advanced as indispensable preliminaries—as conditions, without which he would do nothing. The parliament, in recommending the marriage, recommended also that their young queen should, on no account, be sent into England; and they made, with jealous care, sundry regulations for preserving the national independence under all circumstances.[3]

Henry flew into a paroxysm of rage when he heard the turn this affair had taken; his ambassador or political agent Sir Ralph Sadler was instructed to reprimand Angus and his associates. Sadler, who would not have doubted lightly of the success of those intrigues of which he was so expert a manager, wrote to one of the English ministers, that, in his opinion, "the Scots would rather suffer any extremity than come to the obedience and subjection of England—that they would have their own realm free, and live within themselves after their own laws and customs."[4] Henry then attempted to terrify or cajole the Regent Arran—a weak and corrupt man, but

---
[1] Sadler: State Papers.
[2] State Papers. Letter from the Earl of Angus and Sir George Douglas to the English Lord Lisle.
[3] Acts of the Parliament of Scotland.
[4] State Papers.

not wholly destitute of honour and national feeling. He promised that he would give his daughter Elizabeth in marriage to Arran's son; but here a consideration of a selfish nature intervened; for Arran contemplated uniting his son to the young Queen Mary. The regent's passion for church reform was not overlooked; but here, again, Arran could hardly agree with the English king, who continued to maintain the chief dogmas of the Catholic church with fire and fagot; for Arran was at this time a thorough Protestant, entertaining in his house one John Rough, and one Brother William, whom Henry most indubitably would have burned as pestilent heretics. At this very moment Cardinal Beaton recovered his liberty. By what means this was effected is not very clear, but the consequences were soon apparent. The Earl of Lennox, who had served Francis I. in his Italian wars, and who was very nearly related to the royal family of Scotland, was set up as a rival to Arran; and supplies of money and ammunition were brought over from Francis, who undertook to exert himself to the utmost, in order to prevent altogether the English marriage and alliance. But, at the same time, Angus, Sir George Douglas, and the other paid and pensioned agents of Henry, were not idle; and by their advice, Henry relaxed in the harshness of his demands, and agreed to wait the effect of time and intrigue. On the 1st of July his commissioners met Sir George Douglas, the Earl of Glencairn, Sir James Learmont, Sir William Hamilton, and Balnavis, the Scottish secretary, at Greenwich, and there finally arranged a less objectionable treaty. It was agreed that Queen Mary should marry Edward, Prince of Wales, as soon as she was of proper age, and that a perfect peace should be established, from the signing of the treaty, between the two countries; that Mary should remain in Scotland until she completed her tenth year—Henry being permitted to send thither an English nobleman, with his wife and family, to form part of her household; and that two Scottish earls and four barons should be sent forthwith into England as hostages. It was provided in the treaty, and set down as an indefeasible part of it, that in all cases the ancient kingdom of Scotland should keep her name, and be governed by her own laws.[1]

[1] Rymer; Sadler's State Papers.

But, in effect, this outward parchment was but a cover to a scheme of the utmost perfidy—a scheme which must have been suspected by the Scottish statesmen of those days, though it has only been fully brought to light in our own by the research of a national historian.[2] Under the treaty of Greenwich there was what was called a *secret device*—a name which very happily expresses the nature of the thing. By this precious compact, Angus, his brother George, Maxwell, Glencairn, Cassillis, and the rest, bound themselves once more to the service of Henry—undertook, in case of need, to arm in his favour, and to adhere solely to his interests; "so that he should attain all the things then pacted and covenanted, or, at the least, the dominion on this side the Firth;" by which last expression was meant the whole of the south of Scotland.[3]

But the treaty was scarcely concluded, when Cardinal Beaton and the Earl of Huntly collected an army in the north of Scotland, when Argyle and Lennox rose in the west, and Bothwell, Home, and the Laird of Buccleuch mustered their vassals along the Borders. Their manifesto stated that they were forced into these hostile measures by Arran and the Douglases, who threatened their holy church, and who had sold their country to Henry. At this crisis, or a

The Palace of Linlithgow, as now existing.[4]

little later, Arran, who was receiving money from the English court, sent to request the assistance of an English army. Before this, Henry

[2] Mr. Tytler.
[3] State Papers. "Copy of the Secret Device," dated July 1, 1543. Further information as to these treacherous transactions exists in the Hamilton MSS., in the possession of the Duke of Hamilton, and quoted by Mr. Tytler.
[4] The palace of Linlithgow—for several centuries a favourite residence of the Scottish monarchs—was accidentally set on fire in the year 1746, and is now a magnificent ruin.

tried every possible means for seizing Beaton, and getting possession of the person of Queen Mary. The cardinal dreaded his stratagems and the effect of his gold; and he resolved to put the infant Mary in safer keeping. She was living with her mother, Mary of Guise, in the palace of Linlithgow, guarded by a great force appointed by Arran and the Hamiltons. By combined movements, the cardinal brought all the forces of Lennox, Huntly, Argyle, and Bothwell, together with the Buccleuchs and the Kers, to act suddenly at one moment on Edinburgh and the neighbourhood. Arran and the Douglases yielded to the storm; and the infant queen, and the queen-dowager, were given up to Beaton's party, and conveyed for safety to Stirling Castle.[1] Arran, however, retained the office of regent or governor; and in the month of August of the same year (1543) he caused the treaties with England to be ratified by the nobles, and himself swore to their faithful observance.[2] Cardinal Beaton and his party represented, with perfect truth, that this ratification was made contrary to the wishes of the great body of the nation—that it was unauthorized by parliament, and in consequence illegal. Henry chose this very moment for offering a fresh provocation. As soon as the treaty of peace was published, some Scottish merchants ventured to send to sea a number of ships; these ships were driven by stress of weather into an English port, where, by the king's orders, they were seized, and their cargoes confiscated, under pretence that they were carrying provision to his majesty's enemies in France.[3] This measure excited such a fury in Edinburgh, that Sir Ralph Sadler found his life in danger from the populace; upon which Henry threatened the magistrates of that capital with his high displeasure. Angus, Cassillis, Glencairn, and the other pensioners of England, now thought that it would be better to bring matters to a crisis openly, and they strongly recommended Henry to send a main army for the conquest of the realm—the time, they said, being come: but Arran, the regent, seems to have trembled at the exasperation of the Scottish people, and, to the surprise of most men, on the 3d September, only six days after protesting to Sadler that no prince alive should have his heart and service save only the English king, he met the cardinal by appointment at Callendar House, and entirely reconciled himself with that party, agreeing to renounce all former pledges, and even his attachment to the Reformed doctrines. Very soon after, he publicly abjured his heresy in the Franciscan convent of Stirling, and received absolution for his late wandering from the holy Catholic faith. Beaton then applied himself to win over the Earl of Angus and his traitorous associates; but these men seemed determined to earn their pensions, and, withdrawing to Douglas Castle, they assembled their vassals, and drew up a new bond or covenant, to employ their whole strength in fulfilling their engagements with the King of England. Lord Somerville undertook to deliver this bond to Henry, and to concert with him proper warlike measures. Beaton, on the other side, caused the infant queen to be crowned at Stirling, appointed a new council, and made Arran, as governor or regent, take a most solemn oath to govern according to the advice of this council. On a sudden, the Earl of Lennox, whom the cardinal had played off with good effect against Arran, disgusted with the reconciliation that had taken place between Beaton and the regent, and led by other base motives, threw himself into the English interests. Lennox soon showed himself worthy of his new associates. To him had been intrusted the recent negotiations with the French court; and when the Sieur de la Brosse arrived with a few ships, bearing fifty pieces of artillery, some military stores, and 10,000 crowns to be distributed amongst the anti-English party, he anchored at Dumbarton, *because* the town and castle were devoted to his friend the Earl of Lennox. Taking good care not to inform him of his sudden change of politics, Lennox got all the gold, and then left the poor ambassador to discover his mistake. In his eagerness for the money, Lennox lost the rest of the cargo on board the French ships, which landed a Papal legate, Marco Grimani, who was commissioned to confirm Arran in his new zeal for Papistry, and to attend to the affairs of the church generally. The more patriotic of the Scottish nobles entertained this clever and polished Italian with great hospitality.[4] But there wanted no legate from the pope to excite the Scottish people. Somerville was seized, and the traitorous bond recently signed at Douglas Castle was found upon his person, along with other letters, which disclosed the full extent of that treasonable plan. Maxwell, another chief agent of the English party, was seized at the same time. Angus, with the Douglases and others, took up arms; but they were disconcerted by the decisive steps of the regent, who now acted under the control of Cardinal Beaton. Dalkeith and Pinkie, two of the chief places of the Douglases, were occupied by government troops, and Angus was obliged to take refuge in his strong castle of Tantallon, carrying with him his dear friend Sir

---

[1] *Diurnal of Occurrents in Scotland, from Death of James IV. to 1575*, 4to, Edin. 1833—a valuable volume, printed by the Bannatyne Club. [2] *Sadler; State Papers.*
[3] Henry had just declared war against Francis.
[4] *State Papers; Sadler; Diurnal of Occurrents;* Hamilton MSS., as quoted by Tytler (*Hist. Scot.*) and Chalmers (*Life of Mary*).

Ralph Sadler, whose life, by all law, was forfeited to the Scots. The Scottish parliament met in unusual numbers; and Grimani the legate, and the French ambassadors, De la Brosse and Mesnage, were introduced at proper moments. Arran would have hesitated, but Beaton boldly caused Angus, and all his party whose names were to the infamous bond signed at Douglas Castle, to be accused of treason; and, not stopping here, the parliament, under the same energetic direction, declared that the late treaties of peace and marriage with England were void and at an end, in consequence of the unjust conduct of the king in seizing the Scottish ships, promoting incursions on the Borders, and refusing to ratify the peace in proper time. De la Brosse and Mesnage delivered a message from Francis, who was expecting to be invaded by the English, and who was anxious on that account to remind the Scots of their long alliance with France.

Henry had for some time been greatly dissatisfied with his ally Francis. They had never been good friends since the marriage with Anne Boleyn; but it was the steady encouragement given by the French king to the Scots that brought about an open rupture. Before declaring himself, Henry sought a reconciliation with their old and common enemy, the emperor; and Charles, though greatly grown in power and in experience, had still such respect for the might of England as to be ready to make many concessions to her capricious king, in order to obtain her alliance. He was willing to admit that, as his aunt Catherine, and her rival Anne Boleyn, were both in their graves, all causes of difference ought to be buried with them; but still Charles was anxious to remove an insult to his family that had been made permanent in the person of Catherine's daughter, the Princess Mary. Here, as on other occasions, Henry's "subtle devisings" saved his pride, and the service to be done was thrown upon that slave of all-work—the parliament. Without mentioning her legitimacy, which would have been to declare that the king had acted most unlawfully by her mother, they passed an act restoring Mary to her place in the succession, and both her and her half-sister, the Princess Elizabeth, to their civil rights; so that it was now treason to hold the marriages of the king with Catherine of Aragon and Anne Boleyn to be legal—it was treason to hold the children by the said marriages to be illegitimate, it was treason to be silent upon the subject, and it was treason to refuse to take an oath upon it when required.[1] The emperor, who had suffered severe losses in his last campaign, was fain to be satisfied with this very extraordinary act, and a treaty was concluded in the month of February (1543). In the month of June, Francis refused even to listen to the extravagant demands which they had jointly agreed to enforce upon him, and this refusal they considered as a declaration of war. Henry talked largely of campaigns and conquests, but, in effect, he did little more than send 6000 men to the Continent under Sir John Wallop, and this insignificant force acted merely as auxiliary to the army of the emperor, who only thought of recovering some towns he had lost in Flanders, and of reducing the Duke of Cleves, then in close alliance with the French. Instead of taking the field, Henry, after an unusually long widowhood, took to himself a sixth wife, in the person of Catherine Parr, a very matronly, learned, discreet, and sagacious woman, widow to Nevil, Lord Latimer. It is said that Catherine was well versed in the new learning, and a sincere convert to the Protestant faith: it is quite certain that the Protestant party rejoiced at the union; and yet it is equally certain that, only sixteen days after the nuptials, three Sacramentarians or Protestants were burned alive in Smithfield. Catherine seems to have crawled with the axe hung by a thread over her neck, till death relieved her of her dangerous husband.

Sir Thomas Wallop, after failing miserably in the siege of Landreci, and losing a considerable portion of his army, withdrew to winter quarters.[2]

A.D. 1544. With an exhausted exchequer, it was resolved, in the wisdom of the king and his council, to conquer both Scotland and France at one and the same time; and, with an obese body, no longer fit even for the mere parade and spectacular part of war, Henry resolved to take the field in person. By immense and ruinous efforts an army of 30,000 men was raised, and in the month of July, about a year after his late marriage, of which he was probably already tired, the king's gracious majesty, in his royal person, passed the seas from Dover to Calais. A part of the army, led by the Duke of Norfolk and "the gentle Lord Russell," had taken the field, and laid siege to Montreuil, "where they lay a long time, and left the town as they found it." When Henry, "like a very god of war," assumed the command of the English forces and of 15,000 Imperialists sent by Charles to act with him, wonderful things were expected. The plan of the campaign had been nicely defined by the two allies. Charles was to strike across France by Champagne, Henry by Picardy; and neither was to stop till he reached Paris, where, in their united might, they were to dispose of the French monarchy. It was the old plan which had failed twice or thrice already, but this time they were to profit by past experience, and on no account to loiter on their way in besieging towns and castles: and yet the very first thing which Henry did was

---

[1] Raumer.

[2] State Papers; Godwin; Du Bellay.

to sit down with the mass of his army before the town of Boulogne, and to swear one of his biggest oaths, amidst the roar of his biggest guns, that he would do nothing else until he had taken it. In vain Charles implored him to advance: he justified his delay by saying that the emperor, on his side, had stopped to take some castles; and he continued burning an enormous quantity of gunpowder before Boulogne, which badly-fortified city detained him and his great army for nearly two months! When the garrison of Boulogne at last capitulated, and marched out with bag and baggage, "the king's highness having the sword borne naked before him by the Lord Marquis Dorset, like a noble and valiant conqueror rode into the town, and all the trumpeters, standing on the walls of the town, sounded their trumpets at the time of his entering, to the great comfort of all the king's true subjects."[1]

Before Henry had made this solemn entrance Charles had very wisely opened negotiations with the French king, and shortly after (in the month of September) the treaty of Crespi was signed, and fully ratified. His majesty of England, who had refused to be included in it, was left to carry on the war by himself; and Francis and the emperor agreed to forget all former grievances, and to unite their families and their politics by intermarriages. Having garrisoned Boulogne, and destroyed the church of "Our Ladye" there, Henry returned to England sorely impoverished. Nor did Henry gain more glory by his lieutenants in Scotland than he had gained personally on the Continent. Some time before his departure for Boulogne he sent the Viscount Lisle, Admiral of England, and the Earl of Hertford, uncles of Prince Edward, and brothers of the late Queen Jane Seymour, with a fleet of 200 sail, having on board an army of 10,000 men, to make a sudden attack upon Leith and Edinburgh, and to demand the immediate surrender of the young queen and of sundry fortresses. Arran, as regent, had made no suitable preparations; and Cardinal Beaton, by burning some poor people at Perth (for denying the efficacy of prayer to the saints and the Virgin, for treating an image of St. Francis irreverently, for breaking the fast of Lent, and for other heresies), had revived the keen hostility of the reforming party. At the same time the noble pensioners of England were not idle, and there was nothing but division or distrust at a moment when all Scotsmen ought to have been united by the common danger. On the 4th of May the English landed at Leith, which they plundered and occupied with little opposition. Though left almost entirely to themselves, the citizens of Edinburgh barricaded their gates, and determined to defend their ancient town. When Otterburn of Reid Hall, their provost, went with a flag of truce to remonstrate with the English commander, and to propose an amicable adjustment, Hertford told him that he came as a soldier, not as an ambassador—that they must instantly deliver up their young queen; for, if they did not, he was commanded to ravage their country with fire and sword.[2] Otterburn thought proper to remain in the English camp, but the people of Edinburgh chose a new provost, and held out. They even compelled Hertford to re-

THE CASTLE OF BOULOGNE.—From a drawing on the spot by T. S. Boys.

---

[1] *Hall; Du Bellay; Godwin; Rymer.* Rymer gives Henry's own journal, which is a curious document.

[2] Here is part of the infernal commission given by the king to the Earl of Hertford:—"You are there to put all to fire and sword; to burn Edinburgh town, and to raze and deface it, when you have sacked it, and gotten what you can out of it, as that it may remain for ever a memory of the vengeance of God alighted upon it, for their falsehood and disloyalty. . . . Do what you can out of hand, and, *without long tarrying* it was felt that this would not be safe with 10,000 men, to beat down and overthrow the castle, sack Holyroodhouse, and as many towns and villages about Edinburgh as ye conveniently can; sack Leith, and burn and subvert it, and all the rest, *putting man, woman, and child to fire and sword*, without exception, when any resistance shall be made against you; and this done, pass over to the Fife land, and extend like extremities and destructions in all towns and villages whereunto ye may reach conveniently, not forgetting, amongst all the rest, so to spoil and turn upside down the cardinal's town of St. Andrews, *as the upper stone may be the nether*, and not one stick stand by another, *sparing no creature alive* within the same, specially such as either in friendship or blood be allied to the cardinal. . . . *This journey shall succeed most to his majesty's honour*."—Hamilton MSS., as quoted by Mr. Tytler.

treat to Leith, but, when he brought up his heavy artillery, they found it a hopeless attempt to defend their wooden gates; and, removing as much of their property as they could, the citizens for the most part evacuated the town during the night, leaving the brave Hamilton of Stenhouse to hold the castle. The English entered the Canongate, put a few stragglers to the sword, and plundered such property as was left. But Hertford was foiled before Edinburgh Castle; his guns were dismounted by a sure fire from the ramparts, and he beat a retreat, which was covered by the smoke and flame of the city, to which he barbarously set fire. Being reinforced by a motley host of 4000 Borderers, partly English and partly Scots, the retainers of the house of Douglas, he employed himself in executing his king's commission to the letter, burning and destroying all the open country round the Scottish capital. In the vain hope of reconciling that faction, the Earl of Angus and his brother Sir George Douglas, who had been arrested, were set at liberty; upon which Sir George forthwith repaired to Leith, and had a private interview with the Earl of Hertford, to whom he betrayed all that he knew concerning the plans adopted by his countrymen. But the English soon perceived that they could not maintain their ground even at Leith, which they had fortified; and, in the middle of May, as Arran and Cardinal Beaton were marching towards them with a superior force, they abandoned the shores of the Forth, part sailing away with the fleet, and the rest, under Hertford, marching rapidly alongshore towards Berwick. Seton, Haddington, Dunbar, and Renton—all the towns between Edinburgh and Berwick—were plundered and burned, and every village and cottage near the road partook of the same fate. This was too much even for the traitors, and for those Scots who had wished for the presence of an English army in order to curb the fierceness of the Catholic party. The Earl of Angus joined the cardinal, who was the real director of the campaign; and even his brother, Sir George Douglas, was induced to pursue the same course, apparently giving up his English treaties and pensions. Indeed, in a very short time Henry had no traitorous ally in Scotland except Lennox and Glencairn; and the popular feeling of hatred against him and the English amounted almost to a frenzy. Glencairn was defeated in a sanguinary battle near Glasgow; and Lennox, having delivered the castle of Dumbarton into his keeping, fled by sea into England. Lennox soon returned from England with a fleet of eight ships; and, "hanging over the coast of Scotland, like a cloud uncertain where to disburden itself, he deterred the Scots from undertaking anything against England during the absence of the king in France." He took the isles of Arran and Bute; and, according to agreement, delivered them up to Sir Rice Mansel and Richard Broke, who accompanied him in the expedition with a small force of English archers and pikemen. He plundered Cantyre, Kyle, and Carrick, and returned loaded with booty and disgrace to an English port. While he had been plundering like a pirate by sea, Sir Ralph Evre, and other English officers, ravaged the Scottish borders in their whole length, and with a fury that but too plainly showed the intention of making those parts a desert. At the same time the two factions disagreed on every important point, and it was soon discovered, or suspected upon very good grounds, that the Douglases had renewed their plots with the English. Confidence disappeared—the men could not trust their officers—and when Arran took the field, with 6000 men, Angus, Cassillis, and others of the lords who had formerly bound themselves to Henry, would not fight; and the whole force fled disgracefully before 2000 English troops. But Angus and the Douglases were now made really patriotic and true to the national cause, by a report that Henry had promised all their hereditary estates to Sir Ralph Evre, if that officer could conquer them. Angus swore a great oath, that he would give Sir Ralph his *seisin*[1] on his skin, with sharp pens and bloody ink. Nothing deterred, the fierce Englishman in the following year re-entered Scotland, making all the country a desert about Jedburgh and Kyle. His host consisted of English archers, foreign mercenaries collected during the late expedition into France, and 700 or 800 freebooters from the Scottish borders—in all, about 6000 men. They burned the tower of Broom House, and in it a noble old lady with her whole family. They penetrated to Melrose, where they vented their barbarous spite on the beautiful old abbey and the tombs of the Douglases within it.

Angus' temporary patriotism was increased by the last-mentioned deed, and he joined the Regent Arran with all the vassals he could collect. Yet even at this moment his brother, Sir George Douglas, was corresponding with Sir Ralph Evre, and is supposed to have betrayed the movement of his countrymen to the English, who surprised Arran and Angus in an unfavourable position, and forced them to retreat with some loss. After burning Melrose, Sir Ralph Evre turned down the Tweed, being followed or watched in flank by Arran and Angus, who had re-collected their forces behind the Eildon Hills. Their recent successes had made the English

[1] A seisin, in the Scotch law, is the instrument or attestation of a notary, that possession of the land has been actually given by the superior to the vassal: it is the evidence or record of the infeftment or investiture.

commanders confident and careless. They marched upon Jedburgh with very little precaution; but when they came to Ancrum Moor, on the Teviot, they found the Scots drawn up in order of battle. On a near approach, Arran and Angus were disposed to decline battle, on account of the great inequality in numbers; but Sir Walter Scott, the veteran Laird of Buccleuch, galloped up to announce that his followers were close at hand; and Norman Lesly arrived on the field with 800 spears. Still, however, the Scots were very inferior in number, and they had recourse to some skilful manœuvring, which was recommended and directed by Walter Scott. A part of their army was concealed; their horses, mounted by the camp-boys, were posted on the crest of a hill, so as to look like a second army; and every fighting-man put his foot to the heather, having both sun and wind at his back, and in the faces of the enemy. The English advanced in a great hurry on horseback, as if loath to let the Scots escape them: the foremost line of the Scots retreated, but only for a few yards, when the assailants found themselves suddenly chased by a dense phalanx of Scottish pikemen, with spears an ell longer than those of the English.[1] Sir Brian Latoun and Sir Robert Bowes, who led the English van, were thrown back in disorder upon the main body, which was charging up the hill with great assurance under Sir Ralph Evre; and then the battle became general. It was, however, short: as soon as the English began to give way, the Scottish borderers, who had followed their standard, threw away their red crosses and fell upon their former allies. Upon this there ensued a general panic; the English fled in the greatest confusion, and the Scots pursued them with great slaughter. Wheresoever the fugitives turned, they found infuriated enemies in the peasantry, who had suffered so sorely from their recent excesses. Even the women and children joined in the carnage, and all pity was dismissed by their cries of "Remember their cruelty at Broom House!" Eight hundred of the English were killed in this battle, and a thousand, maimed and wounded, were taken prisoners. The joy of the Scots was at its height when they discovered among the dead the bodies of Evre and Latoun.[2]

A.D. 1545. Henry's great conquest of Boulogne, achieved at an expense of £400,000 of English money, was very nearly lost almost as soon as won, and the place was only saved by the gallantry and skill of Sir Thomas Poynings. Francis saw how greatly the English pale in France would be strengthened by the addition of Boulogne, and he made great efforts, both by sea and land, to retake it. Large galleys were built at Rouen, others were ordered round from Marseilles and the French ports on the Mediterranean, and all manner of great ships—Venetians, Aragonese, Italians, or whatsoever they might be—were pressed into the French service either by fair means or foul.[3] When Francis saw this formidable navy safely collected on the coasts of Brittany and Normandy, he conceived the bold notion of striving for the mastery of the sea, and seizing upon the Isle of Wight. Henry received timely warning that Francis intended to attempt an invasion, but he did not know where the blow might fall. His exchequer was very bare, but the people hastened to fortify the banks of the Thames, the coasts of Kent, Sussex, and Hampshire; and sixty ships of war were collected at Portsmouth under the flag of Dudley Lord Lisle, the high-admiral. On the 16th of July, the French fleet, amounting to 136 sail, under the command of Annebaut, put to sea, and two days after, they fell down the channel that separates the Isle of Wight from the main, and cast anchor at St. Helen's. These were not days for heroical achievements: Lisle, after a distant cannonading, retired into Portsmouth harbour, where the king then was, and whence he saw a foreign fleet insulting him to his face, and riding triumphant in the Channel. The next day Annebaut put out his flat-bottomed galleys and vessels that drew little water; and, while these went up to the very mouth of the port, he ravaged the coast and did whatever he could to provoke the English to come out and give battle; but, by Henry's orders, the lord-admiral stirred not. After holding a council of war, the French admiral determined to attack the Isle of Wight, and a descent was made in three several places; but the brave inhabitants drove the invaders back to their ships, though not before much of their property had been plundered or given to the flames. Annebaut sailed away towards Dover, landing occasionally to burn and destroy. In some places, however, his men got worse than they gave, being cut to pieces by the inhabitants, who lay in ambush to receive them. It was now the object of the French admiral, who stood off-and-on in the narrow part of the Channel, to prevent the

---

[1] The length of the Scottish pike or spear was fixed, by act of parliament, in 1471, at six ells—that is, eighteen feet and a half.

[2] The place where the battle was fought received the name of Lilliard's Edge, "from an Amazonian Scottish woman of that name," says Sir Walter Scott, "who is reported by tradition to have distinguished herself in the same manner as Squire Witherington at Chevy Chase. The old people point out her monument, now broken and defaced. The inscription is said to have run thus:—

Fair maid Lylliard lies under this stane;
Little was her stature, but great was her fame.
Upon the English louns she laid many thumps,
And when her legs were cutted off, she fought upon her stumps."

[3] State Papers.

English from victualling Boulogne, and from sending reinforcements of ships from the Thames to Portsmouth: but he executed his commission with very indifferent success: provisions were thrown into Boulogne, which greatly wanted them, almost under the shadow of his own flag; and the lord-admiral at Portsmouth was reinforced with thirty sail. When Dudley received the king's orders to put forth against the enemy, he said, with proper spirit, that he would lose no time in so doing—that he was grateful for being restored to his liberty, having never thought himself in prison till now, since the time of his lying there doing nothing. The watch-word for the fleet in the night was, "God save King Henry!"—to which the answer was, "And long to reign over us!" The two fleets were soon in presence between Brighton and the French coast, but "thought it best to eschew the fight that day for a better day," and, in the end, they did nothing but exchange a few long shots. The English commander went back to Portsmouth, the French withdrew to Brest.

Henry's father had left him the richest sovereign in Europe, but that money had long been gone. The seizure of the church property, after all deductions, had furnished him with immense sums, but they, too, were all gone. The parliament had voted such subsidies as had never been voted before, but they were all spent as soon as raised. In his constant and recurring need he had already adopted all kinds of illegal measures to extract more money from his people. His officers had obtained returns which showed the value of each man's estate; and with this clue he now addressed a royal letter to every person rated at £50 per annum, requesting a certain sum by way of loan. To refuse was dangerous: in most cases he got the money he asked for, and then he made parliament vote him a grant of all the money so raised, as well as whatever sums he had borrowed from any of his subjects since 1539, or the thirty-first year of his reign! After this he had recourse to a benevolence, and the people, who had made a spirited opposition to that illegal mode of raising money in the time of Cardinal Wolsey, were now fain to submit and pay. Henry had long since adopted the common but ruinous system of adulterating the coinage: now he debased it to such an extent that what was called the silver shilling contained twice as much alloy as silver. This practice greatly embarrassed the trade of the country, and tended to dry up his resources at the fountain head. In the month of November he made a very tender appeal to parliament, explaining his increasing wants; and parliament not only voted him an enormous subsidy, but also granted him the disposal of all colleges, charities, and hospitals in the kingdom, with all their manors, lands, and hereditaments, receiving, in return, his gracious promise that they should all be employed to the glory of God and the public good. This was the last grant the tyrant got from his slaves, and he did not live to employ the whole power the act gave him. Had he survived a little while longer, he would not have left an hospital for the care of the sick, or a school for the instruction of youth.

A great deal of the money thus wrung from the loyal English was spent among the traitors of Scotland. The victory of Ancrum had raised the spirits of the Scottish people. It was scarcely gained, however, when Angus, his brother George, Glencairn, Cassillis, and the rest of that vile league, renewed their intercourse with Sir Ralph Sadler, who was appointed treasurer of an army that was levying in the north of England, under the Earl of Hertford. On the 17th of April, Cassillis endeavoured to induce the convention of the Scottish nobility, held at Edinburgh, to ask pardon of the King of England, and to solicit a renewal of the treaty of marriage; but Cardinal Beaton, encouraged by assurance of assistance from Francis, who was then preparing his great naval expedition, kept alive the spirit of the more patriotic among the nobles; the proposals were rejected; the treaty of marriage was declared to be at an end for ever; upon which, Cassillis advised Henry to try a fresh invasion of his native land. But Henry, as we have seen, found other business of more urgency; and fancying that all opposition in Scotland would cease if he could only remove Beaton, he entertained the project for assassinating the cardinal. In the month of May, Cassillis, acting with some of the other noble traitors, sent a letter to Sir Ralph Sadler, very coolly making an offer "for the killing of the cardinal, if his majesty would have it done, and promise, when it was done, a reward." These high-born villains never moved a step without bargaining beforehand. Sadler showed the letter to the Earl of Hertford and the council of the north, who evidently thought the plan a good one, and transmitted it to the king. Henry's reply was worthy of Cassillis' proposal. On the 30th of May, his privy council wrote to the Earl of Hertford:—"His majesty hath willed us to signify unto your lordship, that his highness, reputing the fact not meet to be set forward expressly by his majesty, will not seem to have to do in it; and yet, not misliking the offer, thinketh good that Mr. Sadler, to whom that letter was addressed, should write to the earl, of the receipt of his letter containing such an offer, which he thinketh not convenient to be communicated to

[1] *State Papers; Du Bellay; Holinshed; Godwin; Southey; Naval Hist.*

the king's majesty. Marry to write to him what he thinketh of the matter, he shall say, that if he were in the Earl of Cassillis' place, and were as able to do his majesty good service there, as he knoweth him to be, and thinketh a right good will in him to do it, he would surely do what he could for the execution of it; believing verily to do thereby not only an acceptable service to the king's majesty, but also a special benefit to the realm of Scotland, and would trust verily the king's majesty would consider his service in the same; as you doubt not, of his accustomed goodness to them which serve him, but he would do the same to him."[1] Sir Ralph Sadler accordingly wrote, in the indirect manner pointed out by Henry, to Cassillis; and Thomas Forster, an Englishman of some note, who had recently been a prisoner-of-war in Scotland, at the request of the Scottish conspirators, and by order of Henry, who commanded that no time should be lost, was sent across the Borders, to consult with Cassillis, Angus, and Sir George Douglas. Forster entered Scotland at Wark, and, without provoking much suspicion, reached Dalkeith, where he had an interview with Sir George, who wished him to go to Douglas, where he would cause the Earls of Cassillis and Angus to meet him; for he (Sir George) said he could not get them to Dalkeith without great suspicion. These secret agents, going towards Douglas, met the Earl of Angus at Dumfries, where, as he was hunting, he gave Forster welcome, saying that he would give him hawks and dogs, and he caused him to pass that night with him. And on the morrow, Angus conducted him to Douglas, and that afternoon sent for the Earl of Cassillis, who, riding all night, came thither the next day early in the morning; upon which he and the Earl of Angus went into a chamber together, and called Forster to them, who then declared the "occasion of his coming, by whom he was sent, and the full of his instructions." But Angus and Cassillis were as cunning and cautious as their English friends; and, as Sadler had made no specific proposal and fixed no certain reward, they would not speak to Forster of the murder,[2] but kept to the grand treason of co-operating with the English army of invasion. Cassillis said that he was still the same true man to Henry as he was at parting with his majesty; and Angus promised his cordial assistance, declaring that he would either go to the field or stay at home, as Henry judged it best. But on his departure, Cassillis gave Forster a letter, in cipher, to Sir Ralph Sadler; and Sir George Douglas, in his heat, was betrayed into the following expressions, which he sent as a message from himself to the Earl of Hertford: —"He willed me," says Forster, "to tell my lord-lieutenant, that if the king would have the cardinal dead, if his grace would promise a good reward for the doing thereof, so that the reward were known what it should be, the country being lawless as it is, he thinketh that that adventure would be proved; for he saith, the common saying is, the cardinal is the only occasion of the war, and is smally beloved in Scotland; and then, if he were dead, by what means that reward should be paid."[3] The revelation of these atrocious secrets, which had been concealed for centuries amidst the dust and cobwebs of the State Paper Office, is enough to make the villains turn in their graves! As his majesty of England had still some sense of shame, he hesitated at committing himself so far as to make a direct bargain: he wished the deed done, but in such a manner, that it could never be brought clearly to his own door; and as the most noble Scots would not commit murder otherwise than as they had bargained, Beaton was permitted to live a few months longer, when he was taken off by less conspicuous assassins. Before the journey of Forster into Scotland, the Sieur Lorges de Montgomerie had arrived from France, with a body of 3000 infantry and 500 horse; and in the month of August these foreign auxiliaries, well appointed and disciplined, took the field with an army of about 25,000 Scots. By the advice of Beaton, the whole of this force was thrown across the English borders; but the vanguard was commanded by Angus, who, not a month before, had promised Forster to do what King Henry might think best; and after two days, which were ingloriously employed in plundering and burning a few villages, the army returned, through the deceit of George Douglas and the vanguard.[4] That there might be no mistake in the matter, the lords in the interest of England wrote a letter to claim the whole credit of the failure of the expedition, and to advise the instant advance of an English army.[5]

On the 5th of September, the English put themselves in motion under the Earl of Hertford; but the money-chests were empty; and, at the moment of crisis, several of the Scottish traitors hung back, and, instead of joining the English with all their retainers, they began to think of opposing them. They had requested that the old system of warfare might this time be abandoned; but Hertford burned and destroyed even more savagely than before, employing on this work a vast number of Irish kerns, who had been brought over for the purpose.

[1] *State Papers.*
[2] Sir Ralph Sadler, in obedience to Henry's orders, recommended the assassination as if of himself, and told them that the project had *not* been communicated to King Henry.
[3] *State Papers.*   [4] *Diurnal Occurrents.*
[5] This letter appears in the *State Papers.*

At Kelso the poor monks attempted to defend their abbey, and boldly repulsed some adventurers; but Hertford brought up his heavy guns, made a breach, and carried the church. Retreating to the tower or belfry, the monks there prolonged the struggle, but the tower was battered and stormed, and every monk butchered. As the savage invaders poured through Tweeddale, the abbeys of Melrose and Dryburgh were again plundered and fired, and every village, every farm, castle, or mansion on the pleasant banks of the Tweed was sacked and burned. All this havoc was grateful to the sight of the noble Seymour, who wrote boastingly to his royal master, that he had done more damage in Scotland by fire than had been done for the last 100 years.[1] But this ruthless destroyer could not maintain himself even on the Borders; his army soon felt the effects of the ruin they had spread around them; the country was become a desert, furnishing no food for man or horse; the impoverished government could forward no adequate supply of provisions; and in less than three weeks Hertford retreated and disbanded his starving forces.

The cardinal did not lose heart in the midst of these difficulties. After the retreat of Hertford, he held a parliament at Stirling, and suggested several energetic measures for the defence of the national independence. Seeing, however, the impoverishment and exhaustion of the country, he proposed passing over to France, in order to procure a fresh supply of money and troops. This project was communicated to Henry by one of the most unscrupulous of his agents, Crichton, the Laird of Brunston, in a letter dated from Ormiston House, the 6th of October. After mentioning what is in the wind, the laird expresses some hopes that the intended journey of the cardinal may be cut short; for, that at no time were there more Scottish gentlemen desirous of doing his highness good service. A day or two after, this cautious assassin wrote to Lord Wharton, one of the English wardens, that he was very anxious for a private interview with him, that he might know whether his majesty would be plain with them *what he would have them do, and as to what reward they might count upon.* On the 20th of October he wrote to King Henry himself, requesting a private conference with Sadler at Berwick, where he would communicate such things as should be greatly to the advancing of his majesty's affairs.[2] From all this, it is very evident that the project for murdering Cardinal Beaton had been resumed. It has been usual for historians, wanting the light which has been recently thrown upon these long-hidden transactions, to attribute the assassination of Beaton

[1] *State Papers.*
[2] *Tytler,* from the originals in the State Paper Office.

solely to the fanaticism of certain converts to the new religion, and their desire of avenging the cruelties he had committed upon their persecuted sect; but it now appears very evident that the deed was undertaken and done from baser motives, though some who engaged in the plot at its last stage may have been moved by a desire of destroying the arch-enemy of their faith.

George Wishart, commonly called the Martyr, was a man of obscure or uncertain birth, but of considerable learning. He had been patronized in his youth by John Erskine of Dun, provost of Montrose, one of the first Scotsmen that declared against the Church of Rome. Wishart kept a school at Montrose, where he introduced the teaching of Greek, and made his pupils read the New Testament in the original language. On account of some persecution to which this exposed him, he fled into England, where, in 1538, in the city of Bristol, he preached against the worship paid to the Virgin Mary. In consequence, he was thrown into prison, and he only escaped the penalties of heresy by openly recanting, upon which a fagot was burned instead of himself, and he disappeared from that part of the country. When he next attracted attention it was at Cambridge, where he was admired for his learning, and hated for his zeal and strictness. Some time in 1543, he returned to his native country, where he denounced the Popish doings of Cardinal Beaton, and most closely connected himself with those chiefs who leaned towards the Reformation, namely, the Earls of Cassillis and Glencairn, the earl-marischal, Sir George Douglas, and the Lairds of Brunston, Ormiston, and Calder. Protected by these great lords and lairds, Wishart preached publicly against the errors of Popery and the wickedness of the monks; and his fiery eloquence inflamed the people in sundry places. At Dundee his converts or audience destroyed the houses of the Black and Gray friars; and when he preached at Edinburgh the religious houses were only saved by the prompt interference of the civil authority. In the ears of the people his denunciations of coming vengeance sounded very like prophecy; and when the Earl of Hertford set the south of Scotland in a blaze, it was remembered how the preacher had predicted that event.

For two years the preacher was left at large, for it was not easy to seize one who seldom moved anywhere without being preceded by a trusty disciple bearing a two-handed sword, and watched by other followers with pikes, halberts, and morions. It is said that Cardinal Beaton was, to a certain degree, aware of the plot laid against his own life, and that, in dread of Wishart, he attempted to anticipate him, and laid plots for murdering Wishart. After a time the preacher's popularity declined. Some of his great friends fell from his side, and he was obliged to take refuge in West Lothian with the Laird of Brunston, Sandilands of Calder, and Cockburn of Ormiston, who concealed him by turns in their houses. One night when he was at Ormiston with his friends, expecting the arrival of the Earl of Cassillis, the house was suddenly surrounded by a party of soldiers led by the Earl of Bothwell, who was then devoted to the cardinal. Upon an assurance that his life would be spared, Wishart surrendered. Bothwell took the preacher to his own house of Hailes; but soon after he sold him to Beaton, who summoned a council of the bishops and abbots at St. Andrews, and brought him to trial as an heretic. The assembled clergy found him guilty, and sentenced him to be burned, and he was burned accordingly at St. Andrews. This execution was as impolitic as it was barbarous: the dead Wishart became more formidable than the living preacher; many of his converts, quoting the Old Testament, showed how it would be a virtue to avenge his death, and cut off his wicked persecutor and destroyer; and Cassillis, Glencairn, Sir George Douglas, and their fellow-conspirators, derived great strength from the popular feeling excited against the cardinal, which feeling, however, was confined to certain towns and districts, the vast majority of the nation being as yet attached to the old religion, and seeing nothing very remarkable in the burning of a man who attacked its dogmas.

Being alarmed at the threats of his enemies in Scotland, and rumours of a fresh invasion, Beaton immediately employed masons and carpenters to strengthen his castle of St. Andrews. He also called around him the gentlemen of Fife, to concert means for the defence of the coast. At one of these meetings he had a violent quarrel about a piece of land with Norman Lesly, commonly called the Master of Rothes. After using language not likely to be forgiven, Norman hurried to his uncle, John Lesly, who had already declared that Beaton's blood ought to be shed for the blood of the martyr Wishart. Both uncle and nephew consulted with William Kirkaldy, the Laird of Grange, with James Melville, a religious enthusiast, with Carmichael, and with several others; and at a secret conclave it was determined that the cardinal should die forthwith. On the evening of the 28th of May, Norman Lesly rode into the town of St. Andrews, and in the course of the night he was followed by a whole troop, who stole into the town in small parties, without being perceived, or without exciting any suspicion. At an early hour on the following morning, they surprised the castle by entering with the workmen, and the cardinal was roused from his sleep to meet his death. John Lesly and Carmichael appear to have been the first to stab him, and then Melville, with great gravity, advanced to execute what he called "the judgment of God," and passed his long sword through the body of the unresisting victim several times. Then, covered with the blood of the cardinal, the conspirators, who had taken care to raise the drawbridge and close the gates, ascended to the battlements to address the people of the town, who now, headed by their provost, crowded in alarm around the castle, and shouted that they must restore the lord-cardinal. Norman Lesly dragged up the body, and suspended it by a sheet over the wall. "There," said he, "there is your god; and now that ye are satisfied, get home to your houses!" Kirkaldy of Grange, Norman Lesly, and others of the conspirators, were at the moment receiving pensions from the English king—were described by Henry as his good friends and supporters; and almost as soon as the murder was finished, they opened communications with the king, offered to hold the castle for his behoof, and received from him assurances of assistance and support.[1]

But though the death of Cardinal Beaton was fatal to the Roman church in Scotland, the event was not followed by all that Henry had fondly expected from it. The embarrassments of his government increased daily; and in the month of June he was glad to conclude a treaty of peace with the French king, who insisted that Scotland should be comprehended in it.

The six remaining months of Henry's life were occupied by vile attempts at devising reasons for excluding the Scots from the benefit of the treaty of peace, by the intrigues and struggles of the two great religious factions, and by more executions for treason. The most wretched being, in this most wretched state of things, was the king himself, whose mind and body were alike diseased. In the absence of other pleasures he had given himself up to immoderate eating, and he had grown so enormously fat that he could not pass through an ordinary door, nor could he move about from room to room without the help of machinery, or of numerous attendants. The old issue in his leg had become an inveterate ulcer, which kept him in a constant state of pain and excessive irritability. It was alike offensive to the senses, and dangerous to life and property, to approach this corrupt mass of dying tyranny. The slightest thing displeased him, and his displeasure was a fury and a madness, and nothing on earth could give him a wholesome pleasurable feeling. How his last wife, Catherine Parr, escaped destruction appears almost miraculous: she was more than once in imminent peril.

[1] *Tytler.*

The court, which no longer presented any of the pageantries and gaieties of earlier days, had become a gloomy conventicle, where men, and women too, gave themselves up to polemics. Catherine ventured to read some of the prohibited works put forth by the Reformers, and as the king grew worse and worse, and more and more helpless, she took courage to dispute with him upon faith and doctrine. Henry was greatly exasperated. "A good hearing this," cried he, "when women become such clerks, and a thing much to my comfort, to come in mine old age to be taught by my wife." Gardiner, it is said, took advantage of this state of mind, and received orders, with Wriothesley the chancellor, to prepare articles of impeachment against her. But Catherine was warned in time, and adroitly recovered by flattery the ground she had lost by venturing upon polemical controversy. On the following morning, when the Chancellor Wriothesley came with forty men of the guard to take Catherine into custody, the king's majesty called him knave, an arrant knave, a fool, and a beast, and so dismissed him.[1]

There had long been a bitter rivalry between the old house of Howard and the new house of Seymour, which owed its sudden exaltation to the king's third marriage and the birth of a son, Prince Edward, by Jane Seymour. The Duke of Norfolk, the head of the Howards, was, as we have repeatedly noticed, a zealous Papist: Lord Hertford, the uncle of Prince Edward, and the real founder of the greatness of the Seymours, almost as a natural consequence, leaned towards the Reformation, though he took good care to conceal this fact from the king. The two names became rallying points to the two rival sects. With the evidence we have before us we may confidently pronounce them both to have been men of a cruel and base character, ready to execute if not to suggest some of the worst actions of the king,

THOMAS HOWARD, Duke of Norfolk.—After Holbein.

and to crawl in the dust at his feet at the slightest sign of his displeasure; but the real nature of both has been overlooked by their respective sects. Hertford, in family alliances, connections, and landed property, was far the inferior of Norfolk, but he had the grand advantages of being uncle of the heir to the throne, and of being almost constantly about the court. Favoured by these circumstances, he already aspired to the protectorship of the kingdom during the minority of his nephew; for, though the fact was concealed from the public with all possible care, it was evident that the king was hastening to the grave.[2]

Hertford felt that the grand obstacle to his promotion would be found in the Duke of Norfolk and his son, the accomplished and poetical Earl of Surrey; and mere self-preservation gave him a strong motive to destroy both father and son while there was yet time. Henry, Earl of

---

[1] Lord Herbert.

"It would have been pleasing could we have dwelt on this escape made by the queen as one of the last transactions which illustrate the personal character of this monarch. But short and dark as was the period of life now allotted him, it was to be lighted up by the flames of martyrs, and stained by the blood of the noblest and the most accomplished of his victims. About this time Mrs. Anne Askew, a lady of ancient family, remarkable accomplishments, and great beauty, had embraced the Reformed opinions. Her chief offence seems to have been a denial of transubstantiation; upon which point she was repeatedly brought before the council. Of her examinations, on these occasions, she herself has left a pathetic and interesting account, which has been preserved by Fox, and presents a picture of religious persecution which it is impossible to read without horror. On finding her fixed in the resolution to maintain her belief, the next object of the inquisitors was to discover her accomplices, as the king had been informed she could name, if she were willing, a great number of her sect. Strong suspicions were even entertained that she secretly encouraged by some of the privy council: this, however, she positively denied; upon which, Gardiner and Wriothesley, the lord-chancellor, ordered Knevet, the lieutenant of the Tower, to put her on the rack. She was then let down into the lower dungeon, where she beheld that dreadful instrument, and the jailor standing beside it, his sleeves tucked up, and ready for his office. Still, her courage was unshaken; and the lieutenant, although compelled by his office to obey, was anxious to spare her the extremity of the torture. He commanded the jailer to stretch her on the iron platform, but only to 'pinch' her; after which, being about to take her down, he was reprimanded by Wriothesley and ordered to proceed. This he refused although threatened with the royal displeasure; upon which the other threw off his gown and drew the rack himself, till her bones and joints were almost plucked asunder. She was then untied, and having fainted away from the excess of torture inflicted on her by this legal monster, was removed from the dungeon in a chair or litter. No persuasions, not even the offer of her life, could prevail on her to recant, and she was soon after, with three other Sacramentarians, publicly burned at Smithfield."—Tytler, Life of King Henry VIII., p. 453.

[2] The first notice of the king's failing health—a subject on which Henry was so jealous that those around him seem to have been afraid of mentioning it in writing to their colleagues—occurs in a letter from Yetswelrt to Sir William Paget, dated the 17th of September, 1546. But, in this letter, it is added that his majesty was recovered.—State Papers.

Surrey, upon being superseded in a military command in France by the new man Hertford (and Surrey always expressed a great contempt of the new nobility), was excessively irritated; and it is said that he vowed revenge upon Hertford as soon as the king should be dead. Nothing was so easy as to excite the jealousies and fears of Henry—fears probably increased by the reflection that Hertford, who would be in a manner the natural guardian of his son, was without influence among the high nobility, and was at enmity with Norfolk, the most powerful of them all. There were also men in the king's council, who were Protestants in their hearts, and (as such) ready to go great lengths against the champions of the rival faith. The first blow was struck at Bishop Gardiner, but it was warded off by that prelate. A few days after, on the 12th of December, the Duke of Norfolk and the Earl of Surrey, "upon certain surmises of treason," were sent to the Tower, the one by water, the other by land, and neither aware of the apprehension of the other. From his dungeon, Norfolk, ignorant of the cause of his sudden seizure, wrote to the king. "Undoubtedly," said the duke, "I know not that I have offended any man, or that any man was offended with me, unless it be such as be angry with me for being quick against such as have been accused for sacramentaries." On the 13th day of January, when the king was lying dangerously sick, the gallant and accomplished Surrey, who appears to have been dreaded more than his aged father, was arraigned at Guildhall on a charge of treason, for having borne the royal arms of Edward the Confessor mixed and quartered with the coat of his own family. It may

SURREY'S AUTOGRAPH OF HIS ARMS, quartered with those of the Confessor.—Arundel MS.

seem strange that no more serious charge should be produced; but even this much had been obtained in the most nefarious manner, and in part by means which are not calculated to raise our very low estimate of the domestic virtues of those times. The court, preparatory to the trial, had tampered with and terrified the women of the Howard family. The Duchess of Norfolk had long been on bad terms with her husband, living separated from him; and one of her daughters, the Duchess of Richmond, bore an unnatural hatred to her brother Surrey. On Sunday night, the 12th of December, immediately after the arrest of the duke and his son, Gate, Southwell, and Carew were despatched with all haste to Kenninghall (seven miles from Thetford), the principal house of the Howards, and they arrived there by break of day on Tuesday, "so that the first news of the Duke of Norfolk and the son came thither by them."[1] After taking care "of all the gates and back-doors," they desired to speak with the Duchess of Richmond and her sister, Mrs. Elizabeth Holland, who were found "at that time newly risen, and not ready." The two ladies, however, appeared in the dining-chamber without delay, and the court agents imparted to them "the case and condition wherein the duke and his son, without the king's great mercy, did stand." "Wherewith," continue these respectable gentlemen, "we found the Duchess of Richmond a woman sore perplexed, trembling, and like to fall down; but, coming unto herself again, she was not, we assure your majesty, forgetful of her duty, and did most humbly and reverently, upon her knees, humble herself in all unto your highness: saying that, although nature constrained her sore to love her father and also to desire the well-doing of his son, her natural brother, whom she noteth to be a rash man, yet for her part she would, nor will, hide or conceal anything from your majesty's knowledge, specially if it be of weight, or otherwise, as it shall fall in her remembrance; which she hath promised, for the better declaration of her integrity, to exhibit in writing unto your highness and your honourable council." They then tell the king, whom they address directly, that they desired sight of the chambers and coffers, and got the keys from the Duchess of Richmond. They go on to express their disappointment at the poorness of the prize; but we suspect that, in all these domiciliary visits, the agents concealed a portion of the spoils, and kept it for themselves. "Her coffers and chambers be so bare as your majesty would hardly think; her jewels, such as she had, sold, or lent to gage (pawn), to pay her debts, as she, her maiden, and the almoner do say. We will, nevertheless, for our duty, make a further and more earnest search." When they had done with the duchess' chambers and coffers, they searched those of Mrs. Elizabeth Holland, her sister, where they found divers girdles, beads, buttons of gold, pearls, and rings set with stones of divers sorts, whereof with all other things, they were, they say, making inventories to be sent to his highness. They also report that, hav-

[1] State Papers.

ing made sure of the house and property at Kenninghall, they with all speed, and at one instant, sent some of their most discreet and trusty servants to all the other houses of the duke in Norfolk and Suffolk, not omitting the house of his daughter, Elizabeth Holland, "newly made in Suffolk, which was thought to be well furnished with stuff." The duke's almoner had engaged to deliver into their hands all, or the greater part, of the family plate, "but money of the duke had none, but supposes that the steward upon his last account had such as did remain." As another important duty, the agents had informed themselves as to the clear value of the duke's possessions, and all other his yearly revenue, as near as they could learn, by his books of account and other his records. The Duchess of Richmond and Mrs. Elizabeth Holland they had taken into custody, and would send on their journey towards London on the morrow; but they represented that there remained unattached in the house the Earl of Surrey's wife and children, with certain women in the nursery attending upon them, and they humbly besought his majesty to signify what they were to do with the servants, seeing that the said earl's wife was near her time, and expecting to lie in at Candlemas.[1]

The Duchess of Norfolk was arrested near London, and the three ladies were "travailed with" and examined by some of the council. But though the wife was ready to speak against the husband—the sister against the brother—their depositions amounted to almost nothing. The Duchess of Richmond said that she had heard her brother Surrey speak bitterly against the Earl of Hertford; and these women also stated (what was notorious to all) that Norfolk and his son had quartered the arms of the Duke of Buckingham, a lineal descendant from Edward III.[2] When the council could get no more from the women, they set forward the evidence of two obscure men, who asserted that the Earl of Surrey had entertained certain Italians who were suspected of being spies; that the Duke of Norfolk had expressed great dissatisfaction at the changes in the church, had spoken about the king's diseases, and greatly abused some of the new nobility.

Before the court at Guildhall, Surrey, who, in the words of Lord Herbert, "was a man of deep understanding, sharp wit, and high courage," made a most spirited and eloquent defence. And the cause he had to plead was most simple. He admitted that he had borne the arms of Edward the Confessor, but he exhibited a decision of the heralds which allowed him so to do; and he told them (what most of them must have known perfectly) that he had borne those arms for years, even in the king's presence, without giving any offence. Notwithstanding all this, the court pronounced that there was proof sufficient, in the fact of his wearing the arms, that he had aspired to the throne; and the jury, doing their duty as usual, found him guilty. "And so the flower of the English nobility was, on the 19th of January, beheaded, the king being then in extremity, and breathing his *last* in blood."[3]

Norfolk, from his cell in the Tower, repeatedly requested to be confronted with his accusers, either before his royal majesty, or, if his pleasure should not be to take that pains, then before his council. But it may be questioned whether his letters ever reached the king, who, at the moment (though not aware of it), "was feeling the inevitable necessity of death;" and it had been fully determined by the Seymours and others who surrounded the bed of the expiring tyrant, that no more justice or leniency should be shown to the duke, than *he*, in his days of favour and might, had meted out to others. After several private examinations, the duke, upon some promises tendered to him in the name of the king, consented to write or sign a confession. But even in this document there was nothing that could reasonably be construed into treason; for he only admitted that, during his long and difficult services, he had occasionally communicated to others some of the secrets of the privy council, contrary to his oath; that he had concealed the treasonable act of his son, in assuming the arms of Edward the Confessor; and that he had himself treasonably borne on his shield the arms of England, with the difference of labels of silver, which of right belonged only to Prince Edward. The Seymour party, who had got from Henry a promise that the spoils of Howard should be shared amongst them, and whose promises to the duke were only meant to extract the confession, thought this matter sufficient upon which to proceed to judgment. Norfolk, however, who was well practised in business of this kind, knew perfectly well that, if his estates were divided among many, his family would find a great difficulty in getting them back in case of a reversal of his attainder, and he sent a petition to the king, to implore, as a favour, that all his "good and stately gear" might be settled on Prince

---

[1] *State Papers.*
[2] Norfolk had done this in right of his wife, who was daughter of the unfortunate Duke of Buckingham, executed in the early part of this reign.

[3] *Godwin.* There were other grounds of suspicion against Surrey which it was thought proper to suppress in public. He was suspected of a design upon the king's daughter, the Princess Mary! In the *State Papers* there is a remarkable document, without title or date, in the hand-writing of Wriothesley, the chancellor, with interlineations written by the king himself, in a tremulous hand. It consists of a set of queries evidently preparatory to the prosecution of the Howards.

Edward. This petition was not likely to disarm the enmity of the rival party. Instead of arraigning him before his peers, they proceeded by the system which Cromwell had introduced, and by which Cromwell had himself suffered. A bill of attainder, founded on the confession, was brought into the House of Lords, and read three times on three successive days. The commons did their work with equal despatch—returning the bill, passed, in three days more. It had been usual, even in these murderous times, to wait till the close of the session for the royal assent to such bills of attainder; but two days after the bill had passed, the king grew so much worse, that Norfolk's enemies saw there was no time to lose; and accordingly, on the 27th of January, Wriothesley, the chancellor, informed the two houses of parliament that his majesty had been pleased to appoint certain lords to signify his assent to the bill. And thereupon the commission, under the sign-manual, was read; the royal assent was given by the lords appointed; and, without losing precious moments, an order was despatched to the lieutenant of the Tower to execute the Duke of Norfolk at an early hour on the following morning.

But by the good fortune of Norfolk, and many a better man, the tyrant died in the palace of Whitehall in the intervening night. His last scene of all has been very differently represented by the opposite sects; but the account usually inserted in our histories is supported by respectable authority, and is—at least in part—very like truth. As several persons had been put to death at various times for saying the king was dying or likely to die, the people about him were afraid to tell him of his true condition; and the Seymour party had strong motives for concealing his danger both from himself and the public as long as possible. The physicians, on the approach of certain symptoms, wished his courtiers—friends he had none—to warn him of his state; but they all hung back in affright, like unarmed men in the presence of a wounded and dying beast of prey. At last Sir Anthony Denny undertook the task, and, going directly to the bedside of the fainting monarch, told him that the hope of human help was vain, and recommended him to turn his thoughts to heaven,—an advice not very acceptable to him: but finding it was grounded upon the opinion of his physicians, he submitted to the hard law of necessity, and, reflecting upon the course of his life, which he much condemned, he still professed himself confident that, through Christ, all his sins, though they had been more in number and weight, might be pardoned. He was then asked whether he desired to confer with any divines? "With none other," said he, "but the Archbishop Cranmer, and not with him yet; I will first repose myself a little, and, as I then find myself, will determine accordingly." After a sleep, or stupor, of an hour or two, he felt that he was going; and then he commanded that the archbishop should be sent for in all haste. Cranmer, after being present in the House of Lords on the three several days on which the iniquitous bill of attainder against the Duke of Norfolk was read, had retired for quiet to Croydon, where he was on the evening when he received the royal summons. He posted to court with all possible speed, but before he arrived the king was speechless. It is added that, when he bent over the bed, Henry grasped his hand; that then Cranmer exhorted him to hope for God's mercy, through Christ, on which the king grasped his hand as hard as he could, and expired a few moments after, having lived fifty-five years and seven months, and reigned thirty-seven years, nine months, and six days.

It is generally set down, somewhat vaguely, in our annals, that the party which succeeded to power did not think it advisable to begin a new reign by shedding the blood of the first nobleman of England; but, from the character of the majority of those men, we are inclined to believe that they were deterred merely by the dread of consequences to themselves in case of a failure of their schemes. If Henry had lived two or three hours longer the head of Norfolk would have been upon the block; but then it might have been made to pass as the act of a living king. As it was, Norfolk was respited, and the sentence was never carried into effect, although the aged duke remained in confinement till the accession of Queen Mary. If, in the course of this narrative, our views of certain historical characters, and of their motives of action, be found to vary somewhat from those of preceding writers, the reader should bear in mind that those views have been opened to us and illuminated by the unerring light of the STATE PAPERS.

END OF VOL. I.

BLACKIE AND SON:

GLASGOW:
36, FREDERICK STREET.

EDINBURGH:
5, SOUTH COLLEGE STREET.

LONDON: 44, PATERNOSTER ROW, E.C.

Just completed, in 36 Parts, imperial 4to, 2s. 6d. each; or elegantly half-bound, morocco, gilt edges, £5, 5s.

THE IMPERIAL ATLAS
OF MODERN GEOGRAPHY;

A Series of One Hundred carefully coloured Maps, embracing the most recent Discoveries, and the latest Political Divisions of Territory in all parts of the World. Compiled from the most authentic sources, under the supervision of W. G. BLACKIE, Ph.D., F.R.G.S. With an INDEX, containing References to nearly 120,000 Places.

In fulness and accuracy of information, largeness of scale, and clearness of engraving, this Atlas will compare favourably with the most costly works of the kind extant. It is portable, and can be consulted with ease, being an imperial 4to, measuring when closed 15 inches by 11 inches. The Maps are printed on paper measuring 22 inches by 15, and carefully coloured. The Series extends to Seventy-eight such Sheets, comprising above One Hundred different Maps.

"After a careful perusal of the whole work, we can safely say that we know of no Atlas, published at the same low price, which is so copious and accurate in detail, so clearly printed, and so well engraved; that no maps have been hitherto constructed on scales so carefully adapted to the relative importance of countries, as viewed from the stand-point of English merchants and general readers."—*London Review*.

In 30 Parts, imperial 8vo, 2s. 6d. each.

THE IMPERIAL GAZETTEER:
A GENERAL DICTIONARY OF GEOGRAPHY,

PHYSICAL, POLITICAL, STATISTICAL, and DESCRIPTIVE; including comprehensive Accounts of the Countries, Cities, Principal Towns, Villages, Seas, Lakes, Rivers, Islands, Mountains, Valleys, &c., in the World. Edited by W. G. BLACKIE, Ph.D., F.R.G.S. Illustrated by nearly SEVEN HUNDRED AND FIFTY ENGRAVINGS, printed in the Text, comprising Views, Costumes, Maps, Plans, &c. Two large Volumes, 2670 pages, imperial 8vo, cloth, £4, 6s.

"This excellent book of reference. . . . . . All the articles we have examined, whether long or short, exhibit a greater degree of correctness in minute detail than we should have thought practicable in so comprehensive a work."—*Athenæum*.

"By far the best Gazetteer in our language."—*Critic*.

In 30 Parts, imperial 8vo, 2s. 6d. each.

THE IMPERIAL DICTIONARY,
ENGLISH, TECHNOLOGICAL, AND SCIENTIFIC;

On the Basis of Webster's English Dictionary, with the addition of many Thousand Words and Phrases, including the most generally used Technical and Scientific Terms, together with their Etymology and their Pronunciation. Also a SUPPLEMENT, containing an extensive collection of Words, Terms, and Phrases, not included in previous English Dictionaries. By J. OGILVIE, LL.D. Illustrated by above 2500 Engravings on Wood.

"Dr. Ogilvie has not only produced the *best* English Dictionary that exists, but, so far as the actual state of knowledge permitted, has made some approach towards perfection."—*British Quarterly Review*.

"The most comprehensive work of the kind we possess. We have examined attentively, and can report most favourably of its execution."—*Atlas*.

In 38 Parts, imperial 4to, 2s. 6d. each.

THE IMPERIAL FAMILY BIBLE,

Containing the OLD and NEW TESTAMENTS, according to the most Correct Copies of the Authorized Version. With many Thousand Critical, Explanatory, and Practical Notes; also, References, Readings, Chronological Tables, and Indexes. Illustrated by a Superb Series of Engravings.

The Engraved Illustrations, 74 in number, consist of a Series of Historical Subjects, selected with much care and research from the Works of the Old Masters, and from those of the existing Schools of Painting on the Continent and in Britain. And a Series of Views of important Bible Localities, from authentic drawings; the whole engraved in the most finished manner.

BLACKIE AND SON'S PUBLICATIONS:

Complete in 36 Parts, 2s. each, forming 4 handsome Volumes, super-royal 8vo.

THE COMPREHENSIVE HISTORY OF ENGLAND,

CIVIL and MILITARY, RELIGIOUS, INTELLECTUAL, and SOCIAL: from the Earliest Period to the Suppression of the Sepoy Revolt. By CHARLES MACFARLANE and the Rev. THOMAS THOMSON. Illustrated by above Eleven Hundred Engravings on Wood and Steel—Views, Costumes, Portraits, Maps, Plans, &c. &c.

"We regard this publication as by far the most beautiful, cheap, and really 'comprehensive' history of the nation which has ever yet appeared."—*John Bull.*

"An admirable record, not only of military and political events, but of moral and intellectual progress, thus comprising, in fact, a real History of England."—*Civil Service Gazette.*

"This ought emphatically to be entitled the Family History of England."—*Morning Herald.*

Publishing in Parts, super-royal 8vo, 2s. each.

A COMPREHENSIVE HISTORY OF INDIA,

CIVIL, MILITARY, and SOCIAL, from the first landing of the English, to the suppression of the Sepoy Revolt, including an Outline of the Early History of Hindoostan. By HENRY BEVERIDGE, Esq., Advocate. Illustrated by above Five Hundred Engravings on Wood and Steel. It will extend to 25 Parts.

"This elaborate and able work is indeed more comprehensive than its title would imply, for it gives us with philosophical discrimination the ancient, medieval, and modern history of a most singular people, who were well fed and well clad, who had a written language, and composed metaphysical treatises, when the forefathers of the race that now bears sway over two hundred millions of them were still wandering in the woods of Britain and Germany, all of them savages, and some perhaps cannibals. . . . The numerous engravings on wood and steel, remarkable for their beauty and fidelity, contribute greatly to the interest and even to the instructive power of the work."—*Examiner.*

New and revised edition, in Parts, 2s., and Divisions, 10s. each.

THE POPULAR ENCYCLOPEDIA;
Or, CONVERSATIONS LEXICON.

Being a General Dictionary of Arts, Sciences, Literature, Biography, History, and Politics; with Preliminary Dissertations by distinguished Writers.

The POPULAR ENCYCLOPEDIA has been before the public for many years past, and has met with a large measure of acceptance. The alterations and corrections made for the present edition render the Work a satisfactory exponent of the state of knowledge in the present day. The articles on Botany, Chemistry, and Geology have been wholly re-written, and the scientific articles generally have been carefully revised; and those on Geography, Topography, History, Theology, and Biography have been subjected to a rigid examination.

An entirely new SUPPLEMENT has been written, containing additional biographies, notices of localities newly discovered, or that have risen recently into importance—of substances and processes new in science and the arts—of the great events of the world during the last twenty years—and other subjects of general interest.

The Illustrations of the POPULAR ENCYCLOPEDIA have been augmented fully a half, and extend to One Hundred and Fifty-four Pages of Steel Engravings, and Fourteen Coloured Maps, besides many Engravings on Wood. The whole Work, including Supplement, will be completed in 63 Parts, price 2s. each; or in 14 Divisions, 10s. each.

In 28 Parts, 2s. 6d. each; or 2 large Vols., 2250 pages, super-royal 8vo, cloth, £3, 15s.

MORTON'S CYCLOPEDIA OF AGRICULTURE,
PRACTICAL AND SCIENTIFIC:

In which the Theory, the Art, and the Business of Farming, in all their departments, are thoroughly and practically treated. By upwards of Fifty of the most Eminent Farmers, Land-Agents, and Scientific Men of the Day. Edited by JOHN C. MORTON. With above 1800 Illustrative Figures on Wood and Steel.

The object of this Work is to present to the Agricultural reader the whole of the truth immediately connected with his profession, so far as it is known to the men most familiar with the sciences it involves, the methods it employs, and the risks it incurs. Illustrations on Wood and Steel, of Farm Buildings, Insects, Plants (cultivated and uncultivated), Agricultural Machines, Implements, and Operations, &c., are given wherever they can be useful.

In 35 Parts, Imperial 8vo, 1s. each; or 2 Vols., cloth extra, 38s.

THE HISTORY OF THE BIBLE,

From the Beginning of the World to the Establishment of Christianity; and a connection of Profane with Sacred History. By the Rev. THOMAS STACKHOUSE, M.A. With copious additions from recent Commentators, Critics, and Eastern Travellers; and Complete Indexes. Also, an Appendix on the Illustrations of Scripture derived from the Egyptian and Assyrian Monuments, &c. Illustrated by Fifty highly-finished Engravings.

GLASGOW, EDINBURGH, AND LONDON.

In 46 Parts, medium 8vo, 1s. each; or in Divisions, cloth gilt, 6s. 6d. each.

BIOGRAPHICAL DICTIONARY OF EMINENT SCOTSMEN.

Originally Edited by ROBERT CHAMBERS. In Four Volumes. New and revised Edition. With a Supplemental Volume, continuing the Biographies to the Present Time. By the Rev. THOMAS THOMSON. Illustrated by Eighty-five highly-finished Portraits, and Five Engraved Titles.

In 21 Parts, super-royal 4to, 2s. each.

ITALY:
CLASSICAL, HISTORICAL, AND PICTURESQUE.

Illustrated in a Series of Views, engraved in the most finished manner, from Drawings by Stanfield, R.A.; Roberts, R.A.; Harding, Prout, Leitch, Brockedon, Barnard, &c., &c. With Descriptions of the Scenes, and an Essay on Italy and the Italians, by CAMILLO MAPEI, D.D.

" We do not know a more delightful drawing-room book than this work on Italy, which comprises upwards of sixty exquisite Illustrations of the noblest and most interesting scenery in the world, with corresponding descriptions to record the natural features, and the poetical and historical associations of each spot."—*Inverness Courier.*

Re-issue, with Coloured Plates. In 36 Parts, royal 8vo, 1s. each.

A HISTORY OF THE EARTH AND ANIMATED NATURE.

By OLIVER GOLDSMITH. With numerous Notes from the Works of the most distinguished British and Foreign Naturalists. The Plates contain 2400 Illustrative Figures, of which 250 are carefully coloured.

In 22 Parts, royal 8vo, 1s. each.

A HISTORY OF THE VEGETABLE KINGDOM;

Embracing the Physiology, Classification, and the Culture of Plants; with their various uses to Man and the Lower Animals, and their application in the Arts, Manufactures, and Domestic Economy. Illustrated by Seven Hundred Figures on Wood and Steel, of which One Hundred are beautifully coloured.

In 30 Parts, 1s. each; Divisions, cloth elegant, 6s. each; or 4 Vols., cloth, £2, 4s.

D'AUBIGNE'S HISTORY OF THE REFORMATION.

Translated by D. D. SCOTT, and H. WHITE, B.A. The Translation carefully revised by Dr. MERLE D'AUBIGNE. Large type, numerous Notes, not in any other Edition, and Forty Illustrations, beautifully Engraved on Steel. The Emerald Edition, small 8vo, in 17 Nos., Price 6d. each.

In 20 Parts, 1s. each; or 2 Vols., cloth, £1, 1s.

A HISTORY OF THE PAPACY,

POLITICAL and ECCLESIASTICAL, in the Sixteenth and Seventeenth Centuries. By LEOPOLD RANKE. With Notes by the Translator, and an Introductory Essay by J. H. MERLE D'AUBIGNE, D.D. Illustrated by Twenty highly-finished Portraits.

In 12 Parts, super-royal 8vo, 2s. 6d. each; or 1 Vol., cloth extra, £1, 11s. 6d.

THE GARDENER'S ASSISTANT.

PRACTICAL and SCIENTIFIC. A Guide to the Formation and Management of the Kitchen, Fruit, and Flower Garden, and the Cultivation of Conservatory, Green-house, and Hot-house Plants. By ROBERT THOMPSON, Superintendent of the Horticultural Society's Garden, Chiswick. Illustrated by Twelve beautifully-coloured Engravings, each representing two or more choice Flowers or Fruits, and nearly Three Hundred Engravings on Wood.

GLASGOW, EDINBURGH, AND LONDON.

BLACKIE AND SON'S PUBLICATIONS:

In 25 Parts, 2s. each; or 3 Vols. super-royal 8vo, cloth, £2, 14s.

THE WORKS OF JOHN BUNYAN,
PRACTICAL, ALLEGORICAL, AND MISCELLANEOUS;

First Complete Edition. Carefully collated and printed from the Author's own Editions. With EDITORIAL PREFACES, NOTES, and a MEMOIR OF BUNYAN AND HIS TIMES. By GEORGE OFFOR. Numerous Illustrative Engravings.

SEPARATE ISSUES.

I. THE EXPERIMENTAL, DOCTRINAL, AND PRACTICAL WORKS. Illustrations. In 32 Parts, 1s. each.
II. THE ALLEGORICAL, FIGURATIVE, AND SYMBOLICAL WORKS. Numerous Illustrations. In 18 Parts, 1s. each.

LADIES OF THE REFORMATION.
MEMOIRS OF DISTINGUISHED FEMALE CHARACTERS,

Belonging to the Period of the Reformation in the Sixteenth Century. By the Rev. JAMES ANDERSON, Author of *Ladies of the Covenant*, &c. Nearly Two Hundred Illustrations, from Drawings by J. Godwin, G. Thomas, J. W. Archer, E. K. Johnson, &c.

FIRST SERIES.—ENGLAND, SCOTLAND, and the NETHERLANDS. Small 4to, cloth, antique, 10s. 6d.
SECOND SERIES.—GERMANY, FRANCE, SWITZERLAND, ITALY, and SPAIN. Small 4to, cloth, antique, 10s. 6d.

Cloth, antique, 7s. 6d.; or 14 Nos., 6d. each.

LADIES OF THE COVENANT;

Being Memoirs of Distinguished Scottish Female Characters, embracing the period of the Covenant and Persecution. By the Rev. JAMES ANDERSON, Author of the *Martyrs of the Bass*, &c. Numerous Engravings.

Complete in 28 Nos., 6d. each; or 2 Vols., cloth, gilt, 15s.

THE SHEEPFOLD AND THE COMMON;
OR, WITHIN AND WITHOUT.

Being Tales and Sketches illustrating the Power of Evangelical Religion, and the Pernicious Tendency of the Heresies and Errors of the Day. Illustrated by a Series of Thirty-two Page Engravings.

This Work is a new and much-improved Edition of the *Evangelical Rambler*, a title under which above One Hundred Thousand copies of it were sold. The highest testimony was borne to its excellency when first put forth, and its re-appearance, in a revised and amended form, has met with great approval.

Complete in 20 Parts, imperial 8vo, 1s. each.

THE LIFE OF JESUS CHRIST,

With the Lives of the Apostles and Evangelists. By the Rev. JOHN FLEETWOOD, D.D. Also, the Lives of the most Eminent Fathers and Martyrs, and the History of Primitive Christianity, by WILLIAM CAVE, D.D. With an Essay on the Evidences of Christianity, and numerous Notes not to be found in any other Edition. To which is subjoined, A Concise History of the Christian Church, by the Rev. THOMAS SIMS, M.A. Illustrated by Forty beautiful Engravings.

Complete in 20 Parts, super-royal 8vo, 1s. each; or 1 Vol., cloth, 21s.

THE CHRISTIAN CYCLOPEDIA;
OR, REPERTORY OF BIBLICAL AND THEOLOGICAL LITERATURE.

By the Rev. JAMES GARDNER, M.D., A.M. With numerous Illustrations.

This Work is designed to be a popular compendium of what has hitherto been written on all those subjects which are either involved in, or allied to Christianity. It embraces in its plan the general features both of a Biblical and Theological Dictionary, and a comprehensive digest of the Literature and Biography connected with Christianity. It must be regarded as a Work of high value to the readers and students of the Scriptures.

GLASGOW, EDINBURGH, AND LONDON.

BIBLES AND COMMENTARIES.

THE IMPERIAL FAMILY BIBLE,
See page 1.

THE COMPREHENSIVE FAMILY BIBLE; with Notes and Practical Reflections; also, References, Readings, Chronological and other Tables. By DAVID DAVIDSON, LL.D. With numerous Historical and Landscape Illustrations and Maps. In 36 Parts, super-royal 4to, 2s. each.

COOKE'S BROWN'S SELF-INTER- PRETING BIBLE. With Introduction, Marginal References, and Copious Notes, Explanatory and Practical. By the Rev. HENRY COOKE, D.D., Belfast. Illustrated with Historical Designs, and a Series of Views. In 44 Parts, royal 4to, 1s. each.

HAWEIS' EVANGELICAL EXPO- SITOR; a Commentary on the Holy Bible, with Introduction, Marginal References and Readings, and a Complete Index and Concise Dictionary, by the Rev. JOHN BARR. With Maps, Plans, and other Engravings. 65 Parts, 1s. each.

THE TWOFOLD CONCORDANCE to the Words and Subjects of the Holy Bible; including a Concise Dictionary, a Chronological Arrangement of the Sacred Narrative, and other Tables, designed to facilitate the Consultation and Study of the Sacred Scriptures. In 18 Nos., 6d. each.

The FIRST PART of this Work consists of a careful condensation of Cruden's Concordance, but retaining all that is really valuable. The SECOND PART comprises a Complete Index and Concise Dictionary of the Bible, by the Rev. JOHN BARR.

THE BOOK OF ECCLESIASTES: ITS MEANING AND ITS LESSONS. By the Rev. ROBERT BUCHANAN, D.D. Square 8vo, cloth, 7s. 6d.

ILLUSTRATED POCKET BIBLE; Containing nearly 9000 Critical and Explanatory Notes, and 80,000 References and Readings; also, THIRTY-SEVEN beautiful Engravings. In 24 Nos., 6d. each.

BROWN'S DICTIONARY of the BIBLE. Corrected and Improved. Illustrated by several hundred Engravings. 20 Parts, 1s. each; cloth, £1, 1s.

THE BOOK of COMMON PRAYER. With Notes compiled from the Writings of the most eminent Commentators. Illustrated by 26 beautiful Engravings, including Eight Designs for the Offices, by H. C. SELOUS. *The Rubrics printed in Red.* 16 Nos., 6d. each; and in mor., flexible, 15s.

BARNES' NOTES ON THE NEW TESTAMENT. Illustrated and Annotated Edition. With 38 Steel Plates, 22 Maps and Plans, and 28 Engravings on Wood—in all, *Seventy* separate Plates, from the most authentic source, illustrating the principal Scripture Scenes, and Sites of Celebrated Cities, Towns, &c. The whole complete in 33 Parts, 1s. each; or in 5 double vols., 6s. each, and 1 at 4s. 6d.

BARNES' QUESTIONS ON THE NEW TESTAMENT. For Bible Classes and Sunday Schools. In 1 Vol. (MATTHEW to HEBREWS), cloth, 3s. 6d.; or 6 Parts, 6d. each.

BARNES' NOTES ON THE OLD TESTAMENT. Books of JOB, ISAIAH, and DANIEL. With additional Prefaces and Notes, also Appendixes, Engravings on Steel, and above 150 Illustrations on Wood; most of them to be found in no other Edition. In 19 Parts, 1s. each; or JOB, 1 Vol., cloth, 6s.; ISAIAH, 2 Vols., 7s.; DANIEL, 1 Vol., 6s. 6d.

STANDARD RELIGIOUS WORKS.

BAXTER'S SELECT PRACTICAL WORKS. Including his Treatises on Conversion, The Divine Life, Dying Thoughts, and Saints' Everlasting Rest, and a Memoir of the Author. In 48 Nos., super-royal 8vo, 6d. each.

BAXTER'S SAINTS' EVERLAST- ING REST; The Divine Life, and Dying Thoughts; also, a Call to the Unconverted, and Now or Never. 21 Nos., super-royal 8vo, 6d. each; cloth, 11s. 6d.

FAMILY WORSHIP: A Series of Prayers, with Doctrinal and Practical Remarks on Passages of Sacred Scripture, for every Morning and Evening throughout the Year, by One Hundred and Eighty Clergymen of the Scottish Church. With Twenty-one highly-finished Engravings. 20 Parts, super-royal 8vo, 1s. each; cloth, £1, 1s.

M'GAVIN'S PROTESTANT: A Series of Essays on the Christianity of the New Testament, and the Papal Superstition. New Edition. Medium 8vo, cloth, 14s.; or in 26 Nos., 6d. each.

DWIGHT'S SYSTEM of THEO- LOGY; or, Complete Body of Divinity. In a Series of Sermons. In 20 Parts, 1s. each.

THEOPNEUSTIA; The Bible, its Divine Origin and Entire Inspiration, deduced from Internal Evidence, and the Testimonies of Nature, History, and Science. By L. GAUSSEN, D.D., Geneva. Cloth, 3s.

PSALMS of DAVID: Scottish Met- rical Version. To bind with Family Bibles, various sizes. Imperial 4to, 2s. 6d.; super-royal 4to, 2s.; royal 4to, 2s.; demy 4to, 2s.; 18mo, 6d.

CONTEMPLATIONS on the HIS- TORICAL PASSAGES of the OLD and NEW TESTAMENT. By the Right Rev. JOSEPH HALL, D.D. Numerous Plates. In 15 Parts, 1s. each.

PROFESSION AND PRACTICE; Or, Thoughts on the Low State of Vital Religion among Professing Christians. By G. M'CULLOCH. Cloth, 1s. 6d.

An EXPOSITION of the CONFES- SION of FAITH of the WESTMINSTER ASSEMBLY of DIVINES. By ROBERT SHAW, D.D., Whitburn. Eighth Edition. Cloth, 5s. 6d.

SCOTS WORTHIES; their LIVES and TESTIMONIES. With a Supplement, containing Memoirs of THE LADIES OF THE COVENANT. Upwards of One Hundred Illustrations. In 22 Parts, super-royal 8vo, 1s. each.

THE CHRISTIAN'S DAILY COM- PANION : A Series of Meditations and Short Practical Comments on the most Important Doctrines and Precepts of the Holy Scriptures, arranged for Daily Reading throughout the year. With Twenty-one highly-finished Engravings. 20 Parts, super royal 8vo, 1s. each; cloth, £1, 1s.

WATSON'S BODY of PRACTICAL DIVINITY, in a Series of Sermons on the Shorter Catechism of the Westminster Assembly, with Select Sermons on Various Subjects. The whole Revised and Corrected, with numerous Notes. In 20 Nos., super-royal 8vo, 6d. each.

WILLISON'S PRACTICAL WORKS. With an Essay on his Life and Times. By the Rev. Dr. HETHERINGTON. 20 Parts, super royal 8vo, 1s. each.

BLACKIE AND SON'S PUBLICATIONS:

HISTORY, BIOGRAPHY, &c.

MEMOIRS of NAPOLEON BONAPARTE. By M. DE BOURRIENNE. Numerous Historical and Portrait Illustrations. 23 parts, 1s. each; or 2 vols., £1, 6s.

CABINET HISTORY of ENGLAND, Civil, Military, and Ecclesiastical, from the Landing of Julius Cæsar till the year 1846. 12 vols., bound in cloth, £1, 6s.

SMITH'S CANADA: PAST, PRESENT, and FUTURE. Being an Historical, Geographical, Geological, and Statistical Account of Canada West. Maps, and other Illustrations. 2 Vols., royal 8vo, cloth, 20s.

AIKMAN'S HISTORY of SCOTLAND, from the Earliest Period to the present Time. A New Edition. With NINETY ILLUSTRATIONS, comprising Portraits, Views, and Historical Designs. In 53 Parts, 1s. each.

THE ISRAEL of the ALPS. A Complete History of the Vaudois of Piedmont and their Colonies. Prepared in great part from unpublished Documents. By ALEXIS MUSTON, D.D. Illustrated by a Series of Steel Engravings. In 16½ Parts, 1s. each; or 2 Vols. 8vo, cloth, 18s.

THE WORKS of FLAVIUS JOSEPHUS. With Maps and other Illustrations. Demy 8vo, 22½ Parts, 1s. each; or 4 Vols., cloth, 24s.

NOTES of a CLERICAL FURLOUGH, spent chiefly in the HOLY LAND. By the Rev. ROBERT BUCHANAN, D.D. Illustrated by an Accurate Map of the whole Country, and by various enlarged Sketch Maps, illustrative of individual localities and of particular excursions. Cloth, 7s. 6d.

THE TEN YEARS' CONFLICT; Being the History of the Disruption of the Church of Scotland. By the Rev. ROBERT BUCHANAN, D.D. Illustrated with Portraits on Steel and Designs on Wood. 25 Nos., 6d. each; or 2 Vols. cloth, 14s. The Library Edition, elegantly printed in large type, 2 vols. demy 8vo, cloth, £1, 1s.

ROLLIN'S ANCIENT HISTORY; With Extensive Notes, Geographical, Topographical, Historical, and Critical, and a Life of the Author. By JAMES BELL. Numerous Illustrations. In 24 Parts, medium 8vo, 1s. each.

ROLLIN'S ARTS and SCIENCES of the ANCIENTS. With Notes by JAMES BELL (forming a third Volume to Ancient History). In 10 Parts, 1s. each.

BIOGRAPHICAL DICTIONARY of EMINENT SCOTSMEN. In Four Volumes. New Edition. With a Supplemental Volume, continuing the Biographies to the Present Time. By the Rev. THOS. THOMSON. With 85 Portraits, and 5 Engraved Titles. In 46 Parts, medium 8vo, 1s. each; or Divisions, cloth gilt, 6s. 6d. each.

WORKS ON AGRICULTURE.

CYCLOPEDIA of AGRICULTURE. Practical and Scientific. By upwards of Fifty of the most Eminent Farmers, Land-Agents, and Scientific Men of the day. Edited by JOHN C. MORTON. With above 1800 Illustrative Figures on Wood and Steel. In 28 Parts, 2s. 6d. each; or 2 large Vols., super-royal 8vo, cloth, £3, 15s.

NEW FARMER'S ALMANAC. Edited by JOHN C. MORTON, Editor of the *Agricultural Gazette, Cyclopedia of Agriculture*, &c. Published yearly. Price 1s.

OUR FARM CROPS; Being a popular Scientific Description of the Cultivation, Chemistry, Diseases, and Remedies, &c., of our different Crops, worked up to the high Farming of the present day. By JOHN WILSON, F.R.S.E., Professor of Agriculture in the University of Edinburgh, Member of Council of the Royal Agricultural Society of England, &c., &c. Illustrated with Engravings on Wood. In 2 Vols., crown 8vo, cloth, 13s.; or 12 Parts, 1s. each.

"This Work is probably the most remarkable, and the most useful for the Agriculturist, that has appeared for a long time."—*Guernsey Official Gazette.*

THE GARDENER'S ASSISTANT, Practical and Scientific. A Guide to the Formation and Management of the Kitchen, Fruit, and Flower Garden, and the Cultivation and Management of Conservatory, Green-house, and Hothouse Plants. With a Copious Calendar of Gardening Operations. By ROBERT THOMPSON, Horticultural Society's Garden, Chiswick. Illustrated by numerous Engravings and carefully Coloured Plates. In 12 Parts, 2s. 6d. each, or cloth, £1, 11s. 6d.

Besides the subjects above indicated, the Work contains Chapters on the Physiology of Plants, the Nature and Improvement of Soils, the various kinds of Manures and their Uses, and the Tools, Instruments, &c., employed in Gardening; together with descriptions of the best varieties of Vegetables, Fruits, and Flowers. Profusely Illustrated with Engravings printed in the Text.

HOW to CHOOSE a Good MILK COW. By J. H. MAGNE. With a Supplement on the Dairy Cattle of Britain. Illustrated with Engravings. Cloth, 3s.

FARM INSECTS. Being the Natural History and Economy of the Insects injurious to the Field Crops in Great Britain and Ireland, and also those which infest Barns and Granaries, with suggestions for their destruction. By JOHN CURTIS, F.L.S., &c., &c. Illustrated with many hundred Figures, Plain and Coloured. In 8 Parts, super-royal 8vo, 2s. 6d. each, plain plates, or 3s. 6d. coloured plates; or cloth, £1, 10s.

"We are taught how to anticipate the insects before they attack the crops, so as to weaken the assault, and also to check their progress. For these ends, concise rules are given as to the management of the soil and plant. We know of no greater boon to the agriculturist, in one particular department of his labours, than the publication of this volume."—*Gloucester Chronicle.*

FARMER'S GUIDE. A Treatise on the Diseases of Horses and Black Cattle, with Instructions for the Management of Breeding Mares and Cows. By JAMES WEBB, Veterinary Surgeon. Seventh Edition. Foolscap 8vo, cloth, 3s. 6d.

AGRICULTURIST'S CALCULATOR. A Series of Forty-five Tables for Land-Measuring, Draining, Manuring, Planting, Weight of Hay and Cattle by Measurement, Building, &c. 17 Nos., foolscap 8vo, 6d. each; bound, 9s.

THE HAY and CATTLE MEASURER. A Series of Tables for Computing the Weight of Haystacks and Live Stock by Measurement. Also, Tables showing the Equivalent, in Weight and Price, of the Imperial to the Dutch Stone, and other Local Weights. Foolscap 8vo, cloth, 2s. 6d.

DITCHING and DRAINING: A Manual of Tables for Computing Work done. Suited to the use of Contractors and Employers of Labour. Foolscap 8vo, cloth, 2s.

AGRICULTURIST'S ASSISTANT: A Note-Book of Principles, Rules, and Tables, adapted to the use of all engaged in Agriculture, or the Management of Landed Property. By JOHN EWART, Land-Surveyor and Agricultural Engineer. Plates and Cuts. Foolscap 8vo, cloth, 3s. 6d.

GLASGOW, EDINBURGH, AND LONDON.

BLACKIE AND SON'S PUBLICATIONS: 7

ILLUSTRATED HISTORY OF THE WALDENSES.

In 16½ Parts, 1s. each; or 2 Vols. 8vo, cloth, 18s.

THE ISRAEL OF THE ALPS.

A Complete History of the Vaudois of Piedmont and their Colonies. Prepared in great part from unpublished Documents. By ALEXIS MUSTON, D.D. Illustrated by a Series of Steel Engravings, comprising Scenery in the Valleys, Maps, and Historical Illustrations, prepared by or under the superintendence of the Author, M. MUSTON.

This Work contains the most complete and connected view of the history of the Vaudois. It is the fruit of long and laborious research, and throws new light upon many of the known facts, events, and periods of the Waldensian people in their earnest and protracted struggle for the preservation of the true faith.

WORKS ON MACHINERY, CARPENTRY, &c.

ENGINEER and MACHINIST'S
DRAWING-BOOK: A Complete Course of Instruction for the Practical Engineer; comprising Linear Drawing, Projections, Eccentric Curves, the various forms of Gearing, Reciprocating Machinery, Sketching and Drawing from the Machine, Projection of Shadows, Tinting and Colouring, and Perspective, on the basis of the works of M. Le Blanc and MM. Armengaud. Illustrated by numerous Engravings on Wood and Steel. In 16 Parts, imperial 4to, 2s. each; or 1 Vol. half-morocco, £2, 2s.

ENGINEER and MACHINIST'S
ASSISTANT; Being a Series of Plans, Sections, and Elevations of Steam Engines, Water Wheels, Spinning Machines, Mills for Grinding, Tools, &c., taken from Machines of approved Construction; with detailed Descriptions and Practical Essays on various departments of Machinery. New and Improved Edition. In 28 Parts, imperial 4to, 2s. 6d. each; or 2 Vols. half-morocco, £4, 4s.

RAILWAY MACHINERY. A Treatise
on the Mechanical Engineering of Railways; embracing the Principles and Construction of Rolling and Fixed Plant, in all departments. Illustrated by a Series of Plates on a large scale, and by numerous Engravings on Wood. By D. KINNEAR CLARK, Engineer. In 30 Parts, imperial 4to, 2s. 6d. each; 2 Vols. half-morocco, £4, 15s.

RAILWAY LOCOMOTIVES. Their
Progress, Mechanical Construction, and Performance, with the recent Practice in England and America. Illustrated by an extensive series of Plates, and numerous Engravings on Wood. By D. KINNEAR CLARK, Engineer. In 25 Parts, imperial 4to, 2s. each; 2 Vols., half-morocco, £4.

This Work combines the Locomotive Section of the Author's Work on Railway Machinery, with extensive additions illustrating the practice of English Locomotive Engineers of the present day, and presenting the most recent attainments in American practice. It also includes the consideration of coal-burning, and a variety of other questions bearing upon the economical working and improvement of the Locomotive.

RECENT PRACTICE in the LOCO-
MOTIVE ENGINE; being a Supplement to Railway Machinery; Comprising the most Recent Improvements in English Practice, and Illustrations of the Locomotive Practice of the United States of America. By D. KINNEAR CLARK, Engineer. In 10 Parts, imperial 4to, 2s. 6d. each; half-morocco, 35s.

This Work consists simply of the new portion of Railway Locomotives, announced above. It is published separately for the benefit of those who already possess the Author's Work on Railway Machinery.

LAND-MEASURER'S READY-
RECKONER: Being Tables for ascertaining at sight the Contents of any Field or Piece of Land. Third edition. Bound in roan, 2s.

THE PRACTICAL MEASURER;
Or, Tradesman and Wood-Merchant's Assistant. By ALEXANDER PEDDIE. New Edition, greatly enlarged. In 12 Nos., 6d. each; bound, 6s. 6d.

CARPENTER and JOINER'S
ASSISTANT. Being a Comprehensive Treatise on the Selection, Preparation, and Strength of Materials, and the Mechanical Principles of Framing, with their Applications in Carpentry, Joinery, and Hand Railing; also, a Course of Instruction in Practical Geometry, Geometrical Lines, Drawing, Projection, and Perspective, and an Illustrated Glossary of Terms used in Architecture and Building. By JAMES NEWLANDS, Borough Engineer of Liverpool. Illustrated by an extensive Series of Plates, and many hundred Engravings on Wood. In 24 Parts, super-royal 4to, 2s. each; or 1 Vol., half-morocco, £2, 10s.

This Publication supplies, in a compendious form, a complete and practical Course of Instruction in the Principles of Carpentry and Joinery, with a Selection of Examples of Works actually executed. It includes the most important features of the great works of Emy, Krafft, and others, which, from their cost and foreign languages, are inaccessible to workmen.

"It will be for a long time to come the standard treatise on Carpentry and Joinery."—Mechanic's Magazine.

CABINET-MAKER'S ASSISTANT.
A Series of Original Designs for Modern Furniture, with Descriptions and details of Construction. Complete in 23 Parts, imperial 4to, 2s. 6d. each; half-bound morocco, £3, 5s.

"The Work now before us takes up the subject in a proper spirit, and is calculated to produce a very beneficial effect on the trade to which it is addressed."—Civil Engineer and Architect's Journal.

RURAL ARCHITECTURE. A
Series of Designs for Ornamental Cottages and Villas. Exemplified in Plans, Elevations, Sections, and Details. With Practical Descriptions. By JOHN WHITE, Architect. In 21 Parts, imperial 4to, 2s. each; 1 Vol. half-morocco, £2, 10s.

MECHANIC'S CALCULATOR;
Comprehending Principles, Rules, and Tables, in the various Departments of Mathematics and Mechanics. Nineteenth Edition. Cloth, 5s. 6d.

MECHANIC'S DICTIONARY. A
Note-Book of Technical Terms, Rules, and Tables, useful in the Mechanical Arts. With Engravings of Machinery, and nearly 200 Diagrams on Wood. Thirteenth Edition. Cloth, 9s.

The CALCULATOR and DICTIONARY are published in 27 Nos., 6d. each.

REID'S CLOCK and WATCH-
MAKING, Theoretical and Practical. Illustrated with Twenty Folding Plates, and Vignette Title. In 10 Parts, royal 8vo, 2s. each; or 1 Vol., cloth, 21s.

ORNAMENTAL DESIGN: A Series
of examples of Egyptian, Grecian, Roman, Italian, Gothic, Moorish, French, Flemish, and Elizabethan Ornaments, suitable for Art-workmen and Decorators. With an Essay on Ornamental Art, as applicable to Trade and Manufactures. By JAS. BALLANTYNE, Author of a Treatise on Painted Glass, &c., &c. Forty Plates, imperial 4to, cloth, £1, 2s.

GLASGOW, EDINBURGH, AND LONDON.

POETRY AND LIGHT LITERATURE.

HOGG.—The WORKS of the ETTRICK SHEPHERD, with Illustrations by D. O. Hill, R.S.A.—The Poetical Works, complete in 5 Vols., cloth, 17s. 6d.; the Prose Works, complete in 6 Vols., £1, 1s. Both Series are also published for sale in separate Vols., at 3s. 6d. each.

CASQUET of LITERARY GEMS; Containing upwards of 700 Extracts in Poetry and Prose, from nearly 300 Distinguished Authors. Illustrated by Twenty-five Engravings. In 4 Vols., cloth extra, gilt edges, £1.

BOOK of SCOTTISH SONG. A Collection of the Best and Most Approved Songs of Scotland, with Critical and Historical Notices, and an Essay on Scottish Song. Engraved Frontispiece and Title. 16 Nos., 6d. each; cloth, gilt edges, 9s.

BOOK of SCOTTISH BALLADS. A Comprehensive Collection of the Ballads of Scotland, with Illustrative Notes, and Engraved Frontispieces and Title. 15 Nos., 6d. each; cloth, gilt edges, 9s.

NICOLL'S POEMS and LYRICS, chiefly in the Scottish Dialect. With a Memoir of the Author. New Edition. Small 8vo, cloth, gilt, 3s. 6d.

THE WORKS of ROBERT BURNS. Complete Illustrated Edition, Literary and Pictorial. With Wilson's Essay "On the Genius and Character of Burns," and Dr. Currie's Memoir of the Poet, and 50 Landscape and Portrait Illustrations. 25 Parts, super-royal 8vo, 1s. each. Or with Eight Supplementary Parts, containing 22 Engravings; making in all 82 Illustrations. 2 Vols., cloth extra, £1, 16s.

LAND of BURNS; A Series of Landscapes, Illustrative of the Writings of the Scottish Poet, from Paintings by D. O. Hill, R.S.A. Also, Portraits of the Poet, his Friends, &c. With Descriptions and Biographies, by Robert Chambers; and Essay by Professor Wilson. 2 Vols., 4to, cloth, gilt edges, £2, 2s.

REPUBLIC of LETTERS. A Selection in Poetry and Prose, from the Works of the most Eminent Writers, with many Original Pieces. Twenty-five beautiful Illustrations. 4 Vols., cloth extra, gilt edges, £1.

SANDFORD'S ESSAY on the RISE and PROGRESS of LITERATURE. Foolscap 8vo, cloth, 2s. 6d.

LAING'S WAYSIDE FLOWERS: Being Poems and Songs. Introduction by Rev. Geo. Gilfillan. Third Edition. Cloth, gilt, 2s.

MISCELLANEOUS.

CYCLOPEDIA of DOMESTIC MEDICINE and SURGERY. By Thos. Andrew, M.D. Illustrated with Engravings on Wood and Steel. 17 Parts, royal 8vo, 1s. each; cloth, 18s.

BARR'S SCRIPTURE STUDENT'S ASSISTANT. A Complete Index and Concise Dictionary to the Bible. New Edition, Enlarged, with Pronunciation of Proper Names, Chronological Arrangement of the Scriptures, &c. Post 8vo, cloth, 3s.

BARR'S CATECHETICAL INSTRUCTIONS for YOUNG COMMUNICANTS. With an Address to Young Persons not yet Communicants. 31st Edition, 18mo, sewed, 4d.

BARR'S CATECHETICAL INSTRUCTIONS on INFANT BAPTISM. With an Address to Young Parents. 15th Edition, 18mo, sewed, 3d.

COMMERCIAL HAND-BOOK: A Complete Ready-Reckoner, and Compendium of Tables and Information for the Trader, Merchant, and Commercial Traveller. 310 pp. 48mo, bound in roan, 1s.

TYTLER'S ELEMENTS of GENERAL HISTORY, Ancient and Modern. With considerable additions to the Author's Text, numerous Notes, and a Continuation to the reign of Queen Victoria. Edited by the Rev. Brandon Turner, M.A. Sixth Edition. Cloth, 5s. 6d. Also in Divisions. Div. I., price 2s. 6d.; Div. II., price 3s. 6d.

GERLACH'S COMPREHENSIVE GERMAN DICTIONARY. German and English, and English and German. By J. J. Gerlach, LL.D. Bound, 5s. 6d.

This Dictionary is more copious in the number of its words and meanings than any portable German Dictionary hitherto published.

HARTLEY'S ORATORICAL CLASS-BOOK. With the Principles of Elocution Simplified and Illustrated by suitable examples. Fifteenth Edition, improved. Foolscap 8vo, bound, 2s. 6d.

CHORISTER'S TEXT-BOOK: Containing nearly Two Hundred Psalm and Hymn Tunes, Chants, Anthems, &c., arranged for from Two to Five Voices, with Organ or Pianoforte Accompaniments; preceded by a Comprehensive Grammar of Music. By W. J. P. Kidd. Super-royal 8vo, stiff paper, 5s.; cloth, gilt, 8s.

HAND PLACE-BOOK of the UNITED KINGDOM; Containing References of daily use to upwards of 15,000 Localities in Great Britain and Ireland, and General Statistical Tables. Bound, 2s.

FERGUSON'S INTEREST TABLES, At Fourteen different Rates, from a Quarter to Six and a Half per Cent.; also, Tables of Commission and Brokerage. New Edition, enlarged. Bound, 7s.

LAWRIE'S SYSTEM of MERCANTILE ARITHMETIC; With the Nature, Use, and Negotiation of Bills of Exchange. Fifth Edition. In 2 Parts, bound in roan, with Key, 3s.; or Parts I. and II., in cloth, 1s. each; the Key separately, 1s.

MOFFAT: Its WALKS and WELLS. With Incidental Notices of its Botany and Geology. By William Keddie; and Report on, and Chemical Analysis of, its Mineral Wells, by J. Macadam, F.R.S.S.A. Foolscap 8vo, 1s.

COMSTOCK'S NATURAL PHILOSOPHY: Edited and largely augmented by R. D. Hoblyn, M.A. Oxon. A Manual of Natural Philosophy; in which are popularly explained the Principles of Heat, Mechanics, Hydrostatics, Hydraulics, Pneumatics, the Steam Engine, Acoustics, Optics, Astronomy, Electricity, Magnetism, &c.; with Questions for Examination on each Chapter, and an Appendix of Problems. Illustrated by nearly Three Hundred Engravings on Wood. Foolscap 8vo, cloth, 5s.

M'CRIE'S SKETCHES of SCOTTISH CHURCH HISTORY: Embracing the Period from the Reformation to the Revolution. 2 Vols., demy 12mo, cloth, 4s.

ROBERTSON'S HISTORY of the JEWS, From the Babylonian Captivity to the Destruction of Jerusalem. Cloth, 1s. 6d.

ROBERTSON'S CHART of SCRIPTURE CHRONOLOGY, from the Creation to the Destruction of Jerusalem. In stiff covers, 4d.

STAFFA and IONA DESCRIBED and ILLUSTRATED; With Notices of the Principal Objects on the route from Port Crinan to Oban, and in the Sound of Mull. Many Engravings. Limp cloth, 2s.

GLASGOW, EDINBURGH, AND LONDON.